PROFESSIONAL SILVERLIGHT® 4

PROFESSIONAL

Silverlight® 4

Jason Beres
Bill Evjen
Devin Rader

WILEY
Wiley Publishing, Inc.

Professional Silverlight® 4

Published by
Wiley Publishing, Inc.
10475 Crosspoint Boulevard
Indianapolis, IN 46256
www.wiley.com

Copyright © 2010 by Wiley Publishing, Inc., Indianapolis, Indiana

Published simultaneously in Canada

ISBN: 978-0-470-65092-9

Manufactured in the United States of America

10 9 8 7 6 5 4 3 2 1

Library of Congress Control Number: 2010930723

To my beautiful wife Sheri and our amazing 4-year-old daughter Siena for supporting me during the late nights and weekends that it took to get this book completed.

— Jason Beres

To George — glad you made it to the developer ranks, brother!

— Bill Evjen

To Mom and Dad, thanks for everything!

— Devin Rader

ABOUT THE AUTHORS

 JASON BERES is the Vice President of Product Management, Community, and Evangelism, and spearheads customer-driven, innovative features and functionality throughout all of Infragistics' products. Jason is a Microsoft .NET MVP for 8 years running, a member of the INETA Speakers Bureau, and is the author of 7 books on various .NET technologies, the latest being this one, *Professional Silverlight 4* from Wrox Press.

 BILL EVJEN is an active proponent of .NET technologies and community-based learning initiatives for .NET. He has been actively involved with .NET since the first bits were released in 2000. In the same year, Bill founded the St. Louis .NET User Group (www.stlnet.org), one of the world's first such groups. Bill is also the founder and former executive director of the International .NET Association (www.ineta.org), which represents more than 500,000 members worldwide. Based in St. Louis, Missouri, Bill is an acclaimed author and speaker on ASP.NET and Services. He has authored or coauthored more than 20 books including *Professional C# 4 and .NET 4*, *Professional ASP.NET 4 in VB and C#*, *ASP.NET Professional Secrets*, *XML Web Services for ASP.NET*, and *Web Services Enhancements: Understanding the WSE for Enterprise Applications* (all published by Wiley). In addition to writing, Bill is a speaker at numerous conferences, including DevConnections, VSLive!, and TechEd. Along with these items, Bill works closely with Microsoft as a Microsoft Regional Director and an MVP. Bill is the Global Head of Platform Architecture for Thomson Reuters, Lipper, the international news and financial services company (www.thomsonreuters.com). He graduated from Western Washington University in Bellingham, Washington. When he isn't tinkering on the computer, he can usually be found in his summer house in Toivakka, Finland. You can reach Bill on Twitter at @billevjen.

 DEVIN RADER works at Infragistics where he focuses on delivering great user experiences to developers using their controls. He's done work on all of the .NET platforms, but most recently has been focused on ASP.NET and Silverlight. As a co-founder of the St. Louis .NET User Group, a current board member of the Central New Jersey .NET User Group, and a former INETA board member, he's an active supporter of the .NET developer community. He's also the co-author or technical editor of numerous books on .NET including *Silverlight 3 Programmer's Reference* and *Professional ASP.NET 4 in C# and VB* from Wrox. Follow Devin on Twitter @devinrader.

ABOUT THE CONTRIBUTORS

SHAWN ANDERSON is currently a senior solutions architect with Infragistics and spends much of his time working on designing and developing business solutions and new product lines that utilize cutting edge technology in combination with the latest Infragistics suites and tools. He has a passion for all things technical and has been designing and developing large scale business systems across multiple platforms for over 15 years.

GRANT HINKSON serves as a bridge between design and development in Microsoft's Entertainment Experience Group as an Experience Developer, focused on the Zune PC Client. Grant has a history of uniting design and development and has pioneered integrated workflows across multi-discipline teams. He is an advocate for iterative design and rapid prototyping and believes Silverlight is an enabling technology that supports those processes. Before joining Microsoft, Grant founded and grew the Experience Design Group at Infragistics. He has been honored as a Microsoft Expression MVP and has spoken at Microsoft Mix, Microsoft ReMix, Adobe MAX, and Devscovery. Grant is a contributing author on the Wrox titles *Silverlight 1.0*, *Silverlight 3 Programmer's Reference*, and the Friends of Ed title *Foundation Fireworks CS4*. He has authored a number of utilities for the designer/developer community, notably the Fireworks to XAML exporter. You can find Grant's latest creations at www.granthinkson.com.

DAVID KELLEY has been building targeted customer experiences primarily on the web and offline for over 10 years. David's main focus is on integrating technology into environments, ranging from using sensors to touch screens and Silverlight. David is currently the Principal User eXperience Architect for Wirestone and publishes a blog "Hacking Silverlight" as well as posts related to UX for Interact Seattle. Currently his main focus is in the retail space with touch experiences such as digital price tags and Silverlight-based kiosks. David's other career highlights include the Silverlight Bill Gates demo at TechEd '08, the Entertainment Tonight Emmy Award site for the Silverlight launch, and achievement of a Silverlight MVP in 2009, as well as his work with Wirestone. In his spare time David helps run Interact (Seattle's Designer Developer Interaction Group and the Seattle Silverlight User Group), travels, plays with his kids, Legos, and more.

MIHAIL MATEEV is a senior software development engineer with Infragistics, Inc. He worked as a software developer and team lead on WPF and Silverlight Line of Business production lines of the company and now works as a Technical Evangelist. Over the past 10 years, he has written articles for Bulgarian *ComputerWorld* magazine as well as blogs about .NET technologies. Prior to Infragistics, he worked at ESRI Bulgaria as a software developer and a trainer. For several years Mihail has delivered lectures about geographic information systems for the Sofia University "St. Kliment Ohridski" Faculty of Mathematics and Informatics. Mihail is also a lecturer on computer systems for the University of the Architecture, Civil Engineering and Geodesy in Sofia, Bulgaria, in the Computer Aided Engineering Department. Mihail holds master's degrees in Structural Engineering and Applied Mathematics and Informatics.

TODD SNYDER is a solution architect and developer with over 15 year of experience building enterprise and rich Internet (RIA) applications on the Microsoft platform. He currently is a principal consultant on the Infragistics UI Service team specializing in RIA and Enterprise application architecture. He is the co-leader for the New Jersey .NET user group (`www.njdotnet.net/`) and is a frequent speaker at trade shows, code camps, and Firestarters.

ABOUT THE TECHNICAL EDITORS

STEPHEN ZAHARUK graduated with a B.S. in Computer Science from Susquehanna University in 2004. Since then he's been working at Infragistics, first working in their Developer Support department and soon writing new UI controls for their ASP.NET product line. When Silverlight was announced, Steve joined a new team for the Infragistics Silverlight Line of Business product line as Team Lead and soon after as Product Architect.

TODD SNYDER See Todd Snyder's bio in the preceding "About the Contributors" section.

MATTHEW VAN HORN specializes in rapid development focused on flexible and dynamic code to leverage maximum results with minimal effort. His development tool of choice is Silverlight, which he has used in projects ranging from a clone of Space Invaders for Facebook to back office accounting to a dynamic business intelligence visualization system that turned heads at the Global Gaming (casino) Expo this year in Las Vegas, Nevada.

CRAIG SELBERT currently works for Thomson Reuters, Lipper (`www.lipperweb.com`), as a Senior Software Developer. His primary responsibilities are developing web frameworks and applications using various rich Internet application toolsets like ASP.NET, jQuery, ASP.NET MVC, Silverlight, Unity, and Prism. At Lipper, Craig works on a team that created a framework leveraging the Unity/Prism framework in Silverlight and WPF that has allowed them to build true enterprise module-based applications. He has always been an early adopter of technology that has growing pains, but through perseverance, the software and Craig have always come out better in the end. Craig enjoys spending most of his working time dealing with Microsoft technologies, but keeps a watchful eye on other technologies to make sure he stays well rounded. You can reach Craig on Twitter at `@craigselbert`.

CREDITS

CONTRIBUTORS
Shawn Anderson
Grant Hinkson
David Kelley
Mihail Mateev
Todd Snyder

EXECUTIVE EDITOR
Robert Elliott

SENIOR PROJECT EDITOR
Kevin Kent

DEVELOPMENT EDITOR
Jeff Riley

TECHNICAL EDITORS
Steve Zaharuk
Todd Snyder
Matthew Van Horn
Craig Selbert

SENIOR PRODUCTION EDITOR
Debra Banninger

COPY EDITORS
Kim Cofer
Cate Caffrey

EDITORIAL DIRECTOR
Robyn B. Siesky

EDITORIAL MANAGER
Mary Beth Wakefield

MARKETING MANAGER
Ashley Zurcher

PRODUCTION MANAGER
Tim Tate

VICE PRESIDENT AND EXECUTIVE GROUP PUBLISHER
Richard Swadley

VICE PRESIDENT AND EXECUTIVE PUBLISHER
Barry Pruett

ASSOCIATE PUBLISHER
Jim Minatel

PROJECT COORDINATOR, COVER
Lynsey Stanford

COMPOSITORS
Jeff Lytle, Happenstance Type-O-Rama
Craig Woods, Happenstance Type-O-Rama

PROOFREADER
Nancy Carrasco

INDEXER
Robert Swanson

COVER DESIGNER
Michael E. Trent

COVER IMAGE
© pederk/istockphoto

ACKNOWLEDGMENTS

I WOULD LIKE TO THANK THE ENTIRE TEAM AT WROX, especially Kevin Kent, our Senior Project Editor, and Bob Elliott, our Executive Editor, who kept this book on schedule on a tight timeline. You guys really pulled the team together to make this happen. Thank you. I would recommend Kevin for Project Editor of the Year if there was such an award. I'd also like to thank my two awesome co-authors, Bill and Devin. It was a pleasure working with you on the book, and I hope we can do more in the future. And last but not least, Todd Snyder, Matt Van Horn, Stephen Zaharuk, Craig Selbert, Mihail Mateev, Shawn Anderson, David Kelley, and Grant Hinkson — you guys wrote chapters and gave technical guidance, and without you, this book wouldn't have the backbone that it does. Thanks for the hard work in making this book a reality.

— JASON BERES

THANKS TO KEVIN KENT, BOB ELLIOTT, AND JIM MINATEL for the opportunity to work on such a great book. I also want to thank my co-authors who have also been very longtime friends of mine and guys that have been making this .NET journey with me since the first days. I would also like to thank my family for putting up with another writing project (as this takes away many weekends from their time with me). Thank you, Tuija, Sofia, Henri, and Kalle!

— BILL EVJEN

THANKS TO JIM MINATEL, BOB ELLIOT, KEVIN KENT, PAUL REESE, and everyone at Wrox for helping us make this book happen. Thanks to Shawn Anderson, Grant Hinkson, David Kelley, Mihail Mateev, and Todd Snyder for contributing to the book. Each one of you brought your unique talents to the content of this book, and it's better for that. Thanks to Steve, Todd, Matt, and Craig for your technical feedback and advice. A huge thanks to Jason and Bill. Jason, this is our second Wrox collaboration and, Bill, this is our fifth, and it's awesome working with you guys. Finally a special thanks to my wife, Kathleen, who continues to support and tolerate my writing despite the late nights and long weekends.

— DEVIN RADER

CONTENTS

CONTENTS

INTRODUCTION

TO ABUSE AN ALREADY ABUSED CLICHÉ, we are at a tipping point for the Web and application development in general. The past several years have seen a notable shift away from basic full-page-based, postback-intensive web applications that minimized the use of JavaScript in favor of server-side code for maximum browser compatibility. Today, some amount of AJAX is assumed for any new web application, and every day we see new "Web 2.0" applications and companies popping up.

At the same time, and in part because of this shift, the old "thin client" versus "rich client" dichotomy has increasingly faded. It is entirely possible, and, indeed, it is often the case, for a web-based application using AJAX to truly have a richer experience than most desktop-based applications, be they Windows Forms-, Java-, or MFC-based. In fact, one might say that web applications today set the bar (excluding games, of course).

Enter Windows Presentation Foundation (WPF), the long-awaited, updated Microsoft desktop-application user interface (UI) framework. WPF borrowed from what has been learned on the Web (such as markup-based interface declaration and good separation of UI concerns), unified multiple Windows graphics APIs, and introduced new capabilities to Windows-based applications and new platform features (such as the enriched dependency property system, commanding, triggers, declarative animations, and more). WPF reestablished the desktop as the new "rich client," although not without contest from fairly rich Internet applications (RIAs) that were based on AJAX.

But this book is not about AJAX. Nor is it about WPF, at least not directly. It's about bringing together these two worlds of RIAs and rich WPF-based desktop applications, and that's where Silverlight comes in.

Silverlight was originally codenamed *WPF/e*, meaning "WPF everywhere." That's a pretty good tagline for Silverlight — bringing the good stuff from WPF to all the major platforms today, including OS X and flavors of Linux (via the Linux "Moonlight" implementation).

Silverlight 1.0 was an initial salvo. It brought with it the rich media, the rich UI declarative model, and a subset of WPF's presentation layer capabilities. However, it still depended on JavaScript for the development environment and browsers' JavaScript execution engines. It did not have many of the basic application development facilities that developers today have come to expect and rely on, such as a control model (and controls), data-binding facilities, and a solid development environment with reliable IntelliSense and debugging. Building a truly rich application for Silverlight 1.0 was only marginally better than using AJAX — the key advantages were in the high-quality media player and, of course, animation facilities.

2008 brought Silverlight 2 followed shortly by a respectable update with Silverlight 3. Silverlight 3 was, in a sense, the de facto Microsoft RIA development platform, and not just for the Internet but also (in this author's opinion) for Line of Business solutions, except in cases where the functional or experiential demands call for the greater power of WPF. That said, although dramatically improved over Silverlight 1.0 and light-years better than building on AJAX frameworks, in many ways, even Silverlight 3 was still something of a fledgling RIA platform.

Now in 2010, Microsoft has released a major and monumental release of Silverlight — version 4! This release of Silverlight is so powerful and so well put together that it is drawing hoards of developers to its ranks. When used in combination with ASP.NET, Silverlight 4 provides developers with the tools and technology to build quick-to-market rich Internet applications.

Silverlight 4, in a broad sense, brings pretty much all the goodness of the .NET development platform to the browser. Almost everything you need from the .NET Frameworks that would apply in a browser environment is at your disposal. Oh, and did I mention that includes a CLR especially crafted for RIAs?

Learning Silverlight 4 is taking your learning path in a new and exciting direction. RIAs in themselves introduce a not-exactly-new but new-to-many-developers application model. You are essentially forced into a three-tier model that many, perhaps most, Microsoft developers have only given lip service to. You can no longer simply write ADO.NET code to directly access a database — you must go through a network service, be that HTTP or TCP-based, and for many developers, this will no doubt be something new to learn. However, for those who have been developing true three-tier applications for some time now, though it may not be a stumbling block, they will appreciate the added separation that this model imposes. Silverlight 4 does introduce .NET RIA Services, which goes a long way toward ameliorating this extra complexity.

Silverlight 4 is, as noted, light-years ahead of developing RIAs on AJAX. In some ways, Silverlight does not add much in the way of experiential capability over a rich AJAX framework (or a combination of them). A lot of the basic and not-so-basic animations and, of course, asynchronous capabilities can be had without Silverlight, and certainly it is easier today to build rich AJAX-based applications than in even very recent years past.

Nevertheless, it is still terribly difficult not only to build but also to maintain a truly rich Internet application on AJAX. Although we developers might enjoy the immense technological challenge; the exciting intellectual stimulation of dancing between CSS, HTML, XML, and JavaScript; the sheer joy of screaming at the monitor when the beautiful set of functionality you finally got working in Firefox totally falls apart in Internet Explorer; the exhilaration of dealing with angry customers who have somehow disabled (or had disabled by corporate policy) one of the several technical puzzle pieces your application relies on — we, in the end, could be putting our collective intelligence and valuable time into far more valuable and rewarding — for *everybody* — enterprises.

And this is one of the chief areas where Silverlight 4 rushes to the rescue. By giving you a reliable CLR; .NET Frameworks; the WPF-based presentation core (including controls, data binding, and much more); a better networking stack; local, isolated storage; a rich IDE with rich debugging, IntelliSense, and LINQ (and even a Dynamic Language Runtime, DLR); and WCF RIA Services; Silverlight makes developing rich *interactive* applications far more feasible for everybody, especially our patrons (businesses), who are concerned with the total cost of ownership, not just what's technically feasible. And for developers, except for those few die-hard JavaScripters, Silverlight will undoubtedly be a source of newfound joy in productivity and empowerment.

WHO THIS BOOK IS FOR

This book was written to introduce you to the features and capabilities that Silverlight 4 offers, as well as to give you an explanation of the foundation that Silverlight provides. We assume you have a general understanding of the .NET Framework, C#, and the basics of web technologies.

In addition to these aforementioned items, we also assume that you understand basic programming constructs, such as variables, `for each` loops, and the basics of object-oriented programming.

WHAT THIS BOOK COVERS

This book embodies the Wrox philosophy of programmer to programmer. We are experienced programmers writing for other programmers. We wrote the book with the average business application developer in mind. Certainly, others can derive value — anyone trying to build on or even to just understand the architectural concerns and realities of Silverlight — but this is at its heart a true programmer's companion.

The book explores the release of Silverlight 4. It covers each major new feature in detail. This book consists of 21 chapters, each covering a separate functional area of the Silverlight platform. Additionally five appendixes provide additional ancillary information to the reader.

WHAT YOU NEED TO USE THIS BOOK

To work through these examples, you will need to be using the .NET Framework 4. This version of the framework will run on Windows XP, Windows 2003, Windows 7, and the latest Windows Server 2008 R2. To write any of this code, you will need to have the .NET 4 SDK installed.

Though it is possible to do all this in a simple text editor, you are probably going to want to install Visual Studio 2010. Installing Visual Studio will also install the .NET Framework 4 to your machine. At the time of this writing, you are going to need to go to http://www.silverlight.net and install the latest Silverlight 4 Tools for Visual Studio either using the Microsoft Web Platform Installer or the executable provided on the site. Another install you are probably also going to need from the same website is the WCF RIA Services install.

CONVENTIONS

To help you get the most from the text and keep track of what's happening, we've used a number of conventions throughout the book.

 Boxes with a warning icon like this one hold important, not-to-be-forgotten information that is directly relevant to the surrounding text.

The pencil icon indicates notes, tips, hints, tricks, or asides to the current discussion.

As for styles in the text:

➤ We *highlight* new terms and important words when we introduce them.

➤ We show keyboard strokes like this: Ctrl+A.

➤ We show filenames, URLs, and code within the text like so: `persistence.properties`.

➤ We present code in two different ways:

```
We use a monofont type with no highlighting for most code examples.
We use bold to emphasize code that is particularly important in the present context
or to show changes from a previous code snippet.
```

SOURCE CODE

As you work through the examples in this book, you may choose either to type in all the code manually, or to use the source code files that accompany the book. All the source code used in this book is available for download at `http://www.wrox.com`. When at the site, simply locate the book's title (use the Search box or one of the title lists) and click the Download Code link on the book's detail page to obtain all the source code for the book. Code that is included on the website is highlighted by the following icon:

Available for
download on
Wrox.com

In some cases (for example, when the code is just a snippet), you'll find the filename in a code note such as this:

Code snippet filename

 Because many books have similar titles, you may find it easiest to search by ISBN; this book's ISBN is 978-0-470-65092-9.

Once you download the code, just decompress it with your favorite compression tool. Alternatively, you can go to the main Wrox code download page at www.wrox.com/dynamic/books/download.aspx to see the code available for this book and all other Wrox books.

ERRATA

We make every effort to ensure that there are no errors in the text or in the code. However, no one is perfect, and mistakes do occur. If you find an error in one of our books, like a spelling mistake or faulty piece of code, we would be very grateful for your feedback. By sending in errata, you may save another reader hours of frustration, and at the same time, you will be helping us provide even higher quality information.

To find the errata page for this book, go to www.wrox.com and locate the title using the Search box or one of the title lists. Then, on the book details page, click the Book Errata link. On this page, you can view all errata that has been submitted for this book and posted by Wrox editors. A complete book list, including links to each book's errata, is also available at www.wrox.com/misc-pages/booklist.shtml.

If you don't spot "your" error on the Book Errata page, go to www.wrox.com/contact/techsupport .shtml and complete the form there to send us the error you have found. We'll check the information and, if appropriate, post a message to the book's errata page and fix the problem in subsequent editions of the book.

P2P.WROX.COM

For author and peer discussion, join the P2P forums at p2p.wrox.com. The forums are a web-based system for you to post messages relating to Wrox books and related technologies and interact with other readers and technology users. The forums offer a subscription feature to e-mail you topics of interest of your choosing when new posts are made to the forums. Wrox authors, editors, other industry experts, and your fellow readers are present on these forums.

At http://p2p.wrox.com, you will find a number of different forums that will help you, not only as you read this book, but also as you develop your own applications. To join the forums, just follow these steps:

1. Go to p2p.wrox.com and click the Register link.

2. Read the terms of use and click Agree.

3. Complete the required information to join, as well as any optional information you wish to provide, and click Submit.

4. You will receive an e-mail with information describing how to verify your account and complete the joining process.

You can read messages in the forums without joining P2P, but in order to post your own messages, you must join.

Once you join, you can post new messages and respond to messages other users post. You can read messages at any time on the Web. If you would like to have new messages from a particular forum e-mailed to you, click the Subscribe to this Forum icon by the forum name in the forum listing.

For more information about how to use the Wrox P2P, be sure to read the P2P FAQs for answers to questions about how the forum software works, as well as many common questions specific to P2P and Wrox booParks. To read the FAQs, click the FAQ link on any P2P page.

1

Introduction to Silverlight

WHAT'S IN THIS CHAPTER?

➤ Overviewing Silverlight

➤ Getting the Silverlight Plug-In and SDK

➤ Taking a Silverlight 4 Tour

Silverlight 4, the fourth iteration of the Silverlight platform, continues to deliver on the promise of Adobe Flash–like and Flex-like rich Internet applications (RIAs) built using a standards-based, open approach with HTML and XAML (eXtensible Application Markup Language) using tools like Visual Studio 2010 and Microsoft Expression Blend. Silverlight 4 continues to add excitement to RIA development with the expansion of the capabilities of the Base Class Libraries (BCLs) from the .NET Framework, new user interface (UI) controls, and new libraries for building line-of-business applications. The result is that not only do you have the rich, XAML markup to describe expressive user interfaces, you have the power of the .NET Framework and your language of choice (C#, VB, etc.) to build Silverlight applications. Even with the .NET Framework libraries, Silverlight still retains the cross-browser and cross-plat-form compatibility that it has had since the beginning. This includes Windows 2000, Windows XP, Windows Vista, Windows 7, Macintosh, and, through the Mono Project, various Linux distributions. To give you an idea of the flexibility of the client and server scenarios, you can build a Silverlight application and run it in a Safari web browser on an Apple Macintosh, while being served up from an Apache web server running on Linux.

There is a lot to learn about Silverlight, and you'll gain more and more insight with each chapter in this book.

This chapter does two basic things:

➤ It gives you an introduction to Silverlight.

➤ By covering the essentials on creating Silverlight applications, it sets the groundwork that helps for the rest of the book.

WHAT IS SILVERLIGHT?

Silverlight is a web-based platform for building and running RIAs. The web-based platform part of that equation is essentially the plug-in that runs inside the web browser. Silverlight applications execute within an ActiveX browser plug-in that installs onto the local machine via the web browser in the exact same manner that you install Adobe Flash to run Flash-based animations on web pages. The Silverlight plug-in supports the entire wow factor that you'd expect from an RIA, such as vector-based graphics and animations and full video integration, including Digital Rights Management (DRM) secured audio/video and high-definition video, as well as the tools for building rich line-of-business applications. You can boil down the coolness of Silverlight to the following points:

➤ Silverlight is a cross-platform, cross-browser platform for delivering rich, interactive applications.

➤ Silverlight 4 applications can be built using Expression Blend, Visual Studio, or Eclipse on Windows, and with Eclipse on Apple Macintosh computers.

➤ Silverlight supports playback of native Windows Media VC-1/WMA (with Digital Rights Management) as well as MPEG-4-based H.264 and AAC audio on PCs and Macs with no dependency on Windows Media Player, as well as full online and offline DRM capability for purchase and download, rental, and subscription capabilities.

➤ Silverlight supports playback of 720p+ full-screen HD Video.

➤ Using XAML, HTML, JavaScript, C#, or VB (or your managed language of choice, including dynamic languages like Ruby and Python), Silverlight delivers rich multimedia, vector graphics, animations, and interactivity beyond what AJAX can deliver.

➤ With the Base Class Libraries, you have access to common classes for generics, collections, and threading that you are accustomed to using in Windows client development.

➤ There are more than 60 controls in the Toolbox, and probably five times that many from third-party vendors.

➤ You can deliver out-of-browser experiences with elevated trust that can run any Silverlight 4 application just like a desktop application; including network access, COM interoperability, and local filesystem access.

➤ You can access video and audio resources, giving you the ability to record content that is streaming from an end user's local computer.

➤ There are multiple lines of business features, including a navigation framework, printing, drag-and-drop support, clipboard access, right-click events, and multi-directional text rendering.

➤ RIA Services, or the Business Application template, supply the framework, tools, and services that provide the server context of your application to the client, which simplifies the application model when building Silverlight applications.

➤ The installation package is less than 6MB on Windows and less than 12MB on Macintosh.

➤ Almost all of the same XAML and application logic created for Silverlight applications can be used in Windows Presentation Foundation (WPF) applications with no changes.

The Silverlight player is also known as a *plug-in*, or *control* — these terms are used interchangeably in the book, and you will see these variances when others talk about Silverlight as well. The player is a completely stand-alone environment; there is no dependency version of the .NET Framework on the client or the server to run Silverlight applications. When developing applications for Silverlight, you use tools (like Visual Studio 2010 or Expression Blend) that require or are based on a version of the Common Language Runtime (CLR), but the compiled Intermediate Language (IL) of your Silverlight applications that is parsed by the Silverlight player is not using a specific client version of the .NET Framework. The BCL for Silverlight is entirely self-contained within the player itself. The XAML and BCL used by the Silverlight player are both subsets of their counterparts that are used when building full desktop-based WPF applications. In Silverlight 4, the features in Silverlight and the CLR 4 version of WPF are coming closer together, which gives you more flexibility when designing applications that you intend to target both run times.

You might ask why Microsoft is pushing out another web-based, client-side technology when there is already ASP.NET, ASP.NET AJAX Extensions, and, with CLR 4 and Visual Studio 2010, specific project types that target Dynamic Data, MVC, and the ASP.NET AJAX Framework. The simple answer is that users are demanding an even richer experience on the Web. Even though AJAX does a lot for improved user experience — the postback nightmare of Web 1.0 is finally going away — it does not do enough. There is demand for a richer, more immersive experience on the Web. This has been accomplished with WPF on the Windows client side. WPF provides a unified approach to media, documents, and graphics in a single run time. The problem with WPF is that it is a 30-MB run time that runs only on the Windows OS. Microsoft needed to give the same type of experience that WPF offers, only in a cross-platform, cross-browser delivery mechanism. So what Microsoft did was take the concept of a plug-in model like Adobe Flash and mix it with the .NET Framework and the WPF declarative language in XAML, and they came up with a way to develop highly rich, immersive Web 2.0 applications.

 For a good comparison of what is in WPF and not in Silverlight 4, check out this link:

    http://msdn.microsoft.com/en-us/library/cc903925(VS.96).aspx

The big picture of Silverlight from an architecture perspective is shown in Figure 1-1. Each area is covered in more detail as you read along in the book.

As mentioned earlier, Silverlight can conceivably be fully supported across multiple browsers and operating systems. The current status for browser and OS support is identified in Table 1-1.

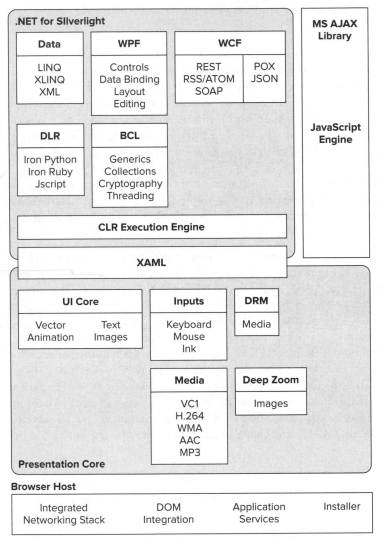

FIGURE 1-1

TABLE 1-1

OPERATING SYSTEM	BROWSER SUPPORTED
Windows Vista Windows Server 2008	Windows Internet Explorer 7, 8 Firefox 2, 3 Google Chrome

OPERATING SYSTEM	BROWSER SUPPORTED
Windows 7	Windows Internet Explorer 8 Firefox 2, 3 Google Chrome
Windows Server 2008 R2	Windows Internet Explorer 8 Google Chrome
Windows XP SP2, SP3	Windows Internet Explorer 6, 7, 8 Firefox 2, 3 Google Chrome
Windows Server 2003 (excluding IA-64)	Windows Internet Explorer 6, 7, 8 Firefox 2, 3 Google Chrome
Mac OS 10.4.8+	Firefox 2, 3 Safari 3 Safari 4

SILVERLIGHT VERSIONS EXPLAINED

If you have been following Silverlight, you might be a little confused over the versions that are available:

➤ **Silverlight 1.0** — Released in September of 2007, this is the first version of Silverlight and supports the JavaScript programming model. This means that your language choice is simple: JavaScript. JavaScript is used to interact with Silverlight objects that are executing within the Silverlight player in the browser. There is no managed language support in Silverlight 1.0, which means no BCL for Silverlight 1.0.

➤ **Silverlight 2** — Released in late 2008, Silverlight 2 brought the ability to create RIA applications with the familiar code-behind programming model used in Windows Forms, ASP.NET, and WPF development. Starting with Silverlight 2, you can use any CLR language to code Silverlight applications, and you have the power of the .NET Framework to interact with Silverlight objects. The ability to use the base class libraries and your .NET language of choice to build Silverlight applications truly revolutionized the way developers and designers looked at this new RIA platform.

➤ **Silverlight 3** — Released in mid-2009, Silverlight 3 included extensive enhancements to Silverlight 2 for building line-of-business applications as well as richer support for graphics and media.

➤ **Silverlight 4** — Released in April of 2010, Silverlight 4 continues with the focus on line-of-business–focused applications, and a more feature-complete RIA Services implementation is included, as well as a richer feature set for accessing local filesystem and COM resources in richer, out-of-browser experiences.

Silverlight uses an auto-update model for the player. When a new version of Silverlight is released, the player running in the browser is updated to the latest version automatically. There is also the commitment of backward compatibility, so your applications will not break when the player moves from version 1.0 to 2, or 2 to 3, and so on.

APPLICATION DEVELOPMENT SCENARIOS

When building Silverlight applications, you are likely to use one of the following scenarios:

➤ Your entire application is written in Silverlight, the player takes up 100 percent of the height and width of the browser, and all UI interaction is done through Silverlight.

➤ You implement an "Islands of Richness" scenario, in which your application is an ASP.NET application (or any other type of HTML-rendered application), and you build islands of your UI with Silverlight. Thus, you add richness to your web applications but you don't build the entire interaction using Silverlight.

➤ You create an out-of-browser (OOB) experience, with the specific need to use elevated permissions on the client machine. This means that you create more of a desktop-like experience and you can access the local filesystem, use COM interoperability, keyboard in full screen mode, and other out-of-browser–only features.

➤ You are building a mobile application that is targeting the Windows 7 Series Phone.

As the adoption of Silverlight grows, the type of application you decide to build most likely depends on the features you need. If you are slowly introducing Silverlight into your applications, the "Islands of Richness" scenario will be used. If you are going all out and need to access the My Documents folder of the client machine, you'll end up building an OOB application.

The area surrounded with the box in Figure 1-2 is an example of an "Islands of Richness" scenario in which Silverlight has been added to an existing web application. In this case, the image strip is a Silverlight control that plays a video in-page when an item is clicked. Silverlight enhances the "Islands of Richness" scenarios by allowing multiple Silverlight plug-ins and an easy way to communicate with each other in the browser. This also works across browsers; for example, a Silverlight application running in a Firefox browser can talk to a Silverlight application running in Internet Explorer 8 on the same machine.

Figure 1-3 shows an OOB experience. Notice that there is no *chrome* around the browser shell, giving the application a desktop-like experience.

Figure 1-4 shows a typical Silverlight application that takes up 100 percent of the viewable browser area, but is not running outside of the browser.

FIGURE 1-2

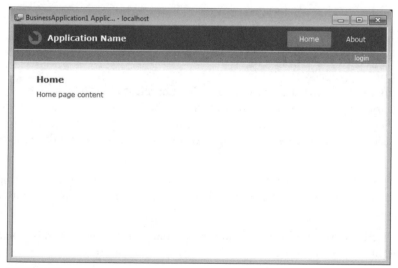

FIGURE 1-3

FIGURE 1-4

GETTING THE SILVERLIGHT PLUG-IN

The first time you navigate to a web page that contains a Silverlight application, the Silverlight player is not installed automatically; installation is similar to the Adobe Flash experience. There is a non-intrusive image on the page where the Silverlight content would have rendered that gives a link to download the player. Silverlight has two different prompts for installation — the standard install and the in-place install.

In a *standard install*, the Get Microsoft Silverlight image tells you that you need to install Silverlight to complete the experience on the web page you have arrived at. Figure 1-5 illustrates a page with the standard install images.

Once you click on the Get Microsoft Silverlight Installation image, one of two scenarios takes place. You are taken to the Silverlight Installation page on the Microsoft site (see Figure 1-6).

Or you are prompted to install Silverlight *in-place* with a download prompt, as shown in Figure 1-7.

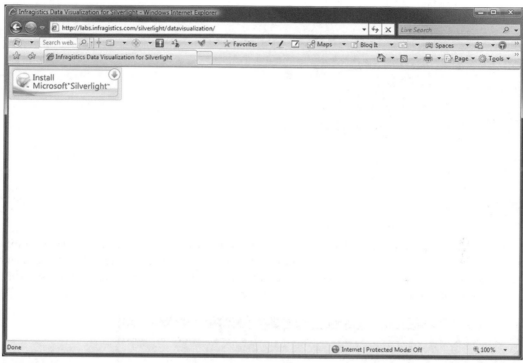

FIGURE 1-5

FIGURE 1-6

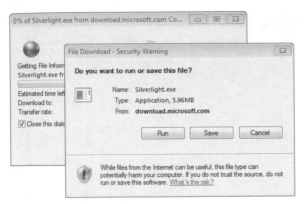

FIGURE 1-7

After the Silverlight player is installed, you never have to install it again. Silverlight also has built-in knowledge of updates, so once a new version of Silverlight is available, you are asked if you would like to install the update to get the latest version of the player. Once you refresh the browser, the Silverlight content is rendered correctly in the browser (see Figure 1-8).

FIGURE 1-8

GETTING THE SILVERLIGHT SDK

To build Silverlight applications, you need more than the Silverlight player. If you have not arrived at a page where you are prompted to install the Silverlight run time, you can easily get it on the Silverlight SDK page. There are also supporting files, help files, samples, and quick starts in the Silverlight Software Development Kit (SDK), which will give you the files you need to start building Silverlight applications. To get the SDK, go to `www.silverlight.net/getstarted/default.aspx`, as shown in Figure 1-9.

On the Get Started page, you can download all of the tools that you need to create Silverlight 4 applications:

➤   Silverlight run times for Mac and Windows operating systems

➤   Silverlight tools for Visual Studio 2010

➤   The latest version of Microsoft Expression Blend

➤   A trial version of Visual Studio 2010

More importantly, this page has links to dozens of videos, tutorials, and samples that will help you learn Silverlight.

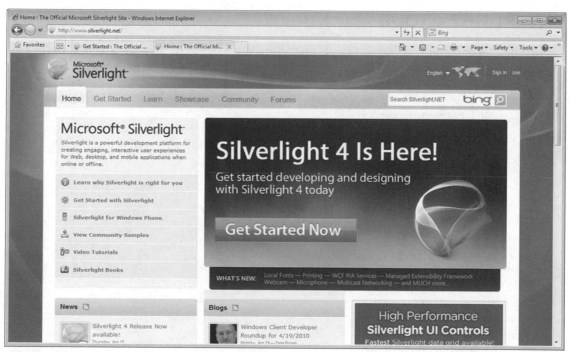

FIGURE 1-9

BUILDING SILVERLIGHT APPLICATIONS

Now that you have the Silverlight player installed and you know how to get the tools for Visual Studio that will give you the project templates, you can start building Silverlight applications. There are several ways to create Silverlight applications:

➤ **Visual Studio 2010 Silverlight Project Templates** — These include Silverlight Application, Silverlight Navigation Application, and Silverlight Class Library, as well as Silverlight Business Application.

➤ **Expression Blend 3 or Expression Blend 4** — This a tool in the Expression suite of products from Microsoft that provides project templates for creating Silverlight and WPF projects and helps create vector-based graphics for your Silverlight user interface as well as aids in screen prototyping with the Sketch Flow feature.

➤ **Eclipse using the Eclipse Plug-In** — There is an Eclipse plug-in for both Windows-based and Apple Macintosh–based operating systems.

In the following chapters, you will get a better understanding of the details for how to build applications using Visual Studio 2010 and Expression Blend.

SILVERLIGHT 4 TOUR

Silverlight 4 continues the improvements that Silverlight 3 delivered over Silverlight 2. In the next sections, we'll look at some of the more important features of Silverlight 4, including:

➤ XAML

➤ .NET Framework support

➤ Graphics and animations

➤ Page layout and design

➤ User interface controls

➤ Audio and video, including capturing audio and video

➤ Local data storage

➤ Out-of-browser capability

➤ Local filesystem access

➤ Navigation Framework

➤ Ink support

➤ Network access

➤ Data binding

➤ Printing

➤ Drag-and-drop

➤ Clipboard access

➤ Deep Zoom technology

Throughout the book, you learn about each of the items listed in much more detail. The following sections are designed to set the stage for what's to come as you explore the full capability of Silverlight 4.

XAML

If you are not familiar with WPF, you are probably not familiar with XAML. Since the dawn of Visual Studio, there has always been code and UI design separation. This means that a developer can write code, while a designer just works on the design and layout aspects of an application. This had never been realized, mostly because developers and designers were always using different tools and different languages. With the introduction of XAML, however, there was finally a unified markup that could not only describe what a control is and how it fits into a page, but also how layout and, more importantly, the overall look and feel of the controls on a page are defined. A designer can use XAML to create a mockup of a page or an application, and a developer can take that XAML markup and use it directly in her project files. Because partial classes and code-behind files in Visual Studio 2010 allow you to separate the code logic from the layout and control definitions, using XAML gives you the opportunity to have this separation of the design from the code.

XAML elements are objects that map to classes in the Silverlight run time. So when you declare a XAML `TextBlock` like this:

```
<TextBlock />
```

you are actually creating a new instance of the `TextBlock` class like this:

```
TextBlock t = new TextBlock();
```

The following code demonstrates a XAML snippet from a Silverlight application that shows *Hello World* in a `TextBlock`:

```
<Canvas>
    <TextBlock>Hello World</TextBlock>
</Canvas>
```

The next code listing shows how the XAML can get more complex, demonstrating adding animations to the `TextBlock` element. In this example, a `RotateTransform` is being applied to a `TextBlock` control via a `DoubleAnimation` in a `StoryBoard` object. This action is triggered when the `UserControl` loads, through the `RoutedEvent Canvas.Loaded`. If you run the XAML, you will see that the text *Hello World* rotates in a 360-degree circle.

 In Chapter 18, you learn how animations work in Silverlight and how they are used to bring your application to life in the Silverlight player.

```
<StackPanel Margin="4"
            HorizontalAlignment="Center"
            Orientation="Horizontal">
    <TextBlock Width="200" Height="150"
               FontSize="24">Hello World

        <TextBlock.Triggers>
            <EventTrigger RoutedEvent="Canvas.Loaded">
                <EventTrigger.Actions>
                    <BeginStoryboard>
                        <Storyboard BeginTime="0"
                                    RepeatBehavior="Forever">
                            <DoubleAnimation
                                Storyboard.TargetName="rotate"
                                Storyboard.TargetProperty="Angle"
                                To="360"
                                Duration="0:0:10"/>
                        </Storyboard>
                    </BeginStoryboard>
                </EventTrigger.Actions>
            </EventTrigger>
        </TextBlock.Triggers>

        <TextBlock.RenderTransform>
            <RotateTransform x:Name="rotate"
                             Angle="0"
                             CenterX="300"
                             CenterY="200"/>
        </TextBlock.RenderTransform>
    </TextBlock>
</StackPanel>
```

In Appendix A, you can gain more insight into XAML and how you can use it to define and create your Silverlight applications. You will also get your fair share of XAML throughout the book, because it is how you create most of the examples and applications that we have created. Tools like Microsoft Expression Blend and Visual Studio 2010 are all Rapid Application Development (RAD) tools that you can use to create your Silverlight applications. Besides using Expression Blend or Visual Studio 2010, you can look to other XAML tools like XAMLPad or Kaxaml to help you learn XAML. In Chapter 2, you will learn more of the specifics on building Silverlight applications using Visual Studio.

.NET Framework Support

A key aspect of Silverlight, and probably the most exciting aspect of this technology, is its support for the CLR and BCL of the .NET Framework. Although these are not the exact set of class libraries you are familiar with using on the desktop, and the CLR might handle memory management and optimizations slightly differently than it does on the desktop or server, they do provide the fundamental capabilities of the .NET Framework for your use in building rich Silverlight applications.

Execution of content targeting the Silverlight player is handled by the CoreCLR. The *CoreCLR* is a smaller, refactored version of the CLR used in full .NET desktop applications. Although the

Microsoft Intermediate Language (MSIL) is exactly the same between the CLRs, the CoreCLR is stripped of the unnecessary scenarios that are not needed for Silverlight 3 development. The CLR is still responsible for managing memory in Silverlight applications, as well as enforcing the common type system (CTS). Some examples of the differences in the CoreCLR versus the full CRL are:

➤ The JIT Compiler in the CoreCLR is enhanced for fast startup time, while the full CLR is enhanced for more complex optimizations.

➤ In ASP.NET applications, the garbage collection mode is tuned for multiple worker threads, whereas the CoreCLR is tuned for interactive applications.

Both the CoreCLR and CLR can run in the same process; therefore, for example, you can have an embedded Silverlight player running in an Office Business application that also includes a full .NET 3.5 plug-in. The isolation of the CoreCLR is why you can run Silverlight applications on machines that do not have any versions of the .NET Framework installed; this is further highlighted by the fact that Silverlight can run on Macintosh operating systems.

The namespaces that contain all of the classes that you interact with in your Code window are the Base Class Libraries, as you have learned. The Silverlight BCL does not contain namespaces and classes that do not make sense for client development, such as code-access security, ASP.NET Web Server–specific classes, and many others.

Graphics and Animations

A big part of why Silverlight is an exciting technology is that it provides a rich, vector-based drawing system as well as support for complex animations. Some key features include:

➤ Perspective three-dimensional (3D) graphics

➤ Pixel-Shader effects, including `Blur` and `DropShadow`

➤ Bitmap Caching to increase the rendering performance

➤ Animation effects like `Spring` and `Bounce`

➤ Local font usage for rendering text

For vector-based drawing, Silverlight supports `Geometry` and `Shape` objects that include support for rendering shapes, such as ellipse, line, path, polygon, polyline, and rectangle. These classes give you the ability to render any type of visual display. For example, the following XAML displays an image in its normal, square shape:

```
<Canvas>
    <Image
        Source="Images/elk.jpg"
        Width="200" Height="150">
    </Image>
</Canvas>
```

Using the `EllipseGeometry` class, you can clip the image into whatever shape you desire. This XAML clips the image into an oval:

```
<Canvas>
    <Image
        Source="Images/elk.jpg"
        Width="200" Height="150">
        <Image.Clip>
            <EllipseGeometry
                RadiusX="100"
                RadiusY="75"
                Center="100,75"/>
        </Image.Clip>
    </Image>
</Canvas>
```

The results are shown in Figure 1-10.

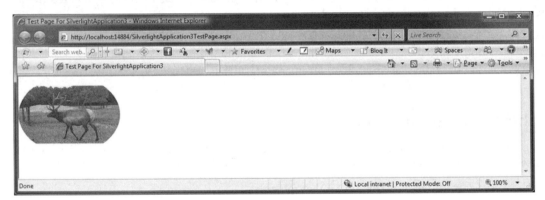

FIGURE 1-10

Once you render your geometries or shapes into something meaningful, you can use `Brushes`, `VideoBrushes`, or `Transforms` to further give life to your UI rendering. The following XAML takes a basic `TextBlock` and adds a `LinearGradientBrush` for some nice special effects:

```
<TextBlock
    Canvas.Top="100"
    FontFamily="Verdana"
    FontSize="32"
    FontWeight="Bold">
    Linear Gradient Brush
    <TextBlock.RenderTransform>
        <ScaleTransform ScaleY="4.0" />
    </TextBlock.RenderTransform>
    <TextBlock.Foreground>
        <LinearGradientBrush StartPoint="0,0" EndPoint="1,1">
            <GradientStop Color="Red" Offset="0.0" />
            <GradientStop Color="Blue" Offset="0.2" />
            <GradientStop Color="Green" Offset="0.4" />
            <GradientStop Color="Olive" Offset="0.6" />
            <GradientStop Color="DodgerBlue" Offset="0.8" />
            <GradientStop Color="OrangeRed" Offset="1.0" />
```

```
            </LinearGradientBrush>
        </TextBlock.Foreground>
    </TextBlock>
```

You can also use an `ImageBrush` to paint an image on your `TextBlock`, as the following code demonstrates:

```xml
<StackPanel>
    <!--TextBlock without an ImageBrush -->
    <TextBlock
        FontSize="72"
        FontFamily="Verdana"
        FontStyle="Italic"
        FontWeight="Bold">
            Rhino Image
        </TextBlock>

    <!--TextBlock with an ImageBrush -->
    <TextBlock
        FontSize="72"
        FontFamily="Verdana"
        FontStyle="Italic"
        FontWeight="Bold">
            Rhino Image
        <!-- Add an Image as the foreground -->
        <TextBlock.Foreground>
        <ImageBrush ImageSource="Images/rhino.jpg"
                Stretch="Fill"/>
        </TextBlock.Foreground>
    </TextBlock>
</StackPanel>
```

The results are shown in Figure 1-11.

Later in this section, you will see a `VideoBrush` applied to text. In Chapter 18, we'll cover graphics and animations in full detail.

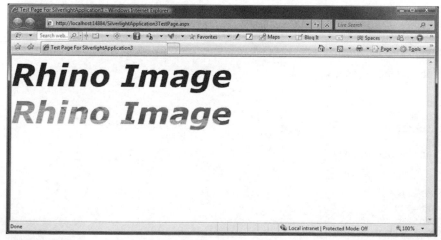

FIGURE 1-11

Page Layout and Design

Silverlight includes several options for doing rich, resolution-independent layout using a `Canvas`, `DockPanel`, `Grid`, `StackPanel`, and `WrapPanel` element. These five major layout panels can be described as:

➤ `Canvas` — An absolute positioning panel that gives you an area within which you can position child elements by coordinates relative to the `Canvas` area. A `Canvas` can parent any number of child `Canvas` objects.

➤ `DockPanel` — Used to arrange a set of objects around the edges of a panel. You specify where a child element is located in the `DockPanel` with the `Dock` property.

➤ `Grid` — Similar to an HTML table, it's a set of columns and rows that can contain child elements.

➤ `StackPanel` — A panel that automatically arranges its child elements into horizontal or vertical rows

➤ `WrapPanel` — Allows the arrangement of elements in a vertical or horizontal list and has elements automatically wrap to the next row or column when the height or width limit of the panel is reached.

Once you decide how you are going to lay out your page using one of the layout types, you can use other means of positioning individual elements as well. For example, you can change margins, set the `ZOrder` or `Border` of an object, or perform `RotateTranforms` to change the position of an object. Chapter 5 covers all layout options in greater detail. Here we'll look at the `Canvas` object and how it behaves.

The `Canvas` essentially becomes the container for other child elements, and all objects are positioned using their X- and Y-coordinates relative to their location in the parent canvas. This is done with the `Canvas.Top` and `Canvas.Left` attached properties, which provide the resolution-independent pixel value of a control's X- and Y-coordinates. The following code shows a `Canvas` object with several child elements absolutely positioned within the `Canvas`:

```
<Canvas>
    <Rectangle
    Canvas.Top ="30"
    Canvas.Left="30"
    Fill="Blue"
    Height="100" Width="100"/>

    <Rectangle
    Canvas.Top ="75"
    Canvas.Left="130"
    Fill="Red"
    Height="100" Width="100"/>

    <Ellipse
    Canvas.Top ="100"
    Canvas.Left="30"
    Fill="Green"
    Height="100" Width="100"/>
</Canvas>
```

Figure 1-12, demonstrates the location of the objects in the canvas.

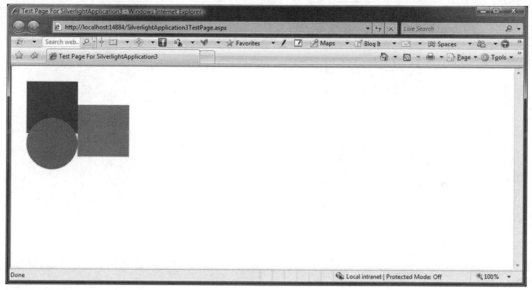

FIGURE 1-12

In the following example from the SDK, you can see how a `DockPanel` can be configured to return the results shown in Figure 1-13:

```
<StackPanel x:Name="LayoutRoot" Background="White">
    <TextBlock Margin="5" Text="Dock Panel" />
    <Border BorderBrush="Red" BorderThickness="2" >
        <controls:DockPanel LastChildFill="true"
                            Height="265">
            <Button Content="Dock: Left"
                    controls:DockPanel.Dock ="Left" />
            <Button Content="Dock: Right"
                    controls:DockPanel.Dock ="Right" />
            <Button Content="Dock: Top"
                    controls:DockPanel.Dock ="Top" />
            <Button Content="Dock: Bottom"
                    controls:DockPanel.Dock ="Bottom" />
            <Button Content="Last Child" />
        </controls:DockPanel>
    </Border>
</StackPanel>
```

 To test out the above code using the `DockPanel`, *you need to install the Silverlight Control Toolkit. You can get this on the same page that you download the Silverlight Tools for Visual Studio at* `http://silverlight.codeplex .com/Release/ProjectReleases.aspx?ReleaseId=36060.`

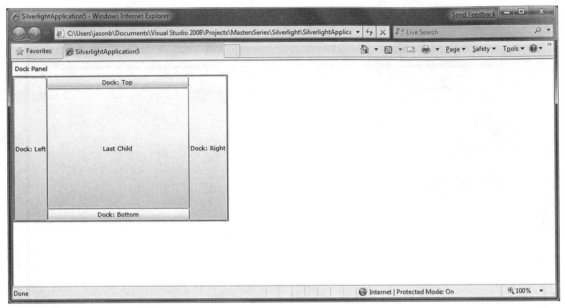

FIGURE 1-13

In Figure 1-13, notice the position of the elements based on the `TextBlock` and `Border` controls that wrap the `DockPanel` in the XAML.

User Interface Controls

Silverlight adds an even greater number of controls to the Toolbox for creating user interfaces. The Toolbox in Visual Studio 2010 is now filled with controls that can be dragged onto forms to build the user interface. The following controls are included for use by the core Silverlight 4 player:

AutoCompleteBox	Ellipse	RadioButton
Border	Frame	Rectangle
Button	Grid	ScrollBar
Calendar	GridSplitter	ScrollViewer
Canvas	HyperlinkButton	Slider
CheckBox	Image	StackPanel
ComboBox	Label	TabControl
ContentControl	ListBox	TextBlock
DataGrid	MediaElement	TextBox
DataPager	MultiScaleImage	TreeView
DatePicker	Password	
DockPanel	ProgressBar	

In addition to the aforementioned controls, the Silverlight Toolkit, which is a separate download from CodePlex, contains several very useful additions to the core list.

When working with any of the controls, remember that they are just like any other control model: The XAML controls in Silverlight can be instantiated in code, and properties can be retrieved or set on them. Over the next several chapters, you learn about the controls and how they can be used with Visual Studio 2010 or Expression Blend.

Using Media in Silverlight

One could argue that the entire reason for Silverlight was to provide rich, multimedia experiences on web pages, which essentially means audio and video on web pages. If you take a look at the top 100 trafficked websites on the Internet, almost all of them have video playing on the home page or use video prevalently throughout. Silverlight 4 continues to add first-class media capability to the player.

Adding Video to Web Pages

To add video or audio to a web page, set the `Source` property on the `MediaElement` object. The following code demonstrates playing the video file car.wmv automatically when the canvas is loaded:

```
<Grid x:Name="LayoutRoot" Background="White">
    <MediaElement Source="Images/video1.wmv" />
</Grid>
```

The `Source` property is the URI of a valid video or audio file. In the preceding code example, the source file is located in the deployment directory of your Silverlight application. Your media files can be located in various locations, including the website folder structure you are running the page from, or from a remote site. In either case, in order to maintain cross-platform support, you must use "/" in place of "\" in your URIs. For example:

```
<MediaElement Source="..\..\car.wmv"></MediaElement>
```

should read:

```
<MediaElement Source="../../car.wmv"></MediaElement>
```

If the `Source` property points to a file on a Windows Media Server using the MMS protocol, the player automatically attempts to stream the video down to the client. The default behavior is a progressive download, which means that the audio or video begins playing immediately and background-loads as you are playing the media. The drawback to progressive downloads is that even if you pause the video, it still downloads the media file, even if you never intended to continue playing it. With streaming media, the only data that is downloaded is the data that you actually play, which is a more efficient use of network resources.

Supported Audio and Video Formats

The `MediaElement` supports the Advanced Stream Redirector (ASX) playlist file format, as well as the audio and video formats listed in Table 1-2.

TABLE 1-2

VIDEO FORMATS	AUDIO FORMATS
WMV1: Windows Media Video 7	WMA 7: Windows Media Audio 7
WMV2: Windows Media Video 8	WMA 8: Windows Media Audio 8
WMV3: Windows Media Video 9	WMA 9: Windows Media Audio 9
WMVA: Windows Media Video Advanced Profile, non-VC-1	WMA 10: Windows Media Audio 10
WMVC1: Windows Media Video Advanced Profile, VC-1	AAC: Advanced Audio Coding — Can only be used for progressive download, smooth streaming, and adaptive streaming. AAC is the LC variety and supports sampling frequencies up to 48 kHz.
H.264 — Can only be used for progressive download, smooth streaming, and adaptive streaming. Supports Base, Main, and High Profiles.	MP3: ISO/MPEG Layer-3 with the following features:
	—Input — ISO/MPEG Layer-3 data stream
	—Channel Configurations — Mono, stereo
	—Sampling Frequencies — 8, 11.025, 12, 16, 22.05, 24, 32, 44.1, and 48 kHz
	—Bitrates — 8–320 Kbps, variable bitrate
	—Limitations — "Free format mode" (ISO/IEC 11172-3, subclause 2.4.2.3) is not supported.

Local Data Storage

Using the *isolated storage* concept, which behaves the same as it does in the full .NET Framework, you can use a client-side cache location to store data. This means that you can take commonly needed data, and, instead of always having to go back to the server to retrieve it, you can store it locally and access it locally. Examples might be a list of states or countries, or Buddy Lists for instant messenger clients. This data is commonly needed for fast access but does not change often enough to warrant constant round-trips back to the server to retrieve it.

By default, Silverlight gives you 1MB of local storage. This can be increased by prompting the user to allow for more local storage or can be accessed via the Silverlight Configuration screen. As its name implies, this is isolated storage, so you cannot access the end user's filesystem or do anything that would break the partial trust sandbox that Silverlight runs in. Storage is granted per application, so, for example, you might have `www.someapp.com`, which is using 10MB of storage, and another application running on the same client computer from a different domain that has its own 20MB of isolated storage. The storage areas are independent of each other; there is no limit to the number of applications that can have isolated storage on a client machine.

Out-of-Browser Experiences

With the enhanced OOB capability in Silverlight, an end user can install your application to the desktop on his or her Windows-based or Apple Macintosh computer. There is no need to install any special assemblies or controls to make this work — it is part of the native Silverlight experience. Using APIs that detect whether an application is running outside of the browser, and that check for the network connected state, an OOB application can react intelligently based on its current state. If you build an OOB application, you can also use elevated permissions on the client machine, which gives you the following features:

➤ Keyboard support in full screen mode

➤ Offline DRM

➤ HTML hosting

➤ Notification window

➤ Local filesystem access

➤ Cross-domain access

 In Chapter 9, you learn how easy it is to actually create this out-of-browser experience and use the features I have mentioned above.

Local Filesystem Access

When running an application with elevated privileges in OOB mode, you can access the client machine's local filesystem. This is limited to the GetSpecialFolder enumeration of the *My* folders, such as My Documents, My Music, and the like. This enumeration does include folders like *Desktop*. However, you cannot access the files on the desktop; you can access only the *My* folders. In Chapter 9, you learn how to access the local filesystem in an out-of-browser application.

Navigation Framework

Silverlight includes two controls that enable complete browser-journal back/forward integration with your application. Using the new Frame and Page controls, you can partition your views into separate XAML files (instead of separate UserControl objects as you did in Silverlight 2) and navigate to each view as simply as you previously navigated to a web page. The Navigation Framework also allows you to implement deep linking support in your Silverlight application, which builds on the SEO (Search Engine Optimization) enhancements added in Silverlight 3.

The following XAML shows the navigation control added to a UserControl:

```
<navigation:Frame x:Name="Frame"
                   Source="/Views/HomePage.xaml"
                   HorizontalContentAlignment="Stretch"
                   VerticalContentAlignment="Stretch"
                   Padding="15,10,15,10"
                   Background="White"/>
```

And the following code demonstrates the Navigate method of the Frame class, which is how you move from Page to Page:

```
private void NavButton_Click(object sender, RoutedEventArgs e)
{
    Button navigationButton = sender as Button;
```

```
        String goToPage = navigationButton.Tag.ToString();
        this.Frame.Navigate(new Uri(goToPage, UriKind.Relative));
}
```

As well as `Navigate`, the `Frame` class includes other useful methods such as `Navigated`, `NavigationFailed`, and `NavigationStopped` that give you complete control over the navigation life cycle of your `Page` object. Chapter 4 talks more about the `Navigation` and `Frame` classes.

Annotation and Ink

Like WPF, Silverlight has full support for ink input in the player. Using the `InkPresenter` object, you can give users an input area where they can use the mouse or an input device to handwrite. Using the application interface for the `InkPresenter` object, the application developer collects the `Stroke` objects that are written and persists them to a location on the server for later use. An example of where ink might be cool on a web page is a simple blog, where text and ink can combine to create a great visual output for whatever the blog is about. The XAML in the following code shows how to create an `InkPresenter` object:

```
<InkPresenter x:Name="inkInput" Cursor="Stylus"
    MouseLeftButtonDown="inkInput_MouseLeftButtonDown"
    MouseMove="inkInput_MouseMove"
    MouseLeftButtonUp="inkInput_MouseLeftButtonUp"/>
```

Notice that events are wired up for the various mouse behaviors. Each action of the mouse — the `Move`, `LeftButtonUp`, and `LeftButtonDown` — has a method in the code-behind that acts on the strokes of the input device. The following code provides an example of how to collect the strokes from the `InkPresenter`:

```
private Stroke MyStroke = null;

private void inkInput_MouseLeftButtonDown
    (object sender, MouseButtonEventArgs e)
{
    inkInput.CaptureMouse();
    StylusPointCollection
        MyStylusPointCollection = new StylusPointCollection();
    MyStylusPointCollection.Add
        (e.StylusDevice.GetStylusPoints(inkInput));
    MyStroke = new Stroke(MyStylusPointCollection);
    inkInput.Strokes.Add(MyStroke);
}

private void inkInput_MouseMove
    (object sender, MouseEventArgs e)
{
    if (MyStroke != null)
    {
        MyStroke.StylusPoints.Add
            (e.StylusDevice.GetStylusPoints(inkInput));
        txtBlock.Text =
            "" + e.StylusDevice.GetStylusPoints(inkInput)[0].X;
        txtBlock.Text =
            "" + e.StylusDevice.GetStylusPoints(inkInput)[0].Y;
```

```
            }

        }

    private void inkInput_MouseLeftButtonUp
        (object sender, MouseButtonEventArgs e)
    {
        MyStroke = null;
    }
```

Once you have the ink data collected, you can store it locally on the client machine, put it into a database, or even save the ink as an image.

Accessing the Network

To access network resources in Silverlight, use the classes in the `System.Net` namespaces and the `System.Net.Sockets` namespace. The namespace you choose depends on the type of network access you are trying to achieve. For basic HTTP or HTTPS access to URI-based resources, you can use the `WebClient` class in the `System.Net` namespace. Some examples of this type of network access are:

➤ Retrieving XML, JSON, RSS, or Atom data formats from a URI then parsing it on the client

➤ Downloading resources such as media or data to the browser cache

Using `WebClient`, you can perform the types of asynchronous operations that are common in browser-based applications. The following code demonstrates a simple method that grabs an image file from a network resource and downloads it to the browser cache:

```
    void DownloadFile(string imgPart)
    {
        WebClient wc = new WebClient();
        wc.OpenReadCompleted +=
            new OpenReadCompletedEventHandler
            (wc_OpenReadCompleted);
        wc.OpenReadAsync(new Uri("imgs.zip",
            UriKind.Relative), imgPart);
    }
```

If you need more flexibility in how you access HTTP or HTTPS resources, use the `HttpWebRequest` and `HttpWebResponse` classes.

If you need more direct and constant access to network resources or if you are working in a situation in which multiple clients are "listening" for the same server data, use the classes in the `System.Net.Sockets` namespace. Although both `Sockets` and `WebClient` allow asynchronous communication using the TCP protocol, `Sockets` gives you the ability to write *push-style* applications, where the server can communicate with the client in a more client–server manner. Imagine the unnecessary overhead when using basic AJAX timers (polling) to look for updated data on the server. If you were using sockets instead of this type of timer-based polling, you would reduce the amount of wasted bandwidth and would achieve tighter control of the data passing between the client and the server.

No matter how you choose to work with the network, both the `System.Net` and `System.Net .Sockets` namespaces support the ability to access network resources from other URIs than the originating domain. By default, a Silverlight application can always access resources from its origi-nating domain. Using a policy file, an application can access resources from different domains from the one containing its original URL. This cross-domain access is controlled by policy files that dic-tate the type of network domain access an application has. For `WebClient` requests, the same format used by Adobe Flash is supported. The following code is an example of a crossdomain.xml file:

```xml
<?xml version="1.0"?>
<! DOCTYPE cross-domain-policy
    SYSTEM "http://www.macromedia.com/xml/dtds/cross-domain-policy.dtd">
<cross-domain-policy>
    <allow-access-from domain="*" />
</cross-domain-policy>
```

In Chapter 10, you are fully exposed to various ways of accessing network resources.

Data Binding

Similarly to the data-binding features in WPF, Silverlight supports data-bound controls, XAML markup extensions, and support for data context binding. Most of the time, your bindings are set up in XAML, which is where the markup extensions come into play. In the following XAML, the `Text` property of the `TextBlock` element uses the `Binding` markup extension to bind the `Title` field from the data source:

```xml
<TextBlock x:Name="Title"
 Text="{Binding Title, Mode=OneWay}" />
```

The field `Title` from the original data source is retrieved from the data content of the control's par-ent element; in this case, the `TextBlock` could be contained in a `Canvas` or `Grid` object. Once you set the `DataContext` property for the parent element, the data contained in that object is available for binding to anything it contains. A more complete example of this data binding looks like this:

```xml
<Canvas x:Name="rootCanvas" Background="White" >
    <TextBlock x:Name="Title"
    Text="{Binding Title, Mode=OneWay }" />

    <TextBlock x:Name="Name"
    Text="{Binding Title, Mode=OneWay }" />
</Canvas>
```

You would then set the context in the code as follows:

```
LayoutRoot.DataContext = dataList;
```

The `dataList` object is an object that contains the data you are binding to the controls. In the case of simple `TextBlock` objects, you must handle the navigation between elements yourself. If you want a richer, tabular data display, use the `Grid` that is included with Silverlight. The XAML for the `DataGrid` control is as follows:

```xml
<data:DataGrid x:Name="dataGrid1"
    Height="120" Width="450"
    AutoGenerateColumns="True" />
```

The same `dataList` object can be bound to the grid in code such as this:

```
dataGrid1.ItemsSource = dataList;
```

All of the binding could be accomplished in code, but using the combination of XAML and code gives you greater flexibility when you build Silverlight applications. An interesting area of data binding in Silverlight is where the data actually comes from. Since the Silverlight player is a complete client-side solution, you are not creating connections to SQL Server or other data sources and then dumping that data into a data set in your code-behind. You will use technologies like WCF to access services on the Internet and then put the data you retrieve into objects that are bound to controls in Silverlight. In Chapter 7, you learn about the various types of data access, how to interact with different data formats, and how the data-binding mechanism works in Silverlight.

Printing

One of the most requested features is the ability to print the contents of the Silverlight control. Using the `PrintDocument` class's `Print` method, you can print whatever content is in the `PageVisual` property. By setting the `PageVisual` property to the root visual element, you can print the entire Silverlight control. Or by setting `PageVisual` to the named `UIElement` in the XAML of your page, you can print a portion of the Silverlight control.

Drag-and-Drop

Another highly anticipated feature of Silverlight 4 is its ability to handle a `Drop` event on a control. Using the `DragEventArgs` class, you can handle the following events when `AllowDrop` is set to `True` on any `UIElement`:

➤ `DragEnter`

➤ `DragLeave`

➤ `DragOver`

➤ `Drop`

This means that you can enable scenarios like allowing users to drag multiple files from their My Documents folder onto a Silverlight upload application or allowing users to drag-and-drop pictures from My Pictures onto a photo-editing application built in Silverlight.

Clipboard Access

You can now programmatically access the shared Clipboard object to Get or Set Unicode text information. It is important to note that in Silverlight, you are going to encounter a few differences from the Clipboard access that you might be used to in WPF and Windows Forms:

➤ You can access only Unicode text. You cannot access bitmap objects or streams.

➤ The end user is prompted one time per session to allow for access in partial trust mode, which is the default experience of a Silverlight application.

➤ Clipboard access is not valid from a Loaded event handler or from a constructor and access attempts throw exceptions.

Deep Zoom Graphics

Deep Zoom is a multi-scale image-rendering technology that partitions a very large image, or set of images, into smaller *tiles* that are rendered on demand to the Silverlight player. When an image is first loaded, it is in the lowest-resolution tiles. As the user zooms into the image using the mouse wheel or keyboard, higher-resolution images are loaded based on the area that is being zoomed into. To check this out yourself, take a look at the "CMA Be This Close" web site at yourself at http://www.cmafest.com/silverlight/bethisclose/. Firefly Logic , a design consultancy, built this application which lets users explore high-resolution images of their favorite country music artists at the annual Country Music Festival held in Nashville, Tennessee. The wow factor of Deep Zoom was shown off at Mix '08 in April 2008. In Figure 1-14, you can see the initial page loaded into the browser.

FIGURE 1-14

Once you start zooming in with the mouse wheel, you move to the higher-resolution images. Figure 1-15 shows the detail of a portion of the larger image seen in Figure 1-14.

FIGURE 1-15

SUMMARY

Silverlight brings a lot to the table for RIA development. It has progressed from its original release into much more than just a simple media player. Silverlight is a platform for developing rich line-of-business applications that have the data and input capability of ASP.NET with the media and interactive capabilities usually reserved for Adobe Flex applications.

2

Building Applications with Visual Studio

WHAT'S IN THIS CHAPTER?

> ➤ Creating a Silverlight application in Visual Studio 2010

> ➤ Using the various tools and property editors available for Silverlight projects

> ➤ Learning how the project structure and deployment works with Silverlight

> ➤ How to attach a Silverlight application to an existing Silverlight application

> ➤ Learning how partial classes and event handlers work

> ➤ Debugging a Silverlight application, including the steps for remote debugging on an Apple Macintosh computer

Now that you have a grasp on what Silverlight is, and what it can offer you as an RIA developer, it's time to get into the details of building Silverlight applications.

CREATING A BASIC SILVERLIGHT APPLICATION

The best way to understand how Silverlight works in Visual Studio is by building an application, so go ahead and open up Visual Studio 2010.

You'll notice that Visual Studio 2008 and earlier versions are not mentioned when discussing an IDE for building Silverlight 4 applications. Microsoft made a decision to support only Silverlight 4 in Visual Studio 2010, so you cannot use an earlier version of Visual Studio to design or compile Silverlight 4 applications. Note that you can multi-target with Visual Studio 2010 — you can choose to target a Silverlight 3 or Silverlight 4 application. You see where that comes in a little later in this chapter.

Once you've started Visual Studio, go ahead and start a new project. You can create a new project in one of several ways, highlighted in Figure 2-1:

➤ Select File ➪ New Project from the main menu.

➤ Hit Ctrl+Shift+N on your keyboard.

➤ Click New Project from the newly redesigned Start Page.

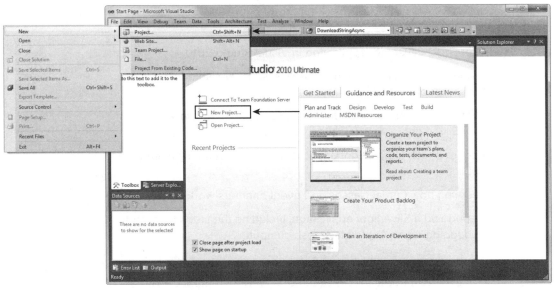

FIGURE 2-1

Once you perform one of those actions, you're prompted with the New Project dialog. In the Installed Templates pane (the left of the dialog), you should see Silverlight listed along with the other major template categories under the default language that you have chosen. Once you select Silverlight, you'll see five project templates, as shown in Figure 2-2.

Table 2-1 describes each project type and its purpose.

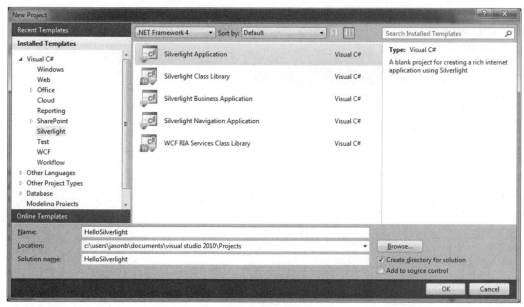

FIGURE 2-2

TABLE 2-1

PROJECT TYPE	DESCRIPTION
Silverlight Application	Basic Silverlight application with a default `MainPage.xaml` starting page that has no default content or navigation scheme
Silverlight Class Library	Standard class library project
Silverlight Business Application	Feature-rich Silverlight application that includes the WCF RIA Services features as well as a default `MainPage.xaml` with a built-in navigation
Silverlight Navigation Application	Basic Silverlight application that includes a `MainPage.xaml` with built-in navigation as well as several navigation views
WCF RIA Services Class Library	Standard class library project that includes additional references to WCF RIA Services–specific functionality
Silverlight Unit Test Application	Basic unit test stub project

For this very first application, do the following:

1. Select Silverlight Application from the New Project dialog.

2. Change the Name to HelloSilverlight.

3. Click OK.

Once you click OK, you are prompted with the New Silverlight Application dialog, which has some additional questions about the type of Silverlight application you want Visual Studio to create, as shown in Figure 2-3.

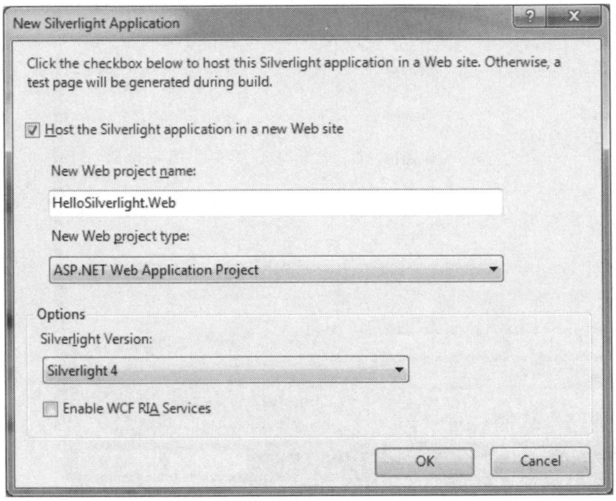

FIGURE 2-3

Because Silverlight is a client technology that runs inside of a web browser, the initial question this dialog is asking, Host the Silverlight application in a new Web site, lets Visual Studio know if you want to create a Silverlight application plus an ASP.NET project that will host the Silverlight application. If you uncheck this option, a stand-alone Silverlight project is created with no accompanying web application.

If you create a stand-alone Silverlight application, or someone e-mails a Silverlight project to you and you want to associate it with a new or existing ASP.NET application, follow these steps:

1. Create a new ASP.NET project or open an existing one.

2. Add the Silverlight project to the solution by right-clicking on the solution name and selecting Add ⇨ Existing Project from the context menu.

3. View the ASP.NET project's properties by right-clicking the project name and selecting Properties from the menu, by hitting Alt+Enter, or by selecting the Project ⇨ Properties.

Once the Properties window is open, you'll notice a Silverlight tab on the left side. If you select this tab, you'll see various options for adding a new or existing Silverlight project to the existing ASP.NET application.

In this case, make sure you leave the default values checked, and then click OK to create the solution and projects.

In Chapter 8, you learn about the details of WCF RIA Services, which is also an option in the New Silverlight Application dialog.

Once Visual Studio churns for a second to create the solution, based on your settings, you will see something similar to Figure 2-4.

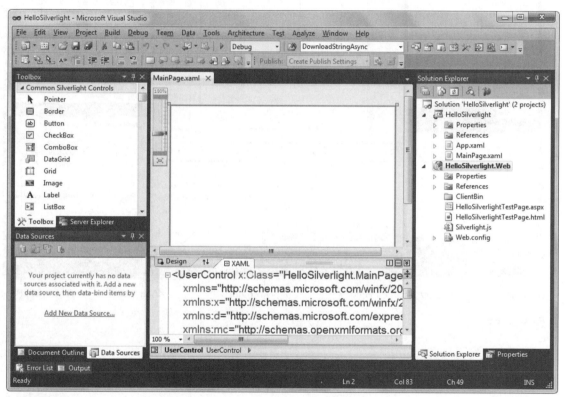

FIGURE 2-4

Using Silverlight Designer for Visual Studio

At this point, you have created a basic Silverlight application. It doesn't do anything yet; you will add functionality later. This section looks at what Visual Studio offers for Silverlight developers, as well as some of the details on how projects run inside of Visual Studio. As you have probably noticed, Visual Studio 2010 has the same feel as previous versions and the same basic layout. I have my Visual Studio set up with the default C# Developer settings, so on the right side, I see my Solution Explorer and Properties pane, and in the main area of the screen I have the default MainPage.xaml in a split view. Figure 2-5 highlights the various areas of Visual Studio as it pertains to Silverlight development.

Toolbox   Design Surface Zoom   Silverlight Design Surface   Split View   Solution Explorer

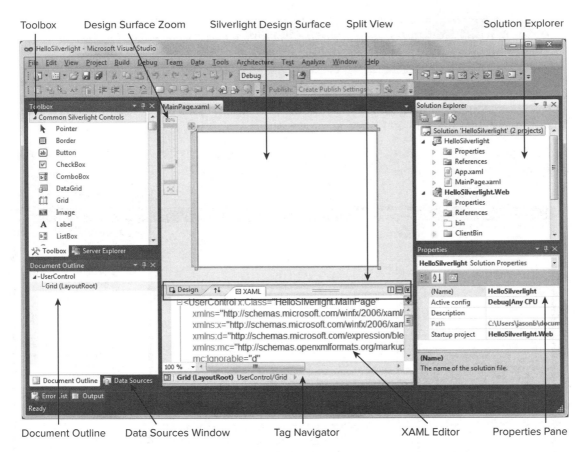

Document Outline   Data Sources Window   Tag Navigator   XAML Editor   Properties Pane

FIGURE 2-5

Table 2-2 looks at these key areas and describes what purpose they serve.

TABLE 2-2

VISUAL STUDIO FEATURE	DESCRIPTION
Silverlight Design Surface	The Design Surface is the visual surface where you design the layout for your application as well as drag controls or user controls from the Toolbox to create the user interface for your application. Everything displayed on the Design Surface is reflected in the XAML view.
Solution Explorer	The Solution Explorer contains the Silverlight project(s) and the ASP.NET web application projects.
Properties Pane	Using the Properties pane you set property values on controls that are selected on the Design Surface or in the XAML editor. Figure 2-6 highlights some of the key features of the Properties pane.

VISUAL STUDIO FEATURE	DESCRIPTION
XAML Editor	The XAML Editor is a synchronized XML view of the Design Surface. The XAML Editor includes IntelliSense, auto-formatting, syntax highlighting, and tag navigation.
Split View bar	The Split View bar lets you control the relative sizes of Design view and XAML view. You can also swap views, specify whether split view is horizontal or vertical, and collapse either view.
Tag Navigator	The Tag Navigator appears below the XAML view and lets you move to any parent tag of the currently selected tag in XAML view. When you move the mouse pointer over a tag in the Tag Navigator, a thumbnail preview is displayed for that element.
Data Sources Window	The Data Sources window allows you to drag any Entity Data Model tables onto the design surface. This process creates the business logic and data bindings automatically.
Document Outline	The Document Outline window provides a hierarchical view of the currently opened Design Surface.
Toolbox	The Toolbox contains Silverlight controls and components that can be dragged on the Design Surface or XAML Editor.
Design Surface Zoom	The Design Surface Zoom control gives you the ability to zoom the design surface down to 10% of its original size up to 20X its original size. If the design surface is zoomed in, and horizontal or vertical scroll-bars appear, you can pan to view parts of the design surface that are off-screen by pressing the spacebar and dragging the Design Surface. Note that in the lower left of the XAML Editor you can access the XAML Editor Zoom control. The XAML Editor will zoom from 20 percent of the original size to 400 percent of the original size of the displayed text.

Several interesting tools are available (all free, which is even better) that can either help you be more productive with XAML or help you learn/test out XAML snippets:

➤ `http://xamlcodesnippets.codeplex.com/` — This tool helps you create XAML snippets as well as gives you a nice integration with Visual Studio to insert XAML snippets into the XAML Editor.

➤ `http://blog.nerdplusart.com/archives/` `silverlight-code-snippets` — This website has several really useful XAML snippets, plus it is a great resource for learning various aspects of Silverlight.

➤ `http://kaxaml.com/` — This is a great tool that gives you a XAML Editor, complete with IntelliSense, to write and test XAML.

Using the Properties Pane

As Figure 2-6 demonstrates, several features on the Properties pane help you modify, find, and navigate to control properties.

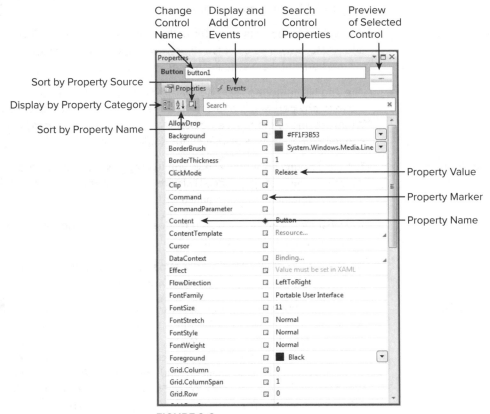

FIGURE 2-6

New to the Silverlight Designer for Visual Studio 2010 are enhanced tools on the Properties pane that make it easier to work with the richer visual features of Silverlight controls. As Figure 2-6 demonstrates, the first column displays the property name, the right column is the property value, and new to Visual Studio 2010 is the middle column, which contains the property marker. The property marker indicates whether there is a data binding or a resource applied to the property. When you click the property marker, you can open the Data Binding Builder or the Resource Picker. Figure 2-7 shows what the property marker context menu looks like.

Table 2-3 shows each type of custom Property Editor and their description.

TABLE 2-3

PROPERTY EDITOR	DESCRIPTION
Data Binding Builder	The Data Binding Builder lets you create data bindings without typing any XAML. You can create bindings to resources, data contexts, and element properties as well as apply value converters (see Figure 2-8).
Resource Picker	The Resource Picker lets you find and assign resources to properties in the Properties pane (see Figure 2-9).
Brush Editor	The Brush Editor gives you a UI similar to Expression Blend to set colors and create gradients for objects (see Figure 2-10).

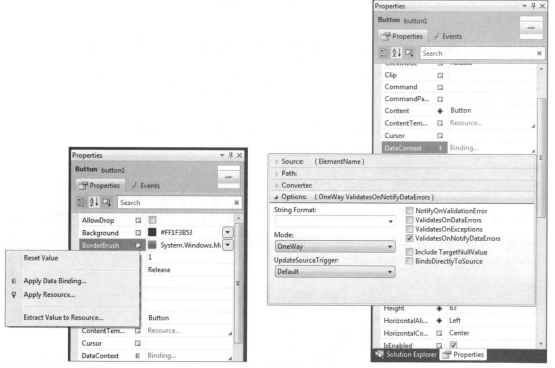

FIGURE 2-7   FIGURE 2-8

Before you go any further, take a look at the files in the projects that were created.

FIGURE 2-9

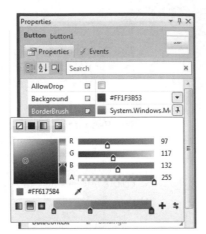

FIGURE 2-10

Creating Silverlight Project and Web Application Project Files

When you create a new Silverlight solution, and you choose the default option of creating a Silverlight project and a web application project to host the Silverlight project, Visual Studio generates a series of different files in each project.

Table 2-4 describes the Silverlight project files that are created by Visual Studio.

TABLE 2-4

FILENAME	DESCRIPTION
AppManifest.xml	This is the application manifest file that is required to generate the `.xap` file.
AssemblyInfo.cs or AssemblyInfo.vb	This file contains the name and version metadata that is embedded into the generated assembly.
References	mscorlib.dll System.dll System.Core.dll System.Net.dll System.Windows.dll System.Windows.Browser.dll System.Xml.dll
App.xaml	The `App` class is required by a Silverlight application to display the application user interface. The `App` class is implemented by using `App.xaml` and `App.xaml.cs` or `App.xaml.vb`. The `App` class is instantiated by the Silverlight plug-in after the application package (`.xap` file) is created.
MainPage.xaml	The `MainPage` class is used to create the user interface for the Silverlight application. The `MainPage` class derives from `UserControl`.

Expression Blend and Visual Studio share the same project and solution file structure, so any Silverlight project that is created in Visual Studio can be opened in Expression Blend, and vice versa.

Table 2-5 describes the web application project files that are created by Visual Studio.

TABLE 2-5

FILENAME	DESCRIPTION
AssemblyInfo.cs or AssemblyInfo.vb	This file contains the name and version metadata that is embedded into the generated assembly.
Client Bin folder	This is the deployment folder for the XAP file, which is created when you build the application. The details of a XAP file are covered later in this chapter.
HelloSilverlightTestPage.aspx	An `.aspx` file that is the default startup web page. The name of this file is a concatenation of the name of the Silverlight application project and the text "TestPage.aspx".
HelloSilverlightTestPage.html	An HTML file that is used to configure and instantiate the Silverlight plug-in, which downloads and runs the Silverlight application. The name of this file is a concatenation of the name of the Silverlight application project and the text "TestPage.html".
Silverlight.js	A JavaScript helper file that contains functions to initialize Silverlight plug-in instances and functions for determining the client's installed version of the plug-in.
Web.config	A website configuration file.

Using the Silverlight Design Surface

The split view by default will have the screen you are working with on the top half of the window, and the XAML for that screen on the lower half of the window. If you are coming from Windows Forms or ASP.NET development, the spilt screen exists, but you may not be used to a split screen by default. The main reason the split screen exists is that in previous versions of Visual Studio, there was no WYSIWYG designer for Silverlight. When you created the UI for your application, it was all done by typing XAML. The design surface was considered a Previewer rather than a drag-and-drop surface. Visual Studio 2010 is the first version of Visual Studio that brings this RAD capability to building Silverlight applications. As you learned in Chapter 1 and can further examine in Appendix A, XAML is a declarative markup language that defines the user interface and binds the user interface to the code that drives the interactions with the user. When designing screens, you can:

➤ Drag controls from the Toolbox onto the design surface

➤ Drag controls from the Toolbox onto the XAML Editor

➤ Write the XAML in the editor to create the user interface

Because this chapter is focused on Visual Studio, I want to get across the RAD features of the tool. Drag some controls from the Toolbox onto the design surface to create the Hello Silverlight application. To make this happen:

1. If the Toolbox is not showing, click the Toolbox tab on the left side of Visual Studio to open it. For convenience, click the pushpin to pin the Toolbox open. Your IDE should look something like Figure 2-11.

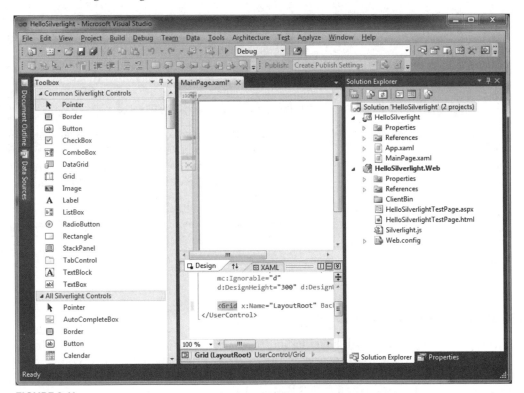

FIGURE 2-11

2. From the Toolbox, drag-and-drop a `Button` onto the design surface.

3. Using the mouse, drag the button to the upper left of the screen using the snap lines as a guide. Figure 2-12 demonstrates what you should see.

4. Review the XAML in the split window. Note the `Button` element was added inside of the `Grid` layout element. As you drop controls onto the design surface, the XAML is simultaneously updated.

```
<Grid x:Name="LayoutRoot" Background="White">
    <Button Content="Button" Height="23"
        HorizontalAlignment="Left" Margin="12,12,0,0" Name="button1"
        VerticalAlignment="Top" Width="75" />
</Grid>
```

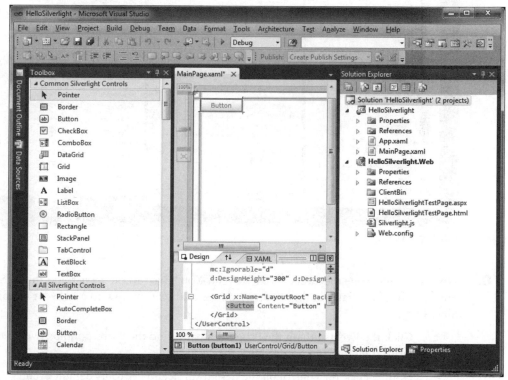

FIGURE 2-12

5. From the Toolbox, drag-and-drop a `TextBlock` onto the design surface and line it up under the `Button` control using the snap lines.

6. Select the `Button` control with the mouse and press the F4 key on your keyboard. This brings up the Properties pane for the `Button` control.

7. Change the Content property to Click Me! and press the Enter key as Figure 2-13 shows. Note that this isn't the Text or Caption property. Because XAML is based on the concept of composable controls, you can embed almost any control inside of another control. The "content" in this example is a string value. It could have also been a `MediaElement` control or a `ListBox` control. You are not limited to strings as the content for controls.

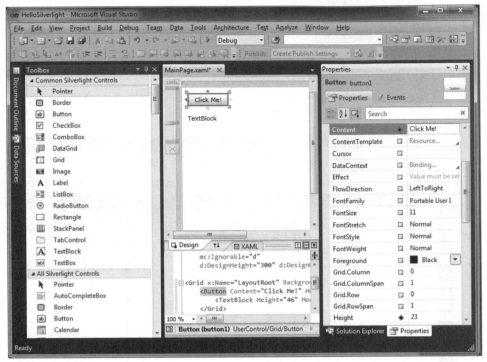

FIGURE 2-13

8. Now add some code the `Button`'s click event. You have several ways to do this in Silverlight. Here is a brief list (later in the chapter, you see examples of how to add event handlers in Silverlight):

➤ Click the Events tab on the Properties pane, find the corresponding event you want to write code for, and double-click the event name.

➤ Double-click the control on the design surface to get to its default event.

➤ Type the event name in the XAML element and add a new event handler, as Figure 2-14 demonstrates. Selecting New Event Handler from the IntelliSense creates a default event handler name. To get to the event handler, you can either hit the F7 key to jump to code-behind, or right-click the event handler name and select Navigate to Event Handler from the context menu. Use one of these methods to get to the event handler.

9. You should now be looking at the code-behind for this form. Add the following code to the `button1_Click` event handler:

```
textBlock1.Text = "Hello Silverlight World";
```

10. The next step is to build the application. Before doing a build, note the ClientBin folder in the HelloSilverlight.Web project as shown in Figure 2-15. Now press the F6 key to build the solution. If you look in the ClientBin folder now, you'll see something similar to Figure 2-16 — there is a file named `HelloSilverlight.xap` in the folder. You learn what the XAP (pronounced ZAP) file is a little later in this chapter.

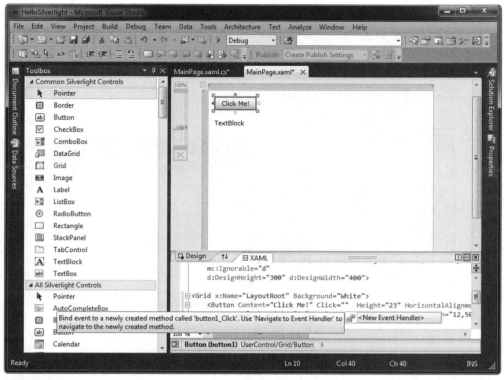

FIGURE 2-14

FIGURE 2-15

FIGURE 2-16

11. Right-click `HelloSilverlightTestPage.html` and select View in Browser as demonstrated in Figure 2-17.

12. Once the browser window opens, click the Click Me! button, and you should see something like Figure 2-18.

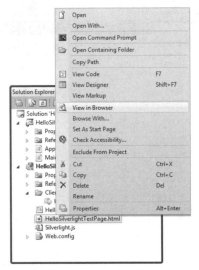

FIGURE 2-17

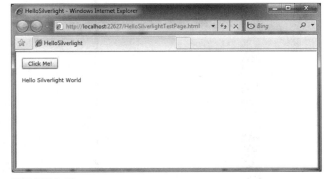

FIGURE 2-18

Congratulations! You just completed your first, albeit simple, Silverlight application. But what just happened? Remember that Silverlight is a client technology; there is no server-side piece to Silverlight. So when you built the solution, the HelloSilverlight project, the Silverlight project code and XAML, was compiled down to IL (intermediate language) and packaged in a XAP file, which was then deployed to a website. In this case, the website is the web application that you linked to the Silverlight project when you first created the HelloSilverlight solution. Visual Studio links these projects together, so every time you build, the XAP that is created from the Silverlight project is automatically deployed to the ASP.NET project. Figure 2-19 describes this visually.

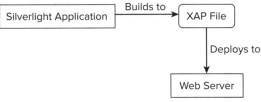

FIGURE 2-19

The next obvious question is: How did `HelloSiverlightTestPage.html` show the Silverlight form you just worked with? As you learned in Chapter 1, Silverlight is a browser plug-in, so `HelloSilverlightTestPage.html` has an object tag that loads the plug-in onto the HTML page. The following HTML snippet is the object tag for `HelloSilverlightTestPage.html`:

```
<object data="data:application/x-silverlight-2,"
  type="application/x-silverlight-2" width="100%" height="100%">
    <param name="source" value="ClientBin/HelloSilverlight.xap"/>
    <param name="onError" value="onSilverlightError" />
    <param name="background" value="white" />
    <param name="minRuntimeVersion" value="4.0.50331.0" />
    <param name="autoUpgrade" value="true" />
```

```
    <a href="http://go.microsoft.com/fwlink/?LinkID=149156&v=4.0.50331.0"
      style="text-decoration:none">
        <img src="http://go.microsoft.com/fwlink/?LinkId=161376"
          alt="Get Microsoft Silverlight" style="border-style:none"/>
    </a>
</object>
```

Like any other plug-in, there is an object that describes the type of plug-in and there are one or more `param` elements, which are key-value pair property settings for the object that is being loaded. Notice the bold line of code:

```
<param name="source" value="ClientBin/HelloSilverlight.xap"/>
```

This is where the XAP file comes into play. The content that this plug-in needs to run is in the ClientBin folder and is named `HelloSilverlight.xap`.

Understanding the XAP File

A XAP file is a unit of deployment for a Silverlight application. The XAP file is essentially a ZIP file format using a XAP file extension, which means that multiple files can be contained within a XAP file. When a browser navigates to a page that has a Silverlight object tag on it, the Silverlight plug-in is activated, and the XAP file specified in the source parameter in the HTML page begins to download. Once the XAP file is downloaded to the browser cache, the Silverlight plug-in reads the `AppManifest.xaml` file in the XAP container and gleans some key pieces of information:

➤ The assembly name that the Silverlight plug-in should load

➤ The entry point of the application class to load

➤ The minimum version of Silverlight that this application is targeting

If you locate the `HelloSilverlight.xap` file on your filesystem (hint: find the ClientBin folder for your web project), rename it to `HelloSilverlight.zip`, and extract the contents, you'll see something like Figure 2-20.

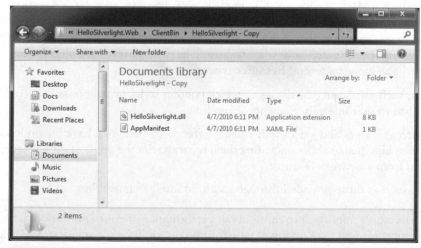

FIGURE 2-20

Go ahead and open up the `AppManifest.xaml` file, and you'll see this:

```
<Deployment xmlns="http://schemas.microsoft.com/client/2007/deployment"
            xmlns:x="http://schemas.microsoft.com/winfx/2006/xaml"
            EntryPointAssembly="HelloSilverlight"
            EntryPointType="HelloSilverlight.App"
            RuntimeVersion="4.0.50331.0">
  <Deployment.Parts>
    <AssemblyPart x:Name="HelloSilverlight" Source="HelloSilverlight.dll" />
  </Deployment.Parts>
</Deployment>
```

Note the `Deployment.Parts` section in `AppManifest.xaml`. Each assembly that is compiled as a Resource in your project will be listed as an `AssemblyPart` in the manifest. For example, if I right-click the References folder in my HelloSilverlight project and add an assembly that is not part of the core assemblies, it will be added to my XAP file when I build, and `AppManifest.xaml` will be updated to include the additional `AssemblyPart` elements. In the following example, I added the `Microsoft.Expression.Interactions.dll` and its dependent assembly `System.Windows.Interactivity.dll`:

```
<Deployment xmlns="http://schemas.microsoft.com/client/2007/deployment"
            xmlns:x="http://schemas.microsoft.com/winfx/2006/xaml"
            EntryPointAssembly="HelloSilverlight"
            EntryPointType="HelloSilverlight.App"
            RuntimeVersion="4.0.50331.0">
  <Deployment.Parts>
    <AssemblyPart x:Name="HelloSilverlight" Source="HelloSilverlight.dll" />
    <AssemblyPart x:Name="Microsoft.Expression.Interactions"
                  Source="Microsoft.Expression.Interactions.dll" />
    <AssemblyPart x:Name="System.Windows.Interactivity"
                  Source="System.Windows.Interactivity.dll" />
  </Deployment.Parts>
</Deployment>
```

Note the two additional `AssemblyPart` elements for each of the assemblies added.

You'll also notice that `HelloSilverlight.dll` is a fairly small 8kb file. So far, this only contains a very small amount of IL: the XAML and code for this simple Silverlight application. If you were to add additional artifacts to your Silverlight project (like images, for example), they would be compiled as a Resource by default, so you can dramatically increase the size of your DLL, and thus your XAP file, by adding artifacts like images or video as Resources, as well as third-party assemblies from component vendors. Silverlight supports several Resource types:

➤ XAML resources, such as resource dictionaries, which contain styles or templates that could be shared or applied to user interface elements at run time

➤ Resource files, such as images and videos that you can refer to by URI. You have the option of embedding resource files in assemblies, including them separately in the application package, or retrieving them from a network resource.

➤ Resource strings, such as those provided through localized satellite assemblies

When dealing with Resources, it's important to think about performance of your application. The larger your XAP file, the longer it will take to download. Your goal should be the smallest XAP file possible, giving your application a fast startup time. This does not mean you can't have rich, interactive applications that use various media artifacts and third-party components. You just need to be smart about how you get those application pieces down to the client. If you have images or video files, you may want to deploy them to the web server's ClientBin folder, and reference them in your code using the fully qualified URI, or you can asynchronously download files or assemblies as they are needed on the client. Either way, you have multiple good options for keeping a small XAP file and a responsive application.

To make it easier to unzip the XAP file of your application, you can associate the XAP extension with the Shell Zip application. To do this, follow these steps:

1. Open a Command Prompt with Administrative permissions as Figure 2-21 shows.

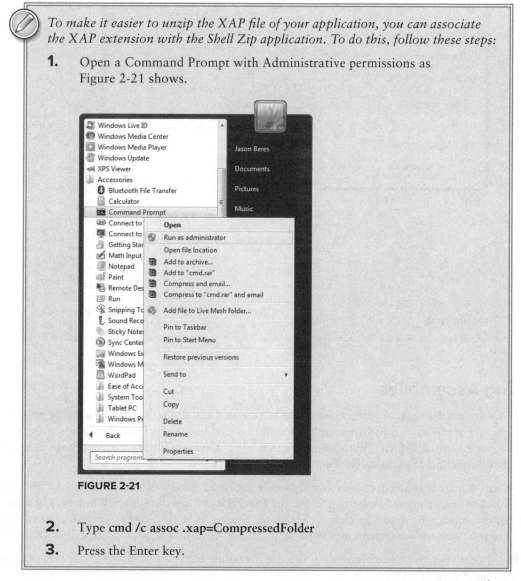

FIGURE 2-21

2. Type **cmd /c assoc .xap=CompressedFolder**

3. Press the Enter key.

continues

(continued)

Now if you right-click a `.xap` extension, you can extract the contents to a folder as shown in Figure 2-22.

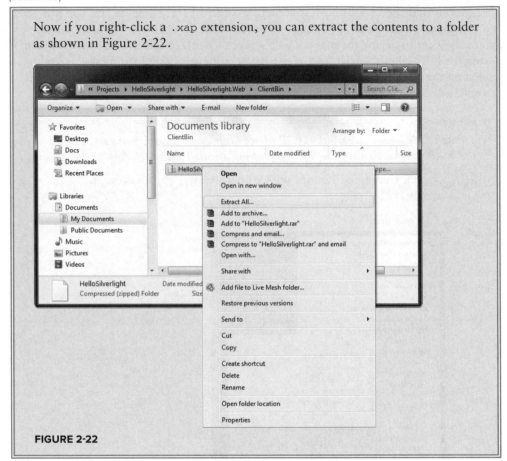

FIGURE 2-22

Caching Assemblies

Since we are on the topic of performance, one feature that can dramatically improve the performance of an application is by using application library caching. This means that when a user revisits your website running a Silverlight application that has application library caching enabled, the overall startup time increases, because the assemblies are already on the client.

When this feature is enabled, certain assemblies are packaged outside of the project's XAP file when it's built. For example, the Infragistics.Silverlight.Excel library uses the System.Windows.Data assembly. For my application to use application library caching to cache the System.Windows.Data assembly down to the client for subsequent uses without needing to be downloaded, I would follow these steps:

1. Right-click the HelloSilverlight project in the Solution Explorer and select Properties to open the Properties window.

2. On the Silverlight tab, click Reduce XAP size by using application library caching, as demonstrated in Figure 2-23.

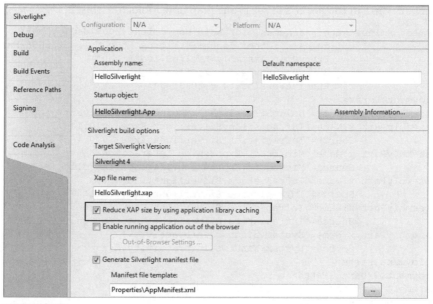

FIGURE 2-23

3. Add a reference to a third-party assembly, such as the Infragistics.Silverlight.Excel assembly or an assembly that ships with Silverlight but is not part of the core run time, such as the System.Windows.Controls.Data assembly.

4. Build the application.

When the project is built, the build packages the System.Windows.Data assembly into a separate zip file as Figure 2-24 shows.

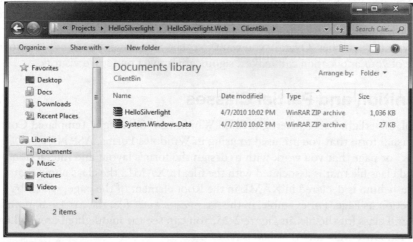

FIGURE 2-24

The `AppManifest.xaml` in the `HelloSilverlight.xap` now looks like this:

```xml
<Deployment xmlns="http://schemas.microsoft.com/client/2007/deployment"
            xmlns:x="http://schemas.microsoft.com/winfx/2006/xaml"
            EntryPointAssembly="HelloSilverlight"
            EntryPointType="HelloSilverlight.App"
            RuntimeVersion="4.0.50331.0">
  <Deployment.Parts>
    <AssemblyPart x:Name="HelloSilverlight" Source="HelloSilverlight.dll" />
    <AssemblyPart x:Name="Infragistics.Silverlight.Excel.v10.1"
                  Source="Infragistics.Silverlight.Excel.v10.1.dll" />
    <AssemblyPart x:Name="Microsoft.Expression.Interactions"
                  Source="Microsoft.Expression.Interactions.dll" />
    <AssemblyPart x:Name="Infragistics.Silverlight.v10.1"
                  Source="Infragistics.Silverlight.v10.1.dll" />
    <AssemblyPart x:Name="Infragistics.Silverlight.Compression.v10.1"
                  Source="Infragistics.Silverlight.Compression.v10.1.dll" />
    <AssemblyPart x:Name="System.Windows.Interactivity"
                  Source="System.Windows.Interactivity.dll" />
  </Deployment.Parts>
  <Deployment.ExternalParts>
    <ExtensionPart Source="System.Windows.Data.zip" />
  </Deployment.ExternalParts>
</Deployment>
```

 You cannot use application library caching and out-of-browser support in the same application. In Chapter 9 you learn about out-of-browser applications, and the requirement that its startup assemblies are all contained in its XAP file.

When a user first visits your web page, the XAP and all of the ZIP files indicated in the `ExternalParts` section are added to the browser cache so that they can be reused on subsequent visits. Keep in mind that Silverlight caching is subject to the caching configuration settings on the server and in the browser. Files are typically downloaded only if they are not in the cache or if they are newer than the cached versions. Application library caching is beneficial for libraries that do not change that often, such as third-party tools or non-core System assemblies. Overall, you want to cache as much as you can; performance or perceived performance of your application can make a significant impact on return visitors.

Adding Class Definition and Partial Classes

A Silverlight User Control, Silverlight Page, Silverlight Child Window, or Silverlight Templated Control is no different than any visual form that you are used to using in Windows Forms, ASP.NET, or WPF. There is a "design surface" or page that you work with to design the form's layout and interactions, and there is a code-behind class file that is associated with the file. In XAML, the class name that glues the form to the code-behind is declared in XAML in the Root element of the page, which by default is set to a Build Action as Page. For example, in the `MainPage.xaml` file, the `x:Class` modifier indicates the namespace and class for the file. In Figure 2-25, you can see the highlighted area, which shows the namespace is HelloSilverlight and the class is `MainPage`.

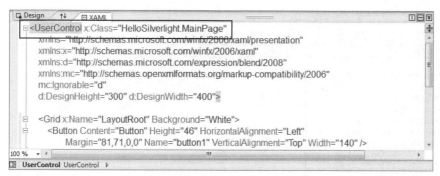

FIGURE 2-25

The partial class file for this page, as indicated by the hierarchical structure in Visual Studio (see Figure 2-26) derives from the type of the class used to define the root element of the page.

So for example, if you added a new UserControl, the derived type is UserControl, as shown in Figure 2-27.

If you added a new Child Window or Page, the corresponding type derived in the partial class is going to match ChildWindow or Page. As with any partial class, it must be declared as public so the partial class and the XAML page are aware of each other and can build properly.

You'll also notice in Figure 2-27 the call to InitializeComponent in the constructor. Similar to other platforms,

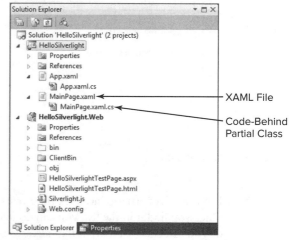

FIGURE 2-26

InitializeComponent points to a generated code file that is created when the page associated with the code-behind is markup-compiled, which is responsible for rendering the UI as well as connecting the objects declared with an x:Name modifier in the XAML page with the object definitions in the partial class. The code generated file is normally in the obj folder of your project after your project is compiled. If you look in the obj folder, you'll see a file that has a .g between the filename and the extension.

Adding Events to a Partial Class

This section is a review if you are a seasoned Visual Studio developer, and a must read if you are new to using Visual Studio. In any event-driven programming model, you write code that responds to interactions on the screen. So how do you link up the action with re-action of the code? You have several ways to do this in Visual Studio when creating Silverlight applications:

➤ From the design surface, double-click the object. This takes you to the code-behind file and the default event handler for the object. For example, if you double-click a button, you are taken to the Button's Click event.

Partial Class Derived Type

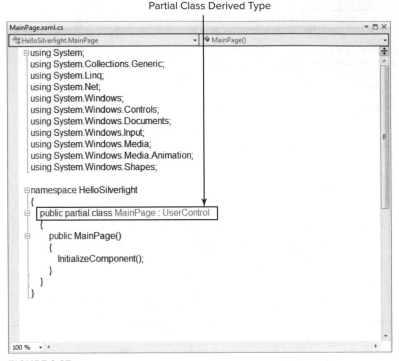

FIGURE 2-27

➤ From the Properties pane, click the Events tab and find the event you want to write code for. Once you find it in the list, you can double-click the name of the event to get to the code-behind, or you can choose an event that already exists from the drop-down control to the right of the event name.

➤ From the partial class, you can add an event handler manually by typing *object.eventname* **+=** and then pressing the Tab key twice to add the event and event handler as shown in Figure 2-28.

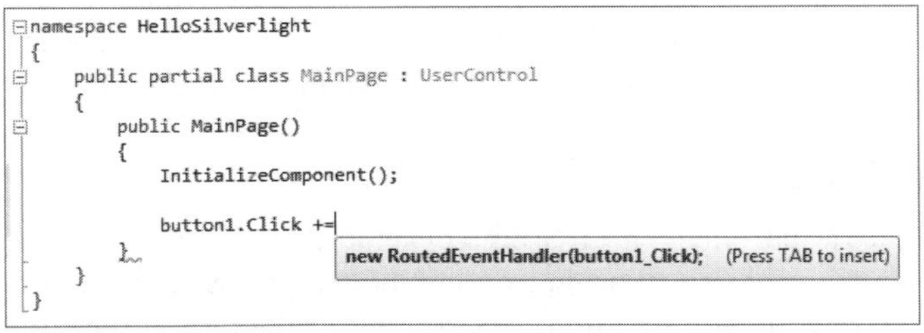

```
namespace HelloSilverlight
{
    public partial class MainPage : UserControl
    {
        public MainPage()
        {
            InitializeComponent();

            button1.Click +=|
                            new RoutedEventHandler(button1_Click);   (Press TAB to insert)
        }
    }
}
```

FIGURE 2-28

➤ From the XAML page, use the IntelliSense feature to add the event on the object. For example, in the `Button` markup, type **Click=** and let IntelliSense take over to add the event declaration in XAML and the code-behind. This IntelliSense interaction is show in Figure 2-29.

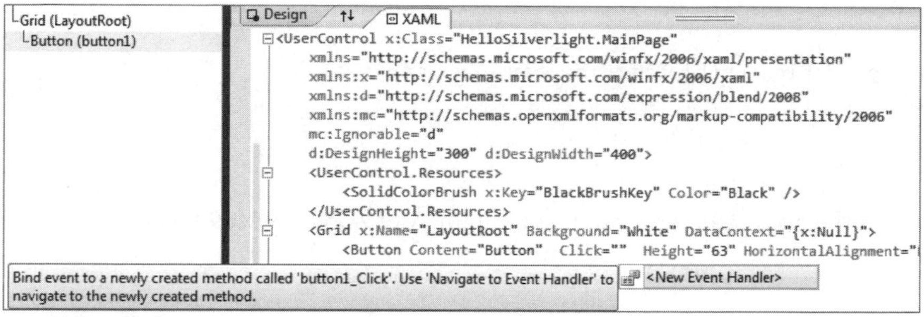

FIGURE 2-29

By default, when you add an event handler, the scope is private to the partial class. You can modify the scope to non-public, but for events that are specific to an object this is not recommended. If you need to repeat the same code block multiple times, you should create a public or static class with events that have public modifiers and call those events from the private event.

UNDERSTANDING THE APPLICATION LIFE CYCLE

As mentioned earlier, the `AppManifest.xaml` file contains the key information needed by the Silverlight plug-in to load your application. The `EntryPointType` property contains the namespace and type name of the class that contains the `Application` entry point for your application. This `Application` class contains the following key elements:

➤ Application `Startup` and `Exit` events

➤ Interaction with the Silverlight plug-in and the host web page

➤ Resource management

➤ Centralized exception handling

All Silverlight applications contain one class, which is derived from `Application`. By default, this code is in the `App.xaml.cs` code file. So for example, if you want to write custom code for when your application is initialized or is exiting, you would write code in the `Startup` and `Exit` events:

```
public App()
{
    this.Startup += this.Application_Startup;
    this.Exit += this.Application_Exit;
    this.UnhandledException
        += this.Application_UnhandledException;

    InitializeComponent();
}

private void Application_Startup(object sender, StartupEventArgs e)
{
    this.RootVisual = new MainPage();
```

```
        }

        private void Application_Exit(object sender, EventArgs e)
        {

        }
```

Note this line of code in the `Application_Startup` event of your `App.xaml.cs` file:

```
        this.RootVisual = new MainPage();
```

Now look at the first line of XAML in the `MainPage.xaml` file:

```
        <UserControl x:Class="HelloSilverlight.MainPage"
```

The class name for this object is `MainPage`, which is the `RootVisual`, or startup visual class, for this application. If you add a new `UserControl` to your Silverlight project, named `NewPage` for example, and change the `Application_Startup` to this:

```
        this.RootVisual = new NewPage();
```

the `NewPage.xaml` file will be loaded when the application starts. So as you are experimenting with Silverlight, you may use various pages for startup, and can easily swap out the startup file in the `App` class. To better understand the life cycle of this process, examine Figure 2-30.

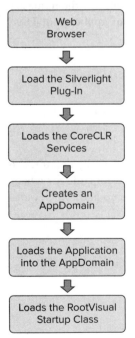

FIGURE 2-30

DEBUGGING SILVERLIGHT APPLICATIONS

Because the application is now built, you should understand some of the debugging techniques available to you. I won't go into general debugging features that are available in Visual Studio, such as the Locals, Watch, Immediate, Call Stack, or Intellitrace features, but rather look at how to attach to a running instance of your application in a browser and how to remote debug from an Apple Mac computer.

Attaching to a Process to Debug

Using the Attach to Process dialog in Visual Studio, you can attach to the instance of your browser that has a Silverlight application running from IIS.

To attach to a process, either:

➤ Select Attach to Process from the Tools menu

➤ Or press and hold Ctrl+Alt+P

This menu is shown in Figure 2-31.

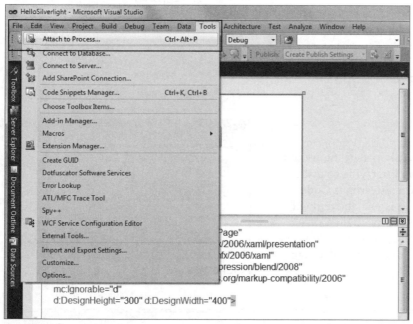

FIGURE 2-31

Once the dialog is shown, you will see multiple instances of Internet Explorer in the list, based on how many browser instances and tabs you have open. To attach to the right process, find the instance that has Silverlight as the type. This is the parent instance of the browser, not the tab that has Silverlight running.

Figure 2-32 shows the Attach to Process dialog with the Silverlight process and the instance tab displayed.

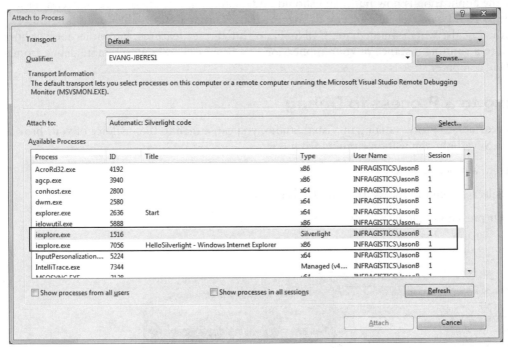

FIGURE 2-32

The debugger automatically tries to figure out what type of process you are trying to attach to. You should see Automatic:Silverlight Code in the Attach To box, which is just above the list of processes. If you don't see Silverlight Code in that box, click the Select button to show the Select Code Type dialog and select Silverlight as shown in Figure 2-33.

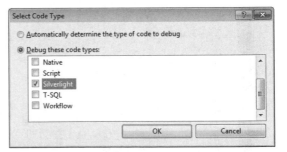

FIGURE 2-33

 You can debug JavaScript code in the host web page by using an Attach To value of Script. However, you cannot debug your Silverlight code and your JavaScript code at the same time.

Attaching to a Remote Macintosh Process

You can also attach the debugger to a remote Macintosh browser process running a Silverlight-based application. This requires some additional configuration steps on both computers, and is supported only between a computer running Windows and a Macintosh computer.

 When debugging a remote process, the Disassembly and Registers windows are not available.

All of the tools to remote debug an application running on an Apple Mac computer are installed with Visual Studio and when you install Silverlight on the Apple Mac, you'll need to go through just a few configuration steps to get it set up. The process of remote debugging occurs over an SSL-encrypted TCP channel between the debugger (the Windows computer running the Visual Studio instance) and the target computer (the Mac running your Silverlight application). The initial configuration is setting up the correct TCP port as well as a private/public key pair so the machines can communicate.

Follow these steps to set up the remote debugging:

1. From Apple Mac, run the Silverlight Debugging Configuration application located in the /Applications directory.

2. Click the Generate New Configuration button, which does three things:

   ➤ Populates the Network Port (TCP IPv4) field with a randomly generated port number between 49152 and 65535.

   ➤ Creates a per-user configuration directory, `~/Library/Application Support/ SilverlightDebuggingConfig1.0/`, which contains the `Certificate.dat`, `PrivateKey.dat`, and `Settings.dat`.

   ➤ Creates a per-user launch agent at `~/Library/LaunchAgents/com.microsoft .silverlight.debugproxy.plist`.

3. In the Encryption Password text box, specify an 8- to 25-character password and then duplicate it in the Verify Password text box.

4. In the Replicator Path text box, specify a path and `.exe` filename for the PC configuration, or accept the default value.

5. Click the Generate PC Configuration button.

A dialog box will confirm the creation of the PC configuration `.exe` file at the location you specified in Step 4. You can use this file with any computer running Windows that you want to use to debug Silverlight on the Macintosh computer. Your Apple Mac is now configured for remote debugging. The next step is to configure the Windows computer with the configuration information you just created.

To configure the computer running Windows, follow these steps:

1. Close any open instances of Visual Studio.

2. Copy the `.exe` file you just created on the Apple Mac to your Windows computer and run the `.exe`.

3. Enter the password you specified in the previous procedure.

4. Click OK in the dialog box that indicates that the Windows configuration has completed successfully.

Now both computers are configured for remote debugging. You can now establish the connection between the computers to start debugging:

1. On your Macintosh computer, start the Silverlight-based application that you want to debug.

2. On your computer running Windows, use Visual Studio to open the Silverlight project that corresponds to the application that is running on your Macintosh computer.

3. On the Debug menu, select Attach to Process.

4. In the Transport drop-down list, select Silverlight Remote Cross-Platform Debugging.

5. In the Qualifier combo box, specify the fully qualified domain name or IP address of your Macintosh computer.

6. The Available Processes window displays a list of processes running on your Macintosh.

7. Select your Silverlight-based application process. You can use the Type column to identify the Silverlight processes.

8. Click Attach.

To remove the Macintosh debugging configuration, you can do the following from the Command Prompt:

➤   On Windows Vista and Windows 7:

```
rmdir /s /q %LOCALAPPDATA%\Microsoft\SilverlightDebuggingConfig1.0
```

➤   On Windows XP:

```
rmdir /s /q "%USERPROFILE%\Local Settings\Application
    Data\Microsoft\SilverlightDebuggingConfig1.0"
```

➤   On the Macintosh computer, open a terminal window and then run the following commands:

```
rm -rf ~/Library/Application\
 Support/SilverlightdebuggingConfig1.0
cd ~/Library/LaunchAgents
launchctl unload
  ~/Library/LaunchAgents/com.microsoft.silverlight.debugproxy.plist
rm
  ~/Library/LaunchAgents/com.microsoft.silverlight.debugproxy.plist
```

The Visual Studio debugger is now attached to the target process on the Macintosh. At this point, you can use Visual Studio to perform normal debugger tasks, such as setting breakpoints, stepping through code, and examining the call stack.

CONFIGURING SILVERLIGHT MIME TYPES

Now that your application is written and debugged, and you have a pretty good idea about what you can do in the IDE with Visual Studio and Silverlight, you should know how to get the server properly configured to serve up your Silverlight application. MIME, or Multipurpose Internet Mail Extensions, is an Internet standard that describes content for browsers to consume. In general, MIME types include audio, video, text, HTML, and of course, Silverlight. The way MIME handling works is when a browser downloads a file, it goes through steps to validate that the type of the file matches the MIME type declared by the HTTP server. Based on your web server, you may need to add support for the Silverlight MIME type.

Adding MIME Support to IIS

If you are using IIS 7 in Windows Server 2008, Windows 7, or Windows Vista SP1, the MIME types needed to support Silverlight are already added by default. If you are running Windows Vista or Windows Server 2003 IIS 6.0, follow these steps to add the Silverlight MIME type:

1. Open IIS Manager.

2. Click MIME Types.

3. Click Add.

At this point, add the following MIME types (repeat steps 1 through 3 to add each MIMI type):

➤ `.xap` — `application/x-silverlight-app`

➤ `.xaml` — `application/xaml+xml`

➤ `.xbap` — `application/x-ms-xbap`

Figure 2-34 shows this dialog.

In addition to adding MIME types via the IIS Manager, you can add MIME types to the `<staticConent>` section of the `applicationHost.config` file located at `%windir%\system32\inetsrv\config\applicationHost.config`.

Add these mappings in the `<staticContent>` section for Silverlight:

➤ `<mimeMap fileExtension=".xaml" mimeType="application/xaml+xml" />`

➤ `<mimeMap fileExtension=".xap" mimeType="application/x-silverlight-app" />`

➤ `<mimeMap fileExtension=".xbap" mimeType="application/x-ms-xbap" />`

It's that easy to set up MIME types to ensure your Silverlight content is served up correctly.

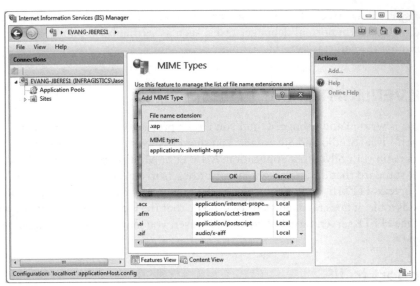

FIGURE 2-34

SUMMARY

In this chapter you learned the basics of creating a Silverlight application with Visual Studio and the life cycle of a Silverlight application. You learned how to add controls to the design surface, how to change properties on controls, how to add code to events, and how to build an application. You were also introduced to concepts such as application library caching, which can improve the performance of your application, as well as debugging and configuring your server to handle the Silverlight MIME types.

3

Building Applications with Expression Blend 4

WHAT'S IN THIS CHAPTER?

➤ Understanding the key Expression Blend IDE elements

➤ Creating a project in Silverlight using Expression Blend

➤ Creating and using Behaviors in Expression Blend

➤ Visual states, the Visual State Manager, and custom control templates in Expression Blend

➤ Importing and working with Design Elements not created in Expression Blend

➤ Understanding other elements of the Expression Suite as they relate to Expression Blend

This chapter gets you (the Silverlight Developer) up-and-working with Expression Blend; it helps you understand what Expression Blend does and doesn't do and how it works in conjunction with Visual Studio.

If you have done any Silverlight work lately, you most likely have heard of Expression Blend. *Expression Blend* is the premier WYSIWYG (What You See Is What You Get) tool for working with XAML (eXtensible Application Markup Language)–based design elements in Windows Presentation Foundation (WPF) and Silverlight. Designed specifically for designers or those developers that tend to work more in the UI rather than the backend, Expression Blend has been built out so well as to be a crucial tool for all developers, and in some cases, when used with SketchFlow, it can also be a valuable tool for other types of workers such as information architects (IAs) and project managers. Part of what makes Expression Blend crucial in your development process is that both Visual Studio and Expression Blend can work against the same solution at the same time. This allows your developers and designers to work together in ways never before possible. If you are one of those developers that span both the front-end and back-end worlds of application development, you will find that when provided with dual monitors, you will have Expression Blend in one while you are working on the same solution in Visual Studio in the other. Next, this chapter will help you get started by getting you introduced to the basics of Expression Blend.

LEARNING EXPRESSION BLEND BASICS

Since you are most likely a developer reading this book, it is important to note that Expression Blend is a dedicated integrated development environment (IDE) for designing WPF and Silverlight applications. However, keep in mind that it has been designed specifically as a designer-friendly tool for working with XAML assets. Designers will not be calling it an IDE, but as a developer, it might be easier for you to understand it as an IDE. With that in mind, Expression Blend has evolved to the point of doing this better than Visual Studio, not just from a WYSIWYG standpoint but in functionality — for example, doing key frame animations using Expression Blend's Timeline tools is a natural task, but in Visual Studio, it's not so easy.

IDE Tour

When you have created or otherwise started an Expression Blend project for the first time, your screen looks something like what is presented here in Figure 3-1 after the splash screen and the start up dialog which you will read about later.

If you look closely, you can see that Expression Blend is divided into five key areas, namely, four columns and the top Menu bar. The Menu bar is great for finding help or drilling into things — much like Visual Studio — but for the sake of this discussion, focus on the four columns first. The *columns*, from left to right, are:

➤ The toolbar

➤ The Objects timeline plus the Project, Assets, and States views

➤ The design surface

➤ The Properties pane

Each section might have additional tabs and functionality, but this should be what you see before you customize Expression Blend. You can also disconnect each section and rearrange the UI to fit just about any way you might want to lay out the application; but assume you are using this default screen.

To dive a bit deeper into the UI, consider each section separately, starting on the far left with the toolbar.

Toolbar

Figure 3-2 shows the toolbar up close with all 13 icons, each with its own function(s); some of the icons can also change behavior or change to icons that are not visible when initially launched.

Toolbar   Object Timeline/Projects/Assets
           and States View   Design Surface   Properties Pane   Menu Bar

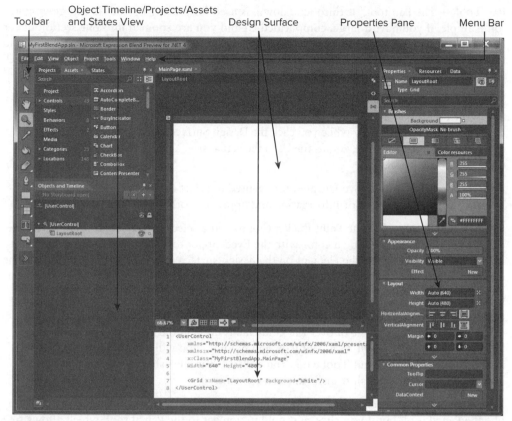

FIGURE 3-1

If you click-and-hold many of the icons — for example, the magnifying glass icon in the figure — it opens up an additional selection of tools to replace the default icon, and the selected tool is shown with a lighter box around it. Icons that have a small triangle in the lower-right corner are the ones that contain different icons or tools, other than the default, that can be selected. Another way to show the additional options is to right-click the icon and select from the menu that comes up.

> ➤ **Selection Tool** — The first icon at the top of the list is the Selection tool, which is used to select objects and groups of objects. A typical operation using this tool would be to click-and-drag over the UI.

> ➤ **Direct Selection Tool** — Often you might be looking at a group of objects that make up part of a complex UI so that selecting a specific grouped item can be difficult at best. But using this tool, you can select discretely so that a typical operation is a standard left-click on the target.

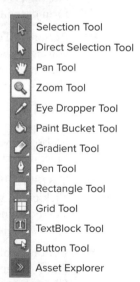

Selection Tool

Direct Selection Tool

Pan Tool

Zoom Tool

Eye Dropper Tool

Paint Bucket Tool

Gradient Tool

Pen Tool

Rectangle Tool

Grid Tool

TextBlock Tool

Button Tool

Asset Explorer

FIGURE 3-2

➤ **Pan Tool** — The Pan tool, or third icon down, is used for *picking up* the UI and moving it; for example, if you have a large, complicated UI and you are zoomed into one section of very fine details, you might need to *move* to another section of the UI. This tool allows you to do that. Along with moving the UI Design view around, if you double-click the Pan tool, the UI will be centered.

➤ **Zoom Tool** — If you need to zoom in and out, you can use the next icon down, called the *Zoom tool*. When the Zoom tool is selected, the design surface zooms in if you click anywhere on it. If you hold down the Alt key while you click the Design Surface, the UI zooms out. Double-clicking the Zoom tool, then, zooms the UI to the actual size. You can also zoom in and out using the mouse wheel.

➤ **Eye Dropper Tool** — The Eye Dropper tool is used to select colors from the Design view. This allows you to copy color information and apply it to other elements in your design.

➤ **Paint Bucket Tool** — Use the Paint Bucket tool to add a selected color to an element on the design surface. After selecting a color with the Eyedropper tool, you then can use the Paint Bucket tool by clicking on the element on the design surface to which you want to apply the selected color.

➤ **Gradient Tool** — The Gradient tool is the first tool that can be swapped out. The Gradient tool itself is used to apply or create gradients as a part of elements on the design surface. (Once applied, discrete control over the gradients is done in the Properties pane, discussed later on.) By clicking on the Gradient icon and holding, you will get a small pop-up menu that holds another Gradient Tool icon. You will also get a Brush Transform tool, which allows you to apply a brush transform to an element.

➤ **Pen Tool** — The Pen tool is used to draw line paths with Bezier curves and is not free-form, like the Pencil tool; but if you click-and-hold it, you get to the Pencil tool, which allows free-form drawing.

➤ **Rectangle Tool** — The Rectangle tool creates rectangular objects on the design surface. If you right-click and hold it, you can also get a Line tool or an Ellipse tool. The Line tool lets you draw straight lines, and the last object you can select in this set is the Ellipse tool to draw ellipses. In all three cases, detailed properties can be edited from the Properties pane.

➤ **Grid Tool** — When you click-and-hold the Grid tool, you can select from six different layout controls that can be clicked and added to the design surface. The default is the Grid, but there is also Canvas, StackPanel, ScrollViewer, Border, and ViewBox. All of these have the same functionality as described.

➤ **TextBlock Tool** — The TextBlock tool allows you to add text by selecting this tool and then clicking on the UI. Also, if you click-and-hold on this icon, you can select from TextBlock, Textbox, and the Password box. All the icons have the same basic behavior for adding text controls.

➤ **Button Tool** — When you select the Button tool, you can add a button by clicking anywhere in the design surface. If you double-click on this icon, the default size button is added to the UI design surface. As a designer, you can find additional tools by clicking on the Button icon and holding it to get a list, which includes the Check box, Combo box, List box, Radio button, Scrollbar, and Slider. Each control typically has events or behaviors tied to it.

➤ **Asset Explorer** — When you click-and-hold the Asset Explorer tool, it opens a library of assets (such as controls, behaviors, and other objects) that you may want to add to the design surface. The default assets that Expression Blend provides are significant. Figure 3-3 shows the pop-up Asset Explorer.

FIGURE 3-3

You'll note that Asset Explorer has a Search box at the top, and just to the right of it are two icons. The Grid Mode icon is selected, and the other changes the results to a List view. Once you type in the Search field, you can click the Search icon or hit Enter to get results laid out according to the layout selected. You will note that on the left of the results is the Asset Tree. Feel free to explore all the additional controls from data grids and grid splitters to pop-ups and rating controls. All you do is select one and click on the design surface.

To the right of the toolbar is the next section — the Project Explorer.

Project Explorer

The Project Explorer is just to the right of the toolbar, or left of the design surface. This area can be split into top and bottom by default such that the top section is the Project Explorer and the bottom section is Objects and Timelines. At the top of the Project Explorer area are several tabs. The first tab is Projects, the second Assets, and then the next one States. See Figure 3-4.

The Assets tab is the Asset Explorer discussed earlier, and the States tab is for working with the Visual State Manager in Visual Studio.

Project Explorer itself (see Figure 3-5) is basically the same tool as Visual Studio's Solution Explorer. The control is a tree control that at the top level is a solution and as a tree is broken out according to the project file structure. Although not all the files are editable in Expression Blend, you can see them. These are XAML files that you can click on and edit; you can also right-click and get a full menu, including start and edit in Visual Studio if you have Visual Studio installed. If you have both Expression Blend and Visual Studio installed, this also works in Visual Studio when you right-click a XAML file or project.

Project Explorer Assets Tab States Tab

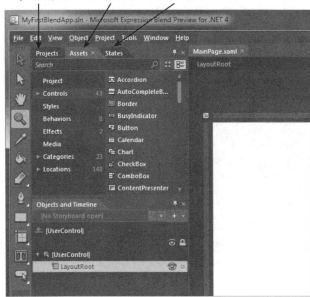

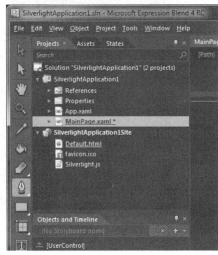

FIGURE 3-4   **FIGURE 3-5**

One of the newest features in Expression Blend is a basic code editor. It is not as robust as Visual Studio in that it's not designed to be a rich editor, but it does allow you to be dangerous to yourself and others, enabling you to do basic code editing, program event handlers, and the like. You can also integrate Expression Blend with Team Foundation Server (TFS) for source control similar to Visual Studio. Having source control integration also means that you can check stuff in and out of source control from Project Explorer.

Object Explorer

The bottom half of the Project Explorer section in Figure 3-6 is called *Objects and Timeline* in the tab. Besides being an object explorer, at the time of this writing, this is also the place to see timeline information. Object Explorer is a representation of the current Visual Tree in the form of an object hierarchy. This representation of what can be in your Visual Tree lets you turn elements on and off (i.e. add or remove from Visual Tree) and helps you identify the elements you are looking for. Look at the simple tree in Figure 3-6.

In the object tree, objects are nested based on their parent and have an icon based on their type. Names are based on type, such as canvas or path, but if they are named elements — meaning that they specifically have the x:Name property set — then that name is what will show as opposed to their type value in the tree. You can tell which elements are "named" elements by the lack of square brackets that contain types used in the tree. In Figure 3-6, you can see the top-level element is [UserControl], which is not named and thus is in brackets. [UserControl] has one child called LayoutRoot, which is named and so does not have brackets around it. The same applies to all elements in the visual tree represented here.

Object Tree   Visual Tree Elements

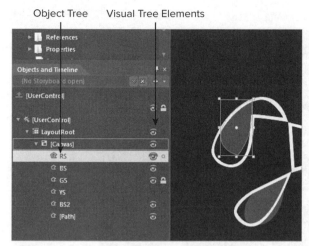

FIGURE 3-6

Another key aspect of the object tree tool is that it can make any element of the tree visible or not. This is done by clicking the eye icon, or the spot where the eye icon should be, to cause an element to switch its visible state. In this way, you can better focus on the elements you are working with currently.

The next section focuses on the design surface.

Design Surface

The design surface is where you see our XAML rendered, or at least, rendered in as much as Expression Blend can render it without it running. You can draw here, animate things here — everything is here for the current XAML page or view. The design surface can actually be shown in one of three ways: Design view, Split view (which includes the Design view and Code view), and Code view.

 You will find many developers who work in Expression Blend use the Split view because it gives you the design surface but also allows you to tweak the XAML without messing with the design surface in Design view. If you know XAML, this can be really helpful.

Figure 3-7 shows the Split view with some simple content.

This figure gives you a good idea of what to expect in Expression Blend. Along the top, you see two tabs, but there can be any number of tabs for each open document. Right above the VerticalScrollbar to the right of the design surface are the mode icons. The Design mode icon is on top, the middle icon is for XAML only, and the bottom one is for Split mode. You may find it easier to work in Split mode, and the code section is very small. For the most part, if you know XAML, this allows you to tweak the XAML. Another great feature in Expression Blend is that it color-codes the XAML the same way Visual Studio does so you know what is what. Keep in mind that this book is not in color so some elements such as color-coding do not show as well as in Expression Blend.

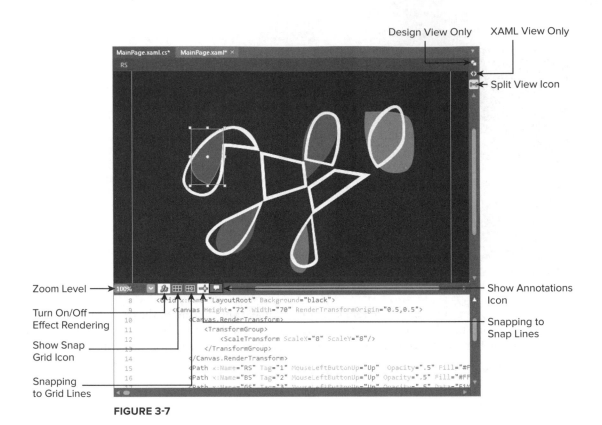

FIGURE 3-7

Looking closely, you can also see some icons to the left of the horizontal scrollbar below the Design view. The first icon on the left is actually a drop-down arrow you can use to size. (In this figure, the sizing is set at 100 percent. You can change this level of zoom much like using the Zoom tool but with this drop down.) The next icon is the Render Effect icon. Sometimes render effects (for example, pixel shaders) interfere with design work; this allows you to turn items off.

The next three icons are grid-related. One is to turn the snap grid overlay on and off. The second is to turn the snapping to grid lines button on and off, and the third one is to turn the snap-to-snap lines functionality on and off. After these icons is one more button used to turn annotations on and off, which is great for design review notes right in the assets.

Properties Pane

The Properties pane, to the far right of Expression Blend (see Figure 3-8), can be broken into three tabs — the Properties, the Resources, and the Data tabs. One of the cool features in Expression Blend is that it supports the idea of *design time data* that can be managed from the Data tab. The Resources tab is much like the Object Explorer. Nevertheless, the most important item is the Properties tab.

Whenever you select an object on the design surface, all the possible properties of that object that can be tweaked appear in the Properties tab. Keep in mind that each "type" of UIElement object you select in the Design view of the currently selected XAML page can have different properties and the chapter will cover them here generically. Starting at the top, you have the Name, the Type, and the Search field for when you cannot find the property you are interested in using. Just to the right of the Search field are two icons that let you change the Properties tab into the Events tab so that you can see all the events associated with the selected item; this also allows you to create event handlers and other items with this particular item.

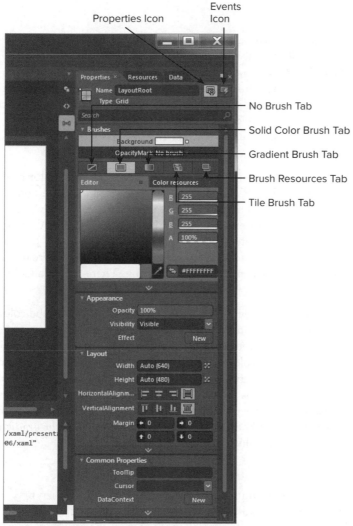

FIGURE 3-8

The Properties tab is broken down into Brushes, Appearance, Layout, Common Properties, Transform, and Miscellaneous sections, all of which are all collapsible, and Expression Blend automatically collapses the default view elements until you customize any of the properties for a given element. As for most of the Expression Blend UI, there is bubble help, so for most if not all of the items, if you hover the mouse over them, a small description will come up.

This part of the chapter discusses each of these sections in turn, with the exception of transforms, which merits its own discussion later in the chapter after I have covered the other sections here.

Brushes

Taking a closer look at the top section labeled *Brushes*, you can start applying brushes to the selected item from the Design view. The top shows the three types of brushes because you clicked a path element in the Design view that can be applied, namely, Fill, Stroke, and OpacityMask; each can have a value, and here you see the state of each. Just under this are the Brush tabs, which display the details of each of the three types and also are used to remove a brush or look at brush resources. For example, if the Fill brush is selected, then the tab lets you set that to Empty or "No brush," a solid color brush, a gradient brush, or a tile brush; you can also see that brush's specific resources. Each one of these has its own set of tools.

Click the No brush tab to set the brush type to No brush. The next element is the solid color brush with an Editor showing the color palette, matching RGB and Alpha settings, and the color code with the current selection. Left clicking on the RGBA area of the color palette will actually allow you to switch between different color algorithms (for example, HLS, HSB, and CMYK). At the bottom of the color palette, a bar shows the current selected color with a "last color" button. Just to the right of that is a color eyedropper, which can be used to select another color from anywhere on your screen. Right below that is a small arrow bar that opens the opacity setting. There is also a Color resources tab that you can use as well.

The next Brush tool is the brush gradient color editor. The top part of this is similar to the solid color brush editor. There are two tabs at the top of this section that work the same as the last section. The tab on the right is the Color resources tab with the color editor selected. On the right side of the color editor are the RGB and Alpha values of the current selected color. Below that is the hex value of the RGB and Alpha. Along the left is the color palette/picker, and at the bottom of that are Select Color, Last Color, and the Color Eyedropper tool. Below the color editor is the gradient selector with two gradient stops set at both ends. You can set additional stops or remove them to manipulate the gradient shown by the brush selected. Last, below this, is the Gradient Type button for linear or radio gradients, the gradient Stop Switch button, and the Stop selector and offset values.

Appearance

The next section of the Properties pane is the Appearance section (Figure 3-9). When open by default, you will see five values that you can set including Opacity, Visibility, Data, Effect, and Stroke Thickness. However, at the bottom in the middle is a collapsed section that contains an additional set of more obscure items dealing with stroke. Normally you would leave these settings to their default values. The top values are the ones that people usually edit, and some properties are different depending on the type. For example, a rectangle doesn't have Data but does have RadiusX and RadiusY instead.

Starting back at the top of the section, Opacity is how much another item can show through the element or object selected, whereas Visibility basically lets something be in the Visual Tree altogether. If you are turning something on or off entirely, then Visibility is the better setting. Effect allows you to pick bitmap effects to be applied to the item by clicking the New button to find the effect to apply. Built-in you have the BlurEffect and DropShadowEffect but other pixel shaders can be used if included in the project. The BlurEffect does just that, it "blurs" whatever it is applied to and DropShadowEffect creates an object drop shadow on the applied element.

FIGURE 3-9

Layout

The next section is the Layout section (Figure 3-10), which, as implied, is used to manipulate layout settings such as height, width, grid-related settings, margins, and ZIndex. The Layout section is a bit less visual than the earlier ones, with lots of settings, but mostly they are straightforward to understand. The top two (Width and Height) are just that. These can be set to doubles (a "double" precision floating-point number) like *100.5* and can be set to *Auto* using the icon to the right. Below these are the four standard grid settings for Row, Column, RowSpan, and ColumnSpan; these can be set to `int` values only, which means that you can't have something like *column 1.5*. Under the grid settings is ZIndex.

ZIndex is basically the location in the Visual Tree. If you have two rectangles, and Rectangle A is set to ZIndex 5 and Rectangle B is set to ZIndex 10, and both have `click` events and are in the same spot, then Rectangle B is the only one that will get the `click` event. But if you change the ZIndex around, then you also change which rectangle gets the event.

FIGURE 3-10

Below the ZIndex are two sets of Alignment icons — one for HorizontalAlignment and the other for VerticalAlignment. Both of these values are used to set alignment in the context of their container. After the Alignment icons are the four margins. Each Margin setting has an arrow showing which Margin it is; these can be set to values of type double.

The Layout section of the Properties pane also has an arrow for extended layout settings, including values such as MinWidth, MinHeight, MaxWidth, and MaxHeight as well as scroll-related settings and layout rounding. UseLayoutRounding, which is set to `true`, is good to know about when animating image motion, especially as this value can affect smoothness by ignoring sub pixel rendering. By default, this value is set to `true`, which means animations will not move at a resolution of less than 1 pixel. This can make images look especially choppy when you animate them or otherwise place it in motion.

Common Properties

Next on the Properties pane could be (depending on the type of UIElement selected on the design surface) the Common Properties section. This normally includes features or properties such as:

➤ **ToolTip** — A pop-up like the tooltips in Expression Blend

➤ **Cursor** — Defines a standard cursor other then the default.

➤ **DataContext** — You use this for binding.

This section might also feature the following:

➤ **Text** — Appears only for controls that have properties like a text box.

➤ **IsHitTestVisible** — Appears if you are using drag-and-drop and need to ensure that something is not going to interact with the cursor on a drag.

➤ **Tag** — Sets an undefined text value of anything to any UIElement so that it can be used in any way you like.

The next section you could see is the text formatting property box if the selected control supports text (Figure 3-11). Otherwise, this area doesn't appear. The section contains three tabs — one for the text's regular text and font properties, one for paragraph properties, and the last one for text alignment. All the standard settings are there, including font, font manager, font weight, point size, and so on. Under the Paragraph tab is Line Height, Paragraph Spacing, and Paragraph Alignment. The last tab has Right, Left, and Centered justification settings. Past this tabbed section at the bottom are the additional text settings including FontStretch, FontStyle, FontWeight, LineHeight, TextAlignment, TextTrimming, TextWrapping, and LineStackingStrategy.

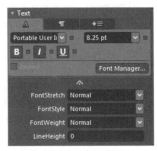

FIGURE 3-11

 Some settings are duplicated primarily to make them easy for designers to use. For example, the tabbed area features icons for Bold, Italic, and Underlined, where these values will be reflected in FontWeight and the like.

In general, it is best to leave settings in their default states. Notice that settings, not only here but also everywhere, only appear if you change the default. Manipulating typography using this box is great but you need to consider design practices when you deal with text.

Depending on the selected UIElement on the design surface, the next possible section of the Properties pane, is the Transform property box. This box is sufficiently complicated that it is covered in greater detail in the next section.

Miscellaneous Settings

The last element of the Properties pane is the Miscellaneous settings box. This is for all the settings that do not fit anywhere else. Here you will find settings like AllowDrop, CacheMode, Clip, FontSource, Inlines, RenderTransformOrigin, and Style.

AllowDrop is a true or false setting that is used for drag-and-drop operations. Clip is a popular setting that is used to add a geometric shape defined by a path or other shape object that *clips* the contents of a given control. RenderTransformOrigin is used to set the center point of any transforms you might use (see the next section to learn more about transforms). Style is the last value you typically see in this section, which is used to apply predefined styles to a given control.

Now that you have taken a look at all those sections of the Properties pane, it is time to take a closer look at the Transform section.

Transform(s)

The topic of transforms could probably be a book in itself, especially if you want to get into matrix transforms; but for the most part, Expression Blend hides this complexity with a nice Transform tool in the Properties pane. Start by looking at the Transform tool shown in Figure 3-12.

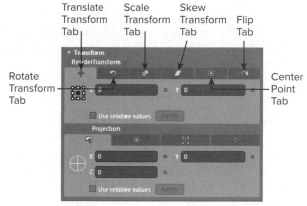

You can see that the Transform section is broken down into two subsections — RenderTransform and Projection, sometimes referred to as *2.5D* or *Fake 3D*. Let's start with the RenderTransform section.

Right above the RenderTransform tabs is the title *RenderTransform*, and there is a small box to the right of the text. If a RenderTransform of any kind is applied, this little box will be a white box. (The same is true of the Projection section below it.) Sticking to the RenderTransform section, it is good to note that under the covers (that is, from a compiler rendering engine standpoint) these are all *Matrix Transforms* — for all the super math geeks. Expression Blend has broken this down, and, in fact, XAML generally hides this. You can still do *Matrix* transforms, but that is abstracted from us by XAML language constructs and Expression Blend. What you have here is the set of tabs that correspond to all the kinds of things you would normally do using transforms.

FIGURE 3-12

The tabs each have their own set of properties or tools related to the specific kind of transform you might want to do to the selected element on the design surface. The tabs are in the following order: Translate, Rotate, Scale, Skew, Center Point, and Flip transforms. Center Point is not so much a transform but an element of a transform that manipulates how a given transform is applied.

The Translate transform is used to effectively move a selected object based on x/y values and a given center point. To the very left of the area is a 9-point map that represents the key points on the object; based on that center point, an object is moved the set x and y values. If you use relative values and click that checkbox, then your x and y values are lost. Anytime you are manipulating these values and you click Apply, then the current values are thus applied to the selected object.

The second tab is the Rotate transform tab, which has an angle tool that is a circle along the left side (see Figure 3-13). You can click the line in the middle that goes from the inner circle to the edge of the angle indicator and move that line around the circle to get the angle you want. If you try this in Expression Blend, you will also see that the bar next to this angle tool shows the angle in degrees, and you can move the

FIGURE 3-13

slider in this box to adjust it as well. Here also, if you use relative values, your degree/angle setting will be lost. If you do not see changes on the design surface immediately, you can click the Apply button here as well after "Use relative values" is clicked.

The Scale transform is used to change the size from what would normally be the size of the selected object. The resize is calculated for you by an x and y value applied by the Scale transform. What this means is that if x and y are set to 1 (a double type in this case), nothing changes; but if you change both values to 2, the object will be rendered twice as big. This can be used also to only render the transform on one axis by changing only one of the values, but this will *skew* the object on either the x or the y axis. You can set relative values here as well and apply them using the Apply button.

The Skew transform works like the Scale transform but moves the opposite sides of the object on the axis on diametrically opposed vectors on that axis — meaning if you have a square and set the x value to 2 of the skew, then the rectangle looks slightly like a parallelogram with the bottom moved slightly to the right and the top moved slightly to the left. You can use negative numbers to do the opposite. You can use relative values and apply them with the Apply button as with the other transforms.

The Transform Center Point is for setting the center point of all transforms. This is done using an x and y value that is a double, where 0.5 represents the center point of the given object on the selected axis. For example, if you set the x and y values to 0, then the center point would be the upper-left corner, and if you applied the Skew transform, then the difference would be that the top face of the rectangle would stay where it is and only the bottom would move.

The Flip transform is really just a Scale transform using one axis with a negative number. A designer does not care to know *how* it happened — they just want to flip something and not think about it.

A good activity to really get your head around what these Transform tools do is to open Expression Blend in Split view and play with these; see what happens in XAML and visually on the design surface.

One of the big things that many Silverlight Developers like to do is three-dimensional (3D) effects, but because the Silverlight run time needed to be small and there is just so much space in the binary, 3D (as in WPF) was left out. Owing to a need or want for the look of 3D, however, you have the ability to do PlaneProjection, which allows us to do things that *look* 3D without all the heavy lifting built into WPF. Look at the projection in Figure 3-14.

FIGURE 3-14

The Projection section next to the title *Projection* also has a small box that is white if you have a Projection Transform applied. The first Projection tab is the one that actually sets the 2.5D transform based on a set of *x*, *y*, and *z* points. You also get a small 3D-looking line globe next to the three point values that allows you to manipulate the PlaneProjection settings using your mouse to figure out the angle you want. This can have relative values applied like the regular transforms as well.

The last three tabs of the Projection area are used to set the center of rotation, global offset, and local offset. These values are all used to change how the PlaneProjection transform is applied.

The States Tab

Lastly, when you select the States tab, you can see that it is mostly blank. This section is actually part of a feature in Expression Blend that allows you to manipulate the control template of a given selected element. This section is used to manipulate and customize the look and feel of controls via control templates and the VSM (Visual State Manager), where the VSM is used to manage transitions between visual states that are listed in the States tab. You will learn more about the States tab later when the chapter talks about Templates and Customizing Visual States.

Now you are ready to create your first project in Expression Blend.

Creating Your Own Silverlight Project

Now that you have gone through Expression Blend, it is time to walk through the process of building out a Silverlight project in Expression Blend. In principle, building out a Silverlight project in Expression Blend is similar to doing so in Visual Studio. You start with the Startup screen, as seen in Figure 3-15, and then you have the File menu. For the most part, the differences are not so much in creating your project but in the design interaction once you get the project loaded.

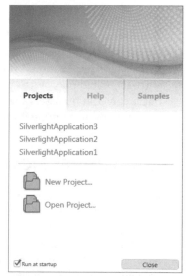

FIGURE 3-15

Expression Blend Startup Dialog

Figure 3-15 shows the Startup screen's three tabs with the Projects tab selected. The selected Project tab shows a list of the most recent projects as well as the "New Project" and "Open Project" icons. Selecting one of these projects opens that project if the project is still where the project was when you last opened it. The "New Project" and "Open Project" icons are straightforward as well: New Project opens the "New Project" dialog and Open Project opens a file dialog so you can navigate to an existing project and open it in Expression Blend. Keep in mind that you can open any Silverlight project in Expression Blend by finding the project and clicking on the solution file or by right-clicking and selecting the "Open with" menu item and selecting Expression Blend.

This gets you into a project, but there are also two items at the bottom that you should know about, namely, the "Run at startup" checkbox and the Close button. The Close button closes this dialog, and the "Run at startup" checkbox lets you *not* have this dialog show up at all when you start Expression Blend.

The Help tab includes User Guide, Online Tutorials, and Online Community. Each is designed to access helpful resources. User Guide opens a CHM or local help file that you can use to explore all the details of working in Expression Blend.

The Samples tab is particularly interesting because it features samples that came with Expression Blend. They were installed on your machine so you can check out some of the great Expression Blend project samples that help you see most of the key Expression Blend features used in the real world.

Now let's get back to building our first project in Expression Blend.

New Project in Expression Blend

When you click the New Project button in the Startup dialog, you get the "New Project" dialog. One thing that should be quickly pointed out is that Expression Blend does, in fact, also support other types of projects than those specific to Silverlight (namely WPF, which is for Windows-based desktop applications). For the context of this book, the chapter will refer specifically to Silverlight, but you need to be aware that Expression Blend goes beyond Silverlight.

With Silverlight selected, you have several project types that you can build in Expression Blend. The three main ones you will probably care about are "Silverlight (v.X) Application + Website," "Silverlight (v.X) Application," and "Silverlight (v.X) Control Library."

The first one builds a Silverlight project but also creates a website project, binds the Silverlight application to it, and creates base pages that load the Silverlight application. If you create just a "Silverlight Application," you are not getting the prebuilt web project; when you run it, you get an auto-generated one. With "Silverlight (v.X) Control Library, this project can't really be run as such but it can contain assets that can be consumed in the Silverlight UI. If you create this kind of project, you will not be running it unless you consume it to some other Silverlight application.

USING EXPRESSION BLEND BEHAVIORS

Behaviors are a cool way of adding functionality to objects in Expression Blend. The idea is that some rich programmatically implemented functionality that would be hard for a designer to do can be wrapped in a control that can then be used as a drag-and-drop feature to add the functionality like magic to an element in Expression Blend. A *Behavior* is just a class that implements a certain base class and member so that it can be easily consumed in Expression Blend as a drag-and-drop behavior. Therefore, in this case, to build one you need to start in or get to Visual Studio.

Implementing Behaviors

Implementing a Behavior is straightforward but can be as complicated as you like. To start with, you will need Expression Blend installed so that you have the Expression Blend assets needed to make a Behavior work within Expression Blend. If you are already in Expression Blend (from following along in this chapter), right-click the project and click "Open in Visual Studio," which implies correctly that you need both Expression Blend *and* Visual Studio installed to create a Behavior. Once the project is opened in Visual Studio, right-click and select "Add New." Then in the "Add New" dialog, select Class. Give the class a name, and then you need to get the Expression Blend Library into your project.

To get the library, you must add a reference to the System.Windows.Interactivity.dll that comes with Expression Blend. This will not show with the other libraries in Visual Studio, so when you right-click and select "Add Reference," you need then to click the Browse tab. You will find the DLL in the Programs folder normally on your C drive under Microsoft SDKs, then under the Expression folder, the Blend folder, then ../Interactivity/Libraries/Silverlight/. Once the DLL is included, you are ready to build out the class you created into a Blend Behavior. You need to start by adding the namespace at the top like this:

```
using System.Windows.Interactivity;
```

This gets the base library you need so you can inherit from the behavior class which is the base class that you need. Next, of course, you need to set up the base class and make your class look like this:

```
public class SomeBehavior : TargetedTriggerAction<FrameworkElement>
{
}
```

TargetedTriggerAction is our base class, where you will be able to apply it to a class of type FrameworkElement For the purposes of this example, the Behavior will also be targeted specifically at Shape objects. The next step is to implement Invoke, which is what is fired when the Behavior is applied to the target. Invoke needs to look like this block:

```
Protected override void Invoke(object parameter)
{
}
```

From this point, you need to get a reference to the object that you need and do to the object whatever is necessary to make the object do what you want it to do. In this case, you typically would add a member to be the reference to the associated object, like this:

```
Shape TargetElementItem1;
```

Now when Invoke is called, you would get your reference, cast it to a Shape and place it into the member reference:

```
TargetElementItem1 = (Shape)(this.AssociatedObject);
```

This code then needs to be in the Invoke member. At this point, the implementation for each Behavior will be increasingly different for each Behavior that you build. This example changes the color back and forth between two colors when a user clicks on the shape. Next, you need to add these members to the Behavior class like this:

```
Brush Color1;
Brush Color2 = new SolidColorBrush(Color.FromArgb(0,0,0,0));
```

This gives you a color to switch to and the reference to the base color of the class. To populate Color1 with the base or start color of the object, add this second line to the Invoke method:

```
Color1 = (Brush)(TargetElementItem1.Fill);
```

Now that the Behavior has a reference to the colors and the Shape is typed and referenced, you can add our behavior logic. In this example, add two event bindings to the Shape reference like this:

```
TargetElementItem1.MouseLeftButtonDown += new
    MouseButtonEventHandler(TargetElementItem1_MouseLeftButtonDown);
TargetElementItem1.MouseLeftButtonUp += new
    MouseButtonEventHandler(TargetElementItem1_MouseLeftButtonUp);
```

These lines actually work until you add the two methods, which should look like this:

```
void TargetElementItem1_MouseLeftButtonUp(object sender, MouseButtonEventArgs e)
{
    TargetElementItem1.Fill = Color1;
}
void TargetElementItem1_MouseLeftButtonDown(object sender, MouseButtonEventArgs e)
{
    TargetElementItem1.Fill = Color2;
}
```

This completes the Behavior. You should now be able to use it in Expression Blend.

Consuming Behaviors

Besides visual behaviors, you can also add nonvisual functionality as you might in a command. Therefore, if you are familiar with commanding, a good way to look at Behaviors is as "commands for designers in Expression Blend." Using Expression Blend to work on an element, you need to be able to see the element that you want a Behavior to be applied to. For example, in the last section, you built out a simple behavior. Now you need a Shape to apply the Behavior to. You can start by dragging a rectangle from the toolbar onto the design surface. Then you need to set the fill to a solid color brush using the Properties pane. The XAML code might look like this:

```
<Rectangle Fill="Green" />
```

Now you should open the Asset Explorer from the toolbar. On the left side of the Asset Explorer, select Behavior, and you will see that your behavior is one of the Behaviors listed, as well as other built-in Behaviors. Select the Behavior you want and drag it onto the object, in this case `Rectangle`, and you are finished. The XAML code will appear like this:

```
<Rectangle Fill="Green" >
    <i:Interaction.Triggers>
        <i:EventTrigger>
            <local:SomeBehavior/>
        </i:EventTrigger>
    </i:Interaction.Triggers>
</Rectangle>
```

If you look at this closely, you will note that there are a couple of namespaces referenced here. You will find these referenced at the top of the XAML document that were inserted by Expression Blend dynamically. A designer is not going to care, but as a developer, it is important for you to realize this.

Behaviors, as you can see, are a way to provide rich functionality that is bound to controls in XAML that also, and more importantly, are easy for designers and developers to use in building, maintaining, and customizing the UX/Design of views in Silverlight applications.

Now that you can use Behaviors and build custom behaviors, you can review Visual States in Expression Blend and the Visual State Manager.

USING THE VISUAL STATE MANAGER

Part of the job of the designer that you typically see being done in Expression Blend is skinning and templating controls, views, and other objects. For the most part, all controls have built-in templates, and in Visual Studio it is very difficult to get at these as they are part of the framework and not exposed. Expression Blend has a great tool to help you get at the templates by creating copies of templates for any control, putting them into your code and allowing you to edit them in the Designer using the Visual State Manager area labeled *States* that was mentioned earlier.

This States tab, and moreover the entire Visual State Manager infrastructure, was built as part of Expression Blend but has been added to the underlying framework as of Silverlight 4. You can tweak the code in Visual Studio, but the VSM was designed for use in Expression Blend or specifically to make it easier for designers to work with visual states of objects. Here, you will use the VSM to create a custom skin or *template* and then use the VSM to help build or change the default animations and transitions between states.

Start by creating your custom control template.

Creating a Control Template(s)

Since control templates are baked-in, sometimes creating a control template can be very difficult to extrapolate independently without Expression Blend. In Expression Blend it's really simple.

1. Start by selecting the control. At the top of the design surface, you see a breadcrumb that shows the control in question as the root item. If you select the breadcrumb, you will get a drop-down menu that lets you select either Edit Template or Edit Additional Template.

2. Normally you select Edit Template, which displays an additional menu consisting of Edit Current, which will be disabled; Add Resource, which will also be disabled; as well as Edit a Copy or Create Empty. You will also generally want to select Edit a Copy, at least until you understand the templates enough to build them from scratch and know what "states" are available. For most people, it is easier to just edit a copy of the default template.

3. When you select Edit a Copy, the Control Template dialog appears (see Figure 3-16). Because a control template is a style resource, a box comes up so you can give the resource a proper name.

   All the correct settings are there by default. You do have the option to have the new control template put into the application or you can also create a new resource dictionary and have the control template go there.

4. Once you select the settings you want, click the OK button. All of the underlying code required to support this new custom template (that is a copy of the one baked in) is added to your project; in addition, the control is bound to this new custom template. Now you click the States tab and you will see something like Figure 3-17.

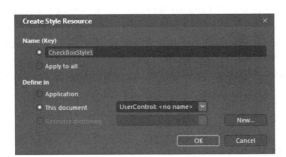

FIGURE 3-16

FIGURE 3-17

In Figure 3-17, all the states and transitions to each state are divided into what is a tree. When you select any of these, that state is applied visually in the design surface. In addition, the state properties show in the Properties pane so that they can be customized as needed visually without going into code. However, you can open the project in Visual Studio and edit the template if you want to. You will also note that the Visual Tree shows all the elements of the template for you to select as well, and you can remove any element you do not need to complete your custom control template.

> *The Visual Tree is a representation of your UI and how it is rendered visually —*
> *how the underlying engine renders elements to the screen. Some things might*
> *not be in the Visual Tree because they are in a collapsed state. In other words,*
> `Visibilty='Collapsed'` *rather than* `Opacity='0'` *where the* `Opacity='0'` *is*
> *considered to still be in the Visual Tree.*

Customizing Visual States

When customizing elements of your control template, you generally are going to use the VSM States tab and the Visual Tree in the Objects and Timeline viewer, as well as the design surface and Properties pane. (You can also edit it in the raw XAML if you are comfortable with that but, keep in mind that some default templates can be very complex.) Often when you are customizing the control, the entire look and feel needs to change. When you select your control, you can go to the Visual Tree and delete anything you do not want or entirely replace it by pasting in whatever it is you want or editing it on the design surface.

To change the state, select the correct state in the VSM State tab, which turns on the State Recorder, and change the control however you like. For example, if you select the state of a button, that state is shown on the control on the design surface. You then can select the element of the control in the object tree of the control that you want customized and edit it — say, change the color or add a transform.

There is also in the VSM tab on each element, a Transitions drop-down that you can select to add specific transitions to one state or the other as needed. Right on the transition, you can set the timing of the transition as well; however, the transition details are edited elsewhere. The last important element of working with transitions that you will need to know is that when you select a transition, you get the Timeline view next to the object tree. This allows you to do custom keyframe animations, which are covered in the Chapter 18.

In the next section, you will import design assets.

IMPORTING DESIGN ASSETS

One of the great features of Expression Blend is that it allows better integration with other tools in Team Foundation Server for Source control, Visual Studio, Adobe Illustrator, and Photoshop. Blend allows closer integration of teams, design assets, and tools. Many design shops have designers who work with other tools so outside the realm of Microsoft application development that even the idea of using a Microsoft tool is offensive. Expression Blend allows those design assets to be easily imported into Expression Blend and used to build Silverlight applications. This allows stronger development (lower to market development costs) by Expression Blend's ability to integrate with Visual Studio as well from a tooling standpoint with regard to other tools.

The two most popular tools that designers and developers concerned with design use outside of Expression Design are Adobe Photoshop and Adobe Illustrator. Though these applications are from the same company, both tools are radically different under the covers. However, both Illustrator and Photoshop are the best in their respective areas. Photoshop is about pixel manipulation. It's about the pixel. Illustrator, on the other hand, is about paths and vectors, which is the same kind of thing as XAML.

Let's start with Photoshop.

Importing PhotoShop (PSD) Assets

Photoshop, then, is about *pixels*. Expression Blend is about *blending* design assets such as PSD into XAML that can be used in Silverlight and WPF application development. When importing PSDs, it is important to note that because Photoshop is pixel-based, it does not import into Expression Blend as smoothly. Frequently what you will find is that what is imported into Expression Blend comprises graphics and images and less scalable Path information. This means that the imported PSD is going to be larger in memory than all-Path-based XAML and also isn't scalable. So resizing the imported assets from Expression Blend will not be as easy, straightforward, or performant.

All of that detail aside, you can now get started importing some assets into Expression Blend.

1. The Photoshop import tool is under the File menu, so to start, open the File menu and choose Import Adobe Photoshop File.

2. This brings up the Select File dialog box; select a Photoshop or PSD file. Once you have selected the file, click Open.

3. You will now have the Import dialog come up, which shows the PSD image on one side with a Zoom icon and a Zoom Level drop-down box (Figure 3-18). The important part is on the right side: a tree of the layers that the image contains. Uncheck elements you don't want to import; drill down and select even single items to import or not to import. By default, all the elements in the layers are imported, except a special element at the bottom called the *compatibility image*, which shows you what the complete view of the PSD file looks like rendered up front. If you select this, it is included in the import.

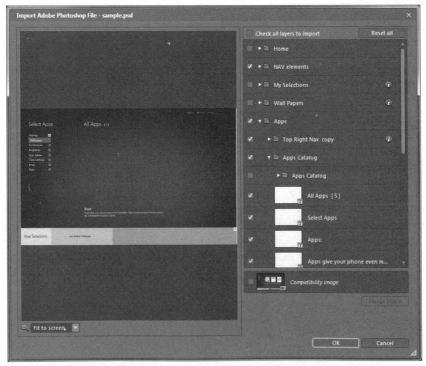

FIGURE 3-18

4. It is a good idea to create a separate user control or *view* in Expression Blend and import a different layer or element into each view so that these elements are broken out and easier to work with in XAML. Otherwise the generated XAML will contain all of the elements from the imported file and can thus be overly complicated and difficult to work with. Lastly, when selecting and unselecting elements in the layers, you can reselect the "Check all layers to import" checkbox to get all the elements checked or unchecked again. You can also use the "Reset all" button to do the same thing.

Now it's time to talk about vectors.

Importing Illustrator (AI) Files

Importing Illustrator (AI) files is much the same process as importing Photoshop files. Unlike Photoshop, however, Illustrator imports almost entirely as Path- or vector-based data, which really improves the design integration process when working with teams, building apps, and making the UI scalable. Using Illustrator to build design assets is almost as good as building them straight up in Expression Blend.

1. The Illustrator import tool is under the File menu. So to start, open the File menu and choose Import Adobe Illustrator File.

2. This brings up the Select File dialog box; select an Illustrator (.AI) file. Once you have selected the file, click Open.

3. You should now have the Import dialog come up, which shows the PSD image on one side with a Zoom icon and a Zoom Level drop-down box. The important part is on the right side: a tree of the layers that the image contains. Uncheck elements you don't want to import; drill down and select even single items to import or not to import. By default, all the elements in the layers are imported, except a special element at the bottom called the *compatibility image*, which shows you what the complete view of the AI file looks like rendered up front. If you select this, it is included in the import.

4. Like with the PSD files you should create a separate user control or *view* in Expression Blend and import a different layer or element into each view so that these are broken out and easier to work with in XAML. An AI file that is a complete UI will normally be extremely complicated XAML if entirely decomposed into a single XAML file. Lastly, when selecting and unselecting elements in the layers, you can reselect the Check all layers to import checkbox to get all the elements checked or unchecked again. You can also use the Reset all button to do the same thing.

Once imported, all the Paths will now be great XAML assets that allow you to scale them really well. What of other design assets?

Importing Fonts and Images Assets

In addition to AI and PSD assets, fonts and images are the only assets that are typically pulled into Expression Blend. Images in Silverlight can be PNGs or JPGs and can be dragged onto the design surface, where Expression Blend copies them into the project and adds them to the current view that is on the design surface. You can then manipulate the images any way you like.

The other common import is fonts that you will want to include in your projects for any custom font and typography you are doing. Fonts don't require a special tool. You can drag a font TFF into your Project Explorer. To use the font you might include a `TextBlock` control from the toolbar and go to the Text section of the Properties pane, where you'll find the Font Manager button. Click this button to find the font you added to the project (see Figure 3-19). Select it and then select that font from the Font drop-down list to the upper left of the Font Manager button.

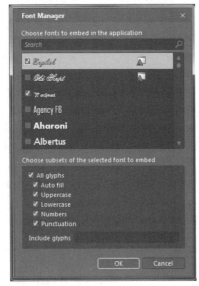

FIGURE 3-19

The XAML code that is generated will look something like this:

```
<TextBlock Margin="155,175,237,237" TextWrapping="Wrap" Text="TextBlock"
FontFamily="Fonts.zip#Digital Readout"/>
```

This code shows the `FontFamily` property, where Expression Blend has added a reference to a zip file that it generates with your project fonts and references the included font. This works in Visual Studio well enough but only because Expression Blend has the resources required to make this work. In Visual Studio, this is usually done differently unless it has been worked with in Expression Blend, which adds the additional resources.

Without getting into the more esoteric topic of designing in Expression Blend, you next learn about the rest of the Expression Suite of tools.

USING THE EXPRESSION SUITE

Expression Blend is the most important tool of a suite of tools from Microsoft for working with Silverlight and WPF. That being the case, there are three common situations when other parts of the Expression Suite are more effective at creating or preparing elements for your Silverlight applications:

➤ The first is graphics generation, which most designers and developers who do design work do when referring to the Expression Suite in *Expression Design* (a rich Photoshop-like tool that is used for the same).

➤ The second scenario is when you need to transcode media to get it into a format that can be consumed easily in Silverlight. This tool is called the *Expression Encoder*.

➤ The third typical scenario is when you need to build multi-scale images that can be generated from images using *Expression Deep Zoom*.

Expression Design is a topic for its own book, and just a basic walk-through would fill a chapter; but it is important to note that Expression Design doesn't use native XAML but exports to XAML. Then you can dive into a basic scenario using Expression Encoder.

Expression Encoder

Expression Encoder as part of the Expression Suite is specifically designed to take media content and either transcode or encode that media or *produce* it in a form that can be consumed online by a Silverlight media player and Windows Media Video (WMV) to integrate it into your existing Silverlight application. Expression Encoder has several built-in templates you can select as part of the output of Expression Encoder and that you can use to quickly build Silverlight media players.

Once you get Expression Encoder running, you need to import your media file. To do so, go to the File menu and select Import, navigate to the video file you want, select it, and then click Open. Next, you need to select a template, which you can do by clicking the Output tab at the top and then, under the section "Job Output," selecting one of the templates. It should look like Figure 3-20.

Click the button in the middle on the bottom labeled 'Encode', and Expression Encoder will "go to town." Now this is all good and Expression Encoder has a variety of other features regarding setting up markers, but the key thing is that it gets video content into a nice format, one that Silverlight can consume easily.

Deep Zoom Composer

Expression Deep Zoom is the key tool for building out MultiScaleImages that you will use in Silverlight. Deep Zoom is a simple tool like Encoder, for example, that allows you to import images and produce the multi-layer image collections; it auto-generates the underlying tile structure used by Deep Zoom (MultiScaleImages) that thus can be used in Silverlight to produce the effect of efficiently having an infinite ability to zoom in and out without performance issues. When you open Deep Zoom Composer for the first time, you will get a dialog like that of Expression Blend that lets you create a new project or select an old one. Since this is your first time, you need to create a new one.

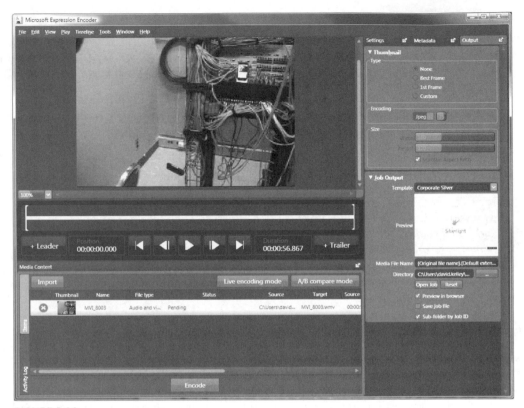

FIGURE 3-20

Deep Zoom Composer then creates a new Deep Zoom Project in which you import all the high-resolution images you want to use. Then you can compose your collection of images, and it will export and build all of your multi-layer image collections, tiles, and other bits as configured so you can use them in your Silverlight applications.

Now you need to get familiar with the user interface. Initially there is just going to be a File menu at the top and then three buttons centered below that — Import, Compose, and Export (Figure 3-21). Import is selected by default. To the right, just below that level, is the Add Image button — the only other item that is important on the UI." When you click "Add Image," you can select as many images as you want to add to the collection. Once they are added, you will see a list of the images as thumb names below the button; you can select one at a time, and the selected image is shown in the larger gray area to the left in high resolution, with the image details at the bottom.

Next, click Compose and the view shown in Figure 3-22 displays.

Here the user interface still has the Menu bar and the three buttons. However, you can also see a toolbar to the left, the images laid out in the center, the image collection at the bottom, and the Layers and Properties to the far right, along with the small button menu between the design surface in the center and the Layers and Properties box.

FIGURE 3-21

Images can be dragged into the center and laid out as you like. The toolbar to the left can be used to manipulate the design surface with Zoom, Pan, and Selection tools as well as various alignment tools. The bottom-left corner of the design surface features a higher-level view that allows you to move the viewable area around the design surface. This is helpful when you are zoomed in and there are lots of images.

The buttons to the right are for creating specialized elements in the Deep Zoom project, including creating a slide show out of your images, creating a menu navigator for your images, and creating internal links or external links within the Deep Zoom design surface. Once you are done and your images are laid out as you want the multi-scaled image to work, click the Export button at the top.

The Export section (Figure 3-23) shows a preview area as well as a dual-tabbed section for either creating a DeepZoomPix account or Custom. Select Custom and you can set the output type, which should be "Silverlight Deep Zoom." Then you have an area to give it a name and location with a Browse button that opens a Folder dialog box. Below that are the "Deep Zoom Settings." The settings include the Export type, which can be a composition or image, and a Collection. If you select Collection — which is the most typical selection — a template drop-down includes the default template as well as an Expression Blend Behavior-based template, a classic with source template, an empty project template, and a tag browser template. Below this area are the Image settings for setting the fidelity of the images in the generated project.

Images that can be added to the design surface for composition

Design surface for composing images into a deep zoom composite

Export Button

Selection Tool

Pan Tool

Zoom

Fit To Screen Tool

Alignment Tools

Arrange Icons

Size Matching Icons

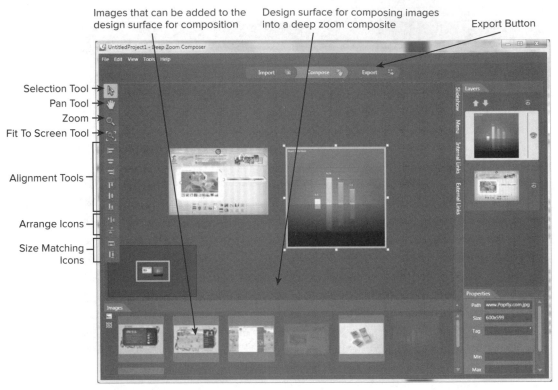

FIGURE 3-22

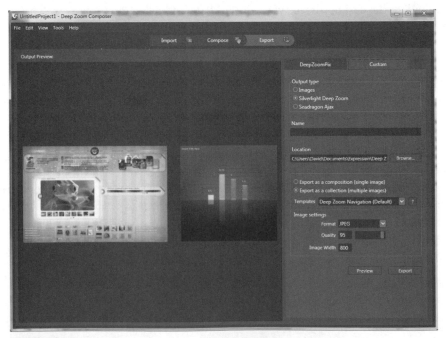

FIGURE 3-23

When you click Export, the Export in Progress dialog displays. When the export process is complete, the Completed dialog displays, where you can preview the project in a browser, open the image folder, view the project folder, and learn more or just close it. If you open the Folder view in Expression Encoder, you can then open your project in Expression Blend to do further customization or in Visual Studio.

SUMMARY

In this chapter, you reviewed the Expression Blend IDE including all the key sections and how those sections behave with regard to your Silverlight view when it is selected on the design surface. You should now be able to find and change properties, including complex transitions, as well as navigate the Visual Tree using the Objects and Timeline tab and find and drag controls off the toolbar.

You learned the process of creating a new project in Expression Blend and how to transition from Visual Studio to Expression Blend. You also learned the process of building custom Behaviors in Visual Studio and how those custom Behaviors are consumed and used in the Expression Blend IDE. You also learned how to import Photoshop (PSD) files and Adobe Illustrator (AI) files, as well as how to include images and fonts in your project.

You also learned how to use the Visual State Manager in the Expression Blend IDE, including how to use the State tab and how to customize elements. You learned how Expression Blend provides custom control templates for you to edit based on the existing built-in template used by the framework (as opposed to Visual Studio, which has no concept of getting at the base control templates that are part of the framework).

Even if you do not have the skill and eye of a designer, you should be able to work with the Expression Blend — the main design tool for Silverlight — to help you build better application UIs.

Working with the Navigation Framework

WHAT'S IN THIS CHAPTER?

> ➤ Understanding the Navigation Framework

> ➤ Using the Navigation Application template

> ➤ Using a custom menu control

> ➤ Caching navigation pages

Silverlight 3 introduced the Navigation Framework, which is an API used in conjunction with the `Frame` control in the `System.Windows.Controls.Frame` class in the `System.Windows.Controls.Navigation` assembly, which enables you to add an ASP.NET-like navigation scheme to your applications. Silverlight 4 further enhances the Navigation Framework with additional extensibility points. Some of the key concepts in the Navigation Framework in Silverlight are:

> ➤ You can implement URI routing.

> ➤ You can achieve navigation declaratively or via code.

> ➤ You can link page navigation into the browser's journal history.

The `Frame` control is at the center of the navigation capability, which works in conjunction with the `Page` class to give you navigation features.

USING THE NAVIGATION TEMPLATE

To get started quickly with navigation, open Visual Studio and from the New Project dialog select the Navigation Application template for Silverlight as shown in Figure 4-1.

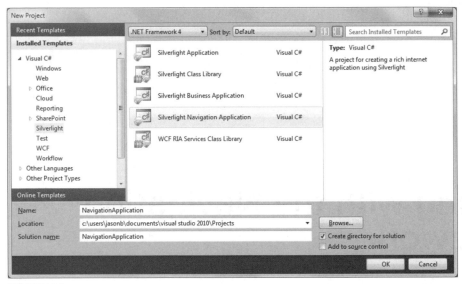

FIGURE 4-1

Once you click OK and accept the default options on the New Project dialog, you should see something like Figure 4-2, which is the default `MainPage.xaml` for a new project based on the Navigation template.

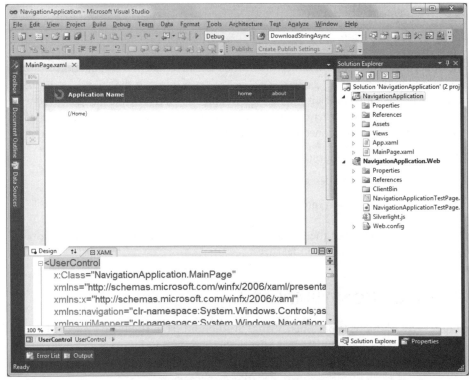

FIGURE 4-2

You'll notice that, different from a standard Silverlight application template, the Navigation template has a decent looking style on the `MainPage.xaml`, and two additional folders named Assets and Views in the Solution Explorer for the Silverlight project:

➤ **Assets** — Contains the default `ResourceDictionary` named `Styles.xaml`, which contains the visual styles used in this application.

➤ **Views** — Contains the About, ErrorWindow, and Home XAML pages derived from the `Page` class that consist of the stock pages set up in the default navigation scheme for this template.

If you expand the References folder, you will see two additional assembly references that are not included in the default Silverlight template:

➤ `System.Windows.Controls` — Contains the `Frame` control, which is used to navigate to Silverlight `Page` controls, either programmatically or through a user action, via a valid URI.

➤ `System.Windows.Controls.Navigation` — Contains the `UriMapper` class, which stores a collection of `UriMapping` objects to use for converting a requested URI to another URI. You define the `UriMapper` object and its collection of `UriMapping` objects for a `Frame` control by assigning the `UriMapper` object to the `UriMapper` property of the `Frame` control.

To see this in action, examine the XAML in the `MainPage.xaml` page. It contains two namespace references to the aforementioned assemblies:

```
xmlns:navigation="clr-namespace:System.Windows.Controls;assembly=
System.Windows.Controls.Navigation"
xmlns:uriMapper="clr-namespace:System.Windows.Navigation;assembly=
System.Windows.Controls.Navigation"
```

In the XAML for the page itself, the `Frame` and `UriMapping` objects are defined with various properties set:

```
<navigation:Frame x:Name="ContentFrame"
                   Style="{StaticResource ContentFrameStyle}"
                   Source="/Home"
                   Navigated="ContentFrame_Navigated"
                   NavigationFailed="ContentFrame_NavigationFailed">
    <navigation:Frame.UriMapper>
        <uriMapper:UriMapper>
        <uriMapper:UriMapping
            Uri=""
            MappedUri="/Views/Home.xaml"/>
        <uriMapper:UriMapping
            Uri="/{pageName}"
            MappedUri="/Views/{pageName}.xaml"/>
        </uriMapper:UriMapper>
    </navigation:Frame.UriMapper>
</navigation:Frame>
```

In the `Frame`, three key properties are set in this default template (ignoring the `Style` property):

➤ `Source` — The default page to navigate to when loaded

➤ `Navigated` — The event that is fired when the `Frame` is navigated to

➤ `NavigationFailed` — The event that is fired when a navigation failure occurs

In the `Frame.UriMapper` object, there is a collection of `UriMappings`. Each mapping contains two properties:

➤ `Uri` — Gets or sets the pattern to match when determining whether the requested URI is converted to a mapped URI. This is typically set to a user-friendly value, such as `Home`, and you set the `MappedUri` property to the actual file to use for the request, such as `/Views/HomePage.xaml`.

➤ `MappedUri` — Gets or sets the URI that is navigated to instead of the originally requested URI.

To set up navigation declaratively, you are adding as many `UriMapping` objects that contain the `Uri` and `MappedUri` as pages you need to navigate to in your application. You may have multiple folders that contain `Page` controls, or many subfolders that contain pages that you need to navigate to. Using the `UriMapping` objects, you can define the navigation scheme for your application. In this default template, the `UriMapping` is simple:

➤ If the Uri is empty (`Uri=""`), navigate to the Views folder and load the `Home.xaml` page (`MappedUri="/Views/Home.xaml"/`).

➤ If the Uri contains a forward slash and then a Page name variable (`Uri="/{pageName}"`), navigate to the Views folder and replace the Page name variable, add the `.xaml` file extension (`MappedUri="/Views/{pageName}.xaml"`), and navigate to that page.

To trigger the navigation, the default Navigation template adds two `HyperlinkButton` controls to the top right of the page as shown here:

```
<HyperlinkButton x:Name="Link1"
                 Style="{StaticResource LinkStyle}"
                 NavigateUri="/Home"
                 TargetName="ContentFrame"
                 Content="home"/>

<HyperlinkButton x:Name="Link2"
                 Style="{StaticResource LinkStyle}"
                 NavigateUri="/About"
                 TargetName="ContentFrame"
                 Content="about"/>
```

Using the `NavigateUri` property and the `TargetName` property, you can declaratively set the content of the defined `Frame` control with the `Uri` in the `NavigateUri` property. Note that the `TargetName` is set to `ContentFrame`, which is the unique `x:Name` identifier for the `Frame` control on this page. If you run the application, you'll see that the default `Page` loads in the `Home.xaml`, which is located in the Views folder as shown in Figure 4-3.

If you click the About `HyperlinkButton`, the `Frame` is replaced with the new `NavigateUri` target, the `/About` page. The `UriMapping`'s `Uri` property sees the `/{pageName}` as `/About` and points to the `MappedUri` of `/Views/{pageName}.xaml`, which in this case, is `/Views/About.xaml`. Figure 4-4 shows the About page content once the About `HyperlinkButton` is clicked.

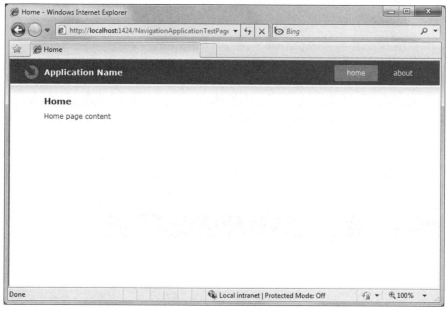

FIGURE 4-3

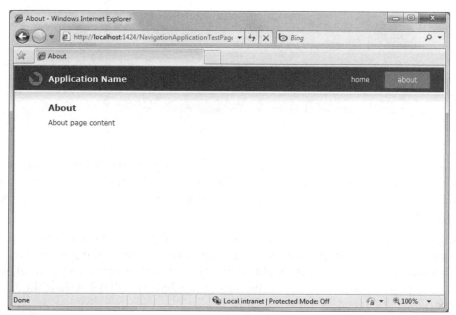

FIGURE 4-4

You can also navigate to URIs that are not Page classes in your application. If you set the Uri property to a valid URL, and the TargetName to _new, clicking the HyperlinkButton opens a new browser window to the URL specified (Listing 4-1).

LISTING 4-1: Navigating to a valid URL

```
<HyperlinkButton NavigateUri="http://www.infragistics.com"
    Content="Infragistics Home"
    TargetName="_new" />
```

What's even cooler is that when you click the Home and About HyperlinkButtons a few times and then click the browser's Back button, you'll notice that the MappedUris show up in the browser's journal history as shown in Figure 4-5.

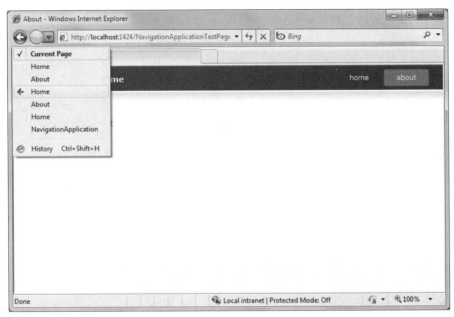

FIGURE 4-5

The name that shows up in the browser's journal history is the Title property that you set for the Page that loads. For example, Figure 4-6 shows the Title property for the About page. If you want to display a friendlier name in the journal history, simply be as descriptive as you'd like to be in the Title property of your Page.

To make this work, the Frame class includes a JournalOwnership property that is set to Automatic by default, which means the frame integrates with the browser's journal history if it is a top-level frame. If you are building an application that should not integrate in with the browser's journal, set the JournalOwnership property to OwnsJournal and the browser history will not include the journal history from the Silverlight application.

To support navigation history, the web page that contains the Silverlight object must include an iframe named _sl_historyFrame. By default, this iframe is included in the web page when you create a new Silverlight application. If you want to add journaling to an existing Silverlight application that does not include it, simply add the following HTML snippet to the page that hosts your Silverlight plug-in:

```
<iframe id="_sl_historyFrame"
        style="visibility:hidden;height:0px;width:0px;border:0px">
</iframe>
```

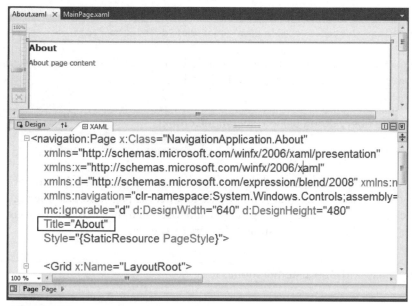

FIGURE 4-6

 Browser-integrated navigation is not possible for an out-of-browser applica-tion. When integrated with the browser, the forward and back buttons of the web browser navigate to requests within the navigation history for the top-level frame. Through the forward and back buttons of the web browser, the user can navigate to a different Silverlight page. With browser-integrated navigation, the user can type a URI directly into the browser window and the page representing that URI is displayed in the Silverlight application. Therefore, a user can book-mark a URI or share a hyperlink that corresponds to not just the Silverlight application, but the application in a specific state.

CREATING PARAMETERIZED QUERY STRINGS

Most applications that you build have common user interface patterns where there is a list of objects, and when a user clicks an item in the list, you either navigate to a details page or pop up a details page. This scenario can be easily accomplished with the same pattern that you use in an ASP.NET application: You pass a parameter to a new page, that page checks the query string for an ID of some sort, and your application code does the database lookup based on the parameter in the query string. Using the UriMapper, you could do something like what is shown in Listing 4-2.

LISTING 4-2: Passing a custom query string to a MappedUri

```
<uriMapper:UriMapping Uri="Customer/{customerId}"
        MappedUri="/Views/CustomerDetails.xaml?customerId={customerId}" />
```

In the specified CustomerDetails page, you grab the parameter in the onNavigatedTo event handler using the NavigationContext of the page like this (Listing 4-3).

LISTING 4-3: Retrieving the query string using NavigationContext

```
var id = this.NavigationContext.QueryString["customerId"];
```

To implement this scenario, in this section you update the Home.xaml page to list a collection of objects, and when one of those objects is clicked, you navigate to a details page and pass the tag of the clicked object so you can retrieve the query string. To get started, add a new class file to your project named Customers and add the code in Listing 4-4 to create the class.

LISTING 4-4: Customer class and GetCustomer method

```
using System;
using System.Collections.Generic;
using System.Linq;

namespace CustomerUriApp
{
    public class Customers
    {
        public List<Customer> GetAllCustomers()
        {
            List<Customer> c = new List<Customer>();
            c.Add(new Customer()
                { CustomerId = 1,
                CompanyName = "Microsoft" });
            c.Add(new Customer()
                { CustomerId = 2,
                CompanyName = "Infragistics" });
            c.Add(new Customer()
                { CustomerId = 3,
                CompanyName = "Apple" });
            return c;
        }

        public Customer GetCustomer(int customerId)
        {
            var customer =
```

```
                            from c in GetAllCustomers()
                            where c.CustomerId == customerId
                            select c;

            return customer.First();
        }
    }

    public class Customer
    {
        public int CustomerId { get; set; }
        public string CompanyName { get; set; }
    }
}
```

The `Customers` class has two fields, `CustomerId` and `CompanyName`, which are populated with a few data records in the `GetAllCustomers` method. The `GetCustomer` method takes the `customerId` parameter and does a simple LINQ statement to get the `Customer` object based on the `customerId` parameter.

In `MainPage.xaml`, add the following `UriMapping` (Listing 4-5) to the existing `UriMapper` collection. This mapping takes the nice and readable `Customer/customerId` URI and maps it to the `CustomerDetails` page in the Views folder, with the appended query string of `customerId={passed variable customerId}`.

LISTING 4-5: Setting up a custom Uri and MappedUri

Available for
download on
Wrox.com

```
<uriMapper:UriMapping Uri="Customer/{customerId}"
        MappedUri="/Views/CustomerDetails.xaml?customerId={customerId}" />
```

In the `Home.xaml` page, add the following XAML (Listing 4-6) for a `TextBlock` and an `ItemsControl` inside the `StackPanel` that is inside of the `ScrollViewer`.

LISTING 4-6: ItemsControl and TextBlock for Home.xaml

Available for
download on
Wrox.com

```
<TextBlock FontSize="24">Customers List</TextBlock>
<!-- add an ItemsControl that will hold the Customers -->
<ItemsControl x:Name="CustomersList">
    <ItemsControl.ItemTemplate>
        <DataTemplate>
            <StackPanel Orientation="Horizontal">
                <HyperlinkButton FontSize="24"
                            Content="{Binding CompanyName}"
                            Tag="{Binding CustomerId}"
                            Click="HyperlinkButton_Click" />
            </StackPanel>
        </DataTemplate>
    </ItemsControl.ItemTemplate>
</ItemsControl>
```

In the code-behind for the `Home.xaml` page, register a `Loaded` event handler in the `IntializeComponent` for the `Loaded` event (Listing 4-7).

LISTING 4-7: Registering the Loaded event in the Home class file

```
public Home()
{
    InitializeComponent();
    Loaded += new RoutedEventHandler(Home_Loaded);
}
```

Then add the code in the `Home_Loaded` event handler (Listing 4-8) that creates a new instance of `Customer` and sets the return collection of `Customers` to the `CustomerList` `ItemsControl` on the page.

LISTING 4-8: The Home_Loaded event handler

```
void Home_Loaded(object sender, RoutedEventArgs e)
{
    Customers c = new Customers();
    CustomersList.ItemsSource = c.GetAllCustomers();
}
```

Once the `ItemsSource` of the `CustomersList` is set, the XAML that you added earlier for the `ItemsControls` adds the `HyperlinkButton` for each of the `Customer` objects returned from `GetAllCustomers`. The `CompanyName` is rendered, the `CustomerId` is data bound to the `Tag` property of the `HyperlinkButton` control, and on the `Click` event, the `HyperlinkButton_Click` will execute. See Listing 4-9.

LISTING 4-9: Setting the Click event on the HyperlinkButton

```
<HyperlinkButton FontSize="24"
    Content="{Binding CompanyName}"
    Tag="{Binding CustomerId}"
    Click="HyperlinkButton_Click" />
```

Add the following to the `HyperlinkButton_Click` event (Listing 4-10). This code casts the sender, or the actual button that was clicked, to the type `HyperlinkButton`. The reason for this is so you can correctly extract the `Tag` property from the button that was clicked.

LISTING 4-10: Using NavigationService in the Click event handler

```
private void HyperlinkButton_Click
    (object sender, RoutedEventArgs e)
{
    HyperlinkButton hyperlink = sender as HyperlinkButton;
```

```
            string customerId = hyperlink.Tag.ToString();

            this.NavigationService.Navigate
                (new Uri
                    (string.Format("Customer/{0}", customerId), UriKind.Relative));
        }
```

Once you have the `Tag`, which represents the bound `CustomerId`, you navigate to the `Customer` page passing the `customerId` variable. To navigate, you call `NavigationService.Navigate`. The `NavigationService` class enables you to access the navigation service used by the hosting frame and launch new navigation requests. You can retrieve the navigation action service through the `NavigationService` property of the `Page` class. In this case, you are telling the `NavigationService` to navigate to the `Customer/{0}` page, which will map to the `CustomerDetails.xaml` page. To add the `CustomerDetails.xaml` page, right-click the Views folder and add a new `Page` named `CustomerDetails`.

In the `CustomerDetails.xaml` page, add the code in Listing 4-11 to XAML in the `Grid` element:

LISTING 4-11: XAML for the CustomerDetails.xaml Page

```
<StackPanel>
    <TextBlock x:Name="CustomerId" FontSize="24"></TextBlock>
</StackPanel>
```

In the code-behind in `CustomerDetails.xaml`, in the `OnNavigatedTo` event handler, add the code in Listing 4-12 to retrieve the ID that is passed in the query string.

LISTING 4-12: CustomerDetails OnNavigateTo event handler

```
// Executes when the user navigates to this page.
protected override void OnNavigatedTo(NavigationEventArgs e)
{
    CustomerId.Text = this.NavigationContext.QueryString["customerId"];
}
```

This looks at the `NavigationContext` of the page and extracts out the `customerId` parameter in the query sting. If you are building an application that has some all-purpose or generic pages that should behave in a certain way based on the action passed in the query string, you can do something slightly more interesting based on the `QueryString.ContainsKey` variable, as shown in Listing 4-13.

LISTING 4-13: Richer example using OnNavigatedTo event handler

```
protected override void OnNavigatedTo(NavigationEventArgs e)
{

    if (this.NavigationContext.QueryString.ContainsKey("action"))
```

continues

LISTING 4-13 *(continued)*

```
    {
        switch (this.NavigationContext.QueryString["action"])
        {
            case "getCustomerDetails":
                // do something for customer details
                break;
            case "getCompanyDetails":
                // do something for company details
                break;
            case "getOrders":
                // do something for orders list
                break;
            case "getOrderDetails":
                // do something for order details
                break;
        }
    }
}
```

In the sample you are building here, once the `customerId` variable is retrieved, you set the `Text` property of the `TextBlock` that you added to the page. If this were a database-driven application, you would have a method named `GetCustomerDetails`, which takes the `customerId` parameter and returns an object with more fields pertaining to this customer. If you run the application, you see something like Figure 4-7.

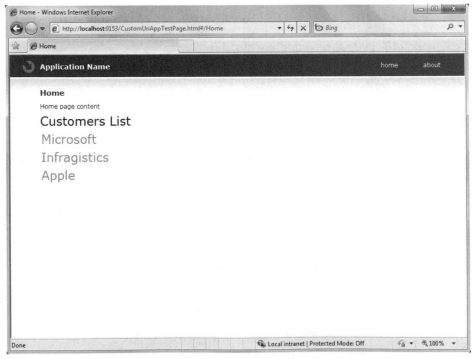

FIGURE 4-7

Once you click one of the company name links, the HyperlinkButton_Click code executes and navigates to the CustomerDetails page as shown in Figure 4-8.

FIGURE 4-8

These URI's also behave very nicely with browser-integrated navigation for deep linking on a website. If you navigate directly to a page in the website, like this:

```
http://localhost:9153/CustomUriAppTestPage.html#Customer/2
```

you are taken directly to the correct CustomerDetails page. You do not have to remember long URLs like this:

```
http://localhost:9153/CustomUriAppTestPage/Views/CustomerDetails.xaml?customerId=2
```

You can test this easily by simply copying the user-friendly browser URL after you navigate to a CustomerDetails page and pasting the URL into another browser session or a different browser.

Using the Frame Class

Now that you have seen the various ways to handle navigation, this section looks at the Frame class and its members. You should already be somewhat familiar with the Frame class; this is the main object you will use whenever you are building applications that have anything beyond basic navigation. The following key methods, properties, and events help you determine what you can do to traverse Page objects in a Silverlight application.

Frame Class Methods

This section covers the methods in the `Frame` class.

➤ `GoBack` — Navigates to the most recent entry in the back navigation history, or throws an exception if no entry exists in back navigation (Listing 4-14).

LISTING 4-14: The GoBack method

```
private void GoBackLink_Click
    (object sender, RoutedEventArgs e)
{
    if (ContentFrame.CanGoBack)
    {
        ContentFrame.GoBack();
    }
}
```

➤ `GoForward` — Navigates to the most recent entry in the forward navigation history, or throws an exception if no entry exists in forward navigation. Use the `CanGoForward` property to check whether there is an entry in the navigation history to go forward to (Listing 4-15).

LISTING 4-15: The GoForward method

```
private void GoForwardLink_Click
    (object sender, RoutedEventArgs e)
{
    if (ContentFrame.CanGoForward)
    {
        ContentFrame.GoForward();
    }
}
```

➤ `Navigate` — Navigates to the content specified by the uniform resource identifier (URI) (Listing 4-16).

LISTING 4-16: The Navigate method

```
private void NavigateLink_Click
    (object sender, RoutedEventArgs e)
{
    ContentFrame.Navigate
        (new Uri("/views/about.xaml", UriKind.Relative));
}
```

➤ `Refresh` — Reloads the current page (Listing 4-17). By default, navigation to the page that is currently loaded will not reload the content.

LISTING 4-17: The Refresh method

```
private void RefreshLink_Click
    (object sender, RoutedEventArgs e)
{
    ContentFrame.Refresh();
}
```

➤ `StopLoading` — Stops asynchronous navigations that have not yet been processed by raising the `NavigationStopped` event (Listing 4-18).

LISTING 4-18: The StopLoading method

```
private void CancelNavigationLink_Click
    (object sender, RoutedEventArgs e)
{
    ContentFrame.StopLoading();
}
```

Frame Class Properties

The following key properties are in the `Frame` class:

➤ `CacheSize` — Specifies how many pages can be retained in a cache. When a page is cached, an instance of the page is reused for each navigation request rather than re-creating the page for each request. The `CacheSize` property is used only when you set the `NavigationCacheMode` property of the `Page` class to `Enabled`. If you set the `NavigationCacheMode` property to `Required`, the page is cached regardless of the number of cached pages specified in the `CacheSize` property. Pages marked as `Required` do not count against the `CacheSize` total. See Listing 4-19.

LISTING 4-19: Setting the CacheSize property

```
<navigation:Frame x:Name="ContentFrame"
                   CacheSize="10"
                   Style="{StaticResource ContentFrameStyle}"
                   Source="/Home"
                   Navigated="ContentFrame_Navigated"
                   NavigationFailed="ContentFrame_NavigationFailed">
```

In the in the `Page` class, set the `NavigationCacheMode` to `Enabled`, `Required`, or `Disabled` (Listing 4-20).

LISTING 4-20: Setting the NavigationCacheMode property

```
<navigation:Page x:Class="NavigationApplication.About"
    ...
    Title="About"
    NavigationCacheMode="Required" >
```

➤ `CanGoBack` — Gets a value that indicates whether there is at least one entry in the back navigation history (Listing 4-21). If true is returned, there is at least one entry in the back navigation history; otherwise, false is returned.

LISTING 4-21: Checking the CanGoBack property

```
private void GoBackLink_Click
    (object sender, RoutedEventArgs e)
{
    if (ContentFrame.CanGoBack)
    {
        ContentFrame.GoBack();
    }
}
```

➤ `CanGoForward` — Gets a value that indicates whether there is at least one entry in the forward navigation history (Listing 4-22). If there are no entries in the forward navigation history, the-`GoForward` method throws an `InvalidOperationException`. Use the `CanGoForward` property to determine whether there is at least one entry in the forward navigation history.

LISTING 4-22: Checking the CanGoForward property

```
private void GoForwardLink_Click
    (object sender, RoutedEventArgs e)
{
    if (ContentFrame.CanGoForward)
    {
        ContentFrame.GoForward();
    }
}
```

➤ `ContentLoader` — Gets or sets the object responsible for providing the content that corresponds to a requested URI. The default is a `PageResourceContentLoader` instance. To get a complete example of using the advanced `ContentLoader` property, review the article at `http://www.davidpoll.com/tag/contentloader/`.

➤ `CurrentSource` — Gets or sets the URI of the content that is currently displayed (Listing 4-23).

LISTING 4-23: Using the CurrentSource property

```
private void ContentFrame_Navigated
    (object sender, NavigationEventArgs e)
{
    ApplicationNameTextBlock.Text =
        ContentFrame.CurrentSource.ToString();
    }
}
```

➤ `JournalOwnership` — Gets or sets whether a frame is responsible for managing its own navigation history, or whether it integrates with the web browser Journal. Use the `JournalOwnership` enumeration when setting the `JournalOwnership` property of the `Frame` class to specify whether the frame integrates with the browser Journal. When a frame is integrating with the browser Journal, the browser's navigation history includes navigation that has occurred within the frame. Only top-level frames can integrate with the browser Journal.

➤ `Source` — Gets or sets the URI of the current content or the content that is being navigated to (Listing 4-24). When the `Source` property is set to a value that is different from the content being displayed, the frame navigates to the new content.

LISTING 4-24: Setting the Source property

```csharp
private void SetSource_Click
    (object sender, RoutedEventArgs e)
{
    ContentFrame.Source = new Uri("/About", UriKind.Relative);
}
```

➤ `UriMapper` — Gets or sets the object to manage converting a URI to another URI for this frame.

Frame Class Events

This section covers the events in the `Frame` class.

➤ `FrameNavigation` — Occurs when navigation to a content fragment begins.

➤ `Navigated` — Occurs when the content that is being navigated to has been found and is available (Listing 4-25).

LISTING 4-25: Auto-generated Navigated event code from the Home.cs class

```csharp
private void ContentFrame_Navigated
    (object sender, NavigationEventArgs e)
{

    CurrentNavigatedSource.Text =
        ContentFrame.CurrentSource.ToString();

    // After the Frame navigates, ensure the
    // HyperlinkButton representing the current page is selected
    foreach (UIElement child in LinksStackPanel.Children)
    {
        HyperlinkButton hb = child as HyperlinkButton;
        if (hb != null && hb.NavigateUri != null)
        {
            if (hb.NavigateUri.ToString().Equals(e.Uri.ToString()))
            {
                VisualStateManager.GoToState(hb, "ActiveLink", true);
            }
```

continues

LISTING 4-25 *(continued)*

```
            else
            {
                VisualStateManager.GoToState(hb, "InactiveLink", true);
            }
        }
    }
}
```

➤ `Navigating` — Occurs when a new navigation is requested (Listing 4-26).

LISTING 4-26: Using the Navigating event

```
void ContentFrame_Navigating
    (object sender, NavigatingCancelEventArgs e)
{

    MessageBox.Show("you have navigating using mode "
        + e.NavigationMode);

    // cancel the navigation
    e.Cancel = true;
}
```

➤ `NavigationFailed` — Occurs when an error is encountered while navigating to the requested content (Listing 4-27).

LISTING 4-27: Using the NavigationFailed event

```
private void ContentFrame_NavigationFailed
    (object sender, NavigationFailedEventArgs e)
{
    e.Handled = true;
    ChildWindow errorWin = new ErrorWindow(e.Uri);
    errorWin.Show();
}
```

➤ `NavigationStopped` — Occurs when a navigation is terminated by calling the `StopLoading` method or when a new navigation is requested while the current navigation is in progress (Listing 4-28).

LISTING 4-28: Using the NavigationStopped event

```
void ContentFrame_NavigationStopped
    (object sender, NavigationEventArgs e)
{
    MessageBox.Show("navigation was cancelled or stopped");
}
```

USING A CUSTOM MENU CONTROL

In the previous examples, navigation was triggered by clicking a `HyperlinkButton` control. In some cases, you will use other types of controls to trigger navigation. The basic concept is the same no matter what type of control you use. In this example, you see how to implement navigation using a third-party menu control, the `xamWebMenu` from the Infragistics Silverlight controls toolset. The `XamWebMenu` easily integrates into the Navigation Framework by simply setting a few properties on the control and its menu items. Listing 4-29 is an example where I have taken the default `MainPage.xaml` template that is created when you start a Silverlight Navigation Application and I have added the `XamWebMenu` control to the page.

LISTING 4-29: Adding the Infragistics XamWebMenu for navigation

```
<!-- Default controls for navigation, this section would be removed
(everything inside the Border control if you replace
navigation with a custom menu control -->
<Border
        x:Name="LinksBorder"
        Style="{StaticResource LinksBorderStyle}">
    <StackPanel
                x:Name="LinksStackPanel"
                Style="{StaticResource LinksStackPanelStyle}">
        <HyperlinkButton x:Name="Link1"
                        Style="{StaticResource LinkStyle}"
                        NavigateUri="/Home"
                        TargetName="ContentFrame"
                        Content="home"/>
        <Rectangle
            x:Name="Divider1"
            Style="{StaticResource DividerStyle}"/>
        <HyperlinkButton
            x:Name="Link2"
            Style="{StaticResource LinkStyle}"
            NavigateUri="/About"
            TargetName="ContentFrame"
            Content="about"/>
    </StackPanel>
</Border>
<!--  This is the custom menu control - note the NavigationElement
is bound to the ContentFrame control, and the XamWebMenuItems
use the NavigationUri to navigate to the Uri in the
UriMapping collection -->
<ig:XamWebMenu
            NavigationElement="{Binding ElementName=ContentFrame}"
            Height="27"
            HorizontalAlignment="Left"
            Margin="214,6,0,0" Name="xamWebMenu1"
            VerticalAlignment="Top"
            Width="232" >

    <ig:XamWebMenuItem
```

continues

LISTING 4-29 *(continued)*

```
                  Header="Select a Nav Target">
          <ig:XamWebMenuItem
              NavigationOnClick="True"
              NavigationUri="/Home"
              Header="Home">
          </ig:XamWebMenuItem>

          <ig:XamWebMenuItem
              NavigationOnClick="True"
              NavigationUri="/About"
              Header="About"  />
          </ig:XamWebMenuItem>
      </ig:XamWebMenu>
```

You can see that on the main `XamWebMenu` control I use the `NavigationElement` property to tell the menu which element it should target when a menu item is clicked. In this case, I am binding to the `Frame` element on the page. Then, on each `XamWebMenuItem`, I have set two properties: the `NavigationOnClick` property and the `NavigationUri` property. The `NavigationOnClick` property, when set to `True`, tells the menu that I want to use the Silverlight Navigation framework when a menu item is clicked. The `NavigationUri` property tells the menu what URI I want the target `Frame` to navigate to when I click the menu item. When you run the project, you can see that as expected, clicking the menu items causes the content in the `Frame` to change. Figure 4-9 shows what the menu should look like based on the XAML added to the preceding page.

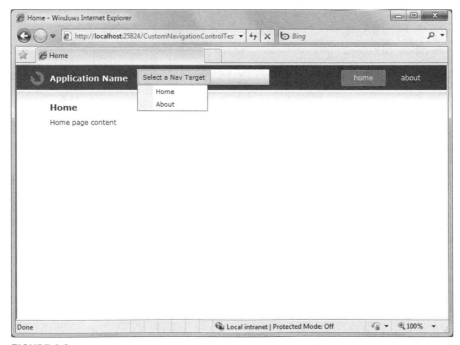

FIGURE 4-9

To get the `XamWebMenu`, download the Infragistics Silverlight controls at this link: `http://www` `.infragistics.com/dotnet/netadvantage/silverlight/line-of-business.aspx#Overview`.

ADDING NAVIGATION ANIMATIONS

One of the compelling features of Silverlight is its animations capabilities. You can flip, rotate, skew, bounce, shrink, grow, and a lot more on any object that is rendered on the screen. The same goes for the pages that you are navigating to via the Navigation Framework. This could be done in several ways, but the simplest is to use a control in the Silverlight Control Toolkit that you can download here:

`http://silverlight.codeplex.com/`

Once you download and install the Toolkit, you can run the samples that demonstrate its various features. One of the controls in the Toolkit is the `TransitioningContentControl`.

 The Silverlight Control Toolkit is licensed under MS-PL, or the Microsoft Permissive License. This means you are free to use the controls and source code for anything that you choose to, as long as the license reference is included in what you are redistributing. Note that these controls are not supported by Microsoft, so the only available support is via the various public forums on CodePlex and Silverlight.net.

The `TransitioningContentControl` is a `ContentControl` that provides four transition animations that are triggered when the `Content` property of the control is changed. The following four transitions are available:

➤ `DefaultTransition`

➤ `Normal`

➤ `UpTransition`

➤ `DownTransition`

To use the `TransitioningContentControl` to animate the content changes of the `Frame` control, you need to update the `ContentFrameStyle` in the `Styles.xaml` Resource Dictionary of a Navigation Application template, which is located in the Assets folder as shown in Figure 4-10.

To get this going, add a reference to the `System.Windows.Controls.Layout.Toolkit` assembly as shown in Figure 4-11. I chose to download the `.zip` file of the Silverlight Control Toolkit, so I browsed to the Bin folder on my machine where I unzipped the file. If you chose to install the MSI of the Silverlight Control Toolkit, look in the `\Program Files\Microsoft SDKs\Silverlight` folder.

Once this reference is added, add the following namespace reference to the `Styles.xaml` Resource Dictionary:

`xmlns:layout="http://schemas.microsoft.com/winfx/2006/xaml/presentation/toolkit"`

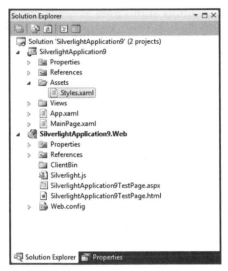

FIGURE 4-10

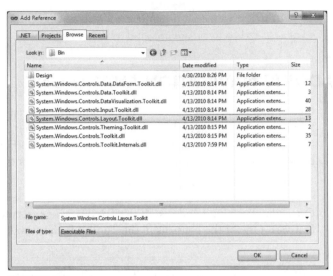

FIGURE 4-11

In the `Styles.xaml` file, locate the `ContentFrameStyle` (it is near the top of the file, or you can hit Ctrl+F to launch the Find dialog). Once you have located the `ContentFrameStyle`, update the `Setter` value for the `ControlTemplate` as shown in Listing 4-30.

Available for download on Wrox.com

LISTING 4-30: Updating the ContentFrameStyle in the Styles.xaml file

```xml
<!-- Content Frame Style -->
<Style x:Key="ContentFrameStyle"
      TargetType="navigation:Frame">
   <Setter Property="Background"
      Value="Transparent"/>
   <Setter Property="BorderBrush"
      Value="Transparent"/>
   <Setter Property="Padding"
      Value="58,15,58,15"/>
   <Setter
      Property="VerticalContentAlignment"
      Value="Stretch"/>
   <Setter
      Property="HorizontalContentAlignment"
      Value="Stretch"/>
   <Setter Property="Template">
      <Setter.Value>
         <ControlTemplate
               TargetType="navigation:Frame">
            <Border>
               <layout:TransitioningContentControl
                  <!-- The control supports the following
                       Transition values
                    DefaultTransition
```

```
                    Normal
                    UpTransition
                    DownTransition
                    -->
                      Transition="DownTransition"
             Content="{TemplateBinding Content}"  />
                 </Border>
             </ControlTemplate>
          </Setter.Value>
       </Setter>
    </Style>
```

If you look at the `Frame` control in the `MainPage.xaml`, you will see the `Style` property is set to `ContentFrameStyle`, which you have just modified:

```
<navigation:Frame x:Name="ContentFrame"
                  Style="{StaticResource ContentFrameStyle}"
```

The `Frame` control contains a `ContentPresenter`, which is replaced with the `TransitioningContentControl` when the `ContentFrameStyle` is merged with the page. Once the content of the `Frame` changes when a user triggers a navigation event, the specified transition executes based on the `Transition` property that you set in the style. You can experiment with the various `Transition` options to determine what works best for your application.

SUMMARY

This chapter gave you the information you need for fundamental navigation scenarios in Silverlight. You learned how to use and manipulate the Navigation Application template, how to create parameterized queries for real work Line of Business applications, and how to extend your application to use a richer, third party menu like the Infragistics `XamWebMenu` control. Finally, you learned how to add finishing touches to your navigation application, using a `TransitioningContentControl` to animate the transitions of the `Frame` control.

5

Controlling Layout with Panels

WHAT'S IN THIS CHAPTER?

➤   Measuring and arranging

➤   Sizing elements

➤   Using and making layout panels

Controlling the layout of an application's user interface (UI) is a problem that has long plagued developers. Over the years, rich-client developers have written thousands of lines of code solely devoted to reposition UI elements in the application as its window size changes. Web developers have long struggled with the multitude of positioning schemes available to them, starting with HTML tables and progressing to CSS layout, and — adding insult to injury — dealing with different browser interpretations of these layout schemes.

Microsoft looked to address many of the basic problems in application user interface layout with Windows Presentation Foundation (WPF) by creating a powerful, flexible, and highly extensible new layout system. Thankfully, they have brought most of those layout concepts into the world of Silverlight. Through the use of layout containers and panels, the Silverlight layout system gives you a level of layout control that was previously difficult, if not impossible, to achieve.

In this chapter, you first learn the basics of the Silverlight layout system and how it works to create flexible application user interfaces, and ways that you can influence how individual UI elements are sized and positioned. Next, you will learn about the different layout panels included in Silverlight that implement these layout concepts. You also learn how simple it is to take advantage of the layout system by building your own custom layout panel that includes your own layout logic. Finally, you learn how external influences such as browser rendering can influence the layout of your Silverlight application.

MEASURE, THEN ARRANGE

The basis of the Silverlight layout system is a two-pass measure and arrangement concept. While all UI elements participate in this system, most of the work is done by layout panels, so in this section, we talk about the layout system in the context of a panel.

When a layout panel in the application changes size or location, this invalidates the layout of the panel and triggers one or more passes of the Silverlight layout system. Panels can also be manually invalidated using the InvalidateMeasure and InvalidateArrange methods.

> *In order for an element to participate in the layout system, it must be added to the Visual Tree. The* Visual Tree *is the internal hierarchy of UI elements that Silverlight maintains. When a Silverlight application executes, the Visual Tree is constructed based on the XAML elements defined in the user interface. Elements can be added or removed from the tree at run time by manipulating a panel's* Children *collection. If you are creating UI elements at run time, make sure you add them to some panel's* Children *collection so that it is added to the Visual Tree.*

Once a panel becomes invalid, Silverlight initiates the Measure pass, which is shown in Figure 5-1.

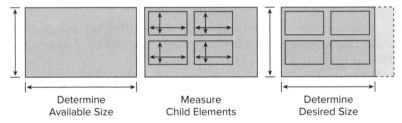

Determine Available Size   Measure Child Elements   Determine Desired Size

FIGURE 5-1

In the Measure pass, the invalid panel is told how much size it has available to it. The panel then has all of its child elements measure themselves, calculating how much space they would like to take based on the panel's available size. The size an element would like to be is called the element's DesiredSize and is usually based on the size of its content or a hard-coded Height or Width value.

> *Note that if a panel is the child of certain elements, such as the* ScrollViewer, *it can be told in the Measure pass that it has infinite height and/or width. This can affect how a panel renders its children, allowing them to take infinite height or width.*

The term *desired* size is used because although an element may desire a specific size, other factors in the user interface may cause the Silverlight layout system to force the element to be rendered with a different size. When all of the panel's children have completed measuring themselves, the panel can determine how much of the available size it would like to use and returns that value to the Silverlight layout system.

Once the Measure pass completes, Silverlight calculates the final size available to the panel and the second pass of the layout system, the Arrange pass (see Figure 5-2) is executed.

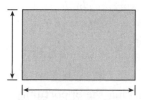

1. Determine Pre-Arrangement Final Size

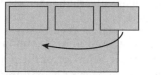 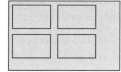

2. Arrange Child Elements Based on Panel Logic

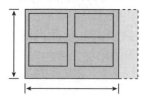

3. Determine Post-Arrangement Final Size

FIGURE 5-2

During the Arrange pass, the panel has the opportunity to arrange each of its children based on its panel-specific logic and by asking the child elements for their final size. Based on the arrangement of the children, the panel returns its final size to the layout system before being rendered.

The final height and width of the panel is called its `ActualWidth` and `ActualHeight`.

> *When querying an element for its current size, you should always use the* `ActualHeight` *and* `ActualWidth` *properties since the element's parent can alter the element's height and width regardless of any explicit height and width values that might be set. Also note that the* `ActualHeight` *and* `ActualWidth` *properties can return a value of zero. This can happen if the element is either not in the Visual Tree or has not gone through a layout pass.*

Later in this chapter you will look at the different `Panels` available in Silverlight, and the arrangement logic used by each, as well as how you can create panels with your own custom measure and arrangement logic.

Each time a UI element changes size or position, it has the potential to trigger a new pass of the layout system, which can cascade down the Visual Tree invalidating children of the original invalid element. If the Visual Tree is large, this can be an expensive process. To help reduce the amount of work performed by the layout system, Silverlight will cache arranged versions of the Visual Tree. As the invalidation of elements cascades down, if Silverlight determines that a specific child element's size and position have not changed, it will use the cached version of the elements, rather than triggering the measure and arrange passes for it.

As mentioned earlier, during the Arrange pass of the layout system, a panel has the opportunity to arrange its children based on its arrangement logic. When positioning elements, the panel is in reality positioning a rectangle called a *layout slot*, which contains the element. Silverlight surrounds every UI element with this rectangle to simplify the arrangement process.

The size of the layout slot is determined by the layout system, giving consideration to the amount of available screen space, constraints like margin and padding, and the unique behavior of the parent `Panel`. It is up to the parent container to determine the size of the layout for each of its children. You can get the `Rectangle`, and through that the size of the layout slot, by using the static `System .Windows.Controls.LayoutInformation.GetLayoutSlot` method.

If an element extends outside of its allocated layout slot, the layout system will begin to clip the element. You can get the dimensions of the visible portion of the element by calling the `System .Windows.Controls.LayoutInformation.GetLayoutClip` method.

ELEMENT SIZING CHARACTERISTICS

Every `FrameworkElement` includes several properties that can help the element influence its size and position within the layout container. These properties are:

➤ `Height` and `Width`

➤ `Alignment`

➤ `Margin`

➤ `Padding`

This section looks at these different properties and how you can use them to control how elements of your user interface are arranged.

Height and Width

The most direct way to control a `FrameworkElement`'s size is to use its `Height` and `Width` properties. These properties allow you to set specific pixel values for the element's height and width, and depending on the `FrameworkElement`'s layout container, these values will usually override any other size properties set on the element.

For users who have set their OS DPI to a value other than the default 96 DPI, browsing the Web can be difficult. This is because most browsers are not DPI-aware and cannot take advantage of Windows DPI Scaling features to improve the readability of their content. Internet Explorer 8 (IE 8) helps off-set this issue by automatically increasing its zoom level based on the OS DPI setting, but Silverlight itself is not DPI-aware (pixels are always rendered at a fixed 1/96th of an inch), and therefore it will not automatically scale its own content. To work around this problem, you can use a scale transform based on the actual size of the Silverlight plug-in object, which will be scaled by IE. Or if you are targeting only Internet Explorer to host your application, you can detect the OS DPI using the Silverlight DOM Bridge to get the value of the `deviceXDPI` *property of the Internet Explorer DOM.*

By default, `FrameworkElement`s have their `Width` and `Height` properties set to `Double.NaN`, which is interpreted by the layout system as "Auto." Auto layout generally means that the layout system will size the element to fill whatever space is available in the layout, rather than sizing to any specific pixel value. This is shown in Figure 5-3, where a button with no height or width set has been added to a `Grid`.

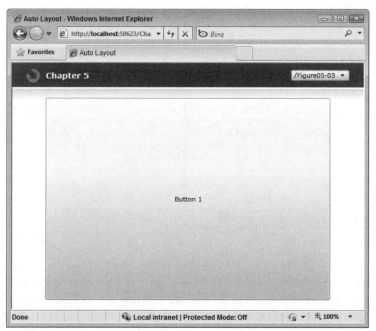

FIGURE 5-3

You can clearly see that the `Button` consumes all the available space in the `Grid`.

Although not necessary, you can explicitly set the Width *and* Height *properties to Auto in XAML. It is also possible to reset a* FrameworkElement's *height and width value back to Auto by assigning the property a value of* Double.NaN *in code.*

Note that in Figure 5-3, neither the Grid nor its container, the UserControl, have Width and Height properties set; therefore, they too default to Auto size. This explains why the Grid is consuming all available space of its layout container, the UserControl, and the UserControl is consuming all available space of its container, the Silverlight plug-in.

Setting an explicit width or height on the Button will constrain its size within the Grid, as shown in Figure 5-4, where the Button now has its Width property set to 150.

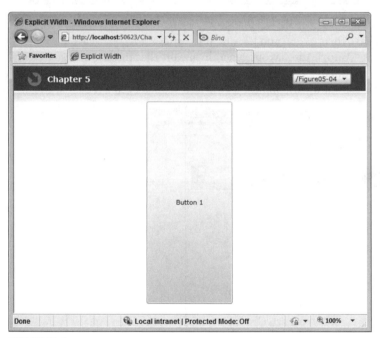

FIGURE 5-4

Also, by default the button has its HorizontalAlignment and VerticalAlignment properties set to stretch. This means that the Button is going to stretch to fill its parent container. Setting these properties to a different value, such as center, changes the layout behavior of the Button so that it sizes itself based on the size of its content.

Leaving a control's Height or Width as Auto allows its containing Panel to influence how the control is ultimately rendered. For example, if you take the code from the previous listing and substitute a StackPanel for the Grid as the Button's layout container, you will see that the Button's height is rendered differently. This is because of the different arrangement logic used by the StackPanel compared to the Grid, which will be explained in greater detail when we examine the StackPanel layout container later in this chapter.

In addition to setting explicit height and width values, every `FrameworkElement` can also have height and width thresholds set on it. Using the `FrameworkElement`'s `MinWidth`, `MinHeight`, `MaxWidth`, and `MaxHeight` properties, you can dictate to the layout system that the element should never exceed certain height or width values. Setting these values will even override the `FrameworkElement`'s `Width` or `Height` properties if they are explicitly set to values outside the minimum or maximum ranges.

In cases in which the size given to the `FrameworkElement`'s layout container is less than the `MinWidth` or `MinHeight` of the `FrameworkElement`, the container will begin to clip the element rather than reduce the element's size.

Alignment

`FrameworkElements` can have a horizontal or vertical alignment set on them. The alignment properties include the standard alignment values — `Left`, `Right`, and `Center` for horizontal alignment and `Top`, `Center`, and `Bottom` for vertical alignment — but by default, an element's alignment is set to a fourth option, called `Stretch`. `Stretch` tells the element that it should attempt to fill its parent's entire layout slot.

Margin and Padding

Finally, there are two additional properties you can use to influence the size and position of UI elements in your application, `FrameworkElement`'s `Margin` property and `Control`'s `Padding` property.

Margin

The `Margin` property allows you to add space to the outside of the element, between it and any other elements that surround it. You can set an element's margin as a single uniform value:

```
<Button Margin="10" />
```

You can also control the margin for each side of the element individually. In XAML, you can set the margin for each side of the element by specifying a comma-delimited list. The order of the `Margin` values is `Left`, `Top`, `Right`, `Bottom`:

```
<Button Margin="10,5,10,5" />
```

When a `FrameworkElement`'s container has no size constraints, the margins will push the Layout Slot boundaries outward. Figure 5-5 demonstrates this by placing a `Button` with explicitly set `Height` and `Width` properties and a margin size of `40` into a `Grid` that has no explicit height or width set.

By setting the `Grid`'s `Background` to `LightGray` and its `HorizontalAlignment` and `VerticalAlignment` to `Center`, you can see that the button's margin pushes the grid outward beyond the boundaries of the button.

If the Silverlight layout system determines that space is not available to add the margin to the `FrameworkElement`, the system attempts to constrain, or even clip, the element's content in order to display the full margins. If the `FrameworkElement` has an explicit height or width set, the content of the element will be clipped. This is shown in Figure 5-6, where an explicit width and height has been set on the grid and the content of the button is now clipped when a margin is added.

FIGURE 5-5

FIGURE 5-6

It is also possible to set margin values to negative values. Doing this allows you to position elements outside of their normal position.

If the `FrameworkElement` does not have an explicit size set, Silverlight attempts to constrain the element content in order to display the full margins.

Padding

The `Padding` property allows you to add space around the inside of an element. Figure 5-7 demonstrates this by showing two `Border` controls inside of a two-column grid. Both `Border` controls contain a rectangle. The `Border` control on the left has no `Padding` set, while the one on the right has had its `Padding` property set to increase the buffer between it and the child rectangle.

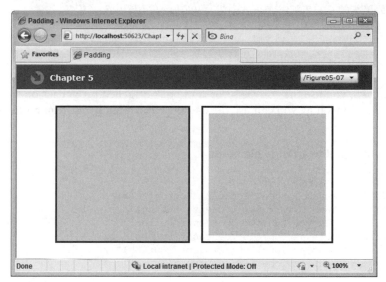

FIGURE 5-7

As with the `Margin` properties, if the parent element has no explicit size set, the element increases in size in order to accommodate the padding.

`Margin` and `Padding` are cumulative, meaning that if the parent element has `Padding` defined and the inner element has `Margin` defined, Silverlight displays both.

Finally, unlike `Margin`, `Padding` cannot be set to negative values.

USING LAYOUT PANELS

Now that you have a basic understanding of how the Silverlight layout system works, you can begin to use some of the layout panels that are native to Silverlight or are available in the Silverlight Toolkit that leverage this system. Each of these panels provides a unique layout mechanism you can leverage in your application.

Additionally, there are numerous third-party and open source layout panels available that you can leverage in your application.

Canvas

The Canvas layout panel provides you with a way to position elements using an explicit coordinate system. Elements contained in the Canvas are positioned relative to the top-left corner of the panel, which is considered position 0,0.

While this layout panel may feel the most familiar to developers who are coming from the Windows Forms world, for the most part, you should avoid using Canvas *in your applications (or at least use it sparingly) because it forces you to do most of the work to control the position of your UI elements, rather than allowing the layout system to do this for you. An excellent explanation of why the use of* Canvas *should be avoided can be found here:* http://blogs.msdn .com/devdave/archive/2008/05/21/why-i-don-t-like-canvas.aspx.

To position elements on the Canvas, you use the Canvas's Top and Left attached properties on its child elements. Listing 5-1 demonstrates how you can use the Canvas to absolutely position buttons.

LISTING 5-1: Using the Canvas panel to arrange elements

```
<Canvas>
    <Button Canvas.Left="0" Canvas.Top="0" Content="Button1" />
    <Button Canvas.Left="50" Canvas.Top="25" Content="Button1" />
    <Button Canvas.Left="100" Canvas.Top="50" Content="Button1" />
    <Button Canvas.Left="150" Canvas.Top="75" Content="Button1" />
    <Button Canvas.Left="200" Canvas.Top="100" Content="Button1" />
    <Button Canvas.Left="250" Canvas.Top="125" Content="Button1" />
</Canvas>
```

Figure 5-8 shows how the buttons are absolutely positioned within the Canvas when the application is run.

While Canvas is useful when you need to explicitly position elements in your user interface — for example, if your application performs some type of physics-based rendering or drawing — it does mean that your user interface becomes less dynamic and will not be able to scale properly as the available space in the UI changes. Canvas does not consider some of the basic element characteristics like HorizontalAlignment and VerticalAlignment when positioning children because Canvas is based on absolute positioning.

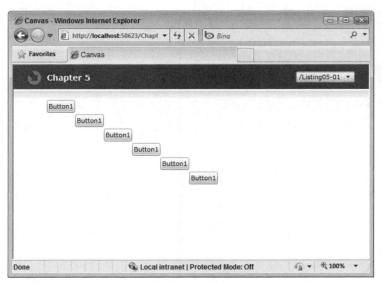

FIGURE 5-8

StackPanel

As the name implies, the StackPanel simply stacks elements vertically or horizontally. Listing 5-2 demonstrates using the StackPanel to create a vertical stack of elements.

Available for download on Wrox.com

LISTING 5-2: Using StackPanel to stack elements

```
<StackPanel>
    <Button Content="Button" />
    <TextBlock>Lorum Ipsum</TextBlock>
    <Slider></Slider>
    <HyperlinkButton Content="HyperlinkButton" />
    <CheckBox />
</StackPanel>
```

As you can see in Figure 5-9, when child elements are added to the StackPanel, the panel simply stacks them in a vertical orientation by default. Using the StackPanel's Orientation property, you can change the panel to stack elements horizontally.

When the StackPanel's orientation is set to Vertical, the control sets its available height to Infinity, allowing its children to take an infinite amount of vertical space if they have no explicit size set. If the orientation is horizontal, then the panel's width is set to Infinity.

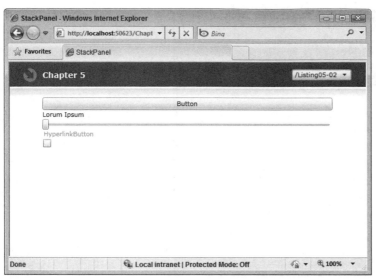

FIGURE 5-9

This is one reason why the StackPanel works well in conjunction with the ScrollViewer control. As a StackPanel's children begin to exceed the amount of vertical or horizontal space available to the panel, the ScrollViewer allows you to start scrolling them into view, rather than adjusting their own size.

Additionally, as with every other element, StackPanel can have its height and width set. If no width is set, the StackPanel will make itself as wide as its widest child. If no height is set, it takes enough height to display all of its children.

VirtualizingStackPanel

The VirtualizingStackPanel offers the same basic element stacking arrangement as the StackPanel, but because it is derived from the VirtualizingStackPanel, it leverages virtualization to help reduce the number of UI elements created in your application.

Working with an ItemsControl like ListBox, the VirtualizingStackPanel can determine which items in the list are currently visible on screen, and generates only the UI elements needed for those items that can help you increase the performance of your application.

> *Starting in Silverlight 3, the* ListBox *default items panel is the* VirtualizingStackPanel, *so if you are using this control, you will automatically see the benefits of the virtualization. In order for the* ListBox *to determine the number of items visible, the control needs to be able to calculate some height value. If your* ListBox *is inside of a* ScrollViewer, *you will need to either set an explicit height on the* ListBox *or turn off the* VerticalScrollBarVisibility.

In addition to ListBox, you can use the VirtualizingStackPanel to increase the performance of the ComboBox. Listing 5-3 demonstrates using the VirtualizingStackPanel with the ComboBox control.

LISTING 5-3: Using the VirtualizingStackPanel with the ComboBox

Available for
download on
Wrox.com

```
<ComboBox x:Name="comboBox1">
    <ComboBox.ItemsPanel>
        <ItemsPanelTemplate>
            <VirtualizingStackPanel />
        </ItemsPanelTemplate>
    </ComboBox.ItemsPanel>
</ComboBox>
```

As you can see, to use the VirtualizingStackPanel, you simply assign it to the ComboBox's ItemsPanel property.

Grid

Perhaps the most powerful layout container in Silverlight is the Grid layout panel. As the name implies, the Grid allows you to define a grid of rows and columns in which you can position child elements.

Listing 5-4 demonstrates a simple Grid layout container.

LISTING 5-4: Defining rows and columns in a Grid layout panel

Available for
download on
Wrox.com

```
<Grid Background="White" ShowGridLines="True">
    <Grid.RowDefinitions>
        <RowDefinition />
        <RowDefinition />
    </Grid.RowDefinitions>
    <Grid.ColumnDefinitions>
        <ColumnDefinition />
        <ColumnDefinition />
    </Grid.ColumnDefinitions>

    <TextBlock Text="Grid Cell 1" Grid.Row="0" Grid.Column="0" />
    <TextBlock Text="Grid Cell 1" Grid.Row="0" Grid.Column="1" />
    <TextBlock Text="Grid Cell 1" Grid.Row="1" Grid.Column="0" />
    <TextBlock Text="Grid Cell 1" Grid.Row="1" Grid.Column="1" />
</Grid>
```

In the previous sample, a grid structure consisting of two rows and two columns is created using the grid's RowDefinitions and ColumnDefinitions collections. Once the structure is defined, several TextBlocks are added to the grid. Using the grid's Row and Column attached properties, you can dictate which grid cell each TextBlock element should be positioned in.

If you add children to the Grid, but do not explicitly set a Row or Column value, the grid automatically assumes they will be in row zero, column zero.

The `Grid` also exposes `RowSpan` and `ColumnSpan` attached properties that you can use to alter how an element is positioned in the `Grid`. Listing 5-5 demonstrates using these attached properties to allow a `TextBlock` to span two grid columns.

LISTING 5-5: Using a ColumnSpan with a TextBlock

```
<Grid Background="White" ShowGridLines="True">
    <Grid.RowDefinitions>
        <RowDefinition />
        <RowDefinition />
    </Grid.RowDefinitions>
    <Grid.ColumnDefinitions>
        <ColumnDefinition />
        <ColumnDefinition />
    </Grid.ColumnDefinitions>

    <TextBlock Grid.Row="0" Grid.Column="0"
            Grid.ColumnSpan="2" TextWrapping="Wrap">
        Lorem ipsum dolor sit amet, consectetuer adipiscing elit.
        Sed ultricies lectus et dui. Quisque vulputate facilisis nisl.
        Nulla sed turpis. Pellentesque ultricies mi ac velit. Praesent
        id turpis. Nunc mattis pharetra enim. In leo eros, sollicitudin
        vitae, ultricies accumsan, luctus quis, justo.
    </TextBlock>
    <TextBlock Text="Grid Cell 1/0" Grid.Row="1" Grid.Column="0" />
    <TextBlock Text="Grid Cell 1/1" Grid.Row="1" Grid.Column="1" />
</Grid>
```

The `Grid` also allows you to set properties on the individual rows and columns that affect their layout. The `RowDefinition` and `ColumnDefinition` classes expose properties that allow you to set their `Height` or `Width`.

Unlike a standard element's `Width` and `Height` properties, which only accept pixel measurements or the `Auto` keyword, `Grid` `Row` and `Column` size properties accept a special measurement type called `GridLength`. This type not only offers the standard size units (`Pixels` or `Auto`), but also includes an additional measurement type call `Star`. The `Star` unit allows you to provide a value that expresses a size as a weighted proportion of available space. To specify a `Star` value, you simply provide the literal `*` character as the value for the `Width` property. You can also specify a factor by placing an integer preceding the `*`, for example, `3*`.

Listing 5-6 demonstrates the use of the `Star` sizing in a `Grid`.

LISTING 5-6: Using Star sizing with the Grid

```
<Grid Background="White" ShowGridLines="True">
    <Grid.RowDefinitions>
        <RowDefinition />
        <RowDefinition />
    </Grid.RowDefinitions>
    <Grid.ColumnDefinitions>
        <ColumnDefinition Width="100" />
```

```
        <ColumnDefinition Width="*" />
        <ColumnDefinition Width="2*" />
        <ColumnDefinition Width="*" />
    </Grid.ColumnDefinitions>
</Grid>
```

In this sample, the first `ColumnDefinition` has an explicit pixel width set, while the rest use `Star` size values. The third `ColumnDefinition` includes a factorial value that specifies that the width given to this column should be two times that given to the other columns. Figure 5-10 shows the resulting grid rendered.

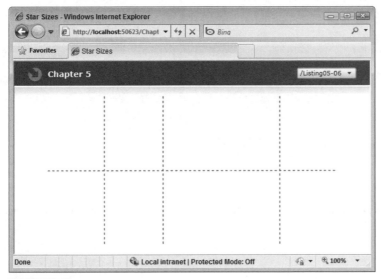

FIGURE 5-10

In this case, the `Grid` has had its `ShowGridLines` property set to `True` in order to show the column widths.

WrapPanel

The `WrapPanel`, included in the Silverlight Toolkit, allows you to create a layout that wraps UI elements when they begin to exceed the width of the wrap panel. Listing 5-7 demonstrates the use of the `WrapPanel`.

Available for
download on
Wrox.com

LISTING 5-7: Using the Silverlight Toolkit's WrapPanel

```
<my:WrapPanel>
    <Button Content="Button" />
    <TextBlock>Lorum Ipsum</TextBlock>
    <Slider></Slider>
    <HyperlinkButton Content="HyperlinkButton" />
    <CheckBox />
</my:WrapPanel>
```

You can see that using the `WrapPanel` is virtually identical to using the `StackPanel`. As the width of the panel changes, the elements within it will wrap to new lines, as shown in Figure 5-11.

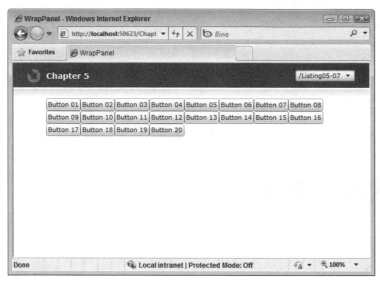

FIGURE 5-11

If there are enough elements to begin to exceed the height of the panel, it will begin to show a vertical scrollbar.

DockPanel

The `DockPanel`, also included in the Silverlight Toolkit, allows you to dock elements to the edge of the panel. If you are familiar with Windows Forms, the `DockPanel` provides a layout behavior similar to the `Dock` property of Windows Forms controls.

Listing 5-8 shows how you can use the `DockPanel`, using the panel's attached properties on its child elements to control their dock behavior.

LISTING 5-8: Using the Silverlight Toolkit's DockPanel

```
<controlsToolkit:DockPanel>
    <Button Content="Left" controlsToolkit:DockPanel.Dock="Left" />
    <Button Content="Top" controlsToolkit:DockPanel.Dock="Top" />
    <Button Content="Right" controlsToolkit:DockPanel.Dock="Right" />
    <Button Content="Bottom" controlsToolkit:DockPanel.Dock="Bottom" />
    <Button Content="Center" />
</controlsToolkit:DockPanel>
```

You can see that in this listing, the `DockPanel` contains four `Button`s. Each `Button` has the `DockPanel`'s `Dock` property set on it, dictating the side of the panel the `Button` is docked to.

Finding Third-Party Panels

In addition to the layout panels available as native Silverlight panels or as part of the Silverlight Toolkit, there are many other places to find layout panels. Third-party component vendors offer a variety of layout panels with different panels, and a quick Bing search demonstrates that there are many other sources of layout panels, from developers posting panels in a blog to open source projects hosted on CodePlex.

One of the more interesting open source projects is Blacklight, which is hosted on CodePlex (`www.codeplex.com/blacklight`). This project contains two interesting layout panels: the Drag Dock Panel and the Animated Layout Panel. The Drag Dock Panel allows you to create a series of content panels that the end user can reorder through drag-and-drop gestures. The Animated Layout Panel allows you to define an animation that is used when new elements are shown or hidden in the panel.

Listing 5-9 demonstrates how you can use the Drag Dock Panel.

Available for download on Wrox.com

LISTING 5-9: Using the Blacklight Drag Dock Panel

```
<Grid x:Name="LayoutRoot">
    <blacklight:DragDockPanelHost Margin="50">
        <blacklight:DragDockPanel>
            <Button Content="Button 1" />
        </blacklight:DragDockPanel>
        <blacklight:DragDockPanel>
            <Button Content="Button 2" />
        </blacklight:DragDockPanel>
        <blacklight:DragDockPanel>
            <Button Content="Button 3" />
        </blacklight:DragDockPanel>
        <blacklight:DragDockPanel>
            <Button Content="Button 4" />
        </blacklight:DragDockPanel>
        <blacklight:DragDockPanel>
            <Button Content="Button 5" />
        </blacklight:DragDockPanel>
    </blacklight:DragDockPanelHost>
</Grid>
```

As the listing shows, to use the panel, simply create a `DragDockPanelHost` and then add as many `DragDockPanels` as you want. Each `DragDockPanel` contains the unique elements you want to show in that panel.

CREATING CUSTOM PANELS

As stated earlier in the chapter, the layout system included in Silverlight is not only highly flexible but very extensible. It is quite easy to leverage the layout system to create your own custom layout panels that contain your own unique arrangement logic. In order to show this, this section demonstrates how to create a version of the `WrapPanel` control shown earlier called `SimpleWrapPanel`.

The layout logic for the panel will stack its child elements from left to right, starting in the upper-left corner of the panel. When the child elements begin to exceed the width of the panel, the panel will automatically begin to wrap the elements to a new row.

To get started creating a custom panel, simply create a new Silverlight Class Library in your project. Once the class file has been created, change the class so that it derives from the base `Panel` object. This is shown in Listing 5-10.

LISTING 5-10: Deriving from the base Panel

```
using System;
using System.Windows;
using System.Windows.Controls;

namespace SimpleWrapPanelSample
{
    public class SimpleWrapPanel : Panel
    {
    }
}
```

Next, you must override two methods from the base `Panel` — `MeasureOverride` and `ArrangeOverride`. This is shown in Listing 5-11.

LISTING 5-11: Overriding the MeasureOverride and ArrangeOverride methods

```
public class SimpleWrapPanel : Panel
{
    protected override Size MeasureOverride(Size availableSize)
    {
    }

    protected override Size ArrangeOverride(Size finalSize)
    {
    }
}
```

Now all that is left to do is for you to implement your own layout logic in the `Measure` and `Arrange` methods. The logic for the `SimpleWrapPanel`'s `MeasureOverride` method is shown in Listing 5-12.

LISTING 5-12: MeasureOverride logic for SimpleWrapPanel

```
protected override Size MeasureOverride(Size availableSize)
{
    Size size = new Size();

    foreach (UIElement element in this.Children)
    {
        if (element != null)
```

```
        {
            element.Measure(availableSize);
            Size desiredSize = element.DesiredSize;

            size.Width = Math.Max(size.Width, desiredSize.Width);
            size.Height += desiredSize.Height;
        }
    }

    return size;
}
```

The first step in the method is to loop through all of the panel's child elements and call `Measure` on each one of them, passing in the `availableSize` parameter. This causes the child elements to calculate their own desired sizes.

Next, in the same loop, the `Panel` control attempts to identify the amount of space needed by the panel for the layout. This is calculated by finding the width of the widest element in the panel and by calculating the sum height of all elements in the panel. Once the size is determined, it is returned as the result of the method. The value returned from this method is the panel's Desired Size, as discussed earlier in the chapter.

Once the layout system has completed the Measure pass, it then executes its Arrange. The Arrange pass is when the panel actually positions its child elements in the final space allocated to the panel by the layout system. The positioning of the child elements is done by calling the `Arrange` method on each child of the `Panel`, passing the child its final desired size and position by using a `Rectangle` object.

Listing 5-13 shows the panel's `ArrangeOverride` method, which includes the positioning logic for the panel.

LISTING 5-13: ArrangeOverride logic for SimpleWrapPanel

```
protected override Size ArrangeOverride(Size finalSize)
{
    Point point = new Point(0, 0);

    double top = 0.0;
    double left = 0.0;

    double maxheight = 0.0;
    double rowheight = 0.0;
    double width = 0.0;

    foreach (UIElement element in this.Children)
    {
        if (element != null)
        {

            left += width;
```

continues

LISTING 5-13 *(continued)*

```
        width = element.DesiredSize.Width;

        //Check to see if this element will be rendered outside of
        //the panels width and if so, create a new row in the panel
        if ((left + element.DesiredSize.Width) >
                finalSize.Width)
        {
            left = 0.0;

            maxheight += rowheight;
            top = maxheight;
            rowheight = 0.0;
        }

        //Find the tallest element in this row
        if (element.DesiredSize.Height > rowheight)
            rowheight = element.DesiredSize.Height;

        element.Arrange(
            new Rect(left, top,
                    element.DesiredSize.Width,
                    element.DesiredSize.Height)
        );
    }
}

    return finalSize;
}
```

The logic in the `Arrange` method for this panel is relatively simple. First, several internal members are defined which help the `Panel` track information about the positioned elements. The `Panel` needs to track three things: the cumulative width of all elements it has positioned in the current row, the height of the tallest element in the current row, and the cumulative height of all rows in the panel.

The cumulative width is used to correctly position the next element in the row. The tallest element in the current row is used to determine the overall row height. As each element is positioned, the `Panel` checks to see if its height is greater than any other element that has been positioned in the row before it. The cumulative row height of all rows in the panel is used to determine the position of the next row.

Next, the method begins to enumerate each child element of the panel, calculating the position for each child element and calling its `Arrange` method. As the `Panel` enumerates each element, it sets the `Width` and `Height` and `X` and `Y` properties of the positioning rectangle using the data from the internal members.

The `Panel` also checks to determine if the element, when positioned, will exceed the width of the panel. If this is found to be true, the `Panel` resets the `Rectangle`'s `X` and `Y` properties to reposition the element onto a new row.

Finally, the child elements' `Arrange` method is called. A new `Rectangle` object is created, which is used to provide the panel's children with the information they need to position themselves within the panel.

> *Note that in the `ArrangeOverride` method, if you try to make the height or width of a child element smaller than its desired size, the size passed into the child's `Arrange` method is ignored, and the element continues to render at its desired size. If you want to keep the smaller size, then you may need to apply a clip to that element so that it won't overspill its layout slot. Or earlier during the panel's Measure phase you can pass in the size that you actually want it to be.*

Figure 5-12 shows the results of the panel once it is rendered.

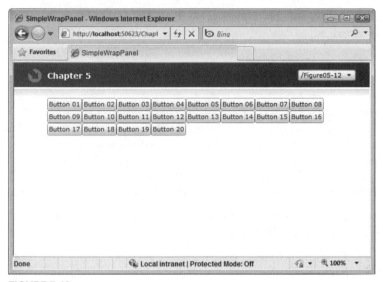

FIGURE 5-12

While the Wrap Panel is a simple example of a custom panel, every panel that you create will follow the same basic Measure and Arrange principles.

SILVERLIGHT PLUG-IN SIZING

As described earlier, at its core, Silverlight is a browser plug-in, which is added to the page using a standard HTML `<object>` tag. This means that when mixed into a page that contains other HTML, CSS, and JavaScript, the specific way the browser renders this content can have significant influence over how the Silverlight plug-in is sized and positioned.

To control the size of the browser plug-in, you can set a `Height` and a `Width` attribute on the `object` tag in HTML, as shown in Listing 5-14.

LISTING 5-14: Setting the Silverlight plug-in's Height and Width

```
<object data="data:application/x-silverlight-2,"
        type="application/x-silverlight-2" width="100%" height="100%">
  <param name="source" value="ClientBin/Chapter5.xap"/>
  <param name="onError" value="onSilverlightError" />
  <param name="background" value="white" />
  <param name="minRuntimeVersion" value="3.0.40818.0" />
  <param name="autoUpgrade" value="true" />
  <a href="http://go.microsoft.com/fwlink/?LinkID=
          149156&v=3.0.40818.0" style="text-decoration:none">
    <img src="http://go.microsoft.com/fwlink/?LinkId=161376"
        alt="Get Microsoft Silverlight" style="border-style:none"/>
  </a>
</object>
```

As with other HTML `Height` and `Width` attributes, you can provide either percent values, like those shown in the sample, or fixed pixel values.

SUMMARY

Silverlight provides a new and innovating user interface layout system that allows you to create highly flexible user interfaces that easily adjust to and accommodate changes in application and content size. This chapter introduced you to the basics of this new layout system, starting with an overview of the new Measure, Arrange, and Render pattern used by Silverlight to intelligently render UI elements. This two-pass system allows Silverlight first to evaluate the amount of space that each UI element needs, and then to arrange each of these elements in the actual amount of space available.

The layout system allows you to influence this process by setting various sizing characteristics such as the height, width, alignment, and margin on UI elements.

The chapter then introduced you to the available `Panel` control, which is responsible for most of the element arrangement that happens in Silverlight. You can choose a panel that uses a layout scheme that meets your layout needs, be it `Grid`, `StackPanel`, or `Canvas`; or as the chapter showed, you can create your own custom panel with your own custom layout scheme.

Finally, the chapter looked briefly at how the browser itself can influence how Silverlight renders its content and how you can use the object tag to configure the Silverlight object size.

6

Working with Visual Controls

WHAT'S IN THIS CHAPTER?

➤ Finding Silverlight controls

➤ Using UI controls

➤ Creating custom controls

Like most other Microsoft platforms, Silverlight allows developers to use controls to define an application's user interface (UI). Controls allow developers to be more productive by encapsulating reusable chunks of behavior and a UI into a single package that makes it easy to add the user interface to your application. Rather than being responsible for drawing every detail and coding every behavior, controls allow you to focus more on the specific requirements of your application and less on developing those lower-level capabilities.

Silverlight provides a rich set of native controls as part of the platform. Additionally, there are many other sources of controls including the Silverlight SDK, Silverlight Toolkit, third-party vendors, and open source projects. This chapter will introduce you to many of the controls across all of these resources. The chapter is not intended to be an in-depth guide to every single control included in Silverlight, however, because many of the controls are fairly self-explanatory. Additionally, although this chapter will touch on certain controls such as `MediaElement` and `TextBlock`, they are discussed in much greater detail in other, more applicable chapters of the book.

> *Because of the large number of Silverlight controls that are available from a variety of sources, it can be difficult to know what assembly a specific control is contained in. To make navigating this information easier, Appendix E contains a table that maps the controls discussed in this chapter with the assemblies they are found in.*

Finally, this chapter focuses primarily on the visual user interface controls you can use in Silverlight. Another set of items that appears in Visual Studio and Blend is layout panels like the `Grid` and `StackPanel`. Those are discussed in greater detail in Chapter 5.

WHERE TO FIND CONTROLS

As stated in the introduction to this chapter, there are many places where you can look to find a wide variety of useful controls. Before beginning to dive into the specific controls, it's useful to understand where you can find different controls and the consequences of choosing controls from different sources.

Controls for Silverlight can be found in the following general sources:

➤ Native Silverlight Platform

➤ Silverlight SDK

➤ Silverlight Controls Toolkit

➤ Third-party vendors

➤ Open source projects

➤ Custom controls

Each of these sources has different strengths and weaknesses. Obviously, controls that are included in the native platform are the easiest to leverage, but the number of controls in that set is limited. Controls included in the Silverlight SDK are also convenient to use, but because they are not part of the native platform, using them requires you to add additional assemblies to your application, which will increase the size of the application XAP.

In addition to the controls that Microsoft includes in the native platform and Silverlight SDK, an additional set of controls is available through the Silverlight Controls Toolkit. These controls are made available outside the Silverlight release cycle and are made available with full source code via the Microsoft CodePlex website: `www.codeplex.com/Silverlight`.

Having a separate set of controls outside of Silverlight allows Microsoft to release new controls more frequently and at differing levels of quality than are required for controls in the SDK. The Toolkit uses three quality bands to describe the status of the controls. The quality bands are explained in Table 6-1.

TABLE 6-1

BAND	DESCRIPTION
Mature	Mature components are ready for full release, meeting the highest levels of quality and stability. Future releases of mature components will maintain a high-quality bar with no breaking changes except when such changes are necessary to make them more secure or guarantee future compatibility. Customers should be confident using mature components, knowing that when they upgrade from one version of the Silverlight Toolkit to a newer version, it will be a quick and easy process. Owing to the heavy focus on backward compatibility between versions, the bar for fixing bugs found in mature components is also considerably higher than for any other quality band.

BAND	DESCRIPTION
Stable	Stable components are suitable for the vast majority of usage scenarios and will have incorporated most major design and functionality feedback. They are designed to address more than 90 percent of customer scenarios and will continue evolving via limited bug fixes and fit-and-finish work. *Stable* is similar to *Beta* in other projects. Stable components will have a very small number of breaking APIs or behavior changes when feedback demands it.
Preview	Preview components are intended to meet most basic usage scenarios. While in the Preview Quality Band, these components may have a moderate number of breaking APIs or behavior changes in response to customer feedback and as we learn more about how they will be used. Customers are likely to encounter bugs and functionality issues for non-mainline scenarios. *Preview* is similar to *Alpha* quality in many traditional projects.
Experimental	Experimental components are intended for evaluation purposes. The main goal of these components is to provide an opportunity for feedback during the earliest stages of development. This feedback will help decide the future of these components. Development of an experimental component may end at any point, so it may not be included in future releases.

Before you choose to use a control from the Silverlight Toolkit, you should carefully consider the current quality band of the control. You can find which quality band a Toolkit control is currently assigned to by visiting the Toolkit website on CodePlex (`http://silverlight.codeplex.com/Wikipage`).

Beyond the Microsoft-developed set of controls, the Silverlight ecosystem includes many options for commercial and open source controls. The controls cover a wide range of user interface patterns, from data grids to maps.

Purchasing controls from a third-party vendor often has the advantage of providing you with some level of developer support for using the controls and some level of assurance that bugs in the controls will be fixed in a timely manner.

Open source controls are a great alternative to commercial controls. Many open source control projects exist, with a large number hosted on Microsoft's CodePlex website. Table 6-2 lists some of the open source control projects that can be found on CodePlex.

TABLE 6-2

PROJECT	URL
Silverlight Contrib — Various Controls	`http://silverlightcontrib.codeplex.com`
DeepEarth — Multi-provider Mapping Control	`www.codeplex.com/deepearth`
Silverlight SDK for Bing	`http://silverbing.codeplex.com/`
Interactive Timeline Control	`http://timeline.codeplex.com/`

continues

TABLE 6-2 *(continued)*

PROJECT	URL
Cover Flow Control	http://silverlightcoverflow.codeplex.com/
Silverlight Media Player	http://silverlight30.codeplex.com/
Advance Tooltip Service	http://tooltipservice.codeplex.com/

Although this chapter highlights open source Silverlight control projects that you can use in your application, be aware that the quality of open source projects can vary widely. Simply because an open source control or project is included in this chapter, that does not guarantee the quality of the control or project. You should make sure to perform adequate quality testing on the controls just as you would on any other part of your application.

Additionally, when choosing an open source control, you should make sure you understand how the specific license the control is released under can affect your application. There are a variety of open source licenses that controls can be licensed under, and each has specific rules and provisions that may affect how your application can be distributed or licensed.

USING TEXT DISPLAY CONTROLS

Silverlight includes several controls that you can use to display text. The text capabilities of Silverlight are discussed in detail in Chapter 19, but two controls you can use to display text are introduced in this chapter: TextBlock and Label.

TextBlock

The TextBlock is the basic control used to display read-only text. You can use the Text property to provide the control a value, or simply add text as the control content:

```
<TextBlock Text="Lorum Ipsum" />
```

The TextBlock also allows you to specify Runs and LineBreaks as its content. Runs and LineBreaks give you more control over formatting of individual sections of the text. Listing 6-1 shows how you can use Runs and LineBreaks within a TextBlock.

Available for
download on
Wrox.com

LISTING 6-1: Using Runs and LineBreaks on a TextBlock

```
<TextBlock>
    <Run Foreground="Green">Line 1: Lorum</Run>
    <LineBreak />
    <Run FontFamily="Courier New">Line 2: Ipsum</Run>
</TextBlock>
```

In this listing, the foreground color of the first run of text is changed to green, a line break is inserted, and the font face of the second line is changed to Courier.

Label

The Label control can be used in more targeted text display scenarios. It is typically used in conjunction with a form field when you need to display a field caption, required field indication, or a validation error.

A simple use of the caption is shown in Listing 6-2 as a caption of a form field.

LISTING 6-2: Using the Label control with a TextBox

Available for
download on
Wrox.com

```
<StackPanel>
    <sdk:Label Content="First Name:" IsRequired="True" />
    <TextBox x:Name="TextBox1" Text="John" />
</StackPanel>
```

To indicate to the end user that the TextBox is a required field, the Label has had its IsRequired property set to True. This causes the Label to display its content in a bold font.

The Label control can also be bound to another control in the form, allowing the Label to automatically configure itself based on the value of that control. Listing 6-3 demonstrates binding the Label to a TextBox that has had its Text property bound to an object.

LISTING 6-3: Binding the Label to a TextBox

Available for
download on
Wrox.com

```
<StackPanel>
    <sdk:Label Target="{Binding ElementName=TextBox1}" />
    <TextBox x:Name="TextBox1" Text="{Binding FirstName, Mode=TwoWay,
             ValidatesOnExceptions=true, NotifyOnValidationError=true}" />
</StackPanel>
```

If the target control has multiple bindings, you can specify the specific property the Label should be bound to by using its PropertyPath property.

Notice that the binding set on the Text property's ValidatesOnException attribute is set to True. If the binding attempts to set the property to a new value and the property returns an exception, the Label automatically detects the exception and shows its content in red, indicating a data validation error, as shown in Figure 6-1.

The Label also automatically detects data attributes on the object bound to the TextBox like the DisplayAttribute's Name property and the RequiredAttribute.

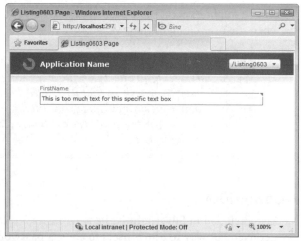

FIGURE 6-1

If the `Name` property is set, the `Label` automatically uses that value as its content. If the `RequiredAttribute` is `true`, the content will be displayed in a bold font.

USING INPUT EDITOR CONTROLS

Most applications at some point require some type of input from the end user. While you could simply use a simple Text Box editor, this does not provide an optimal experience for the end user and also requires you to validate his or her input to make sure it meets your application requirements. Silverlight includes a variety of controls that make editing input, including text, numbers, dates, and times, easy.

Text

The most basic input control is the `TextBox`. The `PasswordBox` and `AutoCompleteBox` extend the basic `TextBox` features, adding password masking and Google-style auto-complete behavior, respectively.

For more advanced text entry capabilities, Silverlight 4 adds a new `RichTextBox` control.

For displaying text, Silverlight includes the `TextBlock` element. For a more basic text display option, the Silverlight Toolkit includes a basic `Label` control.

TextBox

Silverlight includes a `TextBox` control, which provides the same basic text input capabilities you are used to receiving from the HTML `<input>` element. The control offers single-format, multi-line input capabilities with automatic text wrapping, as well as integration with the clipboard. An undo/redo stack is also included. The following code demonstrates using the `TextBox`:

```
<TextBox Text="Lorum Ipsum" />
```

For those creating applications for international audiences, the control supports IME Level 3 when run on Windows and Level 1 when run on a Mac. It also includes international keyboard support.

As you might expect, the `TextBox` exposes a `TextChanged` event that you can use to be notified when the user changes the `TextBox`'s text.

 An interesting property on the `TextBox` *is the* `Watermark` *property, though you may have to search to find it. That is because it has been hidden from Visual Studio's property grid and from IntelliSense. Unfortunately, the Microsoft documentation for the property explicitly states you should not use this property in Silverlight 4.*

PasswordBox

Also included in Silverlight is the `PasswordBox`. Related to the `TextBox`, the `PasswordBox` gives you a convenient way to allow users to enter a password into your application:

```
<PasswordBox PasswordChar="#" Password="password" />
```

As shown in the previous code snippet, you can get or set the value of the control by using the `Password` property. You can change the character used to mask the password using the `PasswordChar` property.

Unlike the `TextBox`, the `PasswordBox` accepts only a single line of text, but like the `TextBox`, it includes an event, the `PasswordChanged` event, that you can use to be notified when the end user changes the control's value.

AutoCompleteBox

Originating from the Silverlight Toolkit and added to the SDK for Silverlight 4, the `AutoCompleteBox` control allows you to add Google-suggest style auto-complete capabilities to your application, as shown in Figure 6-2.

FIGURE 6-2

Listing 6-4 shows how you can configure the `AutoCompleteBox` by assigning an `ItemsSource` that contains the values that the control will search as the end user enters text into the control.

LISTING 6-4: Configuring the AutoCompleteBox

```xml
<my:AutoCompleteBox ItemsSource="{Binding}"
                    ValueMemberPath="FirstName"
                    FilterMode="Contains"
                    IsTextCompletionEnabled="True">
    <my:AutoCompleteBox.ItemTemplate>
        <DataTemplate>
            <TextBlock Text="{Binding FirstName}" />
        </DataTemplate>
    </my:AutoCompleteBox.ItemTemplate>
</my:AutoCompleteBox>
```

The `AutoCompleteBox` also includes several properties that allow you to configure the Filter mode used by the control. The `FilterModes` property supports several derivations of a `Contains` filter, a `StartsWith` filter, and an `Equals` filter.

Finally, the control also allows you to enable text completion. Setting the `TextCompletion` property to `True` directs the control to automatically complete the currently entered text with the first match found in the auto-complete list.

RichTextBox

Silverlight 4 introduces a new `RichTextBox` control that allows you to display and edit richly formatted text in your application. While an in-depth look at the `RichTextBox` is included in Chapter 19, Listing 6-5 demonstrates a simple use of the `RichTextBox`.

LISTING 6-5: Display and edit rich text

```
<RichTextBox>
    <Paragraph>
        <Run>The quick brown </Run>
        <InlineUIContainer>
            <Image
                Source="/Chapter6;component/Assets/fox.png" Width="100" />
        </InlineUIContainer>
        <Run> jumped over the lazy </Run>
        <InlineUIContainer>
            <Image
                Source="/Chapter6;component/Assets/dog.png" Width="100"/>
        </InlineUIContainer>
        <Run>.</Run>
    </Paragraph>
</RichTextBox>
```

In this sample, several text `Run`s are shown in the `RichTextBox`, as well as several inline UI elements containing `Image` elements. You can see the `RichTextBox` content in Figure 6-3.

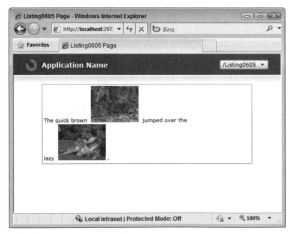

FIGURE 6-3

Using Numeric Editor Controls

Silverlight and the Silverlight Toolkit offer several controls designed to make adding numeric-editable capabilities to your application easier, including the `Slider` control, `NumericUpDown` control, and `Rating` control.

Slider

The `Slider` control allows you to add the familiar slider UI pattern to your application. Sliders provide a simple way for end users to edit numerical values and allow you to ensure that those values remain constrained in a range. Listing 6-6 shows how you can configure the `Slider`'s value range by using the `Minimum` and `Maximum` properties.

LISTING 6-6: Displaying Slider property values in TextBlocks

```
<StackPanel>
    <Grid>
        <Grid.ColumnDefinitions>
            <ColumnDefinition Width="Auto" />
            <ColumnDefinition />
            <ColumnDefinition Width="Auto" />
        </Grid.ColumnDefinitions>
        <TextBlock
            Text="{Binding ElementName=Slider1, Path=Minimum}"
            Grid.Column="0" />

        <Slider x:Name="Slider1" Minimum="0" Maximum="100"
                Value="50" Grid.Column="1" />

        <TextBlock
            Text="{Binding ElementName=Slider1, Path=Maximum}"
            Grid.Column="2" />
    </Grid>
    <TextBlock
        Text="{Binding ElementName=Slider1, Path=Value}"
        HorizontalAlignment="Center" />
</StackPanel>
```

The `Slider` also includes properties that allow you to change the `LargeChange` and `SmallChange` values, as well as a `ValueChanged` event to notify you when the control's value changes. Figure 6-4 shows the Slider.

Notice that even though the `Slider`'s range has been defined using `Integers`, the `Value` is returned as a `Double`, so you may need to round or cast the value.

NumericUpDown

Part of the Silverlight Toolkit, the `NumericUpDown` control allows end users to easily increment numerical values by set steps using `Spin` buttons. This can be especially useful when users need to adjust existing values or you want to simplify adjusting values by certain steps.

```
<my:NumericUpDown Increment="3"
                  DecimalPlaces="4"
```

```
Maximum="1000"
Minimum="-1000"
Value="3.3333" />
```

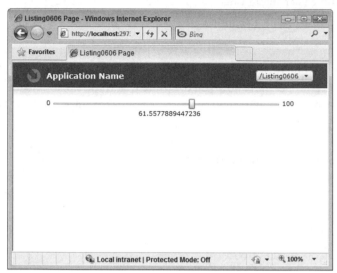

FIGURE 6-4

The control allows you to set minimum and maximum value limits, as well as configure the number of decimal places shown.

Additionally, users can continuously increase or decrease the control's value by clicking and holding the spin buttons. This causes the control to continue to change its value until the click is released.

Rating

Finally, as applications introduce more social network integration and personal preference tracking, the ability to rate content in your application becomes more important. The Silverlight Toolkit contains a Rating control, which allows you to add a simple rating IU to your application. Listing 6-7 shows how you can use the Rating control to show a simple five-star rating.

Available for download on Wrox.com

LISTING 6-7: Using the Rating control

```
<inputToolkit:Rating x:Name="Rating1" Value="0.6" ItemCount="5" />
<Slider
    Minimum="0" Maximum="1"
    SmallChange="0.1"
    Value="{Binding Path=Value, ElementName=Rating1, Mode=TwoWay}" />
```

By default, the Rating control shows its value using stars, as shown in Figure 6-5.

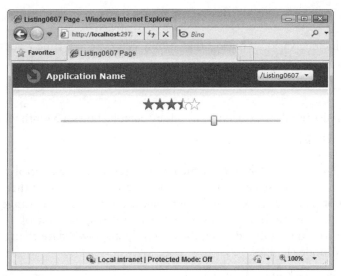

FIGURE 6-5

In its most simple configuration, to use the `Rating` control you provide a value for the `ItemCount` property, which indicates the number of stars to show.

You can change the default star display by restyling the `RatingItem` control. Once you restyle the control, you can use the `ItemContainerStyle` property to assign the style to all `RatingItem` controls displayed in the `Rating` control or assign the style individually to `RatingItem` controls in the `Rating` control.

Listing 6-8 shows how you can define individual `RatingItem` controls in the `Rating` control and assign each of them a separate custom style.

LISTING 6-8: Assigning custom styles to RatingItems

```
<inputToolkit:Rating x:Name="Rating1" Value="0.6">
    <inputToolkit:RatingItem
        Style="{StaticResource myThumbDownRatingItemStyle}" />
    <inputToolkit:RatingItem
        Style="{StaticResource myThumbAngleLowRatingItemStyle}" />
    <inputToolkit:RatingItem
        Style="{StaticResource myThumbSidewaysRatingItemStyle}" />
    <inputToolkit:RatingItem
        Style="{StaticResource myThumbAngleUpRatingItemStyle}" />
    <inputToolkit:RatingItem
        Style="{StaticResource myThumbUpRatingItemStyle}" />
</inputToolkit:Rating>
```

Note that if you define the `RatingItems` explicitly, you do not need to provide a value for the `ItemCount` property.

Dates and Time

Silverlight and the Silverlight Toolkit include various controls that simply edit date and time values, including the `Calendar`, `DatePicker`, `TimePicker`, and `GlobalCalendar`.

Calendar and GlobalCalendar

The `Calendar` control, as the name implies, renders a calendar, which by default shows a Month view.

```
<sdk:Calendar SelectedDate="{Binding StartDate}" />
```

The control supports both Year and Decade calendar views, which can be set using the control's `DisplayMode` property. You can also control the selection behavior of the control by setting the `SelectionMode` property, which supports No Selection, Single Date Selection, Single Date Range Selection, and Multiple Date Range Selection modes. Also, as with other controls, the control exposes a variety of events that allow you to be notified when the currently displayed date changes, a selected date changes, or the display mode changes.

Figure 6-6 shows the `Calendar` control in each of its display modes.

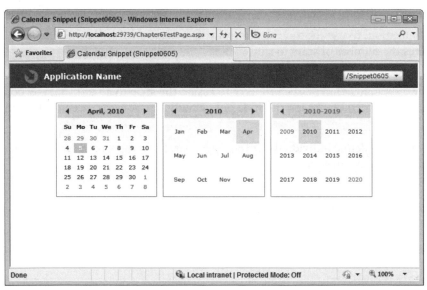

FIGURE 6-6

The control will automatically detect the culture of the host operating system and will display the calendar with appropriate localized text and date arrangement. Figure 6-7 shows the calendar with the Japanese culture.

The `GlobalCalendar` control extends the calendar by providing additional APIs for styling individual days and displaying modified customer Gregorian calendar systems.

Listing 6-9 shows how you can assign your own `CultureInfo` object to the `GlobalCalendar` using the `CalendarInfo` property.

FIGURE 6-7

Available for
download on
Wrox.com

LISTING 6-9: Assigning a CultureInfo object to the GlobalCalendar

```
CultureInfo culture = new CultureInfo("Fr-fr");
CulturedCalendar.CalendarInfo = new CultureCalendarInfo(culture);
```

The control also includes a `CalendarDayButtonSelectorStyle`, which allows you to style specific days in the control, such as holidays or events.

DatePicker and TimePicker

The `DatePicker` control displays a simple text input field with an attached calendar pop-up, as shown in Figure 6-8.

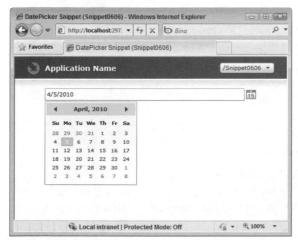

FIGURE 6-8

Unlike the `Calendar` control, which allows date ranges to be selected, the `DatePicker` control allows for only a single date to be selected at one time. As with `Calendar`, there are events you can use to be notified when the selected date changes.

```
<sdk:DatePicker SelectedDateFormat="Short" />
```

The control allows you to configure the format you want the selected date to be returned as. The `SelectedDateFormat` property allows you to choose to receive the selected date in Long or Short format.

The `DatePicker` also supports the validation using the `ValidatesOnException` binding attribute; however, by default the control does not include the validation visual states needed to show the result of an invalid value. If you want to use validation with the `DatePicker`, you will need to change the control's default template to include these additional states.

Like the `DatePicker` control, the `TimePicker` provides a simplified way for end users to select times. The `TimePicker` functions much like the `DatePicker`, associating a text entry field with a pop-up. The `TimePicker` offers two different pop-up experiences, the `RangeTimePickerPopup` or the `ListTimePickerPopup`, which you assign to the `TimerPicker` using its `Popup` property.

Listing 6-10 demonstrates using the `TimePicker` control with both `Popup` options.

LISTING 6-10: Using the TimePicker control

```xml
<StackPanel Orientation="Horizontal">
    <inputToolkit:TimePicker x:Name="TimePicker1"
                    PopupButtonMode="Press" Format="hh:mm:ss"
                    PopupTimeSelectionMode="AllowSecondsSelection"
                    PopupMinutesInterval="5"
                    PopupSecondsInterval="15">
        <inputToolkit:TimePicker.Popup>
            <inputToolkit:RangeTimePickerPopup />
        </inputToolkit:TimePicker.Popup>
    </inputToolkit:TimePicker>

    <inputToolkit:TimePicker x:Name="TimePicker2" PopupButtonMode="Press"
                    PopupTimeSelectionMode="AllowSecondsSelection"
                    PopupMinutesInterval="5"
                    PopupSecondsInterval="15">
        <inputToolkit:TimePicker.Popup>
            <inputToolkit:ListTimePickerPopup />
        </inputToolkit:TimePicker.Popup>
    </inputToolkit:TimePicker>
</StackPanel>
```

Figure 6-9 shows the result of running Listing 6-10.

The `TimePicker` control also includes options that allow you to configure whether the control allows only hours and minutes to be selected, or hours, minutes, and seconds. Additionally, you can configure the minute and second intervals that the end user can select using the pop-up.

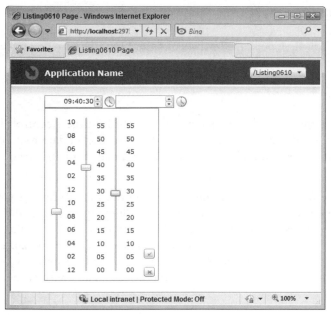

FIGURE 6-9

Finally, like the `DatePicker`, the `TimePicker` automatically uses the appropriate culture, but you can assign customized culture information to the control through its `TimeGlobalizationInfo` property. Additionally, although the control uses a robust time parser by default, you can also supply your own parser by deriving from the `TimeParser` class and adding the derived class to the control's `TimeParsers` collection.

TimeUpDown

Like the `NumericUpDown` control described earlier, the `TimeUpDown` control allows users to increment or decrement time values using the familiar spin button metaphor.

Listing 6-11 demonstrates the use of the `TimeUpDown` control.

Available for download on Wrox.com

LISTING 6-11: Using the TimeUpDown control

```
<inputToolkit:TimeUpDown x:Name="TimeUpDown1"
                         Format="hh:mm:ss"
                         IsCyclic="False"
                         Value="8:00:00"
                         Minimum="8:00:00"
                         Maximum="17:00:00" />
```

As you can see, the control includes a variety of configuration properties, including the `Format` property, which allows you to dictate the time format shown by the control, the minimum and maximum values allowed, and whether the control should allow the end user to roll from the maximum value to the minimum using the `IsCyclic` property.

USING LISTS AND ITEMS CONTROLS

Silverlight includes a wide array of controls designed to show lists of data. From the `ListBox` to the `DataGrid`, these controls are designed to give you a powerful and flexible means of showing data.

DataGrid

Perhaps the most important control for application developers building Line-of-Business controls is the Silverlight `DataGrid` control. This control allows you to easily bind a collection of data to it and have it automatically display the data and allow the end user to edit the data and manipulate the data display.

When running the `DataGrid` even in the simplest configuration, you will notice that it provides you with a lot of capabilities right out-of-the-box. For example, clicking on a column header sorts the column data; dragging a column header allows you to change the column display order; hovering over the edge of a column header allows you to resize the column width; and double-clicking a cell places that cell into Edit mode, allowing you to change the cell data. As you learn later in this section, the `DataGrid` exposes properties that allow you to control all of these behaviors both at the control level and on a per-column level.

Data Binding

To get started using the `DataGrid`, you simply need to provide it with some data by setting its `ItemsSource` property to some type of enumerable object, either in XAML or in code. The following code snippet shows how you can bind the `DataGrid` to data that has been assigned to the `DataContext` in XAML:

```
<my:DataGrid ItemsSource="{Binding}" />
```

Once you set the `ItemsSource` property, the `DataGrid` control automatically interrogates the data source and generates the appropriate column structure based on public members exposed by the objects on the data source. Figure 6-10 shows an example of a basic `DataGrid` with automatically generated columns.

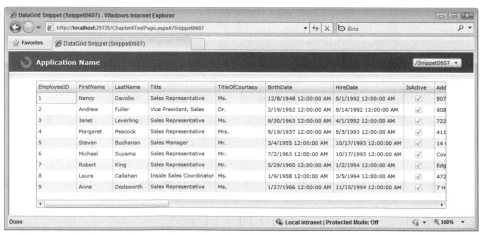

FIGURE 6-10

You can control whether or not the control automatically generates columns for you by using the `AutoGenerateColumns` property. If you choose to set this property to `False`, you need to manually define a set of columns for the `DataGrid` to display, using the control's Columns collection. The different types of columns you can add are described later in this section.

It is also possible to use the Visual Studio Data Sources window to add a `DataGrid` to your application. The Data Sources window allows you to easily manage the sources of data available in your application. Once a data source is identified, the window displays all of the attributes of the data source and allows you to create UI elements based on those attributes. Figure 6-11 shows the Data Sources window, which is showing a single data source.

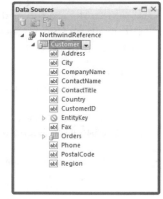

If the active document in Visual Studio is a XAML document, the Data Sources window allows you to drag enumerable properties directly onto the design surface. Visual Studio will automatically create a `CollectionViewSource` representing the data and configure the appropriate XAML bindings to connect the `CollectionViewSource` to the `DataGrid`. Additionally, a template of code is dropped into the code-behind, which allows you to connect the `CollectionViewSource` to your data.

FIGURE 6-11

The `DataGrid` also automatically honors data annotation attributes that may be on the objects in the `ItemsSource`. This allows the grid to automatically mark certain columns as hidden, or read only, or provide a friendlier column header label. Data annotations are typically used when you are using WCF RIA Services as the source of grid data.

If you want to insert your own logic into the column generation process, you can use the grid's `AutoGeneratingColumn` event. Using this event, you can access the column currently being created and alter its properties.

Another entry point into the binding process is the `Grid's` `LoadingRow` event. This event allows you to access each row as it is being created in the grid and alter the data ultimately shown by the grid. If you choose to use this event, it's important to understand how the grid's internal UI virtualization affects it.

In order to maintain an acceptable level of performance the grid uses UI virtualization to only create the UI elements that are needed to display information on the screen. If a row moves out of the visible area of the control, its resources are recycled to show new rows entering the visible area of the control.

Because of this UI virtualization, the `LoadingRow` event will not fire for each object in the `ItemsSource` when the control loads. Instead the event fires as rows move in and out of the visible area of the control. If you use the `LoadingRow` event to customize a row, you will have to use the `UnloadingRow` event to undo your changes. This is event is fired when a `DataGridRow` is freed for reuse.

The `Grid` also supports the selection of rows in the grid, supporting Single and Extended Selection modes. *Single Selection mode* allows end users to select only a single row at any given time. *Extended Selection mode* allows them to select multiple rows by holding down the Ctrl or Shift keys while clicking rows. You can change the current selection mode by setting the control's `SelectionMode` property, as well as access the currently selected item(s) by using the `SelectedItem` or `SelectedItems` properties.

Grid Columns

The `DataGrid` control includes three different column types that you can add to the Columns collection: `Text`, `CheckBox`, and `Template`. Each column allows you to bind a field from the data source to it, using the column's `Binding` property.

If you configure the grid to automatically generate columns, the grid tries to choose the correct column type to use based on the structure of the data. For example, if the bound data contains a Boolean property, the grid automatically uses a `DataGridCheckBoxColumn` to show that data.

Of course, if you have disabled auto-generation of columns, then you need to define them yourself. Listing 6-12 shows how you can use the Columns collection to display data in the `DataGrid`.

LISTING 6-12: Using the Columns collection to display data

```
<my:DataGrid ItemsSource="{Binding}" AutoGenerateColumns="False">
    <my:DataGrid.Columns>
        <my:DataGridTextColumn Binding="{Binding FirstName}" />
        <my:DataGridTextColumn Binding="{Binding LastName}" />
        <my:DataGridTextColumn Binding="{Binding Address}" />
        <my:DataGridTextColumn Binding="{Binding City}" />
    </my:DataGrid.Columns>
</my:DataGrid>
```

Notice that when defining columns you use standard Silverlight binding syntax in each column's `Binding` property to indicate which property of the `ItemsSource` the column is bound to. Because the columns use this syntax, you can take advantage of any of its features, such as value converters and formatting. The columns will also use standard two-way binding to allow data in column cells to be edited.

To control the order in which the columns are displayed, you can use the column's `DisplayIndex`.

When rendered, grid columns also include a header. To provide text for the header, columns expose a string `Header` property. If the grid is automatically generating the columns, the control will by default use the property names of the item source as the columns' header text, which you can override using the `Header` property. If you manually define columns, then you need to explicitly define the text that should be used for the column header.

Unfortunately, the `DataGrid` does not provide a `DataTemplate` for the header, but if you do want to change the default style of a column header, you can create your own `DataGridColumnHeader` style and assign it to the column's `HeaderStyle` property.

If you are defining your own columns, in addition to the `DatasGridTextBoxColumn` shown in Listing 6-12, you can also include the `DataGridCheckBoxColumn` or `DataGridTemplateColumn` in your Columns collection. Listing 6-13 shows how to add a `DataGridCheckBoxColumn` and bind it to a Boolean property in the `ItemsSource`.

LISTING 6-13: Adding a DataGridCheckBoxColumn

```
<sdk:DataGrid ItemsSource="{Binding}" AutoGenerateColumns="False" >
    <sdk:DataGrid.Columns>
        <sdk:DataGridCheckBoxColumn Binding="{Binding IsActive}" />
        <sdk:DataGridTextColumn Binding="{Binding FirstName}" />
        <sdk:DataGridTextColumn Binding="{Binding LastName}" />
        <sdk:DataGridTextColumn Binding="{Binding Address}" />
        <sdk:DataGridTextColumn Binding="{Binding City}" />
    </sdk:DataGrid.Columns>
</sdk:DataGrid>
```

Figure 6-12 shows the checkbox column in the `DataGrid`.

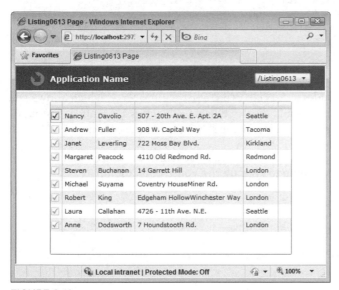

FIGURE 6-12

The `DataGridCheckBoxColumn` not only allows you to use a standard two-state checkbox, but by setting the `IsThreeState` property, you also can have the checkbox behave like a tri-state checkbox. This allows you to set the `IsChecked` property to `True`, `False`, or `Null`.

As the name suggests, the `DataGridTemplateColumn` allows you to take control of the contents of cells in a column. The `CellTemplate` property accepts a `DataTemplate`, which is used to define the contents of the column while not being edited. Listing 6-14 demonstrates using the `DataGridTemplateColumn` to show an `Image` in a column.

LISTING 6-14: Using the DataGridTemplateColumn to show an image

```
<Grid x:Name="LayoutRoot" Background="White">
    <Grid.Resources>
        <DataTemplate x:Key="myEmployeeImageTemplate">
```

continues

LISTING 6-14 *(continued)*

```
            <Grid>
                <Image Source="{Binding PhotoPath}" />
            </Grid>
        </DataTemplate>
    </Grid.Resources>
        <sdk:DataGrid ItemsSource="{Binding}" AutoGenerateColumns="False" >
            <sdk:DataGrid.Columns>
                <sdk:DataGridCheckBoxColumn Binding="{Binding IsActive}" />
                <sdk:DataGridTextColumn Binding="{Binding FirstName}" />
                <sdk:DataGridTextColumn Binding="{Binding LastName}" />
                <sdk:DataGridTextColumn Binding="{Binding Address}" />
                <sdk:DataGridTextColumn Binding="{Binding City}" />
                <sdk:DataGridTemplateColumn
                CellTemplate="{StaticResource myEmployeeImageTemplate}" />
            </sdk:DataGrid.Columns>
        </sdk:DataGrid>
    </Grid>
```

The `DataGridTemplateColumn` also includes a `CellEditingTemplate` property, which allows you to specify a `DataTemplate` that the column should display when a cell enters Edit mode. Listing 6-15 shows how you can use the `CellEditingTemplate` to change the value of the column.

LISTING 6-15: Using the CellEditingTemplate to change the value of a column

```
<Grid x:Name="LayoutRoot" Background="White">
    <Grid.Resources>
        <DataTemplate x:Key="myEmployeeImageTemplate">
            <Grid>
                <Image Source="{Binding PhotoPath}" />
            </Grid>
        </DataTemplate>
        <DataTemplate x:Key="myEditableEmployeeImageTemplate">
            <Grid>
                <TextBox Text="{Binding PhotoPath}" />
            </Grid>
        </DataTemplate>
    </Grid.Resources>
    <sdk:DataGrid ItemsSource="{Binding}" AutoGenerateColumns="False">
        <sdk:DataGrid.Columns>
            <sdk:DataGridCheckBoxColumn Binding="{Binding IsActive}" />
            <sdk:DataGridTextColumn Binding="{Binding FirstName}" />
            <sdk:DataGridTextColumn Binding="{Binding LastName}" />
            <sdk:DataGridTextColumn Binding="{Binding Address}" />
            <sdk:DataGridTextColumn Binding="{Binding City}" />
            <sdk:DataGridTemplateColumn
            CellTemplate="{StaticResource myEmployeeImageTemplate}"
            CellEditingTemplate=
                    "{StaticResource myEditableEmployeeImageTemplate}"/>
        </sdk:DataGrid.Columns>
    </sdk:DataGrid>
</Grid>
```

As you can see in the listing, the `CellEditingTemplate` property is used to provide a custom template that contains completely different content from the standard `CellTemplate`, and content that is appropriate for allowing the end user to edit the object's `PhotoPath` property.

Sorting

As shown previously, in its default state the grid automatically enables column sorting. Users can sort individual columns by clicking on the column header or by holding down the Ctrl or Shift keys while clicking on successive columns, sorting each.

Various `Grid` properties give you control of the `Grid`'s sorting behavior. At the control level, you can change whether or not you want to enable sorting in the entire grid by using the `CanUserSortColumns` property. Using the column's `CanUserSort` property, you can control the sorting behavior for an individual column.

By overriding the `DataGridColumnHeader` style as described earlier, you can also control the sort indicator shown in the column header.

Finally, using `SortMemberPath`, you can configure a column to sort itself based on a different field from the one configured in the column's `Binding` property.

Data Grouping

A common task users want to perform in `DataGrids` is to group data together based on the values of a specific property of the data source. While the `DataGrid` itself does not have grouping built in, you can group data using the `PagedCollectionView` object and then display this in the `DataGrid`.

Listing 6-16 show how you can add a `PropertyGroupDescription` to the `PagedCollectionView`, then set that as the `DataGrid`'s `ItemsSource`.

LISTING 6-16: Grouping data using PagedCollectionView

```
PagedCollectionView myView =
    new PagedCollectionView(Assets.DemoData.Employees);

myView.GroupDescriptions.Add(new PropertyGroupDescription("Title"));

this.grid1.ItemsSource = myView;
```

Column Resizing

`DataGrid` includes properties that allow you to set column widths on each column and heights on rows. Like the standard Grid panel included in Silverlight, `DataGrid` gives you various options for specifying size units by using a special object called `DataGridLength`. When setting size properties on the `DataGrid`, you set its `Height` and `Width` properties as a value of this object.

The `DataGridLength` includes five sizing options:

➤ `Auto` — This option sizes the column or row to the size of the largest visible header or cell.

➤ `SizeToHeader` — This option sizes the column or row to the size of the header, ignoring the size of the cell contents.

Because the `DataGrid` virtualizes its UI, it cannot know ahead of time what the largest cell contents in the grid will be. This means that as you scroll rows, if the grid encounters a cell with content that is larger than the current cell width, it expands that cell's column width. Once the column's size has increased, the grid won't revert back to a smaller size if that row scrolls out of view.

➤ `SizeToCells` — This option sizes the column or row to the size of the largest visible cell. It also behaves like the `Auto` option, meaning that the column or row size may change as rows are scrolled.

➤ `Pixel` — This option allows you to set a specific pixel base value.

➤ `Star` — New to Silverlight 4, the `Star` sizing option allows you to use the same proportional sizing behavior as is available in the Grid layout panel.

By default, end users can also resize columns at run time. Like other grid behaviors, you can control this behavior for the entire grid by setting the `CanUserResizeColumns` property on the `DataGrid`. You can also control this on a per-column basis by setting the `CanUserResize` property on an individual column.

The `DataGrid` also allows you to set minimum and maximum column width values, again both at the grid level — using the `DataGrid`'s `MinColumnWidth` and `MaxColumnWidth` properties — and on the column level — using the `MinWidth` and `MaxWidth` properties.

Column Freezing

The Freezing column feature of the grid replicates the Excel Frozen column behavior, which allows you to freeze (or *fix*) a certain number of columns to the left side of the `DataGrid`. This means that if the grid is displaying a horizontal scrollbar, the frozen columns will remain fixed to the left side of the grid, while the remaining columns are free to scroll horizontally.

You can set the number of columns you want to be included in the freeze using the `Grid`'s `FrozenColumnCount` property. The `Grid` will then freeze that number of columns, starting from the left side of the grid.

Column Moving

As described earlier, `DataGrid` allows you to set the order in which columns are displayed by using the `DisplayIndex` property. The control, also by default, allows users to reorder columns in the grid at run time. To do this, the user simply clicks on and drags a column header to a new position in the headers. Users are given visual cues to help them determine where the column will be inserted when dropped.

If the user reorders columns at run time, this will reset the `DisplayIndex` property of all other grid columns.

You can control this behavior for the entire grid by using the control's `CanUserReorderColumns` property on the root control or individually on a column, using its `CanUserRender` property. You can also use the series of events exposed by the DataGrid to be notified when the end user initiates and completes a column move.

Row Details

As discussed in previous sections, the DataGrid control includes three column types that you can use to control how data is shown, including a template column that allows you to add custom content to cells in a column.

Often, though, you may need to customize the layout of an entire row, or show additional detail information in each row. The DataGrid includes a built-in mechanism for this, called the RowDetailsTemplate. This feature allows you to specify a DataTemplate in which you can define a custom layout attached to each row that includes additional details for the currently selected row.

Listing 6-17 demonstrates how you can use the RowDetailsTemplate.

LISTING 6-17: Using the RowDetailsTemplate

Available for
download on
Wrox.com

```xml
<Grid x:Name="LayoutRoot" Background="White">
    <Grid.Resources>
        <DataTemplate x:Key="myRowDetailsTemplate">
            <StackPanel>
                <StackPanel Orientation="Horizontal">
                    <TextBlock Text="{Binding EmployeeID}" />
                    <TextBlock Text=" - " />
                    <TextBlock Text="{Binding FirstName}" />
                    <TextBlock Text=" " />
                    <TextBlock Text="{Binding LastName}" />
                    <TextBlock Text=", " />
                    <TextBlock Text="{Binding Title}" />
                </StackPanel>

                <TextBlock Text="{Binding Address}" />

                <StackPanel Orientation="Horizontal">
                    <TextBlock Text="{Binding City}" />
                    <TextBlock Text=", " />
                    <TextBlock Text="{Binding State}" />
                    <TextBlock Text="  " />
                    <TextBlock Text="{Binding PostalCode}" />
                </StackPanel>

                <StackPanel Orientation="Horizontal">
                    <TextBlock Text="{Binding HomePhone}" />
                    <TextBlock Text=" x" />
                    <TextBlock Text="{Binding Extension}" />
                </StackPanel>

                <TextBlock Text="{Binding Notes}" />
            </StackPanel>
        </DataTemplate>
```

continues

LISTING 6-17 *(continued)*

```
        </Grid.Resources>
        <sdk:DataGrid ItemsSource="{Binding}"
            RowDetailsTemplate="{StaticResource myRowDetailsTemplate}"
            RowDetailsVisibilityMode="VisibleWhenSelected"
            AutoGenerateColumns="False">
            <sdk:DataGrid.Columns>
                <sdk:DataGridTextColumn Binding="{Binding FirstName}"  />
                <sdk:DataGridTextColumn Binding="{Binding LastName}" />
            </sdk:DataGrid.Columns>
        </sdk:DataGrid>
    </Grid>
```

 It's interesting to note that when you are using a StackPanel *inside of a template used with the* RowDetailsTemplate, *the panel's* VerticalAlignment *property defaults to* Top. *This will cause problems if you try to add space above the panel using a top margin. Instead of expanding the template, this situation causes the* StackPanel's *content to simply be clipped. You can work around this problem by placing the* StackPanel *inside of a* Border *and setting the* Border's Margin *property.*

To configure when the template is shown by the DataGrid, use the RowDetailsVisibilityMode property. This property allows you to configure the RowDetailsTemplate to always be collapsed for every row, always be visible for every row, or only be visible for the currently selected row. Use the RowDetailsVisibilityChanged event to be notified when the RowDetailsTemplate is changed.

DataForm

While the DataGrid is perfect for viewing and editing tabular data, often users prefer viewing and editing data as a form, rather than in a tabular grid. The DataForm control is the perfect control for these scenarios.

The DataForm shares a lot of the same capabilities as the DataGrid. Just as with the DataGrid, you can start using the DataForm control simply by binding a collection of data to the control:

```
<my:DataForm ItemsSource="{Binding}" />
```

The DataForm shares the same auto-generation capabilities as the Grid, but instead of generating columns, the control generates DataFields. Also notice that rather than column headers, the control automatically adds Labels to each field. You can control the position of the Labels using the LabelPosition property. You can also have the control add a description to each field. The position of the description can be controlled using the DescriptionViewerPosition property.

As with the DataGrid, you can disable auto-generation of DataFields and manually define the fields you need to display for your application. This is shown in Listing 6-18.

LISTING 6-18: Disabling auto-generation of DataFields and manually defining fields

```
<dataFormToolkit:DataForm ItemsSource="{Binding}"
                          AutoGenerateFields="False">
    <dataFormToolkit:DataForm.ReadOnlyTemplate>
        <DataTemplate>
            <Grid>
                <Grid.ColumnDefinitions>
                    <ColumnDefinition Width="Auto" />
                    <ColumnDefinition />
                </Grid.ColumnDefinitions>
                <Grid.RowDefinitions>
                    <RowDefinition Height="Auto" />
                    <RowDefinition Height="Auto" />
                    <RowDefinition Height="Auto" />
                    <RowDefinition />
                </Grid.RowDefinitions>
                <TextBlock Text="First Name:"
                           Grid.Row="0" Grid.Column="0" />
                <TextBlock Text="Last Name:"
                           Grid.Row="1" Grid.Column="0" />
                <TextBlock Text="Title:"
                           Grid.Row="2" Grid.Column="0" />
                <TextBlock Text="{Binding FirstName}"
                           Grid.Row="0" Grid.Column="1" />
                <TextBlock Text="{Binding LastName}"
                           Grid.Row="1" Grid.Column="1" />
                <TextBlock Text="{Binding Title}"
                           Grid.Row="2" Grid.Column="1" />
            </Grid>
        </DataTemplate>
    </dataFormToolkit:DataForm.ReadOnlyTemplate>
</dataFormToolkit:DataForm>
```

You can see in Listing 6-18 that the ReadOnlyTemplate is used to define the DataFields included in the DataForm. The control also includes the EditTemplate, which allows you to define the content shown when a record enters Edit mode; a NewItemTemplate, which allows you to define the content shown when a new data object is added to the ItemsSource via the DataForm; and the HeaderTemplate, which defines the content shown in the control's header.

The DataForm can be configured to place records in Edit mode automatically by setting the AutoEdit property to True. If records are not automatically in Edit mode, end users can place them in Edit mode by clicking the Edit command button.

The DataForm includes a variety of built-in command buttons, including Add, Edit, Delete, Commit, Cancel, and Navigation. Use the CommandButtonsVisibility property to control which of these buttons are shown by the control.

ListBox, ComboBox, and TabControl

Despite their different user interfaces, the ListBox, ComboBox, and TabControl controls are all derived from the same base class (System.Windows.Controls.ItemsControl) and allow you to display a list of items and select items in that list. Because they all share the same base class, the controls share many of the same properties and basic behaviors.

The ListBox control allows you to display items in a single flat list, specifying the list items either manually or bound from a data source, using the control's ItemsSource property. The number of items visible is dictated by the size of the control.

By default, when items are bound using ItemsSource, the control will simply output the objects in that list as strings. You can, however, create a DataTemplate and provide a far more complex layout for each list item using the ItemTemplate property. Listing 6-19 demonstrates the use of the ListBox, including the use of a DataTemplate to define the list items display.

LISTING 6-19: Using the ListBox

```xml
<Grid x:Name="LayoutRoot" Background="White">
    <Grid.Resources>
        <DataTemplate x:Key="myTemplate">
            <Grid>
                <TextBlock Text="{Binding FirstName}" />
            </Grid>
        </DataTemplate>
    </Grid.Resources>
    <ListBox
        ItemTemplate="{StaticResource myTemplate}"
        ItemsSource="{Binding}" />
</Grid>
```

Figure 6-13 shows the ListBox from Listing 6-19.

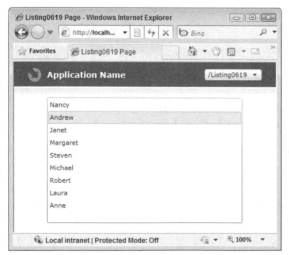

FIGURE 6-13

Another interesting feature of the `ListBox` is the `ItemsPanel` property. This property allows you to specify the layout panel you want the `ListBox` to use when arranging its children. By default, the `ListBox` uses a simple `StackPanel`, but you can create your own layout panel and provide it to the `ListBox`. Listing 6-20 demonstrates this by providing the `ListBox` with a new `StackPanel` with its `Orientation` property changed.

LISTING 6-20: ListBox with Orientation changed

```xml
<Grid x:Name="LayoutRoot" Background="White">
    <Grid.Resources>
        <DataTemplate x:Key="myTemplate">
            <Grid>
                <TextBlock Text="{Binding FirstName}" />
            </Grid>
        </DataTemplate>
    </Grid.Resources>
    <ListBox
        ItemTemplate="{StaticResource myTemplate}"
        ItemsSource="{Binding}">
        <ListBox.ItemsPanel>
            <ItemsPanelTemplate>
                <StackPanel Orientation="Horizontal" />
            </ItemsPanelTemplate>
        </ListBox.ItemsPanel>
    </ListBox>
</Grid>
```

The `ComboBox` works much in the same way as the `ListBox`, although rather than displaying items in a flat list, the `ComboBox` displays them in a pop-up display.

Listing 6-21 demonstrates the use of the `ComboBox` control using the same data source as Listing 6-20.

LISTING 6-21: Using the ComboBox control

```xml
<ComboBox x:Name="ComboBox1"
          ItemsSource="{Binding}"
          DisplayMemberPath="FirstName">
</ComboBox>
```

Figure 6-14 shows the `ComboBox` from Listing 6-21.

You can access the currently selected item of either control by using the `SelectedItem` property. Both controls can also notify you when the current selected item changes, using the `SelectionChanged` event.

Silverlight 4 adds two new properties to the base `Selector` class from which both `ComboBox` and `ListBox` are derived that make it easier to set and get the current selected item — the `SelectedValue` and `SelectedValuePath` properties. Listing 6-22 shows how you can use the `SelectedValuePath` property.

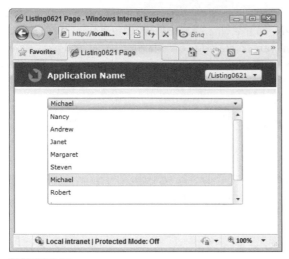

FIGURE 6-14

LISTING 6-22: Using the SelectedValuePath property

```
<StackPanel>
    <ComboBox x:Name="ComboBox1"
        ItemsSource="{Binding}"
        DisplayMemberPath="FirstName"
        SelectedValuePath="LastName" />
    <TextBox Text="{Binding ElementName=ComboBox1, Path=SelectedValue}" />
</StackPanel>
```

The `TabControl` again works much the same way as the `ComboBox` and `ListBox` controls. By using the `ItemsSource` property, you can assign a list of objects as the control's tabs. However, unlike `ListBox` and `ComboBox`, `TabControl` does require a bit of extra work. By default, `TabControl` does not know how to convert the objects in your list into tabs. To help it out, you can create a `ValueConverter`, which is shown in Listing 6-23.

LISTING 6-23: Creating a ValueConverter

```
public class TabConverter : IValueConverter
{
    public object Convert(object value, Type targetType, object parameter,
                          System.Globalization.CultureInfo culture)
    {
        List<Employee> source = value as List<Employee>;

        FrameworkElement root =
```

```
                (FrameworkElement)Application.Current.RootVisual;

        if (root!=null)
        {
            DataTemplate template =
                (DataTemplate)root.Resources["myTemplate"];

            if (source != null)
            {
                List<TabItem> result = new List<TabItem>();
                foreach (Employee e in source)
                {
                    result.Add(new TabItem()
                    {
                        Header = string.Format("{0} {1}",
                                                e.FirstName, e.LastName),
                        ContentTemplate = template,
                        DataContext = e
                    });
                }
                return result;
            }
        }
        return null;
    }

    public object ConvertBack(object value, Type targetType,
                            object parameter,
                            System.Globalization.CultureInfo culture)
    {
        throw new NotImplementedException();
    }
}
```

The `ValueConverter` converts each object in the `TabControl`'s item source into a tab and assigns the header text, the `DataTemplate`, and a `DataContext` to each tab.

Once you have created the `TabConverter`, you can use it to bind your data to the `TabControl`. This is shown in Listing 6-24.

LISTING 6-24: Using the TabConverter to bind data

```
<Grid x:Name="LayoutRoot">
    <Grid.Resources>
        <local:TabConverter x:Key="myTabConverter" />
        <DataTemplate x:Key="myTabTemplate">
            <StackPanel>
                <StackPanel Orientation="Horizontal">
                    <TextBlock Text="{Binding EmployeeID}" />
                    <TextBlock Text=" - " />
                    <TextBlock Text="{Binding FirstName}" />
                    <TextBlock Text=" " />
                    <TextBlock Text="{Binding LastName}" />
```

continues

LISTING 6-24 *(continued)*

```xml
                    <TextBlock Text=", " />
                    <TextBlock Text="{Binding Title}" />
                </StackPanel>

                <TextBlock Text="{Binding Address}" />

                <StackPanel Orientation="Horizontal">
                    <TextBlock Text="{Binding City}" />
                    <TextBlock Text=", " />
                    <TextBlock Text="{Binding State}" />
                    <TextBlock Text="  " />
                    <TextBlock Text="{Binding PostalCode}" />
                </StackPanel>

                <StackPanel Orientation="Horizontal">
                    <TextBlock Text="{Binding HomePhone}" />
                    <TextBlock Text=" x" />
                    <TextBlock Text="{Binding Extension}" />
                </StackPanel>

                <TextBlock Text="{Binding Notes}" />
            </StackPanel>
        </DataTemplate>
    </Grid.Resources>

    <sdk:TabControl
        ItemsSource="{Binding Converter={StaticResource myTabConverter}}"
        ItemTemplate="{StaticResource myTabTemplate}">
    </sdk:TabControl>
</Grid>
```

Of course, as with the `ListBox` and `ComboBox` controls, you can also create tabs manually. The Listing 6-25 code demonstrates creating tabs directly in XAML using the `TabItem` object.

LISTING 6-25: Creating tabs directly in XAML

```xml
<sdk:TabControl>
    <sdk:TabControl.Items>
        <sdk:TabItem Header="See a Button Here">
            <Button Content="I am a Button!" Margin="10" />
        </sdk:TabItem>
        <sdk:TabItem Header="See an Image Here">
            <Image
                Source="/Chapter6;component/Assets/dog.png" Margin="10" />
        </sdk:TabItem>
    </sdk:TabControl.Items>
</sdk:TabControl>
```

As with `ComboBox` and `ListBox`, the `TabControl` exposes a `SelectedItem` property that allows you to determine which tab is selected, as well as an event that allows you to be notified when the selected tab changes.

Also note that unlike `ComboBox` and `ListBox`, because the `TabControl` does not derive from the `Selector` class, it does not include the `SelectedValuePath` and `SelectedValue` properties.

DataPager

If you are using `List` controls in your application, like the `DataGrid` or the `ListBox`, then it is likely that you are displaying a lot of data. To help users navigate that data, a common pattern is to enable paging in the grid. Silverlight includes a special control called `DataPager` that you can use to enable paging in `List` controls.

Listings 6-26 and 6-27 show how you can use the `DataPager` and `ListBox` with the `PagedCollectionView` to allow users to page through the list data.

LISTING 6-26: Creating the PagedCollection

```
// Executes when the user navigates to this page.
protected override void OnNavigatedTo(NavigationEventArgs e)
{
    PagedCollectionView itemListView =
        new PagedCollectionView(Assets.DemoData.Employees);

    this.DataContext = itemListView;
}
```

Listing 6-26 demonstrates how in the page's `OnNavigated` event, the `PagedCollectionView` is created using an existing collection of `Employees`. The view is then assigned as the page's `DataContext`.

LISTING 6-27: Binding a ListBox and DataPager to a PagedCollection

```
<ListBox x:Name="ListBox1"
         ItemsSource="{Binding}"
         DisplayMemberPath="FirstName" />
<sdk:DataPager
    DisplayMode="FirstLastNumeric"
    Source="{Binding}" PageSize="5" />
```

Once the `PagedCollectionView` is created, as Listing 6-27 shows, you can simply bind the view as the `ItemsSource` of both the `ListView` and the `DataPager`.

If you run the sample, Figure 6-15 shows how the `DataPager` can now be used to page data in the `ListView`.

FIGURE 6-15

Accordion

The `Accordion` control is an additional `ItemsControl` that is available as part of the Silverlight Toolkit. The control allows you to replicate the familiar Closable Panels UI pattern seen in many popular applications. Like other item controls, the `Accordion` supports both a Data-Bound mode and a manually defined Content mode.

Listing 6-28 demonstrates binding an `ItemsSource` to the `Accordion` control.

LISTING 6-28: Binding an ItemsSource to the Accordion control

```xml
<layoutToolkit:Accordion ItemsSource="{Binding}">
    <layoutToolkit:Accordion.ItemTemplate>
        <DataTemplate>
            <sdk:Label Content="{Binding FirstName}"/>
        </DataTemplate>
    </layoutToolkit:Accordion.ItemTemplate>
    <layoutToolkit:Accordion.ContentTemplate>
        <DataTemplate>
            <StackPanel>
                <StackPanel Orientation="Horizontal">
                    <TextBlock Text="{Binding EmployeeID}" />
                    <TextBlock Text=" - " />
                    <TextBlock Text="{Binding FirstName}" />
                    <TextBlock Text=" " />
                    <TextBlock Text="{Binding LastName}" />
                    <TextBlock Text=", " />
                    <TextBlock Text="{Binding Title}" />
```

```
                    </StackPanel>

                    <TextBlock Text="{Binding Address}" />

                    <StackPanel Orientation="Horizontal">
                        <TextBlock Text="{Binding City}" />
                        <TextBlock Text=", " />
                        <TextBlock Text="{Binding State}" />
                        <TextBlock Text="  " />
                        <TextBlock Text="{Binding PostalCode}" />
                    </StackPanel>

                    <StackPanel Orientation="Horizontal">
                        <TextBlock Text="{Binding HomePhone}" />
                        <TextBlock Text=" x" />
                        <TextBlock Text="{Binding Extension}" />
                    </StackPanel>

                    <TextBlock Width="300" Text="{Binding Notes}" />
                </StackPanel>
            </DataTemplate>
        </layoutToolkit:Accordion.ContentTemplate>
    </layoutToolkit:Accordion>
```

In the listing, `DataTemplates` are used to define the content that will be shown in the control at run time. The `ItemTemplate` is used to define the content shown in each `Accordion` header, and the `ContentTemplate` to define the content in each content section.

Figure 6-16 shows the result of running Listing 6-28.

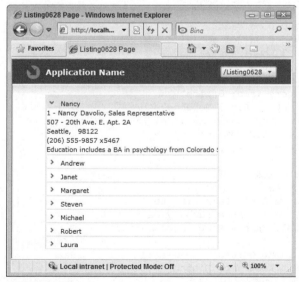

FIGURE 6-16

You can change the default style of the `Accordion` headers by re-templating the `AccordionItem` control. This control contains the `AccordionButton` control and `ExpandableContentControl` as its two primary UI elements.

TreeView

The `TreeView` control is, as it sounds, a control that allows you to add tree UIs to your application. As with all other `List` and `Item` controls, it allows you to define items explicitly or bind data to the control.

Listing 6-29 shows how you can create a set of explicitly defined nodes in a `TreeView`.

LISTING 6-29: Creating a set of explicitly defined TreeView nodes

```
<sdk:TreeView x:Name="TreeView1">
    <sdk:TreeViewItem Header="Books">
        <sdk:TreeViewItem Header="Books" />
        <sdk:TreeViewItem Header="Textbooks"/>
        <sdk:TreeViewItem Header="Magazines"/>
    </sdk:TreeViewItem>
    <sdk:TreeViewItem Header="Music, Movies &amp; Games">
        <sdk:TreeViewItem Header="Movies &amp; TV"/>
        <sdk:TreeViewItem Header="Blu-Ray"/>
        <sdk:TreeViewItem Header="Video On Demand"/>
    </sdk:TreeViewItem>
    <sdk:TreeViewItem Header="Music">
        <sdk:TreeViewItem Header="MP3 Downloads"/>
        <sdk:TreeViewItem Header="Musical Instruments"/>
    </sdk:TreeViewItem>
    <sdk:TreeViewItem Header="Digital Downloads">
        <sdk:TreeViewItem Header="Video On Demand"/>
        <sdk:TreeViewItem Header="MP3 Downloads"/>
        <sdk:TreeViewItem Header="Game Downloads"/>
    </sdk:TreeViewItem>
    <sdk:TreeViewItem Header="Computers &amp; Office">
        <sdk:TreeViewItem Header="Laptops &amp; Notebooks" />
        <sdk:TreeViewItem Header="Desktops &amp; Servers" />
        <sdk:TreeViewItem Header="Computer Components" />
        <sdk:TreeViewItem Header="Computer Accessories" />
    </sdk:TreeViewItem>
    <sdk:TreeViewItem Header="Electronics">
        <sdk:TreeViewItem Header="TV &amp; Video" />
        <sdk:TreeViewItem Header="Home Audio &amp; Theater" />
        <sdk:TreeViewItem Header="Camara, Phone &amp; Video" />
        <sdk:TreeViewItem Header="Cell Phones &amp; Accessories" />
    </sdk:TreeViewItem>
    <sdk:TreeViewItem Header="Home &amp; Garden">
        <sdk:TreeViewItem Header="Kitchen &amp; Dining" />
        <sdk:TreeViewItem Header="Bedding &amp; Bath" />
        <sdk:TreeViewItem Header="Home Appliances" />
        <sdk:TreeViewItem Header="Vacuums &amp; Storage" />
```

```
        </sdk:TreeViewItem>
    </sdk:TreeView>
```

As you can see in Listing 6-29, to create tree nodes, you use the `TreeViewItem` element. The `TreeViewItem` element exposes a variety of properties that allow you to control how it is shown by the tree including setting the node's text using the `Header` property and setting its expanded state by using the `IsExpanded` property. Or, if you want to add more complex content to a node, you can use the `HeaderTemplate` property to provide a `DataTemplate`. This is shown in Listing 6-30.

LISTING 6-30: Using the HeaderTemplate property

```
<sdk:TreeViewItem Header="Books">
    <sdk:TreeViewItem.HeaderTemplate>
        <DataTemplate>
            <StackPanel Orientation="Horizontal">
                <CheckBox />
                <Image Source="/Chapter6;component/Assets/Book.png" />
                <TextBlock Text="Books"/>
            </StackPanel>
        </DataTemplate>
    </sdk:TreeViewItem.HeaderTemplate>
</sdk:TreeViewItem>
```

Figure 6-17 shows the `TreeView` from Listing 6-30.

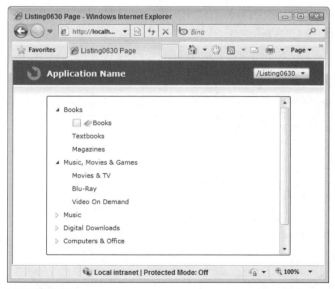

FIGURE 6-17

If you have data that you want to bind to the `TreeView`, you can use the `HierachicalDataTemplate`. Listing 6-31 demonstrates the most basic way to use the `HierarchicalDataTemplate`.

LISTING 6-31: Using the HierarchicalDataTemplate

```
<Grid.Resources>
    <common:HierarchicalDataTemplate
        x:Key="myTreeViewHierarchicalTemplateLevel"
        ItemsSource="{Binding Children}" >

        <TextBlock Text="{Binding Name}" />
    </common:HierarchicalDataTemplate>
</Grid.Resources>
<sdk:TreeView x:Name="TreeView1" ItemsSource="{Binding}"
        ItemTemplate="{StaticResource myTreeViewHierarchicalTemplate}" />
```

In the listing, you can see that a new HierachicalDataTemplate has been created as a Grid resource. The template's ItemsSource is set to the name of the property on the objects in the TreeView's ItemsSource that returns the collection. The HierachicalDataTemplate uses this to walk the nested object structure in the ItemsSource and create a TreeViewItem for each object. The content used to show each node is contained within the HierachicalDataTemplate.

The HierachicalDataTemplate resource is assigned to the TreeView's ItemTemplate property.

You can define different layouts for each level of the tree by defining a series of HierachicalDataTemplates and setting the ItemTemplate property of each. This is shown in Listing 6-32, where a HierarchicalDataTemplate has been defined for each level of the ItemsSource.

LISTING 6-32: Defining different layouts for each level of a tree

```
<Grid.Resources>
    <common:HierarchicalDataTemplate
      x:Key="myTreeViewHierarchicalTemplateLevel0"
      ItemsSource="{Binding Children}"
      ItemTemplate="{StaticResource myTreeViewHierarchicalTemplateLevel1}">
      <TextBlock Text="{Binding Name}" Foreground="Blue" />
    </common:HierarchicalDataTemplate>

    <common:HierarchicalDataTemplate
      x:Key="myTreeViewHierarchicalTemplateLevel1"
      ItemsSource="{Binding Children}"
      ItemTemplate="{StaticResource myTreeViewHierarchicalTemplateLevel2}">
      <TextBlock Text="{Binding Name}" Foreground="Red" />
    </common:HierarchicalDataTemplate>

    <common:HierarchicalDataTemplate
      x:Key="myTreeViewHierarchicalTemplateLevel2"
      ItemsSource="{Binding Children}" >
      <TextBlock Text="{Binding Name}" Foreground="Green" />
    </common:HierarchicalDataTemplate>
</Grid.Resources>
<sdk:TreeView x:Name="TreeView1" ItemsSource="{Binding}"
        ItemTemplate="{StaticResource myTreeViewHierarchicalTemplate0}" />
```

Once you've added nodes to the tree, you can use the control API to programmatically interact with nodes of the tree. The control includes a `SelectedItemChanged` event that allows you to access the currently selected `TreeView` item.

It is also possible to walk the tree nodes by using the `ItemsControl`'s `ContainerFromIndex` method (`TreeView` is derived from `ItemsControl`). Listing 6-33 shows how you can recursively walk through all of the nodes included in a `TreeView` control.

LISTING 6-33: Walking the Items included in a TreeView control

```
public void WalkTreeViewItems(TreeView treeView)
{
    for (int i = 0; i < treeView.Items.Count; i++)
    {
        WalkAllTreeViewItems((TreeViewItem)
            treeView.ItemContainerGenerator.ContainerFromIndex(i));
    }
}

private void WalkAllTreeViewItems(TreeViewItem currentTreeViewItem)
{
    for (int i = 0; i < currentTreeViewItem.Items.Count; i++)
    {
        TreeViewItem child =
            (TreeViewItem)currentTreeViewItem.ItemContainerGenerator.
                        ContainerFromIndex(i);
        WalkAllTreeViewItems(child);
    }
}
```

You can see that the listing includes two methods, the first of which loops the root methods and the second which recursively walks all of the child tree items. Each method uses the `ContainerFromIndex` method to retrieve the `TreeViewItem` object, which wraps each item included in the `TreeView`.

You could expand these methods to perform actions like expanding or collapsing all nodes programmatically.

USING BUTTON CONTROLS

Next to the `TextBlock` and `CheckBox`, `Button` controls are probably one of the most basic controls used in applications. Silverlight includes a standard `Button` control, as well as two additional `Button` controls that extend the basic capabilities of the `Button` — the `HyperlinkButton` and the `ToggleButton`.

Button

The basic `Button` control included in Silverlight offers the basic behaviors that you would expect a button to, such as `Normal`, `MouseOver`, and `Pressed` states, and a `Click` event, but unlike buttons on other platforms like Windows Forms, the Silverlight `Button` control uses the power of XAML to allow you to transform the normal gray button into something completely different.

You can first see this if you try to find a `Text` property on the `Button`, which you would expect to be there in order to allow you to set the button's text. This is where the power of Silverlight begins to kick in. Rather than a basic `Text` property, the `Button` control offers a `Content` property that — unlike `Text`, which only accepts a `String` — accepts a more generic `Object`. Using this, you can set the `Content` property to very complex elements such as a checkbox or even another button.

A more realistic example might be placing an image as the `Button`'s content rather than text. In platforms like Windows Forms, you would need to draw this yourself, or in HTML, you would have to use an Image button, both of which have significant drawbacks. But in Silverlight, this is simple to achieve. Listing 6-34 demonstrates using the `Content` property to use an image as the `Button`'s content.

LISTING 6-34: Using an image as a Button's content

```
<Button x:Name="Button1" Click="Button1_Click">
    <Button.Content>
        <Border Margin="20" BorderBrush="Black" BorderThickness="3" >
            <Image Source="/Chapter6;component/Assets/dog.png" />
        </Border>
    </Button.Content>
</Button>
```

Figure 6-18 shows the button with an image as its content.

FIGURE 6-18

This example only replaces the content area of the `Button`, but you can replace the entire default user interface for the `Button` if you want to. When you run the code in Listing 6-34, you will see that even though the content is different, the control still fires its normal events, like the `Click` event.

Another interesting feature of the `Button` control is the `ClickMode` property. Using this property, you can set when the `Button`'s `Click` event should fire: when the mouse is hovered, when the mouse is pressed, or when the mouse is released.

HyperlinkButton

The `HyperlinkButton` extends the basic `Button` to allow you to provide the button with a URI value using the `NavigateUri` property. You can provide either absolute or relative URIs, although the behavior of the control will depend on the value of the Silverlight object's `EnableNavigation` property. If the property is set to `None`, then the `HyperlinkButton` will permit only relative links.

The control also includes a `TargetName` property that allows you to specify the window or frame the URI should open in. If you have specified a relative URI, then the `TargetName` property should be given the *x:Name* of the Silverlight Navigation Frame element you want to target.

 Chapter 4 includes more information on using the Frame element with the Silverlight Navigation framework.

If you have provided an absolute URL, then you can provide the standard HTML Target attribute values such as _blank or _top. The code in Listing 6-35 demonstrates the use of the `HyperlinkButton` with an absolute URI.

 LISTING 6-35: Using the HyperlinkButton

Available for download on Wrox.com

```
<HyperlinkButton
    ClickMode="Release"
    TargetName="_blank"
    NavigateUri="http://www.silverlight.net">
    <HyperlinkButton.Content>
        <TextBlock Text="Click Me!" TextDecorations="Underline" />
    </HyperlinkButton.Content>
</HyperlinkButton>
```

ToggleButton

Silverlight 4 also contains a new `ToggleButton` control. This control combines the basic behaviors of a button with the behavior of a checkbox, allowing your `Button` control to have a checked state.

Listing 6-36 demonstrates the use of the `ToggleButton`.

 LISTING 6-36: Using the ToggleButton

Available for download on Wrox.com

```
<ToggleButton x:Name="ToggleButton1"
    Content="Toggle Me!" IsChecked="true"
    Height="100" Width="100" />
```

The `ToggleButton` control serves as the base for other controls that have a checked state such as `CheckBox` and `RadioButton` and therefore supports the same capabilities, including supporting a three-state checked option.

USING THE GRIDSPLITTER CONTROL

The `Grid` panel, which is discussed in detail in Chapter 5, is a great way to lay out your application's user interface. A common pattern when using a grid is to allow the user to resize grid columns or rows. While the `Grid` panel itself does not have this capability, Silverlight includes the `GridSplitter` control, which allows you to add this capability to it.

Listing 6-37 demonstrates the use of the `GridSplitter` control, splitting a column containing two columns.

LISTING 6-37: Using the GridSplitter to split a two-column Grid

```
<Grid x:Name="LayoutRoot">
    <Grid.ColumnDefinitions>
        <ColumnDefinition />
        <ColumnDefinition />
    </Grid.ColumnDefinitions>
    <sdk:GridSplitter />
</Grid>
```

To control the orientation of the `GridSplitter` control, use its `Horizontal` and `Vertical` alignment properties. If `HorizontalAlignment` is set to `Stretch`, then the grid splits between rows; if `VerticalAlignment` is set to `Stretch`, then the control splits columns. Listing 6-38 demonstrates using the `GridSplitter` control in two different configurations — one splitting a grid vertically, and one splitting a grid horizontally.

LISTING 6-38: Using the GridSplitter in horizontal and vertical orientation

```
<Grid x:Name="LayoutRoot">
    <Grid.ColumnDefinitions>
        <ColumnDefinition />
        <ColumnDefinition />
    </Grid.ColumnDefinitions>

    <Grid x:Name="HorizontalOrientation" Background="Gray"
        Grid.Column="0" Margin="10" ShowGridLines="True">
        <Grid.RowDefinitions>
            <RowDefinition />
            <RowDefinition Height="Auto" />
            <RowDefinition />
        </Grid.RowDefinitions>

        <sdk:GridSplitter
            HorizontalAlignment="Stretch"
```

```
                    VerticalAlignment="Center" Grid.Row="1" />

            <Button Grid.Row="0" Content="Top" Margin="5" />
            <Button Grid.Row="2" Content="Bottom" Margin="5" />
        </Grid>

        <Grid x:Name="VerticalOrientation" Background="Gray"
            Grid.Column="1" Margin="10" ShowGridLines="True">
            <Grid.ColumnDefinitions>
                <ColumnDefinition />
                <ColumnDefinition Width="10" />
                <ColumnDefinition />
            </Grid.ColumnDefinitions>

            <sdk:GridSplitter
                HorizontalAlignment="Center"
                VerticalAlignment="Stretch" Grid.Column="1" />

            <Button Grid.Column="0" Content="Left" Margin="5" />
            <Button Grid.Column="2" Content="Right" Margin="5" />

        </Grid>
    </Grid>
```

If both are set to Stretch and GridSplitter has an actual height less than its actual width, then it splits rows. If the actual height is greater than the width, then columns are split.

Setting the alignment properties to Left, Right, Top, or Bottom, you can control the direction in which the splitter resizes its column or row. Setting a property to Center means to resize in both directions.

GridSplitter always drags the entire Column or Row, even if it only visually appears in one cell. You can use the Grid's RowSpan and ColumnSpan properties on the GridSplitter to make it appear in multiple cells.

Also, by default, when the GridSplitter is repositioned, the content of the grid is resized in real time. You can use the GridSplitter's ShowsPreview property to configure the control to show a preview first of the new GridSplitter position, and then resize it when the user releases the splitter.

USING THE IMAGE CONTROL

The Image element is a simple control that allows you to show images in your applications. Listing 6-39 shows the basic usage of the Image control.

LISTING 6-39: Using the Image control

Available for download on Wrox.com

```
<Image Source="/Chapter6;component/Assets/fox.png"
       Stretch="Uniform"
       ImageFailed="Image_ImageFailed"
       ImageOpened="Image_ImageOpened" />
```

The listing loads a PNG image that has been included as a Resource in the applications XAP. The `Image` element can load images in PNG and JPEG formats from a variety of locations including relative (as shown above), absolute URIs, or a stream.

When setting the `Image`'s source in XAML, as shown in Listing 6-39, you can provide a URI directly as a property value. Silverlight automatically converts the value to a `Uri` object that is used to create a new `ImageSource` object. When loading from an absolute URI, cross-domain URIs are permitted. Relative URLs are relative to the XAP, not the hosting page location.

When setting the `Image`'s source property in code, you need to create a new instance of a `BitmapSource` object and assign that to the property. You can use the `SetSource` method of the `BitmapSource` to create an image from a stream.

The `Image` control exposes two events that can help you determine if an image was loaded successfully or not. The `ImageOpened` event is fired when the image file has been successfully downloaded and decoded. The `ImageFailed` event is fired if either of those two processes fails.

USING DATA VISUALIZATION CONTROLS

The Silverlight Toolkit includes two controls that are designed to make visualizing data easy. The `TreeMap`, which is similar to a `Heatmap`, is designed to visually display hierarchical data structures. The `Chart` control allows you to render data visually as one of seven different common chart types.

TreeMap

Tree maps are a relatively recent visualization technique that is specifically designed for showing hierarchical data. Points in the tree map are sized based on their value, relative to all the other values in the bound items source. Additionally, a second dimension of data can be shown by using a gradient color within each node rendered in the map.

Listing 6-40 shows a basic usage of the `TreeMap` control to visualize the number of wins for each team in the 2009 season of Major League Baseball's American League teams.

LISTING 6-40: Using the TreeMap control to visualize baseball game wins

```
<my:TreeMap ItemsSource="{Binding}">
    <my:TreeMap.ItemDefinition>
        <my:TreeMapItemDefinition ValuePath="Wins">
            <DataTemplate>
                <Border x:Name="Border1" Background="AliceBlue"
                        BorderBrush="Black" BorderThickness="1">
                    <TextBlock Text="{Binding Name}"
                               VerticalAlignment="Center"
                               TextAlignment="Center"
                               TextWrapping="Wrap"/>
                </Border>
            </DataTemplate>
        </my:TreeMapItemDefinition>
```

```
            </my:TreeMap.ItemDefinition>
        </my:TreeMap>
```

As you can see from Listing 6-40, using the control is fairly straightforward. You create a `DataTemplate` within the `TreeMapItemDefinition` that defines the contents of each node in the `TreeMap`. You use the `ValuePath` property to identify the property in the control's `ItemsSource` that should be used as the node value.

Running Listing 6-40 results in the tree map shown in Figure 6-19.

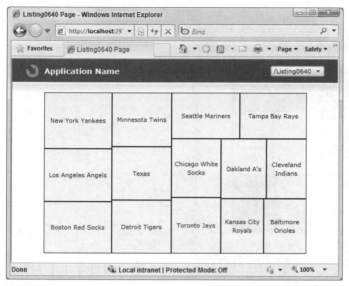

FIGURE 6-19

As you can see, a node has been created for each team, and the nodes have been sized according to their values.

As mentioned previously, a second dimension can be added to the tree map by creating a gradient color to fill each node. To do this, you can use the `TreeMap` control's `Interpolators` collection, which accepts either a `SolidColorBrushInterpolator` or a `DoubleInterpolator`. Listing 6-41 demonstrates how to use the `SolidColorBrushInterpolator` to add an additional dimension showing the streak for each team.

LISTING 6-41: Using the SolidColorBrushInterpolator

Available for
download on
Wrox.com

```
<my:TreeMap.Interpolators>
    <my:SolidColorBrushInterpolator
        TargetName="Border1"
        TargetProperty="Background"
        DataRangeBinding="{Binding Streak}"
        From="White"
        To="DarkRed" />
</my:TreeMap.Interpolators>
```

In this case, the `SolidColorBrushInterpolator` colors each tile a shade from `White` to `DarkRed` depending on the value of the streak. To tell the `TreeMap` which element in the `TreeMapItemDefinition`'s `DataTemplate` to assign the color to, use the `Target` and `TargetProperty` properties, in this case, telling the control to assign the color to the `Border`'s `Background` property. The result of adding the `SolidColorBrushInterpolator` is shown in Figure 6-20.

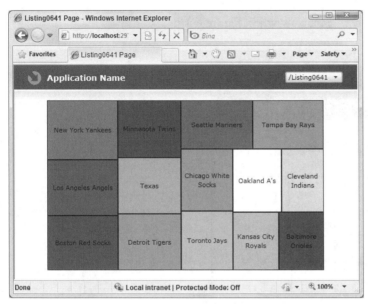

FIGURE 6-20

It is also possible to have more than one segment of data defined in the `TreeMap`. For example, the listings so far have shown the 2009 season statistics for only the American League teams. What if you wanted to add in the National League teams and color them from blue to white? You can do that by creating a custom `TreeMapItemDefinitionSelector`, which allows you to define multiple `TreeMapItemDefinitions` within the control and tells the control how to divide up the data.

Listing 6-42 shows how to derive a custom class from the `TreeMapItemDefinitionSegment`.

LISTING 6-42: Using the TreeMapItemDefinitionSelector

```
[ContentProperty("Children")]
public class LeagueItemDefinitionSelector : TreeMapItemDefinitionSelector
{
    public Collection<TreeMapItemDefinition> Children { get; private set; }

    public LeagueItemDefinitionSelector() {
        Children = new Collection<TreeMapItemDefinition>(); }

    public override TreeMapItemDefinition
```

```
            SelectItemDefinition(TreeMap treeMap, object item, int level)
    {
        if (item is Chapter6.Views.Listing0643.League)
        {
            return Children[0];
        }

        if (item is Chapter6.Views.Listing0643.TeamStats)
        {
            Chapter6.Views.Listing0643.TeamStats node =
                item as Chapter6.Views.Listing0643.TeamStats;

            if (Children.Count > 0 &&
                node != null &&
                node.League.Length > 0)
            {
                switch (node.League)
                {
                    case "American":
                        return Children[1];
                    case "National":
                        return Children[2];
                }

                return null;
            }
        }

        return null;
    }
}
```

The code for creating a custom selector class is fairly straightforward. First, you create a collection to hold the TreeMapItemsDefinitions. You need to create a separate definition for each segment you want to show. Next, you simply override the SelectItemDefinition method and insert the logic that determines how this selector should select the TreeMapItemDefinition for each node in the control. In the previous listing, the logic first checks to see what type of object is being passed in. If the type is a League object, the first template is returned. If the type is a TeamStats object, then the League property is checked and a template returned based on its value.

Once your selector is created, add this to the TreeMap control by assigning it to the ItemTemplateSelector property. You can also create additional interpolators to color the different segments. Listing 6-43 shows how the TreeMap is modified to leverage the selector and interpolators.

LISTING 6-43: Modifying the TreeMap

```
<my:TreeMap ItemsSource="{Binding}">
    <my:TreeMap.Interpolators>
        <my:SolidColorBrushInterpolator
            TargetName="Border1"
```

continues

LISTING 6-43 *(continued)*

```
                TargetProperty="Background"
                DataRangeBinding="{Binding Streak}"
                From="White"
                To="DarkRed" />
            <my:SolidColorBrushInterpolator
                TargetName="Border2"
                TargetProperty="Background"
                DataRangeBinding="{Binding Streak}"
                From="White"
                To="DarkBlue" />
        </my:TreeMap.Interpolators>
        <my:TreeMap.ItemDefinitionSelector>
            <local:LeagueItemDefinitionSelector>
                <my:TreeMapItemDefinition ItemsSource="{Binding Teams}"
                                          ValueBinding="{Binding Value}">
                    <DataTemplate>
                        <Border x:Name="Border0" Background="AliceBlue"
                         BorderBrush="Black" BorderThickness="1">
                        </Border>
                    </DataTemplate>
                </my:TreeMapItemDefinition>

                <my:TreeMapItemDefinition ItemsSource="{Binding Children}"
                                          ValueBinding="{Binding Wins}">
                    <DataTemplate>
                        <Border x:Name="Border1" Background="AliceBlue"
                        BorderBrush="Black" BorderThickness="1">
                            <TextBlock Text="{Binding Name}"
                            VerticalAlignment="Center"
                            TextAlignment="Center"
                            TextWrapping="Wrap"/>
                        </Border>
                    </DataTemplate>
                </my:TreeMapItemDefinition>

                <my:TreeMapItemDefinition ItemsSource="{Binding Children}"
                                          ValueBinding="{Binding Wins}">
                    <DataTemplate>
                        <Border x:Name="Border2" Background="AliceBlue"
                        BorderBrush="Black" BorderThickness="1">
                            <TextBlock Text="{Binding Name}"
                            VerticalAlignment="Center"
                            TextAlignment="Center"
                            TextWrapping="Wrap"/>
                        </Border>
                    </DataTemplate>
                </my:TreeMapItemDefinition>
            </local:LeagueItemDefinitionSelector>
        </my:TreeMap.ItemDefinitionSelector>
    </my:TreeMap>
```

Figure 6-21 shows the result of adding the selector and interpolators to the TreeMap.

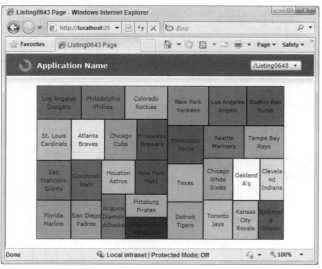

FIGURE 6-21

Chart

The Chart control is the second data visualization control included in the Silverlight Toolkit. It supports seven chart types:

➤ Area

➤ Bar

➤ Column

➤ Line

➤ Scatter

➤ Pie

➤ Bubble

Listing 6-44 demonstrates using the Chart control to show a simple Line chart.

LISTING 6-44: Using the Chart control

```xml
<chartingToolkit:Chart>
    <chartingToolkit:Chart.Series>
        <chartingToolkit:LineSeries
            ItemsSource="{Binding}"
            DependentValueBinding="{Binding Y}"
            IndependentValueBinding="{Binding X}" />
    </chartingToolkit:Chart.Series>
</chartingToolkit:Chart>
```

As shown in Listing 6-44, to create the chart you simply add a `LineSeries` to the charts series collection. On the `LineSeries` you provide an `ItemsSource` and configure the `Dependent` and `Independent` values. You can think of the `Dependent` value as the chart's X-axis and the `Independent` value as the Y-axis.

Running Listing 6-44 results in the Chart shown in Figure 6-22.

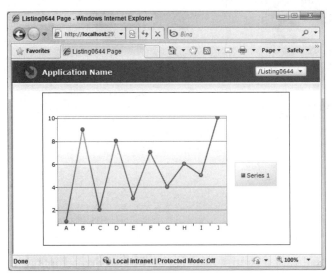

FIGURE 6-22

Notice that the chart automatically adds the appropriate axes and a legend.

You can show multiple sets of data in the chart simply by adding additional series objects to the `Chart`'s `Series` collection. Listing 6-45 shows how you can create a column chart with multiple series.

LISTING 6-45: Creating a column chart with multiple series

```
<chartingToolkit:Chart Title="Automobile Manufacturer Annual Sales">
    <chartingToolkit:Chart.Series>
        <chartingToolkit:ColumnSeries
            Title="Ford"
            DataContext="{Binding PointsA}"
            ItemsSource="{Binding}"
            DependentValueBinding="{Binding Y}"
            IndependentValueBinding="{Binding X}" />
        <chartingToolkit:ColumnSeries
            Title="Toyota"
            DataContext="{Binding PointsB}"
            ItemsSource="{Binding}"
            DependentValueBinding="{Binding Y}"
            IndependentValueBinding="{Binding X}" />
    </chartingToolkit:Chart.Series>
</chartingToolkit:Chart>
```

Figure 6-23 shows the results of adding multiple column series to the Chart.

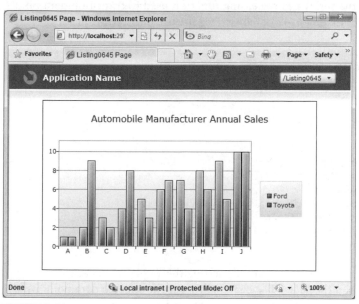

FIGURE 6-23

By default each series in the chart adds an item to the legend. You can change the text shown in the legend for the series by setting the Title property.

Additionally, as you add each series, the chart automatically selects a new unique series color and adds the series to the legend. You can control the collection of colors the chart can use to color series using the chart's Palette collection. Listing 6-46 shows how you can create a ResourceDictionaryCollection that contains the different colors you want the chart to use to color the series.

LISTING 6-46: Creating a ResourceDictionaryCollection

```xml
<chartingToolkit:Chart.Palette>
    <visualizationToolkit:ResourceDictionaryCollection>
        <ResourceDictionary>
            <Style x:Key="DataPointStyle" TargetType="Control">
                <Setter Property="Background" Value="Red" />
            </Style>
        </ResourceDictionary>
        <ResourceDictionary>
            <Style x:Key="DataPointStyle" TargetType="Control">
                <Setter Property="Background" Value="Green" />
            </Style>
        </ResourceDictionary>
    </visualizationToolkit:ResourceDictionaryCollection>
</chartingToolkit:Chart.Palette>
```

Series objects expose a variety of other properties that let you configure features like the animation sequence used to initially display the series and the easing function used to transition data points as values in the `ItemsSource` change. Listing 6-47 demonstrates the use of these properties.

LISTING 6-47: Using properties to configure series features

```
<chartingToolkit:ColumnSeries
    Title="Ford"
    DataContext="{Binding PointsA}"
    ItemsSource="{Binding}"
    DependentValueBinding="{Binding Y}"
    IndependentValueBinding="{Binding X}"
    AnimationSequence="FirstToLast"
    TransitionDuration="5000">
    <chartingToolkit:ColumnSeries.TransitionEasingFunction>
        <ElasticEase EasingMode="EaseIn" />
    </chartingToolkit:ColumnSeries.TransitionEasingFunction>
</chartingToolkit:ColumnSeries>
```

Series also support the notion of selecting a data point. By setting the `IsSelectionEnabed` property to `True`, users can click data points in the chart. The chart will show the selected data point using a different style, which you can change by restyling the data point, and expose the currently selected data point through the `SelectedItem` property. Additionally, you can listen to the `SelectionChanged` event to get notified when the selected data point changes.

As mentioned earlier, by default, the chart automatically selects the appropriate axes to use based on the series included in the chart. You can, however, manually add and configure axes to the chart's Axes collection. The chart includes three axis types — `LinearAxis` for numeric data, `CategoryAxis` for string data, and a `DateTimeAxis` for `DateTime` data. Listing 6-48 shows how to use the `Axes` collection to add linear and category axes for a `LineSeries`.

LISTING 6-48: Using Axes to add linear and category axes

```
<chartingToolkit:Chart>
    <chartingToolkit:Chart.Axes>
        <chartingToolkit:LinearAxis x:Name="yaxis" Orientation="Y"
            ShowGridLines="False" Title="Y Axis Values"
            Minimum="-100" Maximum="100" Interval="50"/>
        <chartingToolkit:CategoryAxis x:Name="xaxis" Orientation="X"
            Title="X Axis Values"  />
    </chartingToolkit:Chart.Axes>
    <chartingToolkit:Chart.Series>
        <chartingToolkit:LineSeries
            DataContext="{Binding PointsB}"
            ItemsSource="{Binding}"
            DependentValuePath="Y"
            DependentRangeAxis="{Binding ElementName=yaxis}"
            IndependentValuePath="X"
            IndependentAxis="{Binding ElementName=xaxis}" />
    </chartingToolkit:Chart.Series>
</chartingToolkit:Chart>
```

Finally, one of the great aspects of the Chart control is that Microsoft has unsealed the primary charting classes in the control. This means that it is now much easier to extend the control to add additional functionality, such as additional series to support different chart types, or more complex axes, like a logarithmic axis. An example of creating a custom series can be found at the following URL:

www.codeproject.com/KB/silverlight/SLTCandlestickChart2.aspx

USING OTHER MISCELLANEOUS CONTROLS

This section covers a few other miscellaneous controls you will find useful as you develop your Silverlight applications.

ViewBox

The ViewBox control, previously included in the Silverlight Toolkit, has been promoted to the Silverlight 4 SDK. The ViewBox is designed to scale XAML content appropriately based on the size of the viewbox. Figure 6-24 demonstrates an ellipse shown inside four ViewBox controls.

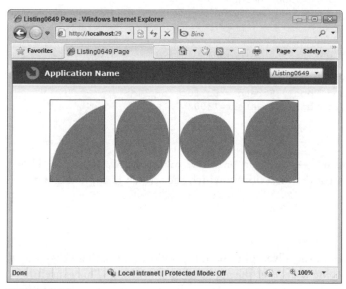

FIGURE 6-24

In the figure, the ellipse has its size fixed at 300 × 300. The ViewBox property scales the ellipse based on the value of the Stretch property. Listing 6-49 shows the code used to generate Figure 6-24.

LISTING 6-49: Using the ViewBox control to show an ellipse in four segments

Available for
download on
Wrox.com

```
<Border BorderBrush="Black" BorderThickness="1"
        HorizontalAlignment="Left" VerticalAlignment="Top">
```

continues

LISTING 6-49 *(continued)*

```
        <Viewbox x:Name="ViewBox6" Width="100" Height="150"
                StretchDirection="Both" Stretch="None">
            <Ellipse Fill="Red" Width="300" Height="300" />
        </Viewbox>
    </Border>
    <Border BorderBrush="Black" BorderThickness="1"
            HorizontalAlignment="Left" VerticalAlignment="Top"
            Margin="120,0,0,0">
        <Viewbox x:Name="ViewBox1" Width="100" Height="150"
                StretchDirection="Both" Stretch="Fill">
            <Ellipse Fill="Red" Width="300" Height="300" />
        </Viewbox>
    </Border>
    <Border BorderBrush="Black" BorderThickness="1"
            HorizontalAlignment="Left" VerticalAlignment="Top"
            Margin="240,0,0,0">
        <Viewbox x:Name="ViewBox4" Width="100" Height="150"
                StretchDirection="Both" Stretch="Uniform" >
            <Ellipse Fill="Red" Width="300" Height="300" />
        </Viewbox>
    </Border>
    <Border BorderBrush="Black" BorderThickness="1"
            HorizontalAlignment="Left" VerticalAlignment="Top"
            Margin="360,0,0,0">
        <Viewbox x:Name="ViewBox5" Width="100" Height="150"
                StretchDirection="Both"  Stretch="UniformToFill">
            <Ellipse Fill="Red" Width="300" Height="300" />
        </Viewbox>
    </Border>
```

The `Stretch` property allows four values — `Uniform`, `UniformToFill`, `Fill`, and `None`. The default is `Uniform`. You can also control the direction in which the stretch is applied using the `StretchDirection` property.

BusyIndicator

The `BusyIndicator`, which is included in the Silverlight Toolkit, provides you with an easy way to add an effect to your application notifying users that the application is working. This is useful if your application executes long-running tasks, such as remote server calls, or complex calculation routines. Listing 6-50 shows how you can use the `BusyIndicator` while the application attempts to validate user credentials.

LISTING 6-50: Using the BusyIndicator

```
<Grid x:Name="LayoutRoot"
    VerticalAlignment="Center" HorizontalAlignment="Center">
    <Grid>
        <Grid.RowDefinitions>
            <RowDefinition />
```

```
            <RowDefinition />
            <RowDefinition />
        </Grid.RowDefinitions>
        <Grid.ColumnDefinitions>
            <ColumnDefinition />
            <ColumnDefinition />
        </Grid.ColumnDefinitions>

        <sdk:Label Content="Username: " Margin="5"
                Grid.Column="0" Grid.Row="0"/>
        <TextBox x:Name="txtUsername" Width="150"  Margin="5"
                Grid.Column="1" Grid.Row="0"/>

        <sdk:Label Content="Password: " Margin="5"
                Grid.Column="0" Grid.Row="1" />
        <TextBox x:Name="txtPassword" Width="150" Margin="5"
                Grid.Column="1" Grid.Row="1"/>

        <Button Content="Login" Click="Button_Click"
                Grid.Row="2" Grid.ColumnSpan="2"
                HorizontalAlignment="Center" Margin="5"  />
    </Grid>
    <controlsToolkit:BusyIndicator
        x:Name="BusyIndicator1"
        BusyContent="Validating credentials..."
        VerticalAlignment="Stretch"
        HorizontalAlignment="Stretch" />
</Grid>
```

Listing 6-50 sets up a simple login form with two input fields and a button inside a Grid panel. At the bottom, you can see that the `BusyIndicator` control has also been added. The control has been given some content, and its alignment properties have been set to `Stretch`. Setting the alignment properties to `Stretch` allows it to overlay the login form while shown.

Figure 6-25 shows the form with its `BusyIndicator` showing.

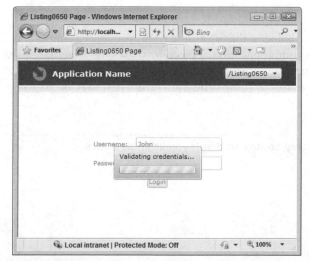

FIGURE 6-25

To show the `BusyIndicator`, simply set the `IsBusy` property to `True`. Normally, you would do this before you start your long-running process. Once the process completes, simply set the property back to `False` to hide the indicator.

Expander

The `Expander` control is a simple control that allows end users to expand or collapse a section of content. Listing 6-51 shows how you can use the `Expander`.

LISTING 6-51: Using the Expander control

```
<StackPanel>
    <controlsToolkit:Expander ExpandDirection="Down"
                                Header="Expand Content Down">
        <Button Content="Expand Content Down" />
    </controlsToolkit:Expander>
    <controlsToolkit:Expander ExpandDirection="Up"
                                Header="Expand Content Up">
        <Button Content="Expand Content Up" />
    </controlsToolkit:Expander>
    <controlsToolkit:Expander ExpandDirection="Left"
                                Header="Expand Content Left">
        <Button Content="Expand Content Left" />
    </controlsToolkit:Expander>
    <controlsToolkit:Expander ExpandDirection="Right"
                                Header="Expand Content Right">
        <Button Content="Expand Content Right" />
    </controlsToolkit:Expander>
</StackPanel>
```

Listing 6-51 shows four `Expanders`, each with a single `Button` as content. Each `Expander` has its `ExpandDirection` property set to one of the four possible values.

ValidationSummary

The `ValidationSummary` control, which is included in the Silverlight SDK, provides a simple way to display a summary of data input errors to your application. The control uses the Silverlight data binding validation properties to receive notification of data input errors that happen. Listing 6-52 shows how to use the `ValidationSummary` control to show validation errors that may occur when entering data into the `TextBox` controls.

LISTING 6-52: Using the ValidationSummary control to display validation errors

```
<Grid x:Name="LayoutRoot">
    <Grid.RowDefinitions>
        <RowDefinition />
        <RowDefinition />
    </Grid.RowDefinitions>

    <StackPanel>
```

```
            <TextBox x:Name="txtFirstName" Text="{Binding FirstName,
                Mode=TwoWay, NotifyOnValidationError=True,
                ValidatesOnExceptions=True}"/>
            <TextBox x:Name="txtLastName" Text="{Binding LastName,
                Mode=TwoWay, NotifyOnValidationError=True,
                ValidatesOnExceptions=True}"/>
        </StackPanel>

        <sdk:ValidationSummary Grid.Row="1" />
    </Grid>
```

It is also possible to restyle the look of the errors shown by the `ValidationSummary` control by creating a new `Style` and assigning it to the control's `ErrorStyle` property.

Tooltip

As its name implies, the `Tooltip` control allows you to add tooltips to UI elements in your application. The control is exposed through the `TooltipService` attached property, which allows you to add a tooltip to any UI Element.

To add content to the control you use the `TooltipService`'s `ToolTip` property. You can set content directly in the property, or you can create a new `Tooltip` object explicitly and place content within it. Listing 6-53 shows how you can add a tooltip to a button by setting content directly on the `TooltipService`'s `ToolTip` property.

LISTING 6-53: Adding a ToolTip to a Button

```
<Button Content="This is a button" Height="100" Width="100"
        ToolTipService.Placement="Mouse"
    <ToolTipService.ToolTip>
        <Grid>
            <TextBlock Text="This is the buttons tooltip" />
        </Grid>
    </ToolTipService.ToolTip>
</Button>
```

Note that the content of the tooltip cannot be interacted with or receive focus, so while you can place elements like `Buttons` in the tooltip, users will not be able to click them.

It is also possible to completely control the look of the tooltip by retemplating the control. Listing 6-54 shows how to retemplate the tooltip from Listing 6-53.

LISTING 6-54: Retemplating the ToolTip control

```
<Grid x:Name="LayoutRoot">
    <Grid.Resources>
        <ControlTemplate TargetType="ToolTip" x:Key="MyToolTipTemplate">
            <Border BorderBrush="Black" BorderThickness="4"
                CornerRadius="8">
```

continues

LISTING 6-54 *(continued)*

```
                <Grid>
                    <ContentPresenter Content="{TemplateBinding Content}"
                        ContentTemplate="{TemplateBinding ContentTemplate}"
                        Margin="{TemplateBinding Padding}" />
                </Grid>
            </Border>
        </ControlTemplate>
    </Grid.Resources>
    <Button Content="This is a button" Height="100" Width="100"
        ToolTipService.Placement="Mouse">
        <ToolTipService.ToolTip>
            <ToolTip Template="{StaticResource MyToolTipTemplate}">
                <ToolTip.Content>
                    <TextBlock Text="This is the buttons tooltip" />
                </ToolTip.Content>
            </ToolTip>
        </ToolTipService.ToolTip>
    </Button>
</Grid>
```

ScrollViewer

The `ScrollViewer` control is a very simple control that allows you to add scrollbars to content elements in your application. The control will add both horizontal and vertical scrollbars as an element's content begins to exceed its available space.

Listing 6-55 demonstrates how you can use the `ScrollViewer` with a `StackPanel` to allow content that exceeds the height given to the `StackPanel` to be scrolled into view.

Available for download on Wrox.com

LISTING 6-55: Using a ScrollViewer to scroll content in a StackPanel

```
<Grid x:Name="LayoutRoot" Height="100" VerticalAlignment="Top">
    <ScrollViewer>
        <StackPanel>
            <TextBlock Text="A" />
            <TextBlock Text="B" />
            <TextBlock Text="C" />
            <TextBlock Text="D" />
            <TextBlock Text="E" />
            <TextBlock Text="F" />
            <TextBlock Text="G" />
            <TextBlock Text="H" />
            <TextBlock Text="I" />
            <TextBlock Text="K" />
            <TextBlock Text="L" />
            <TextBlock Text="M" />
            <TextBlock Text="N" />
            <TextBlock Text="O" />
            <TextBlock Text="P" />
```

```
            <TextBlock Text="Q" />
            <TextBlock Text="R" />
            <TextBlock Text="S" />
            <TextBlock Text="T" />
            <TextBlock Text="U" />
            <TextBlock Text="V" />
            <TextBlock Text="W" />
            <TextBlock Text="X" />
            <TextBlock Text="Y" />
            <TextBlock Text="Z" />
        </StackPanel>
    </ScrollViewer>
</Grid>
```

The `ScrollViewer` control includes properties that allow you to control the visibility of the horizontal and vertical scrollbar. By default the control makes the horizontal scrollbar disabled and the vertical scrollbar visible.

Keep in mind that when you are wrapping elements inside of a `ScrollViewer`, the `ScrollViewer` will tell those controls that they have infinite height and width. This can cause controls that virtualize their UI based on their size, like the `DataGrid`, to fail to utilize their virtualization logic since they no longer have a fixed height.

For controls like `ListBox` that automatically leverage the `ScrollViewer` control, `ScrollViewer` is also an attached property that you can add to these controls to control how the scrollbars are displayed (Listing 6-56).

LISTING 6-56: Using the ScrollViewer attached property with ListBox

```
<ListBox ScrollViewer.VerticalScrollBarVisibility="Hidden">
        <TextBlock Text="A" />
        <TextBlock Text="B" />
        <TextBlock Text="C" />
        <TextBlock Text="D" />
        <TextBlock Text="E" />
</ListBox>
```

CREATING CUSTOM CONTROLS

So far in this chapter, we have looked at the wide variety of controls that are available from Silverlight, the Silverlight SDK, and the Silverlight Toolkit; but there will certainly be times when none of these controls provides the UI you need for your application. In those cases, you may choose to build your own custom controls. In this section you will walk though creating a custom login form control to learn how you can use Silverlight's control API's to build custom controls.

Getting started building custom controls in Silverlight is a fairly simple process. Visual Studio includes a file template named *Silverlight Templated Control* that can get you started quickly creating a new control. Figure 6-26 shows the template selected in the Add New Item dialog.

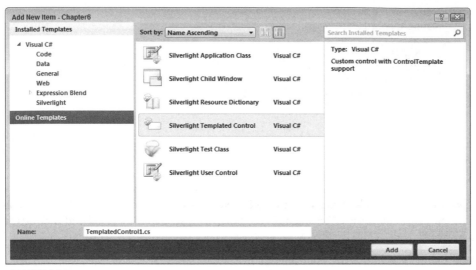

FIGURE 6-26

When you add the Silverlight Templated Control to your application, Visual Studio creates several new assets. First, the basic class file derived from `Control` is created. Second, a new XAML file called Generic.xaml is added to a Themes folder that is created in your project. Generic.xaml is where the XAML used to create the control's UI is stored. Figure 6-27 shows the application structure once you've added the Templated Control.

FIGURE 6-27

 The names of the folder and XAML file created when adding a new Templated Control are very important. Silverlight is hard coded to look for the default style of your custom control in a file called Generic.xaml in folder called Themes. Changing the names of either of these will cause Silverlight to fail to find your control's default style.

The control class and XAML file are connected by setting the `DefaultStyleKey` property in the class constructor. This is done for you automatically when the class is created by Visual Studio. This also enables controls to follow the States and Parts model, which dictates that there is a strict separation between the visual elements of a control and the logical behavior of a control. Later in this chapter you will see how designing controls in this manner makes it easy to change their appearance without affecting their behavior.

By default, the Templated Control file template creates a control derived from the Silverlight `Control` base class, but there are several other useful base classes you might choose to derive from. See Table 6-3.

TABLE 6-3

BASE CLASS	DESCRIPTION
ItemsControl	Represents a control that can be used to present a collection of items.
HeaderedItemsControl	Represents a control that contains multiple items and has a header.
ContentControl	Represents a control with a single piece of content.
HeaderedContentControl	Provides the base implementation for all controls that contain single content and have a header.

Once Visual Studio completes its setup of the control's class and XAML file, you can start adding some style and functionality to the new control. Start by creating the base UI for your control by adding content to Style's ControlTemplate in Generic.xaml. Listing 6-57 shows the base control template used for the login form control.

LISTING 6-57: Defining the default ControlTemplate of a custom control

```
<ResourceDictionary
    xmlns="http://schemas.microsoft.com/winfx/2006/xaml/presentation"
    xmlns:x="http://schemas.microsoft.com/winfx/2006/xaml"
    xmlns:vsm="clr-namespace:System.Windows;assembly=System.Windows"
    xmlns:local="clr-namespace:MyCustomSilverlightControl">

    <Style TargetType="local:LoginForm">
        <Setter Property="Template">
            <Setter.Value>
                <ControlTemplate TargetType="local:LoginForm">

                    <Border Background="{TemplateBinding Background}"
                        BorderBrush="{TemplateBinding BorderBrush}"
                        BorderThickness="{TemplateBinding BorderThickness}">

                        <Grid>
                            <Grid.RowDefinitions>
                                <RowDefinition Height="Auto" />
                                <RowDefinition Height="Auto" />
                                <RowDefinition Height="Auto" />
                                <RowDefinition Height="Auto" />
                                <RowDefinition Height="Auto" />
                            </Grid.RowDefinitions>
                            <Grid.ColumnDefinitions>
                                <ColumnDefinition Width="Auto" />
                                <ColumnDefinition Width="Auto" />
                            </Grid.ColumnDefinitions>

                            <TextBlock x:Name="lblTitle"
```

continues

LISTING 6-57 *(continued)*

```
                                    Grid.ColumnSpan="2"/>

                        <TextBlock x:Name="lblUsername"
                            Text="Username:" Margin="5" Grid.Column="0"
                            Grid.Row="1" VerticalAlignment="Center"/>
                        <TextBox x:Name="txtUsername" Width="150"
                            Margin="5" Grid.Column="1" Grid.Row="1"/>

                        <TextBlock x:Name="lblPassword"
                            Text="Password:" Margin="5" Grid.Column="0"
                            Grid.Row="2" VerticalAlignment="Center" />
                        <PasswordBox x:Name="txtPassword" Width="150"
                            Margin="5" Grid.Column="1" Grid.Row="2"/>

                        <StackPanel Grid.Row="3" Grid.ColumnSpan="2"
                            HorizontalAlignment="Center" Margin="5"
                            Orientation="Horizontal">
                            <Button x:Name="btnClear" Content="Clear"
                                    Margin="0,0,2,0"/>
                            <Button x:Name="btnSubmit" Content="Login"
                                    Margin="2,0,0,0" />
                        </StackPanel>

                        <TextBlock x:Name="lblError"
                            Visibility="Collapsed" Grid.Row="4"
                            Grid.ColumnSpan="2"
                            Text="{TemplateBinding ErrorMessage}"
                            HorizontalAlignment="Center"
                            FontWeight="Bold" Foreground="Red" />
                    </Grid>
                </Border>
            </ControlTemplate>
        </Setter.Value>
    </Setter>
    </Style>
</ResourceDictionary>
```

You can see that within the `Style`, which has its `TargetType` set to `LoginForm` (the name of the custom control class), the `ControlTemplate` property is defined that contains the default visual appearance of the control. In the control template `TemplateBindings` are used to bind elements of the `Template` to properties of the control.

Once the control's default UI is created, you can begin to write the logic that manipulates the controls content. Start by getting references to the control defined in the XAML by overriding the control's `OnApplyTemplate` method and using the `GetTemplateChild` method. This method accepts as an input parameter the name of the control in the control template that you want to reference. Listing 6-58 shows how you can get references to the controls from the control template shown in Listing 6-57.

LISTING 6-58: Referencing default control template UI elements in code

```csharp
public class LoginForm : Control
{
    TextBox _username = null;
    PasswordBox _password = null;
    Button _submit = null;
    Button _clear = null;

    public LoginForm()
    {
        this.DefaultStyleKey = typeof(LoginForm);
    }

    public bool IsLoggedIn { get; set; }
    public string ErrorMessage { get; set; }

    public override void OnApplyTemplate()
    {
        base.OnApplyTemplate();

        if (_clear != null) { _clear.Click -= _clear_Click; }
        if (_submit != null) { _submit.Click -= _submit_Click; }

        _username = GetTemplateChild("txtUsername") as TextBox;
        _password = GetTemplateChild("txtPassword") as PasswordBox;
        _submit = GetTemplateChild("btnSubmit") as Button;
        _clear = GetTemplateChild("btnClear") as Button;

        if (_submit != null)
        {
            _submit.Click += new RoutedEventHandler(_submit_Click);
        }

        if (_clear != null)
        {
            _clear.Click += new RoutedEventHandler(_clear_Click);
        }

    }
}
```

As you can see in Listing 6-58, the `OnApplyTemplate` method is also a good place to attach event handlers to the control's UI elements. Note that the `OnApplyTemplate` method can be called multiple times, so it is very important to check to see if you need to do some cleanup work before you call `GetTemplateChild`. You should check to see if the local element variable is already assigned, and if it is, make sure to remove any existing control event handlers before attaching new handlers.

Also note that before you attach an event, you should check to make sure that the element you are attaching the event to is not `null`. This is because there is no guarantee that the element actually exists in the default template, and if it does not exist, the `GetTemplateChild` method will simple return `null`.

At this point you have a basic custom control that you can add to your application. Figure 6-28 shows the simple control built in this section running in an application.

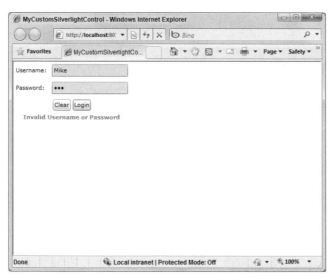

FIGURE 6-28

Template Parts

Once you have the default UI of your control XAML, you can identify elements in the template that you want to designate as control Parts. Parts are generally the UI elements of your control that are critical to the experience your control provides, and therefore have significant amounts of logic tied to them.

While designating UI elements as Parts is not required to run the control, it is generally a good practice for developing custom controls. By designating a control in your template as a Part, you are creating a contract between your control and a developer who wants to change the default style of your control. The contract states that the control will allow the developer to change its default template as long as they ensure that the control designated as a Part is present and named a well-known name. Additionally, tools like Expression Blend have been designed to look for and expose elements marked with the attribute and will inform developers and designers that they are required by the controls.

To mark elements as Parts you use the `TemplatePart` attribute on your custom control's class. The `TemplatePart` attributes allow you to communicate the type of UI elements that your control expects to be in its template and the name that should be given to that element. Listing 6-59 shows how you can add a `TemplatePart` attribute to the class.

LISTING 6-59: Adding TemplatePart attributes

Available for
download on
Wrox.com

```
[TemplatePart(Name = "txtUsername", Type = typeof(TextBox))]
[TemplatePart(Name = "txtPassword", Type = typeof(PasswordBox))]
```

```
[TemplatePart(Name = "btnSubmit", Type = typeof(Button))]
[TemplatePart(Name = "lblError", Type = typeof(TextBlock))]
public class LoginForm : Control
```

Note that using `TemplatePart` attributes simply allows you to expose your *intentions* to other designers and developers. It remains their prerogative to actually provide those elements in the controls template. As mentioned earlier, you should always make sure that you check for the existence of template controls before trying to access them in your control.

Visual States

Another key part of building custom controls that use the States and Parts model is using Visual States to allow the control to change its appearance based on its current state. Visual States are managed in your control using the Visual State Manager (VMS). Using Visual States also makes your control Expression Blend friendly because Expression Blend can expose the states in its UI, allowing designers to easily change the look of a control for a given state without needed to understand or change its behavior, or dig into code.

To demonstrate using Visual States, you can add a `Normal` and an `Invalid` state to the custom control shown in the previous section. The `Invalid` state will be shown by the control when an invalid login attempt occurs. Listing 6-60 shows how you add the states to the default control template.

LISTING 6-60: Creating Visual States using VisualStateManager

Available for download on Wrox.com

```
<vsm:VisualStateManager.VisualStateGroups>
    <vsm:VisualStateGroup x:Name="CommonStates">
        <vsm:VisualState x:Name="Normal">
            <Storyboard x:Name="NormalStoryboard">
                <ColorAnimation Duration="0:0:0.5" To="#FFFFD7D7"
                    Storyboard.TargetProperty="(Control.Background).
                                                (SolidColorBrush.Color)"
                                Storyboard.TargetName="txtUsername"/>
                <ColorAnimation Duration="0:0:0.5" To="#FFFFD7D7"
                    Storyboard.TargetProperty="(Control.Background).
                                                (SolidColorBrush.Color)"
                    Storyboard.TargetName="txtPassword"/>
                <ObjectAnimationUsingKeyFrames
                    Storyboard.TargetProperty="(UIElement.Visibility)"
                    Storyboard.TargetName="lblError">
                    <DiscreteObjectKeyFrame KeyTime="0:0:0.5">
                        <DiscreteObjectKeyFrame.Value>
                            <Visibility>Collapsed</Visibility>
                        </DiscreteObjectKeyFrame.Value>
                    </DiscreteObjectKeyFrame>
                </ObjectAnimationUsingKeyFrames>
                <DoubleAnimation Duration="0:0:0.5" To="0"
                    Storyboard.TargetProperty="(UIElement.Opacity)"
                    Storyboard.TargetName="lblError"/>
            </Storyboard>
```

continues

LISTING 6-60 *(continued)*

```
        </vsm:VisualState>
        <vsm:VisualState x:Name="Invalid">
            <Storyboard x:Name="InvalidStoryboard">
                <ColorAnimation Duration="0:0:0.5" To="#FFFFD7D7"
                    Storyboard.TargetProperty="(Control.Background).
                                                (SolidColorBrush.Color)"
                    Storyboard.TargetName="txtUsername"/>
                <ColorAnimation Duration="0:0:0.5" To="#FFFFD7D7"
                    Storyboard.TargetProperty="(Control.Background).
                                                (SolidColorBrush.Color)"
                    Storyboard.TargetName="txtPassword"/>
                <ObjectAnimationUsingKeyFrames
                    Storyboard.TargetProperty="(UIElement.Visibility)"
                    Storyboard.TargetName="lblError">
                    <DiscreteObjectKeyFrame KeyTime="0:0:0.5">
                        <DiscreteObjectKeyFrame.Value>
                            <Visibility>Visible</Visibility>
                        </DiscreteObjectKeyFrame.Value>
                    </DiscreteObjectKeyFrame>
                </ObjectAnimationUsingKeyFrames>
                <DoubleAnimation Duration="0:0:0.5" To="100"
                    Storyboard.TargetProperty="(UIElement.Opacity)"
                    Storyboard.TargetName="lblError"/>
            </Storyboard>
        </vsm:VisualState>
    </vsm:VisualStateGroup>
</vsm:VisualStateManager.VisualStateGroups>
```

As you can see in Listing 6-60 the `VisualStateManager` exposes a `VisualStateGroups` property. This allows you to define several related states as a group. The native controls often contain a `VisualStateGroup` called `CommonStates`, which can contain states such as `Normal`, `MouseOver`, `Focused`, and `Disabled`.

For the `LoginForm` control, a single `VisualStateGroup` called `CommonStates` is created. Within that group, two states are defined, `Normal` and `Invalid`. Each state contains a storyboard with multiple animations that target different controls in the controls default template.

If you are going to use Visual States in your control's default template, you must set the `VisualStateManager` attached property on the root element of the `ControlTemplate`. In the case of the `LoginForm` control that means attaching it to the `Border` control.

To trigger a change in the state of your control, you can use the `GoToState` method. The best way to do this is to create a method in your control that is responsible for determining the current state of your application and then calls the `GoToState` method with the appropriate state name. In the `LoginForm`, Boolean properties are used to indicate the current state of the control. Listing 6-61 shows how you can create a method called `EnsureCurrentState` in your control. Using the Boolean flags, the method checks the current state and calls the `GoToState` method.

LISTING 6-61: EnsureCurrentState method

```
public void EnsureCurrentState()
{
    if (_isNormal)
    {
        VisualStateManager.GoToState(this, "Normal", false);
        return;
    }

    if (_isInvalid)
    {
        VisualStateManager.GoToState(this, "Invalid", false);
        return;
    }
}
```

SUMMARY

This chapter introduced you to many of the most important and complex controls that are available in Silverlight, the Silverlight SDK, and the Silverlight Toolkit, as well as introducing you to a variety of different open source control projects. From the Silverlight TextBox, which makes it easy to begin to take data input from end users, to perhaps the most complex control, the DataGrid, you learned how you can take advantage of all of these controls to make your applications more useful and make you more productive in your development. Finally, you learned how to create your own custom Silverlight controls.

7

Accessing Data

WHAT'S IN THIS CHAPTER?

➤ Working with XML using LINQ and the XmlReader object

➤ Working with data binding and user interfaces

➤ Dealing with data when it changes

➤ Communicating with services (REST, WCF)

One of the most prominent and compelling aspects of rich Internet applications is unfettered access to data. Therefore, it should be no surprise that Silverlight provides a rich, pervasive model that allows you to create dynamic data-driven applications. Silverlight provides a host of facilities for retrieving, displaying, manipulating, and storing data from a variety of data sources.

If you are accustomed to using classes within System.Data to query databases directly, you are in for a rude surprise with Silverlight, because none of these services are available. This chapter looks at how you can use Silverlight to deal with services, both ASP.NET Web Services and the newer Windows Communication Foundation services.

This chapter also looks at dealing with XML, data binding, and RESTful-based services — starting with working with XML.

 WCF RIA Services is covered in Chapter 8.

PROCESSING XML DATA

Although a developer might actually enjoy seeing XML presented directly in an application, it is far more likely that you will need to massage the XML data into some strongly typed objects that will be presented to the user. For instance, you would probably not want to expose the end user to the raw XML presented in Listing 7-1.

LISTING 7-1: Raw XML

```xml
<?xml version="1.0" encoding="utf-8" ?>
<destinations>
  <destination name="St. Croix" population="70000"
               averageAirfare="300" averageHotel="300"
               bestKnownFor="Beaches" />
  <destination name="St. Barths" population="8450"
               averageAirfare="600" averageHotel="800"
               bestKnownFor="Shopping"  />
  <destination name="St. Lucia" population="160765"
               averageAirfare="400" averageHotel="400"
               bestKnownFor="Rainforests"  />
</destinations>
```

Silverlight provides both the low-level `XMLReader` class and LINQ to XML for working with raw XML. Either framework can be used to transform XML into a strongly typed class that represents the data. This example has a `Destination` class (shown in Listing 7-2), which exposes some of the important factors you might consider when deciding where to spend your next vacation. This class should be placed within the Silverlight client project of your solution.

LISTING 7-2: The Destination class

Available for
download on
Wrox.com

```csharp
public class Destination
{
    public string Name { get; set; }
    public int Population { get; set; }
    public double AverageAirfare { get; set; }
    public double AverageHotel { get; set; }
    public string BestKnownFor { get; set; }
}
```

Next, this chapter takes a look at how you can use both LINQ to XML and the `XMLReader` classes to grab the information found in XML and create a set of `Destination` objects.

LINQ to XML

LINQ to XML provides a clean, consistent syntax for accessing XML data. Begin by adding references to `System.Xml` and `System.Xml.Linq`. Once the `WebClient` object completes downloading the data, you will need to construct a new `XDocument` for LINQ to query.

> *The* `WebClient` *object is covered in more detail in Chapter 10.*

When the new XDocument object is created and you make use of LINQ to query this object, you can map the XML file to a list of strongly typed objects. The code to do this is demonstrated in Listing 7-3.

LISTING 7-3: Using the XDocument to work with the Destinations XML document

```csharp
using System;
using System.Collections.Generic;
using System.Linq;
using System.Net;
using System.Windows;
using System.Windows.Controls;
using System.Xml.Linq;

namespace SilverlightXML
{
    public partial class MainPage : UserControl
    {
        private IEnumerable<Destination> _destinationsList;

        public MainPage()
        {
            InitializeComponent();
            this.Loaded += Page_Loaded;
        }

        private void Page_Loaded(object sender, RoutedEventArgs e)
        {
            // Construct a new WebClient object
            WebClient client = new WebClient();

            // Configure an event handler for when the Download is complete
            client.DownloadStringCompleted += client_DownloadCompleted;

            // Request an XML document located adjacent to the XAP
            Uri xmlUri = new Uri("Destinations.xml", UriKind.Relative);
            client.DownloadStringAsync(xmlUri);
        }

        private void client_DownloadCompleted(object sender,
            DownloadStringCompletedEventArgs e)
        {
            // If no error, sends results to a ListBox
            if (e.Error == null)
            {
                parseDestinationsXml(e.Result);
            }
            else
            {
                MessageBox.Show(e.Error.Message);
            }
        }
```

continues

LISTING 7-3 *(continued)*

```
            private void parseDestinationsXml(string xmlContent)
            {
                // Create an xml document from the content
                XDocument doc = XDocument.Parse(xmlContent);

                // Create a Linq query which maps the document to Destination objects
                _destinationsList =
                    from destination in doc.Descendants("destination")
                    select new Destination
                    {
                        Name = (string) destination.Attribute("name"),
                        Population = (int) destination.Attribute("population"),
                        AverageAirfare =
                            (double) destination.Attribute("averageAirfare"),
                        AverageHotel =
                            (double) destination.Attribute("averageHotel"),
                        BestKnownFor =
                            (string) destination.Attribute("bestKnownFor")
                    };

                DestinationsListBox.ItemsSource = _destinationsList;
            }
        }
    }
```

To make this work, you need to make a reference to the `System.Xml.Linq` namespace within your Silverlight client project. The only thing that you need on the `MainPage.xaml` page is a simple `ListBox` control with the name of `DestinationsListBox`. In the `ListBox` control, you will also want to add the `DisplayMemberPath` property and give it a value of `"Name"`.

Using an XmlReader

You are also free to parse the data through the `XmlReader` API; just do not expect all the bells and whistles of LINQ. An example of using the `XmlReader` object is demonstrated in Listing 7-4.

LISTING 7-4: Using the XmlReader object

```
private void parseDestinationXml(StringReader xmlContent)
{
  // Create a list to hold our destinations
  _destinationsList = new List<Destination>();

  // Create a new XmlReader to walk through the document
  XmlReader reader = XmlReader.Create(xmlContent);

  while (reader.Read())
  {
    if (reader.NodeType == XmlNodeType.Element)
    {
```

```
        if (reader.Name == "destination")
        {
          Destination d = new Destination
          {
            Name = reader["name"],
            Population = int.Parse(reader["population"]),
            AverageAirfare = double.Parse(reader["averageAirfare"]),
            AverageHotel = double.Parse(reader["averageHotel"]),
            BestKnownFor = reader["bestKnownFor"]
          };
          _destinationsList.Add(d);
        }
      }
    }
    DestinationsListBox.ItemsSource = _destinationsList;
}
```

BINDING A USER INTERFACE TO DATA

Silverlight provides a flexible data-binding model for connecting a user interface to data objects. Built around the `Binding` object, it facilitates both presenting and processing updates to data. The binding model is not tied to a specific data provider; instead, it is centered around connecting a property from a source object to a property on a target object. Silverlight's architecture enables and encourages a high degree of separation between the presentation and business layers of an application.

Establishing a Data-Binding Connection

To establish a binding, you need to specify both the object that will communicate via the binding and the properties on those objects that should be connected. Bindings can be established at run time through code or can be specified statically in XAML markup.

Before diving into the details, consider a simple scenario of binding a few `TextBlock` elements to a single object. You will continue to use the `Destination` object discussed earlier in this chapter. You can begin by adding binding statements to the properties on the target object that map to select properties on the source object. This is shown in Listing 7-5.

LISTING 7-5: Binding to the Destination object

```xml
<Grid x:Name="LayoutRoot" Background="White">
  <StackPanel>
    <TextBlock Text="{Binding Name}"></TextBlock>
    <TextBlock Text="{Binding Population}"></TextBlock>
  </StackPanel>
</Grid>
```

Next, provide the source object for both `TextBlocks` by specifying the `DataContext` for the `Grid` as illustrated in Listing 7-6.

LISTING 7-6: Creating and assigning the Destination object in MainPage.xaml.cs

```csharp
public partial class Page : UserControl
{
  public Page()
  {
    InitializeComponent();
    this.Loaded += new RoutedEventHandler(Page_Loaded);
  }

  void Page_Loaded(object sender, RoutedEventArgs e)
  {
    Destination d = new Destination { Name = "St. Croix", Population = 70000 };
    LayoutRoot.DataContext = d;
  }
}
```

In the preceding case, each `TextBlock` is the target of a binding, and a single `Destination` object acts as the source.

Valid Binding Target Types

Silverlight's binding model is able to establish communication among a wide variety of objects. Whereas the binding source can be of any type for one-way and one-time binding, the target must be both a member of a `FrameworkElement` object and a dependency property. This restriction is of greater concern when building custom controls because it is essential for supporting data binding.

Specifying the Source Object

Because a binding's target must be a `FrameworkElement`, you can take advantage of the `DataContext` property to specify the source object for a binding. `DataContext` is inherited from parents in the object tree, which eliminates the need to specify the source for a group of UI elements that present information for the same data object. This is why, in the first example, you only needed to specify the `DataContext` for the `StackPanel` instead of on each `TextBlock` element.

If you do not want the binding source to be inherited by children, you can specify the source property on the binding object itself. In this example, you establish the binding in code. Listing 7-7 first shows the required XAML code.

LISTING 7-7: The XAML code from MainPage.xaml

```xml
<Grid x:Name="LayoutRoot" Background="White">
  <StackPanel>
    <TextBlock x:Name="NameTextBlock"></TextBlock>
    <TextBlock x:Name="PopulationTextBlock"></TextBlock>
  </StackPanel>
</Grid>
```

With that in place, the next step is to databind to this from the code-behind of the page as illustrated in Listing 7-8.

LISTING 7-8: The code-behind for MainPage.xaml.cs

```csharp
public partial class MainPage : UserControl
{
  public MainPage()
  {
    InitializeComponent();
    this.Loaded += new RoutedEventHandler(Page_Loaded);
  }

  void Page_Loaded(object sender, RoutedEventArgs e)
  {
    // The object which will be used as the source
    Destination d = new Destination { Name = "St. Croix", Population = 70000 };

    // Create a Binding in code for the Name
    System.Windows.Data.Binding nameBinding =
        new System.Windows.Data.Binding("Name");
    nameBinding.Source = d;
    nameBinding.Mode = BindingMode.OneTime;

    // Connect the binding to the TextBox's Text property
    NameTextBlock.SetBinding(TextBlock.TextProperty, nameBinding);

    // Create a Binding in code for the Population
    System.Windows.Data.Binding popBinding = new Binding("Population");
    popBinding.Source = d;
    popBinding.Mode = BindingMode.OneTime;
    PopulationTextBlock.SetBinding(TextBlock.TextProperty, popBinding);
  }
}
```

Selecting a Property from the Source Object

The binding object's Path property allows you to specify the property from the Source object. For members on the Source object, you can simply specify the name of the property:

```
<Binding Path="SourceProperty" />
```

Because Path is of type PropertyPath, it also allows for specifying properties of sub-objects on the source as well as collections. In Silverlight, you can traverse sub-objects using a period in between the property names:

```
<Binding Path="SourceProperty.SubObjectProperty" />
```

If your Source object offers collection properties that have additional collections nested beneath them, you can use a forward slash to traverse the relationship:

```
<Binding Path="SourceCollectionProperty/SubCollectionProperty" />
```

Binding to Collections with ItemsControl

Up to this point, you have looked at bindings in the context of a single source data object. An equally common, and more interesting, use case is binding to collections of data. Any ItemsControl can be used to apply a DataTemplate for presenting each item in a Source object's collection. IEnumerable is all that is required on the Source object for basic collection-binding behavior.

The ItemsSource property on ItemsControl is used to specify the Collection to which the control is bound. This can be specified programmatically or set through a binding. If no ItemTemplate is provided for the control, you can take advantage of the DisplayMemberPath property to select which source property will be rendered. The following ItemsControl will be bound to a collection found in the effective DataContext and will render the Name property of each item in that collection. Listing 7-9 shows this in action.

LISTING 7-9: Using the DisplayMemberPath property

```
<Grid x:Name="LayoutRoot" Background="White">
  <ItemsControl ItemsSource="{Binding}" DisplayMemberPath="Name" />
</Grid>
```

Accessing the source collection through the ItemsSource will give you only read access. If you want to modify the source collection, make sure to do so through a direct reference.

Because you have created a binding for the ItemsSource, the ItemsControl will honor the effective DataContext, so creating the binding is straightforward. Listing 7-10 illustrates this in action.

LISTING 7-10: Using DataContext

```
public partial class MainPage : UserControl
{
  public MainPage()
  {
    InitializeComponent();
    this.Loaded += new RoutedEventHandler(Page_Loaded);
  }

  void Page_Loaded(object sender, RoutedEventArgs e)
  {
    List<Destination> destinations = new List<Destination>();
    destinations.Add(new Destination { Name = "St. Croix" });
    destinations.Add(new Destination { Name = "St. John" });
    destinations.Add(new Destination { Name = "St. Thomas" });

    LayoutRoot.DataContext = destinations;
  }
}
```

Specifying an ItemTemplate

If you want to override the default rendering for each item, you can create a DataTemplate and set it as the ItemsTemplate for the ItemsControl. Note that the source of each Binding defined within the Template will be an item in the Collection to which the ItemsControl is bound as illustrated in Listing 7-11.

LISTING 7-11: Using a DataTemplate

```xml
<Grid x:Name="LayoutRoot" Background="White">
  <ItemsControl ItemsSource="{Binding}" >
    <ItemsControl.ItemTemplate>
      <DataTemplate>
        <StackPanel Orientation="Horizontal">
          <TextBlock Text="{Binding Name}" ></TextBlock>
          <TextBlock Text="{Binding Population}" ></TextBlock>
        </StackPanel>
      </DataTemplate>
    </ItemsControl.ItemTemplate>
  </ItemsControl>
</Grid>
```

With the XAML in place, Listing 7-12 shows the code-behind to set the DataContext.

LISTING 7-12: Setting the DataContext to the DataTemplate

```csharp
public partial class Page : UserControl
{
  public Page()
  {
    InitializeComponent();
    this.Loaded += new RoutedEventHandler(Page_Loaded);
  }

  void Page_Loaded(object sender, RoutedEventArgs e)
  {
    List<Destination> destinations = new List<Destination>();
    destinations.Add(new Destination { Name = "St. Croix", Population = 70000 });
    destinations.Add(new Destination { Name = "St. John", Population = 5000 });
    destinations.Add(new Destination { Name = "St. Thomas", Population = 50000 });

    LayoutRoot.DataContext = destinations;
  }
}
```

Providing a Custom ItemsPanel

By default, ItemsControl uses a StackPanel with an orientation set to Vertical to arrange the elements rendered for each item. Continuing to highlight the Silverlight pattern of flexibility, you can adjust this by setting the ItemsPanel to a custom ItemsPanelTemplate as demonstrated in Listing 7-13.

LISTING 7-13: Changing the ItemsPanel

```xml
<Grid x:Name="LayoutRoot" Background="White">
  <ItemsControl ItemsSource="{Binding}" >
    <ItemsControl.ItemTemplate>
      <DataTemplate>
        <StackPanel Orientation="Horizontal">
          <TextBlock Text="{Binding Name}" ></TextBlock>
          <TextBlock Text="{Binding Population}" ></TextBlock>
        </StackPanel>
      </DataTemplate>
    </ItemsControl.ItemTemplate>
    <ItemsControl.ItemsPanel>
      <ItemsPanelTemplate>
        <StackPanel Orientation="Horizontal"></StackPanel>
      </ItemsPanelTemplate>
    </ItemsControl.ItemsPanel>
  </ItemsControl>
</Grid>
```

Using a Relative Source Binding

Silverlight includes the ability to specify the source of a Binding relative to the target. For instance, you can create a Binding with the source specified as the target's TemplatedParent. Listing 7-14 demonstrates using a RelativeSource binding to bind the Text property of a TextBlock to the content of the parent Button element.

LISTING 7-14: Using the RelativeSource binding

```xml
<Grid x:Name="LayoutRoot" Background="White">
    <StackPanel>
        <Button Content="SampleContent">
            <Button.Template>
                <ControlTemplate>
                    <StackPanel>
                        <TextBlock Text="{Binding RelativeSource=
                        {RelativeSource TemplatedParent},
                        Path=Content}" />
                    </StackPanel>
                </ControlTemplate>
            </Button.Template>
        </Button>
    </StackPanel>
</Grid>
```

Element-to-Element Binding

Silverlight also includes the ability to specify an element as the source for a Binding through the ElementName property. This easily used feature can come in handy when building interactive interfaces where one Element should reflect changes to another. Currently, the target of such binding must be a FrameworkElement. The example in Listing 7-15 demonstrates binding the Text property of a TextBlock to the current value of a Slider.

LISTING 7-15: Using ElementName property

```xml
<Grid x:Name="LayoutRoot" Background="White">
    <StackPanel>
        <Slider x:Name="Slider1" Minimum="0" Maximum="100" />
        <TextBlock Text="{Binding ElementName=Slider1, Path=Value}" />
    </StackPanel>
</Grid>
```

Handling Data Updates

Silverlight's binding object provides three distinct binding modes, which determine the way that data flows between the source and target objects:

➤ OneWay — Changes to the Source are reflected on the Target as they occur.

➤ OneTime — The Target property is only set when the binding is initialized.

➤ TwoWay — Changes to the Source are reflected on the Target, and updates to the Target are propagated to the Source.

Both OneWay and TwoWay functionality come at the cost of restricting the types of object that can participate in the binding. Silverlight relies on the DependencyObject infrastructure and several Notification-based interfaces to support the processing of DataBinding updates.

Working with the INotifyPropertyChanged Interface

The INotifyPropertyChanged interface offers a single event to broadcast when a property has been modified on the object. The expectation is that this will be triggered any time a property is adjusted.

The code in Listing 7-16 has an IslandTimer class, which reflects a slower pace of life. Note that it fires PropertyChanged events both from within the Name property and from the read-only ElapsedTime property, a value that is managed internally.

> *This example that the* DispatcherTimer *object is used rather than* System .Timers.Timer *as the* DispatcherTimer *object is not run on the UI thread.*

LISTING 7-16: Using INotifyPropertyChanged

```csharp
using System;
using System.ComponentModel;
using System.Windows.Threading;

namespace Wrox.Silverlight.Data.NotifyChanges
{
    public class IslandTimer : INotifyPropertyChanged
```

continues

LISTING 7-16 *(continued)*

```csharp
{
    private readonly DispatcherTimer _timer;
    private TimeSpan _elapsedTime;
    private string _name;

    public IslandTimer()
    {
        _elapsedTime = new TimeSpan();

        // Create a timer which fires every few seconds
        _timer = new DispatcherTimer();
        _timer.Interval = TimeSpan.FromSeconds(2);
        _timer.Tick += timer_Tick;
    }

    public TimeSpan ElapsedTime
    {
        get { return _elapsedTime; }
    }

    public string Name
    {
        get { return _name; }
        set
        {
            _name = value;
            OnPropertyChanged("Name");
        }
    }

    #region INotifyPropertyChanged Members

    public event PropertyChangedEventHandler PropertyChanged;

    #endregion

    public void StartTimer()
    {
        if (!_timer.IsEnabled)
        {
            _timer.Start();
        }
    }

    public void StopTimer()
    {
        _timer.Stop();
    }

    private void timer_Tick(object sender, EventArgs e)
    {
        _elapsedTime += TimeSpan.FromSeconds(1);
```

```
            OnPropertyChanged("ElapsedTime");
        }

        // Helper method to fire PropertyChanged Events
        private void OnPropertyChanged(string propName)
        {
            if (PropertyChanged != null)
                PropertyChanged(this, new PropertyChangedEventArgs(propName));
        }
    }
}
```

Using Collection Update Notifications

The INotifyCollectionChanged interface is implemented on interfaces that want to participate in full data binding. Similarly to INotifyPropertyChanged, it exposes one event for when the collection is modified, CollectionChanged.

Thankfully, Silverlight includes ObservableCollection<T>, which is a generic collection that implements this interface. If you have a collection that you expect to be updated during the life of your application, it is highly recommended that you use this type.

Using OneTime Bindings

The simplest and best performing binding mode, OneTime, specifies that the binding should be applied only when the application starts or when the effective DataContext is adjusted. This is most appropriate when the source object is not manipulated during the life of the application and when the target object does not accept user input.

Using OneWay Bindings

If you anticipate that the source object may change during the life of the application, you can rely on Silverlight data binding to automatically update target object properties when in the OneWay mode. The OneWay mode is the default action if you do not specify a mode.

Now that you have an object capable of letting Silverlight know that its properties are changing, you can attach it as the source for a OneWay binding as demonstrated in Listing 7-17 and Listing 7-18.

LISTING 7-17: The XAML for MainPage.xaml

```xml
<Grid x:Name="LayoutRoot" Background="White">
  <StackPanel>
    <Button x:Name="StartButton" HorizontalAlignment="Center">
      <TextBlock>Start Timer</TextBlock>
    </Button>
    <StackPanel Orientation="Horizontal" HorizontalAlignment="Center">
      <TextBlock>Elapsed Island Time: </TextBlock>
      <TextBlock Text="{Binding ElapsedTime, Mode=OneWay}" />
    </StackPanel>
  </StackPanel>
</Grid>
```

The code-behind for this is shown in Listing 7-18.

LISTING 7-18: Using one-way binding

```
using System.Windows;
using System.Windows.Controls;

namespace Wrox.Silverlight.Data.NotifyChanges
{
    public partial class MainPage : UserControl
    {
        private readonly IslandTimer _timer;

        public MainPage()
        {
            InitializeComponent();
            this.Loaded += Page_Loaded;
            // Remember that there will be a pause here ... Island Time.
            _timer = new IslandTimer {Name = "MyTimer"};

            StartButton.Click += StartButton_Click;
        }

        private void Page_Loaded(object sender, RoutedEventArgs e)
        {
            LayoutRoot.DataContext = _timer;
        }

        private void StartButton_Click(object sender, RoutedEventArgs e)
        {
            _timer.StartTimer();
        }
    }
}
```

Using TwoWay Bindings

TwoWay bindings are the most powerful mode and offer bidirectional update support for property value changes. They make sense in scenarios in which you use controls that accept users' inputs and are bound to dynamic data objects.

Here, you allow the user to adjust the name of the Timer. Note the use of static bindings to configure the bindings completely in XAML. The code for this is presented in Listing 7-19.

LISTING 7-19: Using two-way binding

```
<Grid x:Name="LayoutRoot" Background="White">
  <StackPanel>
    <Button x:Name="StartButton" HorizontalAlignment="Center">
      <TextBlock>Start Timer</TextBlock>
    </Button>
```

```
    <StackPanel Orientation="Horizontal" HorizontalAlignment="Center">
      <TextBlock>Elapsed Island Time:</TextBlock>
      <TextBlock Text="{Binding ElapsedTime, Mode=OneWay}"></TextBlock>
    </StackPanel>
    <StackPanel Orientation="Horizontal" HorizontalAlignment="Center">
      <TextBlock>Timer Name:</TextBlock>
      <TextBox Text="{Binding Name, Mode=TwoWay}" Width="100" />
    </StackPanel>
  </StackPanel>
</Grid>
```

Validating Data

Data validation is driven by the binding framework's capability to capture exceptions that take place while a binding is in process. Silverlight provides a set of controls with distinct VisualStates that visually indicate that a validation error has occurred.

Handling Binding Exceptions

In a TwoWay binding, exceptions can occur as data flows from the Target back to the Source property. The Binding object provides two properties that allow you to adjust the way these exceptions are handled:

➤   ValidatesOnExceptions

➤   NotifyOnValidationError

If ValidatesOnExceptions is set to true, any exceptions thrown by the setter of the source property or by a converter will be handled by the Binding object.

If NotifyOnValidationError is also true, the Binding will raise the BindingValidationError as exceptions are encountered. Somewhat counterintuitive, the BindingValidationError event will also fire once the binding is able to successfully send the data to the source property. You can therefore use this event to determine both when a validation error has occurred and when it has been resolved.

The Action property of the ValidationEventArgs indicates the state of the Validation error. As a binding encounters exceptions when applying the data updates, the Action will be VaidationErrorEventAction.Added. Once the binding is able to successfully update the source object, the event will be raised with VaidationErrorEventAction.Removed.

In the example shown in Listing 7-20, you adjust the foreground color of the target object based on the Action of the ValidationError. Because the ValidationErrorEvent is routed up the chain of parent elements, you are able to catch it from the LayoutRoot.

LISTING 7-20: Using validation

```
<Grid x:Name="LayoutRoot"
      BindingValidationError="LayoutRoot_BindingValidationError" Background="White" >
  <Grid.RowDefinitions>
        <RowDefinition Height="0.113*"/>
        <RowDefinition Height="0.887*"/>
```

continues

LISTING 7-20 *(continued)*

```
        </Grid.RowDefinitions>
        <Grid.ColumnDefinitions>
            <ColumnDefinition Width="0.462*"/>
            <ColumnDefinition Width="0.538*"/>
        </Grid.ColumnDefinitions>
        <TextBlock Text="Destination Name"/>
        <TextBlock Grid.Column="1" Text="Population" />
        <TextBlock Text="{Binding Name, Mode=OneWay}" Grid.Row="1" />
        <TextBox Text="{Binding Population, Mode=TwoWay,
            ValidatesOnExceptions=true, NotifyOnValidationError=true}"
            VerticalAlignment="Top" Grid.Column="1" Grid.Row="1" Width="200" />
    </Grid>
```

When executed, the application adjusts the color of the TextBox when an error is encountered, converting the text value to the integer value expected by the destination's Population property. This is shown in Listing 7-21.

LISTING 7-21: The code-behind for dealing with validation

```
using System.Windows;
using System.Windows.Controls;
using System.Windows.Media;

namespace Wrox.Silverlight.Data.Validation
{
    public partial class MainPage : UserControl
    {
        public MainPage()
        {
            InitializeComponent();
            this.Loaded += Page_Loaded;
        }

        private void Page_Loaded(object sender, RoutedEventArgs e)
        {
            Destination d = new Destination {Name = "St. Croix",
                Population = 70000};
            LayoutRoot.DataContext = d;
        }

        private void LayoutRoot_BindingValidationError(object sender,
            ValidationErrorEventArgs e)
        {
            // Adjust the foreground color base on the Action
            if (e.Action == ValidationErrorEventAction.Added)
            {
                TextBox tb = (TextBox) e.OriginalSource;
                tb.Foreground = new SolidColorBrush(Colors.Red);
            }
            else
```

```
                    {
                        TextBox tb = (TextBox) e.OriginalSource;
                        tb.Foreground = new SolidColorBrush(Colors.Black);
                    }
                }
            }
        }
```

Using Visual States That Reflect Validation Errors

Silverlight provides a variety of core controls so that they can indicate when a binding validation exception has occurred. This is enabled through the Validation class, which offers attached properties for data validation that are then used to determine the appropriate visual state of the control.

A common scenario for offering a visual indicator when a validation error occurs is on a data entry form. Because the Silverlight TextBox contains visual states that respond to validation errors, all that is required is establishing the binding with ValidatesOnExceptions set to true as shown in Listing 7-22.

LISTING 7-22: Using ValidatesOnExceptions

XAML

```
<Grid x:Name="LayoutRoot" Background="White">
  <StackPanel>
    <TextBlock x:Name="DestinationName" Text="{Binding Name}" />
    <TextBox x:Name="PopulationTextBox"
     Text="{Binding Population, Mode=TwoWay, ValidatesOnExceptions=true}"
    />
    <Button Content="Ok" />
  </StackPanel>
</Grid>
```

CODE-BEHIND

```
public partial class MainPage : UserControl
{
  public MainPage()
  {
    InitializeComponent();
    this.Loaded += Page_Loaded;
  }

  private void Page_Loaded(object sender, RoutedEventArgs e)
  {
    Destination d =
        new Destination { Name = "St. Croix", Population = 70000 };
    LayoutRoot.DataContext = d;
  }
}
```

Converting Data Types

In many instances the source and destination property types will not align. In these cases, the binding attempts to perform a data conversion that may result in a format that is less than ideal. Fortunately, Silverlight provides a baked-in mechanism for converting data as it passes through a binding.

DateTime objects often call for some conversion to display them in a meaningful way to the user. To demonstrate this, add the PeakSeasonStart property to the Destination object and bind it to a TextBlock. Without a converter, this results in a string such as 12/1/2010 12:00:00 AM as shown in Listing 7-23. The first step for this example is to have the following class file.

LISTING 7-23: The Destination class

```
public class Destination
{
  public string Name { get; set; }
  public int Population { get; set; }
  public double AverageAirfare { get; set; }
  public double AverageHotel { get; set; }
  public string BestKnownFor { get; set; }
  public DateTime PeakSeasonStart { get; set; }
}
```

Then for your Silverlight page, use the XAML shown in Listing 7-24.

LISTING 7-24: The XAML for MainPage.xaml

```
<Grid x:Name="LayoutRoot" Background="White">
  <TextBlock Text="{Binding PeakSeasonStart}" />
</Grid>
```

Finally, the code-behind for this page is presented in Listing 7-25.

LISTING 7-25: The code-behind for MainPage.xaml.cs

```
public partial class MainPage : UserControl
{
  public MainPage()
  {
    InitializeComponent();
    this.Loaded += Page_Loaded;
  }

  private void Page_Loaded(object sender, RoutedEventArgs e)
  {
    Destination d = new Destination() { Name = "St. Croix",
      PeakSeasonStart = new DateTime(2009, 12, 1) };
    LayoutRoot.DataContext = d;
  }
}
```

To adjust this behavior with the string value coming out incorrect, follow these steps:

1. Create a class that implements IValueConverter.

2. Include an instance of that class in a Resource.

3. Specify a Converter in the binding.

Using the IValueConverter Interface

The IValueConverter interface defines two straightforward methods to enable conversion: Convert() and ConvertBack(). As their names suggest, they allow conversion back and forth between two types. If you need only to support OneWay binding, the ConvertBack() method is not invoked.

In Listing 7-26 you see a basic implementation of IValueConverter that adjusts the way that a DateTime object is converted to a String. You will find IValueConverter in the System.Windows .Data namespace.

LISTING 7-26: Using the IValueConverter interface

```
// Class for converting between DateTime and string objects
public class DateConverter : IValueConverter
{
  // Convert DateTime to a string without time info
  public object Convert(object value, Type targetType,
    object parameter, System.Globalization.CultureInfo culture)
  {
    DateTime date = (DateTime)value;
    return (date.ToShortDateString());
  }

  public object ConvertBack(object value, Type targetType,
    object parameter, System.Globalization.CultureInfo culture)
  {
    string s = (string)value;
    return (DateTime.Parse(s));
  }
}
```

Adding the Converter to a Binding

The Binding object provides a Converter property for specifying the object that should serve as the intermediary between the source and target. Here, you include the Converter as a resource and reference it from the binding for the binding between a DateTime source and String target object. The code in Listing 7-27 provides a slightly more pleasing representation of your date, which omits the time information.

LISTING 7-27: Using the Converter property

```xaml
<UserControl x:Class="Wrox.Silverlight.Data.Convertion.Page"
    xmlns="http://schemas.microsoft.com/winfx/2006/xaml/presentation"
    xmlns:x="http://schemas.microsoft.com/winfx/2006/xaml"
    xmlns:data="clr-namespace:Wrox.Silverlight.Data.Convertion"
    Width="400" Height="300">
  <UserControl.Resources>
    <data:DateConverter x:Key="DateConverter" />
  </UserControl.Resources>
  <Grid x:Name="LayoutRoot" Background="White">
    <TextBlock Text="{Binding PeakSeasonStart,
        Converter={StaticResource DateConverter}}" />
  </Grid>
</UserControl>
```

Using the ConverterParameter Property

The `Binding` object provides an additional property, which allows you to feed a parameter to the `IValueConverter`. This can be useful if you want to employ a converter in several related scenarios that are slightly different. Those familiar with formatting strings in .NET should be no stranger to the variety of `FormatStrings` available for built-in data types. The following example leverages the `ConverterParameter` to provide a `FormatString`.

Listing 7-28 passes in the .NET short date format string `'{0:d}'` for display of the destination's start of peak season.

LISTING 7-28: Using ConverterParameter to provide a FormatString

XAML

```xaml
<UserControl x:Class="Wrox.Silverlight.Data.Convertion.Page"
    xmlns="http://schemas.microsoft.com/winfx/2006/xaml/presentation"
    xmlns:x="http://schemas.microsoft.com/winfx/2006/xaml"
    xmlns:data="clr-namespace:Wrox.Silverlight.Data.Convertion"
    Width="400" Height="300">
  <UserControl.Resources>

    <data:FormatStringConverter x:Key="FormatStringConverter" />
  </UserControl.Resources>
  <Grid x:Name="LayoutRoot" Background="White">
    <StackPanel>
      <TextBlock Text="{Binding PeakSeasonStart,
        Converter={StaticResource FormatStringConverter},
        ConverterParameter='{0:d}'}" />
    </StackPanel>
  </Grid>
</UserControl>
```

CODE-BEHIND

```
// Class for converting to a string based on the provided FormatString
public class FormatStringConverter : IValueConverter
{
  public object Convert(object value, Type targetType,
    object parameter, System.Globalization.CultureInfo culture)
  {
    string formatString = (string)parameter;
    return String.Format(formatString, value);
  }

  public object ConvertBack(object value, Type targetType,
    object parameter, System.Globalization.CultureInfo culture)
  {
    throw new NotImplementedException();
  }
}
```

WORKING WITH SERVICES

It is a diverse world. In a major enterprise, very rarely do you find that the entire organization and its data repositories reside on a single vendor's platform. In most instances, organizations are made up of a patchwork of systems — some based on UNIX, some on Microsoft, and some on other systems. There probably will not be a day when everything resides on a single platform where all the data moves seamlessly from one server to another. For that reason, these various systems must be able to talk to one another. If disparate systems can communicate easily, moving unique data sets around the enterprise becomes a simple process — alleviating the need for replication systems and data stores.

When XML (eXtensible Markup Language) was introduced, it became clear that the markup language would be the structure to bring the necessary integration into the enterprise. XML's power comes from the fact that it can be used regardless of the platform, language, or data store of the system using it to expose DataSets.

XML has its roots in the Standard Generalized Markup Language (SGML), which was created in 1986. Because SGML was so complex, something a bit simpler was needed — thus the birth of XML.

XML is considered ideal for data representation purposes because it enables developers to structure XML documents as they see fit. For this reason, it is also a bit chaotic. Sending self-structured XML documents between dissimilar systems does not make a lot of sense — you would have to custom build the exposure and consumption models for each communication pair.

Vendors and the industry as a whole soon realized that XML needed a specific structure that put some rules in place to clarify communication. The rules defining XML structure make the communication between the disparate systems just that much easier. Tool vendors can now automate the communication process, as well as provide for the automation of the possible creation of all the components of applications using the communication protocol.

The industry settled on using SOAP (Simple Object Access Protocol) to make the standard XML structure work. Previous attempts to solve the communication problem that arose included component technologies such as Distributed Component Object Model (DCOM), Remote Method

Invocation (RMI), Common Object Request Broker Architecture (CORBA), and Internet Inter-ORB Protocol (IIOP). These first efforts failed because each of these technologies was either driven by a single vendor or (worse yet) very vendor-specific. Implementing them across the entire industry was, therefore, impossible.

SOAP enables you to expose and consume complex data structures, which can include items such as DataSets, or just tables of data that have all their relations in place. SOAP is relatively simple and easy to understand. Like ASP.NET, XML Web Services are also primarily engineered to work over HTTP. The DataSets you send or consume can flow over the same Internet wires (HTTP), thereby bypassing many firewalls (as they move through port 80).

So what is actually going across the wire? ASP.NET Web Services generally use SOAP over HTTP using the HTTP Post protocol. An example SOAP request (from the client to the web service residing on a web server) takes the structure shown in Listing 7-29.

LISTING 7-29: A SOAP request

```
POST /MyWebService/Service.asmx HTTP/1.1
Host: www.wrox.com
Content-Type: text/xml; charset=utf-8
Content-Length: 19
SOAPAction: "http://tempuri.org/HelloWorld"

<?xml version="1.0" encoding="utf-8"?>
<soap:Envelope xmlns:xsi="http://www.w3.org/2001/XMLSchema-instance"
 xmlns:xsd="http://www.w3.org/2001/XMLSchema"
 xmlns:soap="http://schemas.xmlsoap.org/soap/envelope/">
  <soap:Body>
    <HelloWorld xmlns="http://tempuri.org/" />
  </soap:Body>
</soap:Envelope>
```

The request is sent to the web service to invoke the `HelloWorld` WebMethod. Listing 7-30 shows the SOAP response from the web service.

LISTING 7-30: A SOAP response

```
HTTP/1.1 200 OK
Content-Type: text/xml; charset=utf-8
Content-Length: 14

<?xml version="1.0" encoding="utf-8"?>
<soap:Envelope xmlns:xsi="http://www.w3.org/2001/XMLSchema-instance"
 xmlns:xsd="http://www.w3.org/2001/XMLSchema"
 xmlns:soap="http://schemas.xmlsoap.org/soap/envelope/">
  <soap:Body>
    <HelloWorldResponse xmlns="http://tempuri.org/">
      <HelloWorldResult>Hello World</HelloWorldResult>
    </HelloWorldResponse>
  </soap:Body>
</soap:Envelope>
```

In the examples from Listings 7-29 and 7-30, you can see that what is contained in this message is an XML file. In addition to the normal XML declaration of the `<xml>` node, you see a structure of XML that is the SOAP message. A SOAP message uses a root node of `<soap:Envelope>` that contains the `<soap:Body>` or the body of the SOAP message. Other elements that can be contained in the SOAP message include a SOAP header, `<soap:Header>`, and a SOAP fault, `<soap:Fault>`.

> *For more information about the structure of a SOAP message, be sure to check out the SOAP specifications. You can find them at the W3C website,* `www.w3.org/tr/soap`.

Building an ASP.NET Web Service

The next thing that this chapter looks at is how to build an ASP.NET Web Service that can then be later consumed by your Silverlight application. The .NET Framework provides you two major options for building services: ASP.NET Web Services and the newer Windows Communication Foundation (WCF) services. WCF services are covered later in this chapter. Before looking at WCF, you will build a simple ASP.NET Web Service.

Building an XML Web Service means that you are interested in exposing some information or logic to another entity either within your organization, to a partner, or to your customers. In a more granular sense, building a web service means that you, as a developer, simply enable for SOAP communication one or more methods from a class.

You can use Visual Studio 2010 to build an XML Web Service. The first step is to actually create a new website by selecting File ➪ New ➪ Web Site from the IDE menu. The New Web Site dialog opens. You will want to create a typical ASP.NET application (ASP.NET Empty Web Site). Then you will be able to add an ASP.NET Web Service file to the solution as shown in Figure 7-1.

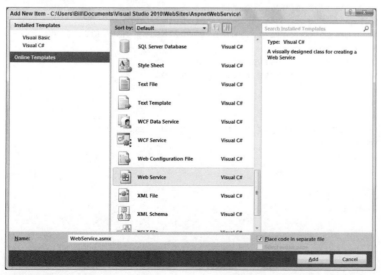

FIGURE 7-1

Adding the file `WebService.asmx` creates a single XML Web Service to your solution. You will find its code-behind file, `WebService.cs`, in the App_Code folder (see Figure 7-2).

FIGURE 7-2

Looking at the Base Web Service Class File

Now look at the `WebService.cs` file — the code-behind file for the XML Web Service. By default, a structure of code is already in place in the `WebService.cs` file, as shown in Listing 7-31.

LISTING 7-31: Default code structure provided by Visual Studio for your web service

```
using System;
using System.Collections.Generic;
using System.Linq;
using System.Web;
using System.Web.Services;

[WebService(Namespace = "http://tempuri.org/")]
[WebServiceBinding(ConformsTo = WsiProfiles.BasicProfile1_1)]
// To allow this Web Service to be called from script, using ASP.NET AJAX,
// uncomment the following line.
// [System.Web.Script.Services.ScriptService]
public class WebService : System.Web.Services.WebService
{
    public WebService () {

        //Uncomment the following line if using designed components
        //InitializeComponent();
    }

    [WebMethod]
    public string HelloWorld() {
        return "Hello World";
    }

}
```

Some minor changes to the structure have been made since the release of the .NET Framework 3.5. You will notice that the `System.Linq` namespace is now included in the C# solution. In addition, the other change in this version is the inclusion of the commented `System.Web.Script.Services .ScriptService` object to work with ASP.NET AJAX scripts.

The other addition is the `<WebServiceBinding>` attribute. It builds the XML Web Service responses that conform to the WS-I Basic Profile 1.0 release (found at `www.ws-i.org/Profiles/ BasicProfile-1.0-2004-04-16.html`).

Exposing Data as SOAP

To build your own web service example, delete the `WebService.asmx` file and create a new file called `Contacts.asmx`. This web service will expose parts of the `Person.Contact` table from the Adventure Works SQL Server database file.

> *You can find the Adventure Works sample database at* `http://msftdbprodsamples.codeplex.com/`.

The idea here is that you will write a service that connects to the `Person.Contact` table and exposes some of the contents of the database as a `List<string>` object, which in turn is converted to an array of strings. The code for this is presented in Listing 7-32.

LISTING 7-32: An XML Web Service that exposes the Contact table from AdventureWorks

```
using System.Collections.Generic;
using System.Data;
using System.Data.SqlClient;
using System.Web.Services;

[WebService(Namespace = "http://www.wrox.com/contacts")]
[WebServiceBinding(ConformsTo = WsiProfiles.BasicProfile1_1)]
public class Contacts : System.Web.Services.WebService
{
    [WebMethod]
    public List<string> GetContacts()
    {
        const string cmdString = "Select FirstName, LastName from Person.Contact";

        SqlConnection conn =
            new SqlConnection(
                @"Data Source=.\SQLEXPRESS;AttachDbFilename=
                |DataDirectory|AdventureWorks_Data.mdf;Integrated
                 Security=True;User Instance=True");
        SqlCommand cmd = new SqlCommand(cmdString, conn);
```

continues

LISTING 7-32 *(continued)*

```
        conn.Open();

        SqlDataReader sqlDataReader;
        List<string> myContacts = new List<string>();

        sqlDataReader = cmd.ExecuteReader(CommandBehavior.CloseConnection);

        while (sqlDataReader.Read())
        {
            myContacts.Add(sqlDataReader["FirstName"] + " " +
                sqlDataReader["LastName"]);
        }

        return myContacts;
    }
}
```

Using the WebService Attribute

All web services are encapsulated within a class. The class is defined as a web service by the
`WebService` attribute placed before the class declaration. Here is an example:

```
[WebService(Namespace = "http://www.wrox.com/contacts")]
```

The `WebService` attribute can take a few properties. By default, the `WebService` attribute is
used in your web service along with the `Namespace` property, which has an initial value of `http://
tempuri.org/`. This is meant to be a temporary namespace and you should replace it with a more
meaningful and original name, such as the URL where you are hosting the XML Web Service. In
the example, the `Namespace` value was changed to `www.wrox.com/contacts`. Remember that the
value does not have to be an actual URL; it can be any string value you want. The idea is that it
should be unique. Using a URL is common practice because a URL is always unique.

Other possible `WebService` properties include `Name` and `Description`. `Name` enables you to change
how the name of the web service is presented to the developer via the ASP.NET test page. `Description`
allows you to provide a textual description of the web service. The description is also presented on the
ASP.NET Web Service test page. If your `WebService` attribute contains more than a single property,
separate the properties using a comma. Here is an example:

```
[WebService(Namespace="http://www.wrox.com/contacts", Name="GetContacts")]
```

Using the WebMethod Attribute

In Listing 7-32, the class called `Contacts` has only a single `WebMethod`. A `WebService` class can
contain any number of `WebMethods`, or a mixture of standard methods along with methods that
are enabled to be `WebMethods` via the use of the attribute preceding the method declaration. The
only methods that are accessible across the HTTP wire are the ones to which you have applied the
`WebMethod` attribute.

As with the `WebService` attribute, `WebMethod` can also contain some properties, which are described in the following list:

➤ `BufferResponse` — When `BufferResponse` is set to `true`, the response from the XML Web Service is held in memory and sent as a complete package. If it is set to `false`, the default setting, the response is sent to the client as it is constructed on the server.

➤ `CacheDuration` — Specifies the number of seconds that the response should be held in the system's cache. The default setting is `0`, which means that caching is disabled. Putting an XML Web Service's response in the cache increases the web service's performance.

➤ `Description` — Applies a text description to the `WebMethod` that appears on the `.aspx` test page of the XML Web Service.

➤ `EnableSession` — Setting `EnableSession` to `true` enables session state for a particular `WebMethod`. The default setting is `false`.

➤ `MessageName` — Applies a unique name to the `WebMethod`. This step is required if you are working with overloaded `WebMethods`.

➤ `TransactionOption` — Specifies the transactional support for the `WebMethod`. The default setting is `Disabled`. If the `WebMethod` is the root object that initiated the transaction, the web service can participate in a transaction with another `WebMethod` that requires a transaction. Other possible values include `NotSupported`, `Supported`, `Required`, and `RequiresNew`.

Working with the XML Web Service Interface

The Contacts web service from Listing 7-32 has only a single `WebMethod` that returns an array of strings containing the names of everyone in the `Person.Contacts` table from the SQL Server AdventureWorks database.

Running `Contacts.asmx` in the browser pulls up the ASP.NET Web Service test page. This visual interface to your web service is really meant either for testing purposes or as a reference page for developers interested in consuming the web services you expose. Figure 7-3 shows the page generated for the Contacts Web Service.

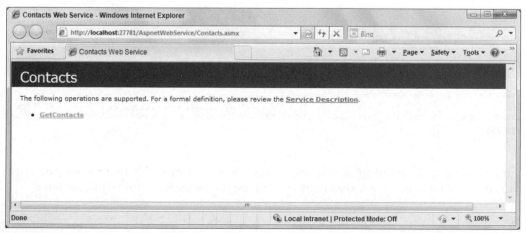

FIGURE 7-3

The interface shows the name of the web service in the blue bar (the dark bar in this black-and-white image) at the top of the page. By default, the name of the class is used unless you changed the value through the `Description` property of the `WebService` attribute, as defined earlier. A bulleted list of links to all of the web service's `WebMethod`s is displayed. This example has only one `WebMethod`: `GetContacts()`.

A link to the web service's Web Services Description Language (WSDL) document is also available (the link is titled "Service Description" in the figure). The WSDL file is the actual interface with the Contacts web service. The XML document (shown in Figure 7-4) is not really meant for human consumption; it is designed to work with tools such as Visual Studio, informing the tool what the web service requires to be consumed. Each web service requires a request that must have parameters of a specific type. When the request is made, the web service response comes back with a specific set of data defined using specific data types. Everything you need for the request and a listing of exactly what you are getting back in a response (if you are the consumer) is described in the WSDL document.

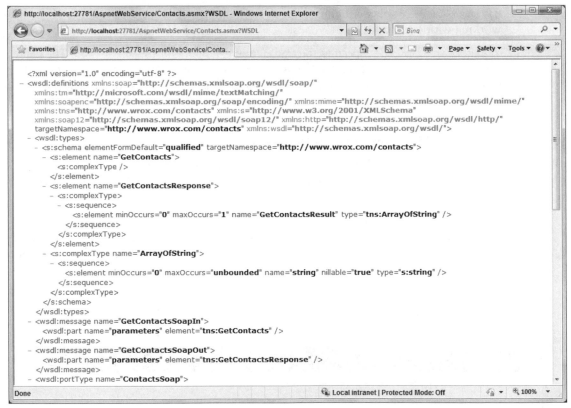

FIGURE 7-4

Clicking the `GetContacts` link gives you a new page, shown in Figure 7-5, that not only describes the `WebMethod` in more detail but also allows you to test the `WebMethod` directly in the browser.

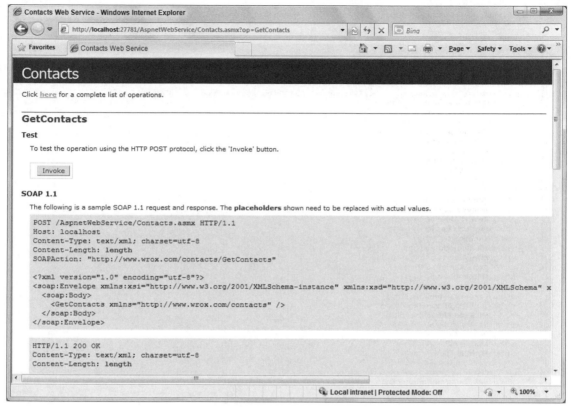

FIGURE 7-5

At the top of the page is the name of the XML Web Service (Contacts); below that is the name of this particular WebMethod (GetContacts). The page shows you the structure of the SOAP messages that are required to consume the WebMethod, as well as the structure the SOAP message takes for the response. Below the SOAP examples is an example of consuming the XML Web Service using HTTP Post (with name/value pairs). Using this method of consumption instead of using SOAP is possible.

You can test the WebMethod directly from the page. In the Test section, you find a form. If the WebMethod you are calling requires an input of some parameters to get a response, you see some text boxes included so you can provide the parameters before clicking the Invoke button. If the WebMethod you are calling does not require any parameters, you see only the Invoke button and nothing more.

Clicking Invoke actually sends a SOAP request to the web service, causing a new browser instance with the result to appear, as illustrated in Figure 7-6.

Now that everything is in place to expose the XML Web Service, you can consume it in a Silverlight application.

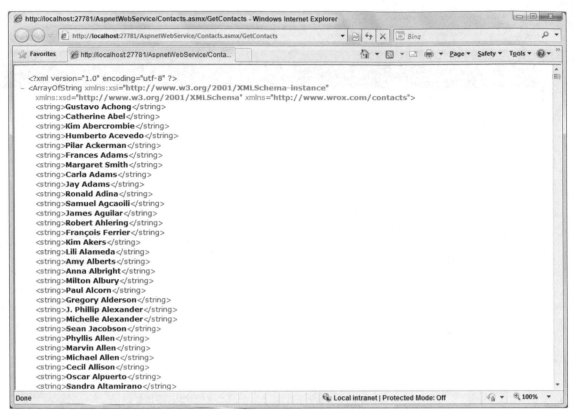

FIGURE 7-6

Consuming a Simple XML Web Service

So far, you have seen only half of the XML Web Service story. Exposing data and logic as SOAP to disparate systems across the enterprise or across the world is a simple task using .NET and particularly ASP.NET. The other half of the story is the actual consumption of an XML Web Service into a Silverlight application.

You are not limited to consuming XML Web Services only into Silverlight applications; but because this is a Silverlight book, it focuses on that aspect of the consumption process. Consuming XML Web Services into other types of applications is not that difficult and, in fact, is rather similar to how you would consume them using Silverlight. Remember that the web services you come across can be consumed in Windows Forms, ASP.NET applications, mobile applications, databases, and more. You can even consume XML Web Services with other web services so you can have a single web service made up of what is basically an aggregate of other web services.

Adding a Web Reference

To consume the Contacts web service that you just created in this chapter, create a new Silverlight application called `SilverlightConsumer`. The first step in consuming an XML Web Service in a

Silverlight application is to make a reference to the remote object — the web service. You do so by right-clicking the root node of your project from within the Visual Studio Solution Explorer and selecting Add Service Reference. The Add Service Reference dialog box appears, shown in Figure 7-7.

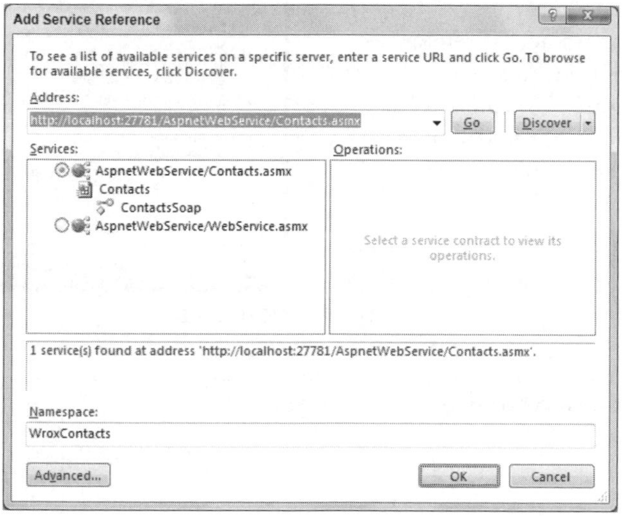

Add Service Reference

To see a list of available services on a specific server, enter a service URL and click Go. To browse for available services, click Discover.

Address:

```
http://localhost:27781/AspnetWebService/Contacts.asmx
```
[Go] [Discover]

Services:

- AspnetWebService/Contacts.asmx
  - Contacts
    - ContactsSoap
- AspnetWebService/WebService.asmx

Operations:

Select a service contract to view its operations.

1 service(s) found at address 'http://localhost:27781/AspnetWebService/Contacts.asmx'.

Namespace:

WroxContacts

[Advanced...]   [OK] [Cancel]

FIGURE 7-7

The Add Service Reference dialog box enables you to point to a particular .asmx file to make a reference to it. Understand that the Add Service Reference dialog box is really looking for WSDL files. Microsoft's XML Web Services automatically generate WSDL files based on the .asmx files themselves. To pull up the WSDL file in the browser, simply type the URL of your web service's .asmx file and add a ?WSDL at the end of the string. For example, you might have the following construction (this is not an actual web service, but simply an example):

```
http://www.wrox.com/MyWebService/Contacts.asmx?WSDL
```

Because the Add Service Reference dialog box automatically finds where the WSDL file is for any Microsoft-based XML Web Service, you should simply type the URL of the actual WSDL file for any non–Microsoft-based XML Web Service.

 If you are using Microsoft's Visual Studio and its built-in web server instead of IIS, you will be required to also interject the port number the web server is using into the URL. In this case, your URL would be structured similar to http://localhost:5444/MyWebService/Contacts.asmx?WSDL.

In the Add Service Reference dialog box, change the reference from the default name to something a little more meaningful. If you are working on a single machine, the web reference might have the name of localhost; if you are actually working with a remote web service, the name is the inverse of the URL, such as com.wrox.www. In either case, renaming it so that the name makes a little more sense and is easy to use within your application is best. In the example here, the web reference is renamed WroxContacts.

Clicking OK causes Visual Studio to make an actual reference to the web service and create a new configuration file in your Silverlight application (shown in Figure 7-8) called ServiceReferences.ClientConfig. You might find some additional files under the App_WebReferences folder — such as a copy of the web service's WSDL file.

Your consuming application's ServiceReferences.ClientConfig file contains the reference to the web service. Listing 7-33 shows the created file.

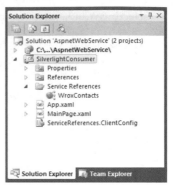

FIGURE 7-8

Available for download on Wrox.com

LISTING 7-33: The config file after making a reference to the web service

```
<configuration>
    <system.serviceModel>
        <bindings>
            <basicHttpBinding>
                <binding name="ContactsSoap" maxBufferSize="2147483647"
                 maxReceivedMessageSize="2147483647">
                    <security mode="None" />
                </binding>
            </basicHttpBinding>
        </bindings>
        <client>
            <endpoint
             address="http://localhost:27781/AspnetWebService/Contacts.asmx"
                binding="basicHttpBinding" bindingConfiguration="ContactsSoap"
                contract="WroxContacts.ContactsSoap" name="ContactsSoap" />
        </client>
    </system.serviceModel>
</configuration>
```

You can see that the contract and the binding have been defined. Once this is in place, you are ready to code to this interface.

Invoking the Web Service from the Client Application

Now that a reference has been made to the XML Web Service, you can use it in your Silverlight application. Using MainPage.xaml in your project, you can consume the query made against the Contacts table from the remote AdventureWorks database directly into your application. The data is placed in a ListBox control.

On the design part of the page, place a simple ListBox control. The idea is that when the Silverlight view is loaded, the application sends a SOAP request to the Contacts web service and gets back a SOAP response containing the contact's names, which is then bound to the ListBox control on the view. Listing 7-34 shows the code for this simple application.

> **LISTING 7-34:** Consuming the Contacts web service in your Silverlight application

```csharp
using System.Windows;
using System.Windows.Controls;
using SilverlightConsumer.WroxContacts;

namespace SilverlightConsumer
{
    public partial class MainPage : UserControl
    {
        public MainPage()
        {
            InitializeComponent();

            ContactsSoapClient ws = new ContactsSoapClient();
            ws.GetContactsCompleted += ws_GetContactsCompleted;
            ws.GetContactsAsync();
        }

        private void ws_GetContactsCompleted(object sender,
            GetContactsCompletedEventArgs e)
        {
            if (e.Error != null)
            {
                MessageBox.Show(e.Error.ToString());
            }
            else
            {
                listBox1.ItemsSource = e.Result;
            }
        }
    }
}
```

The view being loaded causes the Silverlight application to send a SOAP request to the remote XML Web Service. The returned array of strings is bound to the ListBox control, and the page is created, as shown in Figure 7-9.

The Contacts web service is invoked by the instantiation of the ContactsSoapClient proxy object:

```csharp
ContactsSoapClient ws = new ContactsSoapClient();
```

Then you can use the ws object like any other object within your project. In the code example from Listing 7-34, the results of the ws.GetContactsAsync() method call results in the array of strings being bound to the ListBox control:

```csharp
listBox1.ItemsSource = e.Result;
```

As you develop or consume more web services within your applications, you will see more of their power and utility.

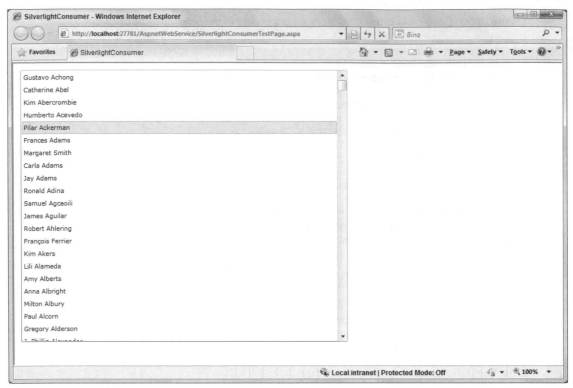

FIGURE 7-9

Working with Windows Communication Foundation (WCF)

Since the introduction of the .NET Framework 3.0, Microsoft has made available a new way to build web services beyond the ASP.NET-based Web Services presented in this chapter.

Until the .NET Framework 3.0 came out, building components that were required to communicate a message from one point to another was not a simple task because Microsoft offered more than one technology that you could use for such an action.

For instance, you could have used ASP.NET Web Services (as just discussed), Web Service Enhancements 3.0 (WSE), MSMQ, Enterprise Services, .NET Remoting, and even the `System` `.Messaging` namespace. Each technology has its own pros and cons. ASP.NET Web Services (also known by some as *ASMX Web Services*) provided the capability to easily build interoperable web services. The WSE enabled you to easily build services that took advantage of some of the WS-* message protocols. MSMQ enabled the queuing of messages, which made working with solutions that were only intermittently connected easy. Enterprise Services, provided as a successor to COM+, offered an easy means to build distributed applications. .NET Remoting was a fast way to move messages from one .NET application to another. Moreover, these are Microsoft options only. These options do not include all the ones available in other environments, such as the Java world.

With so many options available to a Microsoft developer, deciding which path to take with the applications you are trying to build can be tough. With this in mind, Microsoft has created the Windows Communication Foundation (WCF).

WCF is a relatively new framework for building service-oriented applications. Microsoft wanted to provide its developers with a framework to quickly get a proper service-oriented architecture up-and-running. Using the WCF, you can take advantage of all the items that make distribution technologies powerful. WCF is the answer and the successor to all these other message distribution technologies.

Understanding the Larger Move to SOA

Upon examining WCF, you will find that it is part of a larger movement that organizations are making toward the much-talked-about *service-oriented architecture*, or *SOA*. An SOA is a message-based service architecture that is vendor-agnostic. As a result, you have the ability to distribute messages across a system, and the messages are interoperable with other systems that would otherwise be considered incompatible with the provider system.

Looking back, you can see the gradual progression to the service-oriented architecture model. In the 1980s, the revolution arrived with the concept of everything being an object. When object-oriented programming came on the scene, it was enthusiastically accepted as the proper means to represent entities within a programming model. The 1990s took that idea one step further, and the component-oriented model was born. This model enabled objects to be encapsulated in a tightly coupled manner. It was only recently that the industry turned to a service-oriented architecture because developers and architects needed to take components and have them distributed to other points in an organization, to their partners, or to their customers. This distribution system needed to have the means to transfer messages between machines that were generally incompatible with one another. In addition, the messages had to include the ability to express the metadata about how a system should handle a message.

If you ask 10 people what an SOA is, you'll probably get 11 different answers, but some common principles are considered to be foundations of a service-oriented architecture:

➤ **Boundaries are explicit** — Any data store, logic, or entity uses an interface to expose its data or capabilities. The interface provides the means to hide the behaviors within the service, and the interface front-end enables you to change this behavior as required without affecting downstream consumers.

➤ **Services are autonomous** — All the services are updated or versioned independently of one another. Thus, you do not upgrade a system in its entirety; instead, each component of these systems is an individual entity within itself and can move forward without waiting for other components to progress forward. Note that with this type of model, after you publish an interface, that interface must remain unchanged. Interface changes require new interfaces (versioned, of course).

➤ **Services are based on contracts, schemas, and policies** — All services developed require a contract regarding what is required to consume items from the interface (usually done through a WSDL document). Along with a contract, schemas are required to define the items passed in as parameters or delivered through the service (using XSD schemas). Finally, policies define any capabilities or requirements of the service.

➤ **Service compatibility that is based upon policy** — The final principle enables services to define policies (decided at run time) that are required to consume the service. These policies are usually expressed through WS-Policy.

If your own organization is considering establishing an SOA, the WCF is a framework that works on these principles and makes implementing it relatively simple. The next section looks at what the WCF offers. Then you can dive into building your first WCF service.

Understanding WCF

As previously stated, WCF is a means to build distributed applications in a Microsoft environment. Although the distributed application is built upon that environment, this does not mean that consumers are required to be Microsoft clients or to take any Microsoft component or technology to accomplish the task of consumption. On the other hand, building WCF services means you are also building services that abide by the principles set forth in the aforementioned SOA discussion and that these services are vendor-agnostic — thus, they can be consumed by almost anyone.

You can build WCF services using Visual Studio 2010. Note that because this is a .NET Framework 3.0 or greater component, you are actually limited to the operating systems in which you can run a WCF service. Whereas the other Microsoft distribution technologies mentioned in this chapter do not have too many limitations on running on Microsoft operating systems, an application built with WCF can run only on Windows XP SP2, Windows Vista, Windows 7, or Windows Server 2008.

If you are already familiar with WCF, it is interesting to note that some improvements have been made to WCF within the .NET Framework 4 release. A lot of focus was put on increasing the productivity of developers and providing quick options for common tasks such as creating syndicated services, as well as better debugging and serialization options. You will find that the performance for WCF has increased, especially when hosted in IIS7. Other new features include new support for working with the ADO.NET Entity Framework, improvements to the configuration editor, and more.

Building a WCF Service

Building a WCF service is not hard to accomplish. The assumption here is that you have installed the .NET Framework 4 for the purpose of these examples. If you are using Visual Studio 2010, the view of the project from the New Project dialog box is as shown in Figure 7-10.

Name the project **WcfService1**. The example you run through here demonstrates how to build the WCF service by building the interface, followed by the service itself.

Creating the Services Framework

The first step is to create the services framework in the project. To do this, right-click the project and select Add New Item from the provided menu. From the Add New Item dialog box, select WCF Service, and name the service **Service1.svc**, as illustrated in Figure 7-11.

This step creates a `Service1.svc` file, a `Service1.cs` file, and an `IService1.cs` file. The `Service1.svc` file is a simple file that includes only the page directive, whereas the `Service1.cs` file does all the heavy lifting. The `Service1.cs` file is an implementation of the `IService1.cs` interface.

FIGURE 7-10

FIGURE 7-11

Working with the Interface

To create your service, you need a service contract. The service contract is the interface of the service. This consists of all the methods exposed as well as the input and output parameters that are required to invoke the methods. To accomplish this task, turn to the `IService1.cs` file. You are going to want to refactor this name and rename it to `IIslands.cs`. Listing 7-35 presents the interface you need to create.

LISTING 7-35: Creating the interface

```csharp
using System.Collections.Generic;
using System.Runtime.Serialization;
using System.ServiceModel;

namespace WcfService1
{
    [ServiceContract]
    public interface IIslands
    {
        [OperationContract]
        List<Destination> GetIslands();
    }

    [DataContract]
    public class Destination
    {
        [DataMember]
        public string Name { get; set; }

        [DataMember]
        public int Population { get; set; }

        [DataMember]
        public double AverageAirfare { get; set; }

        [DataMember]
        public double AverageHotel { get; set; }

        [DataMember]
        public string BestKnownFor { get; set; }
    }
}
```

This is pretty much the normal interface definition you would expect, but with a couple of new attributes included. To gain access to these required attributes, you must make a reference to the `System.ServiceModel` namespace. This gives you access to the `[ServiceContract]` and `[OperationContract]` attributes.

Use the `[ServiceContract]` attribute to define the class or interface as the service class, and it needs to precede the opening declaration of the class or interface. In this case, the example in the preceding code is based on an interface:

```csharp
[ServiceContract]
public interface IIslands
{
    // Code removed for clarity
}
```

Within the interface, four methods are defined. Each method will be exposed through the WCF service as part of the service contract. For this reason, each method is required to have the [OperationContract] attribute applied:

```
[OperationContract]
List<Destination> GetIslands();
```

Utilizing the Interface

The next step is to create a class that implements the interface. Not only is the new class implementing the defined interface, but it is also implementing the service contract. For this example, add this class to the same Service1.cs file. The code in Listing 7-36 shows the implementation of this interface.

LISTING 7-36: Implementing the interface

```
using System.Collections.Generic;

namespace WcfService1
{
    public class Service1 : IIslands
    {
        #region IIslands Members

        public List<Destination> GetIslands()
        {
            List<Destination> destinations = new List<Destination>();
            destinations.Add(new Destination {Name = "St. Croix"});
            destinations.Add(new Destination {Name = "St. John"});
            destinations.Add(new Destination {Name = "St. Thomas"});

            return destinations;
        }

        #endregion
    }
}
```

From these new additions, you can see that you don't have to do anything different to the Service1 class. It is a simple class that implements the IIslands interface and provides an implementation of the GetIslands() method.

Reviewing the Service

Now that the service is in place, you can right-click the .svc file and select the View in Browser option from the provided menu. You will then be presented with what is shown in Figure 7-12.

The page presented in Figure 7-12 is the information page about the service. In the image, notice the link to the WSDL file of the service. As with ASP.NET Web Services, a WCF service can also auto-generate the WSDL file. Clicking the WSDL link shows the WSDL in the browser, as illustrated in Figure 7-13.

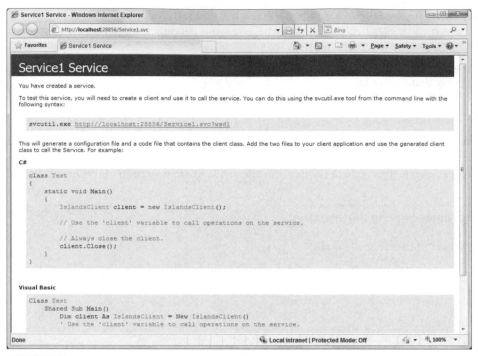

FIGURE 7-12

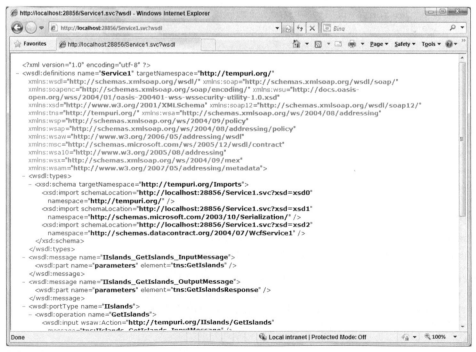

FIGURE 7-13

Building a Silverlight Consumer

Now that an HTTP service is out there, which you built using the WCF framework, the next step is to build a consumer application in Silverlight that uses the simple `Service1` service. The consumer sends its request via HTTP using SOAP. This section describes how to consume this service. From the same solution, add a new Silverlight project called **SilverlightWcfConsumer**. You will also have the customary `SilverlightWcfConsumer.Web` project contained within the same solution.

After you have laid out your Silverlight view with a `ListBox` control, make a reference to the new WCF service. You do this in a manner quite similar to how you do it with XML Web Service references. Right-click the solution name from the Visual Studio Solution Explorer and select Add Service Reference from the dialog box that appears.

The Add Service Reference dialog box (see Figure 7-14) asks you for two things: the Service URI or Address (basically a pointer to the WSDL file) and the name you want to give to the reference. The name you provide the reference is the name that will be used for the instantiated object that enables you to interact with the service.

This adds to your project a Service Reference folder containing some proxy files, as shown in Figure 7-15.

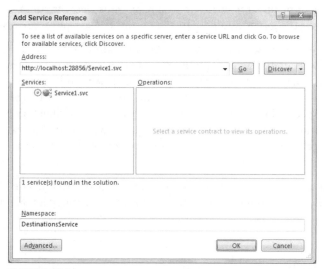

FIGURE 7-14

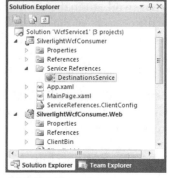

FIGURE 7-15

Changing Configuration Files

Looking at the `ServiceReference.ClientConfig` file, you can see that Visual Studio has placed information about the service inside the document, as illustrated in Listing 7-37.

Available for download on Wrox.com

LISTING 7-37: The created ServiceReference.ClientConfig file

```
<configuration>
    <system.serviceModel>
```

continues

LISTING 7-37 *(continued)*

```xml
        <bindings>
            <basicHttpBinding>
                <binding name="BasicHttpBinding_IIslands"
                    maxBufferSize="2147483647"
                    maxReceivedMessageSize="2147483647">
                    <security mode="None" />
                </binding>
            </basicHttpBinding>
        </bindings>
        <client>
            <endpoint address="http://localhost:28856/Service1.svc"
                binding="basicHttpBinding"
                bindingConfiguration="BasicHttpBinding_IIslands"
                contract="DestinationsService.IIslands"
                name="BasicHttpBinding_IIslands" />
        </client>
    </system.serviceModel>
</configuration>
```

The important part of this configuration document is the `<client>` element. This element contains a child element called `<endpoint>` that defines the *where* and *how* of the service consumption process.

The `<endpoint>` element provides the address of the service — `http://localhost:28856/Service1` `.svc` — and it specifies which binding of the available WCF bindings should be used. In this case, the `BasicHttpBinding` is the required binding. Even though you are using an established binding from the WCF framework, from the client side you can customize how this binding behaves. The settings that define the behavior of the binding are specified using the `bindingConfiguration` attribute of the `<endpoint>` element. In this case, the value provided to the `bindingConfiguration` attribute is `BasicHttpBinding_IIslands`, which is a reference to the `<binding>` element contained within the `<basicHttpBinding>` element.

As demonstrated, Visual Studio 2010 makes the consumption of these services fairly trivial. The next step is to code the consumption of the service interface into the GUI that you created as one of the first steps of this section.

Consuming the Service Interface

Now that everything is in place, the next step is to interact with this proxy in your Silverlight project. The idea here is that when the view is loaded, the service will be invoked and the result will be populated into the `ListBox` control. This action is demonstrated in Listing 7-38.

LISTING 7-38: Calling the Service1 web service

```csharp
using System.Collections.Generic;
using System.Windows;
using System.Windows.Controls;
using SilverlightWcfConsumer.DestinationsService;

namespace SilverlightWcfConsumer
```

```
    {
        public partial class MainPage : UserControl
        {
            public MainPage()
            {
                InitializeComponent();

                IslandsClient client = new IslandsClient();

                client.GetIslandsCompleted += client_GetIslandsCompleted;
                client.GetIslandsAsync();
            }

            private void client_GetIslandsCompleted(object sender,
                GetIslandsCompletedEventArgs e)
            {
                if (e.Error != null)
                {
                    MessageBox.Show(e.Error.Message);
                }
                else
                {
                    ICollection<Destination> result = e.Result;

                    foreach (var destination in result)
                    {
                        listBox1.Items.Add(destination.Name);
                    }
                }
            }
        }
    }
```

This code is quite similar to what is done when working with web references from the XML Web Services world. First is an instantiation of the proxy class, as shown with the creation of the svc object:

```
    IslandsClient client = new IslandsClient();
```

Working with the client object now, the IntelliSense options provide you with the appropriate GetIslandsAsync() and GetIslandsCompleted() methods. Remember that with Silverlight, you are not allowed to invoke services synchronously.

Working with REST-Based Services

It is very easy to build REST-based services using .NET. Using WCF Data Services, you can quickly expose interactions with the application's underlying data source as RESTful-based services. The current version of WCF Data Services allows you to work with the data stores using JSON or Atom-based XML.

WCF Data Services works to create a services layer to your back-end data source. Doing so yourself, especially if you are working with a full CRUD model, means a lot of work. WCF Data Services allow you to get a service layer that is URI-driven.

To work through the creation and consumption of a REST-based service, create a typical Silverlight application called SilverlightRest. This will also create the standard SilverlightRest.Web project within the same solution. This is where you will put the WCF Data Service.

Creating a WCF Data Service

Figuring out how to build a complete services layer to your database for all create, read, update, and delete functions would take some serious time and thought. However, WCF Data Services makes this task much more feasible, as you will see as you work through this example.

Because this example of a WCF Data Service works from an underlying database, you will need to add one. For this example, add the `AdventureWorks_Data.mdf` database as you previously used in this chapter. Place this database within the App_Data folder of your project.

Adding Your Entity Data Model

After you have the database in place, you next create an Entity Data Model that WCF Data Services will work with. To do this, right-click your project and select Add ➪ New Item from the list of options in the provided menu.

The Add New Item dialog appears. Add an ADO.NET Entity Data Model to your project. Name your ADO.NET Entity Data Model file `AdventureWorks.edmx`. When you create the `AdventureWorks.edmx` file by clicking Add, the Entity Data Model Wizard appears, offering you the option of creating an empty EDM or creating one from a pre-existing database (shown in Figure 7-16).

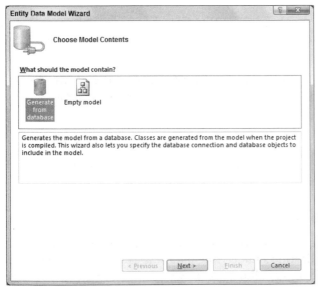

FIGURE 7-16

For this example, choose the option to create one from the pre-existing (AdventureWorks_Data) database (shown in Figure 7-17). Then click Next.

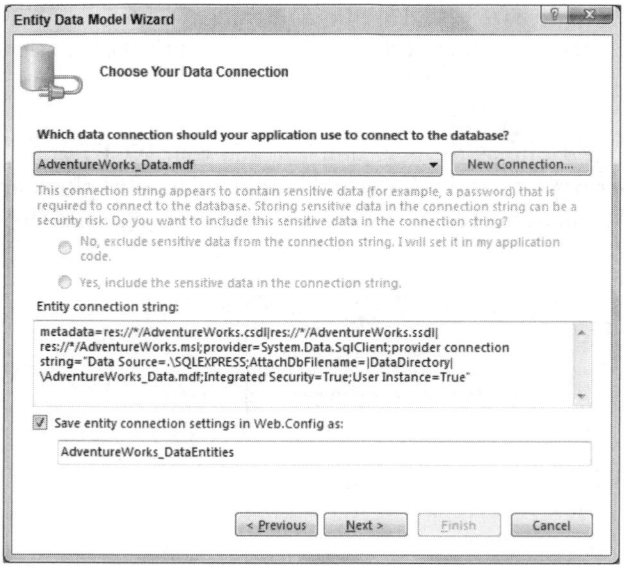

FIGURE 7-17

In Figure 7-17, notice that the connection string and the locations of the mapping details will be stored within the `Web.config` file. You can also see on this screen that you are naming the instance of the model **AdventureWorks_DataEntities** in the text box at the bottom of the wizard. This name is important to note because you will use it later in this example.

The next screen allows you to select the tables, views, or stored procedures that will be part of the model (Figure 7-18). For this example, select the checkbox next to the Table item in the tree view to select all the tables in the database.

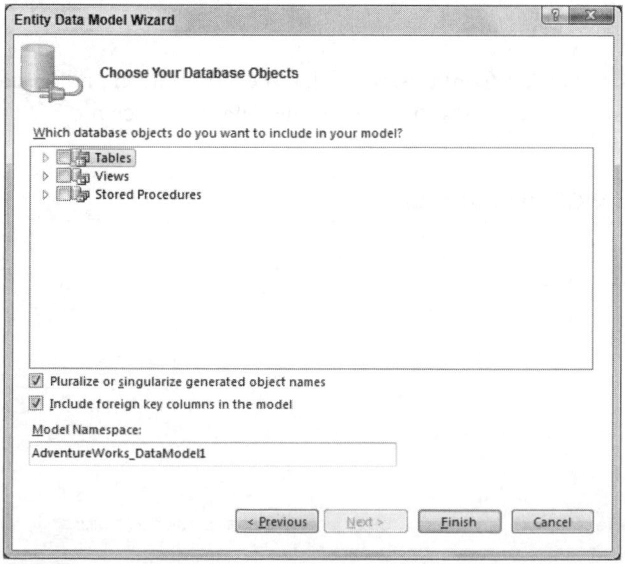

FIGURE 7-18

After selecting the Tables checkbox, click Finish to have Visual Studio create the EDM for you. You will notice that Visual Studio creates a visual representation of the model for you in the O/R Designer.

Creating the Service

Now that the EDM is in place along with the database, the next step is to add your WCF Data Service. To accomplish this, right-click your project within the Visual Studio Solution Explorer and select Add ⇨ New Item from the provided menu. The Add New Item dialog appears again; select WCF Data Service as shown in Figure 7-19.

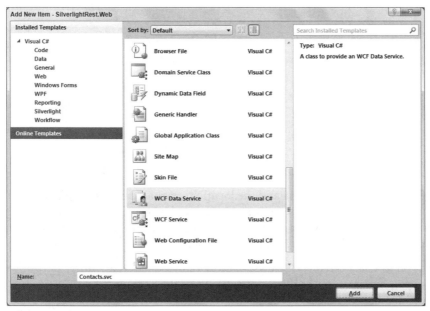

FIGURE 7-19

As shown in the figure, name your WCF Data Service **Contacts.svc**. Click the Add button and Visual Studio generates a WCF service for you. Listing 7-39 shows the code of the default service file.

LISTING 7-39: The default .svc file for a WCF Data Service

```
using System;
using System.Collections.Generic;
using System.Data.Services;
using System.Data.Services.Common;
using System.Linq;
using System.ServiceModel.Web;
using System.Web;

namespace SilverlightRest.Web
{
    public class Contacts : DataService< /* TODO: put your data source class
                                            name here */ >
    {
```

```
            // This method is called only once to initialize service-wide policies.
            public static void InitializeService(DataServiceConfiguration config)
            {
                // TODO: set rules to indicate which entity sets and service
                // operations are visible, updatable, etc.
                // Examples:
                // config.SetEntitySetAccessRule("MyEntityset",
                //     EntitySetRights.AllRead);
                // config.SetServiceOperationAccessRule("MyServiceOperation",
                //     ServiceOperationRights.All);
                config.DataServiceBehavior.MaxProtocolVersion =
                    DataServiceProtocolVersion.V2;
            }
        }
    }
```

The code generated here is the base framework for what you are going to expose through WCF Data Services. It will not work, however, until you accomplish the big TODO that the code specifies. The first step is to put in the name of the EDM instance using the code presented in Listing 7-40.

LISTING 7-40: Changing the WCF Data Service to work with your EDM

```
namespace SilverlightRest.Web
{
    public class Contacts : DataService<AdventureWorks_DataEntities>
    {
        // Code removed for clarity
    }
}
```

Now your application is at a state in which the database, the EDM, and the service to work with the EDM are in place. Upon compiling and pulling up the `NorthwindDataService.svc` file in the browser, you are presented with the following bit of XML:

```
<?xml version="1.0" encoding="utf-8" standalone="yes" ?>
<service xml:base="http://localhost:14057/Contacts.svc/"
 xmlns:atom="http://www.w3.org/2005/Atom"
 xmlns:app="http://www.w3.org/2007/app"
 xmlns="http://www.w3.org/2007/app">
  <workspace>
    <atom:title>Default</atom:title>
  </workspace>
</service>
```

If you don't see this XML, you need to turn off the feed-reading capabilities of your IE browser by selecting Tools ➪ Internet Options. From the provided dialog, select the Content tab and within the Feeds section, click the Select button. From there, uncheck the Turn on Feed Reading checkbox.

The result of the earlier XML is supposed to be a list of all the available sets that are present in the model, but by default, WCF Data Services locks everything down. To unlock these sets from the model, go back to the `InitializeService()` function and add the following bolded code as illustrated in Listing 7-41.

LISTING 7-41: Opening up the service for reading from the available tables

```
using System.Data.Services;
using System.Data.Services.Common;

namespace SilverlightRest.Web
{
    public class Contacts : DataService<AdventureWorks_DataEntities>
    {
        public static void InitializeService(DataServiceConfiguration config)
        {
            config.SetEntitySetAccessRule("*", EntitySetRights.AllRead);
            config.DataServiceBehavior.MaxProtocolVersion =
                DataServiceProtocolVersion.V2;
        }
    }
}
```

In this case, every table is opened up to access. Everyone who accesses the tables can read from them but they can't write or delete them. All tables are specified through the use of the asterisk (*) and the right to the underlying data is set to read-only through the `EntitySetRights` enum being set to `AllRead`.

Now when you compile and run this service in the browser, you see the following bit of XML:

```
<?xml version="1.0" encoding="utf-8" standalone="yes" ?>
<service xml:base="http://localhost:14057/Contacts.svc/"
 xmlns:atom="http://www.w3.org/2005/Atom"
 xmlns:app="http://www.w3.org/2007/app" xmlns="http://www.w3.org/2007/app">
<workspace>
  <atom:title>Default</atom:title>
    <collection href="Addresses">
      <atom:title>Addresses</atom:title>
    </collection>
    <collection href="AddressTypes">
      <atom:title>AddressTypes</atom:title>
    </collection>
    <collection href="Contacts">
      <atom:title>Contacts</atom:title>
    </collection>
    <collection href="ContactTypes">
      <atom:title>ContactTypes</atom:title>
    </collection>
    <collection href="CountryRegions">
      <atom:title>CountryRegions</atom:title>
    </collection>
    <collection href="StateProvinces">
      <atom:title>StateProvinces</atom:title>
    </collection>
  </workspace>
  </service>
```

Consuming the WCF Data Service in Silverlight

The next step is to consume this REST-based service. Keep in mind that consuming a WCF Data Service in all types of .NET applications is obviously possible, but this chapter focuses on using this technology within Silverlight itself.

To start, change the UI of the `MainPage.xaml` page so that it is similar to Listing 7-42.

LISTING 7-42: The XAML from MainPage.xaml

```xaml
<UserControl x:Class="SilverlightRest.MainPage"
    xmlns="http://schemas.microsoft.com/winfx/2006/xaml/presentation"
    xmlns:x="http://schemas.microsoft.com/winfx/2006/xaml"
    xmlns:d="http://schemas.microsoft.com/expression/blend/2008"
    xmlns:mc="http://schemas.openxmlformats.org/markup-compatibility/2006"
    mc:Ignorable="d"
    d:DesignHeight="300" d:DesignWidth="400">

    <Grid x:Name="LayoutRoot" Background="White">
        <ListBox Height="276" HorizontalAlignment="Left" Margin="12,12,0,0"
          Name="listBox1" VerticalAlignment="Top" Width="376">
            <ListBox.ItemTemplate>
                <DataTemplate>
                    <StackPanel Orientation="Horizontal">
                        <TextBlock Text="{Binding FirstName}" Margin="3" />
                        <TextBlock Text="{Binding LastName}" Margin="3" />
                    </StackPanel>
                </DataTemplate>
            </ListBox.ItemTemplate>
        </ListBox>
    </Grid>
</UserControl>
```

With this in place, you then want to make a standard Service reference to the service. Figure 7-20 shows the Add Service Reference dialog.

FIGURE 7-20

Once added, the code-behind of the `MainPage.xaml` page is presented in Listing 7-43.

LISTING 7-43: The code-behind for MainPage.xaml

```csharp
using System;
using System.Data.Services.Client;
using System.Linq;
using System.Windows.Controls;
using SilverlightRest.ContactsRest;

namespace SilverlightRest
{
    public partial class MainPage : UserControl
    {
        private readonly DataServiceCollection<Contact> _contacts;

        public MainPage()
        {
            InitializeComponent();

            AdventureWorks_DataEntities svc =
                new AdventureWorks_DataEntities(new
                    Uri("http://localhost:14057/Contacts.svc"));
            _contacts = new DataServiceCollection<Contact>();
            _contacts.LoadCompleted += contacts_LoadCompleted;

            var query = from c in svc.Contacts
                        orderby c.LastName
                        select c;

            _contacts.LoadAsync(query);
        }

        private void contacts_LoadCompleted(object sender,
            LoadCompletedEventArgs e)
        {
            if (_contacts.Continuation != null)
            {
                _contacts.LoadNextPartialSetAsync();
            }
            else
            {
                listBox1.ItemsSource = _contacts;
                listBox1.UpdateLayout();
            }
        }
    }
}
```

When you run this page, you are presented with an alphabetical list of the contacts in the database.

SUMMARY

Silverlight truly provides the core infrastructure needed to allow pervasive data in your applications. Silverlight makes few assumptions about where your data lives and the format it takes, which opens up exciting opportunities to work with data across a variety of platforms and from disparate providers.

You should now be able to retrieve data from Silverlight, provide compelling data-bound interfaces with bindings, and work with a wide variety of different service layer types. The core options for accessing and manipulating data presented in this chapter are a great foundation for exploring the wealth of options available to all Silverlight developers.

8

WCF RIA Services

WHAT'S IN THIS CHAPTER?

➤ Working with entity data models

➤ Using domain services

➤ Paging content

➤ Filtering content

If you are building a business application that needs to move content from servers down to your Silverlight application, WCF RIA Services is going to be one of the most important resources in your arsenal. WCF RIA Services provides your presentation tier with quick and easy access to the services and data that are made available from the middle tier of your larger application.

Many of the developers that are making their way into the Silverlight ranks are from the ASP.NET world, where dealing with logic and data between the tiers was quite a bit simpler. In the ASP.NET world, it was simpler because the presentation tier and the middle tier were usually on the same server, or even in the same co-location. The generated presentation tier, once completed, and after working with the middle tier for any type of logic or data, was then shot down to the client as HTML, JavaScript, and the like. Any further interactions between the client and the middle tier could then be done with a complete page refresh, or using AJAX to make connections to the middle tier in the cloud.

Silverlight brings a more stark separation between the presentation and middle tiers of your application. The code for the application is actually residing on the client. The client then will need to have a means to communicate back to the middle tier for the logic and data that are required. WCF RIA Services is a means to make the process of n-tier communications between what is on the client and what is back on your server just that much easier. Specifically designed for rich Internet applications, this new approach is something that will make it easier for you to bring these two tiers closer together.

UNDERSTANDING WCF RIA SERVICES

Again, most people are quite used to working in various web technologies where you will find the close proximity of the presentation tier and the middle tier is quite advantageous. An example of this is shown in Figure 8-1.

From this figure, you can see that traditional applications created and manipulated the presentation within the presentation tier and then, in effect, shipped down the finalized UI to the client to be displayed (for example, in the browser).

Silverlight changes all of this. Now the client is running the application code on the client and, for the most part, the entire presentation tier is residing on the client as well. This means that the client will need to somehow interact over the Internet to deal with the middle tier and, in turn, gain access to the data tier. This model is shown in Figure 8-2.

From this figure, you can see that the presentation tier is now on the client and WCF RIA Services is the glue between the middle tier and this presentation tier. Really, there is still a gap between the middle tier and the presentation tier, but now with WCF RIA Services, you have a programmatic view that they are still in the same place.

WCF RIA Services is exactly what the name states. It is a technology, like WCF Data Services, that is built upon the Windows Communication Foundation stack. Though WCF RIA Services works to simplify your life as a developer and make it easy to work with your data and capabilities up and down the application stack, it still does provide you with the capabilities you might need to dig deep into WCF and take full advantage of everything that WCF brings to the table. Using WCF RIA Services does not limit you in your abilities in working with WCF overall. The nice thing, though, is that if you have usually found that WCF was complex to begin with and you are not

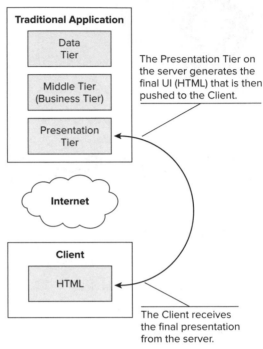

The Presentation Tier on the server generates the final UI (HTML) that is then pushed to the Client.

The Client receives the final presentation from the server.

FIGURE 8-1

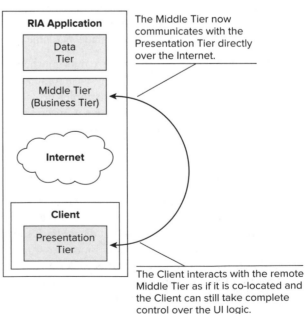

The Middle Tier now communicates with the Presentation Tier directly over the Internet.

The Client interacts with the remote Middle Tier as if it is co-located and the Client can still take complete control over the UI logic.

FIGURE 8-2

too interested in digging in the weeds of this technology, you will still like working with WCF RIA Services because it works to obfuscate this complexity from you as best as possible.

BUILDING A SIMPLE RIA SERVICES APPLICATION

At the time of this writing, WCF RIA Services is a separate download that you can find at www.silverlight.net/getstarted/riaservices. On this page, you will find the Visual Studio additions that you need to install to work through the examples in this chapter.

Once installed, you will find some new WCF RIA Service capabilities contained within Visual Studio. The example in this chapter uses Visual Studio 2010. For the first step in creating a project that works with this new technology, open up Visual Studio and create a new Silverlight project that is going to work with WCF RIA Services. To do this, select File ➪ New ➪ Project from the Visual Studio menu. The New Project dialog appears. Select Silverlight from the list of installed templates and you will see a list of your Silverlight project options, as shown in Figure 8-3.

FIGURE 8-3

If you just installed the WCF RIA Services, you will notice some new options. One new project option is the Silverlight Business Application. This is a sample WCF RIA Services business application. Another option is the WCF RIA Services Class Library. This option allows you to create a project that is a WCF RIA Services class library that can then be utilized by any of your Silverlight applications.

Select the option Silverlight Business Application project. By default, the name of the project is BusinessApplication1. For this example, you can keep this in place.

Reviewing the Business Application Solution

Once you have created the BusinessApplication1 solution, you will find two projects for this. The two projects and the entire output of this project, as shown in the Visual Studio Solution Explorer, are shown in Figure 8-4.

BusinessApplication1 is the Silverlight application, and BusinessApplication1.Web is the server-side solution that will contain your WCF RIA Services. At this point, there is not a WCF RIA Service in place to work with, because you will have to construct that portion yourself.

However, you will notice that a stub of an application is in place for you. Microsoft built out a sample application in a structure that it deems appropriate for working with WCF RIA Services. This is an approach Microsoft likes to call a "prescriptive architecture" — or an architecture that it prescribes to developers building applications using its technologies. You as the developer can follow this prescription, but you can also rip it apart and set things up exactly as you see fit.

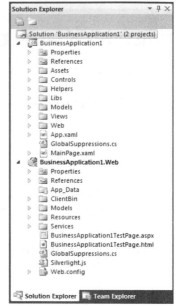

FIGURE 8-4

If you compile and run the BusinessApplication1 as it is now, you will notice (shown in Figure 8-5) that you are presented with a basic Silverlight application with some basic navigation. At this point, no WCF RIA Services are being utilized. The next step is to change that and build a WCF RIA Service within this solution.

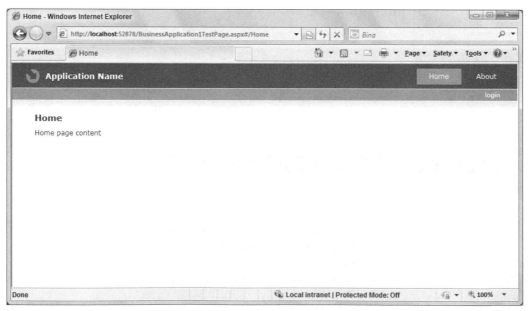

FIGURE 8-5

Building an Entity Data Model

The first step is to build an entity data model and expose that model out from the server-side solution. You are not always required to use entity data models to work with WCF RIA Services. You are also able to use LINQ to SQL, plain old XML (POX) objects, and standard-based web services. For this example, you build a WCF RIA Service that makes use of the entity framework.

To accomplish this task, you first need to add a data store to work with. The one used in a few places within this book is the Microsoft AdventureWorks sample database located at msftdbprodsamples .codeplex.com. Add the AdventureWorks database to the App_Data folder within the project, as shown in Figure 8-6.

FIGURE 8-6

Once you have the database in place, add an ADO.NET Entity Data Model to your project. You will find this in the Data section of installed templates within Visual Studio 2010. Name your ADO.NET Entity Data Model **AdventureWorks.edmx** as shown in Figure 8-7.

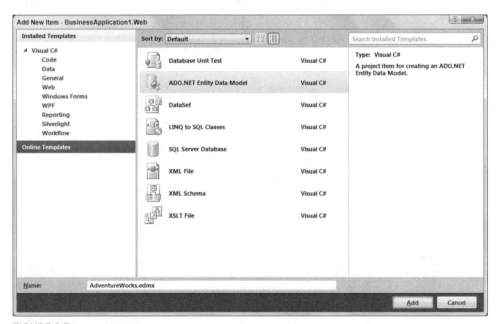

FIGURE 8-7

Click the Add button in the Add New Item dialog and the Entity Data Model Wizard appears (shown in Figure 8-8).

You can create your entity models directly from code or from reading and understanding the contents of a database. In this case, make sure that you choose the database option. Clicking the Next button in the dialog presents you with the second step of the wizard, as shown in Figure 8-9.

In this screen, select the underlying data store that you are using. You will notice that the connection string is defined for you and you can choose to name the connection string within the project's Web.config file. Click Next.

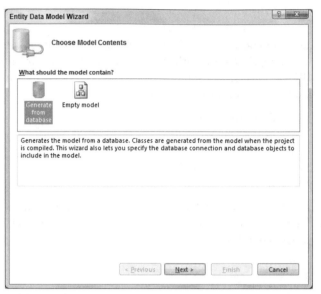

FIGURE 8-8

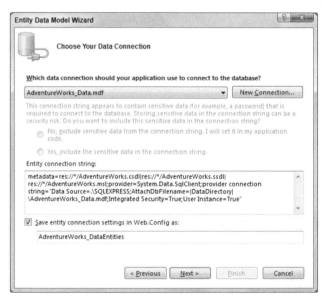

FIGURE 8-9

On the next screen of the wizard, select the database objects that you want to be a part of the model that you are creating. In this case, select all the tables associated with the Human Resources section of the database. This is shown in Figure 8-10.

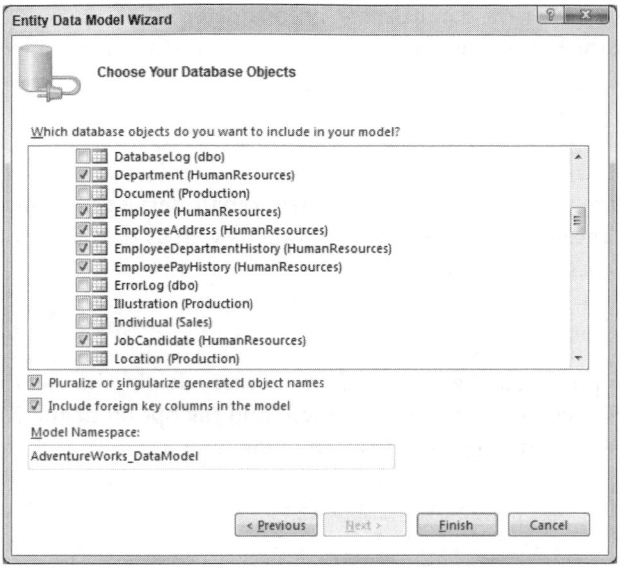

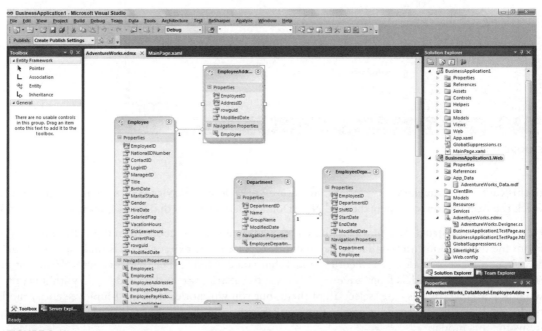

FIGURE 8-10

In addition, you can see from this figure that you also need to provide a model namespace. In this case, it is named `AdventureWorks_DataModel`.

Click Finish. You are presented with a visual view of your model directly in Visual Studio. This view is shown in Figure 8-11.

FIGURE 8-11

You will also notice that the connection string for the database has been added to the `Web.config` file as was stated in the wizard. Now that the entity model is in place, compile the application. Now you are ready to build the Domain Service.

Building a Domain Service

Now that you have the entity model in place, it's time to build your first domain service. A domain service allows you to expose the pieces of the entity models that you want as well as the operations over those models that you need for your client application.

Adding the Domain Service Class

Working in the BusinessApplication1.Web project, add a Domain Service Class. Right-click on the project and choose the option to add a new item to the project. You will find the option to add a Domain Service Class within the Add New Item dialog, as illustrated in Figure 8-12.

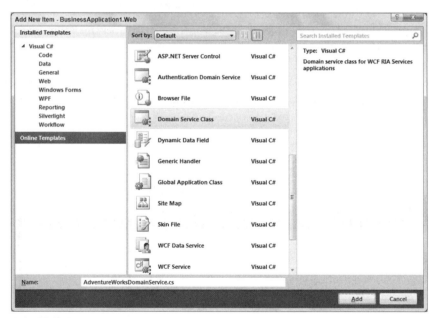

FIGURE 8-12

In this case, name the data service class **AdventureWorksDomainService.cs** as shown in Figure 8-12. Click the Add button to display the Add New Domain Service Class dialog, as shown in Figure 8-13.

Here you are constructing a new class based on what you want to get at from the entity model. From the dialog, you can see that the `AdventureWorksDomainService` class is making use of the `AdventureWorks_DataEntities` entity model that you created earlier in this chapter. Visual Studio reads all the entity models from `AdventureWorks_DataEntities` and provides you with a list of what is available. In this case, select all of them, but you will notice that the Employee entity model is also enabled for editing. This means that you are exposing the ability to insert, update, or delete items for this model.

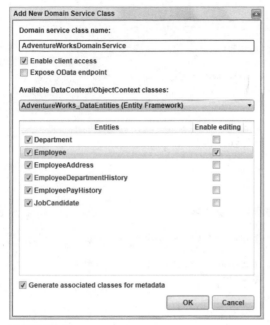

FIGURE 8-13

The other important item to pay attention to in this dialog is the checkbox to enable client access to the domain service. Make sure that this is checked in order for your Silverlight client to get access to what is being constructed here.

Click the OK button in this dialog to produce a new class file within your project, AdventureWorksDomainService.cs. This new class file is presented in Listing 8-1.

LISTING 8-1: The new domain service class — AdventureWorksDomainService.cs

```
namespace BusinessApplication1.Web
{
    using System;
    using System.Collections.Generic;
    using System.ComponentModel;
    using System.ComponentModel.DataAnnotations;
    using System.Data;
    using System.Linq;
    using System.ServiceModel.DomainServices.EntityFramework;
    using System.ServiceModel.DomainServices.Hosting;
    using System.ServiceModel.DomainServices.Server;

    // Also consider adding roles to restrict access as appropriate.
    // [RequiresAuthentication]
    [EnableClientAccess()]
    public class AdventureWorksDomainService :
```

continues

LISTING 8-1 *(continued)*

```
LinqToEntitiesDomainService<AdventureWorks_DataEntities>
{
    public IQueryable<Department> GetDepartments()
    {
        return this.ObjectContext.Departments;
    }

    public IQueryable<Employee> GetEmployees()
    {
        return this.ObjectContext.Employees;
    }

    public void InsertEmployee(Employee employee)
    {
        if ((employee.EntityState != EntityState.Detached))
        {
            this.ObjectContext.ObjectStateManager.ChangeObjectState
              (employee, EntityState.Added);
        }
        else
        {
            this.ObjectContext.Employees.AddObject(employee);
        }
    }

    public void UpdateEmployee(Employee currentEmployee)
    {
        this.ObjectContext.Employees.AttachAsModified(currentEmployee,
            this.ChangeSet.GetOriginal(currentEmployee));
    }

    public void DeleteEmployee(Employee employee)
    {
        if ((employee.EntityState == EntityState.Detached))
        {
            this.ObjectContext.Employees.Attach(employee);
        }
        this.ObjectContext.Employees.DeleteObject(employee);
    }

    public IQueryable<EmployeeAddress> GetEmployeeAddresses()
    {
        return this.ObjectContext.EmployeeAddresses;
    }

    public IQueryable<EmployeeDepartmentHistory>
       GetEmployeeDepartmentHistories()
    {
        return this.ObjectContext.EmployeeDepartmentHistories;
```

```
        }

        public IQueryable<EmployeePayHistory> GetEmployeePayHistories()
        {
            return this.ObjectContext.EmployeePayHistories;
        }

        public IQueryable<JobCandidate> GetJobCandidates()
        {
            return this.ObjectContext.JobCandidates;
        }
    }
}
```

Many of the code comments were removed from this code, but this is a class file generated for you that exposes out the objects you chose from your entity model. You can see that this class file makes use of the underlying RIA Services framework using the `System.ServiceModel.DomainServices` namespace.

While looking at what is presented in the class structure, you should make note of some important items.

```
[EnableClientAccess()]
public class AdventureWorksDomainService :
    LinqToEntitiesDomainService<AdventureWorks_DataEntities>
{

    // Code removed for clarity

}
```

First, the class that is created for you is called `AdventureWorksDomainService` and it inherits from an abstract base class called `LinqToEntitiesDomainService<T>`. The `LinqToEntitiesDomainService<T>` is part of the RIA Services framework and will expose the entity model you want. You put the entity model in place of `<T>` and in this case, it becomes `LinqToEntitiesDomainService<AdventureWorks_DataEntities>`. Remember that `AdventureWorks_DataEntities` was something that you built earlier in this chapter.

The other important aspect of this is that this class has been enabled for client access (from checking the checkbox earlier from the Add New Domain Service Class dialog). This is accomplished by adding the class attribute `[EnableClientAccess()]` to the class.

Looking into the class, you can see that a series of methods have been created for you that expose the entities from the model. The first one (the one that you work with in this example), is the `GetEmployees()` method as shown here:

```
public IQueryable<Employee> GetEmployees()
{
    return this.ObjectContext.Employees;
}
```

You can see from this code snippet that the `GetEmployees()` method call returns an `IQueryable<T>` interface of `IQueryable<Employee>`, which is a list of employees. `IQueryable<T>` is from the `System.Linq` namespace. From this bit of code, you can see it returned all the employees found in the table. You could, if you wanted, change the output to provide any filtering or sorting to what is output directly in this method.

Reviewing the Operations

In addition to the `GetEmployees()` method call, because you have checked the edit option when setting up the class you are provided with `Insert`, `Update`, and `Delete` options for the `Employees` object as well:

```
public void InsertEmployee(Employee employee)
{

    // Code removed for clarity

}

public void UpdateEmployee(Employee currentEmployee)
{

    // Code removed for clarity

}

public void DeleteEmployee(Employee employee)
{

    // Code removed for clarity

}
```

Once you have the domain service in place, compile your solution. Now that this is in place, it is time to turn your attention to the client application.

Connecting the Silverlight Client to Your Domain Service

At this point, everything is in place on the server-side project. This project now includes an entity model and the model is exposed to the client through a domain service. Working with BusinessApplication1 now, you can make the connection to this domain service.

Start by displaying a full list of the employees from the Employee table using the `GetEmployees()` method call. To do this, create a new Silverlight page called `Employees.xaml`. Place this view within the Views folder along with the `About.xaml` and the `Home.xaml` files.

You can open both the `About.xaml` and the `Home.xaml` files to look at how you want to set up the `Employees.xaml` page to make it fit in with the rest of the application. At the end of the day, you want the `Employees.xaml` page to show a grid of all the employees that are provided via the domain service. The `Employees.xaml` page is presented in Listing 8-2.

LISTING 8-2: The page to present a list of employees

```xml
<navigation:Page
  xmlns:my="clr-namespace:System.Windows.Controls;
            assembly=System.Windows.Controls.Data"
  xmlns:sdk="clr-namespace:System.Windows.Controls;
            assembly=System.Windows.Controls.Data.Input"
  x:Class="BusinessApplication1.Employees"
            xmlns="http://schemas.microsoft.com/winfx/2006/xaml/presentation"
            xmlns:x="http://schemas.microsoft.com/winfx/2006/xaml"
            xmlns:d="http://schemas.microsoft.com/expression/blend/2008"
            xmlns:mc="http://schemas.openxmlformats.org/markup-compatibility/2006"
            mc:Ignorable="d"
            xmlns:navigation="clr-namespace:System.Windows.Controls;
              assembly=System.Windows.Controls.Navigation"
            d:DesignWidth="640" d:DesignHeight="480"
            Title="Employees Page">
    <Grid x:Name="LayoutRoot">
        <ScrollViewer x:Name="PageScrollViewer"
         Style="{StaticResource PageScrollViewerStyle}">

            <StackPanel x:Name="ContentStackPanel"
              Style="{StaticResource ContentStackPanelStyle}">

                <TextBlock x:Name="HeaderText"
                  Style="{StaticResource HeaderTextStyle}"
                           Text="Employees"/>

                <my:DataGrid x:Name="gridEmployees" />

            </StackPanel>

        </ScrollViewer>
    </Grid>
</navigation:Page>
```

From this, you can see that there is not much to this page besides some header text and a `DataGrid` control. The `DataGrid` control's name is `gridEmployees`.

Connecting the Two Solutions

With this in place, now you can turn your attention to the code-behind for this page. The first step is to add a new `using` statement to the top of the code-behind file. At the bottom of the list of `using` statements, add a reference to the other project as illustrated in Listing 8-3.

LISTING 8-3: Adding a using statement to BusinessApplication1.Web

```csharp
using System;
using System.Collections.Generic;
using System.Linq;
using System.Net;
```

continues

LISTING 8-3 *(continued)*

```
using System.Windows;
using System.Windows.Controls;
using System.Windows.Documents;
using System.Windows.Input;
using System.Windows.Media;
using System.Windows.Media.Animation;
using System.Windows.Shapes;
using System.Windows.Navigation;
using BusinessApplication1.Web;
```

Once you have this in place, compile the entire solution. Then you have made the tie between the client and the server applications in regard to the domain service.

You probably are looking now to see what changed in your client project. It appears as if nothing changed when looking at the project directly in Visual Studio. However, you can see the changes that were made directly to the BusinessApplication1 project by clicking the Show All Files button from the toolbar of the Visual Studio Solution Explorer. You are then presented with what is shown in Figure 8-14.

Looking over this image from Figure 8-14, you can see that there is a new folder now called Generated_Code. Contained within this folder is a file called `BusinessApplication1 .Web.g.cs`. This file contains all the methods that interact with the methods from the domain service. It also contains the entity models that were defined.

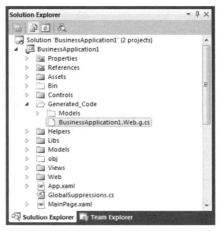

FIGURE 8-14

You will see a lot in this class — too much to show here (it is more than 3,000 lines of code). Some interesting parts, though, are that you can see some overloaded `DomainContext` instances:

```
public AdventureWorksDomainContext() :
            this(new WebDomainClient<IAdventureWorksDomainServiceContract>
            (new
            Uri("BusinessApplication1-Web-AdventureWorksDomainService.svc",
            UriKind.Relative)))
{
}
```

Also, within the `IAdventureWorksDomainServiceContract`, you can see the asynchronous service calls such as `BeginGetEmployees()` and `EndGetEmployees()`:

```
/// <summary>
/// Asynchronously invokes the 'GetEmployees' operation.
/// </summary>
/// <param name="callback">Callback to invoke on completion.</param>
/// <param name="asyncState">Optional state object.</param>
```

```
/// <returns>An IAsyncResult that can be used to monitor the request.</returns>
[FaultContract(typeof(DomainServiceFault),
 Action="http://tempuri.org/AdventureWorksDomainService/
 GetEmployeesDomainServiceFault", Name="DomainServiceFault",
 Namespace="DomainServices")]
[OperationContract(AsyncPattern=true,
 Action="http://tempuri.org/AdventureWorksDomainService/GetEmployees",
 ReplyAction=
   "http://tempuri.org/AdventureWorksDomainService/GetEmployeesResponse")]
[WebGet()]
IAsyncResult BeginGetEmployees(AsyncCallback callback, object asyncState);

/// <summary>
/// Completes the asynchronous operation begun by 'BeginGetEmployees'.
/// </summary>
///<param name="result">The IAsyncResult returned from 'BeginGetEmployees'.</param>
///<returns>The 'QueryResult' returned from the 'GetEmployees' operation.</returns>
QueryResult<Employee> EndGetEmployees(IAsyncResult result);
```

Working with the Domain Context

You will find a lot more in the `BusinessApplication1.Web.g.cs` class. Now, you can make use of this in the code-behind of your `Employees.xaml` file. This is accomplished in Listing 8-4.

LISTING 8-4: Employess.xaml.cs

```csharp
using System.Windows;
using System.Windows.Controls;
using System.Windows.Navigation;
using BusinessApplication1.Web;

namespace BusinessApplication1
{
    public partial class Employees : Page
    {
        public Employees()
        {
            InitializeComponent();
            Loaded += Employees_Loaded;
        }

        private void Employees_Loaded(object sender, RoutedEventArgs e)
        {
            AdventureWorksDomainContext context = new
              AdventureWorksDomainContext();
            gridEmployees.ItemsSource = context.Employees;
            context.Load(context.GetEmployeesQuery());
        }
    }
}
```

In this case, create an instance of the `AdventureWorksDomainContext` and assign the `DataGrid` control's `ItemsSource` property to the value of `context.Employees`. From there, load the `context` object with a query to `GetEmployeesQuery()`. This will load everything in the entity model based on what was defined earlier in this chapter.

As you work with the code in the `Employees_Loaded()` method, you will notice that from the context object, you have everything you would expect via IntelliSense as illustrated in Figure 8-15.

FIGURE 8-15

When you run this code, you will notice the pause as the content gets loaded into the view, but once loaded, you are presented with something similar to what is presented in Figure 8-16.

WCF RIA Services allowed the client to make a service call to a remote service location and get at content and capabilities that resided on the server. The nice thing about this was that in working in code within the client project, it was as if you were working with local objects rather than through a service layer. You can see from this example just how simple WCF RIA Services makes the entire process.

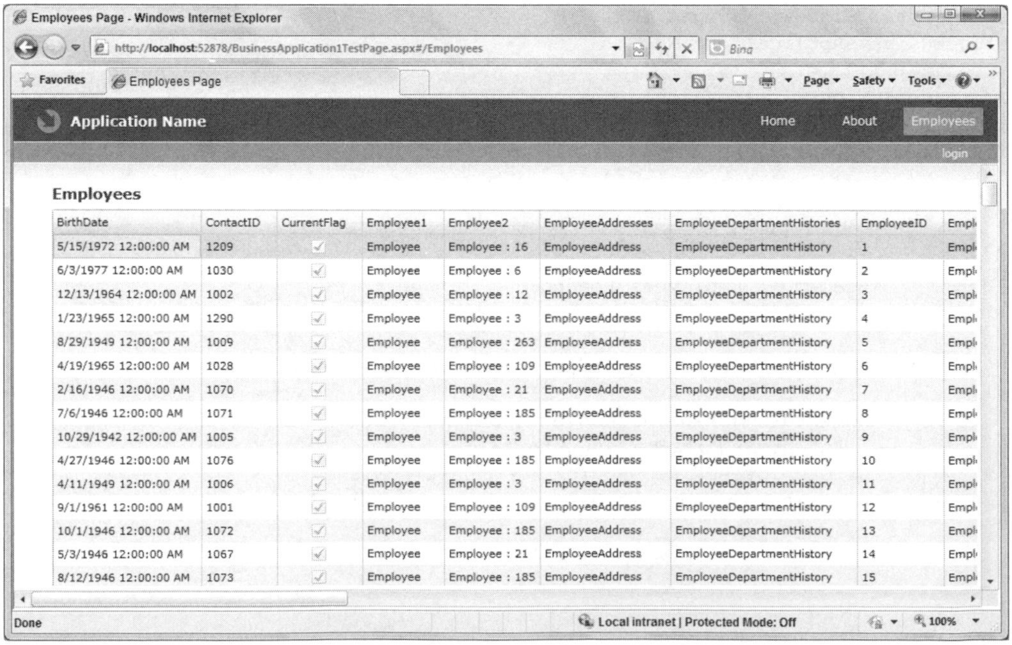

FIGURE 8-16

Connecting to the Domain Service through XAML

So far, you have seen what it is to connect with the domain service through code and work with the underlying data that is retrieved. The next step is to look at solving much of the same problem, except this time you will be doing it using declarative coding using XAML.

Creating Your Entity Data Model

For this example, create a new entity data model within the same BusinessApplication1.Web project. Call this model **Customers.edmx**. Attach only the Customer table from the Adventure Works database. This gives you a simple data model as presented in Figure 8-17.

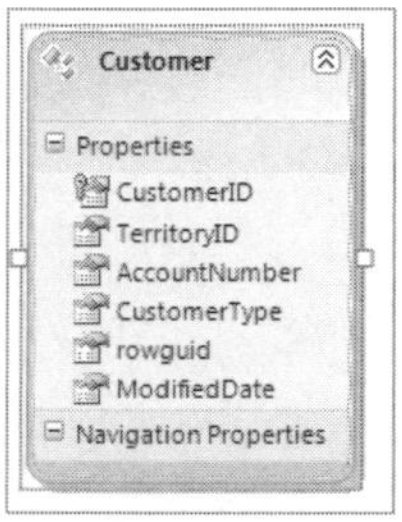

Creating the Domain Service

When you have created this entity data model, be sure to compile the solution first before proceeding with any additional steps. With this data model in place and available throughout the application, it's time to create your domain service. Create a new domain service and give it the name of CustomerDomainService.cs. When you are presented with the dialog of the entities that you are going to want to work with in creating this domain service, you will notice that there are now two options contained within the drop-down. Select the one that contains the Customer table and check the Edit box to enable it for editing.

FIGURE 8-17

From there, open the CustomerDomainService.cs class file and make a small change. Listing 8-5 shows you in bold the change you must make to the generated file.

LISTING 8-5: Having the customers come out of the database ordered by their account number

```csharp
namespace BusinessApplication1.Web
{
    using System;
    using System.Collections.Generic;
    using System.ComponentModel;
    using System.ComponentModel.DataAnnotations;
    using System.Data;
    using System.Linq;
    using System.ServiceModel.DomainServices.EntityFramework;
    using System.ServiceModel.DomainServices.Hosting;
    using System.ServiceModel.DomainServices.Server;

    [EnableClientAccess()]
    public class CustomerDomainService :
       LinqToEntitiesDomainService<AdventureWorks_DataEntities1>
    {
        public IQueryable<Customer> GetCustomers()
        {
            return this.ObjectContext.Customers.OrderBy(c => c.AccountNumber);
        }

        public void InsertCustomer(Customer customer)
```

continues

LISTING 8-5 *(continued)*

```
    {
        if ((customer.EntityState != EntityState.Detached))
        {
            this.ObjectContext.ObjectStateManager.ChangeObjectState(customer,
            EntityState.Added);
        }
        else
        {
            this.ObjectContext.Customers.AddObject(customer);
        }
    }

    public void UpdateCustomer(Customer currentCustomer)
    {
        this.ObjectContext.Customers.AttachAsModified(currentCustomer,
            this.ChangeSet.GetOriginal(currentCustomer));
    }

    public void DeleteCustomer(Customer customer)
    {
        if ((customer.EntityState == EntityState.Detached))
        {
            this.ObjectContext.Customers.Attach(customer);
        }
        this.ObjectContext.Customers.DeleteObject(customer);
    }
    }
}
```

In this small change of code, you are returning the customers in the GetCustomers() call so that they are ordered by their account numbers simply by adding OrderBy(c => c.AccountNumber). You need this type of ordering in place when you start paging results as they come out of the service. This is demonstrated shortly.

When you have finished creating the domain service, compile the application one more time.

Creating Customers.xaml

If you have made it this far, the server-side of the solution to work with your customers is accomplished. The next step is to create a new Silverlight page called Customers.xaml. For the purposes of working with this example, place this page with the other pages within the Views folder of the project.

The first step is to get the page to a point where it is like the other pages you have been working with so far. Listing 8-6 provides you with the XAML code to place within this file.

LISTING 8-6: The start of the Customers.xaml page

```xml
<navigation:Page x:Class="BusinessApplication1.Views.Customers"
        xmlns="http://schemas.microsoft.com/winfx/2006/xaml/presentation"
        xmlns:x="http://schemas.microsoft.com/winfx/2006/xaml"
```

```
            xmlns:d="http://schemas.microsoft.com/expression/blend/2008"
            xmlns:mc="http://schemas.openxmlformats.org/markup-compatibility/2006"
            mc:Ignorable="d"
            xmlns:navigation="clr-namespace:System.Windows.Controls;
                assembly=System.Windows.Controls.Navigation"
            d:DesignWidth="640" d:DesignHeight="480"
            Title="Customers Page"
            xmlns:sdk="http://schemas.microsoft.com/
                winfx/2006/xaml/presentation/sdk" >
    <Grid x:Name="LayoutRoot">
        <ScrollViewer x:Name="PageScrollViewer"
         Style="{StaticResource PageScrollViewerStyle}">

            <StackPanel x:Name="ContentStackPanel"
             Style="{StaticResource ContentStackPanelStyle}">

                <TextBlock x:Name="HeaderText"
                 Style="{StaticResource HeaderTextStyle}"
                        Text="Customers"/>
                <sdk:DataGrid Name="dataGrid1" />

            </StackPanel>

        </ScrollViewer>
    </Grid>
</navigation:Page>
```

You will notice that this page is not much different from the other pages you have seen so far. There is a `TextBlock` control on the page and `DataGrid` control that will later contain your list of customers.

When you add the WCF RIA Services to Visual Studio, you will also notice that there is a new control available to you via the Visual Studio Toolbox. Here you will find a control called `DomainDataSource`. For this example, you want to make use of this. To do this, just drag-and-drop the control onto the design surface of your Silverlight page. You will notice that a few changes happened to your XAML code. First, a new namespace was added to deal with the control. Second, you will see the new control on the page:

```
<riaControls:DomainDataSource />
```

The idea here is that you are going to declaratively define the details of the domain service that you are going to work with and tie the `DataGrid` control to this new control on the page. Listing 8-7 shows you the changes you need to make to the `Customers.xaml` page.

LISTING 8-7: Adding a DomainDataSource control to the page

```
<navigation:Page x:Class="BusinessApplication1.Views.Customers"
        xmlns="http://schemas.microsoft.com/winfx/2006/xaml/presentation"
        xmlns:x="http://schemas.microsoft.com/winfx/2006/xaml"
        xmlns:d="http://schemas.microsoft.com/expression/blend/2008"
        xmlns:mc="http://schemas.openxmlformats.org/markup-compatibility/2006"
        mc:Ignorable="d"
```

continues

LISTING 8-7 *(continued)*

```
        xmlns:navigation="clr-namespace:System.Windows.Controls;
          assembly=System.Windows.Controls.Navigation"
        d:DesignWidth="640" d:DesignHeight="480"
        Title="Customers Page" xmlns:sdk="http://schemas.microsoft.com/
                              winfx/2006/xaml/presentation/sdk"
            xmlns:riaControls="clr-namespace:System.Windows.Controls;
              assembly=System.Windows.Controls.DomainServices"
            xmlns:domain="clr-namespace:BusinessApplication1.Web"
            xmlns:Views="clr-namespace:BusinessApplication1.Views">
    <Grid x:Name="LayoutRoot">
        <ScrollViewer x:Name="PageScrollViewer"
         Style="{StaticResource PageScrollViewerStyle}">

          <StackPanel x:Name="ContentStackPanel"
           Style="{StaticResource ContentStackPanelStyle}">

              <TextBlock x:Name="HeaderText"
               Style="{StaticResource HeaderTextStyle}"
                     Text="Customers"/>
              <sdk:DataGrid Name="dataGrid1"
               ItemsSource="{Binding Data, ElementName=domainDataSource1}" />
              <riaControls:DomainDataSource Name="domainDataSource1"
               LoadSize="10" QueryName="GetCustomers" AutoLoad="True">
                  <riaControls:DomainDataSource.DomainContext>
                      <domain:CustomerDomainContext />
                  </riaControls:DomainDataSource.DomainContext>
              </riaControls:DomainDataSource>
          </StackPanel>

        </ScrollViewer>
    </Grid>
</navigation:Page>
```

Here, the DomainDataSource control is placed on the page and is set to query the GetCustomers()
method using the property QueryName. The LoadSize property is set to 10, meaning that the Silverlight
page will make calls 10 at a time to the service rather than calling for everything at once.

The domain context to use is defined using <riaControls:DomainDataSource.DomainContext />
and assigning the context to the CustomerDomainContext.

From there, the DataGrid is bound to this data source control through the ItemsSource property.

Reviewing the Behavior of the Results

When you compile and run this page, you are presented with a grid of 10 results, as you would expect.
This is demonstrated in Figure 8-18.

As stated, when this page is pulled up, 10 results are quickly displayed. However, after a slight pause,
another 10 results are called for and bound to the grid. The grid continues to do this until all the
results are bound to it.

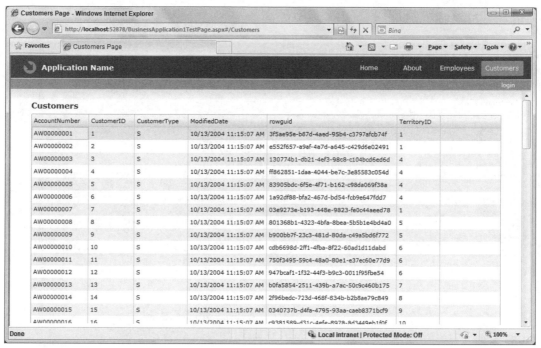

FIGURE 8-18

This is actually the correct behavior and, in some cases, something you might want to achieve if you wanted to display the entire dataset in one view. You can modify this behavior by simply adding a `DataPager` control to your XAML page. This small control is presented in Listing 8-8.

LISTING 8-8: Adding a DataPager control

```
<sdk:DataPager Height="26" Name="dataPager1" PageSize="10"
  Source="{Binding Data, ElementName=domainDataSource1}" />
```

Now with this `DataPager` control in place, when you run the page you are presented with a grid containing a page of only 10 items. This is illustrated in Figure 8-19.

Now the page size is set to `10` and the load size through the `DomainDataSource` control is also set to `10`. This means that for each new page called, a new call is made to the underlying service. If the `DomainDataSource`'s `LoadSize` property was set to `20`, there would only be a new call made for each odd page in the grid because the client application would already contain the first 20 in memory.

Filtering Results

There is a lot you can do with WCF RIA Services — more than can be covered in this single chapter. One interesting item, in addition to pulling pages of content, is filtering the items that are coming back from the service.

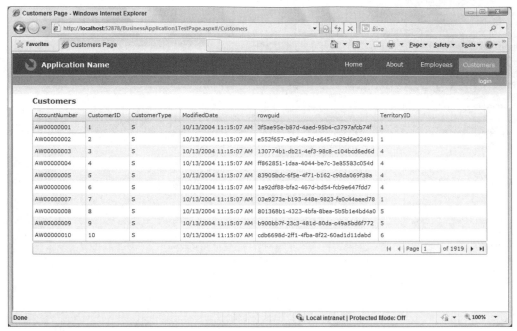

FIGURE 8-19

You can apply filtering options to the `Customers.xaml` page by adding some new controls and changing how the `DomainDataSource` control works. This is illustrated in Listing 8-9.

LISTING 8-9: Adding filtering to the DomainDataSource control

Available for
download on
Wrox.com

```
<navigation:Page x:Class="BusinessApplication1.Views.Customers"
         xmlns="http://schemas.microsoft.com/winfx/2006/xaml/presentation"
         xmlns:x="http://schemas.microsoft.com/winfx/2006/xaml"
         xmlns:d="http://schemas.microsoft.com/expression/blend/2008"
         xmlns:mc="http://schemas.openxmlformats.org/markup-compatibility/2006"
         mc:Ignorable="d"
         xmlns:navigation="clr-namespace:System.Windows.Controls;
            assembly=System.Windows.Controls.Navigation"
         d:DesignWidth="640" d:DesignHeight="480"
         Title="Customers Page"
         xmlns:sdk="http://schemas.microsoft.com/
            winfx/2006/xaml/presentation/sdk"
                xmlns:riaControls="clr-namespace:System.Windows.Controls;
                  assembly=System.Windows.Controls.DomainServices"
                xmlns:domain="clr-namespace:BusinessApplication1.Web"
                xmlns:Views="clr-namespace:BusinessApplication1.Views">
    <Grid x:Name="LayoutRoot">
        <ScrollViewer x:Name="PageScrollViewer"
          Style="{StaticResource PageScrollViewerStyle}">

            <StackPanel x:Name="ContentStackPanel"
```

```
                  Style="{StaticResource ContentStackPanelStyle}">

                     <TextBlock x:Name="HeaderText"
                      Style="{StaticResource HeaderTextStyle}"
                               Text="Customers"/>

                     <StackPanel x:Name="filterStackPanel"
                      Orientation="Horizontal" Height="40">
                        <sdk:Label Name="lblFilter"
                         Content="Filter by Territory ID " />
                        <ComboBox Height="23" Name="comboBox1" Width="120">
                           <ComboBoxItem Content="1" />
                           <ComboBoxItem Content="2" />
                           <ComboBoxItem Content="3" />
                        </ComboBox>
                     </StackPanel>

                     <sdk:DataGrid Name="dataGrid1" ItemsSource="{Binding Data,
                      ElementName=domainDataSource1}" />
                     <riaControls:DomainDataSource Name="domainDataSource1"
                      LoadSize="10" QueryName="GetCustomers" AutoLoad="True">
                        <riaControls:DomainDataSource.DomainContext>
                           <domain:CustomerDomainContext />
                        </riaControls:DomainDataSource.DomainContext>
                        <riaControls:DomainDataSource.FilterDescriptors>
                           <riaControls:FilterDescriptor
                            PropertyPath="TerritoryID"
                            Operator="IsEqualTo"
                            Value="{Binding ElementName=comboBox1,
                            Path=SelectedItem.Content}" />
                        </riaControls:DomainDataSource.FilterDescriptors>
                     </riaControls:DomainDataSource>
                     <sdk:DataPager Height="26" Name="dataPager1" PageSize="10"
                      Source="{Binding Data, ElementName=domainDataSource1}" />
                  </StackPanel>

            </ScrollViewer>
         </Grid>
      </navigation:Page>
```

In this case, a ComboBox control was added and this will be the control that the end user makes use of to filter the contents found in the DataGrid control. With this simple control in place, the only additional change required is to provide a `<riaControls:DomainDataSource.FilterDescriptors>` section to the DomainDataSource control. Here you provide a PropertyPath property, which points to the item in the entity model that you are looking to filter by. From there, you will need to provide an operator to utilize. The Operator property in this sample is set to IsEqualTo, but it can be set to several other things, such as:

➤ Contains

➤ EndsWith

➤ IsContainedIn

➤ IsEqualTo

➤ IsGreaterThan

➤ IsGreaterThanOrEqualTo

➤ IsLessThan

➤ IsLessThanOrEqualTo

➤ IsNotEqualTo

➤ StartsWith

From there, you need only to set the binding to what is presented in the ComboBox control and then compile and run the page. You are then presented with the results as shown in Figure 8-20.

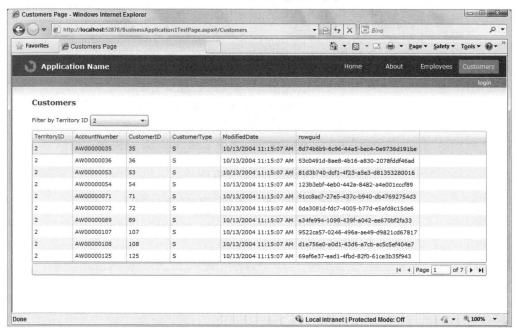

FIGURE 8-20

SUMMARY

This chapter looked at working with WCF RIA Services within your Silverlight applications. Most developers coming from the ASP.NET world will be wondering how to bring the data and logic from the middle tier of their application stacks down to the presentation tier if the entire presentation tier is residing on the client. WCF Data Services makes this task quite simple in that it provides you with the means to code your client applications as if the middle tier resides directly on the client itself. Instead, behind the scenes, calls are being made up to a WCF service layer.

WCF RIA Services is a new feature available to Silverlight developers, and you will find that it is a useful tool in your tool belt when building business applications.

Out-of-Browser Experiences

➤ Configuring and installing an out-of-browser application

➤ Detecting network connectivity

➤ Creating a trusted application

➤ Implementing COM automation

➤ Customizing windows

An out-of-browser application, or OOB for simplicity, is a Silverlight-based application that can be installed from the host browser from which it is running onto a user's local computer. Once installed locally, it can be launched from a local, application-specific icon located on the desktop or Start menu. From a user's perspective, the installed application is launched just like any other application: there is an application-specific icon, and double-clicking that icon opens up the application for execution.

CREATING AN OUT-OF-BROWSER APPLICATION

An OOB application is really no different than an application that is hosted within a browser. You use Visual Studio to build out a user interface, you write code that responds to events, and you use features like isolated storage and printing to deliver expected Line of Business or rich Internet applications (RIA) features. From a security perspective, an OOB is subject to the same security sandbox restrictions as ordinary in-browser applications. To increase the features that Silverlight has available, such as COM automation support and local filesystem access, you can remove some sandbox restrictions by configuring your application to require elevated trust. Elevated trust is a new feature to Silverlight 4, and its implications are covered later in the chapter.

To enable an in-browser application to run outside of the browser, you can do either one of the following:

➤ Set OOB-specific properties in the Properties window in Visual Studio.

➤ Edit the application's manifest to set OOB properties.

Once you perform one of the aforementioned operations, there is an additional menu option when you right-click your Silverlight application that enables you to install the application locally to run outside of the browser as Figure 9-1 shows.

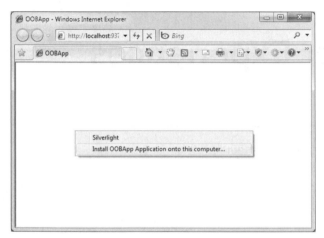

FIGURE 9-1

When an application is installed outside of the browser, it is still accessing the Internet for its network resources. If you are accessing data from a service, or doing some sort of authentication, you need to make sure you handle any network connection issues gracefully. Using the network detection API built into Silverlight, you can deal with these issues effectively. This also allows you to create applications that can run successfully without a network connection. You can use local files or isolated storage to read and write data, and when a connection is available, you can allow your application to sync with a server. Later in this chapter you learn how you can detect network connectivity and deal with situations in which the network is not available.

Out-of-Browser Application Features

You may decide to create an OOB application just to have a more interesting experience for your application; for example, you may be after a desktop-like look and feel, which the OOB application gives you. You have other good reasons to choose an OOB application. The following features are available to your Silverlight application only if it is running outside of the browser.

➤ **Window Manipulation** — At run time, you can change the window size, set it as the topmost window, and minimize or maximize the window programmatically. You also have the ability to handle the `Window_Closing` event, which you can cancel except when the computer is shutting down or the user is logging off. The `Closing` event enables you to perform actions such as displaying a warning if the user has unsaved changes in the application data.

➤ **Window Customization** — Trusted applications can hide the title bar and border of the out-of-browser application window to provide a completely customized user interface. The `Window` class provides APIs that trusted applications can use to replace the title bar buttons and enable mouse dragging to move or resize the window.

➤ **HTML Hosting** — You can display HTML content within your out-of-browser application to replace functionality provided by a host web page.

➤ **Notification Windows** — Out-of-browser applications can display a toaster (or pop-up) notification similar to what displays when a new e-mail arrives in Outlook. The notification window displays in the lower right of the screen.

➤ **Digital Rights Management (DRM)** — DRM support is available for offline media files.

➤ **Elevated Trust** — Trusted applications can integrate with native functionality, such as cross-domain access, and are not subject to the same security restrictions as normal Silverlight-based applications.

➤ **Filesystem Access** — Trusted applications can use the `System.IO` types and related types to enable read and write access to files in user folders on the local computer.

> *OOB applications can access network resources over HTTPS when a connection is available, but OOB applications are no more secure than their host websites. Therefore, users must rely on the security of the host site when installing or updating an out-of-browser application. If your application handles sensitive information, you should use HTTPS for the application URI and for secure communications. Note that the URI (including protocol) of the original application is always used when the application checks for updates.*

Now that you have a basis for what an OOB application is and why you might create one, the next step is to learn how to create an OOB application.

Configuring an Out-of-Browser Application in Visual Studio

You can enable your existing Silverlight application to run outside of the browser in two ways:

➤ Modify the properties on the Out-of-Browser Settings dialog, which is launched from the Properties window of your Silverlight project.

➤ Modify the Out-of-Browser settings in the `AppManifest.xaml` file.

To configure OOB support via the Out-of-Browser Settings dialog, follow these steps:

1. In Solution Explorer, select the Silverlight project for which you want to enable OOB support.

2. On the Project menu, select *project name* Properties.

3. On the Silverlight tab, select Enable running application out of the browser as demonstrated in Figure 9-2.

4. Click Out-of-Browser Settings to launch the Out-of-Browser Settings dialog box, as shown in Figure 9-3.

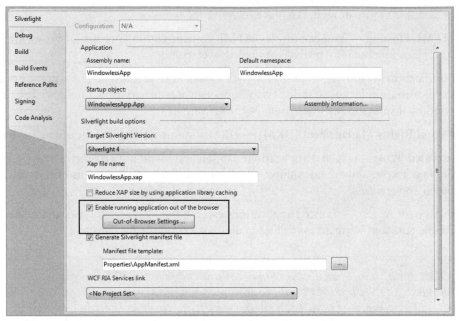

FIGURE 9-2

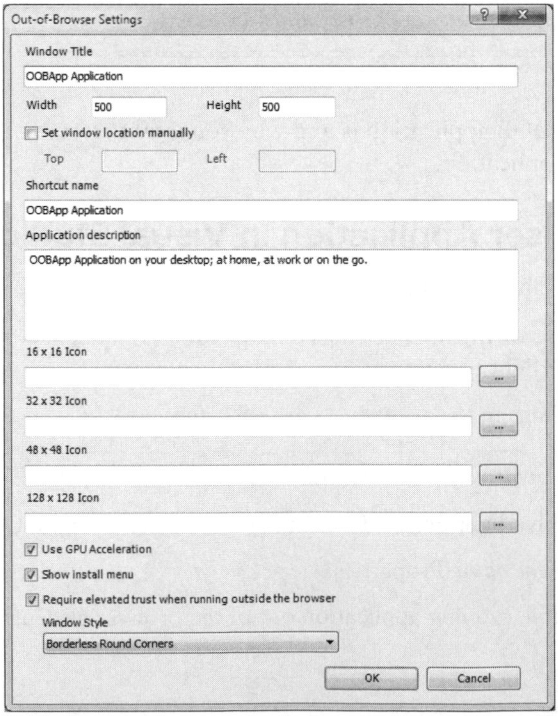

FIGURE 9-3

Table 9-1 describes each property of the `OutOfBrowserSettings` or `WindowSettings` class that are available in the Out-of-Browser Settings dialog.

TABLE 9-1

FIELD	PROPERTY	DESCRIPTION
Window Title (required)	Title	Appears in the title bar of the OOB application window.
Width and Height	Width and Height	Indicates the initial dimensions of the OOB application window. If you do not specify this property, the window defaults to 800x600.
Set Window Location Manually	WindowStartupLocation	Indicates whether the initial position of the OOB application window will be centered or positioned according to the specified Top and Left values.
Top and Left (not supported in Silverlight 3)	Top and Left	Indicates the initial location of the OOB application window. These fields are disabled if you do not select Set Window Location Manually.
Shortcut Name (required)	ShortName	Appears in the OOB installation dialog box and on the installed application shortcut or shortcuts.
Application Description (required)	Blurb	Appears as a tooltip on the installed application shortcuts.
Icon fields	Icons	The operating system chooses the most appropriate icon to display in the following locations: • The installation dialog box • The application window • Windows Explorer • Windows taskbar • Macintosh dock bar Icons must be of type PNG and have their Build Action property set to Content. If you do not specify an icon, a default will be used. If you do specify an icon, you should include an icon for each size (16x16, 32x32, 48x48, and 128x128).

continues

TABLE 9-1 *(continued)*

FIELD	PROPERTY	DESCRIPTION
Use GPU Acceleration	EnableGPUAcceleration	Indicates whether graphics performance is enhanced by using hardware acceleration.
Show Install Menu	ShowInstallMenuItem	Indicates whether the install option should appear on the application right-click menu.
Require Elevated Trust When Running Outside the Browser (not supported in Silverlight 3)	SecuritySettings	Indicates whether the application runs with relaxed security restrictions.
Window Style (not supported in Silverlight 3)	WindowStyle	Indicates the appearance of the title bar and border for the OOB application window.

Once you set the property values in the Out-of-Browser Settings dialog, the values are reflected in the OutOfBrowserSettings.xaml file as demonstrated in Figure 9-4.

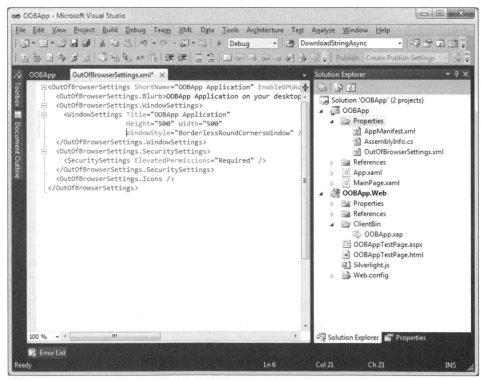

FIGURE 9-4

As mentioned earlier, the other option for enabling OOB in an application is to modify the `AppManifest.xml` file, which is created by default when you create a Silverlight application. The `AppManifest.xml` file has a `DeploymentParts` section, where you can insert the property settings for the OOB configuration. The following code demonstrates an `AppManifest.xml` file set up for an OOB experience:

```xml
<Deployment xmlns="http://schemas.microsoft.com/client/2007/deployment"
        xmlns:x="http://schemas.microsoft.com/winfx/2006/xaml">
    <Deployment.Parts>
    </Deployment.Parts>
    <Deployment.OutOfBrowserSettings>
        <OutOfBrowserSettings
            ShortName="Out of Browser Sample Application"
            EnableGPUAcceleration="True"
            ShowInstallMenuItem="True">
            <OutOfBrowserSettings.Blurb>
                This is the description of an OOB Application
            </OutOfBrowserSettings.Blurb>
            <OutOfBrowserSettings.Icons>
                <Icon Size="16,16">icons/16x16.png</Icon>
                <Icon Size="32,32">icons/32x32.png</Icon>
                <Icon Size="48,48">icons/48x48.png</Icon>
                <Icon Size="128,128">icons/128x128.png</Icon>
            </OutOfBrowserSettings.Icons>
            <OutOfBrowserSettings.WindowSettings>
                <WindowSettings
                    Title="Out of Browser Sample Application"
                    Height="500" Width="500"
                    Left="0" Top="0" WindowStartupLocation="Manual"
                    WindowStyle="SingleBorderWindow"/>
            </OutOfBrowserSettings.WindowSettings>
            <OutOfBrowserSettings.SecuritySettings>
                <SecuritySettings ElevatedPermissions="Required" />
            </OutOfBrowserSettings.SecuritySettings>
        </OutOfBrowserSettings>
    </Deployment.OutOfBrowserSettings>
</Deployment>
```

 If you use the Out-of-Browser Settings dialog box, you cannot specify out-of-browser settings in the `AppManifest.xml` file. This creates duplicate information in the manifest, which raises an exception when your application runs.

Installing an Out-of-Browser Application

As shown in Figure 9-1, the default installation experience of an OOB application is that you right-click the application that is running in the web browser and select the Install <application name> menu option to initiate the install process. Clicking this menu item launches the Install application dialog shown in Figure 9-5.

This is a fairly simple process. The user is prompted to install, and once he or she clicks the OK button on the Install application dialog, the application is deployed locally to an out-of-browser cache located in the user's local profile folder. The process that occurs is as follows:

FIGURE 9-5

1. The user clicks Install <application name> from the right-click menu.

2. The Install application dialog launches.

3. The user clicks OK.

4. A new HTTP request is made to the originating domain and the XAP is downloaded to the user's local profile folder.

5. The application is launched locally using `sllauncher.exe` (passing it a unique ID assigned to the OOB application) using the width, height, and title bar text specified when the OOB application was configured.

If you close the OOB application that is running, you can launch it from the desktop shortcut or the Start menu shortcut, which then launches the application again using the `sllauncher.exe` application. If you are giving your user an additional UI to install your application, such as a button or custom menu item, you can use the following code to install your application out-of-browser:

```
App.Current.Install();
```

Once this code is executed, it initiates the same confirmation dialog as the install option from the right-click menu. Before you actually run any code to install the application, you should check the `InstallState` of the application:

```
if (App.Current.InstallState == InstallState.Installed)
{
    // do not show an install button, or indicate app is installed
}
```

Once you have determined whether the application is installed, you can check whether it's running outside of the browser with the `IsRunningOutOfBrowser` property check (see Listing 9-1).

LISTING 9-1: Checking if an application is running outside of the browser

Available for download on Wrox.com

```
if (!App.Current.IsRunningOutOfBrowser)
{
    // let user know they need to install your app OOB
}
else
{
    // Not running outside of browser, let user know
}
```

No matter which technique you use to install your application out-of-browser, users are always prompted with the confirmation dialog to ensure that they actually want to install your application. You are prohibited from installing an application without the user initiating the process.

Once the application is installed, various techniques are available to enable a complete client application, which caches data locally to the local filesystem or to isolated storage, and accesses network resources only as needed. If you do need to access the network, you can call the `GetIsNetworkAvailable` method before attempting to access a network resource. Listing 9-2 demonstrates how to call `GetIsNetworkAvailable`.

LISTING 9-2: Determining if a network connection is available

Available for
download on
Wrox.com

```
if (NetworkInterface.GetIsNetworkAvailable())
{
    // Access the network resource
}
else
{
    // Notify user that Internet connection is not available
    MessageBox.Show("This application requires an Internet connection");
}
```

During the execution of your application, you may want to let the user know if the network is available, or the application may need to know if there is a connection dropped once a connection is open. To do this, you handle the `NetworkChange.NetworkAddressChanged` event in the `System .Net.NetworkInformation` namespace (see Listing 9-3).

LISTING 9-3: Using the NetworkAddressChanged event

Available for
download on
Wrox.com

```
public MainPage()
{
    InitializeComponent();

    // Add event handler to check the network status
    NetworkChange.NetworkAddressChanged +=
        new NetworkAddressChangedEventHandler(NetworkChange_NetworkAddressChanged);
}

void NetworkChange_NetworkAddressChanged(object sender, EventArgs e)
{
    if (NetworkInterface.GetIsNetworkAvailable())
    {
        MessageBox.Show("Network is available");
    }
    else
    {
        MessageBox.Show("Network is not available");
    }
}
```

In the following sections, you learn how to uninstall your application and update your OOB application.

Uninstalling an Out-of-Browser Application

You remove an OOB application the same way you install one — by right-clicking the application that is running in the web browser and selecting the Remove This Application menu option to initiate the uninstall process. This menu option is shown in Figure 9-6.

Once the menu option is selected, the dialog shown in Figure 9-7 is launched.

FIGURE 9-6

FIGURE 9-7

By default, an OOB application will not be listed in the list of programs to uninstall in the Programs and Features dialog in the Control Panel. If you suppressed the right-click application menu by handling the MouseRightButtonDown *event in your OOB application, you need to uninstall the application from the Programs and Features page in the Control Panel (Windows 7).*

Updating an Out-of-Browser Application

If you consider that your OOB application is just like any other web application, you've chosen this platform not only for the RIA experiences it offers, but for the ease of deployment and ease of updating it provides. Because the OOB application is running from a XAP stored in the local cache, there will be times when you update your application and the client will need to download the update to refresh the application with any new features or bug fixes you have added. To check for and retrieve updates, you call CheckAndDownloadUpdateAsync and then handle the `Application.CheckAndDownloadUpdateCompleted` event. In the event handler, the `UpdateAvailable` property is `true` if a newer version of your application was discovered and successfully downloaded. The purpose of this is to let the end users know that a new update has been downloaded and is available once they restart the application. Listing 9-4 shows how to implement the event handler and check for available updates.

LISTING 9-4: Checking for and downloading updates to an application

Available for
download on
Wrox.com

```
public MainPage()
{
    InitializeComponent();

    App.Current.CheckAndDownloadUpdateCompleted +=
        new CheckAndDownloadUpdateCompletedEventHandler
        (Current_CheckAndDownloadUpdateCompleted);
}

void Current_CheckAndDownloadUpdateCompleted(object sender,
    CheckAndDownloadUpdateCompletedEventArgs e)
{
    if (e.UpdateAvailable)
    {
        MessageBox.Show("An application update has been downloaded. " +
            "Restart the application to run the new version.");
    }
    else if (e.Error != null &&
        e.Error is PlatformNotSupportedException)
    {
        MessageBox.Show("An application update is available, " +
            "but it requires a new version of Silverlight. " +
            "Visit the application home page to upgrade.");
    }
    else
    {
        MessageBox.Show("There is no update available.");
    }
}
```

When you check whether there is an available update with the `UpdateAvailable` property, you should also check for the `PlatformNotSupportedException` exception. This occurs when an update is available but uses a newer version of Silverlight than the version that is installed on the local computer.

Silverlight 4 provides support for running OOB applications with elevated trust. Trusted applications cannot use the update mechanism described in this section unless the application and the update have both been signed with the same valid, code-signing certificate. To update a trusted application that does not have a valid signature, users must uninstall the old version and install the new version manually.

INSTALLING TRUSTED APPLICATIONS

A Silverlight application runs in the safety of the partial trust browser sandbox. However, an OOB application can be installed with elevated trust, which gives the application access to local computer resources that you might expect only in a full desktop application. These features include local file-system access, COM automation support, full-screen keyboard support, and cross-domain access, all without getting the user's permission beyond the initial application install.

To enable elevated trust, you can update the `SecuritySettings` in the `AppManifest.xml` file if you are manually configuring your OOB application. Or you can simply check the Require elevated trust when running outside the browser checkbox on the Out-of-Browser Settings dialog as shown back in Figure 9-3.

If your application is configured for elevated trust, a Security Warning dialog box appears when the installation is initiated. This dialog warns users that they should not install applications they do not trust, as shown in Figure 9-8. (Note that I clicked in the More Options expansion indicator on the dialog to show the dialog in its entirety.)

Once the application is installed, it behaves the same as a default OOB application, except you have those additional application options available to you mentioned earlier in this section, such as local filesystem access. Before you execute any code that requires elevated trust, you should check whether your application is installed with elevated permission by checking the `HasElevatedPermissions` property:

FIGURE 9-8

```
if (Application.Current.HasElevatedPermissions)
{
    // perform operation that requires elevated permissions
}
```

Listing 9-5 can be considered a reusable "stub" that you can use for your OOB application. It encapsulates several features that every trusted OOB application needs:

➤ Checking if the application is running outside of the browser

➤ Checking for updates

➤ Checking for elevated permissions

➤ Checking if the network is available

I have bolded the lines of code that you should become familiar with when writing OOB applications:

LISTING 9-5: Checking for elevated permissions and an available network

```
public MainPage()
{
    InitializeComponent();

    if (Application.Current.IsRunningOutOfBrowser)
    {
        // If running out-of-browser, find out whether a newer version is available
        Application.Current.CheckAndDownloadUpdateCompleted
            += new
                CheckAndDownloadUpdateCompletedEventHandler
                (OnCheckAndDownloadUpdateCompleted);
        Application.Current.CheckAndDownloadUpdateAsync();

        if (Application.Current.HasElevatedPermissions)
        {
            if (NetworkInterface.GetIsNetworkAvailable())
            {
                // Perform a trusted feature
            }
            else
            {
                // Let user know there is no Internet connection
                MessageBox.Show("This application requires an Internet connection");
            }
        }
        else
        {
            // Display warning if running without elevated permissions
            MessageBox.Show("This application requires elevated permissions");
        }
    }
    else
    {
        // Display warning if not running OOB
        MessageBox.Show("This application must be run outside
                        the browser with elevated permissions");
    }
}

private void OnCheckAndDownloadUpdateCompleted(object sender,
            CheckAndDownloadUpdateCompletedEventArgs e)
{
    if (e.UpdateAvailable)
    {
        MessageBox.Show("An updated version of this application is available.
            Close the application and restart it to run the new version.",
            "Update Available", MessageBoxButton.OK);
    }
}
```

In the preceding code, a `MessageBox` is used to prompt the user with information. An additional feature available to OOB applications is the ability to show a notification window, or toaster pop-up to notify the user of useful information. A notification window should be familiar to you; it is the pop-up in the lower-right portion of the screen when new mail arrives in Microsoft Outlook. To duplicate this feature in an OOB application, create an instance of a `NotificatoinWindow` class and assign a control or user control to its content control. This is demonstrated in the Listing 9-6.

LISTING 9-6: Displaying a notification window

```
private void AlertDone(string Message)
{
    NotificationWindow notify = new NotificationWindow();
    notify.Width = 329;
    notify.Height = 74;

    TextBlock tb = new TextBlock();
    tb.Text = Message ;
    tb.FontSize = 24;

    notify.Content = tb;
    notify.Show(3000);
}
```

When the `Show` method is called for 3000 milliseconds, the pop-up window appears on the lower right of the screen for 3 seconds.

Note that system administrators can disable the ability to install trusted applications. If this capability is disabled, attempting to install has no effect, and the `Install` method returns `false`. Some additional considerations for elevated trust applications include:

➤ Keyboard support in full-screen mode is available only in a trusted application.

➤ The `WebClient` and `HTTP` classes in the `System.Net` namespace can be used without policy checks. An application installed from one domain using the HTTP protocol can access media files from a cross-domain site using the HTTPS protocol.

➤ Networking and socket communication can be performed without being subject to cross-domain and cross-scheme access restrictions. An application installed from one subdomain using the HTTP protocol can access media files from a separate subdomain using the HTTPS protocol.

➤ Networking `UdpAnySourceMulticastClient` and `UdpSingleSourceMulticastClient` classes in the `System.Net.Sockets` namespace can be used with relaxed policy checks.

➤ A TCP connection can be made to any port on any host without the need for a cross-domain policy file.

➤ A TCP destination port is no longer required to be within the range of 4502–4534.

➤ The `UdpAnySourceMulticastClient` and `UdpSingleSourceMulticastClient` classes can join any multicast group on any port greater than or equal to 1024 without the need for a policy responder to authorize the connection.

➤ User consent is only required for the AudioSink (microphone) and VideoSink (camera) functionality.

➤ Full-screen mode applications will not display the message "Press ESC to exit full-screen mode."

➤ ESC will not exit full-screen mode in trusted applications because trusted applications do not automatically intercept keystrokes and do not have any keyboard restrictions in full-screen mode.

The following sections look at specific elevated trust operations and how to code them.

Accessing the Filesystems

In a non-trusted Silverlight application, filesystem access is allowed only through the `OpenFileDialog` and `SaveFileDialog` classes. In a trusted OOB application, you can access the MyDocuments, MyMusic, MyPictures, and MyVideos user folders using the `System.IO` classes. To obtain the path of these folders and to access their contents, you use the `System.Environment.SpecialFolder` enumeration to construct paths. In the following example (Listing 9-7), the MyDocuments folder is accessed and the files in the folder are added to a `ListBox` control. To make this code work, you should add the `System.IO` namespace to your class.

LISTING 9-7: Enumerating the filesystem

```
if (Application.Current.HasElevatedPermissions)
{
    List<string> folderFilers = new List<string>();
    var files =   Directory.EnumerateFiles(Environment.GetFolderPath
                    (Environment.SpecialFolder.MyDocuments));

    foreach (var item in files)
    {
        folderFilers.Add(item);
    }
    listBox1.ItemsSource = folderFilers;
}
```

Windows 7 Libraries named Documents, Music, Pictures, and Videos combine the contents of the user folders with other folders, such as shared media folders. However, trusted applications cannot access non-user folders except through the `OpenFileDialog` *and* `SaveFileDialog` *classes.*

Using COM Automation

Using the `AutomationFactory` class in the `System.Runtime.InteropServices.Automation` namespace, OOB trusted applications can integrate with some native functionality of the host operating system, including the ability to access Automation APIs on Windows operating systems. The types of automation servers include but are not limited to Microsoft Office applications like Outlook and Excel; system objects like `Scripting.FileSystemObject`; `WScript.Shell`; and `ShellApplication`.

In Listing 9-8, the `AutomationFactory.IsAvailable` property is checked to verify the application is running outside of the browser with elevated permissions before creating the COM Outlook object to send an e-mail using Outlook on the client machine. To get this code to work, add the `System.Runtime.InteropServices.Automation` namespace to your class.

LISTING 9-8: Using COM automation

Available for
download on
Wrox.com

```
private void sendEmail(string fileName)
{
    // Check if application has elevated privileges outside of browser
    if (AutomationFactory.IsAvailable)
    {
        // Send an email
        dynamic outlook =
            AutomationFactory.CreateObject("Outlook.Application");
        dynamic mail = outlook.CreateItem(0);
        mail.Recipients.Add("webmaster@contoso.com");
        mail.Subject = "Hello, Silverlight";
        mail.Body = "This message was sent from Silverlight 4";
        mail.Save();
        mail.Send();
    }
}
```

IntelliSense is not available when using COM automation, so be sure to keep your API reference handy for the automation server you are using.

Support for Window Customization

When you create a trusted OOB application, you have the option to change from a normal border around your window to a borderless window or a borderless window with rounded corners. Figure 9-9 shows the lower portion of the Out-of-Browser Settings dialog, which has the drop-down with your window options.

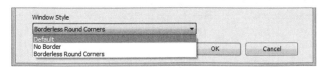

FIGURE 9-9

Behind the scenes, when you hide the title bar and border, Silverlight displays your application content over a white background, which means you cannot create irregularly shaped applications, because the white background is not transparent. To replace the functionality provided by the title bar and border, you can use the Window class members to perform actions like dragging the window or window borders using the DragMove and DragResize methods. You can adjust the window position and size by using the Left, Top, Width, and Height properties. Use the WindowState property to minimize or maximize the window. Listing 9-9 demonstrates some of the code that you would use from the Window class.

LISTING 9-9: Using the Window class

```csharp
private void MoveWindow(object sender, MouseButtonEventArgs e)
{
    if (App.Current.IsRunningOutOfBrowser && App.Current.HasElevatedPermissions)
    {
        App.Current.MainWindow.DragMove();
    }
}

private void ResizeWindowFromBottom(object sender, MouseButtonEventArgs e)
{
    if (App.Current.IsRunningOutOfBrowser && App.Current.HasElevatedPermissions)
    {
        App.Current.MainWindow.DragResize(WindowResizeEdge.BottomRight);
    }
}

private void MinimizeWindow(object sender, MouseButtonEventArgs e)
{
    if (App.Current.IsRunningOutOfBrowser && App.Current.HasElevatedPermissions)
    {
        App.Current.MainWindow.WindowState = WindowState.Minimized;
    }
}

private void RestoreWindow(object sender, MouseButtonEventArgs e)
{
    if (App.Current.IsRunningOutOfBrowser && App.Current.HasElevatedPermissions)
    {
        App.Current.MainWindow.WindowState = WindowState.Normal;
    }
}

private void MaximizeWindow(object sender, MouseButtonEventArgs e)
{
    if (App.Current.IsRunningOutOfBrowser && App.Current.HasElevatedPermissions)
    {
        App.Current.MainWindow.WindowState = WindowState.Maximized;
    }
}
```

To create a simple application that has no border and a custom close button, as well as the ability to move the window around the screen, create a new application based on the Silverlight Navigation Application template. In the Out-of-Browser Settings, change the Window Style to Borderless Round Corners as shown in Figure 9-10.

FIGURE 9-10

In the MainPage.xaml file, add the MouseLeftButtonDown, MouseLeftButtonUp, and MouseMove events (Listing 9-10).

LISTING 9-10: Adding mouse events to the UserControl in MainPage.xaml

```
<UserControl
    x:Class="WindowlessApp.MainPage"
    MouseLeftButtonDown="UserControl_MouseLeftButtonDown"
    MouseLeftButtonUp="UserControl_MouseLeftButtonUp"
    MouseMove="UserControl_MouseMove"
```

From the Toolbox, drag a button to the page, and name it closeButton and add an event handler for the closeButton_Click event. Next, add the code in Listing 9-11 in the code-behind to the event handlers for each of the events you added.

LISTING 9-11: Interacting with a Window object

```
bool dragging = false;

private void UserControl_MouseLeftButtonDown
    (object sender, MouseButtonEventArgs e)
{
    if (Application.Current.IsRunningOutOfBrowser && !dragging)
        dragging = true;
}

private void UserControl_MouseLeftButtonUp
    (object sender, MouseButtonEventArgs e)
{
    if (Application.Current.IsRunningOutOfBrowser && dragging)
        dragging = false;
}

private void UserControl_MouseMove
    (object sender, MouseEventArgs e)
{
    if (dragging)
        Application.Current.MainWindow.DragMove();
}
```

When you run the application, you can drag it around the screen by clicking anywhere on the user control, and you can close the application by clicking the button you added.

Adding Digital Signatures

Adding a digital signature to your trusted application is an important step to help secure the application and increase customer confidence during installation. Additionally, only trusted applications with valid digital signatures can use the out-of-browser update mechanism. To update a trusted application that does not have a valid signature, users must uninstall the old version and install the new version manually.

To add a digital signature to a trusted application, use the `SignTool.exe` utility with an Authenticode X.509 code-signing certificate. For example, you could use the following command line:

```
signtool sign /v /f certificateFile.pfxfileToSign
```

 Code signing is relevant only for trusted applications.

Silverlight verifies the signature and certificate whenever a user installs or updates the application. Users can install a trusted application without a valid signature. However, Silverlight prevents trusted applications from updating unless both the original application and the update are signed with the same valid, verified, code-signing certificate. Additionally, the certificate must not be expired at the time of update. Be sure to take the certificate expiration date into consideration in your deployment and update planning.

INSTALLING A LOCAL SILVERLIGHT APPLICATION

In the same manner that an OOB application is launched using `sllauncher.exe`, you can install an OOB application from a network resource, USB device, or CD-ROM as long as Silverlight is already installed on the local computer. The `sllauncher.exe` application is located in the \program files (x86)\Microsoft Silverlight folder. Note that on a 64-bit machine, Silverlight is installed in the x86 32-bit Program Files folder. The following installs an application locally by running `sllauncher` `.exe` from the location of your XAP file:

```
"%ProgramFiles(x86)%\Microsoft Silverlight\sllauncher.exe" /overwrite /
install:"xapfilename.xap"  /origin:http://www.original_web_location/clientbin/
xapfilename.xap /shortcut:desktop
```

The *original_web_location* is the originating URI and path to the XAP file where the application should look for automatic updates. Even though the application is installed locally, it still needs to get new updates at a URI origin. If you want to run the application after it's installed, use the emulate switch:

```
"%ProgramFiles(x86)%\Microsoft Silverlight\sllauncher.exe" /overwrite /
emulate:"xapfilename.xap"  /origin:http://www.original_web_location/clientbin/
xapfilename.xap /overwrite
```

To uninstall it use the following command:

```
"%ProgramFiles(x86)%\Microsoft Silverlight\sllauncher.exe" /overwrite /
uninstall:"xapfilename.xap"  /origin:http://www.original_web_location/clientbin/
xapfilename.xap /shortcut:desktop
```

The following options can be passed to `sllauncher.exe`:

➤ `/install:"path-toXAP-File"` — Required. Points to the XAP file that you are installing.

➤ `/origin:"URI-to-origin"` — Required. The originating URI of the XAP file.

➤ `/shortcut:desktop+startmenu` — Optional. Indicate `desktop`, `startmenu`, or `desktop+startmenu` for the shortcut location. If you omit this, the user will not be able to launch the application from a shortcut.

➤ `/overwrite` — Optional. Overwrites an existing installation.

SUMMARY

In this chapter, you learned about the experiences you can create in an out-of-browser application. You learned how to configure the application using Visual Studio, or manually by editing the `AppManifest.xml` file. You also learned how trusted applications behave and how to install and uninstall an OOB application. Finally, you learned how to sign your application for an even better UX.

10

Networking Applications

WHAT'S IN THIS CHAPTER?

➤ Using WebClient to call for remote content

➤ Dealing with cross-domain access

➤ Using WCF duplex communications with Silverlight

➤ Working with sockets

Because Silverlight applications are on the client side, this chapter focuses on the communication capabilities these types of applications provide. This chapter is not a guide to computer networking, but an introduction to using the .NET Framework along with Silverlight for network communication.

This chapter covers facilities provided through the .NET base classes for using various network protocols, particularly HTTP and TCP, to access networks and the Internet as a client. It covers some of the lower-level means of getting at these protocols through the .NET Framework. You will also find other means of communicating via these items using technologies such as the Windows Communication Foundation (WCF) or using REST-based services to get at remote capabilities. The two namespaces of most interest for networking are System.Net and System.Net.Sockets. The System.Net namespace is generally concerned with higher-level operations, for example, downloading and uploading files, and making web requests using HTTP and other protocols, whereas System.Net.Sockets contains classes to perform lower-level operations. You will find these classes useful when you want to work directly with sockets or protocols, such as TCP/IP. The methods in these classes closely mimic the Windows Socket (Winsock) API functions derived from the Berkeley sockets interface.

Utilizing these namespaces provides you with the access you will need from Silverlight. With the use of System.Net, you are able to use the simplified WebClient object as well as the more generic but more powerful `HttpWebRequest/Response` objects. Now with these objects, you have libraries that allow for such activities as dealing with RSS/syndication, duplex communications, and downloading.

You also have the ability to access capabilities or underlying data using some kind of a web service from Silverlight. You might have a formal service with an accompanying Web Services Description Language (WSDL) file. If that is the case, you will be able to generate a client proxy for that service and access it remotely using the proxy. Another very common scenario is to access services that are just a Plain-Old XML (POX) and Representational State Transfer (REST) services. For both of these, you can use just the aforementioned `WebClient` or `HttpWebRequest/Response` classes, although Silverlight does provide additional means to access REST services, particularly for WCF Data Services.

THE WEBCLIENT CLASS

If you only want to request a file from a particular URI (Uniform Resource Identifier), you will find that the easiest .NET class to use is `System.Net.WebClient`. This is an extremely high-level class designed to perform basic operations with only one or two commands. You can use the `WebClient` class to retrieve data from a wide variety of endpoints including POX-, JSON-, RSS-, and REST-based services. All requests using `WebClient` are performed asynchronously in Silverlight, which enables your application to still respond even while it is loading data under the covers.

 It is worth noting that the term URL (Uniform Resource Locator) is no longer in use in new technical specifications, and URI (Uniform Resource Identifier) is now preferred. URI has roughly the same meaning as URL, but is a bit more general because URI does not imply you are using one of the familiar protocols, such as HTTP or FTP.

Depending on the format of the data returned by the server, you can choose the appropriate class to parse it into a format for your application to consume. For example, the `XmlReader` class can be used to quickly access data returned from the server in POX.

Using OpenReadAsync()

This first example demonstrates the `WebClient.OpenReadAsync()` method. You will use this to display the contents of a downloaded XML file in a `TextBlock` control on the page. To begin, create a new project as a standard C# Silverlight application called WebClientSolution and add a `TextBlock` control called `textBlock1`. Another possibility would be to use `DownloadStringAsyc()` rather than `OpenReadAsync()`, as this is an XML file. It is interesting to note that `OpenReadAsync()` can work with not only string data, but images, videos, and anything else you can plug into a stream.

Before working with the default `MainPage.xaml` page in detail, create an XML file that you will work with from this application. In the ClientBin folder next to the XAP being accessed, create an XML file called `Persons.xml`. The content of this file is presented in Listing 10-1.

LISTING 10-1: The contents of Persons.xml

```xml
<?xml version="1.0" encoding="utf-8" ?>
<People>
  <Person>
    <FirstName>Bill</FirstName>
    <LastName>Evjen</LastName>
  </Person>
  <Person>
    <FirstName>Devin</FirstName>
    <LastName>Rader</LastName>
  </Person>
  <Person>
    <FirstName>Jason</FirstName>
    <LastName>Beres</LastName>
  </Person>
</People>
```

With this is place, you can now turn your attention to `MainPage.xaml.cs`. At the beginning of this file, you need to add the `System.Net` and `System.IO` namespace references to your list of `using` directives. The code for this page is presented in Listing 10-2.

LISTING 10-2: Calling the server-side XML file using WebClient

```csharp
using System;
using System.IO;
using System.Net;
using System.Windows.Controls;

namespace WebClientSolution
{
    public partial class MainPage : UserControl
    {
        public MainPage()
        {
            InitializeComponent();

            WebClient client = new WebClient();
            Uri uri = new Uri("Persons.xml", UriKind.Relative);
             client.OpenReadCompleted +=
                new OpenReadCompletedEventHandler(client_OpenReadCompleted);

            client.OpenReadAsync(uri);
        }

        void client_OpenReadCompleted(object sender, OpenReadCompletedEventArgs e)
```

continues

LISTING 10-2 *(continued)*

```
            {
                if (e.Error == null)
                {
                    Stream strm = e.Result;
                    StreamReader sr = new StreamReader(strm);
                    textBlock1.Text = sr.ReadToEnd();
                    strm.Close();
                }
                else
                {
                    textBlock1.Text = e.Error.Message;
                }
            }
        }
    }
```

In this example, you connect a `StreamReader` class from the `System.IO` namespace to the network stream. This lets you obtain data from the stream as text through the use of higher-level methods, such as `ReadToEnd()` or `ReadLine()`. In addition, it is important to note that like all other .NET applications, all paths in Silverlight applications are relative to the location of the `.xap` file. Running this example produces a simple page as illustrated in Figure 10-1.

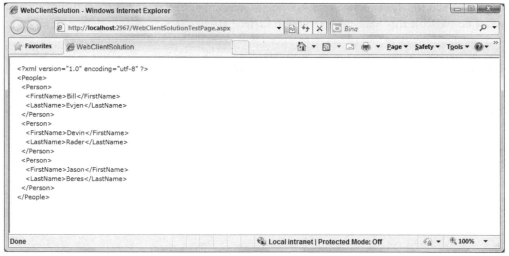

FIGURE 10-1

Downloading Files Using WebClient

In Silverlight 1.0, there was a special Downloader service that simplified downloading items with HTTP GET. Since Silverlight 2.0, the Downloader has been replaced with the `WebClient` class, which is a more general-purpose web client (as its name implies). You can actually use `WebClient` to download all sorts of things including XAML, XML, media, fonts, packages, additional assemblies, and more. This is also done asynchronously over HTTP.

In addition to starting and receiving the download process, you can also use this to monitor the overall progress of the download. The `DownloadProgressChangedEventArgs` object has various members such as bytes and total bytes to receive as well as a progress percentage member that you can use to display meaningful progress to the end user.

To see the progress aspect in action, create a new project called Downloading in Visual Studio. Put a large file in the host solution's ClientBin folder and create a simple XAML page as shown in Figure 10-2.

FIGURE 10-2

The XAML code for this is presented in Listing 10-3.

LISTING 10-3: XAML code for the Downloading solution

```xml
<UserControl x:Class="Downloading.MainPage"
    xmlns="http://schemas.microsoft.com/winfx/2006/xaml/presentation"
    xmlns:x="http://schemas.microsoft.com/winfx/2006/xaml"
    xmlns:d="http://schemas.microsoft.com/expression/blend/2008"
    xmlns:mc="http://schemas.openxmlformats.org/markup-compatibility/2006"
    mc:Ignorable="d"
    d:DesignHeight="300" d:DesignWidth="400"
    xmlns:sdk="http://schemas.microsoft.com/winfx/2006/xaml/presentation/sdk">

    <Grid x:Name="LayoutRoot" Background="White">
        <Button Content="Start downloading ..." Height="23"
          HorizontalAlignment="Left" Margin="12,12,0,0" Name="button1"
          VerticalAlignment="Top" Width="376" Click="button1_Click" />
        <ProgressBar Height="20" HorizontalAlignment="Left"
          Margin="12,41,0,0" Name="progressBar1"
          VerticalAlignment="Top" Width="376" />
        <sdk:Label Height="28" HorizontalAlignment="Left" Margin="12,67,0,0"
          Name="lblPercentComplete" VerticalAlignment="Top" Width="376" />
        <sdk:Label Height="28" HorizontalAlignment="Left" Margin="12,87,0,0"
          Name="lblBytesReceived" VerticalAlignment="Top" Width="376" />
        <sdk:Label Height="28" HorizontalAlignment="Left" Margin="12,107,0,0"
          Name="lblBytesToReceive" VerticalAlignment="Top" Width="376" />
    </Grid>
</UserControl>
```

The idea here is that when the user clicks the only button, the download process starts and the end user is provided with a series of stats on the download that is occurring. The code-behind for this file is presented in Listing 10-4.

LISTING 10-4: Monitoring the download progress

```
using System;
using System.Net;
using System.Windows;
using System.Windows.Controls;

namespace Downloading
{
    public partial class MainPage : UserControl
    {
        public MainPage()
        {
            InitializeComponent();
        }

        private void button1_Click(object sender, RoutedEventArgs e)
        {
            WebClient client = new WebClient();
            Uri uri = new Uri("Big Movie.wmv", UriKind.Relative);


            client.OpenReadCompleted +=
                new OpenReadCompletedEventHandler(client_OpenReadCompleted);
            client.DownloadProgressChanged +=
                new DownloadProgressChangedEventHandler
                (client_DownloadProgressChanged);
            client.OpenReadAsync(uri);
        }

        void client_OpenReadCompleted(object sender, OpenReadCompletedEventArgs e)
        {
            MessageBox.Show("Download completed!");
        }

        void client_DownloadProgressChanged(object sender,
            DownloadProgressChangedEventArgs e)
        {
            progressBar1.Value = e.ProgressPercentage;
            lblPercentComplete.Content = e.ProgressPercentage + "% done";
            lblBytesReceived.Content = e.BytesReceived + " bytes received";
            lblBytesToReceive.Content = e.TotalBytesToReceive + " bytes needed";
        }
    }
}
```

Once the download starts, the `ProgressBar` control is provided with a value of the progress percentage from the `DownloadProgressChangedEventArgs` object. In addition, three `Label` controls are updated with the progress percentage, the total bytes received, and the total number of bytes of the entire file. When you run this solution, you will see results similar to those shown in Figure 10-3.

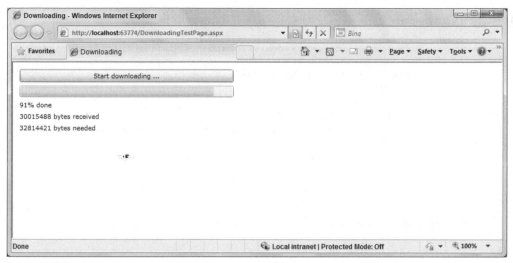

FIGURE 10-3

Uploading Files Using WebClient

In addition to downloading files, you can also allow the end user to upload files to the server. There is a bit of extra work for this, because you are required to create a generic handler on the server for the Silverlight client to interact with in the upload process.

To accomplish this, create a new solution called UploadFiles and the associated UploadFiles.Web. First, this section focuses on the UploadFiles.Web solution. To start, create a generic handler called `FileUpload.ashx` in the root of the solution. Listing 10-5 provides you with the code for the `FileUpload.ashx.cs` file.

LISTING 10-5: A generic handler file for uploading files to the server

```
using System.IO;
using System.Web;

namespace UploadFiles.Web
{
    public class FileUpload : IHttpHandler
    {
        #region IHttpHandler Members

        public void ProcessRequest(HttpContext context)
        {
            string fileuploaded = context.Request.QueryString["uploadedfile"];

            using (FileStream fileStream =
```

continues

LISTING 10-5 *(continued)*

```
            File.Create(context.Server.MapPath("~/Uploads/" + fileuploaded)))
        {
            byte[] bytes = new byte[4096];
            int totalBytesRead;

            while ((totalBytesRead =
               context.Request.InputStream.Read(bytes, 0, bytes.Length)) != 0)
            {
                fileStream.Write(bytes, 0, totalBytesRead);
            }
        }
    }

    public bool IsReusable
    {
        get { return false; }
    }

    #endregion
    }
}
```

From this handler, you can see that it is looking for a querystring object called `uploadedfile` and will take that as the name of the file being uploaded. The upload is occurring in a folder called Uploads that should be created within the UploadFiles.Web solution. You should make sure that there are write privileges to this folder.

Now that you have the handler and the folder ready, the next step is to focus on the Silverlight client and create an application that will make use of this handler.

The actual Silverlight form that you are using is rather simple; it contains a simple button and nothing more. The idea is that when users click the button, they are presented with a file dialog. The file selected will then be the file that is uploaded to the server. Listing 10-6 shows the code-behind file for `MainPage.xaml`.

LISTING 10-6: Uploading a file from a Silverlight client application

```
using System;
using System.IO;
using System.Net;
using System.Windows;
using System.Windows.Controls;

namespace UploadFiles
{
    public partial class MainPage : UserControl
    {
        public MainPage()
        {
            InitializeComponent();
```

```
            }

            private void button1_Click(object sender, RoutedEventArgs e)
            {
                OpenFileDialog openFileDialog = new OpenFileDialog();
                openFileDialog.Multiselect = false;

                bool? userAccepts = openFileDialog.ShowDialog();

                if (userAccepts == true)
                {
                    // Start the upload process
                    // Change the port on the localhost to what
                    // yours is when running in Visual Studio
                    UriBuilder uriBuilder = new
                        UriBuilder("http://localhost:63906/FileUpload.ashx");
                    uriBuilder.Query =
                        string.Format("uploadedfile={0}", openFileDialog.File.Name);

                    WebClient client = new WebClient();

                    client.OpenWriteCompleted += (innerSender, innerE) =>
                        {
                            Stream inputStream = openFileDialog.File.OpenRead();
                            Stream outputStream = innerE.Result;
                            byte[] bytes = new byte[4096];
                            int totalBytesRead;

                            while ((totalBytesRead =
                                inputStream.Read(bytes, 0, bytes.Length)) !=0)
                            {
                                outputStream.Write(bytes, 0, totalBytesRead);
                            }

                            inputStream.Close();
                            outputStream.Close();

                            MessageBox.Show("File Uploaded!");
                        };

                    client.OpenWriteAsync(uriBuilder.Uri);
                }
            }
        }
    }
```

For this application, the OpenFileDialog object is used to bring forth the file dialog that allows the end users to select the file that they are interested in uploading. Notice that using openFileDialog.Multiselect = false; forces only one selection in this process.

A URI is built using the generic handler in conjunction with the querystring uploadedfile. Then the WebClient object's OpenWriteAsync() method is called to upload the file. In the end, a message box is presented saying that the file upload process is complete. When you run this application, you can select a file on the client and then, running through the process, you will notice that the selected file, at the end of it all, is contained within the Uploads folder.

Reusing a Single WebClient Object

If you want to build an application that allows the end user to download a set of files, but you do not want to instantiate different instances of the WebClient object and a separate event handler for each one, you can choose to reuse a single WebClient object to do this instead. Although each download request is made asynchronously, the WebClient class does not support simultaneous requests. You can, however, make additional calls to DownloadStringAsync once the previous calls have completed.

Because each WebClient instance has a single DownloadStringCompleted event, you need a way to distinguish exactly what request has completed in your event handler. You can achieve this by specifying some state with each call to DownloadStringAsync through the userToken parameter. An example of this in action is presented in Listing 10-7.

LISTING 10-7: Allowing for multiple downloads

```
public partial class MainPage : UserControl
{
    // Construct a new WebRequest object as a private member
    WebClient _client = new WebClient();

    public MainPage()
    {
        InitializeComponent();
        this.Loaded += new RoutedEventHandler(Page_Loaded);
    }

    void Page_Loaded(object sender, RoutedEventArgs e)
    {
        // Configure an event handler for when the download is complete
        _client.DownloadStringCompleted += new
            DownloadStringCompletedEventHandler(client_DownloadCompleted);

        // Construct a URI based on files with an indexed naming scheme
        Uri targetUri = new Uri("Destination.xml", UriKind.Relative);

        // Initiate the download passing an integer as the userToken
        _client.DownloadStringAsync(targetUri, 1);
    }

    void client_DownloadCompleted(object sender, DownloadStringCompletedEventArgs e)
    {
        // If no error, process the result
        if (e.Error == null)
```

```
        {
            // Retrieve the state originally specified
            int count = (int)e.UserState;

            // Set the text of the appropriate textbox based on the integer userToken
            switch (count)
            {
                case 1:
                    ResultsTextBlock1.Text = e.Result;
                    break;
                case 2:
                    ResultsTextBlock2.Text = e.Result;
                    break;
                case 3:
                    ResultsTextBlock1.Text = e.Result;
                    break;
            }

            // Fire off requests until you have retrieved three files
            if (count ++ < 3)
            {
                Uri targetUri = new Uri("Destinations" + count + ".xml",
                    UriKind.Relative);

                // Initiate the download passing an integer as the userToken
                _client.DownloadStringAsync(targetUri, count);
            }
        }
    }
}
```

Cross-Domain Access

Silverlight has a few URL access restrictions. For the most part, they are what you would expect from a browser-based technology, but they are worth discussing briefly. They apply to both HTTP-based classes and to other facilities in the .NET Framework that internally use HTTP, such as images, media, font files, XAML source files, and streaming media.

At a high level, three kinds of restrictions exist: those that are based on schemes (HTTP, HTTPS, and FILE), those based on domains (for which Silverlight loosens the standard browser restrictions to enable cross-domain access), and those that are based on zone access (as in Internet Explorer).

For zone-based access, the rule is that you cannot access resources in a zone that is more trusted. For example, you cannot get a resource in Trusted Sites if your application is running in the Internet zone. This zone-based security will override cross-domain policies, so keep this in mind if you find yourself trying to access a site that you know has the correct cross-domain policy. In this case, it does good to ensure that the site you are trying to access is not in a more trusted zone.

Table 10-1 gives a good outline of how the restrictions affect the various kinds of access in Silverlight.

TABLE 10-1

	WEBCLIENT AND HTTP CLASSES	IMAGE, MEDIA ELEMENT (NON-STREAMING)	XAML SOURCE FILES	FONT FILES	STREAMING MEDIA
Allowed Schemes	HTTP, HTTPS	HTTP, HTTPS, FILE	HTTP, HTTPS, FILE	HTTP, HTTPS, FILE	HTTP
Cross-Scheme Access	No	No	No	No	Not from HTTPS
Cross-Domain Access	Only with security policy; Not HTTP, HTTPS	Not HTTP, HTTPS	Not HTTP, HTTPS	No	Not HTTP, HTTPS
Cross-Zone Access (on IE)	Same or less restrictive	Same or less restrictive	Same or less restrictive	Same or less restrictive	Same or less restrictive
Re-Direction Allowed	Same site/scheme or cross-domain with a policy	No cross-scheme	No	No	No

Silverlight enables access to any services that are contained in the same domain as the application. If you want to access services that are located on a different domain, a policy file is required. Assuming that you have root access to your deployment server, adding a Silverlight policy file is actually simple.

Many domains have already been configured to allow cross-domain access from Flash clients via a crossdomain.xml policy file. Thankfully, Silverlight supports the Silverlight (clientaccesspolicy.xml) policy format and the subset of Flash (crossdomain.xml) policy formats. First Silverlight checks to see if the Silverlight policy file, crossaccesspolicy.xml, exists on the server. If it does, Silverlight uses this. However, if not, Silverlight looks for the Flash version of this, crossdomain.xml. In effect, Silverlight supports both. Silverlight doesn't check for crossdomain.xml if crossaccesspolicy.xml exists on the server.

The clientaccesspolicy.xml Silverlight policy file enables classes in the System.Net namespace, such as the WebClient object. It also allows for classes in the System.Net.Sockets namespace to access all the available resources located in the domain. An example of this is presented in Listing 10-8.

Available for download on Wrox.com

LISTING 10-8: The clientaccesspolicy.xml file

```xml
<?xml version="1.0" encoding="utf-8" ?>
<access-policy>
    <cross-domain-access>
        <policy>
            <allow-from http-request-headers="*">
                <domain uri="*" />
            </allow-from>
            <grant-to>
                <resource path="/" include-subpaths="true" />
            </grant-to>
        </policy>
    </cross-domain-access>
</access-policy>
```

The * for the domain URI means that the clients can come from anywhere, whereas using `<domain uri="http://www.thomsonreuters.com" />` means that for the client domain, only www.thomsonreuters.com is allowed along with all of its subpaths.

The crossdomain.xml file is the Flash-based one and is presented in Listing 10-9.

LISTING 10-9: The crossdomain.xml file

```xml
<?xml version="1.0"?>
<!DOCTYPE cross-domain-policy SYSTEM
    "http://www.macromedia.com/xml/dtds/cross-domain-policy.dtd">
<cross-domain-policy>
    <allow-http-request-headers-from domain="*" headers="*" />
</cross-domain-policy>
```

SILVERLIGHT AND WCF DUPLEX COMMUNICATIONS

Duplex communication is a special facility that enables Silverlight clients to connect to a server and effectively keep a channel of communication open so that the server can send updates (sometimes called push) to clients without their having to repeatedly poll for updates. This is especially helpful in cases such as instant communication clients (instant messaging/chat services) as well as server-based monitoring.

 Note that under the covers, there is intermittent polling going on, but it is effectively two-way, because the server keeps the poll connection open until it responds.

The following sample demonstrated next illustrates the basics of setting up duplex (two-way) communications. Be prepared to be mystified if this sort of thing is new to you. It requires jumping through many hoops and does not provide most of the WCF service niceties (like client generation) that you might be used to. First, you set up your Silverlight application as usual and add a website (or link to an existing one). For this example, name your Silverlight application SilverlightDuplex. This also means that the associated web application Visual Studio helps you create will be called SilverlightDuplex.Web. Now that this is set up, instead of first concentrating on the client, you first turn your attention to building the service within the same solution.

Setting Up the Duplex Service

With your Silverlight client in place, you first build the duplex service. To do this, right-click the solution from the Solution Explorer within Visual Studio and select the option to add a new project to the solution. You are presented with the Add New Project dialog. Select the option to add a WCF Service Application as presented in Figure 10-4.

Name the service WCFDuplexServer as is presented in the figure. Once in place, you need to add a reference to `System.ServiceModel.PollingDuplex.dll`, which you will find in a server-side folder within the Silverlight SDK (`C:\Program Files\Microsoft SDKs\Silverlight\v4.0\Libraries\Server`). To do this, right-click the References folder and choose the option to add a reference. The Add Reference dialog displays. Click the Browse tab and use the file dialog to select the appropriate DLL. Once selected, you will see reference to the `PollingDuplex.dll` in your References folder.

From there, create the interface that will be utilized on the server. This interface, `IServerTimeService.cs`, is defined in Listing 10-10.

LISTING 10-10: The server-side interface IServerTimeService.cs

```
using System.ServiceModel;

namespace WCFDuplexServer
```

```
{
    [ServiceContract(Namespace = "Silverlight",
        CallbackContract = typeof (IServerTimeClient))]
    public interface IServerTimeService
    {
        [OperationContract(IsOneWay = true)]
        void GetServerTime();
    }
}
```

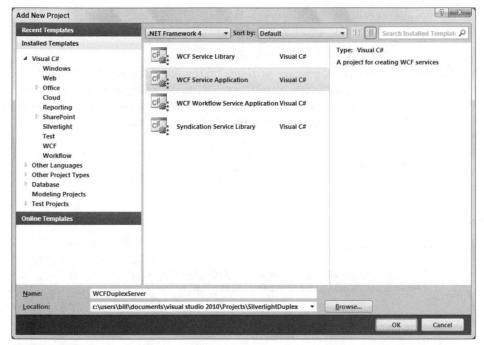

FIGURE 10-4

This code shows that `IServerTimeService` is the server-side contract and `IServerTimeClient` is the client-side contract. What is important here is the `ServiceContract` attribute, because that is how WCF maps the messages sent back and forth to the corresponding code operations. On the server, you just define a Subscribe that clients can call to subscribe to server notifications; the client defines a Notify that the server uses to send notifications to clients. Note the `CallbackContract` on `IServerTimeService`; this indicates the client-side contract that WCF expects for duplex communication.

Now that the server-side interface implementation is in place, add the client-side implementation. This is also done within the WCF service right next to the server-side interface definition. Listing 10-11 provides the code for this interface.

LISTING 10-11: The client-side interface implementation IServerTimeClient

```
using System.ServiceModel;

namespace WCFDuplexServer
{
    [ServiceContract]
    public interface IServerTimeClient
    {
        [OperationContract(IsOneWay = true)]
        void Receive(ServerDateTime serverDateTime);
    }
}
```

Here, you also make use of the `ServiceContract` attribute on the interface, and for the method definition, you make use of the `OperationContract`, setting the `IsOneWay` property to a value of `true`. From this bit of code in Listing 10-11, you can see that the client receives a `ServerDateTime` object back. The next step is to define this complex type as shown in Listing 10-12.

LISTING 10-12: Defining ServerDateTime

```
using System;

namespace WCFDuplexServer
{
    public class ServerDateTime
    {
        public DateTime ServerDateTimeValue { get; set; }
        public ServerDateTimeStatus Status { get; set; }
    }

    public enum ServerDateTimeStatus
    {
        Working,
        Completed
    }
}
```

Here, the class `ServerDateTime` is a simple definition of a `DateTime` object called `ServerDateTimeValue` along with the status of the service, `ServerDateTimeStatus`. Looking at `ServerDateTimeStatus`, you can see that it is actually an `enum` value that tells the clients that the request that they made is either being worked on or it has been completed. This is not really needed for this example, but is put here to make a point that if you had some long-running server-side operations, you might want to consider such an approach on how you would communicate that down to the client.

Now that the interfaces and the type being returned to the client have been created, the next step is to create the actual WCF service that will make use of all of this. For this step, create a new service or use the default `Service1.svc` implementation (though you are going to have to change the code for this). Listing 10-13 shows the code for the `Service1.svc` file that you are going to need to put into place. If you are using the pre-existing `Service1.svc` file, pull up this file by right-clicking the

.svc file (not the .svc.cs file) and selecting Open With. In the Open With dialog, select HTML Editor to view the actual file; otherwise, you will be consistently presented with the code-behind file if you are just double-clicking the .svc file.

LISTING 10-13: The Service1.svc file

```
<%@ ServiceHost Language="C#" Debug="true"
    Service="WCFDuplexServer.ServerTimeService" CodeBehind="Service1.svc.cs" %>
```

Here, make sure that the Service value is actually WCFDuplexServer.ServerTimeService if you have been following along with this example exactly.

With this all in place, it is now time to turn your attention to the code-behind page for this file. This is presented in Listing 10-14.

LISTING 10-14: The code-behind for the service Service1.svc.cs

```csharp
using System;
using System.ServiceModel;
using System.Threading;

namespace WCFDuplexServer
{
    public class ServerTimeService : IServerTimeService
    {
        private IServerTimeClient _client;
        private bool _working;

        public void GetServerTime()
        {
            // Grab the client callback channel.
            _client =
                OperationContext.Current.GetCallbackChannel<IServerTimeClient>();

            // Pretend service is processing and will call client back
            // in 5 seconds.
            using (new Timer(CallClient, null, 5000, 5000))
            {
                Thread.Sleep(11000);
            }
        }

        private void CallClient(object o)
        {
            ServerDateTime sdt = new ServerDateTime();

            if (_working)
            {
                sdt.ServerDateTimeValue = DateTime.Now;
```

continues

LISTING 10-14 *(continued)*

```
                sdt.Status = ServerDateTimeStatus.Completed;
            }
            else
            {
                // Turn the status to working.
                sdt.Status = ServerDateTimeStatus.Working;
                _working = true;
            }

            // Call client back.
            _client.Receive(sdt);
        }
    }
}
```

This service, `ServerTimeService`, implements the `IServerTimeService` interface. This is the server-side implementation. All this code simply sets up a service that sends delayed updates to subscribed clients, telling them what the current server time is. The timer is just there to facilitate the updates; normally you would not do this — you would have something more meaningful to send back to the client that would more likely be event-based than timer-based.

Looking over the example in Listing 10-14, you can see that an instance of the `ServerDateTime` object is returned though the client interface's `Receive()` method.

The next step to take with the WCF service is to configure the `Web.config` file. If you are working with the Visual Studio-generated `Service1.svc` file and `Web.config` file, you most likely want to delete the previous contents of the `Web.config` file and replace it with the contents illustrated in Listing 10-15.

LISTING 10-15: The Web.config file for Service1.svc

```xml
<?xml version="1.0"?>

<configuration>

    <system.web>
      <compilation debug="true" targetFramework="4.0" />
    </system.web>

    <system.serviceModel>
     <extensions>
       <bindingExtensions>
         <add name="pollingDuplexHttpBinding"
         type="System.ServiceModel.Configuration
         .PollingDuplexHttpBindingCollectionElement,
          System.ServiceModel.PollingDuplex, Version=4.0.0.0,
          Culture=neutral, PublicKeyToken=31bf3856ad364e35" />
       </bindingExtensions>
```

```
      </extensions>

      <!-- Create the polling duplex binding. -->
      <bindings>
        <pollingDuplexHttpBinding />
      </bindings>

      <services>
        <service name="WCFDuplexServer.ServerTimeService"
                 behaviorConfiguration="WCFDuplexServer.ServerTimeServiceBehavior">

          <!-- Specify the service endpoints. -->
          <endpoint address=""
                    binding="pollingDuplexHttpBinding"
                    contract="WCFDuplexServer.IServerTimeService">
          </endpoint>
          <endpoint address="mex"
                    binding="mexHttpBinding"
                    contract="IMetadataExchange"/>
        </service>
      </services>

      <behaviors>
        <serviceBehaviors>
          <behavior name="WCFDuplexServer.ServerTimeServiceBehavior">
            <!-- To avoid disclosing metadata information,
             set the value below to false and remove the metadata
             endpoint above before deployment -->
            <serviceMetadata httpGetEnabled="true"/>
            <!-- To receive exception details in faults for debugging purposes,
             set the value below to true.  Set to false before deployment to
             avoid disclosing exception information -->
            <serviceDebug includeExceptionDetailInFaults="false"/>
          </behavior>
        </serviceBehaviors>
      </behaviors>

      <serviceHostingEnvironment multipleSiteBindingsEnabled="true" />
    </system.serviceModel>

    <system.webServer>
       <modules runAllManagedModulesForAllRequests="true" />
    </system.webServer>

</configuration>
```

Some of the main points of this configuration file are that you are declaring a binding of
PollingDuplexHttpBinding. Your version of Visual Studio might not recognize this option,
but it will still work when compiled and run, so don't worry too much about that.

```
<bindings>
  <pollingDuplexHttpBinding />
</bindings>
```

You are also declaring a binding extension pointing to the provided and referenced
`System.ServiceModel.PollingDuplex.dll` from earlier:

```
<extensions>
  <bindingExtensions>
      <add name="pollingDuplexHttpBinding"
        type="System.ServiceModel.Configuration.
                PollingDuplexHttpBindingCollectionElement,
                System.ServiceModel.PollingDuplex, Version=4.0.0.0,
                Culture=neutral,
                PublicKeyToken=31bf3856ad364e35" />
  </bindingExtensions>
</extensions>
```

One of the final points is in creating the endpoint for the service:

```
<endpoint address=""
  binding="pollingDuplexHttpBinding"
  contract="WCFDuplexServer.IServerTimeService">
```

Now that the configuration file is in place, the final step is to create a policy file in the root of the
WCF solution so that your Silverlight application has the appropriate permissioning to make the
call to the service. To accomplish this task, create a new XML file called `clientaccesspolicy.xml`
within the root of the solution. The code for this file is presented in Listing 10-16.

LISTING 10-16: The clientaccesspolicy.xml file

```
<?xml version="1.0" encoding="utf-8" ?>
<access-policy>
  <cross-domain-access>
    <policy>
      <allow-from http-request-headers="*">
        <domain uri="*" />
      </allow-from>
      <grant-to>
        <resource path="/" include-subpaths="true" />
      </grant-to>
    </policy>
  </cross-domain-access>
</access-policy>
```

With this all in place, you are now ready to turn your attention to the client portion of this example.
Therefore, expand the SilverlightDuplex Silverlight project within this solution.

Setting Up the Duplex Client

Now that the server-side capabilities for duplex communication are established, the next step is to create
the client. If you remember, you had to make a server-side reference to the `PollingDuplex.dll` for this
all to work within the WCF project. On the client, you are also going to have to make a similar reference. However, in this case, you will reference the `System.ServiceModel.PollingDuplex.dll` found
at `C:\Program Files\Microsoft SDKs\Silverlight\v4.0\Libraries\Client`. This is obviously

the one that is specifically designed for the client. On another note, you are also going to have to make a reference to the `System.Runtime.Serialization.dll` as well.

After you have the appropriate DLLs referenced, make a *service reference* to the WCF service that you created earlier in this chapter. To accomplish this, right-click the References folder and select Add Service Reference. The Add Service Reference dialog appears. Click the arrow next to the Discover button to search for services that are contained within the same solution. You are presented with the option to reference the service that you just built. This is demonstrated in Figure 10-5.

FIGURE 10-5

In creating the client, the user interface for this is pretty straightforward. Listing 10-17 shows the XAML that is used for the `MainPage.xaml` file.

LISTING 10-17: The MainPage.xaml file

```xml
<UserControl x:Class="SilverlightDuplex.MainPage"
    xmlns="http://schemas.microsoft.com/winfx/2006/xaml/presentation"
    xmlns:x="http://schemas.microsoft.com/winfx/2006/xaml"
    xmlns:d="http://schemas.microsoft.com/expression/blend/2008"
    xmlns:mc="http://schemas.openxmlformats.org/markup-compatibility/2006"
    mc:Ignorable="d"
    d:DesignHeight="300" d:DesignWidth="400">

    <Grid x:Name="LayoutRoot" Background="White">
        <TextBlock Height="276" HorizontalAlignment="Left" Margin="12,12,0,0"
          Name="textBlock1" Text="" VerticalAlignment="Top" Width="376" />
    </Grid>
</UserControl>
```

As you can see from this bit of code, there isn't much to this view. The only thing on the page is a `TextBlock` control. Here you will publish the text that is pushed out of the WCF service using duplex communications. With that small bit of UI in place, the next step is to work with the `MainPage.xaml.cs` file. The code-behind to the `MainPage.xaml` file is represented in Listing 10-18.

LISTING 10-18: The MainPage.xaml.cs file

```csharp
using System;
using System.Windows.Controls;
using System.ServiceModel;
using SilverlightDuplex.ServiceReference1;

namespace SilverlightDuplex
{
    public partial class MainPage : UserControl
    {
        public MainPage()
        {
            InitializeComponent();

            EndpointAddress endpointAddress = new
                EndpointAddress("http://localhost:3737/Service1.svc");
            PollingDuplexHttpBinding pollingDuplexHttpBinding =
                new PollingDuplexHttpBinding();

            ServiceReference1.ServerTimeServiceClient svc =
                new ServerTimeServiceClient
                    (pollingDuplexHttpBinding, endpointAddress);
            svc.ReceiveReceived += new
                EventHandler<ReceiveReceivedEventArgs>(svc_ReceiveReceived);
            svc.GetServerTimeAsync();

            textBlock1.Text += Environment.NewLine +
                "Request made for the server's time";
        }

        void svc_ReceiveReceived(object sender, ReceiveReceivedEventArgs e)
        {
            if (e.Error == null)
            {
                textBlock1.Text += Environment.NewLine +
                    "Request status: " + e.serverDateTime.Status;

                if (e.serverDateTime.Status == ServerDateTimeStatus.Completed)
                {
                    textBlock1.Text += Environment.NewLine +
                        "Server time: " + e.serverDateTime.ServerDateTimeValue;
                }
            }
        }
    }
}
```

This client application creates an instance of the WCF proxy and then applies the endpoint as well as the binding that will be utilized — the `PollingDuplexHttpBinding`. The next bit of important code is in setting the callback for the `ReceiveReceived` event:

```
svc.ReceiveReceived +=
    new EventHandler<ReceiveReceivedEventArgs>(svc_ReceiveReceived);
```

Whenever the server sends a message back to the client, this method is invoked. Through this event handler, you are instructing that the `svc_ReceiveReceived()` method should be invoked. This method deals with the result that comes back from the server. In this case, the `TextBlock` control is populated with status and finally, with the server `DateTime` value.

Once you have this part of the client application in place and considering the fact that you already set up the WCF service as was described earlier in the chapter, you are basically done with this example. You actually don't have to make any changes to the web application that is hosting the Silverlight application. When you compile and run the application, you end up with something similar to what is presented in Figure 10-6.

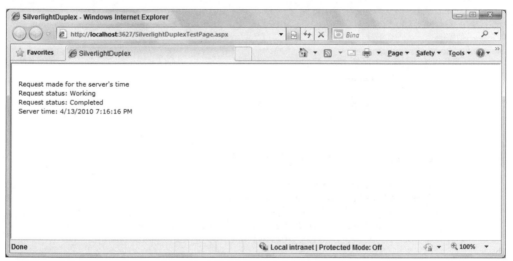

FIGURE 10-6

SOCKETS

Like HTTP-based duplex communication, sockets are likely going to appeal to a limited audience, but they are very useful for those who need them. Silverlight's sockets implementation uses Windows Sockets (Winsock) on Windows and BSD UNIX's sockets on OS X to provide a standard, managed interface. If you need true, real-time duplex communication and can use TCP, this is your solution in Silverlight. The challenge of course is that it uses ports (4502-4532 and 943 for policy) that are less likely to be open in firewalls, so the application of a sockets solution may be limited due to that.

The example that follows is a simple implementation of essentially the same scenario covered in the duplex HTTP section, that is, server notifications. The first thing you'll need to do is create a server; probably the easiest way to do this is via a console application, so you can just add a console application to your solution and call it SocketsServer to get started.

Setting Up the Policy Server

Because sockets require a call access security file (even for site-of-origin calls), you first need to set up a policy server listener. To do this, add a new class file to your console application, calling it PolicyServer.cs. You must use a few namespaces to make things more manageable. The entire set of code for this class is presented in Listing 10-19.

LISTING 10-19: Building PolicyServer.cs

```
using System;
using System.IO;
using System.Net;
using System.Net.Sockets;

namespace SocketsServer
{
    internal class PolicyServer
    {
        private readonly byte[] _policyData;
        private Socket _listener;

        public PolicyServer(string policyFile)
        {
            using (FileStream policyStream =
                new FileStream(policyFile, FileMode.Open))
            {
                _policyData = new byte[policyStream.Length];
                policyStream.Read(_policyData, 0, _policyData.Length);
            }
        }

        public void Start()
        {
            Console.WriteLine("Starting policy server...");
            _listener = new Socket(AddressFamily.InterNetwork,
                SocketType.Stream, ProtocolType.Tcp);
            _listener.Bind(new IPEndPoint(IPAddress.Any, 943));
            _listener.Listen(10);
            _listener.BeginAccept(OnConnection, null);
            Console.WriteLine("Policy server waiting for connections...");
        }

        private void OnConnection(IAsyncResult res)
```

```
        {
            Socket client;

            try
            {
                client = _listener.EndAccept(res);
            }
            catch (SocketException)
            {
                return;
            }

            Console.WriteLine("Policy client connected.");

            PolicyConnection policyConnection =
                new PolicyConnection(client, _policyData);
            policyConnection.NegotiatePolicy();

            _listener.BeginAccept(OnConnection, null);
        }

        public void Close()
        {
            _listener.Close();
        }
    }
}
```

Looking at this code, most of the socket's functionality you'll need is, of course, in `System.Net` `.Sockets`. The namespace `System.IO` is included because you want to read the policy XML file from the local filesystem, as you will see shortly. `System.Net` has the network endpoint classes you will be using.

The `Socket` object created, `_listener`, of course is the listener socket you will set up; the policy data will be an in-memory byte buffer of your policy file data to be shared across connections. The next part of the code, the `PolicyServer()` method, defines a constructor that takes a file path to the location of your policy file. As you can see, this simply reads the policy file data into the afore-mentioned byte buffer. The policy file you will use can be added to your project and called whatever you like; because you will allow all access, you can call it `allow-all.xml`. You could create different policies in different files then and just use some mechanism to specify which policy should apply at any particular time.

The `Start()` method here creates the socket listener and starts listening for requests. Silverlight limits the kinds of sockets you can create — pretty much streams over TCP. Because this is the policy server, you need to bind to the well-known port 943. The `Listen` method starts it listening on that port, allowing up to 10 connections in the queue, which is more than enough in this sample. Finally, attach a handler to the `BeginAccept()` event, such as the `OnConnection()` method.

This handler first gets a reference to the client socket, which is used to send the policy file. To facilitate this, create a `PolicyConnection` class as illustrated in Listing 10-20.

LISTING 10-20: The PolicyConnection class

```csharp
using System;
using System.Net.Sockets;
using System.Text;

namespace SocketsServer
{
    internal class PolicyConnection
    {
        private const string PolicyRequest = "<policy-file-request/>";
        private readonly byte[] _policyData;
        private readonly byte[] _policyRequestBuffer;
        private readonly Socket _connection;
        private int _numBytesReceived;

        public PolicyConnection(Socket client, byte[] policy)
        {
            _connection = client;
            _policyData = policy;
            _policyRequestBuffer = new byte[PolicyRequest.Length];
            _numBytesReceived = 0;
        }

        public void NegotiatePolicy()
        {
            Console.WriteLine("Negotiating policy.");
            try
            {
                _connection.BeginReceive(_policyRequestBuffer, 0,
                                    PolicyRequest.Length,
                                    SocketFlags.None, OnReceive, null);
            }
            catch (SocketException)
            {
                _connection.Close();
            }
        }

        private void OnReceive(IAsyncResult res)
        {
            try
            {
                _numBytesReceived += _connection.EndReceive(res);
                if (_numBytesReceived < PolicyRequest.Length)
                {
                    _connection.BeginReceive(_policyRequestBuffer,
                                        _numBytesReceived,
                                        PolicyRequest.Length -
                                        _numBytesReceived,
                                        SocketFlags.None, OnReceive,
                                        null);
```

```
            return;
        }
        string request =
            Encoding.UTF8.GetString(_policyRequestBuffer, 0,
            _numBytesReceived);
        if (StringComparer.InvariantCultureIgnoreCase.Compare(request,
            PolicyRequest) != 0)
        {
            _connection.Close();
            return;
        }
        Console.WriteLine("Policy successfully requested.");
        _connection.BeginSend(_policyData, 0, _policyData.Length,
                            SocketFlags.None, OnSend, null);
    }
    catch (SocketException)
    {
        _connection.Close();
    }
}

public void OnSend(IAsyncResult res)
{
    try
    {
        _connection.EndSend(res);
    }
    finally
    {
        _connection.Close();
    }
    Console.WriteLine("Policy sent.");
}
    }
}
```

The `System.Net.Sockets` namespace is of course for the sockets work, and the `System.Text` namespace facilitates using the text encoding to read a string from a byte array.

In the case of the fields defined in this file, the `Socket` object will be the connection to the client. `_policyRequestBuffer` will be used to compare the connection request with the expected request, identified in the shared policy request string — this is what Silverlight clients send when looking for a policy file. The number of bytes received is just used to track that the full request is received, as you will see, and the policy data byte array will be a reference to the given policy file data.

The `NegotiatePolicy()` method you called from the `PolicyServer`'s `OnConnection()` handler is used to negotiate the policy for the current connection. It simply starts receiving the request from the client into your buffer, using the `OnReceive()` method as the completion event handler.

Okay, so this is where dealing with sockets can be a little more archaic than what the average .NET developer is probably used to. Because there is no guarantee that the entire request that you are expecting was sent in the first go, you may want to take this approach. Calling `EndReceive()` tells you how many bytes were received. You can then compare that with what you are expecting to see if you are done. In the preceding code, you are expecting to receive a request with the length of the policy request `Length` property; if it is not there yet, call `BeginReceive()` again to (hopefully) get the rest of what you are looking for.

Once you have something that is at least the right length, the next step is to compare that to what you are expecting; however, you first need to read the received bytes into a UTF8 string. You can then compare the actual request contents with the well-known policy request string. If it does not match, just close the connection — this server only handles negotiating server policy according to the Silverlight policy negotiation protocol. If, on the other hand, it is the expected request, just send the server policy data down to the client.

The last thing to do for the policy server is set it up when the console application starts. So go into your `Main()` method (in the `Program` class file, assuming you used the standard Visual Studio Console Application template) and create a policy server instance and start it up as illustrated in Listing 10-21.

LISTING 10-21: The Main() method of the console application

```
namespace SocketsServer
{
    internal class Program
    {
        private static void Main(string[] args)
        {
            PolicyServer ps = new PolicyServer("allow-all.xml");
            ps.Start();
        }
    }
}
```

Looking over this code, you can see that you are passing in the path to your policy file. This is hard-coded in this example for simplicity; you would probably want to let the policy file be passed in via command-line arguments or some other fancier mechanism in real-world code. Also, note that you can simply add that file as a text file to your project and set its Build Action to Content and the Copy to Output Directory to "Copy if newer" so that you can manage the file in your project and have it be in the output location to be consumed while running and debugging.

Unfortunately, that's a lot of boilerplate code that you have to deal with just to enable Silverlight clients to connect to your "real" sockets server; that is, the one that is doing your domain work. On the positive side, your policy server should be the same (code) for all sockets apps, so you can reuse it across them and just tweak your policy files as needed.

Setting Up the Application Sockets Server

In this sample case, the real sockets server just sends notifications, so set that up next by adding a `SocketsServer` class file to your project. The code for this class is presented in Listing 10-22.

LISTING 10-22: The SocketsServer class

```csharp
using System;
using System.Collections.Generic;
using System.Diagnostics;
using System.Net;
using System.Net.Sockets;
using System.Text;
using System.Threading;
using System.Timers;
using t = System.Timers;
using Timer = System.Timers.Timer;

namespace SocketsServer
{
    internal class SocketsServer
    {
        private readonly object _syncRoot = new object();
        private readonly ManualResetEvent _threadCoordinator =
            new ManualResetEvent(false);
        private List<Socket> _clients = new List<Socket>();
        private Socket _listener;
        private Timer _serverTimer;

        public void Start()
        {
            _serverTimer = new Timer(1000);
            _serverTimer.Enabled = false;
            _serverTimer.Elapsed += ServerTimer_Elapsed;

            _listener = new Socket(AddressFamily.InterNetwork,
                SocketType.Stream, ProtocolType.Tcp);
            IPEndPoint serverEndpoint = new IPEndPoint(IPAddress.Any, 4502);
            _listener.Bind(serverEndpoint);
            _listener.Listen(2);

            while (true)
            {
                _threadCoordinator.Reset();
                _listener.BeginAccept(AcceptClient, null);
                Console.WriteLine("Waiting for clients...");
                _threadCoordinator.WaitOne();
            }
        }

        private void AcceptClient(IAsyncResult result)
        {
            try
            {
                _threadCoordinator.Set();

                Socket clientSocket = _listener.EndAccept(result);
                lock (_syncRoot)
                    _clients.Add(clientSocket);
```

continues

LISTING 10-22 *(continued)*

```
            Console.WriteLine("Client connected.");


            if (!_serverTimer.Enabled)
                _serverTimer.Enabled = true;
        }
        catch (ObjectDisposedException ex)
        {
            Trace.WriteLine("Socket closed: " + ex);
        }
        catch (SocketException ex)
        {
            Console.WriteLine(ex.Message);
        }
    }

    private void ServerTimer_Elapsed(object sender, ElapsedEventArgs e)
    {
        byte[] serverTimeBytes = Encoding.UTF8.GetBytes(
            DateTimeOffset.Now.ToString());
        Console.WriteLine("Sending server time.");
        lock (_syncRoot)
        {
            List<Socket> refreshedList = new List<Socket>(_clients.Count);
            foreach (Socket client in _clients)
            {
                if (client.Connected)
                {
                    try
                    {
                        client.Send(serverTimeBytes);
                    }
                    catch (Exception ex)
                    {
                        if (!(ex is SocketException) ||
                            ((SocketException) ex).SocketErrorCode !=
                                SocketError.ConnectionReset)
                            Console.WriteLine("Client Send Error: " + ex);
                        else
                            Console.WriteLine("Client disconnected.");
                        client.Close();
                        return;
                    }
                    refreshedList.Add(client);
                }
            }
            _clients = refreshedList;
            if (_clients.Count == 0)
                _serverTimer.Enabled = false;
        }
    }
}
}
```

Because there is a `System.Threading` timer and a `System.Timers` timer, it is helpful to clarify using the namespace alias setup in the `using` statements, that is, "t." The thread coordinator, sync root, and clients list are all there to facilitate tracking multiple connections and coordinating between them.

In the `Start()` method, the first thing here is the creation of the timer. Note that it is disabled initially — no need for it to be running while no clients are connected. Also, keep in mind that this is just used for simulation purposes; it is safe to assume that you would have more meaningful events and notifications to send to real-world clients than timer-based ones.

The next block of code should look familiar; it is setting up the server socket listener. One thing that is different is that it is listening on port 4502 — one of the ports allowed by Silverlight and not the policy negotiation port of 943. In addition, the code is (arbitrarily) limiting queued connections to two; you need to adjust this to what makes sense for your expected usage and capacity.

The last block here sets up the listener loop. The `ManualResetEvent()` that here is called `_threadCoordinator` is used as a simple way for threads to signal that they are doing or not doing something. `Reset` tells all the threads to hold on while the current thread does its thing. `WaitOne()` tells the current thread to chill until it gets a signal that says go ahead.

In between there, you set up the `AcceptClient()` method to take the next connection that comes in. In this method, the first thing is to let the waiting threads that were previously blocked precede. Then it goes on to get a reference to the connected client socket, synchronizes access to the current list of clients, and adds this one to the list of subscribed clients. Next, enable the server timer now that clients are connected and waiting for notifications. If you recall, you attached the `ServerTimer_Elapsed()` method to the timer's `Elapsed()` method back in the `Start()` method.

This method does the actual sending of notifications to clients, but remember that this is completely arbitrary — you could send updates to clients based on any number of server-side events. Because this sample is timer-based, it makes sense to just send the server time, so that first bit is grabbing the current server time into a byte buffer to be sent to the clients.

The next block goes ahead and synchronizes access to your client list by locking on your sync root object. It then creates a new list of clients that are used to refresh the list of currently connected clients — this way, when clients fall off or unsubscribe, you let go of them on the server side and let their resources get cleaned up. Then for every client still connected, add them to the new list and try to send them the message (the server time).

The last bit of code in this method updates the `_clients` reference with the new, refreshed list of clients and then checks if any clients are still connected. If not, it disables the timer until new clients connect.

The final thing you need to do on the server is create an instance of this class and start it up, so go back to your `Main()` method and add it as is presented in Listing 10-23.

LISTING 10-23: Adding more to the Main() method

```
namespace SocketsServer
{
    internal class Program
    {
        private static void Main(string[] args)
```

continues

LISTING 10-23 *(continued)*

```
        {
                PolicyServer ps = new PolicyServer("allow-all.xml");
                ps.Start();

                SocketsServer s = new SocketsServer();
                s.Start();
        }
    }
}
```

Setting Up the Sockets Client

Now that your server is all set, you need to create a client. To do this, you can create a new
Sockets.xaml user control within a new Silverlight solution. In the code-behind, you need to
set up very little. This is where you will find that sockets are easier than duplex HTTP communications. You can accomplish the same scenario with far fewer methods and trouble.

MainPage.xaml is a simple construction and is provided in Listing 10-24.

LISTING 10-24: The XAML code for MainPage.xaml

```
<UserControl x:Class="SilverlightSockets.MainPage"
    xmlns="http://schemas.microsoft.com/winfx/2006/xaml/presentation"
    xmlns:x="http://schemas.microsoft.com/winfx/2006/xaml"
    xmlns:d="http://schemas.microsoft.com/expression/blend/2008"
    xmlns:mc="http://schemas.openxmlformats.org/markup-compatibility/2006"
    mc:Ignorable="d"
    d:DesignHeight="300" d:DesignWidth="400">

    <Grid x:Name="LayoutRoot" Background="White">
        <StackPanel>
            <Button Content="Subscribe" x:Name="SubscriptionButton"
                Click="SubscriptionButton_Click" />
            <Button Content="Unsubscribe" x:Name="UnsubscriptionButton"
                Click="UnsubscriptionButton_Click" />
            <TextBlock x:Name="SusbscriptionInfo" TextWrapping="Wrap" />
        </StackPanel>
    </Grid>
</UserControl>
```

The code-behind for this simple view is presented in Listing 10-25.

LISTING 10-25: MainPage.xaml.cs

```
using System;
using System.Net;
using System.Net.Sockets;
```

```csharp
using System.Text;
using System.Threading;
using System.Windows;
using System.Windows.Controls;

namespace SilverlightSockets
{
    public partial class MainPage : UserControl
    {
        public MainPage()
        {
            InitializeComponent();
        }

        SynchronizationContext _uiThread;
        Socket _channel;
        DnsEndPoint _remoteEndPoint;
        bool Connected { get { return _channel != null && _channel.Connected; } }

        void AppendServerMessage(object messagePayload)
        {
            string message = messagePayload as string;
            if (!string.IsNullOrEmpty(message))
                this.SusbscriptionInfo.Text += message + Environment.NewLine;
        }

        void SubscriptionButton_Click(object sender, RoutedEventArgs e)
        {
            if (Connected)
            {
                AppendServerMessage("Already subscribed.");
                return;
            }

            AppendServerMessage("Subscribing to server notifications...");
            _uiThread = SynchronizationContext.Current;

            _channel = new Socket(AddressFamily.InterNetwork,
              SocketType.Stream, ProtocolType.Tcp);
            _remoteEndPoint =
              new DnsEndPoint(Application.Current.Host.Source.DnsSafeHost, 4502);

            SocketAsyncEventArgs args = new SocketAsyncEventArgs();
            args.RemoteEndPoint = _remoteEndPoint;
            args.Completed += SocketConnectCompleted;
            _channel.ConnectAsync(args);
        }

        void SocketConnectCompleted(object sender, SocketAsyncEventArgs args)
        {
            if (!_channel.Connected)
            {
                _uiThread.Post(AppendServerMessage,
                  "Could not connect to server.");
```

continues

LISTING 10-25 *(continued)*

```
                _channel.Dispose();
                _channel = null;
                return;
            }

            args.Completed -= SocketConnectCompleted;
            args.Completed += ReceiveData;
            args.SetBuffer(new byte[2048], 0, 2048);
            _channel.ReceiveAsync(args);
            _uiThread.Post(AppendServerMessage, "Waiting for notifications...");
        }

        void ReceiveData(object sender, SocketAsyncEventArgs e)
        {
            if (Connected)
            {
                string notification = Encoding.UTF8.GetString(
                  e.Buffer, e.Offset, e.BytesTransferred);
                _uiThread.Post(AppendServerMessage, notification);
                _channel.ReceiveAsync(e);
            }
        }

        void UnsubscriptionButton_Click(object sender, RoutedEventArgs e)
        {
            if (Connected)
            {
                _channel.Dispose();
                _channel = null;
                AppendServerMessage("Unsubscribed.");
            }
            else
                AppendServerMessage("Not subscribed.");
        }
    }
}
```

The first part of this should look familiar from the duplex HTTP, just ensuring only one subscription for this client at a time and grabbing a reference to the UI thread context. Assuming it is not already connected, this creates a new socket and set up a DnsEndPoint to the site of origin (that is the Application.Current.Host.Source bit) on port 4502. The important thing here is, of course, to connect on the port that the server is listening on. So if this were a real-world app, you would have to somehow publish that information to your clients. Here we are hard coding for simplicity.

Now Silverlight uses the SocketAsyncEventArgs class as a sort of general socket communication facility, so go ahead and create an instance, set the remote endpoint to the one just created, attach to the Completed() event with the SocketConnectCompleted() handler, and call ConnectAsync() on the socket. When the connection completes, it calls SocketConnectCompleted().

If the result of the connection attempt is not successful, dispose of the socket and send a message to the users letting them know that. If it does succeed, move on to the next step — receiving data. Again, the SocketAsyncEventArgs class is used; in fact, you can reuse it to conserve resources as done here. First, remove the SocketConnectCompleted() event handler and attach instead the ReceiveData() handler. Set up a buffer to specify how much to receive at a time; in this case, 2048 is rather arbitrary and actually way more than you need because you know the server is just sending the server time. Set it up to something reasonable that would handle most messages but not so large that it ties up too many resources. Then it puts itself into a state to receive data from the server.

Remember that once this client is connected, the server enables its timer (if no other clients were already connected) and starts sending server-time updates every second, so the ReceiveData() method should be called almost immediately.

The ReceiveData() method just grabs the bytes sent as a UTF8 string, posts those to the UI thread, and tells the socket to receive again (using the same SocketAsyncEventArgs instance). This loop continues as long as the server keeps sending data and, of course, as long as the socket remains open, which leads us to the UnsubscriptionButton_Click() handler.

If connected, this disposes of the socket, clears out your reference to it, and notifies the user accordingly.

To see this in action, right-click the SilverlightSocketsTestPage.html page from Visual Studio's Solution Explorer and choose the option to view the page in a browser.

Once that page is open in the browser, right-click the SocketsServer project and select this as the startup project. Compiling and running this gives you what is presented in Figure 10-7.

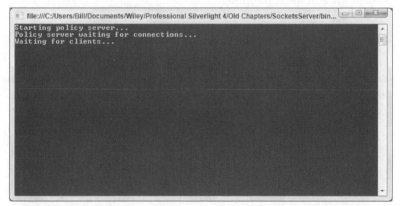

FIGURE 10-7

Once the SocketsServer project is running and waiting, click the Subscribe button back in the view. You are then presented with something similar to what is shown in Figure 10-8.

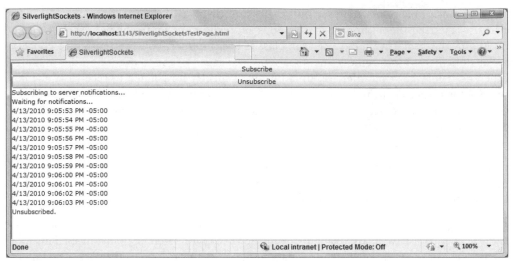

FIGURE 10-8

That about wraps it up for the communications services. As noted, you will see a lot of samples in this book using the standard HTTP- and WCF-style communications, so those were omitted here. But you did learn about the duplex HTTP and sockets in enough depth to give you a good understanding of what is involved in using them. If you have a need for duplex, real-time communication, those are your two best options in Silverlight. If the application is meant to run over the Web, your best bet is duplex HTTP; however, if you can require your clients to open up the right ports, sockets may be a more dependable, perhaps even simpler, solution.

SUMMARY

This chapter covered various services that Silverlight provides to make application development and maintenance easier and, in some cases, possible user scenarios. This chapter looked at communications services such as HTTP-based services, including duplex communication over HTTP, and at sockets communications.

11

Building Line of Business Applications

WHAT'S IN THIS CHAPTER?

➤ Working with the mouse

➤ Printing from a Silverlight application

➤ Drag-and-drop support

➤ Communicating between Silverlight players

➤ Integrating with Microsoft Office applications

➤ Making full-screen applications

It's an exciting new age for software development. Rich Internet applications (RIAs) are quickly becoming the standard architecture chosen by a number of developers. In the past building RIA-based Line of Business (LOB) applications has been very challenging, especially when you to need handle the following key scenarios: printing, localizing, and integrating with Microsoft Office applications.

Silverlight 4 includes several new components and API(s) to address the challenges of building LOB applications to add context-sensitive menus, build a printer-friendly version of your application, integrate with Microsoft Excel or Word, and more. The Silverlight platform makes these and many other typical LOB scenarios easy to implement.

LINE OF BUSINESS BASICS

Silverlight includes several key features for easily building Line of Business applications. You can respond to mouse actions to display context menus, drag-and-drag items, and add Multi-Touch support to your application. The printing support introduced in Silverlight 4 allows you to print the contents of an entire screen, part of the screen or to build a printer friendly version of your screen. With each new release, Silverlight makes it easier to build Line of Business applications that will impress your users.

Responding to Mouse Actions

Silverlight provides a rich set of events for responding to mouse actions such as clicking a button or moving the location of the mouse. In addition, Silverlight 4 supports responding to right-click behaviors and turning stylus input/Multi-Touch input into equivalent mouse actions.

Table 11-1 shows the mouse events you can respond to in your application.

TABLE 11-1

EVENT	DESCRIPTION
LostMouseCapture	Occurs when the UI element loses mouse capture.
MouseMove	Occurs when the coordinate position of the mouse (or stylus) pointer changes.
MouseEnter	Occurs when the mouse (or stylus) enters the bounding area of an object.
MouseLeave	Occurs when the mouse (or stylus) leaves the bounding area of an object.
MouseLeftButtonDown	Occurs when the left mouse button is down or when the tip of the stylus touches the screen.
MouseLeftButtonUp	Occurs when the left mouse button is up or when the tip of the stylus leaves the screen, typically following a MouseLeftButtonDown event.
MouseRightButtonDown	Occurs when the right mouse button is pressed.
MouseRightButtonUp	Occurs when the mouse (or stylus) leaves the bounding area of an object.
MouseWheel	Occurs when the mouse wheel is spun or clicked.

Listing 11-1 shows an example of subscribing to the MouseLeftButtonUp and MouseMove events of a tree view control. The left button event allows you to retrieve the data context of the item clicked, and the MouseMove events expose the current X and Y coordinates of the mouse.

Available for download on Wrox.com

LISTING 11-1: Subscribing to the mouse events

```
using System.Windows;
using System.Windows.Controls;
using System.Windows.Input;

namespace Chapter11.Views
{
    public partial class Listing1101 : UserControl
```

```
    {
        public Listing1101()
        {
            InitializeComponent();

            this.Loaded += new RoutedEventHandler(Sample_Loaded);
        }

        void Sample_Loaded(object sender, RoutedEventArgs e)
        {
            this.DataTree.MouseLeftButtonUp +=
                new MouseButtonEventHandler(DataTree_MouseLeftButtonUp);
            this.DataTree.MouseMove += new
                MouseEventHandler(DataTree_MouseMove);
        }

        void DataTree_MouseMove(object sender, MouseEventArgs e)
        {
            // When you pass null to GetPosition you get the
            // absolute positon of the mouse on the screen
            // if you pass a UIElement you will get a relative offset
            Point point = e.GetPosition(null);
            this.MousePositionX.Text = point.X.ToString();
            this.MousePositionY.Text = point.Y.ToString();
        }

        void DataTree_MouseLeftButtonUp(object sender, MouseButtonEventArgs e)
        {
            FrameworkElement element = (FrameworkElement)e.OriginalSource;
            this.MouseButton.Text = "Left Button Up: " + element.DataContext;
        }
    }
}
```

Listing 11-2 shows an example of subscribing to the MouseWheel events for a slider and image. The MouseWheel event argument includes a Delta property that tracks the factor of the mouse wheel, based on its previous value. In the sample, the image scale is increased or decreased based on when the Delta value is positive or negative. The same condition is used to adjust the value of the slider control.

LISTING 11-2: Subscribing to MouseWheel events

```
using System.Windows.Controls;
using System.Windows.Input;

namespace Chapter11.Views
{
    public partial class Listing1102 : UserControl
    {
        public Listing1102()
        {
            InitializeComponent();
        }
```

continues

LISTING 11-2 *(continued)*

```
private void slImage_MouseWheel(object sender, MouseWheelEventArgs e)
{
    if (e.Delta > 0)
    {
        imageScale.ScaleX *= 1.1;
        imageScale.ScaleY *= 1.1;
    }
    else
    {
        imageScale.ScaleX *= 0.9;
        imageScale.ScaleY *= 0.9;
    }

    e.Handled = true;
}

private void sliderValue_MouseWheel(object sender, MouseWheelEventArgs e)
{
    if (e.Delta > 0)
        slider.Value += 1;
    else
        slider.Value -= 1;

    e.Handled = true;
}
    }
}
```

Enabling Right-Click Support

Many LOB applications require support for context style menus. Typically developers add this feature by enabling right-click support for one or more UI elements. The menu displayed would be context sensitive to its related UI element. In previous versions of Silverlight, you faced many challenges when enabling right-click support. But now, in addition to events for LeftButtonDown and LeftButtonUp, you have RightButtonDown and RightButtonUp events you can use to display context-sensitive menus.

Listing 11-3 shows how to subscribe to the right-click events for a tree view control. In order for the event not to be bubbled up to the default Silverlight context menu, you have to mark it as handled in the MouseRightButtonDown event handler. If this is not done, the MouseRightButtonUp event will not be fired. When the right-click event fires, this code displays a context menu for expanding or collapsing the nodes of the tree view.

LISTING 11-3: Subscribing to right-click events

```
using System.Windows;
using System.Windows.Controls;
using System.Windows.Controls.Primitives;
```

```csharp
using System.Windows.Input;
using Chapter11.Common;

namespace Chapter11.Views
{
    public partial class Listing1103 : UserControl
    {
        public Listing1103()
        {
            InitializeComponent();
        }

        private void DataTree_MouseRightButtonDown(object sender,
            MouseButtonEventArgs e)
        {
            e.Handled = true;
        }

        private void DataTree_MouseRightButtonUp(object sender,
            MouseButtonEventArgs e)
        {
            FrameworkElement element = (FrameworkElement)e.OriginalSource;

            if (element.DataContext != null)
            {
                this.DisplayContextMenu();
            }
        }

        private Popup contextMenu = new Popup();
        private void DisplayContextMenu()
        {
            if (!this.contextMenu.IsOpen)
            {
                ContextMenu menu = new ContextMenu();
                menu.TreeView = this.DataTree;
                menu.ActionClick += (s, e) =>
                    {
                        this.contextMenu.IsOpen = false;
                    };

                this.contextMenu = new Popup();
                this.contextMenu.Child = menu;
                this.contextMenu.VerticalOffset = 150;
                this.contextMenu.HorizontalOffset = 100;

                this.contextMenu.IsOpen = true;
            }
        }
    }
}
```

Handling Multi-Touch

The Silverlight platform includes Multi-Touch support, which enables a wide range of gestures and touch interactions that can be integrated into your application's user experience. However, it's possible to add Multi-Touch features to your application by tracking mouse movements and clicks. Silverlight provides a better mechanism using the Multi-Touch API's FrameReported event. This event will be called when the underling Multi-Touch hardware sends the touch events at run time to your application.

The argument for the FrameReported event includes methods to get the primary touch point plus a list of current touch points. Using either method you get access to the TouchPoint class. The class returns a relative or absolute position based on the offset you passed to the GetTouchPoint method. If you pass in null, the absolute position of the touch point will be returned. The TouchPoint class includes an action property that tells the state of the TouchPoint: Down, Move, or Up. The same sequence will always be followed: first down, then move until the user removes the touch, and then the up action will be fired. The move action is the key piece. It will be fired even if the user is no longer moving any elements. During this state is when you should respond to the gesture by updating the UI element position or size.

To utilize Multi-Touch features in your application you are going to need to run your application on supported Multi-Touch hardware that properly handles sending the WM_TOUCH message to the Windows operating system.

Listing 11-4 shows how to use the FrameReported event to add Multi-Touch features to your application.

LISTING 11-4: Using Multi-Touch support

```csharp
using System.Collections.ObjectModel;
using System.Linq;
using System.Windows;
using System.Windows.Controls;
using System.Windows.Data;
using System.Windows.Input;

namespace MultiTouchTest
{
    public partial class MainPage : UserControl
    {

        ObservableCollection<TouchPoint> currentPoints
            = new ObservableCollection<TouchPoint>();
        TouchPoint primary = new TouchPoint();

        public MainPage()
        {
            InitializeComponent();

            Touch.FrameReported +=
                new TouchFrameEventHandler(Touch_FrameReported);
```

```
            this.Loaded += new RoutedEventHandler(Sample_Loaded);
        }

        void Sample_Loaded(object sender, RoutedEventArgs e)
        {
            PagedCollectionView data = new PagedCollectionView(currentPoints);
            data.GroupDescriptions.Add(new PropertyGroupDescription("Action"));
            this.TouchPointData.ItemsSource = data;
        }

        void Touch_FrameReported(object sender, TouchFrameEventArgs e)
        {
            TouchPointCollection touchPoints = e.GetTouchPoints(this.Host);

            foreach (TouchPoint item in touchPoints)
            {
                switch(item.Action)
                {
                    case TouchAction.Down:
                        this.currentPoints.Add(item);
                        break;
                    case TouchAction.Move:
                        var p = from pts in currentPoints
                        where pts.TouchDevice.Id == item.TouchDevice.Id
                        select pts;

                        this.currentPoints.Remove(p.First());
                        this.currentPoints.Add(item);
                        break;
                    case TouchAction.Up:
                        var c = from pts in this.currentPoints
                        where pts.TouchDevice.Id == item.TouchDevice.Id
                        select pts;

                        this.currentPoints.Remove(c.First());
                        break;
                }
            }
        }
    }
}
```

Drawing with Ink

An exciting feature that the Silverlight platform supports out-of-the-box is the ability to add Tablet PC Ink features to your application. The InkPresenter control provides a drawing surface that enables an end user to use ink to enter input. The InkPresenter control supports displaying one or more UI elements and a stroke collection. The control supports ink input from stylus devices, touch, and mouse input. Input from a mouse has a lower resolution than what can be gathered from a digitizer style input.

```
<InkPresenter x:Name="InkContainer" Background="Transparent" Cursor="Stylus" />
```

The stroke collection supported by the `InkPresenter` is a collection that contains one or more stroke objects. Each stroke corresponds to a stylus -down, stylus-move, and stylus -up sequence. A stroke can be a dot, a straight line, or a curving line. Each stroke object contains a `StylusPointCollection`, which contains one or more `StylusPoints` and their height, width, color, and outline color.

Listing 11-5 shows how to use the `InkPresenter` control to add ink support to your Silverlight application.

LISTING 11-5: Drawing with ink

```
using System.Windows.Controls;
using System.Windows.Ink;
using System.Windows.Input;
using System.Windows.Media;

namespace Chapter11.Views
{
    public partial class Listing1105 : UserControl
    {
        public Listing1105()
        {
            InitializeComponent();
        }

        private Stroke _stroke = null;
        private StylusPointCollection eraserPoints;
        private InkMode _mode = InkMode.Draw;

        public enum InkMode
        {
            Draw,
            Erase
        }

        private void InkContainer_MouseLeftButtonDown(object sender,
            MouseButtonEventArgs e)
        {
            InkContainer.CaptureMouse();
            if (_mode == InkMode.Draw)
            {
                _stroke = new Stroke();
                _stroke.DrawingAttributes.Color = Colors.White;
                _stroke.StylusPoints.Add(
                    e.StylusDevice.GetStylusPoints(InkContainer));

                InkContainer.Strokes.Add(_stroke);
            }
            if (_mode == InkMode.Erase)
            {
                eraserPoints = new StylusPointCollection();
                eraserPoints = e.StylusDevice.GetStylusPoints(InkContainer);
```

```
            }
        }

        private void InkContainer_MouseLeftButtonUp(object sender,
            MouseButtonEventArgs e)
        {
            _stroke = null;
            eraserPoints = null;
            InkContainer.ReleaseMouseCapture();
        }

        private void InkContainer_MouseMove(object sender, MouseEventArgs e)
        {
            if (_mode == InkMode.Draw)
            {
                if (null != _stroke)
                {
                    _stroke.StylusPoints.Add(
                        e.StylusDevice.GetStylusPoints(InkContainer));
                }
            }
            if (_mode == InkMode.Erase)
            {
                if (null != eraserPoints)
                {
                    eraserPoints.Add(
                        e.StylusDevice.GetStylusPoints(InkContainer));
                    StrokeCollection hits =
                        InkContainer.Strokes.HitTest(eraserPoints);

                    for (int cnt = 0; cnt < hits.Count; cnt++)
                    {
                        InkContainer.Strokes.Remove(hits[cnt]);
                    }
                }
            }
        }
    }
}
```

Enabling Clipboard Access

Prior to Silverlight 4 you had to jump through many hoops to get limited Clipboard access support added to your application. Silverlight 4 introduces a cross-browser Clipboard API that allows you to get and send text to and from the user's Clipboard. Using this feature, it's possible to paste the contents of a Word document or other application into your Silverlight application or copy your application contents into Word.

Some limitations are put on the Clipboard API because of security restrictions. You can get Clipboard access only through a user-initiated action (via a keyboard or mouse). Once per session, the user will be prompted to acknowledge that your application wants to access the Clipboard.

Figure 11-1 displays the warning dialog that the end user must accept before your application can access their Clipboard. The user will only be prompted once per session to allow access to their Clipboard.

FIGURE 11-1

The Clipboard API supports only the copying and pasting of text. If the Clipboard contains any other type of data (for example, contents of an image), the call to GetText returns nothing. You can use the ContainsText method to verify whether the Clipboard contains text data.

Listing 11-6 shows an example of using the Clipboard API to copy and paste the contents of one text box into another. While running this sample you should open Notepad or your preferred text editor. First, click the copy button in the application. Then make Notepad the active application, and press Ctrl+P. The text you entered into the text box will appear in Notepad. Change the text in Notepad and copy it (Ctrl+C). Make your Silverlight application active and click the Paste button. The text you typed in Notepad now appears.

Listing 11-6 shows an example of using the Clipboard API to copy and paste text to and from a Silverlight application and external application (for example, Notepad).

LISTING 11-6: Using the Clipboard API

```
using System.Windows;
using System.Windows.Controls;

namespace Chapter11.Views
{
    public partial class Listing1106 : UserControl
    {
        public Listing1106()
        {
            InitializeComponent();
        }

        private void CopyAction_Click(object sender, RoutedEventArgs e)
        {
            Clipboard.SetText(this.Source.Text);
        }

        private void PasteAction_Click(object sender, RoutedEventArgs e)
        {
```

```
                    if (Clipboard.ContainsText())
                    {
                        this.Destination.Text = Clipboard.GetText();
                    }
                }
            }
        }
```

Adding Printing Support

Sooner or later almost all LOB applications have to deal with printing. Whether you have a need to build a sophisticated sales report or just want to provide a printer-friendly view of the current screen, the printing API included in Silverlight 4 provides you with the framework to successfully add print capabilities to your Silverlight application.

The printing API allows you to address simple and complex printing requirements. You can do WYSIWYG printing of the whole or portions of the UI, custom "printer friendly" views, or produce multiple page reports.

To use the printing API, follow these steps:

1. Create a `PrintDocument` object.

2. Attach an event handler for the `PrintPage` event (you can do the same for `BeginPrint` and `EndPrint`).

3. Call the `Print` method. You can optionally pass in the text that will appear in the print queue.

4. In the `PrintPage` event, create one or more visual components you want to print and assign the root element to the `PageVisual` property of the `PrintPageEventArgs` object.

5. You can toggle whether you want to print more than one page by setting the `HasMorePages` property.

As long as there are more pages to print, the `PrintPage` event will be called. Once the `HasMorePages` flag is set to `false`, the event will no longer be called.

Listing 11-7 shows an example of using the printing API to print the contents of the current screen. When the `PrintPage` event fires, the `PageVisual` property is set to the root UI element of the current page. To print only part of the UI set the `PageVisual` property to the UI element you want to print.

LISTING 11-7: Printing the contents of the current page

```csharp
using System;
using System.Windows;
using System.Windows.Controls;
using System.Windows.Printing;

namespace Chapter11.Views
{
    public partial class Listing1107 : UserControl
```

continues

LISTING 11-7 *(continued)*

```
    {
        public Listing1107()
        {
            InitializeComponent();
        }

        private void PrintAction_Click(object sender, RoutedEventArgs e)
        {
            PrintDocument printHandler = new PrintDocument();
            printHandler.PrintPage +=
                new EventHandler<PrintPageEventArgs>(printDoc_PrintPage);
            printHandler.Print("Printing Example");
        }

        void printDoc_PrintPage(object sender, PrintPageEventArgs e)
        {
            e.PageVisual = this.LayoutRoot;
        }
    }
}
```

Listing 11-8 shows an example of using the printing API to create a printer-friendly version of the current screen. Because the PageVisual property can be set to any UI element it's possible to use a tool like Microsoft Expression Blend to build multiple views for the same data.

LISTING 11-8: Building a printer-friendly version of the page

```
using System;
using System.Windows;
using System.Windows.Controls;
using System.Windows.Printing;

namespace Chapter11.Views
{
    public partial class Listing1108 : UserControl
    {
        public Listing1108()
        {
            InitializeComponent();
        }

        private void PrintAction_Click(object sender, RoutedEventArgs e)
        {
            PrintDocument printHandler = new PrintDocument();
            printHandler.PrintPage +=
                new EventHandler<PrintPageEventArgs>(printDoc_PrintPage);
            printHandler.EndPrint +=
```

```
                    new EventHandler<EndPrintEventArgs>(printHandler_EndPrint);

            printHandler.Print("Printing Friendly Example");
        }

        void printHandler_EndPrint(object sender, EndPrintEventArgs e)
        {
            this.Normal.Visibility = Visibility.Visible;
            this.PrinterFriendly.Visibility = Visibility.Collapsed;
        }

        void printDoc_PrintPage(object sender, PrintPageEventArgs e)
        {
            this.Normal.Visibility = Visibility.Collapsed;
            this.PrinterFriendly.Visibility = Visibility.Visible;

            e.PageVisual = this.PrinterFriendly;
        }
    }
}
```

Supporting Drag-and-Drop

For years the Windows operating system has supported the concept of being able to drag-and-drop content from one application to another. In previous versions of Silverlight it was not possible for your application to be a drop target. Silverlight 4 introduces support for drag-and-drop by enabling the AllowDrop property on any UI element. If you use an external application such as Windows Explorer it is now possible to drag one or more selected files into your Silverlight application. By handling the drop event of a particular target element you can access the list of files using the FileInfo class and a stream reader to access the contents of the dropped files.

Currently there are some limitations you need to understand before using the drag-and-drop API. The events for drag-and-drop will not fire if you are in full-screen or windowless mode. In addition, you have to use a JavaScript workaround in the Silverlight player's hosted page to get this feature to work on a Macintosh platform.

Listing 11-9 shows how to respond to the drop event being fired on a ListBox control that has AllowDrop enabled. Using the Data property of DragEventArgs you can get a list of files being dropped. This sample iterates through the list of files and adds them to the ListBox control.

Available for
download on
Wrox.com

LISTING 11-9: Dragging from an external application

```
using System.IO;
using System.Windows;
using System.Windows.Controls;

namespace Chapter11.Views
{
    public partial class Listing1109 : UserControl
    {
```

continues

LISTING 11-9 *(continued)*

```
        public Listing1109()
        {
            InitializeComponent();
        }

        private void ListBox_Drop(object sender, DragEventArgs e)
        {
            IDataObject dataObject = e.Data as IDataObject;
            FileInfo[] files =
                dataObject.GetData(DataFormats.FileDrop)
                as FileInfo[];

            this.FileList.Items.Clear();
            foreach (FileInfo item in files)
            {
                this.FileList.Items.Add(
                    new ListBoxItem { Content = item.Name });
            }

        }
    }
}
```

Using the Web Browser Control

The Web is built around the concept of using HTML to render content. The typical scenario will be to enhance an existing web application by adding an island of richness using Silverlight. Sooner or later, however, you are going to run into a scenario of having to display HTML content from within your Silverlight application.

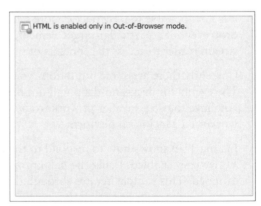

FIGURE 11-2

Silverlight 4 introduces the `WebBrowser` control to make it easier to render HTML content. The control supports displaying string-based HTML content or navigating to a website URL. To use the web browser control, your application needs to be configured for out-of-browser (OOB) mode. If you try to use the control in a normal browser-hosted Silverlight application, the message shown in Figure 11-2 will be displayed.

Listing 11-10 shows how to use the `Navigate` and `NavigateToString` methods of the `WebBrowser` control to tell it to display a specific page or set of HTML content.

LISTING 11-10: Using the WebBrowser control

```csharp
using System;
using System.Text;
using System.Windows;
using System.Windows.Controls;

namespace Chapter11.Views
{
    public partial class Listing1110 : UserControl
    {
        public Listing1110()
        {
            InitializeComponent();
        }

        private void OptionURL_Checked(object sender, RoutedEventArgs e)
        {
            browserControl.Navigate(
                new Uri("http://www.micrsoft.com"));
        }

        private void OptionsHTML_Checked(object sender, RoutedEventArgs e)
        {
            StringBuilder html = new StringBuilder();
            html.Append("<div style='color:blue;width:100;height:100'>");
            html.Append("<b>Silverlight Rocks</b></div>");

            browserControl.NavigateToString(html.ToString());
        }
    }
}
```

ADVANCED SCENARIOS

When building Line of Business applications, it's very common to integrate your application with an external application or product. The most common product you will integrate is Microsoft Office, which offers a rich set of feature that a lot of users are accustomed to using. Silverlight now offers the ability to use COM automation to communicate with Microsoft Office. Another scenario you might run into is the need to communicate between multiple Silverlight players running in the same or even different browsers. As the Silverlight platform continues to mature, it's becoming easier and easier to deal with advanced Line of Business applications.

Communicating between Silverlight Applications

While building a Line of Business application, you may need to use multiple Silverlight players. For example, you may be enhancing an existing web application instead of migrating the entire application to Silverlight all at once. You can add multiple islands of richness to the same page. Then using the Silverlight messaging API you can send and receive asynchronous messages. In addition to communicating between multiple Silverlight players on the same page, the messaging API supports communicating between different Silverlight players across multiple web browser instances.

The following sample walks you through the steps to set up a web application that contains two Silverlight applications that will communicate to each other using the messaging API.

Figure 11-3 displays the UI of the Customer Search and Customer Detail applications. These applications — which you build later in this section — use the Silverlight messaging API to send and receive messages between each other.

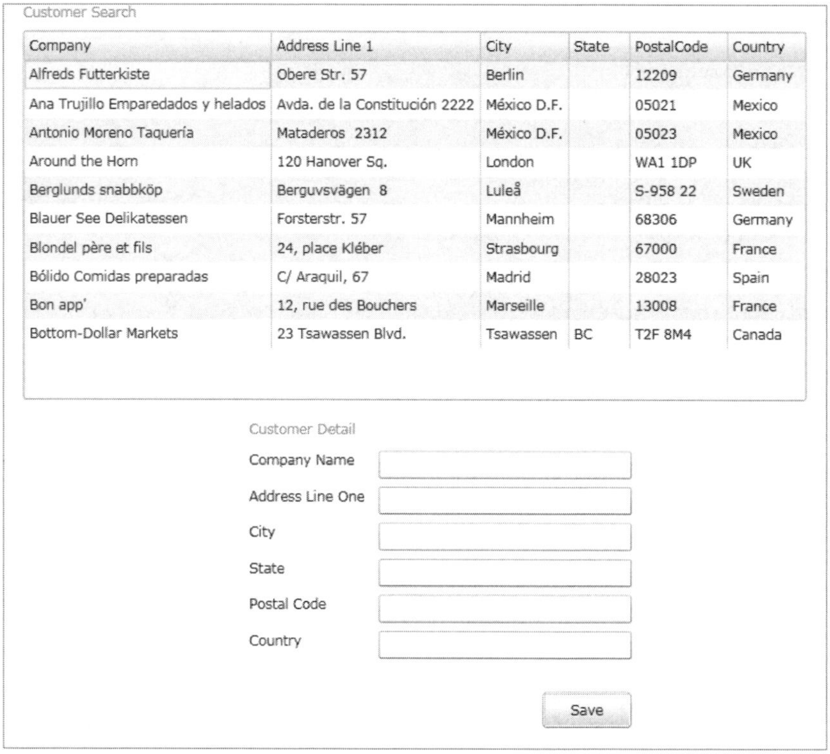

Customer Search

Company	Address Line 1	City	State	PostalCode	Country
Alfreds Futterkiste	Obere Str. 57	Berlin		12209	Germany
Ana Trujillo Emparedados y helados	Avda. de la Constitución 2222	México D.F.		05021	Mexico
Antonio Moreno Taquería	Mataderos 2312	México D.F.		05023	Mexico
Around the Horn	120 Hanover Sq.	London		WA1 1DP	UK
Berglunds snabbköp	Berguvsvägen 8	Luleå		S-958 22	Sweden
Blauer See Delikatessen	Forsterstr. 57	Mannheim		68306	Germany
Blondel père et fils	24, place Kléber	Strasbourg		67000	France
Bólido Comidas preparadas	C/ Araquil, 67	Madrid		28023	Spain
Bon app'	12, rue des Bouchers	Marseille		13008	France
Bottom-Dollar Markets	23 Tsawassen Blvd.	Tsawassen	BC	T2F 8M4	Canada

Customer Detail

Company Name   [_____]

Address Line One   [_____]

City   [_____]

State   [_____]

Postal Code   [_____]

Country   [_____]

[Save]

FIGURE 11-3

The application you are going to build includes two separate Silverlight projects called Customer Search and Customer Detail. Make sure to download the samples for this chapter from www.wrox.com to see the working version of the solution.

To build the solution, you need to understand a couple of concepts. First, you need to understand how the messaging API uses senders and receivers to communicate between different running instances of the Silverlight player. Then you need to understand how to serialize and desterilize data using the JSON API provided by the Silverlight Framework.

To set up communication between different instances of the Silverlight player you use the `LocalMessageSender` to send messages and a `LocalMessageReceiver` to receive messages.

The constructors for both objects accept a string that must identify the name of the receiver/sender the other instance is using. To send a message use the SendAsync(*string value*) method of the sender and to receive a message set up a delegate for the receiver's MessageReceived event. The event argument for this delegate contains a property to receive the message sent.

```
string message = "Hello World";
this.sender = new LocalMessageSender("CustomerDetail");
this.sender.SendAsync(message);

this.receiver = new LocalMessageReceiver("CustomerSearch");
this.receiver.MessageReceived
+= new EventHandler<MessageReceivedEventArgs>(Receiver_MessageReceived);

this.receiver.Listen();

void Receiver_MessageReceived(object sender, MessageReceivedEventArgs e)
{
        string message = e.Message;
}
```

As you may have noticed the message API senders and receivers only allow you to send string messages. At first this may seem to limit what you can do with it, but the Silverlight Framework includes a powerful JSON API for serializing and deserializing objects to and from strings. Though this is possible, it's best to limit to the size of the message and try to only pass simple objects and not complex hierarchical object graphs that contain references to multiple children objects.

To use the JSON API you need to make sure your project has references to the System.SeviceModel.Web and System.Runtime.Serialization assemblies. The JSON API includes methods to read and write data to a stream so you will need to add a using statement to System.IO. The object you want to serialize/deserialize must be annotated with the [DataContact] and [DataMember] attributes. If there are attributes of the class you do not want to serialize, just skip adding the [DataMember] attribute.

Listing 11-11 shows the structure of the Customer class that will be serialized and sent between the Search and Detail applications.

LISTING 11-11: Customer class

Available for
download on
Wrox.com

```
using System.ComponentModel;
using System.Runtime.Serialization;

namespace CustomerViewer.Search
{
    [DataContract]
    public class Customer : INotifyPropertyChanged
    {

        public event PropertyChangedEventHandler PropertyChanged;

        private void NotifyPropertyChanged(string info)
        {
            if (this.PropertyChanged != null)
```

continues

LISTING 11-11 *(continued)*

```csharp
        {
            this.PropertyChanged(this,
                new PropertyChangedEventArgs(info));
        }
    }

    public Customer()
    {
    }

    [DataMember]
    public string CustomerId { get; set; }

    private string companyName;
    [DataMember]
    public string CompanyName
    {
        get { return this.companyName; }
        set
        {
            if (this.companyName != value)
            {
                this.companyName = value;
                this.NotifyPropertyChanged("CompanyName");
            }
        }
    }

    private string addressLineOne;
    [DataMember]
    public string AddressLineOne
    {
        get { return this.addressLineOne; }
        set
        {
            if (this.addressLineOne != value)
            {
                this.addressLineOne = value;
                this.NotifyPropertyChanged("AddressLineOne");
            }
        }
    }

    private string city;
    [DataMember]
    public string City
    {
        get { return this.city; }
        set {
                if (this.city != value)
                {
                    this.city = value;
```

```
                                this.NotifyPropertyChanged("City");
                    }
                }
            }


        private string state;
        [DataMember]
        public string State
        {
            get { return this.state; }
            set
            {
                if (this.state != value)
                {
                    this.state = value;
                    this.NotifyPropertyChanged("State");
                }
            }
        }

        private string postalCode;
        [DataMember]
        public string PostalCode
        {
            get { return this.postalCode; }
            set
            {
                if (this.postalCode != value)
                {
                    this.postalCode = value;
                    this.NotifyPropertyChanged("PostalCode");
                }
            }
        }

        private string country;
        [DataMember]
        public string Country
        {
            get { return this.country; }
            set
            {
                if (this.country != value)
                {
                    this.country = value;
                    this.NotifyPropertyChanged("Country");
                }
            }
        }
    }
}
```

Listing 11-12 shows how to use the `DataContractJsonSerializer` class to serialize and deserialize a customer object converted into JSON data.

LISTING 11-12: Using the JSON Data Contract Serializer

```
string jsonData = string.Empty;

Customer selectedCustomer = new Customer
{
    CustomerId = "TEST001",
    CompanyName = "Test"
};

using (MemoryStream ms = new MemoryStream())
{
    DataContractJsonSerializer json = new
        DataContractJsonSerializer(typeof(Customer));
    json.WriteObject(ms, selectedCustomer);
    ms.Position = 0;

    StreamReader reader = new StreamReader(ms);
    jsonData = reader.ReadToEnd();
    reader.Close();
}


Customer customer = null;
using (MemoryStream ms =
    new MemoryStream(Encoding.Unicode.GetBytes(e.Message)))
{
    DataContractJsonSerializer serializer = new
        DataContractJsonSerializer(typeof(Customer));
    customer = (Customer)serializer.ReadObject(ms);
}
```

Now that you understand the key concept for sending and receiving messages using the messaging API, you are ready to build out the sample solution. The solution will include a web application and two Silverlight projects (Search and Detail). The following steps walk you through building both the Search and Detail applications. The messaging API is used to synchronize changes made in the detail application back to the search application.

Here are the steps to create the sample solution:

1. Create a new web application and add two Silverlight projects (Search and Detail) to the same solution.

2. Add a new page to the web project called `default.aspx`.

3. Set up the object tags for both Silverlight projects.

Listing 11-13 shows the `default.aspx` page for the Customer application with two Silverlight players configured: one running the Customer Search application and one running the Customer Detail application.

LISTING 11-13: Setting up multiple Silverlight players

```
<div id="SearchHost">
            <object data="data:application/x-silverlight-2,"
                type="application/x-silverlight-2" width="100%" height="100%">
              <param name="source" value="ClientBin/CustomerViewer.Search.xap"/>
              <param name="onError" value="onSilverlightError" />
              <param name="background" value="white" />
              <param name="minRuntimeVersion" value="4.0.50331.0" />
              <param name="autoUpgrade" value="true" />
              <a href="http://go.microsoft.com/fwlink/?LinkID=149156&v=
                  4.0.50331.0" style="text-decoration:none">
                <img src="http://go.microsoft.com/fwlink/?LinkId=161376"
                alt="Get Microsoft Silverlight" style="border-style:none"/>
              </a>
            </object>
        </div>
        <div id="DetailHost">
            <object data="data:application/x-silverlight-2,"
                type="application/x-silverlight-2" width="100%" height="100%">
              <param name="source" value="ClientBin/CustomerViewer.Details.xap"/>
              <param name="onError" value="onSilverlightError" />
              <param name="background" value="white" />
              <param name="minRuntimeVersion" value="4.0.50331.0" />
              <param name="autoUpgrade" value="true" />
              <a href="http://go.microsoft.com/fwlink/?LinkID=149156&v=
                  4.0.50331.0" style="text-decoration:none">
                <img src="http://go.microsoft.com/fwlink/?LinkId=161376"
                alt="Get Microsoft Silverlight" style="border-style:none"/>
              </a>
            </object>
        </div>
```

Listing 11-14 shows the XML structure for the customer data used in this sample. The `customers.xml` file must be located in the `ClientBin` folder of the web project. The download for this chapter includes a complete set of data for running the sample.

LISTING 11-14: XML structure for customer data

```
<Customers>
        <CustomerID>ALFKI</CustomerID>
        <CompanyName>Alfreds Futterkiste</CompanyName>
        <ContactName>Maria Anders</ContactName>
        <ContactTitle>Sales Representative</ContactTitle>
        <Address>Obere Str. 57</Address>
        <City>Berlin</City>
        <PostalCode>12209</PostalCode>
        <Country>Germany</Country>
        <Phone>030-0074321</Phone>
        <Fax>030-0076545</Fax>
</Customers>
```

Add a class called `SearchViewModel` to the Search project. This class will contain the logic to download the `customers.xml` file from the web project's ClientBin Folder and to synchronize the changes sent back from the CustomerDetail class.

Listing 11-15 shows the contents of the `SearchViewModel` class.

LISTING 11-15: Building the view model for the Search application

```
using System;
using System.Collections.ObjectModel;
using System.ComponentModel;
using System.IO;
using System.Linq;
using System.Net;
using System.Xml.Linq;

namespace CustomerViewer.Search
{
    public class SearchViewModel : INotifyPropertyChanged
    {
        public event PropertyChangedEventHandler PropertyChanged;

        private ObservableCollection<Customer> customers;

        public SearchViewModel()
        {
            WebClient client = new WebClient();
            client.DownloadStringCompleted +=
                new
                DownloadStringCompletedEventHandler(
                client_DownloadStringCompleted);
                client.DownloadStringAsync(new Uri("Customers.xml",
                UriKind.RelativeOrAbsolute));
        }

        void client_DownloadStringCompleted(object sender,
                        DownloadStringCompletedEventArgs e)
        {
            using (TextReader reader = new StringReader(e.Result))
            {
                XDocument doc = XDocument.Load(reader);
                var dataSource = (from d in doc.Descendants("Customers")
                            select new Customer
                            {
                                CustomerId = d.Element("CustomerID").Value,
                                CompanyName = d.Element("CompanyName").Value,
                                AddressLineOne = d.Element("Address").Value,
                                City = d.Element("City").Value,
                                State = d.Element("Region") != null
                                  ? d.Element("Region").Value : string.Empty,
                                PostalCode = d.Element("PostalCode") != null
```

```
                                  ? d.Element("PostalCode").Value : string.Empty,
                               Country = d.Element("Country").Value,
                           });

               this.customers =
                   new ObservableCollection<Customer>(
                       dataSource.ToList<Customer>());
           }

           this.NotifyPropertyChanged("Customers");
       }

       private void NotifyPropertyChanged(String info)
       {
           if (this.PropertyChanged != null)
           {
               this.PropertyChanged(this,
                   new PropertyChangedEventArgs(info));
           }
       }


       public ObservableCollection<Customer> Customers
       {
           get
           {
               return this.customers;
           }
       }

       public void SyncCustomer(Customer selectedCustomer)
       {
           Customer customer = this.customers.Where(
               q => q.CustomerId == selectedCustomer.CustomerId).Single();

           customer = selectedCustomer;

           this.NotifyPropertyChanged("Customers");
       }

   }
}
```

Add a class called `Customer` to the Search project. This class will contain the attributes for a customer. The same class will need to be created in the Detail project so the data can be properly serialized and deserialized between the two projects.

Open the `MainPage.xaml` in the Search project and add a `DataGrid` control. The data grid will be used to display the list of customers. The code-behind file for `MainPage.xaml` will contain the code for using the messaging API and the `SearchViewModel` class.

Listing 11-16 shows the XAML used to define the UI of the `Customer` Search application.

LISTING 11-16: XAML for the Search application

```xml
<UserControl x:Class="CustomerViewer.Search.MainPage"
    xmlns="http://schemas.microsoft.com/winfx/2006/xaml/presentation"
    xmlns:x="http://schemas.microsoft.com/winfx/2006/xaml"
    xmlns:d="http://schemas.microsoft.com/expression/blend/2008"
    xmlns:mc="http://schemas.openxmlformats.org/markup-compatibility/2006"
    mc:Ignorable="d" d:DesignHeight="352" d:DesignWidth="485"
    xmlns:sdk="http://schemas.microsoft.com/winfx/2006/xaml/presentation/sdk">
    <Grid x:Name="LayoutRoot" Background="White" Width="750">
        <StackPanel Margin="0,0,0,0">
            <TextBlock Text="Customer Search" Margin="29, 5" Foreground="Red" />
            <sdk:DataGrid AutoGenerateColumns="False"
                Height="308" HorizontalAlignment="Left"
                Margin="29,2,0,0" Name="customerView"
                VerticalAlignment="Top"
                ItemsSource="{Binding Customers}" IsReadOnly="true">
                <sdk:DataGrid.Columns>
                    <sdk:DataGridTextColumn Header="Company"
                        Binding="{Binding CompanyName}" />
                    <sdk:DataGridTextColumn Header="Address Line 1"
                        Binding="{Binding AddressLineOne}" />
                    <sdk:DataGridTextColumn Header="City"
                        Binding="{Binding City}" />
                    <sdk:DataGridTextColumn Header="State"
                        Binding="{Binding State}" />
                    <sdk:DataGridTextColumn Header="PostalCode"
                        Binding="{Binding PostalCode}" />
                    <sdk:DataGridTextColumn Header="Country"
                        Binding="{Binding Country}" />
                </sdk:DataGrid.Columns>
            </sdk:DataGrid>
        </StackPanel>
    </Grid>
</UserControl>
```

Listing 11-17 shows the code behind the Customer Search `MainPage.xaml.cs` file.

LISTING 11-17: Search application MainPage.cs

```csharp
using System;
using System.IO;
using System.Runtime.Serialization.Json;
using System.Text;
using System.Windows;
using System.Windows.Controls;
using System.Windows.Messaging;

namespace CustomerViewer.Search
{
    public partial class MainPage : UserControl
    {

        private LocalMessageSender sender { get; set; }
```

```csharp
        private LocalMessageReceiver receiver { get; set; }

    public MainPage()
    {
        InitializeComponent();

        this.sender = new LocalMessageSender("CustomerDetail");
        this.receiver = new LocalMessageReceiver("CustomerSearch");
        this.receiver.MessageReceived += new
            EventHandler<MessageReceivedEventArgs>(Receiver_MessageReceived);
        this.receiver.Listen();

        this.viewModel = new SearchViewModel();
        this.DataContext = this.viewModel;
        this.customerView.SelectionChanged +=
            new SelectionChangedEventHandler(customerView_SelectionChanged);
    }
    private SearchViewModel viewModel;
    void customerView_SelectionChanged(object sender,
            SelectionChangedEventArgs e)
    {
        string jsonData = string.Empty;
        Customer selectedCustomer = e.AddedItems[0] as Customer;

        using (MemoryStream ms = new MemoryStream())
        {
            DataContractJsonSerializer json =
                new DataContractJsonSerializer(typeof(Customer));
            json.WriteObject(ms, selectedCustomer);
            ms.Position = 0;

            StreamReader reader = new StreamReader(ms);
            jsonData = reader.ReadToEnd();
            reader.Close();
        }

        this.sender.SendAsync(jsonData);
    }

    void Receiver_MessageReceived(object sender, MessageReceivedEventArgs e)
    {
        using (MemoryStream ms =
            new MemoryStream(Encoding.Unicode.GetBytes(e.Message)))
        {
            DataContractJsonSerializer serializer =
                new DataContractJsonSerializer(typeof(Customer));
            Customer customer = (Customer)serializer.ReadObject(ms);

            this.viewModel.SyncCustomer(customer);
        }

    }
    }
}
```

At this point you should have everything to run the Search application. The first step for setting up the Detail application is to add the same customer class that the search application uses. For communication to work between applications, you must make sure the same properties are annotated with [DataMember] attributes in both customer classes.

Then add a set of TextBlocks and TextBoxes to the Detail application. These will be used to display and change the selected customer sent from the Search application. In the code behind the MainPage.xaml, add the necessary code to sync changes back to the Search application.

Listing 11-18 shows the XAML used to define the UI of the Customer Detail application.

LISTING 11-18: XAML for the Customer Detail application

```xml
<UserControl x:Class="CustomerViewer.Details.MainPage"
    xmlns="http://schemas.microsoft.com/winfx/2006/xaml/presentation"
    xmlns:x="http://schemas.microsoft.com/winfx/2006/xaml"
    xmlns:d="http://schemas.microsoft.com/expression/blend/2008"
    xmlns:mc="http://schemas.openxmlformats.org/markup-compatibility/2006"
    mc:Ignorable="d"
    d:DesignHeight="316" d:DesignWidth="444">
    <Grid x:Name="LayoutRoot" Background="White" Height="400" Width="370">
        <StackPanel HorizontalAlignment="Left">
            <TextBlock Text="Customer Detail" Margin="29, 5" Foreground="Red" />
            <Grid Height="300">
                <TextBlock Height="23" HorizontalAlignment="Left"
                    Margin="29,5,0,0" Name="CompanyNameCaption" Text="Company Name"
                    VerticalAlignment="Top" />
                <TextBox Height="23" HorizontalAlignment="Left" Margin="138,5,0,0"
                    Name="CompanyName" VerticalAlignment="Top" Width="212"
                    Text="{Binding CompanyName, Mode=TwoWay}" />
                <TextBlock Height="23" HorizontalAlignment="Left"
                    Margin="29,35,0,0" Name="AddressLineOneCaption"
                    Text="Address Line One" VerticalAlignment="Top" />
                <TextBox Height="23" HorizontalAlignment="Left" Margin="138,35,0,0"
                    Name="AddressLineOne" VerticalAlignment="Top" Width="212"
                    Text="{Binding AddressLineOne, Mode=TwoWay}" />
                <TextBlock Height="23" HorizontalAlignment="Left"
                    Margin="29,65,0,0" Name="CityCaption" Text="City"
                    VerticalAlignment="Top" />
                <TextBox Height="23" HorizontalAlignment="Left" Margin="138,65,0,0"
                    Name="City" VerticalAlignment="Top" Width="212" Text="{Binding
                    City, Mode=TwoWay}" />
                <TextBlock Height="23" HorizontalAlignment="Left"
                    Margin="29,95,0,0" Name="StateCaption" Text="State"
                    VerticalAlignment="Top" />
                <TextBox Height="23" HorizontalAlignment="Left" Margin="138,95,0,0"
                    Name="State" VerticalAlignment="Top" Width="212" Text="{Binding
                    State, Mode=TwoWay}" />
                <TextBlock Height="23" HorizontalAlignment="Left"
                    Margin="29,125,0,0" Name="PostalCodeCaption" Text="Postal Code"
                    VerticalAlignment="Top" />
                <TextBox Height="23" HorizontalAlignment="Left"
                    Margin="138,125,0,0" Name="PostalCode" VerticalAlignment="Top"
```

```
                    Width="212" Text="{Binding PostalCode, Mode=TwoWay}" />
                <TextBlock Height="23" HorizontalAlignment="Left"
                    Margin="29,155,0,0" Name="CountryCaption" Text="Country"
                    VerticalAlignment="Top" />
                <TextBox Height="23" HorizontalAlignment="Left"
                    Margin="138,155,0,0" Name="Country" VerticalAlignment="Top"
                    Width="212" Text="{Binding Country, Mode=TwoWay}" />
                <Button Content="Save" Height="30" HorizontalAlignment="Left"
                    Margin="275,205,0,0"
                    Name="SaveButton" VerticalAlignment="Top" Width="75"
                    Click="SaveButton_Click" />
            </Grid>
        </StackPanel>
    </Grid>
</UserControl>
```

Listing 11-19 shows the code behind the Customer Detail `MainPage.xaml.cs` file.

LISTING 11-19: Detail application MainPage.cs

```
using System;
using System.IO;
using System.Runtime.Serialization.Json;
using System.Text;
using System.Windows;
using System.Windows.Controls;
using System.Windows.Messaging;

namespace CustomerViewer.Details
{
    public partial class MainPage : UserControl
    {
        public MainPage()
        {
            InitializeComponent();

            this.sender = new LocalMessageSender("CustomerSearch");
            this.receiver = new LocalMessageReceiver("CustomerDetail");
            this.receiver.MessageReceived +=
                new EventHandler<MessageReceivedEventArgs>
                (Receiver_MessageReceived);
            this.receiver.Listen();
        }

        private LocalMessageSender sender { get; set; }
        private LocalMessageReceiver receiver { get; set; }
        private Customer selectedCustomer;

        private void SaveButton_Click(object sender, RoutedEventArgs e)
        {
            string jsonData = string.Empty;

            using (MemoryStream ms = new MemoryStream())
```

continues

LISTING 11-19 *(continued)*

```
            {
                DataContractJsonSerializer json =
                    new DataContractJsonSerializer(typeof(Customer));
                json.WriteObject(ms, this.selectedCustomer);
                ms.Position = 0;

                StreamReader reader = new StreamReader(ms);
                jsonData = reader.ReadToEnd();
                reader.Close();
            }

            this.sender.SendAsync(jsonData);
        }

        void Receiver_MessageReceived(object sender, MessageReceivedEventArgs e)
        {
            using(MemoryStream ms =
                new MemoryStream(Encoding.Unicode.GetBytes(e.Message)))
            {
                DataContractJsonSerializer serializer =
                    new DataContractJsonSerializer(typeof(Customer));
                this.selectedCustomer = (Customer)serializer.ReadObject(ms);
            }

            this.DataContext = this.selectedCustomer;
        }
    }
}
```

Integrating with Office

It's a very typical scenario in a LOB application to have to interact with one or more of the applications included in the Microsoft Office suite. For example, you may need to import/export data from Excel, generate a report using a Word template, or interface with the object model in Outlook.

Silverlight 4 adds supports for these types of scenarios by using the new COM interop features support in the ComAutomationFactory API. This component allows you to use Office Automation to load data into an Excel spreadsheet and display it to the user. The following code snippet demonstrates the basic steps to making this work:

```
dynamic excel = ComAutomationFactory.CreateObject("Excel.Application");
excel.Visible = true;  // make it visible to the user.
dynamic workbook = excel.workbooks;
workbook.Add();
dynamic sheet = excel.ActiveSheet;
```

To utilize this feature you must build a trusted application with elevated permissions. See Chapter 9 for details on how to build an out-of-browser Silverlight application.

Listing 11-20 shows how to export data stored in a Silverlight `DataGrid` control to Excel using the Office automation API. Make sure to download the source code for this chapter to see the complete working version of the Excel exported application.

Available for download on Wrox.com

LISTING 11-20: Exporting data to Excel

```csharp
using System.Collections;
using System.Runtime.InteropServices.Automation;
using System.Windows;
using System.Windows.Controls;
using ExcelExporter.ViewModel;

namespace ExcelExporter
{
    public partial class MainPage : UserControl
    {
        private ExporterViewModel viewModel;
        public MainPage()
        {
            InitializeComponent();

            this.viewModel = new ExporterViewModel();
            this.DataContext = this.viewModel;

            this.Loaded += new RoutedEventHandler(MainPage_Loaded);
        }

        void MainPage_Loaded(object sender, RoutedEventArgs e)
        {
            this.viewModel.LoadData();
            this.dataView.ItemsSource = this.viewModel.Customers;
        }

        private void ExportToExcel_Click(object sender, RoutedEventArgs e)
        {
            this.ExportDataGrid(this.dataView.ItemsSource);
        }

        private void ExportDataGrid(IEnumerable dataSource)
        {

            // Create Reference to Excel API
            dynamic excel
                = AutomationFactory.CreateObject("Excel.Application");

            excel.Visible = true;  // make it visible to the user.

            // Create Workbook and Sheet to export data
            dynamic workbook = excel.workbooks;
            workbook.Add();
            dynamic sheet = excel.ActiveSheet;

            // Add Header Row
```

continues

LISTING 11-20 *(continued)*

```csharp
            this.AddHeader(sheet);

            // Export Data from data source to excel
            int row = 2;
            foreach (Customer item in dataSource)
            {
                this.AddCell(sheet, row, 1, item.CustomerId, 15);
                this.AddCell(sheet, row, 2, item.CompanyName, 40);
                this.AddCell(sheet, row, 3, item.AddressLineOne, 40);
                this.AddCell(sheet, row, 4, item.City, 20);
                this.AddCell(sheet, row, 5, item.State, 10);
                this.AddCell(sheet, row, 6, item.PostalCode, 10);
                this.AddCell(sheet, row, 7, item.Country, 20);
                row++;
            }
        }

        private void AddHeader(dynamic sheet)
        {
            this.AddCell(sheet, 1, 1, "Customer Id", 15);
            this.AddCell(sheet, 1, 2, "Company Name", 40);
            this.AddCell(sheet, 1, 3, "Address Line One", 40);
            this.AddCell(sheet, 1, 4, "City", 20);
            this.AddCell(sheet, 1, 5, "State", 10);
            this.AddCell(sheet, 1, 6, "Postal Code", 10);
            this.AddCell(sheet, 1, 7, "Country", 20);
        }

        private void AddCell(dynamic sheet, int row, int col,
                             string value, int width)
        {
            dynamic cell = sheet.Cells[row, col];
            cell.Value = value;
            cell.ColumnWidth = width;
        }

    }
}
```

GLOBALIZATION AND LOCALIZATION

When you build a LOB application, adding support for globalization and localization can be one of the most challenging tasks. It's important to understand the needs of your application up front so you can properly handle the localization of your application.

You need to understand which cultures and locales your application must support, how to properly set up a default (fallback) culture, what impact localization will have on how you package and deploy your application, and how to support cultures that require right-to-left reading.

Localizing Your Application

Localization is the process of customizing your application to handle a given culture or locale. This is done by translating the UI elements of your application to display a specific culture or locale, handling complex scripts that must be displayed right to left, and the formatting of data (Numbers, Currency, and DateTime) using the rules for a specific culture or locale.

The approach a developer uses to localize a Silverlight application is very similar to how he would handle localizing an ASP.NET or WinForm application. A developer will create one or more string or image resource files for each culture/language his application needs to support. A hub and spoke model is used to package and deploy localized resources. At run time Silverlight will use the CurrentUICulture of the UI thread to dynamically load culture-specific satellite assemblies. If a satellite assembly is missing for a given culture, the Silverlight run time will default back to the generic region-natural resource files.

Figure 11-4 displays the contents of a Resource file displayed in Visual Studio. To support specific culture or locales, add different Resource files that start with the same name followed by a period and the culture code. It is recommended that you define an invariant resource file for each language plus any culture-specific ones. For example, if you have a strings.resx file you should add a strings.de.resx and a strings.de-DE.resx file. This way if a culture-specific assembly can be found for de-DE, it will fall back to the language invariant version strings.de.resx.

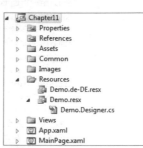

FIGURE 11-4

Using Resource Files

To use resource files to localize your Silverlight UI, you need to add a static resource to your XAML and set up your controls to use data binding to retrieve the strings defined in the resource file. At run time, Silverlight will use the UI threads CurrentUICulture to load the corresponding localized resource strings. By default CurrentUICulture is based on the culture of the end user's machine. For testing you can override this by setting the current thread culture and CurrentUICulture to a specific culture code.

```
Thread.CurrentThread.CurrentCulture
= new System.Globalization.CultureInfo("de-DE");

Thread.CurrentThread.CurrentUICulture
= new System.Globalization.CultureInfo("de-DE");
```

When you are done setting up the data binding for resource strings, you need to update your Silverlight project to set the <SupportedCultures> attribute. The easiest way to do this is to right-click your project in Visual Studio and click Unload Project. Then right-click the project name and click Edit. This opens the metadata for your project. Find the <SupportedCultures> attribute and add all the cultures your application needs to support. The culture/language codes should be separated by a semicolon. The list should not include the default generic fallback culture.

Listing 11-21 shows how to use static resources and data binding to use localized resource strings. To set up your XAML to use localized strings you need to add the namespace (xmlns:res) that points to the local namespace for the resource file, add a static resource to the resources section of the control, and then update all text and content properties of your control to data-bind to the static resource (for example: `Text="{Binding Path=CompanyName, Source={StaticResource Strings}}"`).

Before trying to run this sample, make sure the resource class and all its methods are marked as public instead of internal. The class and all its methods must be marked as public for data binding to work. It's annoying but if you modify the resource file, you will need to reset the class and its methods to public again.

LISTING 11-21: Setting up a Silverlight UI to use resource strings

```xml
<UserControl x:Class="Chapter11.Views.Listing1121"
    xmlns="http://schemas.microsoft.com/winfx/2006/xaml/presentation"
    xmlns:x="http://schemas.microsoft.com/winfx/2006/xaml"
    xmlns:d="http://schemas.microsoft.com/expression/blend/2008"
    xmlns:mc="http://schemas.openxmlformats.org/markup-compatibility/2006"
    xmlns:res="clr-namespace:Chapter11.Resources"
    mc:Ignorable="d"
    d:DesignHeight="300" d:DesignWidh="400">
    <UserControl.Resources>
        <res:Demo x:Key="Strings" />
    </UserControl.Resources>
    <Grid x:Name="LayoutRoot" Background="White">
        <TextBlock Height="23" HorizontalAlignment="Left" Margin="10,10,0,0"
            Name="CompanyNameCaption" VerticalAlignment="Top"
            Text="{Binding Path=CompanyName, Source={StaticResource Strings}}" />
        <TextBox Height="21" HorizontalAlignment="Left" Margin="104,12,0,0"
            Name="CompanyName" VerticalAlignment="Top"
            TextWrapping="Wrap" Width="147" />
        <TextBlock Height="23" HorizontalAlignment="Left" Margin="12,39,0,0"
            Name="ContactNameCaption" VerticalAlignment="Top"
            Text="{Binding Path=ContactName, Source={StaticResource Strings}}" />
        <TextBox Height="25" HorizontalAlignment="Left" Margin="104,37,0,0"
            Name="ContactName" TextWrapping="Wrap"
            VerticalAlignment="Top" Width="147" />
        <TextBlock Height="23" HorizontalAlignment="Left" Margin="12,69,0,0"
            Name="PhoneCaption" VerticalAlignment="Top"
            Text="{Binding Path=Phone, Source={StaticResource Strings}}" />
        <TextBox Height="25" HorizontalAlignment="Left" Margin="104,69,0,0"
            Name="Phone" TextWrapping="Wrap" VerticalAlignment="Top" Width="147" />
        <TextBlock Height="23" HorizontalAlignment="Left" Margin="15,100,0,0"
            Name="EmailCaption" VerticalAlignment="Top"
            Text="{Binding Path=Email, Source={StaticResource Strings}}" />
        <TextBox Height="25" HorizontalAlignment="Left" Margin="104,100,0,0"
            Name="Caption" TextWrapping="Wrap"
                VerticalAlignment="Top" Width="147" />
        <Button Height="23" HorizontalAlignment="Left"
            Margin="176,145,0,0" Name="SaveAction"
                VerticalAlignment="Top" Width="75"
            Content="{Binding Path=Save, Source={StaticResource Strings}}" />
    </Grid>
</UserControl>
```

Packing and Deploying

At run time the Silverlight platform will handle loading the necessary satellite assembly based on the CurrentUICulture. Depending on whether you are running a Silverlight web application or an out-of-browser application, the satellite assemblies will be packaged differently.

For a Silverlight web application the main assemblies and all the culture-specific satellite assemblies will be included in the application's XAP file.

Figure 11-5 uses the contents of the Silverlight web application XAP file. Note that each satellite assembly is stored in a culture-specific subfolder, such as de-DE.

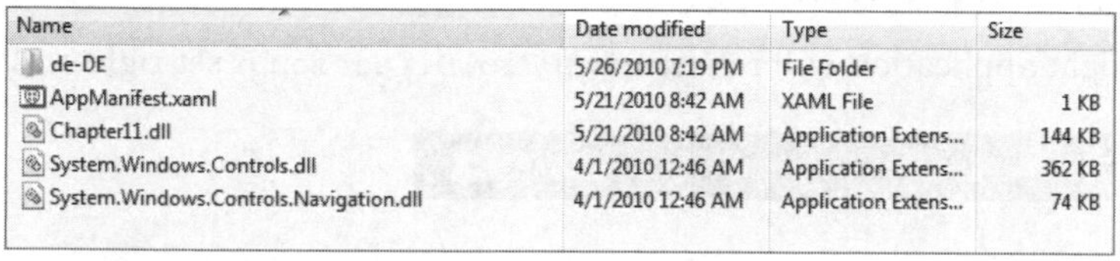

Name	Date modified	Type	Size
de-DE	5/26/2010 7:19 PM	File Folder	
AppManifest.xaml	5/21/2010 8:42 AM	XAML File	1 KB
Chapter11.dll	5/21/2010 8:42 AM	Application Extens...	144 KB
System.Windows.Controls.dll	4/1/2010 12:46 AM	Application Extens...	362 KB
System.Windows.Controls.Navigation.dll	4/1/2010 12:46 AM	Application Extens...	74 KB

FIGURE 11-5

For out-of-browser (OOB) Silverlight applications you have to create separate XAP files for each localized culture or locale your application needs to support. You create separate XAP files by creating new build configurations in Visual Studio. If you want to localize your OOB application window title, shortcut name, and description, you need to create culture-specific versions of the OutofBrowserSettings.xml configuration file.

After you create each culture's OutofBrowserSettings.xml setting file, unload your project file and edit the metadata for the project. Below the <PropertyGroup> attribute add the following code for each culture setting file you created. The culture code should match the name of the culture you used to define the browser setting config file.

```
<OutOfBrowserSettingsFile>
     Properties\OutOfBrowserSettings.culture-code.xml
</OutOfBrowserSettingsFile>
```

After reloading the project in Visual Studio open the OutofBrowserSettings.xml file for each culture and modify the following settings:

➤ ShortName attribute of the <OutOfBrowserSettings> tag, which provides the shortcut name for the application

➤ <OutOfBrowserSettings.Blurb> content, which provides the application description that appears as a tooltip on the installed application shortcuts

➤ Title attribute of the <WindowSettings> tag, which provides the window title

➤ Filenames of icons listed in the <OutOfBrowserSettings.Icons> section, for icons to display in the installation dialog box, Windows Explorer, taskbar, and so on

Supporting Bidirectional Right-to-Left (RTL) Text

Silverlight 4 includes enhancements for localizing your application to support bidirectional text, right-to-left layouts, and complex scripts such as Arabic, Hebrew, Thai, and so on.

To enable right-to-left (RTL), set the `FlowDirection` property on one or more UI elements of your application. Children elements will honor their parent's `FlowDirection` setting. To minimize the impact to your XAML just set your root element's `FlowDirection` property.

When working in RTL mode it's important to understand that the location of the 0 (x) and 0 (y) coordinate is now changed to the upper-right corner. So any settings you defined for margins or padding will be based on the upper-right corner.

Figure 11-6 shows how a Silverlight application will render when `FlowDirection` is set right-to-left.

FIGURE 11-6

Listing 11-22 shows an example of changing the `FlowDirection` property of a control's root element to be `RightToLeft`.

LISTING 11-22: Setting FlowDirection in XAML

```xml
<UserControl x:Class="Chapter11.Views.Listing1122"
    xmlns="http://schemas.microsoft.com/winfx/2006/xaml/presentation"
    xmlns:x="http://schemas.microsoft.com/winfx/2006/xaml"
    xmlns:d="http://schemas.microsoft.com/expression/blend/2008"
    xmlns:mc="http://schemas.openxmlformats.org/markup-compatibility/2006"
    mc:Ignorable="d"
    d:DesignHeight="300" d:DesignWidth="400">
    <Grid x:Name="LayoutRoot" Background="White" FlowDirection="RightToLeft">
        <TextBlock Height="23" HorizontalAlignment="Left" Margin="10,10,0,0"
            Name="CompanyNameCaption" Text="Company Name"
            VerticalAlignment="Top" />
        <TextBox Height="21" HorizontalAlignment="Left" Margin="104,12,0,0"
            Name="CompanyName" TextWrapping="Wrap"
            VerticalAlignment="Top" Width="147" />
        <TextBlock Height="23" HorizontalAlignment="Left" Margin="12,39,0,0"
            Name="ContactNameCaption" Text="Contact Name"
            VerticalAlignment="Top" />
        <TextBox Height="25" HorizontalAlignment="Left" Margin="104,37,0,0"
            Name="ContactName" TextWrapping="Wrap"
```

```
                        VerticalAlignment="Top" Width="147" />
                <TextBlock Height="23" HorizontalAlignment="Left" Margin="12,69,0,0"
                    Name="PhoneCaption" Text="Phone"
                    VerticalAlignment="Top" />
                <TextBox Height="25" HorizontalAlignment="Left" Margin="104,69,0,0"
                    Name="Phone" TextWrapping="Wrap"
                    VerticalAlignment="Top" Width="147" />
                <TextBlock Height="23" HorizontalAlignment="Left" Margin="15,100,0,0"
                    Name="EmailCaption" Text="Email"
                    VerticalAlignment="Top" />
                <TextBox Height="25" HorizontalAlignment="Left" Margin="104,100,0,0"
                    Name="Email" TextWrapping="Wrap"
                    VerticalAlignment="Top" Width="147" />
                <Button Content="Save" Height="23" HorizontalAlignment="Left"
                    Margin="176,145,0,0" Name="SaveAction"
                    VerticalAlignment="Top" Width="75" />
        </Grid>
    </UserControl>
```

Deploying Best Practices

In addition to deciding to enable `RightToLeft` flow direction, you should consider a few things when localizing your application. If your default language is English you need to consider the impact to your UI layout when you need to support multiple languages. Some languages can take up to 40 percent more space to render the same text displayed in English. The following list is just a small subset of the best practices you should follow when localizing an application:

➤ Avoid the `Canvas` control because it requires hard-coded sizes and positions. Instead use the `grid` or `StackPanel` that support automatic layouts.

➤ Use `TextBlocks` or `TextBox` controls instead of `Glyphs`.

➤ Avoid setting the `Width` and `Height` properties of the control.

➤ Make sure `TextWrapping="Wrap"` is set for content that may wrap

FULL-SCREEN APPLICATIONS

In some cases, applications benefit from offering an enhanced experience by being shown as a full-screen application. Silverlight allows applications to be made full-screen using the `IsFullScreen` property. Setting this property to `true` resizes the application to the current screen size and makes the application the topmost application. Listing 11-23 shows how you can use a button's click event to toggle an application between normal and full-screen modes.

Available for download on Wrox.com

LISTING 11-23: Toggling an application between normal and full-screen modes

```
private void btnFullScreen_Click(object sender, RoutedEventArgs e)
{
    App.Current.Host.Content.IsFullScreen = !App.Current.Host.Content.IsFullScreen;
}
```

Because placing an application into full-screen mode has certain security risks, Silverlight places a number of restrictions around putting and keeping an application in full-screen mode, and disables certain features while you're in full-screen mode.

First, placing an application in full-screen mode is only allowed using a user-initiated action like the button click shown in the previous listing. Attempting to set the `IsFullScreen` property to `true` in any other way will result in an exception being thrown. When an application is in full-screen mode, the end user can always use the Escape key (Esc) to exit full-screen mode. There is no way to override the function of this key while in full-screen mode.

Also, as an application enters full-screen mode, Silverlight automatically displays a notice to the end user, reminding them they can use the Escape key to exit. The notice is shown in Figure 11-7.

FIGURE 11-7

The message shown is hard-coded into Silverlight and cannot be changed.

While in full-screen mode, again for security reasons, certain features of Silverlight are restricted:

➤ Attempting to access the `OpenFileDialog` and `SaveFileDialog` while in full-screen mode causes Silverlight to revert to its normal embedded mode.

➤ Keyboard input is greatly restricted. Silverlight allows input from only the arrow keys, spacebar, Tab, Page Up, Page Down, Home, Enter, and End keys. However, Silverlight 4 allows full keyboard input for full-screen applications running as out-of-browser applications with elevated privileges. You can learn more about out-of-browser applications in Chapter 9.

➤ Multi-Touch capabilities of Silverlight are disabled while in full-screen mode. Basic single-touch events remain available.

➤ When running in Safari on Mac, hardware acceleration is not available in full-screen mode because of limitations of the Safari browser.

If you are enabling a full-screen experience in your application, you may want this experience to be different than the application's normal experience. This is especially true for applications that are not already using the full browser frame, but are embedded as an "island of richness" within a larger web page experience.

In this case you need to know when the full-screen state of the application has changed. You can use the FullScreenChanged event to add logic to your application to change the experience. An example of this is shown in Listing 11-24.

LISTING 11-24: Using the FullScreenChanged event

Available for download on Wrox.com

```
void Content_FullScreenChanged(object sender, EventArgs e)
{
    if (App.Current.Host.Content.IsFullScreen)
        btnFullScreen.Content = "Exit Full Screen";
    else
        btnFullScreen.Content = "Make Full Screen";
}
```

In the listing you can see that the application is using the FullScreenChanged event to change the text of the button, although it would be just as simple to make more complex changes to the application UI.

Finally, if you include a full-screen experience in your application, you should consider setting the new FullScreenOptions object to the StaysFullScreenWhenUnfocused value available in Silverlight 4. This allows the application to remain in full-screen mode, even if it loses focus.

```
App.Current.Host.Content.FullScreenOptions =
    System.Windows.Interop.FullScreenOptions.StaysFullScreenWhenUnfocused;
```

Prior to Silverlight 4, if a full-screen application lost focus, it would revert to its embedded mode. Having the ability to keep full-screen mode for the application is especially important for your users with multiple monitors. Setting the FullScreenOptions property allows those users to pin the Silverlight application in full-screen mode on one monitor while continuing to use applications on another monitor.

SUMMARY

In this chapter, you examined several typical Line of Business (LOB) application scenarios from how to build context-sensitive menus, printer-friendly views, integrating with Microsoft Excel or Word, and how to support localizing your application. As more and more developers adopt RIA-based architectures, the Silverlight platform will continue to grow to support additional LOB scenarios.

12

Application Architecture

WHAT'S IN THIS CHAPTER?

➤ Understanding design patterns and principles

➤ Working with the Model View ViewModel pattern

➤ Exploring Silverlight frameworks (MEF and PRISM)

➤ Defining a data access strategy

➤ Designing with performance in mind

When architecting your Silverlight application you need to keep in mind the functional and non-functional requirements.

➤ **Functional requirements** include navigation, workflow, and security.

➤ **Non-functional requirements** include number of concurrent users, performance, scalability, maintainability, and reliability.

Whether your application is configured to run as a web browser plug-in or installed on an end-user machine (out-of-browser application), you need to understand the tradeoffs involved in and best practices for designing an n-tier application. Addressing these functional and non-functional requirements is no small task. A solution that increases performance may impact scalability or the maintainability of your application. Fortunately, n-tier application design is not new and several well-documented approaches exist to address functional and non-functional requirements.

The most proven approach for architecting n-tier application is to focus on building *loosely coupled components*. Each component is focused on a single or small set of responsibilities (features). This approach increases the maintainability of your application and allows you to easily address performance/scalability issues that might come up. For example, if your application has a long-running process, such as creating a report, you can easily set it up to run asynchronously if it's loosely coupled from the rest of your application. Another key principle related to using loosely coupled components is *separation of concerns*. This principle promotes separating responsibility for a feature into several classes that are loosely coupled.

This chapter will introduce you to the common patterns (MVVM) and frameworks (MEF and PRISM) for developing loosely coupled Silverlight applications. The Model View ViewModel (MVVM) pattern has become almost the de facto standard way of building Silverlight applications because of the rich data-binding capabilities built into the platform. The Managed Extensibility Framework (MEF) and the PRISM Composite Application Library (PRISM/CAL) are frameworks you can use to build loosely coupled applications. Both frameworks use the concept of *dependency injection* that allows classes to have their dependencies injected at run time instead of having direct references to concrete classes. One of the most critical design decisions that impacts the performance and scalability of your application is the data access strategy you use. You could choose to build custom Windows Communication Foundation (WCF) services or use one of the data access frameworks (WCF Data Services or WCF RIA Services) available from Microsoft. In some scenarios your data source may be one or more external services to which you subscribe.

The most important thing to remember when architecting a Silverlight or any other n-tier application is that there are no silver bullets. Every choice you make has pros and cons. The golden rule of architecture is "It depends." A well-informed software architect/developer will research the best options for his requirements and focus on building loosely coupled components that can be easily replaced as requirements change.

The download for this chapter includes a Northwind sample application built using the PRISM/CAL Framework and RIA Services. You should download the code ahead of time as you review this chapter. The code listings included in the chapter are simplified to illustrate the topic being discussed without needing the infrastructure of a full-fledged sample. You will need the following items installed to run the Northwind sample.

➤ **SQL Server Express 2008** — `http://www.microsoft.com/express/database/`

➤ **RIA Services** — `http://www.silverlight.net/getstarted/riaservices/`

➤ **PRISM/CAL** — `http://compositewpf.codeplex.com/`

➤ **Unity Application Block** — `http://unity.codeplex.com/`

 If you installed the Silverlight 4 tools you will already have RIA Services installed and the download for PRISM includes the Unity Application Block.

UNDERSTANDING DESIGN PATTERNS

A design pattern is a common solution for dealing with a problem within a specific context. Several well-known design patterns exist but some are more appropriate for data access, whereas others are designed to address separating concerns of a user interface. Before you dive into the inner workings of the MVVM pattern, it is important to get a grasp of what a design pattern is and the design principles applied when using the pattern.

As design patterns have become more popular, developers have adopted a set of design principles called SOLID. SOLID is an acronym for a set of best practices developers use to design loosely coupled applications. When you read the rest of the chapter keep these principles in mind. They are the key to understanding how to properly utilize the MVVM pattern and the frameworks available for building Silverlight applications.

Table 12-1 lists out the SOLID design principles.

TABLE 12-1

ACRONYM	DESCRIPTION
(S) SRP	The single responsibility principle is the notion that a class should have only one reason to change. For example, instead of creating a class that has data access code for several different items you should instead separate the data access for items into a single class.
(O) OCP	The open/closed principle is the notion that a class should be open for extensions but closed to modification. For example, you should be able to add a new behavior to a class without affecting the rest of the code. Instead of adding a new case to a switch statement, you should consider re-factoring the code to use separate classes for each case.
(L) LSP	The Liskov substitution principle is the notion that a derived class must be substitutable for its base class. A good example of this is the .NET stream classes `FileStream` and `MemoryStream`. Both inherit from the `Stream` class but are accessing different types of streams. When you call `Read()` on either class you get the same expected result. If you were to create your own `MyStream` class and override the `Read()` method to write data instead of reading data you would break this principle.
(I) ISP	The interface segregation principle is the notion that it's better to have many specific behavior-related interfaces than one giant monolithic interface. For example, by having `IEnumerable` and `IDisposable` interfaces separate, it's possible for client code to only care about dealing with enumerating a collection or disposing of it and not clutter up either operation by mixing two totally different kinds of behaviors.
(D) DIP	The dependency inversion principle is the notion that you should depend on abstractions and not concretions. For example, when dealing with streams you should be able to read and write data to a file stream or memory stream without having to create or know the underlying stream source.

Exploring the Model View ViewModel (MVVM)

The Model View ViewModel (MVVM) pattern is a User Interface (UI)/Architectural design pattern based on the popular Model View Controller (MVC) and Model View Presenter (MVP) patterns. The MVVM pattern is well-suited for building Silverlight applications because of the rich data binding and commanding abilities built into the Silverlight Platform. All of these patterns promote the same core approach of isolating domain/business logic from the user interface. This approach allows you to change either the UI or the domain logic without affecting the other. For example, in Silverlight it's possible for you to build an application using the out-of-the-box look and feel for buttons and lists. Then later, you can allow a designer to customize the application look and feel without touching the domain logic you wrote.

Figure 12-1 shows the differences between implementing the MVC, MVP, and MVVM patterns. Although each pattern uses a slightly different approach to handle user input, they all share the same core approach of separating concerns across multiple classes. In some advanced scenarios, you may use a combination of these patterns. The most important thing to remember is to build loosely coupled classes that have specific responsibilities.

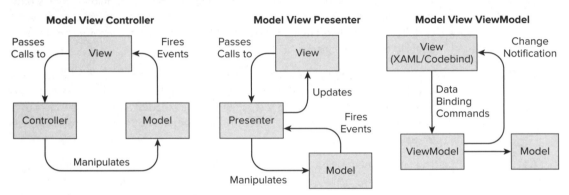

FIGURE 12-1

Now that you have an understanding of what the MVVM pattern is and how it relates to the other popular UI/Architectural patterns, it is time to examine the components of the MVVM pattern and steps for using it in a Silverlight application.

MVVM and Separation of Concerns

Understanding what separation of concerns means is the key to successfully using the MVVM, MVC, or MVP patterns. All three patterns focus on separating the concern of a use case or feature across multiple classes, In MVVM there are three main components that are assigned responsibilities (the Model, View, and ViewModel). In advances scenarios you may use additional controller or service layer classes to limit the responsibility of ViewModel. Using a separation of concern approach has the following advantages over putting all your code in code-behind files.

➤   Each component has a small set of responsibilities.

➤   It is easier to test each component independently.

➤   Isolated code can be replaced without affecting your other code.

➤   It is easier to eliminate duplicate code.

➤   Different developers or teams can work on each component.

Earlier in the chapter, we talked about the SOLID principles. As you use MVVM, it is important to keep these principles in mind and to remember each component is really a layer in your application that has a set of responsibilities assigned to it.

The Responsibility of the Model

A *model* represents the domain/business logic of your application. Several different approaches exist to structure the model. The two most popular approaches are data-centric and domain-driven.

➤ If you use a **data-centric** approach the model is made up of classes that contain only attributes (data points), and your business logic is handled by the ViewModel or another set of classes outside of the model.

➤ In a **domain-driven** design, the model contains behavior and attributes spread across multiple classes that are based on real-world business (domain) concepts.

Both approaches (data-centric and domain-driven) have pros and cons to implementing them, and it is up to you to decide which approach works best for your application.

Figure 12-2 shows a class diagram for a typical customer/order model. In this example, a domain-driven approach was used and the classes contain attributes and behaviors for calculating total sales history and current year sales.

The Responsibility of the View

A *view* represents the screens and controls of your application. The view should focus only on rendering the user interface of your application and have little or no code. In Silverlight a view is made up of the XAML for your screens/controls and their code-behinds. Its main responsibility should be displaying and formatting data for the end user. In a properly designed MVVM application, there is little or no code in your code-behind. Instead, you should rely on the rich data-binding capabilities in Silverlight to set up the binding between UI elements (`TextBoxes`, `Lists`, and so on) and your ViewModel. Silverlight 4 introduces support for `ICommands` so now it is possible to link up commands defined in your ViewModel to button clicks just using XAML. In cases where you need to rely on code-behind (for example, for subscribing to events) you should use the minimal amount of code necessary to communicate with

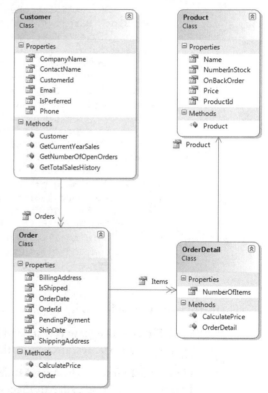

FIGURE 12-2

your ViewModel. If you need to handle the selected event of a list or `DataGrid` event, you should pass the data item returned to the ViewModel. The ViewModel would then be responsible for using the data passed from the code bind to trigger any changes to the view or persisting model to your data store.

Listing 12-1 shows how to set up the XAML for a view to data bind to the properties and commands defined in a ViewModel.

LISTING 12-1: Data binding to a ViewModel

```xml
<Grid x:Name="LayoutRoot" Background="White">
    <TextBlock Margin="14,30,0,0" Text="First Name:"
            Style="{StaticResource Label}" />
    <TextBox Margin="120,30,0,0" Name="FirstName"
            Text="{Binding Mode=TwoWay, Path=FirstName}"
            Style="{StaticResource Data}" />
    <TextBlock Margin="14,60,0,0" Text="Last Name:"
            Style="{StaticResource Label}" />
    <TextBox Margin="120,60,0,0" Name="LastName"
            Text="{Binding Mode=TwoWay, Path=LastName}"
            Style="{StaticResource Data}" />
    <TextBlock Margin="14,90,0,0" Text="Email:"
            Style="{StaticResource Label}" />
    <TextBox Margin="120,90,0,0" Name="EmailAddress"
            Text="{Binding Mode=TwoWay, Path=EmailAddress}"
            Style="{StaticResource Data}" />
    <TextBlock Margin="14,120,0,0" Text="Password:"
            Style="{StaticResource Label}" />
    <PasswordBox Margin="120,120,0,0" Name="Password"
            Password="{Binding Mode=TwoWay, Path=Password}"
            Style="{StaticResource Password}" />
    <TextBlock Margin="14,150,0,0" Text="Repeat Password:"
            Style="{StaticResource Label}" />
    <PasswordBox Margin="120,150,0,0" Name="PasswordRepeated"
            Password="{Binding Mode=TwoWay, Path=PasswordRepeated}"
            Style="{StaticResource Password}" />
    <Button Content="Button" Visibility="{Binding DisplaySave}"
            Margin="119,189,0,0" Name="SaveButton"
            Command="{Binding Save}"
            Style="{StaticResource Button}" />
</Grid>
```

There are two approaches to linking a view to its ViewModel

➤ **View First** — The view is responsible for creating an instance of a ViewModel, via data binding to a static resource or setting the data context in the code-behind file.

➤ **ViewModel First** — The ViewModel creates an instance of the view and sets its data context. This is usually done using an Inversion of Control Container.

The code snippet that follows shows the View First approach of using data binding or code-behind to set the view's data context to its ViewModel.

```xml
<UserControl.Resources>
        <local:SampleViewModel x:Key="ViewModel" />
</UserControl.Resources>

<Grid DataContext="{Binding Path=User,
```

```
                        Source={StaticResource ViewModel}}">
</Grid>

this.DataContext = new SampleViewModel();
```

The code snippet that follows next shows the ViewModel First approach of using dependency injection to create an instance of the view and the ViewModel, setting the data context of the view inside the ViewModel. Later on in the chapter you will learn more about inversion of control and dependency injection and how to use them in your Silverlight application.

```
public interface IMyView
{
    object DataContext { get; set; }
}

public class SampleViewModel
{
    public SampleViewModel(IMyView view)
    {
        view.DataContext = this;
    }
}
```

The Responsibilities of the ViewModel

A *ViewModel* has three main responsibilities:

➤   Abstracting the model from the view

➤   Tracking UI state

➤   Handling user input

You can use several different approaches to design your ViewModel. For simple scenarios, it is okay to have a single ViewModel per screen that exposes each binding type as properties in the ViewModel. For more advanced scenarios you can decide to wrap each model type with a corresponding ViewModel (for example, `CustomerViewModel` will wrap a `Customer` class) or create separate ViewModels for each key component of your UI. For example, if you have a shared search user control it might makes sense to have a `SearchViewModel` that abstracts away the different searchable types. The ViewModel should be responsible for tracking all UI states such as what's selected, hidden, and so on and handling all user input either through `ICommands` or when necessary via methods the view calls.

When you create a ViewModel class, it must implement the `INotifyPropertyChanged` interface. The interface requires you to create an event called `PropertyChanged`. This event is used by the ViewModel to communicate changes to the view via data binding. For example, you have created a property in your ViewModel called `DisplaySave`. In the view's XAML you have bound the `Visibility` property of the Save button to the `DisplaySave` property in the ViewModel. In your ViewModel you change the value of the `DisplaySave` property after a user enters in all the required data. When changing the value you send a notification to the Save button by firing off the `PropertyChanged` event, passing in a parameter equal to `"DisplaySave"`. Silverlight handles the operation of notifying the view about the property changed and changing the `Visibility` of the Save button.

```
<Button Content="Button" Visibility="{Binding DisplaySave}" />

Visibility displaySave = Visibility.Collapsed;

public Visibility DisplaySave
{
    get
    {
        return this.displaySave;
    }
    set
    {
        if (this.displaySave != value)
        {
            this.displaySave = value;
            this.OnPropertyChanged("DisplaySave");
        }
    }
}
```

In real-world scenarios, you should create a base ViewModel class that implements the `INotifyPropertyChanged` interface. This way you can minimize repeating the same notification code in each ViewModel. Silverlight 4 adds support for the `ICommand` interface, which allows you to bind commands exposed by the ViewModel to any UI element that inherits from `ButtonBase`. This new feature allows you to use XAML to bind to a command and pass in parameters to it instead of relying on code-behind events. Using this new feature and having a base ViewModel class will allow you to minimize unnecessary duplicate code.

Listing 12-2 shows a ViewModel class that includes properties and commands. By using the `PropertyChanged` event, the ViewModel can notify any view bound to it that a property has changed. The view will invoke the ViewModel's command when an end user performs an action.

LISTING 12-2: Sample ViewModel

```
using System.ComponentModel;
using System.Windows;
using Chapter12.Commands;

namespace Chapter12.ViewModel
{
    public class SampleViewModel : INotifyPropertyChanged
    {

        public event PropertyChangedEventHandler PropertyChanged;

        protected void OnPropertyChanged(string name)
        {
            if (this.PropertyChanged != null)
            {
```

```
            this.PropertyChanged(this, new PropertyChangedEventArgs(name));
        }
    }


    public SampleViewModel()
    {
        this.firstName = "John";
        this.lastName = "Doe";
        this.emailAddress = "jdoe@company.com";
        this.password = "12345";
        this.passwordRepeated = "12345";

        this.DisplaySave = Visibility.Visible;
    }

    private string firstName;
    public string FirstName
    {
        get
        {
            return this.firstName;
        }
        set
        {
            if (this.firstName != value)
            {
                this.firstName = value;
                this.OnPropertyChanged("FirstName");
            }
        }
    }

    private string lastName;
    public string LastName
    {
        get
        {
            return this.lastName;
        }
        set
        {
            if (this.lastName != value)
            {
                this.lastName = value;
                this.OnPropertyChanged("LastName");
            }
        }
    }

    private string emailAddress;
    public string EmailAddress
    {
        get
        {
```

continues

LISTING 12-2 *(continued)*

```csharp
                return this.emailAddress;
        }
        set
        {
            if (this.emailAddress != value)
            {
                this.emailAddress = value;
                this.OnPropertyChanged("EmailAddress");
            }
        }
    }

    private string password;
    public string Password
    {
        get
        {
            return this.password;
        }
        set
        {
            if (this.password != value)
            {
                this.password = value;
                this.OnPropertyChanged("Password");
            }
        }
    }

    private string passwordRepeated;
    public string PasswordRepeated
    {
        get
        {
            return this.passwordRepeated;
        }
        set
        {
            if (this.passwordRepeated != value)
            {
                this.passwordRepeated = value;
                this.OnPropertyChanged("PasswordRepeated");
            }
        }
    }

    Visibility displaySave = Visibility.Collapsed;
    public Visibility DisplaySave
    {
        get
        {
            return this.displaySave;
```

```
        }
        set
        {
            if (this.displaySave != value)
            {
                this.displaySave = value;
                this.OnPropertyChanged("DisplaySave");
            }
        }
    }

    private SaveCommand saveCommand;
    public SaveCommand Save
    {
        get
        {
            if (this.saveCommand == null)
                this.saveCommand = new SaveCommand(this);

            return this.saveCommand;
        }
    }
}
}
```

Using MVVM Best Practices

As your Silverlight application gets more complex you should keep the following best practices in mind. Always keep separation of concerns and testability in mind. In more complex scenarios, it might make sense to introduce controller or service layer classes to handle interactions with the model or external data access services. Loading the model each time a new screen is displayed can be very costly if you have to call an external data source. This can affect the performance and scalability of your application because you are making multiple run trips to a data source and keep instantiating the same model or, worse yet, keep loading multiple instances of the model. This can lead to a harder to maintain code base. A good solution to this problem is to have a root (shell) ViewModel that keeps a reference to the model and manages properties for the other ViewModel in your application.

More than likely, your Silverlight application will use services to access your data store, so it is important to keep in mind that all service calls are asynchronous and will be executed in a thread outside the UI thread. When the service call is complete, the MVVM pattern is a good way for notifying your user interface that data is ready to be displayed. For example, say your application allows users to search for products. By defining a visibility property in your ViewModel you can control the display of a loading status message. When the service call is kicked off, you would toggle the visibility property to show the message. When the call is complete, you would set the ViewModel property for product search results and set the visibility property to hide the status message.

Listing 12-3 shows an advanced MVVM scenario where the ViewModel displays product search results based on filters the user entered in. It relies on a service layer for calling the search service and loading the model. Once the service call is complete, the service class notifies the ViewModel, which fires off property notification events to the view.

LISTING 12-3: Advanced ViewModel

```csharp
using System.Collections.ObjectModel;
using System.Windows;
using Chapter12.Model;
using Chapter12.Services;

namespace Chapter12.ViewModel
{
    public class ProductSearchViewModel : BaseViewModel
    {

        public ProductSearchViewModel()
        {
        }

        public void LoadData()
        {
            new MockProductService().Execute(Display);
        }

        private void Display(ProductResult result)
        {
            this.Categories = result.Categories;
        }

        private ObservableCollection<Product> products;
        public ObservableCollection<Product> Products
        {
            get
            {
                return this.products;
            }
            set
            {
                if (this.products != value)
                {
                    this.products = value;
                    this.OnPropertyChanged("Products");
                }
            }
        }

        private Product selectedProduct;
        public Product SelectedProduct
        {
            get
            {
                return this.selectedProduct;
            }
            set
            {
                if (this.selectedProduct != value)
                {
```

```
                    this.selectedProduct = value;
                    this.OnPropertyChanged("SelectedProduct");

                    if (this.selectedProduct != null)
                    {
                        this.IsProductSelected = Visibility.Visible;
                    }
                    else
                    {
                        this.IsProductSelected = Visibility.Collapsed;
                    }
                }
            }
        }

        private Visibility isProductSelected = Visibility.Collapsed;
        public Visibility IsProductSelected
        {
            get
            {
                return this.isProductSelected;
            }
            set
            {
                if (this.isProductSelected != value)
                {
                    this.isProductSelected = value;
                    this.OnPropertyChanged("IsProductSelected");
                }
            }
        }

        private ObservableCollection<Category> categories;
        public ObservableCollection<Category> Categories
        {
            get
            {
                return this.categories;
            }
            set
            {
                if (this.categories != value)
                {
                    this.categories = value;
                    this.OnPropertyChanged("Categories");
                }
            }
        }

        private Category selectedCategory;
        public Category SelectedCategory
        {
            get
            {
                return this.selectedCategory;
```

continues

LISTING 12-3 *(continued)*

```
            }
            set
            {
                if (this.selectedCategory != value)
                {
                    this.selectedCategory = value;
                    this.OnPropertyChanged("SelectedCategory");
                    this.DisplayProducts(this.selectedCategory);
                }
            }
        }

        private void DisplayProducts(Category selectedCategory)
        {
            this.Products = selectedCategory.Products;
        }


    }
}
```

Listing 12-4 shows the view (XAML) for the product search view. This is a more complex UI than the previous sample. It shows how to bind a ViewModel to a `ListBox`, `DataGrid`, and multiple `TextBoxes`. When a category is selected, its corresponding products will be displayed.

LISTING 12-4: XAML data bound to ViewModel

```xml
<UserControl x:Class="Chapter12.Views.Listing1204"
  xmlns:data="clr-namespace:System.Windows.Controls;
  assembly=System.Windows.Controls.Data"
  xmlns:sdk="clr-namespace:System.Windows.Controls;
  assembly=System.Windows.Controls"
  xmlns:common="clr-namespace:System.Windows;assembly=System.Windows.Controls"
  xmlns="http://schemas.microsoft.com/winfx/2006/xaml/presentation"
  xmlns:x="http://schemas.microsoft.com/winfx/2006/xaml"
  xmlns:d="http://schemas.microsoft.com/expression/blend/2008"
  xmlns:mc="http://schemas.openxmlformats.org/markup-compatibility/2006"
  mc:Ignorable="d"
  d:DesignHeight="300" d:DesignWidth="400">
    <UserControl.Resources>
        <Style x:Key="Label" TargetType="TextBlock">
            <Setter Property="HorizontalAlignment" Value="Left" />
            <Setter Property="VerticalAlignment" Value="Top" />
        </Style>
        <Style x:Key="Data" TargetType="Control">
            <Setter Property="HorizontalAlignment" Value="Left" />
            <Setter Property="VerticalAlignment" Value="Top" />
            <Setter Property="Width" Value="250" />
            <Setter Property="Height" Value="25" />
        </Style>
        <Style x:Key="Button" TargetType="Button">
```

```xml
                <Setter Property="HorizontalAlignment" Value="Left" />
                <Setter Property="VerticalAlignment" Value="Top" />
                <Setter Property="Width" Value="75" />
                <Setter Property="Height" Value="25" />
        </Style>
    </UserControl.Resources>

    <Grid x:Name="LayoutRoot" Background="White">
        <StackPanel Orientation="Horizontal">
            <ListBox Grid.Column="0"
                Margin="5"
                Height="200"
                VerticalAlignment="Top"
                ItemsSource="{Binding Categories}"
                DisplayMemberPath="Name"
                SelectedItem="{Binding SelectedCategory, Mode=TwoWay}"
                />

            <StackPanel>
                <data:DataGrid AutoGenerateColumns="False"
                        ItemsSource="{Binding Products}"
                        SelectedItem="{Binding SelectedProduct, Mode=TwoWay}">
                    <data:DataGrid.Columns>
                        <data:DataGridTextColumn Header="Name"
                                Binding="{Binding Name}" Width="200" />
                        <data:DataGridTextColumn Header="Price"
                                Binding="{Binding Price}" Width="120" />
                        <data:DataGridTextColumn Header="Number In Stock"
                                Binding="{Binding NumberInStock}" Width="120" />
                        <data:DataGridCheckBoxColumn Header="On Back Order"
                                Binding="{Binding OnBackOrder}" Width="100" />
                    </data:DataGrid.Columns>
                </data:DataGrid>
                <StackPanel VerticalAlignment="Top" Margin="0,10,0,0"
                        Visibility="{Binding IsProductSelected}">
                    <Grid>
                        <Grid.ColumnDefinitions>
                            <ColumnDefinition Width="150" />
                            <ColumnDefinition />
                        </Grid.ColumnDefinitions>
                        <Grid.RowDefinitions>
                            <RowDefinition />
                            <RowDefinition />
                            <RowDefinition />
                            <RowDefinition />
                        </Grid.RowDefinitions>
                        <TextBlock Text="Name:" Grid.Column="0" Grid.Row="0"
                            Style="{StaticResource Label}" />
                        <TextBox Name="Name"  Grid.Column="1" Grid.Row="0"
                            Text="{Binding Mode=TwoWay,
                            Path=SelectedProduct.Name}"
                            Style="{StaticResource Data}" />
                        <TextBlock Text="Amount:" Grid.Column="0" Grid.Row="1"
                            Style="{StaticResource Label}" />
                        <TextBox Name="Price" Grid.Column="1" Grid.Row="1"
```

continues

LISTING 12-4 *(continued)*

```
                          Text="{Binding Mode=TwoWay,
                          Path=SelectedProduct.Price}"
                          Style="{StaticResource Data}"  />
                <TextBlock  Text="Number In Stock:"
                          Grid.Column="0" Grid.Row="2"
                          Style="{StaticResource Label}" />
                <TextBox Name="NumberInStock"
                          Grid.Column="1" Grid.Row="2"
                          Text="{Binding Mode=TwoWay,
                          Path=SelectedProduct.NumberInStock}"
                          Style="{StaticResource Data}"  />
                <TextBlock  Text="On Back Ordered:"
                          Grid.Column="0" Grid.Row="3"
                          Style="{StaticResource Label}" />
                <CheckBox Name="IsBackOrder"
                          Grid.Column="1" Grid.Row="3"
                          IsChecked="{Binding Mode=TwoWay,
                          Path=SelectedProduct.OnBackOrder}"
                          Style="{StaticResource Data}"  />
            </Grid>
          </StackPanel>
        </StackPanel>
      </StackPanel>
    </Grid>
</UserControl>
```

Learning about Inversion of Control/Dependency Injection

When designing the architecture for applications, it is important to understand how different components, layers, and classes depend on each other. To truly achieve separation of concern you must consider how to best isolate different classes. Using the dependency inversion principle is a good place to start. The principle states that you should depend upon abstractions and not concretions.

A related principle to this is the inversion of control (IoC)/dependency injection. This principle allows you to achieve loosely coupled components by relying on third-party containers to create and manage the lifetime of dependencies and at run time inject dependencies into each other. For example, you would use IoC to inject a view into a ViewModel as we previously talked about when you use a ViewModel First approach.

There are several IoC containers available for the Silverlight platform. For the purpose of this book, you will learn about how to use the Managed Extensibility Framework (MEF) and Unity Application Block from the Microsoft Pattern and Practices group. Unity is currently the IoC container used by the PRISM (CAL) framework. Future versions of PRISM will include more integration with MEF. Later on in the chapter, you will learn about each of these frameworks. For now, we are going to focus on the core concepts of IoC.

Listing 12-5 shows the basic implementation of the dependency inversion principle. The `GameViewModel` creates an instance of the `GameService`. Instead of referencing the `GameService` directly, it uses the interface (abstraction) the service implements.

LISTING 12-5: Using abstraction

```
using System.Collections.Generic;
using Chapter12.Model;
using Chapter12.Services;

namespace Chapter12.ViewModel
{
    public class GameViewModel
    {

        public GameViewModel()
        {
        }

        public void LoadData()
        {
            IGameService service = new GameService();

            Game game = service.GetGameById(1);
            IList<Game> game = service.SearchForGames();
        }

    }
}
```

This example is a good starting point. However, there still exists a tight coupling between the ViewModel and its service because the ViewModel is still responsible for creating the service directly. A better approach is to use an IoC Container to inject the dependency at run time. Two popular approaches exist for implementing IoC: dependency injection and service locator.

➤ When you use a service locator, you must specifically ask the container for a dependency.

➤ When you use dependency injection, the container will inject the dependency.

If you use constructor injection, the dependency is injected when the container creates an instance of your class; property injection allows you to have a dependency injected the first time you try to use it. Both approaches require you to register any dependency prior to using them. An exception is raised if a type is not registered. The combination of dependency inversion and the inversion of control principles allows you to design better architected Silverlight applications by loosely coupling classes (components) using abstraction and dependency injection.

Now that you have a basic understanding of IoC, you can examine a few samples of implementing a service locator and dependency injection using the Unity Application Block.

Listing 12-6 shows how to set up a service locator using Unity. When the GameViewModel wants to call the GameService to search for games, it asks the IoC container to locate the class that implements the IGameService interface.

LISTING 12-6: Using Unity as a service locator

```
using System.Collections.Generic;
using Chapter12.Model;
using Chapter12.Services;
using Microsoft.Practices.Unity;

namespace Chapter12.ViewModel
{
    public class GameViewModel
    {

        public GameViewModel()
        {
        }

        private UnityContainer container;
        public GameViewModel(UnityContainer container)
        {
            this.container = container;
        }

        public void UseServiceLocator()
        {
            IGameService service = this.container.Resolve<IGameService>();

            Game game = service.GetGameById(1);
            IList<Game> gameList = service.SearchForGames();
        }

    }
}

using System.Windows;
using System.Windows.Controls;
using Chapter12.Services;
using Chapter12.ViewModel;
using Microsoft.Practices.Unity;

namespace Chapter12.Views
{
    public partial class Listing1206 : UserControl
    {
        private GameViewModel viewModel;
        UnityContainer container;

        public Listing1206()
        {
            InitializeComponent();

            this.container = new UnityContainer();
            this.container.RegisterType<IGameService, GameService>();

            this.viewModel = new GameViewModel(this.container);
```

```
            this.DataContext = this.viewModel;
        }

        private void button1_Click(object sender, RoutedEventArgs e)
        {
            this.viewModel.UseServiceLocator();
        }
    }
}
```

Listing 12-7 shows how to do constructor dependency injection using Unity. The
SportsGameViewModel constructor requires a reference to a class that implements the IGameService.
To have the reference injected into the ViewModel the IGameService must be registered with Unity and
your ViewModel must be created by calling Resolve on the IoC container.

LISTING 12-7: Constructor dependency injection

```
using System.Windows;
using System.Windows.Controls;
using Chapter12.Services;
using Chapter12.ViewModel;
using Microsoft.Practices.Unity;

namespace Chapter12.Views
{
    public partial class Listing1207 : UserControl
    {
        private SportsGameViewModel viewModel;
        UnityContainer container;

        public Listing1207()
        {
            InitializeComponent();

            this.container = new UnityContainer();
            this.container.RegisterType<IGameService, GameService>();

            this.viewModel = container.Resolve<SportsGameViewModel>();
            this.DataContext = this.viewModel;
        }

        private void button1_Click(object sender, RoutedEventArgs e)
        {
            this.viewModel.LoadData();
        }
    }
}

using Chapter12.Model;
using Chapter12.Services;

namespace Chapter12.ViewModel
```

continues

LISTING 12-7 *(continued)*

```
{
    public class SportsGameViewModel
    {
        private IGameService service;
        public SportsGameViewModel(IGameService service)
        {
            this.service = service;
        }

        public void LoadData()
        {
            Game game = this.service.GetGameById(1);
        }

    }
}
```

Listing 12-8 shows how to do property (setter) dependency injection using Unity. The `ActionGameViewModel` contains a property `GameService` that has been annotated with the `[Dependency]` attribute. This allows you to simplify your code instead of adding many dependencies to your constructor, and it delays the loading of a dependency until the first time you use it. You are still required to register the `IGameService` with Unity and create your ViewModel using the `Resolve` method on the IoC container.

LISTING 12-8: Property Dependency Injection

```
using System.Windows;
using System.Windows.Controls;
using Chapter12.Services;
using Chapter12.ViewModel;
using Microsoft.Practices.Unity;

namespace Chapter12.Views
{
    public partial class Listing1208 : UserControl
    {
        private ActionGameViewModel viewModel;
        UnityContainer container;

        public Listing1208()
        {
            InitializeComponent();

            this.container = new UnityContainer();
            this.container.RegisterType<IGameService, GameService>();

            this.viewModel = container.Resolve<ActionGameViewModel>();
            this.DataContext = this.viewModel;
        }

        private void button1_Click(object sender, RoutedEventArgs e)
```

```
            {
                bool isServiceLoaded = this.viewModel.GameService != null;
                this.viewModel.LoadData();
            }
        }
    }

    using Chapter12.Model;
    using Chapter12.Services;
    using Microsoft.Practices.Unity;

    namespace Chapter12.ViewModel
    {
        public class ActionGameViewModel
        {

            public ActionGameViewModel()
            {
            }

            private IGameService service;

            [Dependency]
            public IGameService GameService
            {
                get{return this.service;}
                set{this.service = value;}
            }

            public void LoadData()
            {
                Game game = this.GameService.GetGameById(1);
            }
        }
    }
```

Inversion of Control (IoC) and Dependency Injection (DI) are powerful tools to help you build better architected applications. By using an IoC container to manage dependencies, you create a better separation of concerns between the different classes (or components) of your application. It is important to understand that all dependency injection happens at run time so there is some performance cost that you should consider when using IoC/DI. Later in the chapter, you examine the inner workings of the MEF and PRISM frameworks. Both rely heavily on the concept of IoC/DI so you might want to refer to this section as you read how to use the frameworks.

Exploring the Event Broker Pattern

A key concept to building a Silverlight application is using events. Events allow one class to communicate to one or more other classes that a specific thing happened (for example, a button was clicked or data had been retrieved from a service). The normal way to use an event is for one class to subscribe to the events of another class. This approach works great when each class has direct access to the other and only one class can trigger an event. However, in more advanced scenarios one or more classes may need to send the same event or be notified by events without subscribing directly to the caller event.

As discussed in the previous section on IoC/DI, it is a good idea to use a container for managing dependencies instead of classes having direct access to each other. Events can be treated as another type of dependency and instead of subscribing directly to an event, a container (Event Broker) could be used to manage the subscribers and publishers of an event. When an event occurs, the Event Broker would be responsible for notifying all subscribers that an event occurred. A good example of this is handling the closing of an application. Instead of looping through each control on the screen to check to see if its needs to be saved before your applications closes, an Event Broker could handle notifying each control to save itself. Another example of where an Event Broker would greatly simplify your code is when you need to display a retrieving data status message. The user control for the status message could subscribe to events that a ViewModel publishes: one for when the async call starts and one when it ends. This approach allows the status control to be totally independent of the ViewModel. In fact, the status control and ViewModel do not even know the other one exists. Briefly, an Event Broker allows components to be loosely coupled from the events they need to publish or subscribe to.

USING SILVERLIGHT FRAMEWORKS

When architecting an application it's important to understand how frameworks can help you better design your application. For a simple project, a framework might be overkill. However, for advanced scenarios where you may have several or even dozens of developers it is critical to use or build a framework for your application. By using a framework, you can centralize the plumbing and common services all developers need to use in one place. Even when using an existing framework such as PRISM (Composite Application Library) or the Managed Extensibility Framework (MEF) you should consider building your own application-specific framework on top to increase code reuse and simplify the developer's experience.

Exploring the Managed Extensibility Framework

The Managed Extensibility Framework (MEF) is a new component included in the Silverlight 4 Platform for simplifying the design of extensible applications and components. MEF offers discovery and composition capabilities that you can leverage to load application extensions. MEF now ships with the Silverlight 4 run time. However, there is a version available for Silverlight 3 as a separate download on CodePlex (`http://mef.codeplex.com`). MEF is a key component of the .NET 4.0 platform as well. Therefore, you can now use the same extensibility framework whether you are building a Silverlight, WPF, or ASP.NET application.

It is important to note that there is some overlap between MEF and the PRISM (CAL) Framework. MEF focuses on building extensible applications by providing support for automatic component discovery and compositions. Though PRISM (CAL) is an application framework that is used for building modular composite applications that use UI patterns such as MVVM, MEF will be more integrated into a future version of the PRISM (CAL) Framework.

What Problem Does MEF Solve?

MEF presents a simple solution for addressing run time extensibility. Prior to MEF, any application that wanted to support the plug-in model needed to create its own infrastructure. In many cases, the approaches that developers used were application-specific and could not be easily reused across multiple implementations. Because the MEF model does not require any hard dependencies on a particular application assembly, you can design your extension to be application-specific or generic. This makes it easy to develop a test harness for testing your extension independently of any application. MEF will handle any dependencies between extensions by insuring that they are loaded in the proper order.

How Does MEF Work?

MEF includes a catalog and a composition container. The catalog is responsible for discovering extensions and the composition container is responsible for managing the creation, lifetime, and dependencies for an extension.

`ComposablePart` is a first-class citizen in MEF and offers up one or more exports, and may depend on one or more externally provided services or imports. The default implementation of `ComposablePart` manages an object instance of a given type. However, MEF has built-in extensibility to support additional custom implementations of `ComposableParts` as long as they adhere to import/export contracts.

You define a `ComposablePart` by defining an export contract and then import the `ComposableParts` you want to use in your application. Contracts are the bridge shared between exports and imports. An export contract consists of metadata that can be used to filter the discoverability of the export. A container interacts with a catalog to load the `ComposableParts` your application uses. The container will handle loading any dependencies the `ComposableParts` require. If you want, you can manually add composable part instances directly to a container. By default, MEF uses attribute-based metadata to declare exports and imports. This allows MEF to determine which parts, imports, and exports are available completely through discovery.

Figure 12-3 shows the relationship between the MEF catalog, composition container, and multiple extensions (plug-ins). Each composable part can define export and import contracts and the catalog export provider is extensible enough to support custom export providers. This gives you the ability to build custom providers to better manage extensions if you have custom requirements that do not fit in the default export provider.

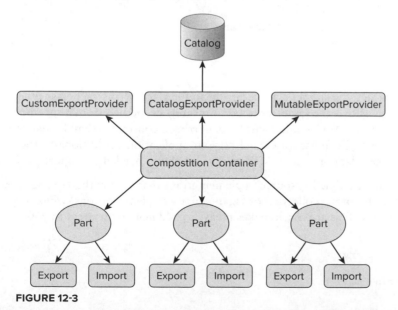

FIGURE 12-3

Using MEF in Your Application

Now that you have a basic understanding of what MEF is and how it works, you can dive into using MEF in your Silverlight application to add extensibility. To use MEF in your application you need to understand how to set up a `ComposablePart` and the import/export contracts for the part.

A `ComposablePart` is a unit within MEF. It exports services that other parts need and imports services from other parts. You use the `[System.ComponentModel.Composition.Import]` and `[System.ComponentModel.Composition.Export]` attributes to declare the imports/exports for a `ComposablePart`. A part must contain at least one export. The default MEF catalog will automatically load `ComposableParts` that have export attributes defined. It is possible to use the catalog to add a `ComposablePart` at run time also.

`ComposableParts` do not depend on each other directly. Instead, they depend on a contract. When defining a contract it's a good idea to use a fully qualified namespace. This will allow `ComposableParts` to be more uniquely defined. The MEF container will handle matching up export and import contracts when a `ComposablePart` is loaded.

The following code snippet shows the different approaches to exporting a contract. If a contract name is not specified, MEF will implicitly use the fully qualified name of the type as the contract.

```
[Export]
public class TextExporter
{
    public TextExporter()
    {
    }
}

[Export(typeof(TextExporterOne))]
public class TextExporterOne
{
}

[Export("Chapter12.MEF.Services.TextExporterTwo")]
public class TextExporterTwo
{
}
```

When defining your export contract you should consider using an interface or abstract class type rather than a concrete class. This allows the importer to be completely decoupled from a specific implementation of an export contract. You should consider deploying a contract assembly that contains the contract types that extenders can use for extending your applications. Additionally, the contract assembly can contain metadata or custom MEF export attributes needed by importers.

The following code snippet shows multiple log source implementations that export the `ILogService` interface. The `LogService` class imports a collection of `ILogService` implementations, which it invokes in the `WriteToLog` method. This approach makes it easy to add new log sources to your application.

```
public interface ILogService
{
    void Write(string value);
```

```
    }

    [Export(typeof(ILogService))]
    public class DatabaseLogService : ILogService
    {
        public void Write(string value)
        {
        }
    }

    [Export(typeof(ILogService))]
    public class FileLogService : ILogService
    {
        public void Write(string value)
        {
        }
    }

    public class LogService
    {
        [ImportMany]
        public IEnumerable<ILogService> Services { get; set; }

        public void WriteToLog(string value)
        {
            foreach (ILogService service in this.Services)
                service.Write(value);
        }
    }
```

Declaring Exports

ComposableParts declare exports through the [System.ComponentModel.Composition.Export] attribute. In MEF you can use several different approaches to declare exports, including at the class level and through properties and methods.

To export a ComposablePart you simply decorate the part with the Export attribute as shown in the following code snippet:

```
    [Export]
    public class TextExporter
    {
        public TextExporter()
        {
        }
    }
```

In addition to exporting itself, a part can export properties or methods. Property exports have several advantages. They allow the exporting of sealed types (such as core CLR types). They allow decoupling the export from how it is created, for example, exporting the existing Html.Document the run time creates for you. Moreover, they allow having a family of related exports in the same ComposablePart, such as the DefaultSendersRegistery ComposablePart that exports a default set of senders as properties.

To export a property, just decorate it with the `Export` attribute as the `ConfigurationService` class does in the following code snippet:

```
public class ConfigurationService
    {
        private int timeout = 60;
        private string serverUri = @"http://www.myserver.com";

        [Export("TimeoutAmount")]
        public int TimeoutAmount
        {
            get { return this.timeout; }
        }


        [Export("ServerUri")]
        public string ServerUri
        {
            get { return this.ServerUri; }
        }


    }
```

Methods are exported as delegates. They have several benefits, including allowing finer grained control as to what is exported. For example, a rules engine might import a set of pluggable methods that shield the caller from any knowledge of the type and that can be generated through simple code generation. Method exports are limited to four arguments because of limitation built into the .NET Framework. They must be defined using a type or string contract name.

The following code snippet shows you how to define a contract for a method export and how a delegate is used for importing the contract:

```
[Export(typeof(Action<Customer>))]
public void Send(Customer data)
{
    // Call Service to save dats
}
[Import(typeof(Action<Customer>))]
public Action<Customer> CallService { get; set; }

public void Save()
{
    CallService(new Customer { ContactName = "John Doe" });
}
```

MEF includes support for base classes/interfaces to define exports that are automatically inherited by subclasses. This is ideal for integration with legacy frameworks that want to take advantage of MEF without requiring modification to existing code. To use this capability you must decorate your class/interface using the `[System.ComponentModel.Composition.InheritedExport]` attribute. In the standard .NET version of MEF, it is possible to discover public and non-public parts, but this behavior is not supported by medium/partial trust environments including the Silverlight 4 Platform.

Declaring Imports

`ComposableParts` declare imports through the `[System.ComponentModel.Composition.Import]` attribute. MEF supports Field, Property, and Constructor importing. Property imports are done by decorating the property using the `[Import]` attribute:

```
[Import]
public IMessageSender MessageSender { get; set; }
```

Instead of listing out multiple imports using properties you can define a constructor that accepts one or more parameters. You have two approaches to define a constructor import. By default, the types for of each parameter will be used when you decorate the constructor using the `[ImportingConstructor]` attribute. It is also possible to explicitly define the import for each parameter using the `[Import]` attribute. An import can be marked as optional by setting the `AllowDefault` import parameter to `true`. If an optional import is not available it will be set to `default(T)` for its type.

The following code snippet shows how to mark one of the import parameters as optional by setting the `AllowDefault` parameter to `true`:

```
private IProductService service;

[ImportingConstructor]
public ProductViewModel([Import(AllowDefault = true)] IProductService
    service)
{
    this.service = service;
}
```

Member variables (fields) can be defined as imports also using the `[Import]` attribute. Importing private fields, properties, and methods is fully supported in a full trust environment, but will be problematic in a medium/partial trust environment like Silverlight because reflection in Silverlight cannot access private or internal members.

```
[Import]
private ILogService service;
```

In addition to single imports, you can import collections using the `[ImportMany]` attribute. This means that all instances of a specific contract will be imported from the container. MEF parts can support recomposition, which means as new exports become available in the container; collections are automatically updated with any new items. You can implement the `IPartImportsSatisfiedNotification` interface to be notified when all imports that could be satisfied are loaded.

```
public class LogManager : IPartImportsSatisfiedNotification
    {

        [ImportMany(AllowRecomposition = true)]
        public IEnumerable<ILogService> Services { get; set; }

        public void WriteToLog(string value)
        {
            foreach (ILogService service in this.Services)
                service.Write(value);
```

```
        }

        public void OnImportsSatisfied()
        {
            // Called when all imports are satisfied
        }
    }
```

Using Catalogs

One of the key value propositions of the MEF attribute-based programming model is the ability to dynamically discover parts via catalogs. Catalogs allow applications to easily consume self-registered exports. Out-of-the-box MEF includes several catalogs that make it easy to consume MEF parts. To use a catalog inside of a container, simply pass an instance of a catalog to the container's constructor:

```
    var container = new CompositionContainer(catalog);
```

AssemblyCatalog allows you to access all the exports available within a specific assembly. For example, use AssemblyCatalog to access the parts available in the currently executing assembly:

```
    Assembly currentAssembly = Assembly.GetExecutingAssembly();
    var catalog = new AssemblyCatalog(currentAssembly);
```

DirectoryCatalog allows you to discover all the exports in all assemblies for a given directory:

```
    var catalog = new DirectoryCatalog("Plugins");
```

AggregateCatalog can be used to combine multiple catalogs into a single catalog. Its constructor can accept a collection of catalogs or you can add catalogs individually to the catalog collection. A common approach is to load the currently executing AssemblyCatalog and DirectoryCatalog for third-party extensions:

```
        Assembly currentAssembly = Assembly.GetExecutingAssembly();

        var catalog = new AggregateCatalog(
                new AssemblyCatalog(currentAssembly),
                new DirectoryCatalog("Plugins")
```

In addition to the previous catalog, there is a TypeCatalog that discovers all the exports in a specific set of types. Silverlight includes a DeploymentCatalog that allows you to design your application using multiple XAP files. The DeploymentCatalog is discussed later in the chapter.

Managing a Part's Lifetime

One of the most important aspects of MEF is understanding how a container manages the lifetime of a part. Because MEF focuses on making your application extensible, you have no control on how many third-party extensions will be created. Lifetime can be explained as being the desired "shareability" of a part, which translates to the policy that a container will use for when a new part is created as well as when the part will be closed or disposed.

The "shareability" of a MEF part is defined using the `CreationPolicy` attribute available only at the class level. The following values are supported:

➤ **Shared** — The part author is telling MEF that only one instance of the part can exist per container.

➤ **NonShared** — The part author is telling MEF that a new instance should be used for each request for the export.

➤ **Any or not supplied** — The part author allows the part to be used in either a `Shared` or `NonShared` way.

```
[PartCreationPolicy(CreationPolicy.NonShared)]
[Export(typeof(IProductService))]
public class ProductService : IProductService
{
    public ProductService()
    {
    }
}
```

The container is always responsible for the ownership of the parts it has created. The ownership will never be transferred to a class that requested it by using the container instance (directly) or through an import (indirectly). An import contract can define or constrain the creation policy used by the container, by your setting the `RequiredCreationPolicy` parameter of the `Import` attribute. By default, this value is set to `Import.Any`, but it can be marked as `Import.Shared` or `Import.NonShared`. You would use this in scenarios where the shareability of a part is relevant to an importer.

Table 12-2 defines the behavior used. If both the part and the importer define "Any," the container will treat the part as shared.

TABLE 12-2

	PART.ANY	PART.SHARED	PART.NONSHARED
Import.Any	Shared	Shared	Non Shared
Import.Shared	Shared	Shared	*No Match*
Import.NonShared	Non Shared	*No Match*	Non Shared

An instance of a container is normally the lifetime holder of parts. A part instance created by the container will have its lifetime conditioned to the container's lifetime. You dispose of a container to signal the end of the container's lifetime. Disposal ordering is not guaranteed in any way and you should avoid using imports from within a dispose method.

The implications of disposing a container are:

➤ Parts that implement `IDisposable` will have the `Dispose` method called.

➤ References to parts held on the container will be cleaned up.

> ➤ Shared parts will be disposed of and cleaned up.

> ➤ Lazy exports won't work after the container is disposed.

> ➤ Operations might throw the `System.ObjectDisposedException`.

The .NET garbage collector is the best thing to rely on for proper clean up of your container and parts. However, there are times when you need deterministic behavior and a container will not hold references to parts it creates unless one of the following conditions is true:

> ➤ The part is marked as `Shared`.

> ➤ The part implements `IDisposable`.

> ➤ One or more imports are configured to allow recomposition.

For those cases when a part reference is kept or when you have many non-shared parts requests that cause memory demand to quickly become an issue, you need to consider one of the following approaches for mitigating the issue.

Some applications like web applications and Windows services vary greatly from desktop applications. They are more likely to rely on short-lived or batched operations. For these types of scenarios, you should either use child containers or release the object graph for your parts early. Releasing early allows the container to clean up non-shared part references. To trigger this operation call the `ReleaseExport` method on the container:

```
var container = new CompositionContainer(catalog);

var logExport = container.GetExport<ILogService>();
var service = logExport.Value;

service.Write("Test Message");
container.ReleaseExport(logExport);
```

Another approach for dealing with this issue is to use container hierarchies. You create child containers by connecting one container to another one. It is important that a child container does not access the same catalog as its parent container. This is necessary so the part references can be properly managed. You should consider filtering a catalog so you can load different filtered catalogs into parent and child containers. A common approach is to have `Shared` parts created in the parent container and `NonShared` ones created in child containers. If a `Shared` part depends on exports in a `NonShared` part, the parent catalog will have to contain the whole set of parts while the child container can still be filtered to only contain `NonShared` parts.

Not all parts are created directly by a container. You have the ability to add and remove parts to a container. When this happens, the container will create any additional parts to satisfy the dependencies for the parts you added. When a part is removed, MEF will handle reclaiming the resources and disposing of any non-shared parts that the part you added used. MEF will never take ownership of an instance you supply, but it does retain ownership of any parts created to satisfy your instance's imports.

Listing 12-9 shows how to add/remove parts to a container. When the `MEFViewModel` part is added to the container, the container will automatically handle importing in the dependencies needed by the `MEFViewModel` instance.

LISTING 12-9: Adding/removing parts to a container

```csharp
using System;
using System.ComponentModel.Composition;
using System.ComponentModel.Composition.Hosting;
using System.ComponentModel.Composition.Primitives;
using System.Windows;
using System.Windows.Controls;

namespace Chapter12.MEF.Views
{
    public partial class Listing1209 : UserControl
    {
        private ComposablePartCatalog catalog;
        private CompositionContainer container;
        private MEFViewModel root;
        private ComposablePart key;

        public Listing1209()
        {
            InitializeComponent();
        }

        private void CreateButton_Click(object sender, RoutedEventArgs e)
        {
            this.catalog = new AssemblyCatalog(
                        typeof(Listing1209).Assembly);

            this.container = new CompositionContainer(catalog);
            this.root = new MEFViewModel();

            this.Status.Text = "Object Created";
        }

        private void LoadButton_Click(object sender, RoutedEventArgs e)
        {
            CompositionBatch batch = new CompositionBatch();
            batch.AddPart(this.root);
            this.key = batch.AddExportedValue<DataService>("DataService",
                    new DataService());
            container.Compose(batch);

            this.Status.Text = root.GetMessage();
        }

        private void UnloadButton_Click(object sender, RoutedEventArgs e)
        {
            CompositionBatch batch = new CompositionBatch();
            batch.RemovePart(this.key);
            container.Compose(batch);

            this.Status.Text = root.GetMessage();
        }
```

continues

LISTING 12-9 *(continued)*

```
    }

    [Export]
    public class MEFViewModel
    {
        public MEFViewModel()
        {
        }

        public string GetMessage()
        {
            string result = "Dependency Not Loaded";

            if (this.Dep != null)
            {
                result = this.Dep.GetMessage();
            }

            return result;
        }

        [Import("DataService", AllowDefault = true,
                AllowRecomposition = true,
                RequiredCreationPolicy = CreationPolicy.NonShared)]
        public DataService Dep { get; set; }
    }

    [Export, PartCreationPolicy(CreationPolicy.NonShared)]
    public class DataService : IDisposable
    {
        public DataService()
        {
        }

        public string GetMessage()
        {
            return "Dependency Loaded";
        }

        public void Dispose()
        {
            Console.WriteLine("Disposed");
        }
    }
}
```

Hosting MEF in Silverlight

The previous sections focused on the key components of the MEF framework. You learned how to set up export and import contracts and how MEF uses containers and catalogs to manage the lifetime of parts. So now, it is time to examine how to use MEF in your Silverlight application.

For desktop applications, you are required to manually configure the composition container and catalogs in order for your application to discover parts. The container often needs to be passed around to all the components of your application that may need it for dynamically composing parts.

In Silverlight, a CompositionInitializer class allows parts to be composed by MEF without having to do a manual bootstrapping. When using the CompositionInitializer MEF will be set up to run on demand when any class that has been created contains imports. This means you can use MEF anywhere within your Silverlight application including XAML markup.

Listing 12-10 shows how to use the CompositionInitializer SatisfyImports method to import the ViewModel for the MainView screen. When the application startup method is called, an instance of the Listing1210 class is passed to the CompositionInitializer to have is imports created. This causes the MainViewModel to be discovered by MEF and inject it with an IProductService. Then the application loads the view and sets its data context to the imported ViewModel.

Notice that the Listing1210 class does not have any exports. SatisfyImports only works with parts that cannot be discovered by the catalog. The method throws an exception if you pass it a class that has an [Export] attribute.

LISTING 12-10: Using CompositionInitializer

```
using System.ComponentModel.Composition;
using System.Windows;
using System.Windows.Controls;
using Chapter12.MEF.ViewModel;

namespace Chapter12.MEF.Views
{
    public partial class Listing1210 : UserControl
    {

        [Import]
        public MainViewModel ViewModel { get; set; }

        public Listing1210()
        {
            InitializeComponent();

            CompositionInitializer.SatisfyImports(this);
            this.DataContext = this.ViewModel;
        }

        private void button_Click(object sender, RoutedEventArgs e)
        {
            this.ViewModel.LoadData();
        }
    }
}

using System.ComponentModel.Composition;
using Chapter12.MEF.Services;
```

continues

LISTING 12-10 *(continued)*

```
using Chapter12.MEF.Model;

namespace Chapter12.MEF.ViewModel
{
    [Export]
    public class MainViewModel : BaseViewModel
    {

        public MainViewModel()
        {
        }

        [Import]
        public IProductService ProductService { get; set; }

        private Product selectedProduct;
        public Product SelectedProduct
        {
            get
            {
                return this.selectedProduct;
            }
            set
            {
                if (this.selectedProduct != value)
                {
                    this.selectedProduct = value;
                    this.OnPropertyChanged("SelectedProduct");
                }
            }
        }

        public void LoadData()
        {
            this.SelectedProduct = this.ProductService.GetProduct();
        }

    }
}
```

`CompositionInitializer` is designed to be called multiple times, which makes it ideal to not only be used within the root application class, but also on elements created in XAML.

Listing 12-11 shows how to use the `CompositionInitializer` from within XAML-created elements. `OrderHeader` and `OrderDetail` are nested controls within the `OrderView`. Both have their own respective ViewModels imported. The `OrderHeader` is directly importing its ViewModel versus having it externally wired by its parent view. This is done to allow the `OrderHeader` control to be dropped within XAML without its containing control having any knowledge of how to wire the `OrderHeader` ViewModel.

LISTING 12-11: Activating CompositionInitializer from XAML

```
using System.ComponentModel.Composition;
using System.Windows.Controls;
using Chapter12.MEF.ViewModel;

namespace Chapter12.MEF.Controls
{
    public partial class OrderHeader : UserControl
    {
        [Import]
        public HeaderViewModel ViewModel { get; set; }

        public OrderHeader()
        {
            InitializeComponent();

            CompositionInitializer.SatisfyImports(this);
            this.DataContext = this.ViewModel;
        }
    }
}
```

There are a few caveats to keep in mind when using the `SatisfyImports` method of the `CompositionInitializer`. By default, only assemblies in the current XAP are discoverable. The next section explores how to override this behavior. All parts created with this method are held around by MEF until the application shuts down. This is not ideal when composing transient multiple-instance parts. In those cases, you should look into using an Export Factory. Classes passed to the method cannot have any exports defined.

MEF creates a default host configuration for `CompositionInitializer` the first time `SatisfyImports` is called. This is ideal for simple applications or ones where all the parts are contained in the current XAP. For more complex scenarios like composite applications, there is a `CompositionHost` class. You have to add a reference to the `System.ComponentModel.Composition.Initialization.dll` to use the `CompositionHost` class. The class allows you to override the default configuration by calling the `Initialize` method of the host class and passing in your own configuration. The `CompositionHost Initialize` method can be called only once when your application is being loaded.

The easiest way to override the default configuration is to call the overload of the `Initialize` method, which accepts one or more catalogs. When you override the host configuration, you take full control, and MEF does not automatically load the parts in the current XAP. To make the current XAP discoverable you create an instance of the `DeploymentCatalog` using its default constructor. This tells MEF to find all the parts in the current XAP.

```
var aggregateCatalog = new AggregateCatalog();
CompositionHost.Initialize(new DeploymentCatalog(), aggregateCatalog);
CompositionInitializer.SatisfyImports(this);
```

In most cases, overriding with catalogs should be fine. For more advanced scenarios such as providing a scoped container strategy, you may need to override the container itself. To do this you create an instance of a `CompositionContainer` and pass it to the `Initialize` method:

```
AggregateCatalog aggregateCatalog = new AggregateCatalog();
aggregateCatalog.Catalogs.Add(new DeploymentCatalog());

CompositionContainer container = new CompositionContainer(
                        aggregateCatalog);

CompositionHost.Initialize(container);
CompositionInitializer.SatisfyImports(this);
```

Partitioning Applications across Multiple XAPs

The default programming model for Silverlight requires all MEF parts to be stored in the current XAP file. This is fine for simple Silverlight applications, but poses severe problems for large applications. The default XAP can get bloated and increase the initial download time for your application. It prevents Silverlight from supporting an extensibility experience similar to what you can have in a desktop application. It can hamper development when multiple teams want to work on the same large application.

The `DeploymentCatalog` was created to address these issues. It supports separating your application into multiple XAP(s) that are hosted on the server. The `DeploymentCatalog` asynchronously downloads XAP files and fires events so you can monitor the download and handle errors. Even though the `DeploymentCatalog` is recomposable, you should override the default configuration for `CompositionInitializer` so the download parts in each XAP can be discoverable.

Listing 12-12 shows the most common approach for using the `DeploymentCatalog` to reduce your application startup footprint and immediately start downloading the other XAPs for your application in the background.

LISTING 12-12: Using the DeploymentCatalog

```
    }

        private void Application_Startup(object sender,
                                        StartupEventArgs e)
        {
            var catalog = new AggregateCatalog();
            catalog.Catalogs.Add(CreateCatalog(
                        "Chapter12.ModuleOne.xap"));
            catalog.Catalogs.Add(CreateCatalog(
                        "Chapter12.ModuleTwo.xap"));

            CompositionHost.Initialize(new DeploymentCatalog(), catalog);
            CompositionInitializer.SatisfyImports(this);

            this.RootVisual = new MainPage();
```

```csharp
        }

        private DeploymentCatalog CreateCatalog(string uri)
        {
            var catalog = new DeploymentCatalog(uri);
            catalog.DownloadCompleted +=
                new System.EventHandler<AsyncCompletedEventArgs>(
                    catalog_DownloadCompleted);
            catalog.DownloadAsync();
            return catalog;
        }

        void catalog_DownloadCompleted(object sender,
                        AsyncCompletedEventArgs e)
        {
            if (e.Error != null)
            {
                MessageBox.Show(e.Error.Message);
            }
        }
    }
```

There are some caveats to consider when using the `DeploymentCatalog`. Cached assemblies are not supported out-of-the-box. Localization is not supported; the `DeploymentCatalog` only downloads assemblies that are defined in the manifest. Loose resources/files outside of the assembly cannot be accessed and downloaded catalogs are not copied to the filesystem.

Exploring PRISM/Composite Application Library

PRISM/Composite Application Library (CAL) is a framework for building modular Windows Presentation Foundation (WPF) or Silverlight applications. PRISM is designed for applications that need to be loosely coupled and evolve over several iterations to adapt to changing requirements. This book focuses on the components and features available in the Silverlight version of the Composite Application Library.

As you review the components available in PRISM, you will start to notice the many similar concepts it shares with MEF. Though similarities exist, it's important to remember that PRISM is an application framework for building composite applications, whereas MEF is an extensibility framework. The technologies complement each other and future versions of PRISM will include more integration with MEF. Currently, PRISM uses the Microsoft Pattern and Practices Unity application framework DI Container. In addition, the PRISM framework includes a set of guidance documentation, quick starts, and videos for building composite Silverlight and WPF applications.

The samples and content for this section are based on earlier versions of the PRISM framework for Silverlight 4. Check the PRISM website — http://compositewpf.codeplex.com — for the latest builds. The October 2009 release is the latest version available for Silverlight 3.

Table 12-3 lists the important terms and definitions for the components used in a PRISM application.

TABLE 12-3

CLASS/TERM	DESCRIPTION
Shell	The shell is the main window of the application where the primary user interface (UI) content is contained. The shell may be composed of multiple windows if desired, but most commonly it is just a single main window that contains multiple views.
View	View is an ordinary .NET Framework user control that is responsible for presenting a part of or the whole model to the user and allowing the user to modify its contents through user interface controls. Typically, the view implements only UI logic, whereas the related client-business logic is implemented in the presenter/controller/ViewModel.
Regions	These are placeholders for content and host visual elements in the shell. These can be located by other components through the `RegionManager` to add content to those regions. Regions can also be hosted in individual views to create discoverable content placeholders.
Modules	These are separate sets of views and services, frequently logically related, that can be independently developed, tested, and optionally deployed. In many situations, these can be developed and maintained by separate teams. In a composite application, modules must be discovered and loaded. In the Composite Application Library, this process consists of populating the module catalog, retrieving the modules if they are remote, loading assemblies into the application domain, and initializing the modules
CompositeCommand	The `CompositeCommand` is a strategy to combine the execution of commands. This allows the command invoker to interact with a single command that affects multiple commands.
EventAggregator	The `EventAggregator` service is primarily a container for events that allow decoupling of publishers and subscribers so they can evolve independently. This decoupling is useful in modularized applications because new modules can be added that respond to events defined by the shell or, more likely, other modules.
Bootstrapper	The Bootstrapper is responsible for the initialization of an application built using the Composite Application Library. By using a Bootstrapper, you have more control of how the Composite Application Library components are wired up to your application.

CLASS/TERM	DESCRIPTION
IModule	Each module consists of a class that implements the `IModule` interface. This interface contains a single `Initialize` method that is called during the module's initialization process.
DelegateCommand<T>	The `DelegateCommand` allows delegating the commanding logic instead of requiring a handler in the code-behind. It uses a delegate as the method of invoking a target handling method.
IServiceLocator	The Composite Application Library provides support for the Unity Application Block (Unity) container, but it is not container-specific. Because the library accesses the container through the `IServiceLocator` interface, the container can be replaced. To do this, your container must implement the `IServiceLocator` interface.
UnityServiceLocatorAdapter	The `UnityServiceLocatorAdapter` is an `IUnityContainer` adapter for the `IServiceLocator` interface. The `UnityServiceLocatorAdapter` is mapped to the `IServiceLocator` interface and the mapping is registered in the `UnityBootstrapper` class.

When designing an application that uses the PRISM framework, you will create a shell and one or more modules. The shell contains the main UI elements of your application plus one or more regions. You use XAML to define the regions of your application that modules use to load their views into at run time. A module is set of views and services that can be developed, tested, and deployed independently. A shell uses a catalog to define what modules to load.

Figure 12-4 shows the high-level design of an application built with the PRISM Framework. The left side shows the custom shell and modules you will create for your application. The right side shows the core components and services that the framework provides for building composite applications.

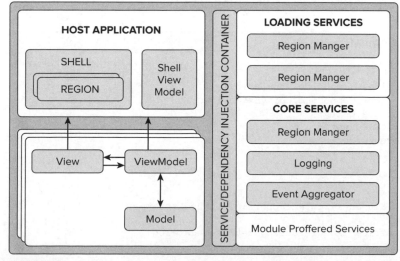

FIGURE 12-4

Using PRISM to Build an Application

When designing an application using PRISM, you need to define a couple of key items up front: how many modules you want to create and what regions your shell will expose for hosting module views. You can take several approaches to define how to partition your application. It might make sense to separate your application into related functionality or to separate it by the different teams that will work on it.

It is always a good idea to start simple and let the shell evolve independently outside the rest of your application. Initially you should create a single region and two modules. You should create a common infrastructure assembly that can be shared across the shell and modules. The shared assembly should include anything that needs to be shared between the different components of your application: model, services, or other shared code. It is a good idea to add a region names class that uses constants to define all your regions. You should avoid adding any unnecessary features to the shell or having modules referencing each other. Instead, always use the dependency injection container included with PRISM for accessing regions, services, and shared events.

Building the Shell and Modules

Once you define the regions and separate your application into modules, it is time to set up the `Bootstrapper` for your shell. A `Bootstrapper` is used to load the module catalog and services exposed by the `Shell` application. In your application startup event, instead of setting the root element to your main UI, create an instance of your custom `Bootstrapper` and call its `Run` method.

```
var bootstrapper = new ShellBootstrapper();
bootstrapper.Run();
```

Listing 12-13 shows how to create a custom `Bootstrapper` by inheriting from the `UnityBootstrapper` base class and overriding the `GetModuleCatalog`, `ConfigureContainer`, and `CreateShell` methods. The `GetModuleCatalog` method is used for loading your modules into the shell's catalog. Each module added to the catalog will be loaded by the PRISM framework. When you add a module, you can specify whether it depends on any other modules. The `ConfigureContainer` method handles registering the shell so it can be dependency injected into the shell ViewModel. The `CreateShell` method uses Unity to resolve the dependencies from the shell presenter and display the shell view.

LISTING 12-13: Creating a PRISM Bootstrapper

```
using System.Windows;
using Microsoft.Practices.Composite.Modularity;
using Microsoft.Practices.Composite.UnityExtensions;
using Microsoft.Practices.Unity;
using NorthWndCal.Model.Customer;
using NorthWndCal.Model.Order;

namespace NorthWndCal
{

    public partial class ShellBootstrapper : UnityBootstrapper
    {
        protected override IModuleCatalog GetModuleCatalog()
```

```
        {
            var catalog = new ModuleCatalog();
            catalog.AddModule(typeof(CustomerModule))
                .AddModule(typeof(OrderModule));
            return catalog;
        }

        protected override void ConfigureContainer()
        {
            Container.RegisterType<IShellView, Shell>();
            base.ConfigureContainer();
        }

        protected override DependencyObject CreateShell()
        {
            ShellPresenter presenter = Container.Resolve<ShellPresenter>();
            IShellView view = presenter.View;

            view.ShowView();

            return view as DependencyObject;
        }
    }
}
```

Defining Region Adapters

Region adapters are used by the shell to define shared UI elements in which module views can be displayed. The region manager is used to define the region adapters your application supports. For Silverlight, PRISM includes the following region adapters: ContentControlRegionAdapter, SelectorRegionAdapter, ItemsControlRegionAdapter, and TabControlRegionAdapter. The TabControlRegionAdapter is available only in the Silverlight version of PRISM because the Silverlight tab control does not derive from the Selector class.

The RegionManager includes the attached properties you can use to define a region using XAML. You can use the RegionManager class to define regions via code, too. The following code snippet shows how to use the RegionName attached property to define a region in your shell:

```xml
<Border x:Name="ContentBorder" Style="{StaticResource ContentBorderStyle}">
    <StackPanel Orientation="Horizontal">
        <StackPanel>
            <ContentControl
                Regions:RegionManager.RegionName="FilterRegion"
                x:Name="ActionControl" >
                <ContentControl.Template>
                    <ControlTemplate>
                        <Grid>
                            <ContentPresenter Margin="10,0,10,0" />
                        </Grid>
                    </ControlTemplate>
                </ContentControl.Template>
            </ContentControl>
        </StackPanel>
```

```
        <StackPanel>
            <ContentControl
                Regions:RegionManager.RegionName="MainRegion"
                x:Name="MainContent" >
                <ContentControl.Template>
                    <ControlTemplate>
                        <Grid>
                            <ContentPresenter Margin="10,0,10,0" />
                        </Grid>
                    </ControlTemplate>
                </ContentControl.Template>
            </ContentControl>
        </StackPanel>
    </StackPanel>
</Border>
```

To share context between multiple views the `RegionManager` includes a `RegionContext` attached property. The `RegionContext` can be any simple or complex object and can be a data-bound value defined to a ViewModel.

```
cal:RegionManager.RegionContext="{Binding Path=SelectedEmployee.EmployeeId}"
```

To override the default behavior or add your own custom region adapters, override the `ConfigureRegionAdapterMapping` method in your custom `Bootstrapper` class:

```
protected override RegionAdapterMappings
    ConfigureRegionAdapterMappings()
{
    RegionAdapterMappings regionAdapterMappings =
            Container.TryResolve<RegionAdapterMappings>();
    if (regionAdapterMappings != null)
    {

        regionAdapterMappings.RegisterMapping(typeof(TabControl),
          this.Container.Resolve
            <CustomTabControlRegionAdapter>());
    }

    return regionAdapterMappings;

}
```

Adding Views to a Region

To use the regions defined in your shell you have to register your view with a region. Views can be created and displayed either automatically using *view discovery* or programmatically using *view injection*.

➤ When you use **view discovery,** you set up a relationship between a view and its region using the `RegionViewRegistry`. When a region is created, it looks for all the `ViewTypes` associated with the region and it automatically instantiates and loads the corresponding views. This approach is simpler than view injection but limits your ability to control when views are loaded and displayed.

➤ When you use **view injection** you programmatically add a view to a region. Typically, this is done when a module is initialized or the result of a user action. In code, you will query the `RegionManager` or a specific region by name and then inject your view into it. This approach gives you the most control over when views are loaded and displayed. You also have the ability remove views from a region, but it is not possible to add a view to a region that has not been created yet.

```
this.regionViewRegistry.RegisterViewWithRegion(RegionNames.SelectionRegion
                        ,typeof(EmployeesView));
```

Using Commands

When a user interacts with your Silverlight application, you typically use commands or events to handle user input and modify your application UI accordingly. For example, when a row in a grid is selected, the `ShowCustomer` command will be fired in your ViewModel to load the details for the selected customer. Although using the basic `ICommand` and events available in Silverlight works great for simple applications, in more advanced applications such as composite applications you need a more loosely coupled approach. PRISM includes the `DelegateCommand<T>` and `CompositeCommand` classes for supporting these scenarios.

Using DelegateCommand<T>

A `DelegateCommand<T>` is a generic command that is used instead of an event. It uses a delegate as the method of invoking a target method. Its constructor takes in a custom action for execution (`Execute`) and as an optional parameter a custom action for its `CanExecute` implementation. Because the class is generic, it enforces compile-time checking on command parameters, which normal WPF and Silverlight commands do not support. In addition, because it uses a generic type, it removes the need for creating new command types for every specific type your application needs.

Listing 12-14 shows how to use the `DelegateCommand<T>` to load customers into a ViewModel after the view is loaded.

LISTING 12-14: Using DelegateCommand<T>

Available for
download on
Wrox.com

```
using System.ComponentModel;
using System.Windows.Input;
using Microsoft.Practices.Composite.Events;
using Microsoft.Practices.Composite.Presentation.Commands;
using NorthWndCal.Model.Models;
using NorthWndCal.Model.Service;

namespace NorthWndCal.Model.CustomerModule.Views
{
    public class CustomerViewModel : BaseViewModel, ICustomerViewModel
    {
        private readonly ICustomerView view;
        private readonly IEventAggregator eventAggregator;
        private readonly ICustomerService service;

        public CustomerViewModel(ICustomerView view,
```

continues

LISTING 12-14 *(continued)*

```
                    ICustomerService service,
                    IEventAggregator eventAggregator)
    {
        this.view = view;
        this.view.Model = this;
        this.service = service;
        this.eventAggregator = eventAggregator;

        this.LoadCustomersCommand =
            new DelegateCommand<object>(LoadCustomers);
    }

    public ICustomerView View
    {
        get { return this.view; }
    }

    public ICommand LoadCustomersCommand { get; set; }

    private ICollectionView customers;
    public ICollectionView Customers
    {
        get
        {
            return this.customers;
        }
        set
        {
            if (this.customers != value)
            {
                this.customers = value;
                this.OnPropertyChanged("Customers");
            }
        }
    }

    protected void LoadCustomers(object parameter)
    {
        this.service.GetCustomers(this.DisplayCustomers);
    }

    protected void DisplayCustomers(ICollectionView dataSource)
    {
        this.Customers = dataSource;
    }

    }
}
```

Using CompositeCommands

The `CompositeCommand` allows you to register and unregister child commands so that when the composite command is invoked all registered commands will be invoked. This is useful when your application has a shared common command that multiple subscribers want their command execution to participate in, such as a Save All command.

Listing 12-15 shows how to use the `CompositeCommand` to execute multiple commands when the close button is clicked by the end user.

LISTING 12-15: Using CompositeCommand

```csharp
using Microsoft.Practices.Composite.Presentation.Commands;

namespace NorthWndCal.Model.Events
{
    public class SharedCommands
    {
        public static readonly CompositeCommand
            ApplicationClosingCommand = new CompositeCommand();

    }
}

using NorthWndCal.Model.Events;

namespace NorthWndCal
{
    public class ShellPresenter
    {
        public ShellPresenter(IShellView view)
        {
            View = view;
            this.View.Model = this;
        }

        public IShellView View { get; private set; }

        public void CloseApplication()
        {
            SharedCommands.ApplicationClosingCommand.Execute(null);
        }

    }
}
using System.Windows.Input;
using Microsoft.Practices.Composite.Events;
using Microsoft.Practices.Composite.Presentation.Commands;
using NorthWndCal.Model.Events;
using NorthWndCal.Model.Models;
using NorthWndCal.Model.Service;

namespace NorthWndCal.Model.CustomerModule.Views
```

continues

LISTING 12-15 *(continued)*

```
{
    public class CustomerViewModel : BaseViewModel, ICustomerViewModel
    {
        private readonly ICustomerView view;
        private readonly IEventAggregator eventAggregator;
        private readonly ICustomerService service;

        public CustomerViewModel(ICustomerView view,
                             ICustomerService service,
                             IEventAggregator eventAggregator)
        {
            this.view = view;
            this.view.Model = this;
            this.service = service;
            this.eventAggregator = eventAggregator;

            this.ApplicationClosing =
                new DelegateCommand<object>(OnClosing);

            SharedCommands.ApplicationClosingCommand.RegisterCommand(
                            ApplicationClosing);
        }

        public ICustomerView View
        {
            get { return this.view; }
        }

        public ICommand ApplicationClosing { get; set; }

        public void OnClosing(object e)
        {
            // Handle closing event
        }

    }
}
```

Using the Event Aggregator

When building a composite application you may run into scenarios that involve multiple components: ViewModels, services, and controllers that exist in different modules need to communicate with one another when some state changes occur or application logic is executed. For example, when data is returned from your application data access service, you may need to notify multiple ViewModels in several different modules that data returned is ready to be displayed.

Because of the loosely coupled design of a composite application you need to use the EventBroker pattern to handle the lack of direct connection between publishers and subscribers and any possible threading issues because the publisher is on a different thread than its subscriber.

The PRISM framework includes the event aggregation (broker) service, which is an implementation of the EventBroker pattern. The service uses a repository to track event objects. An event object uses delegates instead of standard .NET Framework events. One advantage of this approach is that delegates can be created at the time of publishing and immediately released, which does not prevent the subscriber from being garbage collected. Each event object contains a collection of subscribers to publish to. This way, new events can be added to the system without modifying the service and can automatically handle marshaling to the correct thread.

Listing 12-16 shows how the event aggregation service is used to notify multiple ViewModels that data has been retrieved from a data service.

LISTING 12-16: Using the event aggregation service

```
using System.ComponentModel;
using Microsoft.Practices.Composite.Presentation.Events;

namespace NorthWndCal.Model.Events
{
    public class ChangeCustomerEvent
        : CompositePresentationEvent<ICollectionView>
    {
        public ChangeCustomerEvent()
        {
        }
    }
}
using System.ComponentModel;
using System.Windows.Input;
using Microsoft.Practices.Composite.Events;
using Microsoft.Practices.Composite.Presentation.Commands;
using NorthWndCal.Model.Events;
using NorthWndCal.Model.Models;
using NorthWndCal.Model.Service;
using NorthWndCal.Web;

namespace NorthWndCal.Model.CustomerModule.Views
{
    public class CustomerViewModel : BaseViewModel, ICustomerViewModel
    {
        private readonly ICustomerView view;
        private readonly IEventAggregator eventAggregator;
        private readonly ICustomerService service;

        public CustomerViewModel(ICustomerView view,
                            ICustomerService service,
                            IEventAggregator eventAggregator)
        {
            this.view = view;
            this.view.Model = this;
            this.service = service;
            this.eventAggregator = eventAggregator;
```

continues

LISTING 12-16 *(continued)*

```csharp
            this.LoadCustomersCommand =
                new DelegateCommand<object>(LoadCustomers);

            this.ApplicationClosing =
                new DelegateCommand<object>(OnClosing);

            SharedCommands.ApplicationClosingCommand.RegisterCommand(
                            ApplicationClosing);
        }

        public ICustomerView View
        {
            get { return this.view; }
        }

        public ICommand LoadCustomersCommand { get; set; }
        public ICommand ApplicationClosing { get; set; }

        private ICollectionView customers;
        public ICollectionView Customers
        {
            get
            {
                return this.customers;
            }
            set
            {
                if (this.customers != value)
                {
                    this.customers = value;
                    this.OnPropertyChanged("Customers");
                }
            }
        }

        protected void LoadCustomers(object parameter)
        {
            this.service.GetCustomers(this.DisplayCustomers);
        }

        protected void DisplayCustomers(ICollectionView dataSource)
        {
            this.Customers = dataSource;
        }

        protected void DisplayOrders(ICollectionView dataSource)
        {
            this.eventAggregator.GetEvent
                <ChangeCustomerEvent>().Publish(dataSource);
        }

        public void LoadSelectedCustomer(Customer customer)
```

```
        {
            this.service.GetOrdersForCustomer(
                            this.DisplayOrders, customer);
        }

        public void OnClosing(object e)
        {
            // Handle closing event
        }

    }
}
using System.ComponentModel;
using System.Windows.Input;
using Microsoft.Practices.Composite.Events;
using Microsoft.Practices.Composite.Presentation.Commands;
using NorthWndCal.Model.Events;
using NorthWndCal.Model.Models;

namespace NorthWndCal.Model.OrderModule.Views
{
    public class OrderViewModel : BaseViewModel, IOrderViewModel
    {
        private readonly IOrderView view;
        private readonly IEventAggregator eventAggregator;

        public OrderViewModel(IOrderView view,
                        IEventAggregator eventAggregator)
        {
            this.view = view;
            this.view.Model = this;

            this.eventAggregator = eventAggregator;

            this.eventAggregator.GetEvent
                <ChangeCustomerEvent>().Subscribe(
                                    CustomerChanged, true);

            this.ApplicationClosing =
                new DelegateCommand<object>(OnClosing);

            SharedCommands.ApplicationClosingCommand.RegisterCommand(
                ApplicationClosing);
        }

        public IOrderView View
        {
            get { return this.view; }
        }

        public ICommand ApplicationClosing { get; set; }

        private ICollectionView orders;
        public ICollectionView Orders
```

continues

LISTING 12-16 *(continued)*

```
        {
            get
            {
                return this.orders;
            }
            set
            {
                if (this.orders != value)
                {
                    this.orders = value;
                    this.OnPropertyChanged("Orders");
                }
            }
        }

        public void CustomerChanged(ICollectionView dataSource)
        {
            this.Orders = dataSource;
        }

        public void OnClosing(object e)
        {
            // Handle closing event
        }

    }
}
```

DEFINING YOUR DATA ACCESS STRATEGY

When architecting an n-tier application the most important component that impacts the rest of the application is the data access strategy you adopted. Early in the book, the data access and RIA Services chapters (Chapters 7 and 8) walked you through the basic data access approaches for displaying and saving data in your Silverlight application.

This chapter looks at data access from an architecture viewpoint. By reviewing the typical application layers of an application, you can review and consider the best data access strategy options for your application.

Figure 12-5 shows the high-level overview of the typical layers found in an n-tier Silverlight application:

➤ **Presentation Layer (Silverlight Plug-In)** — Includes views, ViewModel, models, and a client service layer. The client service layer is responsible for calling the Windows Communication Foundation (WCF) or external services your application uses.

➤ **Business Layer (Web Server)** — Includes the application service layer, domain model, and business (workflow/components) used by your application. Depending on your application requirements, the client and server domain model may be shared or completely different.

➤ **Data Layer (Web Server)** — Includes the data access components and repositories, Object Relational Mappers (ORM). Examples of an ORM are Entity Framework, LINQ to SQL, and nHibernate.

➤ **Data Stores (Database Server)** — Includes your application databases and any other external data access stores your application may be dependent on.

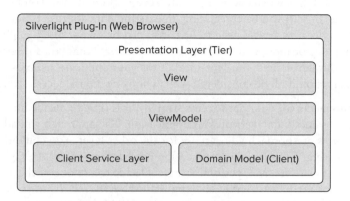

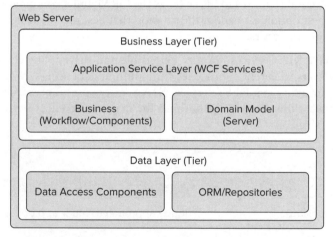

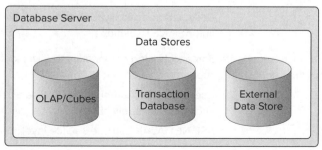

FIGURE 12-5

In a typical n-tier application design each layer (tier) has a core set of responsibilities. This allows you to design each layer to focus on what it is responsible for and not worry about what the other layers are doing. Each layer should be designed to be loosely coupled and dependencies should be based on abstraction. The same set of design principles and concepts (IoC/dependency injection) can be used to design each layer.

You need to consider a number of things when choosing a data access strategy. Will you be using a brand new data source (database) or will you be consuming an existing data source? Is your data source currently exposed as a service and does it need to be consumed by one or many applications? In some cases, you may be using one or more external data sources/services that you subscribe to. Understanding the skill-set of your developers, the time-market for your applications, plus any application-specific requirements should all be considered when choosing a data access strategy.

Once you understand the requirements for your data access strategy, it is time to decide how to design and implement the business and data layers of your application. The approach you adopt for one layer may affect the choices or approach you can use for the other layer. You could decide to build a total custom solution using Windows Communication Foundation (WCF), POCO (Plain old CLR Object), and the Object Relational Mapper nHibernate. Decide to use one of the available frameworks (WCF RIA Services or WCF Data Services) along with the ADO.NET Entity Framework from Microsoft. Build a hybrid solution that uses nHibernate as the ORM and a combination of RIA and custom WCF services. Your best option is to adopt the solution that best meets the needs of your application and the skill set of your developers.

Both WCF Data Services and WCF RIA Services are very extensible and share many common features. However, they use two very different approaches for handling data access. WCF Data Services focuses on exposing your data via a REST service. RIA Services uses a prescriptive approach for building n-tier applications. Table 12-4 outlines the major differences between WCF Data Services and WCF RIA Services.

TABLE 12-4

WCF DATA SERVICES	WCF RIA SERVICES
Uses a RESTful approach for exposing the data source	Prescriptive approach to n-tier app development
Cross Platform interoperability is a goal	Designed specifically for end-to-end Silverlight and ASP.NET solutions
Supported by a number of MS products such as SharePoint 2010, Excel 2010, Azure, and SQL2008 R2	Some technology proprietary to Silverlight (no WPF support) Uses ASP.NET Authentication/Roles across SL and ASP.NET applications. ASP.NET/AJAX can use service layer.
Loosely coupled client and servers	Client and server are designed and deployed together.

WCF DATA SERVICES	WCF RIA SERVICES
Service later exposes raw data source	Opportunity to easily add business logic into service layer • Encourage "domain" concepts. • Strong validation framework • Offline / Sync enabled
Services can be consumer by .NET and non .NET clients including AJAX, PHP, and JAVA	Service can be consumed easily from SL, AJAX, WebForms.
Service's data source must: • Expose at least one `IQueryable` property. • Implement `IUpdateable` for updating.	Service exposes domain objects via convention: • `IQueryable GetX` • `UpdateX/InsertX/DeleteX`
Standardized on `OData` protocol but supports multi-formats including JSON and XML	• SOAP (binary) for SL clients • JSON for AJAX clients • SOAP (XML) for other clients • Will include OData Support.
Hosted as a WCF Service (.svc)	Old version hosted in custom web handler (.axd). New version is WCF service
No client design-time support	Design-time experience with data sources, drag-and-drop, and so on.
More mature — public for more than 2 years; formerly known as "Project Astoria"	Less mature — public for less than a year

HANDLING PERFORMANCE

So far, in this chapter you have looked at the different patterns, frameworks, and data access strategies you can use for building your Silverlight applications. This section switches focus to discuss some best practices to consider when designing and building your n-tier Silverlight applications.

When dealing with the performance of an application it is always important to keep in mind that there are no silver bullets and everything has trade-offs. This is particularly true when dealing with performance versus scalability

Initially it is easy to think both of these work hand-in-hand, but in most applications, the trade-off you make centers around balancing these two. For example, you want to minimize the load time of your application so you choose to limit the data you load up front. This works great for the initial load time, but this could affect the scalability of your application because you have to make multiple calls to retrieve the data the user needs. Another good example of a trade-off is deciding between making one or two large data requests versus making multiple small requests.

The best way to really address application performance or any other non-functional requirements is to try different approaches and test them using real-world hardware and data. An in-depth guide on n-tier application performance is outside the scope of this book. See Table 12-5 for a small subset of scenarios related to the client tier of your application. When dealing with performance and scalability issues it's best to always address them from the perspective of your overall application.

TABLE 12-5

SCENARIO	BEST PRACTICE
Large Result Set.	When returning a large result set you should consider paging the data displayed to users. For overall application performance it's best to offload the paging of data to your data source.
Application Load Time	Consider using multiple XAP files and retrieving only the necessary data the user needs up front.
Memory Footprint	Consider freeing resources and object instances as soon as possible.
Frequently Used Data	Look into caching the data in local storage or memory. If the data is static (for example, drop-down lists) make sure you only load the data once per session.
Heavy Load	If you are experiencing heavy load on your database, consider caching static and non-critical data in memory or a caching server. When possible, utilize isolated storage on the client to cache data needed across sessions.
XAP File Size	Try to eliminate any unnecessary resources; make sure any images are stored as `*.png`. Consider deferred loading of resources until they are needed.
Long Running Process	Use multiple threads to offload the long-running process outside of the UI thread.
Complex Model	Complex models can be very hard to work with and cause performance issues when retrieving or saving data. Lazy loading and the unit of work pattern are two good options for dealing with a complex model.

SUMMARY

In this chapter, you learned how to architect an n-tier Silverlight application. You were introduced to the common design patterns and frameworks available, including the MVVM UI pattern, the Managed Extensibility Framework (MEF), and PRISM (Composite Application Library) guidance framework. This chapter reviewed the different data access strategies and frameworks commonly used when building Silverlight applications. You also learned some options for dealing with performance issues when building your Silverlight application.

13

DOM Interaction

WHAT'S IN THIS CHAPTER?

➤ Configuring the Silverlight plug-in

➤ Interacting with the plug-in using JavaScript

Because Silverlight is a browser plug-in, eventually you must embed the Silverlight player into a host web page. The browser sees the plug-in as any other ordinary object in the Document Object Model (DOM), and, therefore, you can use standard HTML and JavaScript DOM manipulation techniques to configure and interact with the plug-in. This chapter looks at the ways you can configure the plug-in in the browser and how you can use JavaScript to interact with the plug-in. It also looks at a feature of Silverlight called the *HTML Bridge*, which allows you to interoperate between JavaScript and managed code running in the plug-in.

CONFIGURING THE SILVERLIGHT PLUG-IN

When you set up a new web page to host a Silverlight application, you must add the appropriate HTML and JavaScript in order to load and configure the plug-in. If you created a new website when you created the Silverlight application, Visual Studio automatically generates both a test ASP.NET page and test HTML page. These pages include the HTML and JavaScript needed to embed the player.

If you add the Silverlight application to an existing site or page, you can also add this content manually by adding an `<object>` tag to your page, filling in all the appropriate object `<param>` tags, and including the appropriate JavaScript files and code. Listing 13-1 shows the contents of the test ASP.NET page.

LISTING 13-1: Embedding the Silverlight plug-in in an ASP.NET page

```html
<html xmlns="http://www.w3.org/1999/xhtml" >
<head id="Head1" runat="server">
    <title>Chapter13</title>

    <style type="text/css">
    html, body {
        height: 100%;
        overflow: auto;
    }
    body {
        padding: 0;
        margin: 0;
    }
    #silverlightControlHost {
        height: 100%;
        text-align:center;
    }
    </style>
    <script type="text/javascript" src="Silverlight.js"></script>
    <script type="text/javascript">
        function onSilverlightError(sender, args) {
            var appSource = "";
            if (sender != null && sender != 0) {
                appSource = sender.getHost().Source;
            }

            var errorType = args.ErrorType;
            var iErrorCode = args.ErrorCode;

            if (errorType == "ImageError" || errorType == "MediaError") {
                return;
            }

            var errMsg = "Unhandled Error in Silverlight Application " +
                        appSource + "\n";

            errMsg += "Code: " + iErrorCode + "    \n";
            errMsg += "Category: " + errorType + "       \n";
            errMsg += "Message: " + args.ErrorMessage + "       \n";

            if (errorType == "ParserError") {
                errMsg += "File: " + args.xamlFile + "      \n";
                errMsg += "Line: " + args.lineNumber + "     \n";
                errMsg += "Position: " + args.charPosition + "     \n";
            }
            else if (errorType == "RuntimeError") {
                if (args.lineNumber != 0) {
                    errMsg += "Line: " + args.lineNumber + "     \n";
                    errMsg += "Position: " + args.charPosition + "      \n";
                }
                errMsg += "MethodName: " + args.methodName + "       \n";
```

```
                    }

                    throw new Error(errMsg);
                }
        </script>
    </head>

    <body>
        <form id="form1" runat="server" style="height:100%;">
            <div id="silverlightControlHost">
                <object data="data:application/x-silverlight-2,"
                        type="application/x-silverlight-2"
                        width="100%" height="100%">
                    <param name="source" value="ClientBin/Chapter13.xap"/>
                    <param name="onerror" value="onSilverlightError" />
                    <param name="background" value="white" />
                    <param name="minRuntimeVersion" value="4.0.50331.0" />
                    <param name="autoUpgrade" value="true" />
                    <a href="http://go.microsoft.com/fwlink/
                            ?LinkID=149156&v=4.0.50331.0"
                        style="text-decoration: none;">
                        <img src="http://go.microsoft.com/fwlink/
                                ?LinkId=161376"
                            alt="Get Microsoft Silverlight"
                            style="border-style: none"/>
                    </a>
                </object><iframe id="_sl_historyFrame"
                    style='visibility:hidden;height:0;width:0;border:0px'>
                </iframe></div>
        </form>
    </body>
</html>
```

This HTML embeds the Silverlight plug-in in your page using an `<object>` tag, and the JavaScript provides functionality such as detecting whether the plug-in is installed (and proceeds to install if it is not) and what version is installed.

Exploring the HTML markup a bit, you can see that within the object tag are a number of `<param>` tags, which are used to specify the parameters of the player.

Two of the more important parameters of the Silverlight plug-in are `minRumtimeVersion` and `autoUpgrade`. The `minRunTimeVersion` property allows you to specify the minimum Silverlight version the client must have to run your application. As shown in Listing 13-1, the default templates automatically set it to the current Silverlight 4 version. The `autoUpgrade` property tells the control whether or not it should automatically render the appropriate JavaScript needed to automatically upgrade the client's version of Silverlight if it does not meet the minimum version requirement. Using these properties together makes it easy to give your end users a positive experience when they interact with your website.

If the end user has a version of Silverlight installed that is older than the application requires and the Silverlight control is not configured to auto-upgrade, the default template will include content that lets the user know he or she needs to upgrade. You, of course, can customize this content, which is shown in Listing 13-2.

LISTING 13-2: Providing custom content when the Silverlight plug-in is not installed

```
<object data="data:application/x-silverlight-2,"
    type="application/x-silverlight-2" width="100%" height="100%">
    <param name="source" value="ClientBin/Chapter13.xap"/>
    <param name="onerror" value="onSilverlightError" />
    <param name="background" value="white" />
    <param name="minRuntimeVersion" value="4.0.50311.0" />
    <param name="autoUpgrade" value="true" />
    <h1>Whoops!</h1>
    <p>Looks like you don't have the right version of
        Silverlight installed.  This means you&#39;re missing out
        on the greatest thing on the Internet!</p>
    <p>I really suggest that you go download the latest
        version of Silverlight as it will greatly enhance
        your life.</p>
</object>
```

This sample shows custom HTML content added to the object tag, which tells end users about the content they could be viewing if they installed the right version of Silverlight.

A handful of other interesting properties are available on the Silverlight control and are discussed in the following sections.

windowless

The `windowless` parameter (which applies only when running on Windows) enables you to configure the Silverlight plug-in to be displayed directly by the browser rather than having its own render window as it normally would. Running the plug-in in Windowless mode allows the control's content to overlap and better blend with other surrounding HTML content.

Listing 13-3 shows how you can use the `windowless` property to integrate your Silverlight application more seamlessly into its host HTML page. In this case, the Silverlight application has had its root `UserControl`'s background color set to its default transparent color.

LISTING 13-3: Setting the Windowless property

```
<object data="data:application/x-silverlight-2,"
    type="application/x-silverlight-2" width="400" height="300">
    <param name="source" value="ClientBin/Chapter13.xap"/>
    <param name="onerror" value="onSilverlightError" />
    <param name="background" value="transparent" />
    <param name="minRuntimeVersion" value="4.0.50311.0" />
    <param name="autoUpgrade" value="true" />
    <param name="windowless" value="true" />
    <a href="http://go.microsoft.com/fwlink/
            ?LinkID=149156&v=4.0.50311.0"
        style="text-decoration: none;">
        <img src="http://go.microsoft.com/fwlink/?LinkId=161376"
            alt="Get Microsoft Silverlight" style="border-style: none"/>
    </a>
</object>
```

Figure 13-1 shows how enabling and disabling the `windowless` property affects how the plug-in is rendered in the browser.

FIGURE 13-1

With the `windowless` property set to `true`, the underlying `DIV` containing the image shows through.

 By default, the Silverlight plug-in background is set to `White`. *Therefore, to achieve the transparency shown in Figure 13-1, you must explicitly set the plug-in's background parameter to* `Transparent`. *Also note that the Silverlight User Control template in Visual Studio has its root layout element's background property set to* `White` *by default, which you also must change to see the transparency shown in Figure 13-1.*

Use caution when enabling the `windowless` property as performance can be significantly hindered when using the plug-in in Windowless mode. Specifically, complex animations and high-definition video content will not perform as well when running in Windowless mode.

splashScreenSource

The `splashScreenSource` parameter enables you to specify the URI of a XAML file that the Silverlight plug-in should use to replace its default *loading* splash screen. The splash screen is the content that Silverlight displays while downloading and loading its application content, which is typically an XAP file. Replacing the default splash screen enables you to provide a highly customized experience to your users; however, you must note a number of restrictions when providing your own splash screen content. First, unlike the source parameter, which accepts both XAML and XAP files, the splashScreenSource property accepts only a simple XAML file. Second, significant restrictions exist regarding the XAML that is allowed to be run for the splash screen. Only XAML that is exposed by the plug-in's JavaScript API can be used in the splash screen source.

Finally, the splash screen XAML URI must come from the same domain as the Silverlight application and the hosting page. As part of this step, you must make sure your web server is properly configured to serve files with an .xaml extension, which may mean adding a new Multipurpose Internet Mail Extensions (MIME) type to your web server.

To create a new splash screen content XAML file, you can simply add a new Silverlight 1.0 JScript Page to your web application, as shown in Figure 13-2.

FIGURE 13-2

Next, simply add some content to the default canvas of the XAML file. Listing 13-4 shows a simple TextBlock as the content of the XAML file.

Available for
download on
Wrox.com

LISTING 13-4: Simple splash screen XAML content

```
<Canvas xmlns="http://schemas.microsoft.com/client/2007"
        xmlns:x="http://schemas.microsoft.com/winfx/2006/xaml">
  <Canvas x:Name="contentCanvas" Width="240" Height="74" >
    <TextBlock x:Name="textBlock">
      <Run FontSize="48" Text="Loading…"/>
    </TextBlock>
  </Canvas>
</Canvas>
```

Finally, specify the XAML file as the `splashScreenSource` in the Silverlight control (Listing 13-5).

LISTING 13-5: Specifying the splash screen source

```
<object data="data:application/x-silverlight-2,"
    type="application/x-silverlight-2" width="100%" height="100%">
  <param name="source" value="ClientBin/Chapter13.xap"/>
  <param name="onerror" value="onSilverlightError" />
  <param name="background" value="white" />
  <param name="minRuntimeVersion" value="4.0.50311.0" />
  <param name="autoUpgrade" value="true" />
  <param name="splashScreenSource" value="Listing13-4.xaml" />
  <a href="http://go.microsoft.com/fwlink/
        ?LinkID=149156&v=4.0.50311.0"
    style="text-decoration: none;">
        <img src="http://go.microsoft.com/fwlink/?LinkId=161376"
                alt="Get Microsoft Silverlight"
                style="border-style: none"/>
  </a>
</object>
```

When you run your application, you should now see that the default Silverlight splash screen has been replaced by the custom splash screen content.

> *To test your splash screen, make sure the XAP being downloaded is large enough. Silverlight displays the splash screen only if the content load time exceeds 0.5 second. To simulate a longer load time, you can artificially inflate the XAP size by embedding a large resource in your application.*

Although the XAML in Listing 13-4 is completely static, Silverlight does allow you to provide a better experience to your end users by adding animation to the splash screen XAML, and by using two JavaScript events that the plug-in exposes, which provide information relevant to the plug-in's loading process. The `onSourceDownloadProgressChanged` and `onSourceDownloadCompleted` events provide details about the current state of the source download and notification that the download has completed. Using these events in JavaScript, you can provide your end users with download progress information by using the Silverlight JavaScript API to change the splash screen XAML content. Using the JavaScript API to manipulate XAML is discussed in depth later in this chapter.

Note that although the plug-in will fire the `onSourceDownloadCompleted` event, when this point in the plug-in life cycle is reached, the plug-in immediately stops displaying the splash screen content and begins to display main application content. You have no opportunity to provide any type of graceful transition from the splash screen to the main player content.

initParams

The initParams parameter enables you to pass initialization parameters that you can use inside of your application into the Silverlight player. initParams accepts a comma-delimited list of key/value pairs, as shown in Listing 13-6.

LISTING 13-6: Specifying initParams in the Silverlight control

```
<object data="data:application/x-silverlight-2,"
    type="application/x-silverlight-2" width="100%" height="100%">
  <param name="source" value="ClientBin/Chapter13.xap"/>
  <param name="onerror" value="onSilverlightError" />
  <param name="background" value="white" />
  <param name="minRuntimeVersion" value="4.0.50311.0" />
  <param name="autoUpgrade" value="true" />
  <param name="initParams"
        value="DefaultColor=Blue,DefaultStartPoint=Customer" />
  <a href="http://go.microsoft.com/fwlink/
          ?LinkID=149156&v=4.0.50311.0"
    style="text-decoration: none;">
        <img src="http://go.microsoft.com/fwlink/?LinkId=161376"
                alt="Get Microsoft Silverlight"
                style="border-style: none"/>
  </a>
</object>
```

The list of initialization parameters is exposed as a property of type Dictionary<string, string> off the application's Startup event arguments. Listing 13-7 shows how to use initialization parameters to alter the content loaded by the Silverlight application at startup.

LISTING 13-7: Accessing the initParams in the Silverlight application

```
private void Application_Startup(object sender, StartupEventArgs e)
{
    this.RootVisual = new Page();
    switch (e.InitParams["DefaultStartPoint"])
    {
        case "Customer":
            this.RootVisual = new Customer();
            break;
        case "Order":
            this.RootVisual = new Order();
            break;
        default:
            this.RootVisual = new Home();
            break;
    }
}
```

In this listing, the application uses the `initParams` property, which is a member of `StartUpEventArgs`, within the application's `Startup` event. Visual Studio automatically creates the `Startup` event handler in the `App.xaml` file when a new Silverlight application is created.

As mentioned earlier, the `initParams` passed into the plug-in are exposed as a Dictionary, which allows you to access the parameters as key/value pairs, in this case using the value of the `DefaultStartPoint` key to select a specific XAML `UserControl` as the application's `RootVisual`.

enablehtmlaccess

The `enablehtmlaccess` parameter indicates whether the Silverlight player can access the DOM of the host page. The default value allows access to elements from the same domains. Specifying a true value broadens access to any domain, whereas a false value blocks all DOM access.

This property is important if you want to allow or deny communication between the Silverlight plug-in and JavaScript running on a browser, which is discussed later in this chapter.

enableAutoZoom

The `enableAutoZoom` parameter allows you to configure whether the plug-in should respect the zoom settings from its host. For example, in Internet Explorer 8, you can set a zoom level. By default, Silverlight respects this level as it is changed. Using this parameter you can opt out of this behavior.

enableGPUAcceleration

The `enableGPUAcceleration` parameter allows you to indicate that you want to leverage the video hardware for rendering in your application. To enable this feature, you also must set the `CacheMode` property on the XAML elements in your application that you want to accelerate.

You can also use the `enableGPUAcceleration` parameter in conjunction with several other useful diagnostics parameters, such as the `enableCacheVisualization` parameter, which allows you to see what parts of your application are taking advantage of GPU rendering; `enableFramerateCounter`, which adds a display showing the current application frame rate; and the `enableRedrawRegions` parameter, which allows you to see what regions of the plug-in are being redrawn with each frame.

enableNavigation

The `enableNavigation` parameter allows you to control the behavior of the `HyperlinkButton` controls in the application, configuring that application to allow or disallow navigation to external URIs. The parameter accepts two values: `all`, which allows `HyperlinkButtons` to navigate to any URI, and `none`, which prevents this behavior.

Regardless of the parameter setting, relative URIs for internal navigation are always permitted.

allowHtmlPopupWindow

You can use the `allowHtmlPopupWindow` parameter to configure whether managed code running in a Silverlight application can use the `HtmlPage.PopupWindow` method to display new browser windows. You can test the status of this parameter at run time in your application by using the `HtmlPage.IsPopupWindowAllowed` property.

Plug-In API

The Silverlight plug-in also includes a full client-side API that you can use to interact with the control in the browser with JavaScript. You can find a complete description of the plug-in's client-side API at http://msdn.microsoft.com/en-us/library/cc838259(VS.96).aspx.

The plug-in's JavaScript API lets you change various property settings such as the plug-in source, splash screen source, and Scale mode. Additionally, you can use these APIs to handle events raised by the plug-in, such as the OnLoad event.

Table 13-1 lists the events exposed by the Silverlight plug-in as well as a description of the event.

TABLE 13-1

PLUG-IN EVENT	DESCRIPTION
onLoad	Occurs when the plug-in and its content are successfully loaded.
onError	Occurs when something prevents the plug-in or content from loading.
onResize	Occurs when the ActualWidth or ActualHeight properties of the plug-in change.
onFullScreenChanged	Occurs when the player enters or leaves Full Screen mode.
onZoom	Occurs when the plug-in receives a host-generated zoom event.
onSourceDownloadCompleted	Occurs when the plug-in source has been downloaded.
onSourceDownloadProgressChanged	Occurs as the download progress of the plug-in changes.

The default host page template in Visual Studio automatically configures a JavaScript handler for the plug-in's onError event in order to provide a more graceful handling of errors that might happen in the player.

CREATING INTERACTION BETWEEN SILVERLIGHT AND JAVASCRIPT

After a Silverlight control is embedded in a host web page, you can add interaction between your Silverlight application running in the Silverlight plug-in and the host web page running in a browser window. You have two ways to interoperate between the Silverlight plug-in and the browser.

➤ The first option is to use the plug-in's JavaScript APIs. Introduced in Silverlight 1.0, these APIs allow developers to programmatically reach into the Silverlight plug-in and manipulate the plug-in or XAML content running inside of the plug-in.

Although most of the original Silverlight 1.0 JavaScript APIs exist in newer versions of Silverlight, certain features have been removed in favor of managed-code options now available. For example, the original `CreateFromXaml` *method that was available in the Silverlight 1.0 APIs has been removed in favor of using the managed* `XamlReader` *class inside of your Silverlight application.*

The second option is to use the HTML Bridge, which was introduced with Silverlight 2. The HTML Bridge is a set of managed APIs that allows you to reach out from the Silverlight plug-in and access elements of the browser, like the DOM of the host, as well as to expose managed code contained in the plug-in and allow it to be executed from JavaScript running the host page.

JavaScript API

The Silverlight plug-in exposes a set of JavaScript APIs, which allow you to reach into the plug-in and manipulate content running in a Silverlight application. Listing 13-8 shows how you can use the plug-in's `onload` event to access the root element of the application.

LISTING 13-8: Accessing the root visual element using JavaScript

```
<script type="text/javascript" language="javascript">
    function plugin_onload(sender) {
        alert(sender);
    }
</script>
```

As you can see in Listing 13-8, the `onload` event passes a single method parameter that is a reference to the root element of the application. The type of the root element is shown using a JavaScript alert.

After the JavaScript code is written, you still need a way to tell the Silverlight plug-in that it should use the `plugin_onload` function to handle its `Loaded` event. To do this, provide the function name to the plug-in by specifying it in a `<param>` tag:

```
<param name="onload" value="plugin_onload" />
```

Waiting for the plug-in's `Loaded` event to fire before trying to access elements in the Silverlight application is a good idea because trying to access prior content may cause null reference exceptions. Waiting for the `Loaded` event ensures that Silverlight has completed successfully loading all of its content.

While you can use different plug-in events like the `onload` event to access the application's elements, you may need access outside of a plug-in event, for example, a `Button`'s `onclick` event. To do that, you simply need to get a reference to the plug-in object. You do this using the traditional `getElementByID` JavaScript function:

```
<button
    onclick="alert(document.getElementByID('silverlightControl').content.Root);"
    id="Button1">Click Me!</button>
```

Or if you are using a JavaScript Library like jQuery, use its selector syntax:

```
<button
    onclick="alert( $('object#silverlightControl')[0].content.Root );"
    id="btnContent">Click Me!</button>
```

Once you get a reference to the plug-in, you can use the `content` property representing Silverlight's visual tree, which contains a reference to all the visual elements in the Silverlight application. Finally, the code uses the `Root` property to access root visual elements of the application's Visual Tree.

The JavaScript APIs also allow you to access and change element properties. For example, suppose you want to dynamically change the text of a `TextBlock` element in your Silverlight application. You can do this via the JavaScript API by locating the named `TextBlock` element and then setting its `Text` property, as shown in Listing 13-9.

LISTING 13-9: Accessing XAML elements and properties in JavaScript

Available for download on Wrox.com

```
function plugin_onload(sender) {
    var textBlock1 = sender.FindName("textBlock1");

    if (textBlock1 != null) {
        textBlock1.Text = "Hello from the Host!";
    }
}
```

This sample shows the use of the plug-in's `FindName` method to locate the named element `textBlock1` in the element tree. After it is located, you simply set its `Text` property.

You can even get and set dependency properties on elements, although to do that, you must use the `getValue` and `setValue` functions provided by the element. Listing 13-10 shows how to set an attached property on the `TextBlock`.

LISTING 13-10: Setting attached properties in JavaScript

Available for download on Wrox.com

```
function plugin_onload(sender) {
    var textBlock1 = sender.FindName("textBlock1");

    if (textBlock1 != null) {
        textBlock1.Text = "Hello from the Host!";
    }

    var currentColumn = textBlock1.getValue("Grid.Column");
    if (currentColumn == 0) {
        textBlock1.setValue("Grid.Column", 1);
    }
}
```

Being able to access elements contained in the XAML also allows you to connect event handlers to element events.

It's important to note that although the Silverlight 1.0 JavaScript APIs allowed you to access and manipulate every XAML element available in Silverlight 1.0, the same cannot be said of later Silverlight JavaScript APIs. After Silverlight 1.0, a significant number of new XAML elements were added to the platform. These elements make designing and laying out applications much easier; however, not all of those elements have been exposed through the JavaScript API. You can find the full JavaScript API for Silverlight 4 at `http://msdn.microsoft.com/en-us/library/bb979679(VS.96).aspx`. This documentation lists all the XAML elements that have been exposed to the JavaScript APIs.

Also, with the addition of significant new functionality in Silverlight since version 1.0, many XAML elements gained new properties, methods, and events. However, not all of these properties are useful unless used in conjunction with other features available only in the managed API. You can find a list of objects, types, and members that are not accessible via the JavaScript API, or that somehow otherwise expose only limited functionality via the JavaScript API, at `http://msdn.microsoft.com/en-us/library/cc964287(VS.96).aspx`.

HTML Bridge

Although the Silverlight JavaScript APIs can be useful, Silverlight contains a powerful set of managed APIs that allow you not only to manipulate XAML elements from JavaScript, but also to access any managed type, method, property, or event included in the Silverlight application from JavaScript. Additionally, the APIs allow you to access the entire browser DOM (including JavaScript code) from within the Silverlight plug-in. Reaching out from the Silverlight plug-in into the browser allows you to add interesting interoperability capabilities to your application, such as accessing properties of the current browser window or leveraging existing JavaScript libraries you may have.

The HTML Bridge managed-code APIs are contained in the `System.Windows.Browser` namespace (located in the `System.Windows.Browser.dll` assembly). The primary class in the `System.Windows.Browser` namespace that you will work with is the `HtmlPage` class, whose primary function is to allow you to access and manipulate the browser's DOM. The class exposes a variety of static properties that enable you to access the actual HTML document, the browser window, basic browser information such as the name and version, and even the Silverlight plug-in itself. Additionally, as you'll see in the next section, it includes several static methods that help you expose the managed code included in your Silverlight application, via JavaScript APIs.

Exposing Managed Code in JavaScript

Exposing managed code via JavaScript APIs is a powerful tool that helps form a bridge between managed-code developers and developers who are skilled in JavaScript. The easiest way to expose managed types to JavaScript is to use the `ScriptableType` attribute on the class you want to expose. Using this attribute exposes any public member of the class to JavaScript, including methods, properties, and events. Listing 13-11 shows how you can use the `ScriptableType` attribute on a custom Silverlight class.

LISTING 13-11: Exposing a class using the ScriptableType attribute

```
[System.Windows.Browser.ScriptableType()]
public class Employee
```

continues

LISTING 13-11 *(continued)*

```
{
    private bool _status = false;

    public Employee()
    {
    }

    public string FirstName { get; set; }
    public string LastName { get; set; }
    public string Department { get; set; }
    public string SSN { get; set; }
    public DateTime StartDate { get; set; }
    public bool Status { get { return _status; } }

    public void ChangeStatus(bool status)
    {
        this._status = status;
    }

    public string GetFullName()
    {
        return string.Format("{0} {1}", this.FirstName, this.LastName);
    }
}
```

After you have decorated a type with the `ScriptableType` attribute, you must register instances of that type as scriptable objects. Registering the instances allows them to be accessed from the host web page using JavaScript. To register an object instance, use the `RegisterScriptableObject` method of the `HtmlPage` class, as shown in Listing 13-12.

LISTING 13-12: Registering the scriptable type

```
private void Application_Startup(object sender, StartupEventArgs e)
{
    this.RootVisual = new Page();

    Employee employee = new Employee();
    HtmlPage.RegisterScriptableObject("Employee", employee);
}
```

`RegisterScriptableObject` requires two parameters: a `Key`, which represents the name used to register the object, and the actual object instance you want to expose. Although you can call the `RegisterScriptableObject` anywhere in your code, in the preceding sample it is called in the application `Startup` event, allowing you to access this member in JavaScript as soon as the Silverlight application is loaded.

Listing 13-13 shows you how to use the Silverlight plug-in's JavaScript API to access the registered object instance from JavaScript and call its `ChangeStatus` method.

LISTING 13-13: Accessing scriptable objects from JavaScript

```
function plugin_onload(sender) {
    var host = sender.GetHost();

    alert("Current Status: " + host.content.Employee.Status);
    host.content.Employee.ChangeStatus(true);
    alert("Updated Status: " + host.content.Employee.Status);
}
```

Notice that Silverlight exposes the managed type as a property of the plug-in's `content` object. The property name exposed from the `content` object is determined by the `Key` parameter provided in the `RegisterScriptableObject`. Therefore, in Listing 13-12, had you used `Foo` as the key, you would have accessed the object in JavaScript by using `plugin.Content.Foo.Status`.

As stated earlier, applying the `ScriptableType` attribute exposes all public members of a type to the JavaScript API, but you may not want to do that. Thankfully, Silverlight provides the more granular `ScriptableMember` attribute, which allows you to more specifically control which members of a type are exposed through the JavaScript API. The use of this attribute is shown in Listing 13-14. Rather than decorating the entire `Employee` class with the `ScriptableType`, only specific members are exposed by using the `ScriptableMember` attribute.

LISTING 13-14: Exposing specific class properties using the ScriptableMember attribute

```
public class Employee
{
    private bool _status = false;

    public Employee()
    {
    }

    [ScriptableMember]
    public string FirstName { get; set; }
    [ScriptableMember]
    public string LastName { get; set; }
    public string Department { get; set; }
    public string SSN { get; set; }
    [ScriptableMember()]
    public DateTime StartDate { get; set; }
    [ScriptableMember()]
    public bool Status { get { return _status; } }

    public void ChangeStatus(bool status)
    {
        this._status = status;
    }

    public string GetFullName()
```

continues

LISTING 13-14 *(continued)*

```
    {
        return string.Format("{0} {1}", this.FirstName, this.LastName);
    }
}
```

The `ScriptableMember` attribute also enables you to change the name of the member that is exposed through the JavaScript API by setting an alias on the member being exposed. This is shown in the following code, where the `Status` property has been given the alias `CurrentStatus`:

```
[ScriptableMember(ScriptAlias = "CurrentStatus")]
public bool Status { get { return _status; } }
```

In addition to accessing existing type instances, the HTML Bridge allows you to register specific types as creatable types. A *creatable type* is a type that can be instantiated directly in JavaScript. For example, rather than instantiating an instance of the `Employee` type in managed code and registering that specific instance, Silverlight allows you to register the `Employees` type as `Creatable` and instantiate new instances of it directly in JavaScript.

To register a type as creatable using the JavaScript API, call the `HtmlPage` object's `RegisterCreatableType` method, as shown here:

```
HtmlPage.RegisterCreatableType("Employee", typeof(Employee));
```

This method requires two parameters, a `ScriptAlias` and the type to expose. After it is exposed, you can use JavaScript to instantiate the `Employee` class, as shown in Listing 13-15.

LISTING 13-15: Creating managed types in JavaScript

```
function onLoaded(sender) {
    var host = sender.GetHost();
    var employee = host.content.services.createObject("Employee");

    employee.FirstName = "John";
    employee.LastName = "Doe";
}
```

Notice that to create the type in JavaScript, you use the Silverlight JavaScript API's `createObject` function, passing it the `ScriptAlias` provided to the `RegisterCreatableType` method. After it is created, you can set properties and call functions on the object just as you would any other JavaScript object.

Accessing the DOM Using Managed Code

So far in this section, you have seen how you can expose managed code to JavaScript. However, the HTML Bridge is a two-way street, allowing you to also access the browser. Accessing the browser allows you to access the DOM, reference specific elements in the DOM, execute JavaScript functions contained in the host page, or even access aspects of the browser window that contains the host page.

In this section, you learn some of the APIs included in the HTML Bridge that can help you access information about the browser window and the HTML document, beginning with returning to the familiar HtmlPage object, which exposes three important properties, BrowserInformation, Document, and Window.

The BrowserInformation property returns a BrowserInformation object, which, as the name implies, allows you to access basic information about the browser the application is currently running in, such as the browser name, version, and platform.

The Document property returns an HtmlDocument object, which represents the browser's document object. The managed HtmlDocument provides similar functionality to its JavaScript equivalent, allowing you to locate elements in the document using the familiar GetElementByID and GetElementByTagName methods, as well as create new HTML elements and attach and detach events to HTML elements.

When working with existing HTML elements obtained from the HtmlDocument, or when new elements are created, the HTML Bridge uses the HtmlElement object, which represents the managed version of basic HTML elements present in the DOM. As with the HtmlDocument object, the HtmlElement object exposes much of the same functionality as its client-side peer, enabling you to get and set element property and attribute values, and access and manipulate its collection of child elements.

Listing 13-16 demonstrates the use of the HtmlDocument and HtmlElement objects to dynamically manipulate the loaded document structure.

LISTING 13-16: Manipulating the HTML document structure

```
public void AddListItem()
{
    System.Windows.Browser.HtmlElement unorderedlist =
        System.Windows.Browser.HtmlPage.Document.GetElementById(
                                            "demoList");

    if (unorderedlist != null)
    {
        System.Windows.Browser.HtmlElement listitem =
            System.Windows.Browser.HtmlPage.Document.CreateElement(
                                                "li");
        listitem.SetAttribute("Id", "listitem1");
        listitem.SetAttribute("innerHTML", "Hello World!");
        unorderedlist.AppendChild(listitem);
    }
}
```

In this sample, the HtmlDocument's GetElementById method is used to locate a specific unordered list element in the DOM. If it is found, then a new HtmlElement representing an HTML list item is created and its id and innerHTML attributes set. Then, the new list item element is added as a child of the unordered list element.

Finally, the Window property of the HtmlPage object returns an HtmlWindow, which provides you with a managed representation of the browser's window object. The HtmlWindow allows you to do things such as raise Alert and Prompt dialogs, navigate to new URIs or bookmarks, create instances of JavaScript types, and evaluate strings containing arbitrary JavaScript code.

Listing 13-17 demonstrates how to create a managed representation of a JavaScript type.

LISTING 13-17: Creating a JavaScript type in managed code

```
public void Calculate()
{
    var calculator =
        System.Windows.Browser.HtmlPage.Window.CreateInstance(
                                        "Calculator");
    var sum = Convert.ToInt32(calculator.Invoke("add", 5, 1));
    System.Windows.Browser.HtmlPage.Window.Alert(sum.ToString());
}
```

This sample uses the `HtmlWindow` object's `CreateInstance` method, which requires two parameters — a string containing the type you want to create and an object array containing the type's creation parameters. The method returns an instance of a `ScriptObject`, which you can then use to call methods and properties of the JavaScript type.

Finally, take a look at how you can use the `HtmlWindow` object to call a JavaScript function located in the host web page. The following code shows a simple JavaScript function that could be included in the HTML page hosting the Silverlight plug-in:

```
function Add(a, b) {
    return a + b;
}
```

To execute this function, use Silverlight's `Invoke` method, which is exposed from the `HtmlWindow` object, shown here:

```
HtmlWindow window = HtmlPage.Window;
object result = window.Invoke("Add", new object[] {1,2});
```

The `Invoke` method takes two parameters — the name of the function you want to execute and an object array of function parameters — and returns an object type.

SUMMARY

This chapter introduced some of the basic concepts that an ASP.NET developer must know to integrate a Silverlight application into a website and to add interoperability between the Silverlight application and its host web page. The chapter started by introducing the basics of creating a new Silverlight application and the tools that are available for Visual Studio 2010 developers. It showed you how you can automatically have Visual Studio create a new website project to host your Silverlight application or even associate the Silverlight application with an existing website.

Next, you looked at the Silverlight plug-in and how to embed it into a web page. You looked at the configuration parameters exposed by the plug-in that allow you to customize the default Silverlight loading splash screen, and pass initialization parameters into the Silverlight plug-in.

Finally, you explored the different options Silverlight provides for interoperating between JavaScript and managed code. You first looked at how to use the Silverlight plug-in's JavaScript API to reach into a Silverlight application and manipulate its XAML content. This chapter also demonstrated how to use the HTML Bridge to expose managed code contained in a Silverlight application out to the browser via a JavaScript API, to directly access browser properties information from within your Silverlight application, to manipulate the browser's DOM, and to run client-side JavaScript code from within a Silverlight application.

14

Securing Your Applications

➤ Understanding authentication and authorization

➤ Working with ASP.NET authentication types

➤ Exposing ASP.NET application services to Silverlight

Security is a very wide-reaching term. This chapter does not cover each and every thing you can do to build secure applications because this material is covered throughout the entire book. Coding for secure applications is something you should do with every line of code that you write. During every step of the application-building process, you must, without a doubt, be aware of how mischievous end users might attempt to bypass your lockout measures. You must take steps to ensure that no one can take over the application or gain access to its resources. Whether it involves working with basic server controls or accessing databases, you should be thinking through the level of security you want to employ to protect yourself.

This chapter takes a look at security from the standpoint of how you can establish access rules for your Silverlight applications, who can access them, and how to really tell who the user is. Also, this chapter looks at other security aspects in dealing with cryptography and the Security APIs at your disposal. Out-of-browser applications are covered in Chapter 9.

One of the more important aspects of security is in how your applications deal with the end users who come to it. Not every view that you build with Silverlight is meant to be open and accessible to everyone on the Internet. Sometimes, you want to build views that are accessible to only a select group of your choosing. For this reason, you need the security measures explained in this chapter. They can help protect the data behind your applications and the applications themselves from fraudulent use.

How security is applied to your applications is truly a measured process. For instance, a Silverlight application on the Internet, open to public access, has different security requirements than does another Silverlight application that is available to only selected individuals because it deals with confidential information such as credit card numbers or medical information.

The first step is to apply the appropriate level of security for the task at hand. Because you can take so many different actions to protect your applications and the resources, you have to decide for yourself which of these measures to employ.

An important aspect of security is how you handle the authentication and authorization for accessing resources in your applications. Before you begin working through some of the authentication/authorization possibilities in ASP.NET, which is what this chapter covers, you should know exactly what those two terms mean:

➤ *Authentication* is the process that determines the identity of a user. After a user has been authenticated, a developer can determine whether the identified user has authorization to proceed. Giving an entity authorization is impossible if no authentication process has been applied.

➤ *Authorization* is the process of determining whether an authenticated user is permitted access to any part of an application, access to specific points of an application, or access only to specified data sets that the application provides. Authenticating and authorizing users and groups enable you to customize a site based on user types or preferences.

TAKING ADVANTAGE OF ASP.NET

When working with authentication and authorization for your Silverlight applications, remember that Silverlight is a client-side technology and that means that you are required to communicate back to the server to deal with many of the permissioning options that you are going to want to work with.

The nice thing in that regard is that in many cases, you are probably delivering the Silverlight application through an ASP.NET application and therefore can take advantage of some of the security that ASP.NET offers out-of-the-box. However, you have to expose those capabilities in order for your Silverlight application to take advantage of them.

Forms-Based Authentication

Because your Silverlight application is serviced up in an ASP.NET web page for this example, you are able to take advantage of one of the more popular means to provide authentication to your ASP.NET applications — through *forms authentication*.

Forms-based authentication is a means of authenticating users to access your entire Silverlight application or specific server-side resources. Once you have this authentication system in place, you can then interact with it through a regular login form that is located somewhere within your Silverlight application. Using the login form, the end user simply enters his or her username and password into a provided form contained within the Silverlight application itself.

Making use of forms-based authentication in your Silverlight application is easy and relatively straightforward. To begin, you first need to set up the ASP.NET application that will be hosting your Silverlight application.

Create a project called Security and you end up with the default Security Silverlight application along with a Security.Web ASP.NET application. The first changes you must make are to the Security.Web solution. Open up the `Web.config` file and make the following changes as illustrated in Listing 14-1.

LISTING 14-1: Modifying the Web.config file for forms-based authentication

```xml
<?xml version="1.0"?>

<configuration>
    <system.web>
        <compilation debug="true" targetFramework="4.0" />

        <authentication mode="Forms">
          <forms name="Wrox">
            <credentials passwordFormat="Clear">
              <user name="BillEvjen" password="Bubbles" />
            </credentials>
          </forms>
        </authentication>

    </system.web>
</configuration>
```

Using the pattern shown in Listing 14-1, your credentials are stored within the Web.config file of the web application that is hosting the Silverlight application. Within this configuration file, you need to add an <authentication> section (it usually already contains one) and change the mode attribute to have a value of Forms. From there, another sub-element, <credentials>, allows you to specify username and password combinations directly in the Web.config file. You can choose from a couple of ways to add these values.

The <credentials> element has been included to add users and their passwords to the configuration file. <credentials> takes a single attribute — passwordFormat. The possible values of passwordFormat are Clear, MD5, and SHA1. The following list describes each of these options:

➤   Clear — Passwords are stored in clear text. The user password is compared directly to this value without further transformation.

➤   MD5 — Passwords are stored using a Message Digest 5 (MD5) hash digest. When credentials are validated, the user password is hashed using the MD5 algorithm and compared for equality with this value. The clear-text password is never stored or compared. This algorithm produces better performance than SHA1.

➤   SHA1 — Passwords are stored using the SHA1 hash digest. When credentials are validated, the user password is hashed using the SHA1 algorithm and compared for equality with this value. The clear-text password is never stored or compared. Use this algorithm for best security.

The example from Listing 14-1 uses a setting of Clear. This method is not the most secure, but it is used for demonstration purposes. If you want to use this means to provide authentication to your Silverlight application, you can use one of the password encryptions and store the encrypted passwords within the Web.config file. A sub-element of <credentials> is <user>; that is where you define the username and password for the authorized user with the attributes name and password.

Now that the Web.config file is in place, you must create a WCF service that will expose the application of forms authentication to any consuming applications (e.g., your Silverlight application). To the Security.Web project, add a Silverlight-enabled WCF Service called Login.svc. This new service, when completed, is presented in Listing 14-2.

LISTING 14-2: Exposing forms authentication through the Login.svc file

```
using System.ServiceModel;
using System.ServiceModel.Activation;
using System.Web.Security;

namespace Security.Web
{
    [ServiceContract(Namespace = "")]
    [AspNetCompatibilityRequirements(RequirementsMode =
        AspNetCompatibilityRequirementsMode.Allowed)]
    public class Login
    {
        [OperationContract]
        public bool Authenticate(string username, string password)
        {
            if (FormsAuthentication.Authenticate(username, password))
            {
                return true;
            }

            return false;
        }
    }
}
```

Here you have a class called Login that contains a single method called Authenticate(). The Authenticate() method takes a username and password as input (both of type string). In this example, simply use the Authenticate() method to get your ASP.NET page to look at the credentials stored in the Web.config file for verification. If the credential lookup is successful, a value of true is returned from the service.

Storing Encrypted Passwords within the Web.config File

Obviously, it is best not to store your users' passwords in the Web.config file as clear text as the preceding example did. Instead, use one of the available hashing capabilities so you can keep the end user's password out of sight of prying eyes. To do this, simply store the hashed password in the configuration file as shown in Listing 14-3.

LISTING 14-3: Changing the Web.config file to store encrypted passwords

```
<forms name="Wrox">
  <credentials passwordFormat="SHA1">
     <user name="BillEvjen" password="58356FB4CAC0B801F011B397F9DFF45ADB863892" />
  </credentials>
</forms>
```

Using this kind of construct makes it impossible for even the developer to discover a password because the clear-text password is never used in the configuration file or in your code. The Authenticate() method used by the Login.svc service hashes the password using SHA1 (because it is the method specified in the Web.config's <credentials> node) and compares the two hashes for a match. If a match is found, the user is authorized to proceed.

When using SHA1 or MD5, the only changes you make are in the `Web.config` file and nowhere else. You do not have to make any changes to the WCF service or to any other page in the application. To store hashed passwords, however, use the `FormsAuthentication` `.HashPasswordForStoringInConfigFile()` method.

Authenticating Against Values in a Database

Another common way to retrieve username/password combinations is by getting them directly from a data store of some kind. This enables you, for example, to check the credentials input by a user against values stored in Microsoft's SQL Server. Listing 14-4 presents the code for this credentials check.

LISTING 14-4: Checking credentials using SQL Server

Available for
download on
Wrox.com

```
using System.ServiceModel;
using System.ServiceModel.Activation;
using System.Web.Security;

namespace Security.Web
{
    [ServiceContract(Namespace = "")]
    [AspNetCompatibilityRequirements(RequirementsMode =
        AspNetCompatibilityRequirementsMode.Allowed)]
    public class Login
    {
        [OperationContract]
        public bool Authenticate(string username, string password)
        {
            bool returnValue;

            SqlConnection conn;
            SqlCommand cmd;
            string cmdString = "SELECT [Password] FROM [AccessTable] WHERE" +
                " (([Username] = @Username) AND ([Password] = @Password))";

            conn = new SqlConnection("Data Source=localhost;Initial " +
                "Catalog=Northwind;Persist Security Info=True;User ID=sa");
            cmd = new SqlCommand(cmdString, conn);

            cmd.Parameters.Add("@Username", SqlDbType.VarChar, 50);
            cmd.Parameters["@Username"].Value = TextBox1.Text;
            cmd.Parameters.Add("@Password", SqlDbType.VarChar, 50);
            cmd.Parameters["@Password"].Value = TextBox2.Text;
            conn.Open();

            SqlDataReader myReader;

            myReader = cmd.ExecuteReader(CommandBehavior.CloseConnection);

            if (myReader.Read()) {
                returnValue = true;
            }
            else {
                returnValue = false;
```

continues

LISTING 14-4 *(continued)*

```
            }

            myReader.Close();
            return returnValue;
        }
    }
}
```

You can now authenticate usernames and passwords against data stored in SQL Server. In the `Authenticate()` event, a connection is made to SQL Server. (For security reasons, you should store your connection string in the `Web.config` file.) Two parameters are passed in — these will be coming from your Silverlight application. If a result is returned, you can consider the user valid and return `true`.

Now that you have the service in place that exposes the forms authentication required, the next step is to build your Silverlight application so that it can consume this Login service.

Silverlight Consuming the Authenticate() Service

The first step is having your Silverlight application work with the Login service's `Authenticate()` method. To start, create a form for your `MainPage.xaml` file as presented in Figure 14-1.

FIGURE 14-1

The idea here is that the end user inputs his username and password in the form and when he clicks the Login button, the Silverlight application calls the WCF service to authenticate him. The code-behind for the `MainPage.xaml` file is presented in Listing 14-5.

LISTING 14-5: The MainPage.xaml.cs file

```
using System;
using System.Windows;
using System.Windows.Controls;
```

```
using Security.Login;

namespace Security
{
    public partial class MainPage : UserControl
    {
        public MainPage()
        {
            InitializeComponent();
        }

        private void button1_Click(object sender, RoutedEventArgs e)
        {
            Login.LoginClient svc = new LoginClient();
            svc.AuthenticateCompleted +=
              new EventHandler<AuthenticateCompletedEventArgs>
                 (svc_AuthenticateCompleted);
            svc.AuthenticateAsync(textBox1.Text, passwordBox1.Password);
        }

        void svc_AuthenticateCompleted(object sender,
            AuthenticateCompletedEventArgs e)
        {
            if (e.Result)
            {
                label1.Content = "Authenticated!";
            }
            else
            {
                label1.Content = "Not Authenticated!";
            }

        }
    }
}
```

After making a service reference to the Login service in your Silverlight project, you are then able to call the Authenticate() method that the service exposes. Based on the results returned (using e.Result), you then show the appropriate message to the end user.

Now that you have seen using forms authentication from ASP.NET with your Silverlight applications, the next section takes a look at using other forms of authentication.

Windows-Based Authentication

Windows-based authentication is handled between the Windows server where the server application resides and the client machine. In a Windows-based authentication model, the requests go directly to Internet Information Services (IIS) to provide the authentication process. This type of authentication is quite useful in an intranet environment where you can let the server deal completely with the authentication process — especially in environments where users are already logged on to a network. In this scenario, you simply grab and utilize the credentials that are already in place for the authorization process.

IIS first takes the user's credentials from the domain login. If this process fails, IIS displays a pop-up dialog box so the user can enter or re-enter his login information. To set up your Silverlight application to work with Windows-based authentication, begin by creating a new Silverlight application called IntegratedWindows with its respective IntegratedWindows.Web solution. This will host your WCF service that will be locked down.

Within the IntegratedWindows.Web solution, create a new Silverlight-enabled WCF Service called `SimpleMath.svc`. Listing 14-6 shows how your `SimpleMath.svc.cs` file should appear.

LISTING 14-6: Reviewing the SimpleMath service

```
using System.ServiceModel;
using System.ServiceModel.Activation;

namespace IntegratedWindows.Web
{
    [ServiceContract(Namespace = "")]
    [AspNetCompatibilityRequirements(RequirementsMode =
        AspNetCompatibilityRequirementsMode.Allowed)]
    public class SimpleMath
    {
        [OperationContract]
        public int Add(int a, int b)
        {
            return (a + b);
        }
    }
}
```

This is a simple WCF service that exposes a single method called `Add()`, which requires two `int` types that are then added and returned to the consumer. The tricky part with this service is configuring it for working with Windows-based authentication.

Running the WCF Solution in IIS

The first step in configuring the solution is to ensure that the IntegratedWindows.Web solution runs within IIS. You can do this through the solution's property pages. From the property page, select the Web tab and choose the option to Use Local IIS Web Server. You also have the option to generate the virtual directory at this point.

If you are using Windows 7, you will not have IIS installed by default. To install IIS within Windows 7, from the Add/Remove Programs dialog, select the option to Turn Windows features on or off. You are then presented with a dialog that allows you to add or remove additional Windows 7 features. From the provided list, you'll want to select ASP.NET, Internet Information Services, IIS 6 Metabase and IIS 6 Configuration Compatibility.

Authenticating and Authorizing a User in the Web.config

Now create an application that enables the user to enter it. You work with the solution's `Web.config` file to control which users are allowed to access the site and which users are not allowed. You do this in the solution's `Web.config` file. The first step is to enable your WCF service to work with this type of authentication. Listing 14-7 shows the required configuration to the `<system.serviceModel>` section of the configuration file.

LISTING 14-7: Changing the <system.serviceModel> element of the WCF service

```
<system.serviceModel>
    <behaviors>
        <serviceBehaviors>
            <behavior name="">
                <serviceMetadata httpGetEnabled="true" />
                <serviceDebug includeExceptionDetailInFaults="false" />
            </behavior>
        </serviceBehaviors>
    </behaviors>
    <bindings>
        <customBinding>
            <binding name="IntegratedWindows.Web.SimpleMath.customBinding0">
                <binaryMessageEncoding />
                <httpTransport authenticationScheme="Ntlm"/>
            </binding>
        </customBinding>
    </bindings>
    <serviceHostingEnvironment aspNetCompatibilityEnabled="true"
     multipleSiteBindingsEnabled="true" />
    <services>
        <service name="IntegratedWindows.Web.SimpleMath">
            <endpoint address="" binding="customBinding"
             bindingConfiguration="IntegratedWindows.Web.SimpleMath.customBinding0"
             contract="IntegratedWindows.Web.SimpleMath" />
            <endpoint address="mex" binding="mexHttpBinding"
             contract="IMetadataExchange" />
        </service>
    </services>
</system.serviceModel>
```

Looking this over, there is only one minor change to the default generation of configuration code that Visual Studio generates for you when you create a new WCF service in your solution. In your `<bindings>` section, you will notice that the `<httpTransport>` section is normally defined as:

```
<httpTransport />
```

Instead of this, you want to change the line to read:

```
<httpTransport authenticationScheme="Ntlm" />
```

The other options here include None, Digest, Negotiate, Ntlm, IntegratedWindowsAuthentication, Basic, and Anonymous. Using IIS you can design your application to work with all of these when using the appropriate WCF binding.

Once you have this in place, you can then add more to the Web.config to deal with the users you want to access your application. To do this, add the section presented in Listing 14-8 to your Web.config file.

LISTING 14-8: Denying all users through the Web.config file

```
<system.web>
   <authentication mode="Windows" />
   <authorization>
      <deny users="*" />
   </authorization>
</system.web>
```

In this example, the Web.config file is configuring the application to employ Windows-based authentication using the <authentication> element's mode attribute. In addition, the <authorization> element is used to define specifics about the users or groups who are permitted access to the application. In this case, the <deny> element specifies that all users (even if they are authenticated) are denied access to the application. Not permitting specific users with the <allow> element does not make much sense, but for this example, leave it as it is. Figure 14-2 shows the results of this operation.

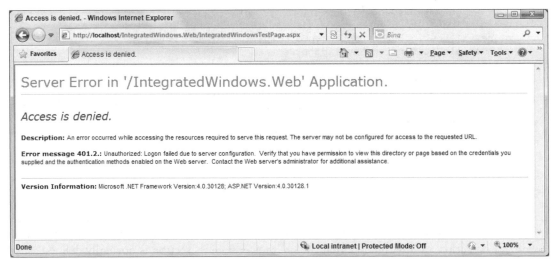

FIGURE 14-2

Any end user — authenticated or not — who tries to access the application sees a large "Access is denied" statement in his or her browser window, which is just what you want for those not allowed to access your application!

In most instances, however, you want to allow at least some users to access your application. Use the <allow> element in the Web.config file to allow a specific user. Here is the syntax:

```
<allow users="Domain\Username" />
```

Listing 14-9 shows how the user is permitted access.

LISTING 14-9: Allowing a single user in through configuration

```
<authentication mode="Windows">
</authentication>

<authorization>
    <allow users="MainLap-PC\BillEvjen"/>
    <deny users="*"/>
</authorization>
```

This section needs to be contained within the <system.web> section of the configuration file. Although all users (even authenticated ones) are denied access through the use of the <deny> element, the definitions defined in the <allow> element take precedence. In this example, a single user — BillEvjen — is allowed.

Now, if you are logged on to the client machine as the user Bill and run the page in the browser, you get access to the application.

Looking Closely at the <allow> and <deny> Nodes

The <allow> and <deny> nodes enable you to work not only with specific users, but also with groups. The elements support the attributes defined in Table 14-1.

TABLE 14-1

ATTRIBUTE	DESCRIPTION
Users	Enables you to specify users by their domain and/or name.
Roles	Enables you to specify access groups that are allowed or denied access.
Verbs	Enables you to specify the HTTP transmission method that is allowed or denied access.

When using any of these attributes, you can specify all users with the use of the asterisk (*):

```
<allow roles="*" />
```

In this example, all roles are allowed access to the application. Another symbol you can use with these attributes is the question mark (?), which represents all anonymous users. For example, if you want to block all anonymous users from your application, use the following construction:

```
<deny users="?" />
```

When using `users`, `roles`, or `verbs` attributes with the `<allow>` or `<deny>` elements, you can specify multiple entries by separating the values with a comma. If you are going to allow more than one user, you can either separate these users into different elements, as shown here:

```
<allow users="MyDomain\User1" />
<allow users="MyDomain\User2" />
```

or you can use the following:

```
<allow users="MyDomain\User1, MyDomain\User2" />
```

Use the same construction when defining multiple roles and verbs.

Authenticating Specific Files and Folders

So far, you have seen how it is possible to lock down the entire Silverlight application and require some sort of authentication for the end user to access it. However, it is also possible to lock down only specific server-side resources that your Silverlight application will use. For example, you might have a public Silverlight application with sections anyone can access without credentials, although you might have an administration section as part of your application that might require authentication/authorization measures.

URL authorization enables you to use the `Web.config` file to apply the settings you need. Using URL authorization, you can apply any of the authentication measures to only specific files or folders. Listing 14-10 shows an example of locking down a single file.

Available for download on Wrox.com

LISTING 14-10: Applying authorization requirements to a single file

```
<configuration>
   <system.web>
      <authentication mode="None" />

      <!-- The rest of your web.config file settings go here -->

   </system.web>

   <location path="SensitiveData.xml">
      <system.web>
         <authentication mode="Windows" />

         <authorization>
            <allow users="MainLap-PC\BillEvjen" />
            <deny users="*" />
         </authorization>
      </system.web>
   </location>
</configuration>
```

This `Web.config` construction keeps the web application open to the general public while, at the same time, it locks down a single file contained on the server-side within the application — the

SensitiveData.xml file. You accomplish this lockdown through the <location> element. <location> takes a single attribute (path) to specify the resource defined within the <system.web> section of the Web.config file.

In the example, the <authentication> and <authorization> elements are used to provide the authentication and authorization details for the SensitiveData.xml file. For this page, Windows authentication is applied, and the only user allowed access to it is BillEvjen in the MainLap-PC domain. You can have as many <location> sections in your Web.config file as you want.

USING ASP.NET APPLICATION SERVICES

In addition to what has been demonstrated thus far, you can also work with users and the roles that they are in through the provided ASP.NET application services such as the ASP.NET membership and role management systems. .NET 4 includes an authentication and authorization management service that takes care of the login, authentication, authorization, and management of users who require access to your Silverlight applications. This outstanding *membership and role management service* is an easy-to-implement framework that works out-of-the-box using Microsoft SQL Server as the backend data store. This framework also includes a service-level API that allows for programmatic access to the capabilities of both the membership and role management services.

These services were offered when ASP.NET 2.0 was released, but ever since the release of the .NET Framework 3.5, you have been able to interact with a new services layer that allows this membership and role management system to be accessible from clients such as ASP.NET AJAX, other AJAX applications, as well as Silverlight applications. This is also something that can be utilized by Windows Forms and Windows Presentation Foundation applications.

Working with Membership on the Server

The first step in working with the underlying ASP.NET membership system from your Silverlight application is to create a WCF service that will act as the interface to this capability. To start, create a new Silverlight application called AspnetAppServices. You are also going to create the standard ASP.NET hosting solution called AspnetAppServices.Web. Within the web portion of the solution, create a new folder called Services and add a simple text file (with a new extension of .svc rather than .txt) called Auth.svc. Open this up in Visual Studio and utilize the small amount of code that is presented in Listing 14-11.

LISTING 14-11: Creating the Auth.svc membership service

```
<%@ ServiceHost Language="C#"
    Service="System.Web.ApplicationServices.AuthenticationService"
    Factory="System.Web.ApplicationServices.ApplicationServicesHostFactory" %>
```

You are not going to need a code-behind for this file. This solution will know how to work with the underlying capabilities that the AuthenticationService provides. You will later use this file and make a reference to it from your consuming Silverlight application.

Now that you have the service in place, the next step is to make some changes to the project's
`Web.config` file. This is illustrated in Listing 14-12.

LISTING 14-12: Working with the membership service from the configuration file

```xml
<?xml version="1.0"?>

<configuration>
    <system.web>
        <authentication mode="Forms" />
        <compilation debug="true" targetFramework="4.0" />
    </system.web>

  <system.web.extensions>
    <scripting>
      <webServices>
        <authenticationService enabled="true"
           requireSSL = "false"/>
      </webServices>
    </scripting>
  </system.web.extensions>

  <system.serviceModel>
    <services>
      <service name="System.Web.ApplicationServices.AuthenticationService"
          behaviorConfiguration="AuthenticationServiceTypeBehaviors">
        <endpoint contract=
        "System.Web.ApplicationServices.AuthenticationService"
          binding="basicHttpBinding"
          bindingConfiguration="userHttp"
          bindingNamespace="http://asp.net/ApplicationServices/v200"/>
      </service>
    </services>
    <bindings>
      <basicHttpBinding>
        <binding name="userHttp">
          <security mode="None" />
        </binding>
      </basicHttpBinding>
    </bindings>
    <behaviors>
      <serviceBehaviors>
        <behavior name="AuthenticationServiceTypeBehaviors">
          <serviceMetadata httpGetEnabled="true"/>
        </behavior>
      </serviceBehaviors>
    </behaviors>
    <serviceHostingEnvironment
      aspNetCompatibilityEnabled="true"/>
  </system.serviceModel>

</configuration>
```

This operation creates a binding with no security applied. The <security> element does allow for the values of None, Transport, Message, TransportWithMessageCredential, and TransportCredentialOnly. In this case, for simplicity, None is selected.

Looking at the top of the configuration file, you can see that forms authentication has been enabled. You will need this in order to work with this membership system.

Before you can start to work with this underlying interface, you need to enable it. This is the purpose of the <system.web.extensions> element in the configuration file:

```
<system.web.extensions>
  <scripting>
    <webServices>
      <authenticationService enabled="true"
        requireSSL = "false"/>
    </webServices>
  </scripting>
</system.web.extensions>
```

Here, the <authenticationService> is turned on using the enabled attribute. In addition, you are setting the SSL requirement to false. Setting this to true requires you to use an SSL certificate and then use https:// to get at the services themselves.

Creating Users

With both the service and the configuration in place, the next step is to create some users that you can work with in your Silverlight application. To add users to the membership service, you can register users into the Microsoft SQL Server Express Edition data store. You can also use any data store that you want and even build a custom provider that interacts with that data store. By default, ASP.NET uses the Microsoft SQL Server Express Edition database.

The Microsoft SQL Server provider for the membership system can use a SQL Server Express Edition file that is structured specifically for the membership service (and other ASP.NET systems, such as the role management system). ASP.NET is set to automatically create this particular file for you if the appropriate file does not exist already. To create the ASPNETDB.mdf file, you work with the ASP.NET Configuration tool that utilizes an aspect of the membership service. When the application requires the ASPNETDB.mdf file, ASP.NET creates this file on your behalf in the App_Data folder.

After the data store is in place, it is time to start adding users to it. To get started with this, highlight the AspnetAppServices project within your Visual Studio Solution Explorer and click the ASP.NET Configuration button in the toolbar of this section. This launches a web-based configuration application for you to use to make the necessary changes. The first page that is presented is shown in Figure 14-3.

From here, select the Security tab and start by clicking the Select Authentication Type link in the provided view. Here you want to change the mode to work from the Internet as is illustrated in Figure 14-4.

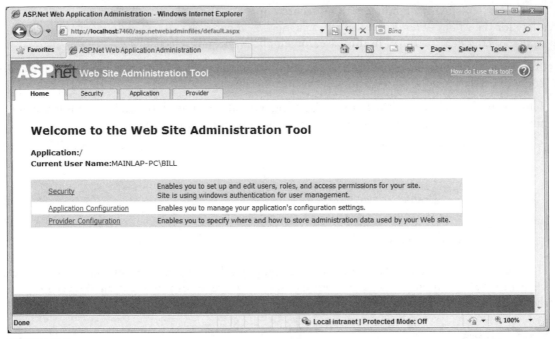

FIGURE 14-3

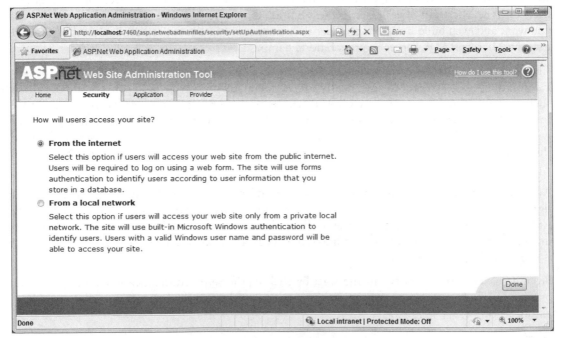

FIGURE 14-4

Once done with that section, you should then create one or more users that will be in the system for you to work with. You do this by clicking the Create User link from the Security tab. You are then presented with the form shown in Figure 14-5 to input a new user.

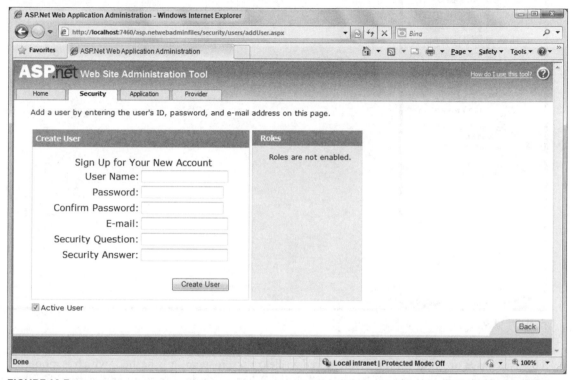

FIGURE 14-5

Notice that there is a pretty strict password requirement here, but that can be corrected later in the Web.config file if you want. Once you have created one or more users, you are ready to work with this membership system from your Silverlight application.

Seeing Where Users Are Stored

Now that you have used the ASP.NET Configuration tool to add a user to the membership service, you might want to then look at where this information is stored. If you used Visual Studio to create the Microsoft SQL Server Express Edition file in which you want to store the user information, the file is created when you complete the form process as shown in the preceding figures. When the example is completed, you will find the ASPNETDB.mdf file, which is located in the App_Data folder of your project. Many different tables are included in this file, but you are interested in the aspnet_ Membership table only.

When you open the aspnet_Membership table (by right-clicking the table in the Server Explorer and selecting Show Table Data), the users you entered are in the system, as illustrated in Figure 14-6.

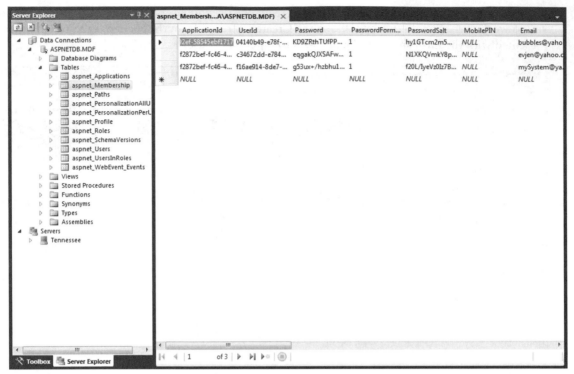

FIGURE 14-6

The user password in this table is not stored as clear text; instead, it is hashed, which is a one-way form of encryption that cannot be reversed easily. When a user logs in to an application that is using the ASP.NET membership service, his or her password is immediately hashed and then compared to the hashed password stored in the database. If the two hashed strings do not compare, the passwords are not considered a match. Storing clear-text passwords is considered a security risk, so you should never do so without weighing the risk involved.

A note regarding the passwords used with the membership system: If you are having difficulty entering users because of a password error, it might be because this system requires strong passwords by default. All passwords input into the system must be at least seven characters and contain at least one non-alphanumeric character (such as [,], !, @, #, or $). Whew! An example password of this combination is

```
Bevjen7777$
```

Although this type of password is a heck of a lot more secure, a password like this is sometimes difficult to remember. You can actually change the behavior of the membership provider so that it doesn't require such difficult passwords by reworking the membership provider in the `Web.config` file, as shown in Listing 14-13.

LISTING 14-13: Modifying the membership provider in Web.config

```
<configuration>
   <system.web>

      <membership>
         <providers>
            <clear />
            <add name="AspNetSqlMembershipProvider"
             type="System.Web.Security.SqlMembershipProvider, System.Web,
                Version=4.0.0.0, Culture=neutral, PublicKeyToken=b03f5f7f11d50a3a"
             connectionStringName="ApplicationServices"
             enablePasswordRetrieval="false"
             enablePasswordReset="true"
             requiresQuestionAndAnswer="false"
             requiresUniqueEmail="true"
             passwordFormat="Hashed"
             minRequiredNonalphanumericCharacters="0"
             minRequiredPasswordLength="3" />
         </providers>
      </membership>

   </system.web>
</configuration>
```

This example shows the membership provider reworked for SQL Server so that it does not actually require any non-alphanumeric characters and allows passwords as small as three characters in length. You do this by using the `minRequiredNonalphanumericCharacters` and `minRequiredPasswordLength` attributes. With these in place, you can now create users with these password rules as set forth in these configuration settings.

The important attributes of the membership provider definition include the `enablePasswordRetrieval`, `enablePasswordReset`, `requiresQuestionAndAnswer`, `requiresUniqueEmail`, and `PasswordFormat` attributes. These are described in Table 14-2.

TABLE 14-2

ATTRIBUTE	DESCRIPTION
enablePasswordRetrieval	Defines whether the provider supports password retrievals. This attribute takes a `Boolean` value, and the default value is `False`. When it is set to `False`, passwords cannot be retrieved although they can be changed with a new random password.
enablePasswordReset	Defines whether the provider supports password resets. This attribute takes a `Boolean` value, and the default value is `True`.
requiresQuestionAndAnswer	Specifies whether the provider should require a question-and-answer combination when a user is created. This attribute takes a `Boolean` value, and the default value is `False`.

continues

TABLE 14-2 *(continued)*

ATTRIBUTE	DESCRIPTION
requiresUniqueEmail	Defines whether the provider should require a unique e-mail to be specified when the user is created. This attribute takes a `Boolean` value, and the default value is `False`. When set to `True`, only unique e-mail addresses can be entered into the data store.
passwordFormat	Defines the format in which the password is stored in the data store. The possible values include `Hashed`, `Clear`, and `Encrypted`. The default value is `Hashed`. Hashed passwords use SHA1, whereas encrypted passwords use Triple-DES encryption.

In addition to having these items defined in the `machine.config` file, you can also redefine them again (thus overriding the settings in the `machine.config`) in the `Web.config` file.

Working with Membership on the Client

Now that the server-side of what you want to do is established, the next step is to build a consuming Silverlight application that will make use of the Auth service.

The first step is to make a service reference to the new Auth service that you created earlier. To do this, right-click the project within the Solution Explorer and select Add Service Reference from the provided options. You are presented with a dialog that allows you to search for services that are contained within the same solution. Here you will find the Auth service. Now that you have the reference in place, the next step is to create the form that interacts with this service.

For this, create a form similar to what is shown in Figure 14-7. This is a simple login form.

FIGURE 14-7

The code-behind for this form is presented in Listing 14-14.

LISTING 14-14: Code-behind for the Silverlight login form

```
using System;
using System.Windows;
using System.Windows.Controls;
using AspnetAppServices.AspnetAuthentication;

namespace AspnetAppServices
{
    public partial class MainPage : UserControl
    {
        public MainPage()
        {
            InitializeComponent();
        }

        private void button1_Click(object sender, RoutedEventArgs e)
        {
            AspnetAuthentication.AuthenticationServiceClient svc =
                new AuthenticationServiceClient();
            svc.LoginAsync(textBox1.Text, passwordBox1.Password,
                string.Empty, false, textBox1.Text);
            svc.LoginCompleted += new EventHandler<LoginCompletedEventArgs>
                (svc_LoginCompleted);
        }

        void svc_LoginCompleted(object sender, LoginCompletedEventArgs e)
        {
            if (!e.Result)
            {
                MessageBox.Show("Unable to login");
            }
            else
            {
                MessageBox.Show("Successfully logged in!");
            }
        }
    }
}
```

Now, when the button is clicked on the client, the username and password are utilized in the LoginAsync() call. A svc_LoginCompleted() event handler is then used to show whether the user was successful in logging in to the application. Running this application produces results similar to what is presented in Figure 14-8.

As you can see, it is straightforward to work with the ASP.NET membership system through WCF. Off the Auth.svc that you created, you will also find methods to logoff and validate the user. In fact, to logoff the user after he has logged in to the application is as simple as what is presented here in Listing 14-15. For this example, simply add another button to the AspnetAppServices application.

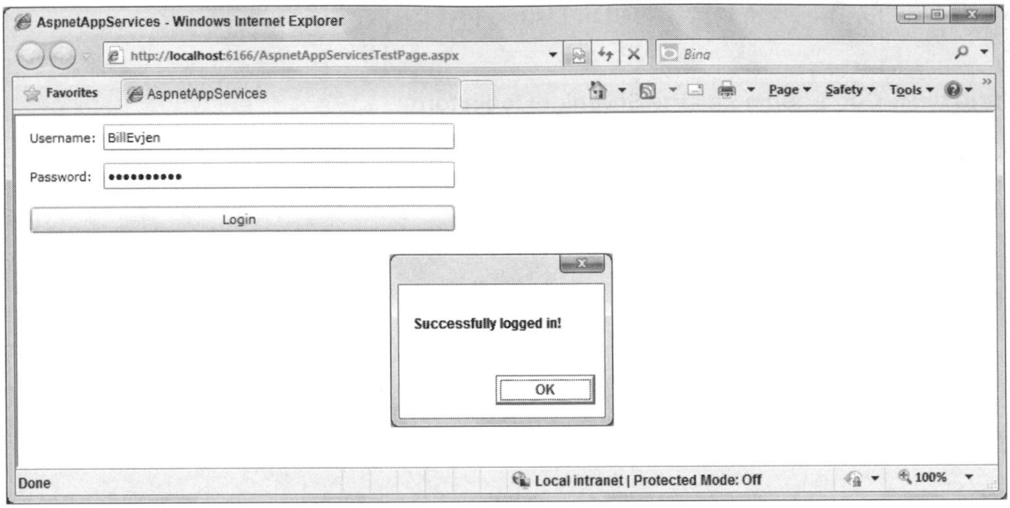

FIGURE 14-8

LISTING 14-15: Logging off the user

```
private void button2_Click(object sender, RoutedEventArgs e)
{
    AspnetAuthentication.AuthenticationServiceClient svc =
        new AuthenticationServiceClient();
    svc.LogoutAsync();
    svc.LogoutCompleted += new EventHandler
        <System.ComponentModel.AsyncCompletedEventArgs>(svc_LogoutCompleted);
}

void svc_LogoutCompleted(object sender,
    System.ComponentModel.AsyncCompletedEventArgs e)
{
    MessageBox.Show("You are now logged off");
}
```

Next, this chapter looks at the role management system that is also part of this same application services story.

Working with Role Management on the Server

After you have authenticated a user, the next step is to look at authorizing the user. You usually do this by figuring out which role that user takes in your system and that role aligns that user with what he is allowed to see or do within your application. These questions are important for any application.

In addition to the membership service just reviewed, the application services system at your disposal provides you with the other side of the end-user management service — the role management service. The membership service covers all the details of authentication for your applications, whereas the role management service covers authorization. Just as the membership service can use any of the data providers listed earlier, the role management service can also use a provider that is focused on SQL Server (SqlRoleProvider) or any custom providers. In fact, this service is comparable to the membership service in many ways.

Making Changes to the <roleManager> Section

The first step in working with the role management service is to change any of the role management provider's behaviors either in the machine.config or Web.config files. If you look in the machine.config.comments file, you will see an entire section that deals with the role management service (see Listing 14-16).

LISTING 14-16: Role management provider settings in the machine.config.comments file

```
<roleManager
 enabled="false"
 cacheRolesInCookie="false"
 cookieName=".ASPXROLES"
 cookieTimeout="30"
 cookiePath="/"
 cookieRequireSSL="false"
 cookieSlidingExpiration="true"
 cookieProtection="All"
 defaultProvider="AspNetSqlRoleProvider"
 createPersistentCookie="false"
 maxCachedResults="25">
   <providers>
      <clear />
      <add connectionStringName="LocalSqlServer" applicationName="/"
       name="AspNetSqlRoleProvider" type="System.Web.Security.SqlRoleProvider,
       System.Web, Version=4.0.0.0, Culture=neutral,
       PublicKeyToken=b03f5f7f11d50a3a" />
      <add applicationName="/" name="AspNetWindowsTokenRoleProvider"
       type="System.Web.Security.WindowsTokenRoleProvider, System.Web,
       Version=4.0.0.0, Culture=neutral, PublicKeyToken=b03f5f7f11d50a3a" />
   </providers>
</roleManager>
```

The role management service documents its settings from within the machine.config.comments file, as shown in the previous code listing. You can make changes to these settings either directly in the machine.config file or by overriding any of the higher-level settings you might have by making changes in the Web.config file itself (thereby making changes only to the application at hand).

Adding Roles to the Database

From the previous example when you were using the membership system, you applied some of the settings for this through the ASP.NET Configuration tool. The first step in this example of working with roles in your Silverlight application is to reopen this tool and go to the Security tab it provides. From this tab, you simply click the Enable Roles link and this gives you the view as presented in Figure 14-9.

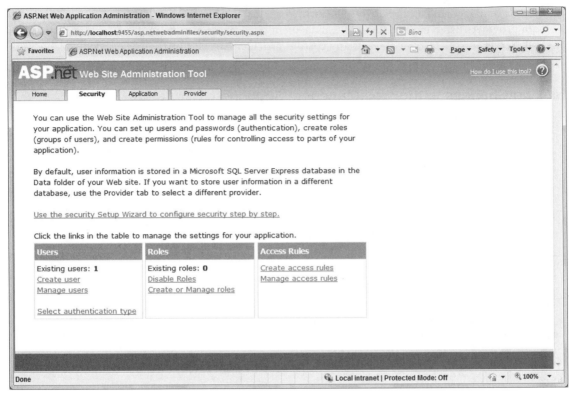

FIGURE 14-9

The role management service, just like the membership service, uses data stores to store information about the users. These examples focus primarily on using Microsoft SQL Server Express Edition as the provider because it is the default provider.

Once you have enabled roles for this section, click the Create or Manage Roles link. You are then presented with a simple textbox where you can enter a role name. This is illustrated in Figure 14-10.

Clicking the Add Role button adds the SilverlightGroup role to your application database. Once added, you can then manage the users that are contained within that role. Clicking the Manage link takes you to a page that allows you to specify this. Figure 14-11 shows adding the user BillEvjen to the SilverlightGroup role.

Once you have added the SilverlightGroup role and assigned some users to this role, create an additional role called Admin and assign some of the same users to this role so that some of your users are in a couple of roles.

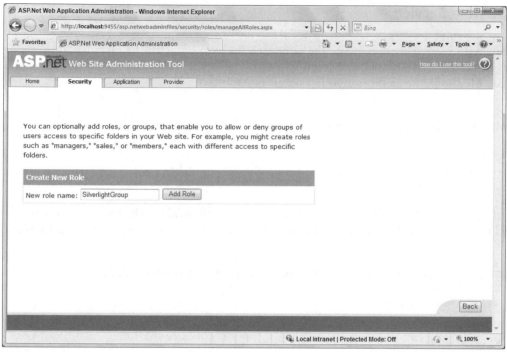

FIGURE 14-10

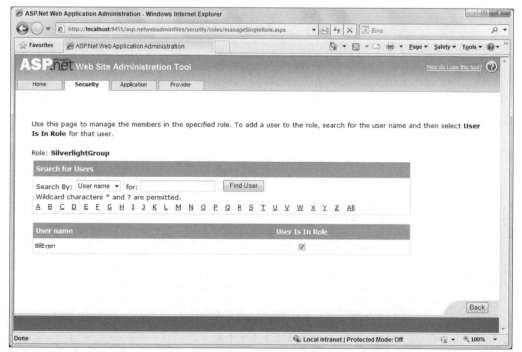

FIGURE 14-11

Creating a Role Service

Now that the roles are in place, create a WCF service in your AspnetAppServices.Web project that deals with roles. For this, follow the same step for working with the membership system. In the Services folder of your solution, create a `Role.svc` file (starting from a text file again). The `Role.svc` file should be as illustrated in Listing 14-17.

LISTING 14-17: Defining the Role.svc file

```
<%@ ServiceHost Language="C#"
    Service="System.Web.ApplicationServices.RoleService"
    Factory="System.Web.ApplicationServices.ApplicationServicesHostFactory" %>
```

Again, there isn't much to this file. It is as simple as what is illustrated. The big changes that you are required to make are made to the project's `Web.config` file. This is presented in Listing 14-18.

LISTING 14-18: Changes required to the Web.config file for working with roles

```
<?xml version="1.0"?>

<configuration>
    <system.web>
        <roleManager enabled="true" />
        <authentication mode="Forms" />
        <compilation debug="true" targetFramework="4.0" />
    </system.web>

  <system.web.extensions>
    <scripting>
      <webServices>
        <authenticationService enabled="true"
          requireSSL="false"  />
        <roleService enabled="true" />
      </webServices>
    </scripting>
  </system.web.extensions>
  <system.serviceModel>
    <services>
      <service name="System.Web.ApplicationServices.AuthenticationService"
         behaviorConfiguration="ApplicationServiceTypeBehaviors">
        <endpoint contract="System.Web.ApplicationServices.AuthenticationService"
          binding="basicHttpBinding"
          bindingConfiguration="userHttp"
          bindingNamespace="http://asp.net/ApplicationServices/v200"/>
      </service>
      <service name="System.Web.ApplicationServices.RoleService"
         behaviorConfiguration="ApplicationServiceTypeBehaviors">
        <endpoint contract=
        "System.Web.ApplicationServices.RoleService"
          binding="basicHttpBinding"
          bindingConfiguration="userHttp"
```

```
                    bindingNamespace="http://asp.net/ApplicationServices/v200"/>
            </service>
        </services>
        <bindings>
            <basicHttpBinding>
                <binding name="userHttp">
                    <security mode="None" />
                </binding>
            </basicHttpBinding>
        </bindings>
        <behaviors>
            <serviceBehaviors>
                <behavior name="ApplicationServiceTypeBehaviors">
                    <serviceMetadata httpGetEnabled="true"/>
                </behavior>
            </serviceBehaviors>
        </behaviors>
        <serviceHostingEnvironment
            aspNetCompatibilityEnabled="true"/>
    </system.serviceModel>

</configuration>
```

The first step here is to ensure that you have roles enabled within the `<system.web>` section of the document:

```
<roleManager enabled="true" />
```

Also, with the `<system.web.extensions>` section, you want to enable the role management system just as you did the membership system:

```
<system.web.extensions>
    <scripting>
        <webServices>
            <authenticationService enabled="true"
                requireSSL="false"  />
            <roleService enabled="true" />
        </webServices>
    </scripting>
</system.web.extensions>
```

Once enabled, the next step is to add a service reference and use the same behavior and binding that the membership service used:

```
<service name="System.Web.ApplicationServices.RoleService"
    behaviorConfiguration="ApplicationServiceTypeBehaviors">
  <endpoint contract="System.Web.ApplicationServices.RoleService"
   binding="basicHttpBinding"
   bindingConfiguration="userHttp"
   bindingNamespace="http://asp.net/ApplicationServices/v200"/>
</service>
```

This is the last step you need to take to enable roles on the server-side. The next step is to turn to the client.

Adding Roles to Your Silverlight Application

Now that the service is in place, you need to make a reference to this service. To accomplish this task, right-click the project in the Visual Studio Solution Explorer and select Add Service Reference from the provided menu. Looking for a service in the same solution produces the Role service. Name the reference AspnetRoles.

To make this simple, add a new button (button3) to your form. When the user clicks the button, that user is presented with all the roles that he or she is part of in the system. The code-behind for the form is presented in Listing 14-19.

LISTING 14-19: Getting the user roles

```
private string _userState;

private void button3_Click(object sender, RoutedEventArgs e)
{
    AspnetRoles.RoleServiceClient svc = new RoleServiceClient();

    if (_userState != string.Empty)
    {
        svc.GetRolesForCurrentUserAsync(_userState);
        svc.GetRolesForCurrentUserCompleted += new EventHandler
            <GetRolesForCurrentUserCompletedEventArgs>(
            svc_GetRolesForCurrentUserCompleted);
    }
}

void svc_GetRolesForCurrentUserCompleted(object sender,
    GetRolesForCurrentUserCompletedEventArgs e)
{
    List<string> userRoles = e.Result.ToList();

    foreach (var userRole in userRoles)
    {
        MessageBox.Show("User is part of " + userRole);
    }
}
```

The Roles service exposes a method called GetRolesForCurrentUserAsync() that allows you to get a full list of all the roles for a particular user. The only parameter required is the user state that was stored in reference when the user logged in to the system. Figure 14-12 shows this in action.

In addition to getting a specific list of roles the user is in, you can also ask if a user is in a particular role:

```
svc.IsCurrentUserInRoleAsync("SilverlightGroup");
```

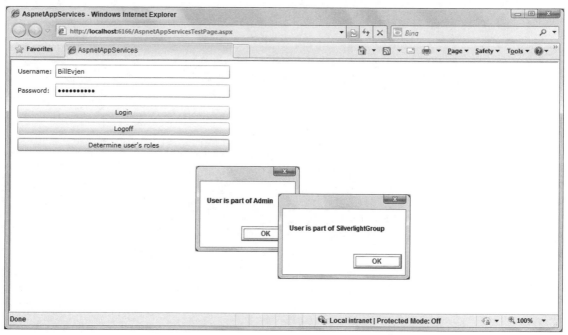

FIGURE 14-12

SUMMARY

This chapter covered some of the basics in dealing with security in the authentication and authorization process. Silverlight applications are no different from other applications. Many of the applications that you build require an understanding of user context in some manner and making choices based upon that context.

15

Accessing Audio and Video Devices

WHAT'S IN THIS CHAPTER?

➤ Capturing a video frame

➤ Capturing an audio stream

➤ Saving a video frame as an image

Silverlight 4 adds new capability for accessing audio and video devices on your computer. You can access the audio from internal and external microphones and you can access video from webcams attached to your computer. This audio/video capability encompasses three key concepts:

➤ Grabbing a video frame and converting it to a static image

➤ Capturing/recording a complete audio or video feed for viewing later

➤ Accessing raw audio or video feeds

With that list, you are probably seeing some interesting scenarios, including streaming the video or audio feed to other computers, using attached video devices to scan barcodes, recording audio for later use or distribution, or even creating an application that takes a photo and displays a security badge for printing using the new printing features in Silverlight 4. This chapter gives you the insight you need to access audio and video devices and work with the data that comes from them.

CONFIGURING PERMISSIONS

In an application that runs in the default sandbox of the browser, Silverlight prompts the user with a permissions dialog if an attempt is made to access microphone or camera devices. Figure 15-1 shows the permissions dialog that launches if your code attempts to access devices.

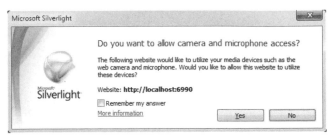

FIGURE 15-1

Several actions can occur based on the user response to this dialog:

➤   User clicks Yes and access to microphone and cameras is allowed.

➤   User checks the Remember My Answer checkbox and clicks Yes. Access is granted to microphone and camera devices for this URI and the user is not prompted again.

➤   User clicks the No button, which cancels the permission request and returns the user to the Silverlight application.

To determine what microphone and camera devices are available on the computer, and to view permissions for these devices, you can right-click the running Silverlight application and click the Silverlight menu item to launch the Silverlight Configuration Settings dialog. In the context of microphone and camera support, two tabs on this form are important:

➤   The Webcam/Mic tab shown in Figure 15-2 lists the available devices on the computer and verifies that the devices are working by displaying the Video Source and Audio Source and their respective current input.

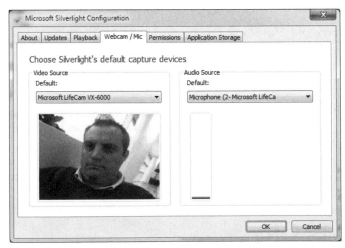

FIGURE 15-2

➤ The Permissions tab shown in Figure 15-3 lists the URIs that have been granted permission to access the audio and video devices from a user-initiated check on the Remember My Answer checkbox on the permissions dialog shown in Figure 15-1. Users can also remove permissions. For example, if they have granted your application access previously, they can open this dialog and remove those permissions later.

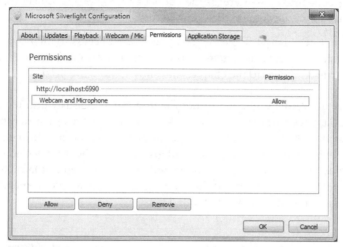

FIGURE 15-3

 If your application is an out-of-browser application that requires elevated trust, the user will not be prompted to access audio and video devices. This permission is implicitly granted when an application is installed with elevated permissions. To learn more about trusted applications and elevated permissions, read Chapter 9.

ACCESSING AUDIO AND VIDEO DEVICES

To get started with accessing audio and video devices, you need to understand the APIs available to you. Two of the most important ones are the CaptureDevice class and the CaptureDeviceConfiguration class. Each is covered in this section.

The CaptureDeviceConfiguration public static class has four methods and one property that return information about the available devices on the system and the state of client permission to access the audio or video devices on the user's system. The following five methods are in this class:

➤ GetAvailableAudioCaptureDevices — Returns a collection of AudioCaptureDevice objects of the available audio capture devices on the client system.

➤ `GetAvailableVideoCaptureDevices` — Returns a collection of `VideoCaptureDevice` objects of the available video capture devices on the client system.

➤ `GetDefaultAudioCaptureDevice` — Returns the `AudioCaptureDevice` object that represents the default audio capture devices on the client system.

➤ `GetDefaultVideoCaptureDevice` — Returns the `VideoCaptureDevice` object that represents the default video capture devices on the client system.

➤ `RequestDeviceAccess` — Returns a Boolean when you request access to all available audio and video capture devices on the client system. This call actually prompts the user with the permissions dialog discussed earlier in the chapter and shown in Figure 15-1.

The `AllowDeviceAccess` property returns whether or not the user has previously granted access. You should call `RequestDeviceAccess` before `AllowDeviceAccess` if you are not sure if permissions have been granted by the user. Keep in mind that `AllowDeviceAccess` is an all-or-nothing property setting. For example, users cannot specify they will give your application access to a certain audio device yet not a certain video device. Also remember that this request launches the permissions dialog discussed earlier in the chapter if the users have not specified to remember their choices or if their applications are not running with elevated trust.

> *For the permissions dialog to launch correctly,* `RequestDeviceAccess` *should be called from the context of a user-initiated event, such as a button click or menu item selection. If the* `RequestDeviceAccess` *is made from a non-user-initiated event, the dialog is not displayed and no exception is thrown. However, if users have previously granted access to the audio and video devices on their systems, the access is still valid even if this exception is thrown.*

Listing 15-1 demonstrates checking the permissions and requesting a list of available devices on the user's machine:

LISTING 15-1: Requesting capture device access

```
if (CaptureDeviceConfiguration.RequestDeviceAccess ||
    CaptureDeviceConfiguration.AllowDeviceAccess())
{
    // Create and configure a capture source
}
```

Once you've made the `CaptureDeviceConfiguration` method calls to return the collections devices and the default devices, you need to use the `CaptureSource` class to interact with audio and video devices. You use the following three methods:

➤ `Start` — Starts the capture from all capture devices that are relevant to this `CaptureSource`.

➤ `Stop` — Stops capture from all capture devices that are relevant to this `CaptureSource`.

➤ `CaptureImageAsync` — Initiates an asynchronous image capture request that retrieves the images returned by handling the `CaptureImageCompleted` event on this `CaptureSource`.

To do a basic video capture, add this XAML (Listing 15-2) to a project that represents a `Button` and `Border` that you'll use to demonstrate the capture features:

Available for
download on
Wrox.com

LISTING 15-2: XAML to set up the camera interactions

```
<Button Content="Start Camera" Height="44" Name="startCamera"
        Width="128" Click="startCamera_Click"
        Margin="12,12,500,648" />

<Border BorderBrush="Silver" BorderThickness="1"
        Height="314" Name="videoRender" Width="433"
        Margin="12,75,195,315" />
```

Listing 15-3 creates a `CaptureSource` object and sets the `VideoCaptureDevice` to the default video capture device and starts the video capture. First you need to create a class-level variable for the `CaptureSource` object that you will assign to the physical video device:

Available for
download on
Wrox.com

LISTING 15-3: Creating a new CaptureSource instance

```
private CaptureSource _cs = new CaptureSource();
```

Next add this code (Listing 15-4) to the `startCamera Click` event. This code listing performs the key operations when attempting to get a video feed; it checks for access, requests it if it is not there, gets the default video capture device, and then starts capturing from it.

Available for
download on
Wrox.com

LISTING 15-4: Retrieving and starting a camera device

```
private void startCamera_Click(object sender, RoutedEventArgs e)
{
    if (CaptureDeviceConfiguration.AllowedDeviceAccess ||
        CaptureDeviceConfiguration.RequestDeviceAccess())
    {
        // Create and configure a capture source
        _cs.VideoCaptureDevice =
            CaptureDeviceConfiguration.GetDefaultVideoCaptureDevice();

        // TODO:  Add source for render

        // Start the capture
        _cs.Start();
    }
}
```

Now that video is being captured, you need to render it onto a VideoBrush. To do this, set the source of a VideoBrush to the CaptureSource. The brush can then be rendered onto almost any object, such as Rectangle, Border, or Button.

The following code sets the source of a VideoBrush to a CaptureSource and displays the video by setting the Fill property on a Border named videoRender. You can add this code (Listing 15-5) under the TODO directive in the previous listing to set up the rendering target before the call to Start.

LISTING 15-5: Setting the VideoBrush to paint the video capture render

```
// Create a VideoBrush to paint the video capture onto
VideoBrush brush = new VideoBrush();
brush.SetSource(_cs);
videoRender.Background = brush;
```

If you run the application, you should see something like Figure 15-4.

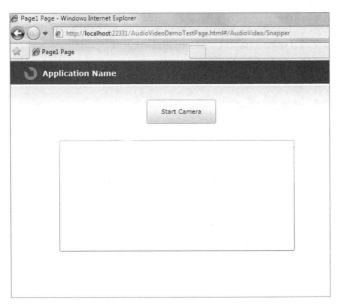

FIGURE 15-4

On the Mac OSX, if an application calls GetDefaultAudioCaptureDevice *or* GetDefaultVideoCaptureDevice *and the default audio and video devices have not previously been set by the user, Silverlight returns the first device found. If a physical device is not connected to this* CaptureDevice, *an* InvalidOperationException *is thrown when* Start *is called. This exception should be caught by the application and the users can then be notified to manually set their default devices in the "Webcam/Mic" section of the Configuration Settings dialog.*

To stop the video capture, add a function that calls `Stop` on the `CaptureSource` (Listing 15-6):

LISTING 15-6: Calling Stop on the video capture device

```
private void StopButton_Click(object sender, RoutedEventArgs e)
{
    // Verify the VideoCaptureDevice is not null then Stop it
    if (_cs.VideoCaptureDevice != null)
    {
        _cs.Stop();
    }
}
```

You'll notice that once you have started a capture and you close the Silverlight application, the capture stops. As good programming practice, you should always clean up any object that you open. So build the `Stop` function into your design.

You can also use the `CaptureSource` to get both the `AudioCaptureDevice` and `VideoCaptureDevice` based on the default values returned from `CaptureDeviceConfiguration` method calls. Listing 15-7 demonstrates this.

LISTING 15-7: Getting both audio and video capture devices

```
CaptureSource _cs = new CaptureSource();

VideoCaptureDevice _webcam =
    CaptureDeviceConfiguration.GetDefaultVideoCaptureDevice();
AudioCaptureDevice _audio =
    CaptureDeviceConfiguration.GetDefaultAudioCaptureDevice();

_cs.VideoCaptureDevice = _webcam;
_cs.AudioCaptureDevice = _audio;
```

Once you have the physical `VideoCaptureDevice` and `AudioCaptureDevice`, you can get the supported video and audio formats of each device by checking the `SupportedFormats` property. The `SupportedFormats` property returns a read-only collection of the `AudioFormat` or `VideoFormat` type.

The following `AudioFormat` properties are available:

➤ `BitsPerSample` — Gets the number of bits that are used to store the audio information for a single sample of an audio format.

➤ `Channels` — Gets the number of channels that are provided by the audio format.

➤ `SamplesPerSecond` — Gets the number of samples per second that are provided by the audio format.

➤ `WaveFormat` — Gets the encoding format of the audio format as a `WaveFormatType` value.

The following `VideoFormat` properties are available:

➤ `FramesPerSecond` — Gets the number of frames per second for the represented video format.

➤ `PixelFormat` — Gets the graphics format information for individual pixels of the video format.

➤ `PixelHeight` — Gets the height of the camera-framing area for the represented video format.

➤ `PixelWidth` — Gets the width of the camera-framing area for the represented video format.

➤ `Stride` — Gets the array stride that is used in the video format.

Up until now, every interaction with an audio or video device has been with the default device. Most systems today have multiple audio and video devices, and you have multiple ways to connect devices to a system. Based on the type of application you are creating, you will either use the default device on the system, such as the attached webcam or built-in microphone, or you may want to give users the option of which devices they prefer to use. An application like Skype, which is a voice over IP software for Windows and Mac computers, allows you to choose the best audio device in its configuration as shown in Figure 15-5. This is useful in scenarios where an attached microphone specifically designed for large rooms or multiple people speaking in to it is more appropriate than the default built-in microphone on the computer.

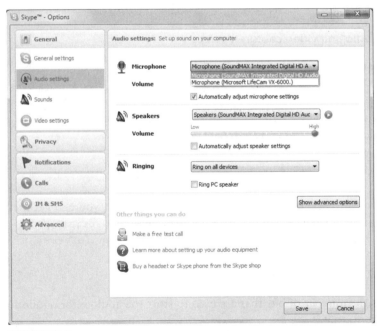

FIGURE 15-5

The following example mimics this configuration behavior, and returns a list of the available audio and video devices on the system. The XAML

    CaptureDevice..::..FriendlyName Property

shows how to set the source of a `ComboBox` to the list of available video devices on the system.

The `FriendlyName` of the device is used to bind to the control (Listing 15-8). An approach like this can be useful if you would like to give users an easy way to choose the media devices they would like to use. You can then listen to the `SelectionChanged` event for the control and set the `CaptureSource` to the appropriate device.

LISTING 15-8: Setting up the combo box for audio and video device lists

```xml
<StackPanel>
    <TextBlock Margin="5,5,5,5">Select an Audio Device</TextBlock>
    <ComboBox x:Name="audioDeviceList">
        <ComboBox.ItemTemplate>
            <DataTemplate>
                <TextBlock Text="{Binding FriendlyName}" />
            </DataTemplate>
        </ComboBox.ItemTemplate>
    </ComboBox>

    <TextBlock Margin="5,5,5,5">Select an Video Device</TextBlock>
    <ComboBox x:Name="videoDeviceList">
        <ComboBox.ItemTemplate>
            <DataTemplate>
                <TextBlock Text="{Binding FriendlyName}" />
            </DataTemplate>
        </ComboBox.ItemTemplate>
    </ComboBox>
</StackPanel>
```

Once the controls are set up in XAML with the `FriendlyName` binding, bind the available devices to the `ComboBoxes` with the following code (Listing 15-9).

LISTING 15-9: Binding the audio and video device lists

```
audioDeviceList.ItemsSource =
    CaptureDeviceConfiguration.GetAvailableAudioCaptureDevices();

videoDeviceList.ItemsSource =
    CaptureDeviceConfiguration.GetAvailableVideoCaptureDevices();
```

The code to set the `AudioCaptureDevice` and `VideoCaptureDevice` based on the user's selection should be added to the `SelectionChanged` event for the `audioDeviceList` and `videoDeviceList` controls and should look like Listing 15-10.

LISTING 15-10: Setting the selected audio and video capture device

```csharp
private void audioDeviceList_SelectionChanged
    (object sender, SelectionChangedEventArgs e)
{
    // set the AudioCaptureDevice to the selected item
    _cs.AudioCaptureDevice =
```

continues

LISTING 15-10 *(continued)*

```
                (AudioCaptureDevice)audioDeviceList.SelectedItem;

        // display the friendly name
        Console.WriteLine(_cs.AudioCaptureDevice.FriendlyName);
    }
    private void videoDeviceList_SelectionChanged
        (object sender, SelectionChangedEventArgs e)
    {
        // set the AudioCaptureDevice to the selected item
        _cs.VideoCaptureDevice =
            (VideoCaptureDevice)videoDeviceList.SelectedItem;

        // display the friendly name
        Console.WriteLine(_cs.VideoCaptureDevice.FriendlyName);
    }
```

That's all there is to getting or setting an audio and video device. You can swap out the `ComboBox` with a `DataGrid` or `ListBox`, or any type of display that fits the experience you are creating. The goal is to make sure users have the option to use their desired devices. You'll also notice when you run this code, you'll see the `FriendlyName` of the selected device in the Console window, which can help you verify the correct device as you are testing.

CAPTURING IMAGES FROM A VIDEO FEED

A common scenario in webcam applications is the ability to snap a photo, or grab the frame, that is currently being rendered by the camera onto a `VideoBrush`. To grab a single frame using the currently started `VideoCaptureDevice`, you use the `CaptureImageAsync` method on the `CaptureSource`, which initiates an asynchronous image capture. Like any asynchronous event, you could have an accompanying `Completed` and `Failed` event to be notified of when the asynchronous call is complete. For the `CaptureImageAsync` method, listen to the `CaptureImageCompleted` event for success and the `CaptureImageFailed` event in case of failure.

To create an example that snaps a photo of the current frame of a video feed, add the XAML in Listing 15-11, which contains two `Button` controls, a `Border` control, and a `ListBox` control.

LISTING 15-11: XAML for the photo snapping user interface

```
<StackPanel>
    <Button Content="Start Camera"
            Height="44" Name="startCamera"
            Width="128"  Margin="10"
            Click="startCamera_Click" />
    <Button Content="Snap Photo"
            Height="44" Name="snapPhoto"
            Width="128" Margin="10"
            Click="snapPhoto_Click" />
    <Border BorderThickness="1"
```

```
            Height="314" Name="videoRender" Width="433" />
    <ListBox Height="226" Name="imageList"
            Width="435" Margin="10" >
        <ListBox.ItemTemplate>
            <DataTemplate>
                <StackPanel Orientation="Horizontal">
                    <Image Source="{Binding}" Margin="5"
                            Stretch="UniformToFill" Height="80" />
                </StackPanel>
            </DataTemplate>
        </ListBox.ItemTemplate>
    </ListBox>
</StackPanel>
```

Now you'll add code to the `Click` events for the buttons and you'll create the event handler for capturing the image asynchronously. First, add two class-level variables, one for the `CaptureSource` and one for the `WriteableBitmap` collection that you'll store the images in as you snap the photos. See Listing 15-12.

LISTING 15-12: Setting up the variables to capture the snapped photos

```
private CaptureSource _cs = new CaptureSource();

ObservableCollection<WriteableBitmap> _images =
            new ObservableCollection<WriteableBitmap>();
```

In the constructor, after the `InitializeComponent` method call, register the `CaptureImageCompleted` event and the `CaptureFailed` event:

```
// register a handler for CaptureImageCompleted event
_cs.CaptureImageCompleted +=
    new EventHandler<CaptureImageCompletedEventArgs>
        (_cs_CaptureImageCompleted);

// register a handler for CaptureFailed event
_cs.CaptureFailed +=
    new EventHandler<ExceptionRoutedEventArgs>(_cs_CaptureFailed);
```

In the `CaptureImageCompleted` event, the `CaptureImageCompletedEventArgs` event argument returns a `WriteableBitmap`. This `WriteableBitmap` can then be displayed, saved, or modified. In this code (Listing 15-13), you'll take the `WriteableBitmap` result and add it to the `_images` collection of `WriteableBitmaps` and bind the collection to the `ListBox`.

LISTING 15-13: The GetImageCompleted event

```
void _cs_CaptureImageCompleted
    (object sender, CaptureImageCompletedEventArgs e)
{
    // add the snapped bitmap to the collection
```

continues

LISTING 15-13 *(continued)*

```
        _images.Add(e.Result);

        // bind collection to ItemsControl
        imageList.ItemsSource = _images;
    }
```

Make sure the `CaptureFailed` event hander is dealt with. In the cases of a failed `CaptureImageAsync`, you may want to prompt the user that the camera may not be connected or there is a problem with the device.

```
    void _cs_CaptureFailed
        (object sender, ExceptionRoutedEventArgs e)
    {
        // handle the exception
    }
```

To initiate the capture, call `CaptureImageAsync` on the `CaptureSource` in the `snapPhoto` `Click` event (Listing 15-14).

LISTING 15-14: Snapping the photo

```
    private void snapPhoto_Click
        (object sender, RoutedEventArgs e)
    {
        // fire the image capture on button click
        _cs.CaptureImageAsync();
    }
```

Finally, add the following (Listing 15-15) to the `startCamera` `Click` event, which verifies the permission to access the video device, sets the `VideoCaptureDevice` to the default device, sets up the render target, and then starts the video capture source.

LISTING 15-15: Starting the camera to capture the photo

```
    private void startCamera_Click(object sender, RoutedEventArgs e)
    {
        if (CaptureDeviceConfiguration.AllowedDeviceAccess ||
            CaptureDeviceConfiguration.RequestDeviceAccess())
        {
            // create and configure a capture source
            _cs.VideoCaptureDevice =
                CaptureDeviceConfiguration.GetDefaultVideoCaptureDevice();

            // create a VideoBrush to paints the video capture onto
            VideoBrush brush = new VideoBrush();
            brush.SetSource(_cs);
            videoRender.Background = brush;

            // start the capture
```

```
        _cs.Start();
    }
}
```

That's all that's needed to snap a photo. If you run the code, and click the Snap Photo button a few times, you should see something similar to Figure 15-6.

FIGURE 15-6

Another technique to use in the `snapPhoto_Click` event handler is to check if the `CaptureSource` is started. If it is, snap the photo. See Listing 15-16.

LISTING 15-16: Updating the SnapPhoto event handler

```
private void snapPhoto_Click
    (object sender, RoutedEventArgs e)
{
    // verify the VideoCaptureDevice is not null and the device is started.
```

continues

LISTING 15-16 *(continued)*

```
        if (_cs.VideoCaptureDevice != null
            && _cs.State == CaptureState.Started)
        {
            _cs.CaptureImageAsync();
        }
    }
```

Saving Images to the Filesystem

In some cases you may want to save the images that you have snapped to the filesystem. You have various ways to accomplish this, some more difficult than others. The easiest way I have found is to use a CodePlex project called .NET Image Tools, which gives you a library of image utilities that lets you save a bitmap as a PNG or as other file formats. To do this, go to the URL — `http://imagetools.codeplex.com/` — and download the Image Tools binaries. Once you unzip the download, add the following assemblies as references to your project:

➤   `ImageTools.dll`

➤   `ImageTools.IO.dll`

➤   `ImageTools.Utils.dll`

Then add the following namespace references:

```
using System.IO;
using ImageTools;
using ImageTools.IO.Png;
```

Add a class-level variable named `Snapshot`. This will be set when the `snapPhoto_Click` event fires and when the user selects an image from the `ListBox`.

```
public WriteableBitmap Snapshot { get; set; }
```

In the user interface, add a `Button` control in XAML that initiates the `SaveFileDialog` to save the image:

```
<Button Content="Save Photo"
    Height="44" Name="savePhoto"
    Width="128" Margin="10"
    Click="savePhoto_Click" />
```

To get to the `savePhoto_Click` event handler, you can either double-click the button you just added or right-click `savePhoto_Click` and select Navigate to Event Handler. In the `savePhoto_Click` event handler, add this code (Listing 15-17).

LISTING 15-17: savePhoto_Click event handler code

```
SaveFileDialog _sfd = new SaveFileDialog
{
```

```
                Filter = "PNG Files (*.png)|*.png|All Files (*.*)|*.*",
                DefaultExt = ".png",
                FilterIndex = 1
        };

        if ((bool)_sfd.ShowDialog())
        {
                var img = Snapshot.ToImage();
                var encoder = new PngEncoder();
                using (Stream stream = _sfd.OpenFile())
                {
                        encoder.Encode(img, stream);
                        stream.Close();
                }
        }
}
```

To set the value of the `Snapshot` variable, update the `CaptureImageCompleted` event to set the `Snapshot` to the `e.Result` `WriteableBitmap` return value (Listing 15-18).

LISTING 15-18: Adding the captured photo to the list

Available for
download on
Wrox.com

```
void _cs_CaptureImageCompleted
        (object sender, CaptureImageCompletedEventArgs e)
{
        // add the snapped bitmap to the collection
        _images.Add(e.Result);

        // set the value of Snapshot to return bitmap
        Snapshot = e.Result;

}
```

At this point, any time the Snap Photo button is clicked, the `Snapshot` value is filled, which means you can always save the last photo taken. If you want to give the user the ability to select an image from the `ListBox` to save, you can set the current value of `Snapshot` by handling the `SelectionChanged` event of the `imageList` `ListBox` control (Listing 15-19).

LISTING 15-19: Setting the selected item in the list

Available for
download on
Wrox.com

```
private void imageList_SelectionChanged
        (object sender, SelectionChangedEventArgs e)
{
        Snapshot = (WriteableBitmap) imageList.SelectedItem;
}
```

At this point, you have a complete process that can view video, take snapshots, and then save those snapshots to an image file on the local system.

CAPTURING AN AUDIO STREAM

Using the `AudioSink` abstract class, you can capture and play back audio. `AudioSink` gives you access to the raw audio stream coming from the audio device, which can then be encoded into a format of your choosing. `AudioSink` has four virtual methods that you will override in your derived class:

➤ `OnCaptureStarted` — Invoked when an audio device starts capturing audio data.

➤ `OnCaptureStopped` — Invoked when an audio device stops capturing audio data.

➤ `OnFormatChange` — Invoked when an audio device reports an audio format change and is the only way to get the correct audio format. The audio format is passed as an `AudioFormat` object, which specifies the bits per second, the number of channels, and the wave format.

➤ `OnSamples` — Invoked when an audio device captures a complete audio sample. The arguments passed into this method are the sample time (in hundreds of nanoseconds), the sample duration (in hundreds of nanoseconds), and the sample data as a byte array. The interval at which `OnSamples` is called depends on the `AudioFrameSize` value for the `AudioCaptureDevice`.

To save an audio stream, you can use the following class (Listing 15-20) derived from `AudioSink`.

LISTING 15-20: Using the AudioSink class

```
namespace AudioRecorder.Audio
{
    public class MemoryAudioSink : AudioSink
    {
        private MemoryStream _stream;
        private AudioFormat _format;

        public AudioFormat CurrentFormat
        {
            get { return _format; }
        }

        protected override void OnCaptureStarted()
        {
            _stream = new MemoryStream(1024);
        }

        protected override void OnCaptureStopped()
        {
        }

        protected override void OnFormatChange
            (AudioFormat audioFormat)
        {
            if (audioFormat.WaveFormat !=
                WaveFormatType.Pcm)
                throw new InvalidOperationException
                    ("MemoryAudioSink supports only PCM
```

```
                    audio format.");

            _format = audioFormat;
        }

        protected override void OnSamples(long sampleTime,
            long sampleDuration, byte[] sampleData)
        {
            _stream.Write(sampleData, 0, sampleData.Length);
        }
    }
}
```

One of the issues with Silverlight is that is does not include audio codecs that make it easy to actually save the audio to a specific format. Hopefully, this will be addressed in the future so that capturing audio is as easy as capturing video. For a great sample that uses some open source code to save an audio stream to PCM format, check out this URL: `http://blog.ondrejsv.com/post/Audio-recorder-Silverlight-4-sample.aspx`.

SUMMARY

This chapter introduced you to working with audio and video with the new Silverlight 4 APIs. You learned how to access the audio and video devices on the local system and how to work with the audio and video that streams from those devices. You were also introduced to an open source image tools library, which gives you helper functions to save images.

16

Working with File I/O

WHAT'S IN THIS CHAPTER?

➤ Working with the OpenFileDialog and SaveFileDialog classes

➤ Examining the class available for file and directory access

➤ Silverlight and file access

➤ Moving, copying, and deleting files

Invariably, most applications built deal with files in some fashion. It might be that your application needs to simply work from an XML configuration file or even store the end users' settings or data on a file on their machines. For this reason, this chapter looks at working with files in your Silverlight applications as well as other means to store content on the client's computer.

You have a couple of different means to work with files and folders with your Silverlight applications. Silverlight does supply file dialogs that allow you to get the end user to specify the actual file that your application is to work with. But, with Silverlight 4, you also have to get programmatic access to specific folders on the end user's system through the `Environment.SpecialFolders` object when running your Silverlight 4 application in an out-of-browser mode with elevated permissions.

THE OPENFILEDIALOG AND SAVEFILEDIALOG CLASSES

In working with files, one of the easiest means has been around even prior to Silverlight 4. Using the `OpenFileDialog` and `SaveFileDialog` classes has allowed you to work with files directly on the end user's desktop. However, working with files in this manner did include some overall limitations that caused Microsoft to further expand upon your overall file management capabilities when it comes to working with the end user's filesystem.

One of the limitations of the OpenFileDialog or the SaveFileDialog class is that it has to be an end-user initiated action. The OpenFileDialog will pop up a file dialog that requires the end user to make a file selection before you can proceed in your application code. In some cases, this might be just fine for your application. If this is the case, this would be the preferred approach because it requires the lowest level of trust for your application.

Listing 16-1 shows an example of using the OpenFileDialog class to open and read a text or XML file. For the UI of this application, all you need is a Button and a TextBox server control on your page.

LISTING 16-1: Using the OpenFileDialog class

```csharp
using System.IO;
using System.Windows;
using System.Windows.Controls;

namespace UsingOpenFileDialog
{
    public partial class MainPage : UserControl
    {
        public MainPage()
        {
            InitializeComponent();
        }

        private void button1_Click(object sender, RoutedEventArgs e)
        {
            OpenFileDialog openFileDialog = new OpenFileDialog();
            openFileDialog.Filter = "Text files (*.txt, *.xml)|*.txt;*.xml";

            bool? userAccepts = openFileDialog.ShowDialog();

            if (userAccepts == true)
            {
                // Open the selected file to read.
                Stream fs = openFileDialog.File.OpenRead();

                using (StreamReader sr = new StreamReader(fs))
                {
                    textBox1.Text = sr.ReadToEnd();
                }

                fs.Close();
            }
        }
    }
}
```

The first step is to instantiate the OpenFileDialog class. In this example, because you want only text or XML files, a filter is placed on the dialog using the Filter property and assigning it a combination of values that limit the dialog to work only with .txt or .xml files.

When end users click the button, they are presented with the dialog shown in Figure 16-1.

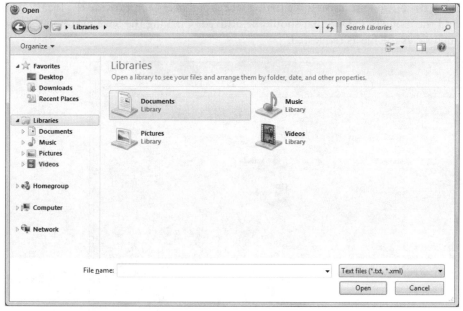

FIGURE 16-1

The SaveFileDialog class does the reverse of this and allows the application to send a file down to the client to be saved on the client's actual machine. Listing 16-2 shows an example of saving a file in this manner.

LISTING 16-2: Saving a file to the client machine

```csharp
private void button2_Click(object sender, RoutedEventArgs e)
{
    SaveFileDialog saveFileDialog = new SaveFileDialog();
    saveFileDialog.Filter = "Only text files (*.txt)|*.txt";

    bool? userAccepts = saveFileDialog.ShowDialog();

    if (userAccepts == true)
    {
        Stream fs = saveFileDialog.OpenFile();
        StreamWriter sw = new StreamWriter(fs);

        sw.WriteLine("Hello World!");

        sw.Flush();
        sw.Close();
    }
}
```

In this case, clicking the button produces a file dialog where end users can provide the location on their computer and the name of the file that should be utilized. Clicking the Save button (as shown in Figure 16-2) then saves the file as requested.

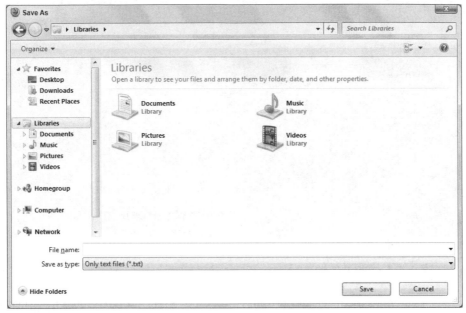

FIGURE 16-2

The rest of this chapter goes beyond the `OpenFileDialog` and the `SaveFileDialog` classes and looks at how to make file operations without the end user's constant permissions being required.

CLASSES FOR MANAGING THE FILESYSTEM

A series of classes are used for managing your abilities to work with files or folders (also known as directories) in .NET. Figure 16-3 shows a diagram of these objects.

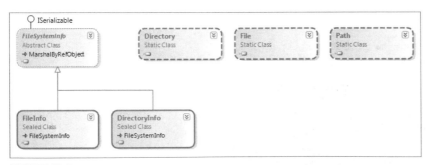

FIGURE 16-3

When you want your Silverlight application to do things like create, copy, delete, move, or open files and directories, you have to build a Silverlight application with elevated trust. This is detailed shortly.

The following list briefly explains the objects presented in the diagram in Figure 16-3.

➤   `FileSystemInfo` — This is the base class that represents any filesystem object.

➤   `FileInfo` and `File` — These classes represent a file on the filesystem.

➤   `DirectoryInfo` and `Directory` — These classes represent a folder or directory on the filesystem.

➤   `Path` — This class contains static members that you can use to manipulate pathnames.

.NET Classes That Represent Files and Folders

You will notice from the previous list that two classes are used to represent a folder and two classes are used to represent a file. The class you use depends largely on how many times you need to access that folder or file:

➤   `Directory` and `File` contain only static methods and are never instantiated. You use these classes by supplying the path to the appropriate filesystem object whenever you call a member method. If you want to do only one operation on a folder or file, using these classes is more efficient because it saves the overhead of instantiating a .NET class.

➤   `DirectoryInfo` and `FileInfo` implement roughly the same public methods as `Directory` and `File`, as well as some public properties and constructors, but they are stateful and the members of these classes are not static. You need to instantiate these classes before each instance is associated with a particular folder or file. This means that these classes are more efficient if you are performing multiple operations using the same object. That's because they read in the authentication and other information for the appropriate filesystem object on construction, and then do not need to read that information again, no matter how many methods and so on you call against each object (class instance). In comparison, the corresponding stateless classes need to check the details of the file or folder again with every method you call.

In this section, you are mostly using the `FileInfo` and `DirectoryInfo` classes, but it so happens that many (though not all) of the methods called are also implemented by `File` and `Directory` (although in those cases these methods require an extra parameter — the pathname of the filesystem object; also, a couple of the methods have slightly different names). For example:

```
string path = Environment.GetFolderPath(Environment.SpecialFolder.MyDocuments);
FileInfo myFile = new FileInfo(Path.Combine(path, "Test.txt"));

string destinationPath =
    Environment.GetFolderPath(Environment.SpecialFolder.MyPictures);
myFile.CopyTo(Path.Combine(destinationPath, "Test.txt"));
```

Doing this has the same effect as performing the following:

```
string path = Environment.GetFolderPath(Environment.SpecialFolder.MyDocuments);
string destinationPath =
```

```
      Environment.GetFolderPath(Environment.SpecialFolder.MyPictures);

   File.Copy(Path.Combine(path, "Test.txt"),
      Path.Combine(destinationPath, "Test.txt"));
```

The first code snippet takes slightly longer to execute because of the need to instantiate a `FileInfo` object, `myFile`, but it leaves `myFile` ready for you to perform further actions on the same file. By using the second example, there is no need to instantiate an object to copy the file.

You can instantiate a `FileInfo` or `DirectoryInfo` class by passing to the constructor a path to the corresponding filesystem object. You have just seen the process for a file. For a folder, the code looks similar:

```
   string path = Environment.GetFolderPath(Environment.SpecialFolder.MyDocuments);
   DirectoryInfo directoryInfo = new DirectoryInfo(path);
```

If the path represents an object that does not exist, an exception will not be thrown at construction, but will instead be thrown the first time you call a method that actually requires the corresponding filesystem object to be there. You can find out whether the object exists and is of the appropriate type by checking the `Exists` property, which is implemented by both of these classes:

```
   string path = Environment.GetFolderPath(Environment.SpecialFolder.MyDocuments);

   FileInfo myFile = new FileInfo(path);
   label1.Content = myFile.Exists.ToString();
```

Note that for this property to return `true`, the corresponding filesystem object must be of the appropriate type. In other words, if you instantiate a `FileInfo` object supplying the path of a folder, or you instantiate a `DirectoryInfo` object, giving it the path of a file, `Exists` will have the value `false`. Most of the properties and methods of these objects return a value if possible — they will not necessarily throw an exception just because the wrong type of object has been called, unless they are asked to do something that really is impossible. For example, the preceding code snippet might first display `false` (because `Environment.SpecialFolder.MyDocuments` is a folder). However, it still displays the time the folder was created because a folder still has that information. If you tried to open the folder as if it were a file, using the `FileInfo.Open()` method, you would get an exception.

After you have established whether the corresponding filesystem object exists, you can (if you are using the `FileInfo` or `DirectoryInfo` class) find out information about it using the properties in Table 16-1.

TABLE 16-1

PROPERTY	DESCRIPTION
CreationTime	The time at which the file or folder was created
DirectoryName	(FileInfo only) The full pathname of the containing folder
Parent	(DirectoryInfo only) The parent directory of a specified subdirectory
Exists	Provides a Boolean of whether a file or folder exists on the client's system

PROPERTY	DESCRIPTION
Extension	The extension of the file. If used on a folder, the return will be empty.
FullName	The full pathname of the file or folder
LastAccessTime	The time at which the file or folder was last accessed
LastWriteTime	The time at which the file or folder was last modified
Name	The name of the file or folder
Root	(DirectoryInfo only) The root portion of the path
Length	(FileInfo only) The size of the file in bytes

You can also perform actions on the filesystem object using the methods in Table 16-2.

TABLE 16-2

METHOD	DESCRIPTION
Create()	Creates a folder or empty file of the given name. For a FileInfo this also returns a stream object to let you write to the file. (Streams are covered later in this chapter.)
Delete()	Deletes the file or folder. For folders, there is an option for the delete to be recursive.
MoveTo()	Moves and/or renames the file or folder.
CopyTo()	(FileInfo only) Copies the file. Note that there is no copy method for folders. If you are copying complete directory trees you will need to individually copy each file and create new folders corresponding to the old folders.
GetDirectories()	(DirectoryInfo only) Returns an array of DirectoryInfo objects representing all folders contained in this folder.
GetFiles()	(DirectoryInfo only) Returns an array of FileInfo objects representing all files contained in this folder.
GetFileSystemInfos()	(DirectoryInfo only) Returns FileInfo and DirectoryInfo objects representing all objects contained in this folder, as an array of FileSystemInfo references.

Note that these tables list the main properties and methods and are not intended to be exhaustive. The preceding tables do not list most of the properties or methods that allow you to write to or read the data in files. This is actually done using stream objects, which are covered later in this chapter. FileInfo also implements a number of methods — Open(), OpenRead(), OpenText(), OpenWrite(), Create(), and CreateText() — that return stream objects for this purpose.

Using the Path Class

The Path class is not a class that you would instantiate. Rather, it exposes some static methods that make operations on pathnames easier. For example, suppose that you want to display the full pathname for a file, Test.txt, in the user's My Documents folder. You could find the path to the file using the following code:

```
string path = Environment.GetFolderPath(Environment.SpecialFolder.MyDocuments);
label1.Content = Path.Combine(path);
```

Using the Path class is a lot easier than using separation symbols manually, especially because the Path class is aware of different formats for pathnames on different operating systems. Path.Combine() is the method of this class that you are most likely to use, but Path also implements other methods that supply information about the path or the required format for it.

Some of the static fields available to the Path class are described in Table 16-3.

TABLE 16-3

PROPERTY	DESCRIPTION
AltDirectorySeparatorChar	Provides a platform-agnostic way to specify an alternative character to separate directory levels. In Windows, a / symbol is used, whereas in UNIX, a \ symbol is used.
DirectorySeparatorChar	Provides a platform-agnostic way to specify a character to separate directory levels. In Windows, a / symbol is used, whereas in UNIX, a \ symbol is used.
PathSeparator	Provides a platform-agnostic way to specify path strings that divide environmental variables. The default value of this setting is a semicolon.
VolumeSeparatorChar	Provides a platform-agnostic way to specify a volume separator. The default value of this setting is a colon.

Using Basic File Objects from Silverlight

This section presents a sample C# application called FileProperties. This application presents a simple user interface that allows you to browse the filesystem and view the creation time, last access time, last write time, and size of files.

 You can download the sample code for this application from the Wrox website at www.wrox.com.

The FileProperties application is a pretty simple application that allows clients to work with the files on their system in the most basic way. Using this application, the end user selects the folder in the main drop-down at the top of the window and clicks the Display button. By selecting one of the special folders and clicking the button, the contents of that particular folder are then listed in the provided list boxes. Figure 16-4 shows the FileProperties sample application in action.

The user can very easily navigate around the filesystem by clicking any folder in the right list box to move down to that folder or by clicking the Up button to move up to the parent folder. Figure 16-4 shows the contents of My Documents folder. The user can also select a file by clicking its name in the list box. This displays the file's properties in the text boxes at the bottom of the application (presented in Figure 16-5).

FIGURE 16-4

FIGURE 16-5

Note that you can also display the creation time, last access time, and last modification time for folders using the `DirectoryInfo` property.

To create this application, create a new Silverlight project called FileProperties. Using Visual Studio 2010, drag the appropriate controls onto the design surface. In the end, you should have something similar to what is presented in Figure 16-6.

In the `MainPage.xaml.cs` page, you need to have the following namespaces as shown in Listing 16-3.

LISTING 16-3: The namespaces to use for the FileProperties project

```
using System;
using System.IO;
using System.Windows;
using System.Windows.Controls;
```

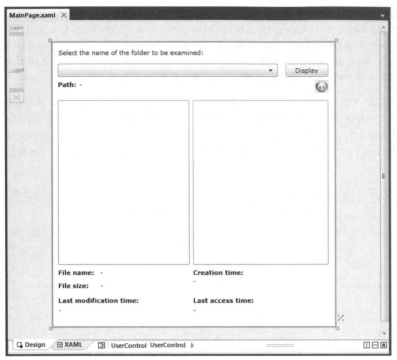

FIGURE 16-6

As you can see from this list of namespaces, you were required to add the System.IO namespace in order to work with files and directories.

You need to do this for all the file-system–related examples in this chapter, but this part of the code will not be explicitly shown in the remaining examples. The next step is to add a member field to the main form as shown in Listing 16-4.

LISTING 16-4: Creating a private member

```
public partial class MainPage : UserControl
{
    private string _currentFolderPath;
```

_currentFolderPath stores the path of the folder whose contents are displayed in the list boxes.

Next, you need to add event handlers for the user-generated events. The possible user inputs are as follows:

➤ **User clicks the Display button** — You need to determine what special folder the user selected from the provided options. Once the user selects the folder they want and has clicked the button, you then list the files and subfolders of this folder in the list boxes.

➤ **User clicks a filename in the Files list box** — You display the properties of this file in the lower part of the form.

➤ **User clicks a folder name in the Folders list box** — You clear all the controls and then display the contents of this subfolder in the list boxes.

➤ **User clicks the Up button** — You clear all the controls and then display the contents of the parent of the currently selected folder.

Before you see the code for the event handlers, here is the code for the methods that do all the work. First, you need to clear the contents of all the controls. This method, shown in Listing 16-5, is fairly self-explanatory.

LISTING 16-5: The method required to clear all the contents

```
private void ClearAllFields()
{
    listBoxFolders.Items.Clear();
    listBoxFiles.Items.Clear();
    lblPathUsed.Content = "";
    lblAccessTime.Content = "";
    lblCreationTime.Content = "";
    lblFileName.Content = "";
    lblFileSize.Content = "";
    lblModificationTime.Content = "";
}
```

Next, you define a method, `DisplayFileInfo()`, that handles the process of displaying the information for a given file in the text boxes. This method takes one parameter, the full pathname of the file as a `String`, and works by creating a `FileInfo` object based on this path as illustrated in Listing 16-6.

LISTING 16-6: The DisplayFileInfo() method

```
private void DisplayFileInfo(string fileFullName)
{
    FileInfo selectedFile = new FileInfo(fileFullName);

    if (!selectedFile.Exists)
    {
        throw new FileNotFoundException("File not found: " + fileFullName);
    }

    lblFileName.Content = selectedFile.Name;
    lblAccessTime.Content = selectedFile.LastAccessTime.ToLongDateString();
    lblCreationTime.Content = selectedFile.CreationTime.ToLongDateString();
    lblModificationTime.Content = selectedFile.LastWriteTime.ToLongDateString();
    lblFileSize.Content = selectedFile.Length + " bytes";
}
```

Note that you take the precaution of throwing an exception if there are any problems locating a file at the specified location. The exception itself will be handled in the calling routine (one of the event handlers). Finally, you define a method, `DisplayFolderList()`, which displays the contents of a given folder in the two list boxes. The full pathname of the folder is passed in as a parameter to this method as demonstrated in Listing 16-7.

LISTING 16-7: The DisplayFolderFileList() method

```
private void DisplayFolderFileList(string folderFullName)
{
    DirectoryInfo folderList = new DirectoryInfo(folderFullName);

    if (!folderList.Exists)
    {
        throw new DirectoryNotFoundException("Folder not found: " + folderFullName);
    }

    ClearAllFields();

    lblPathUsed.Content = folderList.FullName;
    _currentFolderPath = folderList.FullName;

    foreach (var dir in folderList.EnumerateDirectories())
    {
        listBoxFolders.Items.Add(dir);
    }

    foreach (var file in folderList.EnumerateFiles())
    {
        listBoxFiles.Items.Add(file);
    }
}
```

Next, you examine the event handlers. The event handler that manages the event that is triggered when the user clicks the Display button is the most complex because it needs to handle three different possibilities for the text the user enters in the text box. For instance, it could be the pathname of a folder, the pathname of a file, or neither of these. This method is shown in Listing 16-8.

LISTING 16-8: The method for when the Display button is clicked

```
private void button1_Click(object sender, RoutedEventArgs e)
{
    try
    {
        switch (comboBox1.SelectedIndex)
        {
            case 0:
                _currentFolderPath = Environment.GetFolderPath
                    (Environment.SpecialFolder.MyDocuments);
                break;
            case 1:
                _currentFolderPath = Environment.GetFolderPath
                    (Environment.SpecialFolder.MyPictures);
                break;
            case 2:
                _currentFolderPath = Environment.GetFolderPath
```

```
                    (Environment.SpecialFolder.MyVideos);
                break;
            case 3:
                _currentFolderPath = Environment.GetFolderPath
                    (Environment.SpecialFolder.MyMusic);
                break;
        }

        DirectoryInfo directoryInfo = new DirectoryInfo(_currentFolderPath);
        if (directoryInfo.Exists)
        {
            DisplayFolderFileList(directoryInfo.FullName);
            return;
        }

        throw new DirectoryNotFoundException("There is no folder with this name: "
            + lblPathUsed.Content);
    }
    catch (Exception ex)
    {
        MessageBox.Show(ex.Message);
    }
}
```

In this code the first step is to figure out which special folder the user wants to work with. Once the user makes this selection, you then call `DisplayFolderFileList()` to populate the list boxes.

The following code is the event handler that is called when an item in the Files list box is selected, either by the user or, as indicated previously, programmatically. It simply constructs the full pathname of the selected file, and passes it to the `DisplayFileInfo()` method presented earlier. Listing 16-9 shows this in action.

LISTING 16-9: A method for when there is a change to the listBoxFiles control

```
private void listBoxFiles_SelectionChanged(object sender,
    SelectionChangedEventArgs e)
{
    try
    {
        if (listBoxFiles.SelectedIndex != -1)
        {
            string selectedString = listBoxFiles.SelectedItem.ToString();
            string fullFileName = Path.Combine(_currentFolderPath, selectedString);
            DisplayFileInfo(fullFileName);
        }
    }
    catch (Exception ex)
    {
        MessageBox.Show(ex.Message);
    }
}
```

The event handler for the selection of a folder in the Folders list box is implemented in a very similar way, except that in this case you call `DisplayFolderFileList()` to update the contents of the list boxes. Listing 16-10 shows this method.

LISTING 16-10: A method for when there is a change to the listBoxFolders control

```csharp
private void listBoxFolders_SelectionChanged(object sender,
    SelectionChangedEventArgs e)
{
    try
    {
        if (listBoxFolders.SelectedIndex != -1)
        {
            string selectedString = listBoxFolders.SelectedItem.ToString();
            string fullPathName = Path.Combine(_currentFolderPath, selectedString);
            DisplayFolderFileList(fullPathName);
        }
    }
    catch (Exception ex)
    {
        MessageBox.Show(ex.Message);
    }
}
```

Finally, when the Up button is clicked, `DisplayFolderFileList()` must also be called, except that this time you need to obtain the path of the parent of the folder currently being displayed. You do this with the `FileInfo.DirectoryName` property, which returns the parent folder path. Listing 16-11 shows this final method.

LISTING 16-11: The Up button method to change the folder path

```csharp
private void image1_MouseLeftButtonDown(object sender,
    System.Windows.Input.MouseButtonEventArgs e)
{
    try
    {
        if (_currentFolderPath != null)
        {
            string folderPath = new FileInfo(_currentFolderPath).DirectoryName;
            DisplayFolderFileList(folderPath);
        }
    }
    catch (Exception ex)
    {
        MessageBox.Show(ex.Message);
    }
}
```

Applying Settings for an Out-of-Browser Application

With this code in place, you will notice that you cannot run it as is. The main reason for this is that in a basic Silverlight application, you are actually not allowed to work with files and folders as has been shown in the previous code examples.

To have this kind of access to the client's files from your Silverlight application, you need to convert your application to a Silverlight application that runs in the out-of-browser mode. To do this, right-click the project from within Visual Studio Solution Explorer and select Properties. On the Silverlight tab, select the "Enable running application out of the browser" checkbox. This is demonstrated in Figure 16-7.

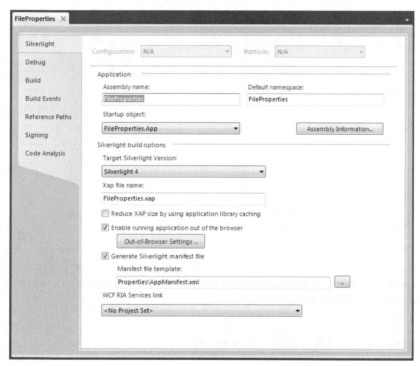

FIGURE 16-7

Now click the Out-of-Browser Settings button on the same page to apply some final settings. In Figure 16-8, you can see some settings that have been applied to work with your out-of-browser version of the FileProperties application.

Building the InstallPage.xaml File

Now that you have established that your FileProperties application will be an out-of-browser application, the next step is to build an Install page that allows end users to trigger this application install themselves.

FIGURE 16-8

For your `InstallPage.xaml` file, simply place a single button on the page and provide the click event for the button as demonstrated in Listing 16-12.

LISTING 16-12: The InstallPage.xaml file's button click event

Available for
download on
Wrox.com

```
private void button1_Click(object sender, RoutedEventArgs e)
{
    Application.Current.Install();
}
```

Now with that simple code in place, the final step is to change your `Application_Startup()` method found in your `App.xaml.cs` file in the same project. This change is demonstrated in Listing 16-13.

LISTING 16-13: Changing the Application_Startup() method of the App.xaml.cs file

Available for
download on
Wrox.com

```
private void Application_Startup(object sender, StartupEventArgs e)
{
    if (Application.Current.IsRunningOutOfBrowser)
```

```
        {
            this.RootVisual = new MainPage();
        }
        else
        {
            this.RootVisual = new InstallPage();
        }
    }
```

From here, you can see that if the FileProperties Silverlight application is not running in out-of-browser mode, the `InstallPage.xaml` page is processed. However, if the application is indeed running in an out-of-browser mode, the `MainPage.xaml` page is run instead. Running FileProperties in an out-of-browser mode is what allows you to work with the client's files as was demonstrated.

Now that you can run the FileProperties application in an out-of-browser mode, you will notice some interesting things. First of all, if you select the special folder of My Documents and you are using Windows, you will see some of the subfolders as well (as shown in Figure 16-9).

Right away, you can see the other special folders of My Music, My Pictures, and My Videos listed as subfolders here. Selecting to dig into one of these folders by highlighting them will not list out the contents of these folders as you would expect. Instead, you are presented with the exception shown in Figure 16-10.

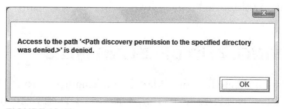

FIGURE 16-9   **FIGURE 16-10**

The reason is that even though these are considered special folders, you are trying to access them through a sub-path of the My Documents folder. If you need to access these folders specifically, you want to access them through the use of `Environment.SpecialFolder.MyPictures`, and so on.

You will also notice that if you are in the root of any of the special folders, you cannot click the Up button to get to `C:\Users\Bill` (or any other user) because you are presented with the exception shown in Figure 16-11.

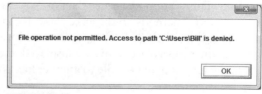

FIGURE 16-11

Finally, when you are looking at the My Pictures folder, you might not find everything you are looking for. For instance, in looking at a fresh operating system install of Windows 7 and selecting the My Pictures special folder, you won't find anything listed. However, looking at Figure 16-12, you can see that I do indeed have some pictures in this folder.

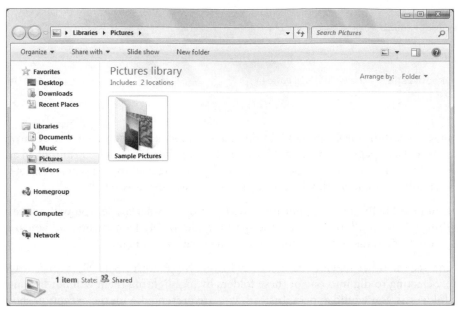

FIGURE 16-12

The reason for this is that the Sample Pictures folder of pictures, though it appears that they are in C:\Users\Bill, is actually contained within C:\Public\Pictures and is a shared resource among all users. Working with the Silverlight file features, you will not be able to programmatically see these items contained within the Public folders.

MOVING, COPYING, AND DELETING FILES

It is possible to move or delete files or folders by making use of the MoveTo() and Delete() methods of the FileInfo and DirectoryInfo classes. The equivalent methods on the File and Directory classes are Move() and Delete(). The FileInfo and File classes also implement the methods CopyTo() and Copy(), respectively. However, no methods exist to copy complete folders — you need to do that by copying each file in the folder.

Using all these methods is quite intuitive — you can find detailed descriptions in the SDK documentation. This section illustrates their use for the particular cases of calling the static Move(), Copy(), and Delete() methods on the File class. To do this, you will build on the previous FileProperties example and call its iteration FilePropertiesAndMovement. This example will have the extra feature that whenever the properties of a file are displayed, the application gives you the option of deleting that file or moving or copying the file to another location.

Extending on the FileProperties Solution

This next example extends on the FileProperties solution that was presented earlier in this chapter. When completed, you will have a user interface as presented in Figure 16-13.

As you can see, the FilePropertiesMore solution is similar in appearance to FileProperties, except for the group of three radio buttons and a folder selection area at the bottom of the window. These controls are enabled only when the example actually displays the properties of a file; at all other times, they are disabled. When the properties of a selected file are displayed, FilePropertiesMore automatically places the full pathname of that file in the bottom part of the dialog allowing the users to edit where they are about to place the file. Users can then click any of the buttons to perform the appropriate operations. When they do, a message box is displayed that confirms the action to be taken by the user (see Figure 16-14).

When the user clicks the Yes button, the action is initiated. Some actions in the form that the user can take will cause the display to be incorrect. For instance, if the user moves or deletes a file, the contents of that file obviously cannot continue to display in the same location. In addition, if you change the name of a file in the same folder, your display will also be out of date. In these cases, FilePropertiesMore resets its controls to display only the folder where the file resides after the file operation.

FIGURE 16-13

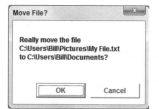

FIGURE 16-14

Using the Move, Copy, and Delete Methods

To code these new capabilities, you need to add the appropriate radio button controls, a button to enable browsing of the user's filesystem, as well as another button to initiate the action.

First, look at the event handler that is called when the user chooses to delete the file that is selected. This is presented in Listing 16-14.

LISTING 16-14: Deleting a file

```
private void DeleteFileOption()
{
    try
    {
        string filePath = Path.Combine(_currentFolderPath,
                                    listBoxFiles.SelectedItem.ToString());
        string query = "Really delete the file\n" + filePath + "?";
        if (MessageBox.Show(query,
            "Delete File?", MessageBoxButton.OKCancel) == MessageBoxResult.OK)
        {
            File.Delete(filePath);
            MessageBox.Show("Deletion of file successful!");
            DisplayFolderFileList(_currentFolderPath);
        }
    }
    catch (Exception ex)
    {
        MessageBox.Show("Unable to delete file.
            The following exception occurred:\n" + ex.Message, "Failed",
            MessageBoxButton.OK);
    }
}
```

The code for this method is contained in a `try` block because of the obvious risk of an exception being thrown if, for example, you do not have permission to delete the file or the if file is moved by another process after it has been displayed but before the user initiates the delete operation. You construct the path of the file to be deleted from the _currentFolderPath field, which contains the path of the parent folder, and the name of the file from the listBoxFiles ListBox control. The delete operation is really done here through the File.Delete(filepath); operation.

The methods to move or copy the files are quite similar. Both of these methods are presented in Listing 16-15.

LISTING 16-15: Moving or copying files

```
private void CopyFileOption()
{
    try
    {
        string filePath = Path.Combine(_currentFolderPath,
            listBoxFiles.SelectedItem.ToString());
        string query = "Really copy the file\n" + filePath + "\nto "
                        + _moveCopyFolderPath + "?";

        if (MessageBox.Show(query,
            "Copy File?", MessageBoxButton.OKCancel) == MessageBoxResult.OK)
        {
            File.Copy(filePath, _moveCopyFolderPath + @"\" +
                listBoxFiles.SelectedItem);
            MessageBox.Show("Copying file successful!");
```

```
                    DisplayFolderFileList(_currentFolderPath);
            }
        }
        catch (Exception ex)
        {
            MessageBox.Show("Unable to copy file. The following exception occurred:\n"
                + ex.Message,
                "Failed", MessageBoxButton.OK);
        }
    }

    private void MoveFileOption()
    {
        try
        {
            string filePath = Path.Combine(_currentFolderPath,
                listBoxFiles.SelectedItem.ToString());
            string query = "Really move the file\n" + filePath + "\nto "
                            + _moveCopyFolderPath + "?";

            if (MessageBox.Show(query,
                "Move File?", MessageBoxButton.OKCancel) == MessageBoxResult.OK)
            {
                File.Move(filePath, _moveCopyFolderPath + @"\" +
                    listBoxFiles.SelectedItem);
                MessageBox.Show("Moving file successful!");
                DisplayFolderFileList(_currentFolderPath);
            }
        }
        catch (Exception ex)
        {
            MessageBox.Show("Unable to move file. The following exception occurred:\n"
                + ex.Message,
                "Failed", MessageBoxButton.OK);
        }
    }
```

These methods also work from the location of `_currentFolderPath` and provide a message box to the end users asking them if they really want to perform this operation. If affirmed, the `File.Move()` or `File.Copy()` methods are executed depending on the operation selected. Both of these methods use a signature that requires the source path and filename followed by the destination path and filename.

There is more to this solution, but these are the main methods you need to understand when moving, copying, or deleting files. For the rest of the solution, please visit www.wrox.com and you will find the solution FilePropertiesMore in the code download.

READING AND WRITING FILES

Another common operation is the task of reading and writing files. Reading and writing to files is in principle very simple; however, it is not done through the `DirectoryInfo` or `FileInfo` objects. Instead, using the Silverlight 4, you can do it through the `File` object. Later in this chapter, you see how to accomplish this using a number of other classes that represent a generic concept called a *stream*.

Reading from a File

For an example of reading from a file, create a Silverlight application that contains a regular `ListBox`, a `Button`, a `TextBlock`, and a `ScrollViewer` server control. In the end, your form should appear similar to Figure 16-15.

FIGURE 16-15

The XAML code for this is presented in Listing 16-16.

LISTING 16-16: The XAML code for the file reader

```
<UserControl x:Class="ReadingFiles.MainPage"
    xmlns="http://schemas.microsoft.com/winfx/2006/xaml/presentation"
    xmlns:x="http://schemas.microsoft.com/winfx/2006/xaml"
    xmlns:d="http://schemas.microsoft.com/expression/blend/2008"
    xmlns:mc="http://schemas.openxmlformats.org/markup-compatibility/2006"
    mc:Ignorable="d"
    d:DesignHeight="600" d:DesignWidth="800">

    <Grid x:Name="LayoutRoot" Background="White" Loaded="LayoutRoot_Loaded">
        <ListBox Height="100" HorizontalAlignment="Left" Margin="12,12,0,0"
         Name="listBox1" VerticalAlignment="Top" Width="568" />
        <Button Content="Read Selected File" Height="100"
         HorizontalAlignment="Left" Margin="586,12,0,0" Name="button1"
         VerticalAlignment="Top" Width="202" Click="button1_Click" />
```

```xml
        <ScrollViewer HorizontalAlignment="Stretch" Margin="12,118,12,12"
         Name="scrollViewer1" HorizontalContentAlignment="Stretch"
         HorizontalScrollBarVisibility="Auto"
         VerticalContentAlignment="Stretch"
         VerticalScrollBarVisibility="Auto">
            <TextBlock HorizontalAlignment="Left" Name="textBlock1" Text="" />
        </ScrollViewer>
    </Grid>
</UserControl>
```

The idea of this form is that the end user selects a specific file from his or her My Documents folder and clicks the Read Selected File button. From there, the application reads the specified file and displays the file's contents in the bottom part of the application. This is illustrated in the code example in Listing 16-17.

LISTING 16-17: Reading from a file

```csharp
using System;
using System.IO;
using System.Windows;
using System.Windows.Controls;

namespace ReadingFiles
{
    public partial class MainPage : UserControl
    {
        private readonly string _filePath =
            Environment.GetFolderPath(Environment.SpecialFolder.MyDocuments);

        public MainPage()
        {
            InitializeComponent();
        }

        private void LayoutRoot_Loaded(object sender, RoutedEventArgs e)
        {
            DirectoryInfo directoryInfo = new DirectoryInfo(_filePath);

            if (directoryInfo.Exists)
            {
                foreach (var file in directoryInfo.EnumerateFiles())
                {
                    listBox1.Items.Add(file);
                }
                return;
            }

            throw new DirectoryNotFoundException(
                "There was an issue opening the My Documents folder.");
        }

        private void button1_Click(object sender, RoutedEventArgs e)
```

continues

LISTING 16-17 *(continued)*

```
        {
            if (listBox1.SelectedIndex != -1)
            {
                string selectedString = listBox1.SelectedItem.ToString();
                string fullPathName = Path.Combine(_filePath, selectedString);

                textBlock1.Text = File.ReadAllText(fullPathName);
            }
        }
    }
}
```

In building this example, the first step is to add the `using` statement to bring in the `System.IO` namespace. From there, simply use the `button1_Click` event for the button on the form to populate the `TextBlock` control with what comes back from the file. You can now access the file's contents by using the `File.ReadAllText()` method. As you can see, you can read files with a single statement. The `ReadAllText()` method opens the specified file, reads the contents, and then closes the file. The return value of the `ReadAllText()` method is a string containing the entire contents of the file specified. The result is something similar to what is shown in Figure 16-16.

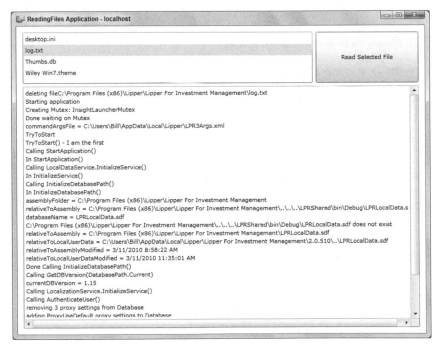

FIGURE 16-16

The `File.ReadAllText()` signature shown in the preceding example is of the following construction:

```
File.ReadAllText(FilePath);
```

The other option is to also specify the encoding of the file being read:

```
File.ReadAllText(FilePath, Encoding);
```

Using this signature allows you to specify the encoding to use when opening and reading the contents of the file. Therefore, this means that you could do something such as the following:

```
File.ReadAllText(textBox1.Text, Encoding.ASCII);
```

Some of the other options for opening and working with files include using the `ReadAllBytes()` and the `ReadAllLines()` methods. The `ReadAllBytes()` method allows you to open a binary file and read the contents into a byte array. The `ReadAllText()` method shown earlier gives you the entire contents of the specified file in a single string instance. You might not be interested in this but instead be interested in working with what comes back from the file in a line-by-line fashion. In this case, you should use the `ReadAllLines()` method because it allows for this kind of functionality and will return a string array for you to work with.

Writing to a File

Besides making reading from files an extremely simple process under the .NET Framework umbrella, the base class library has made writing to files just as easy. Just as the base class library (BCL) gives you the `ReadAllText()`, `ReadAllLines()`, and `ReadAllBytes()` methods to read files in a few different ways, it gives you the `WriteAllText()`, `WriteAllBytes()`, and `WriteAllLines()` methods to write files.

For an example of how to write to a file, create a Silverlight application called WritingFiles. It should appear as shown in Figure 16-17.

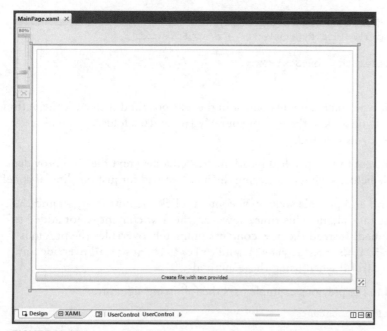

FIGURE 16-17

The code for this is layout is illustrated in Listing 16-18.

LISTING 16-18: The XAML code for the WritingFiles solution

```
<UserControl x:Class="WritingFiles.MainPage"
    xmlns="http://schemas.microsoft.com/winfx/2006/xaml/presentation"
    xmlns:x="http://schemas.microsoft.com/winfx/2006/xaml"
    xmlns:d="http://schemas.microsoft.com/expression/blend/2008"
    xmlns:mc="http://schemas.openxmlformats.org/markup-compatibility/2006"
    mc:Ignorable="d"
    d:DesignHeight="600" d:DesignWidth="800">

    <Grid x:Name="LayoutRoot" Background="White">
        <Button Content="Create file with text provided" Height="23"
          HorizontalAlignment="Left" Margin="12,556,0,0" Name="button1"
          VerticalAlignment="Top" Width="776" Click="button1_Click" />
        <TextBox Height="538" HorizontalAlignment="Left" Margin="12,12,0,0"
          Name="textBox1" VerticalAlignment="Top" Width="776"
          AcceptsReturn="True" TextWrapping="Wrap" />
    </Grid>
</UserControl>
```

The code for the `button1_Click` event handler should appear as shown in Listing 16-19.

LISTING 16-19: Creating a new file

```
private void button1_Click(object sender, EventArgs e)
{
    string filePath = Environment.GetFolderPath
        (Environment.SpecialFolder.MyDocuments) + @"\MyFile.txt";

    File.WriteAllText(filePath, textBox1.Text);
}
```

Build and start the application, type some random content in the text box, and then click the button. Nothing happens visually, but if you look in the root of your My Documents folder, you will see the `MyFile.txt` file with the content you specified.

The `WriteAllText()` method went to the specified location, created a new text file, and provided the specified contents to the file before saving and closing the file. Not bad for just one line of code!

If you run the application again and provide some new content, click the button again and the application performs the same task again. This time, however, the new content is not added to the previous content you specified. Instead the new content completely overrides the previous content. In fact, `WriteAllText()`, `WriteAllBytes()`, and `WriteAllLines()` all override any previous files, so you must be careful when using these methods.

The `WriteAllText()` method in the previous example uses the following signature:

```
File.WriteAllText(FilePath, Contents)
```

You can also specify the encoding of the new file:

```
File.WriteAllText(FilePath, Contents, Encoding)
```

The `WriteAllBytes()` method allows you to write content to a file using a byte array and the `WriteAllLines()` method allows you to write a string array to a file. An example of this is illustrated in the event handler in Listing 16-20.

LISTING 16-20: Using WriteAllLines()

```csharp
private void button1_Click(object sender, EventArgs e)
{
    string[] movies =
        {"Grease",
         "Close Encounters of the Third Kind",
         "The Day After Tomorrow"};

    string filePath =
        Environment.GetFolderPath(Environment.SpecialFolder.MyDocuments)
        + @"\MyFile.txt";

    File.WriteAllLines(filePath, movies);
}
```

Now clicking the button for such an application gives you a `MyFile.txt` file with the following contents:

```
Grease
Close Encounters of the Third Kind
The Day After Tomorrow
```

The `WriteAllLines()` method writes out the string array with each array item taking its own line in the file.

Because data may be written not only to disk but to other places as well (such as to named pipes or to memory), it is also important to understand how to deal with file I/O in .NET using streams as a means of moving file contents around. This is shown in the following section.

USING STREAMS

The idea of a stream has been around for a very long time. A stream is an object used to transfer data. The data can be transferred in one of two directions:

➤ If the data is being transferred from some outside source into your program, it is called *reading* from the stream.

➤ If the data is being transferred from your program to some outside source, it is called *writing* to the stream.

Very often, the outside source will be a file, but that is not always the case. For example, Microsoft has supplied a .NET base class for writing to or reading from memory, the `System.IO.MemoryStream` object.

The advantage of having a separate object for the transfer of data, rather than using the `FileInfo` or `DirectoryInfo` classes to do this, is that separating the concept of transferring data from the particular data source makes it easier to swap data sources. Stream objects themselves contain a lot of generic code that concerns the movement of data between outside sources and variables in your code. By keeping this code separate from any concept of a particular data source, you make it easier for this code to be reused (through inheritance) in different circumstances. For example, the `StringReader` and `StringWriter` classes are part of the same inheritance tree as two classes that you will use later on to read and write text files. The classes will almost certainly share a substantial amount of code behind the scenes.

Figure 16-18 shows the actual hierarchy of stream-related classes in the `System.IO` namespace for Silverlight.

As far as reading and writing files, the classes that concern you most are:

➤   `FileStream` — This class is intended for reading and writing binary data in a binary file. However, you can also use it to read from or write to any file.

➤   `StreamReader` and `StreamWriter` — These classes are designed specifically for reading from and writing to text files.

You might also find the `BinaryReader` and `BinaryWriter` classes useful, although they are not used in the examples here. These classes do not actually implement streams themselves, but they are able to provide wrappers around other stream objects. `BinaryReader` and `BinaryWriter` provide extra formatting of binary data, which allows you to directly read or write the contents of C# variables to or from the relevant stream. Think of the `BinaryReader` and `BinaryWriter` as sitting between the stream and your code, providing extra formatting (see Figure 16-19).

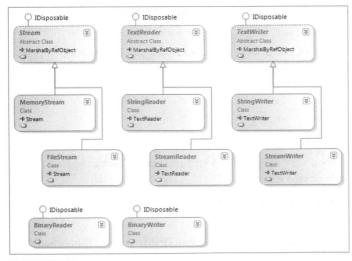

FIGURE 16-18

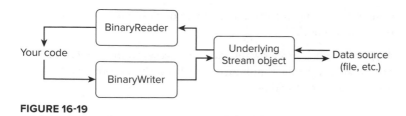

FIGURE 16-19

The difference between using these classes and directly using the underlying stream objects is that a basic stream works in bytes. For example, suppose that as part of the process of saving some document you want to write the contents of a variable of type `long` to a binary file. Each `long` occupies 8 bytes, and if you used an ordinary binary stream, you would have to explicitly write each of those 8 bytes of memory.

In C# code, you would have to perform some bitwise operations to extract each of those 8 bytes from the `long` value. Using a `BinaryWriter` instance, you can encapsulate the entire operation in an overload of the `BinaryWriter.Write()` method, which takes a `long` as a parameter and places those 8 bytes into the stream (and if the stream is directed to a file, into the file). A corresponding `BinaryReader` `.Read()` method extracts 8 bytes from the stream and recovers the value of the `long`. For more information on the `BinaryReader` and `BinaryWriter` classes, refer to the SDK documentation.

Using Buffered Streams

For performance reasons, when you read or write to or from a file, the output is buffered. This means that if your program asks for the next 2 bytes of a file stream, and the stream passes the request on to Windows, Windows will not connect to the filesystem and then locate and read the file off the disk, just to get 2 bytes. Instead, Windows retrieves a large block of the file at one time and stores this block in an area of memory known as a *buffer*. Subsequent requests for data from the stream are satisfied from the buffer until the buffer runs out, at which point, Windows grabs another block of data from the file.

Writing to files works in the same way. For files, this is done automatically by the operating system, but you might have to write a stream class to read from some other device that is not buffered. If so, you can derive your class from `BufferedStream`, which implements a buffer itself. (Note, however, that `BufferedStream` is not designed for the situation in which an application frequently alternates between reading and writing data.)

Reading and Writing Binary Files Using FileStream

Reading and writing to and from binary files can be done using the `FileStream` class. A `FileStream` instance is used to read or write data to or from a file. To construct a `FileStream`, you need four pieces of information:

1. The *file* you want to access.

2. The *mode*, which indicates how you want to open the file. For example, are you intending to create a new file or open an existing file? Also, if you are opening an existing file, should any write operations be interpreted as overwriting the contents of the file or appending to the file?

3. The *access*, which indicates how you want to access the file. For example, do you want to read from or write to the file or do both?

4. The *share* access, which specifies whether you want exclusive access to the file. Or, are you willing to have other streams access the file simultaneously? If so, should other streams have access to read the file, to write to it, or to do both?

The first of these pieces of information is usually represented by a string that contains the full pathname of the file, and this chapter considers only those constructors that require a string here. Besides those constructors, however, some additional ones take an old Windows-API–style Windows handle to a file instead. The remaining three pieces of information are represented by three .NET enumerations called `FileMode`, `FileAccess`, and `FileShare`. The values of these enumerations are listed in Table 16-4 and are self-explanatory.

TABLE 16-4

ENUMERATION	VALUES
FileMode	Append, Create, CreateNew, Open, OpenOrCreate, or Truncate
FileAccess	Read, ReadWrite, or Write
FileShare	Delete, Inheritable, None, Read, ReadWrite, or Write

Note that in the case of `FileMode`, exceptions can be thrown if you request a mode that is inconsistent with the existing status of the file. `Append`, `Open`, and `Truncate` throw an exception if the file does not already exist. `CreateNew` throws an exception if it does. `Create` and `OpenOrCreate` copes with either scenario, but `Create` deletes any existing file to replace it with a new, initially empty, one. The `FileAccess` and `FileShare` enumerations are bitwise flags, so values can be combined with the C# bitwise OR operator, |.

A large number of constructors exist for the `FileStream`. The three simplest ones work as follows:

```
string filePath1 =
    Environment.GetFolderPath(Environment.SpecialFolder.MyDocuments) +
    @"\MyFile1.docx";
string filePath2 =
    Environment.GetFolderPath(Environment.SpecialFolder.MyDocuments) +
    @"\MyFile2.docx";
string filePath3 =
    Environment.GetFolderPath(Environment.SpecialFolder.MyDocuments) +
    @"\MyFile3.docx";
string filePath4 =
    Environment.GetFolderPath(Environment.SpecialFolder.MyDocuments) +
    @"\MyFile4.docx";
string filePath5 =
    Environment.GetFolderPath(Environment.SpecialFolder.MyDocuments) +
    @"\MyFile5.docx";
string filePath6 =
    Environment.GetFolderPath(Environment.SpecialFolder.MyDocuments) +
    @"\MyFile6.docx";
string filePath7 =
```

```
                Environment.GetFolderPath(Environment.SpecialFolder.MyDocuments) +
                @"\MyFile7.docx";

        // Creates a file with read-write access and allows other streams read access
        FileStream fs1 = new FileStream(filePath1, FileMode.Create);

        // As above, but we only get write access to the file
        FileStream fs2 = new FileStream(filePath2,FileMode.Create, FileAccess.Write);

        // As above, but other streams don't get access to the file while fs3 is open
        FileStream fs3 = new FileStream(filePath3, FileMode.Create,
                        FileAccess.Write, FileShare.None);
```

As this code reveals, the overloads of these constructors have the effect of providing default values of `FileAccess.ReadWrite()` and `FileShare.Read()` to the third and fourth parameters depending on the `FileMode` value. It is also possible to create a file stream from a `FileInfo` instance in various ways:

```
        FileInfo myFile4 = new FileInfo(filePath4);
        FileStream fs4 = myFile4.OpenRead();

        FileInfo myFile5= new FileInfo(filePath5);
        FileStream fs5 = myFile5.OpenWrite();

        FileInfo myFile6= new FileInfo(filePath6);
        FileStream fs6 = myFile6.Open(FileMode.Append,
                        FileAccess.Write, FileShare.None);

        FileInfo myFile7 = new FileInfo(filePath7);
        FileStream fs7 = myFile7.Create();
```

`FileInfo.OpenRead()` supplies a stream that gives you read-only access to an existing file, whereas `FileInfo.OpenWrite()` gives you read-write access. `FileInfo.Open()` allows you to specify the mode, access, and file share parameters explicitly.

Of course, after you have finished with a stream, you should close it:

```
        fs.Close();
```

Closing the stream frees up the resources associated with it and allows other applications to set up streams to the same file. This action also flushes the buffer. In between opening and closing the stream, you should read data from it and/or write data to it. `FileStream` implements a number of methods to do this.

`ReadByte()` is the simplest way of reading data. It grabs 1 byte from the stream and casts the result to an `int` that has a value between 0 and 255. If you have reached the end of the stream, it returns -1:

```
        int NextByte = fs.ReadByte();
```

If you prefer to read a number of bytes at a time, you can call the `Read()` method, which reads a specified number of bytes into an array. `Read()` returns the number of bytes actually read — if this value is zero, you know that you are at the end of the stream. Here is an example where you read into a byte array called `ByteArray`:

```
        int nBytesRead = fs.Read(ByteArray, 0, nBytes);
```

The second parameter to `Read()` is an offset, which you can use to request that the `Read` operation start populating the array at some element other than the first. The third parameter is the number of bytes to read into the array.

If you want to write data to a file, two parallel methods are available, `WriteByte()` and `Write()`. `WriteByte()` writes a single byte to the stream:

```
byte NextByte = 100;
fs.WriteByte(NextByte);
```

`Write()`, however, writes out an array of bytes. For instance, if you initialized the `ByteArray` mentioned before with some values, you could use the following code to write out the first `nBytes` of the array:

```
fs.Write(ByteArray, 0, nBytes);
```

As with `Read()`, the second parameter allows you to start writing from some point other than the beginning of the array. Both `WriteByte()` and `Write()` return `void`.

In addition to these methods, `FileStream` implements various other methods and properties related to bookkeeping tasks such as determining how many bytes are in the stream, locking the stream, or flushing the buffer. These other methods are not usually required for basic reading and writing, but if you need them, full details are in the SDK documentation.

Reading and Writing to Text Files

Theoretically, it is perfectly possible to use the `FileStream` class to read in and display text files. Having said that, if you know that a particular file contains text, you will usually find it more convenient to read and write it using the `StreamReader` and `StreamWriter` classes instead of the `FileStream` class. That is because these classes work at a slightly higher level and are specifically geared to reading and writing text. The methods that they implement are able to automatically detect convenient points to stop reading text, based on the contents of the stream. In particular:

➤ These classes implement methods to read or write one line of text at a time, `StreamReader.ReadLine()` and `StreamWriter.WriteLine()`. In the case of reading, this means that the stream automatically determines for you where the next carriage return is and stops reading at that point. In the case of writing, it means that the stream automatically appends the carriage return–line feed combination to the text that it writes out.

➤ By using the `StreamReader` and `StreamWriter` classes, you do not need to worry about the encoding (the text format) used in the file. Possible encodings include ASCII (1 byte for each character), or any of the Unicode-based formats: Unicode, UTF7, UTF8, and UTF32. The convention is that if the file is in ASCII format, it simply contains the text. If it is in any Unicode format, this is indicated by the first 2 or 3 bytes of the file, which are set to particular combinations of values to indicate the format used in the file.

These bytes are known as the *byte code markers*. When you open a file using any of the standard Windows applications, such as Notepad or WordPad, you do not need to worry about this because these applications are aware of the different encoding methods and will automatically read the file correctly. This is also true for the `StreamReader` class, which correctly reads in a file in any of these formats, and the `StreamWriter` class is capable of formatting the text it writes out using whatever encoding technique you request. If you want to read in and display a text file using the `FileStream` class, however, you need to handle this yourself.

Using the StreamReader Class

`StreamReader` is used to read text files. Constructing a `StreamReader` is in some ways easier than constructing a `FileStream` instance because some of the `FileStream` options are not required when using `StreamReader`. In particular, the mode and access types are not relevant to `StreamReader` because the only thing you can do with a `StreamReader` is read! Furthermore, there is no direct option to specify the sharing permissions. However, you have a couple of new options:

> You need to specify what to do about the different encoding methods. You can instruct the `StreamReader` to examine the byte code markers in the beginning of the file to determine the encoding method, or you can simply tell the `StreamReader` to assume that the file uses a specified encoding method.

> Instead of supplying a filename to be read from, you can supply a reference to another stream.

This last option deserves a bit more discussion because it illustrates another advantage of basing the model for reading and writing data on the concept of streams. Because the `StreamReader` works at a relatively high level, you might find it useful if you have another stream that is there to read data from some other source. Instead, you can use the facilities provided by `StreamReader` to process that other stream as if it contained text. You can do so by simply passing the output from this stream to a `StreamReader`. In this way, `StreamReader` can be used to read and process data from any data source — not only files. This is essentially the situation discussed earlier with regard to the `BinaryReader` class. However, in this book you use only `StreamReader` to connect directly to files.

The result of these possibilities is that `StreamReader` has a large number of constructors. Not only that, but there is another `FileInfo` method that returns a `StreamReader` reference: `OpenText()`. The following code illustrates just some of the constructors.

The simplest constructor takes just a filename. This `StreamReader` examines the byte order marks to determine the encoding:

```
string filePath =
    Environment.GetFolderPath(Environment.SpecialFolder.MyDocuments) +
    @"\MyFile.txt";
StreamReader sr = new StreamReader(filePath);
```

Alternatively, you can specify that UTF8 encoding should be assumed:

```
StreamReader sr = new StreamReader(filePath, Encoding.UTF8);
```

You specify the encoding by using one of several properties on a class, `System.Text.Encoding`. This class is an abstract base class, from which a number of classes are derived and which implements methods that actually perform the text encoding. Each property returns an instance of the appropriate class, and the possible properties you can use are:

> `ASCII`

> `Unicode`

> `UTF7`

➤ UTF8

➤ UTF32

➤ BigEndianUnicode

The following example demonstrates how to hook up a `StreamReader` to a `FileStream`. The advantage of this is that you can specify whether to create the file and the share permissions, which you cannot do if you directly attach a `StreamReader` to the file:

```
string filePath =
    Environment.GetFolderPath(Environment.SpecialFolder.MyDocuments) +
    @"\MyFile.txt";
FileStream fs = new FileStream(filePath, FileMode.Open,
                    FileAccess.Read, FileShare.None);
StreamReader sr = new StreamReader(fs);
```

For this example, you specify that the `StreamReader` will look for byte code markers to determine the encoding method used, as it will do in the following examples, in which the `StreamReader` is obtained from a `FileInfo` instance:

```
string filePath =
    Environment.GetFolderPath(Environment.SpecialFolder.MyDocuments) +
    @"\MyFile.txt";
FileInfo myFile = new FileInfo(filePath);
StreamReader sr = myFile.OpenText();
```

Just as with a `FileStream`, you should always close a `StreamReader` after use. Failure to do so results in the file remaining locked to other processes (unless you used a `FileStream` to construct the `StreamReader` and specified `FileShare.ShareReadWrite`):

```
sr.Close();
```

Now that you have gone to the trouble of instantiating a `StreamReader`, you can do something with it. As with the `FileStream`, you will simply see the various ways to read data, and the other, less commonly used `StreamReader` methods are left to the SDK documentation.

Possibly the easiest method to use is `ReadLine()`, which keeps reading until it gets to the end of a line. It does not include the carriage return–line feed combination that marks the end of the line in the returned string:

```
string nextLine = sr.ReadLine();
```

Alternatively, you can grab the entire remainder of the file (or strictly, the remainder of the stream) in one string:

```
string restOfStream = sr.ReadToEnd();
```

You can read a single character:

```
int nextChar = sr.Read();
```

This overload of `Read()` casts the returned character to an `int`. This is so that it has the option of returning a value of `-1` if the end of the stream has been reached.

Finally, you can read a given number of characters into an array, with an offset:

```
// to read 100 characters in.

int nChars = 100;
char [] charArray = new char[nChars];
int nCharsRead = sr.Read(charArray, 0, nChars);
```

nCharsRead will be less than nChars if you have requested to read more characters than are left in the file.

Using the StreamWriter Class

This works in the same way as StreamReader, except that you can use StreamWriter only to write to a file (or to another stream). Possibilities for constructing a StreamWriter include this:

```
string filePath =
    Environment.GetFolderPath(Environment.SpecialFolder.MyDocuments) +
    @"\MyFile.txt";
StreamWriter sw = new StreamWriter(filePath);
```

This uses UTF8 encoding, which is regarded by .NET as the default encoding method. If you want, you can specify alternative encoding:

```
StreamWriter sw = new StreamWriter(filePath, true, Encoding.ASCII);
```

In this constructor, the second parameter is a Boolean that indicates whether the file should be opened for appending. There is, oddly, no constructor that takes only a filename and an encoding class.

Of course, you may want to hook up StreamWriter to a file stream to give you more control over the options for opening the file:

```
FileStream fs = new FileStream(filePath, FileMode.CreateNew,
                    FileAccess.Write, FileShare.Read);
StreamWriter sw = new StreamWriter(fs);
```

FileStream does not implement any methods that return a StreamWriter class.

Alternatively, use the following sequence to create a new file and start writing data to it:

```
FileInfo myFile = new FileInfo(filePath);
StreamWriter sw = myFile.CreateText();
```

Just as with all other stream classes, it is important to close a StreamWriter class when you are finished with it:

```
sw.Close();
```

Writing to the stream is done using any of the many overloads of StreamWriter.Write(). The simplest option to writing out a string:

```
string nextLine = "Groovy Line";
sw.Write(nextLine);
```

You can write out a single character:

```
char nextChar = 'a';
sw.Write(nextChar);
```

And an array of characters:

```
char [] charArray = new char[100];

// initialize these characters

sw.Write(charArray);
```

You can even write out a portion of an array of characters:

```
int nCharsToWrite = 50;
int startAtLocation = 25;
char [] charArray = new char[100];

// initialize these characters

sw.Write(charArray, startAtLocation, nCharsToWrite);
```

USING ISOLATED STORAGE OPTIONS

One nice thing about working with .NET applications is that if you need to store things like user settings or even state from your application, you can make use of a multitude of different options. One of the newest options is termed *isolated storage*.

Think of isolated storage as a virtual disk where you can save items that can be shared only by the application that created them, or with other application instances. Isolated storage provides two means to access it. The first is by application and the second is by site.

When accessing isolated storage by application, there is a single storage location on the machine, which is then accessible on an application-by-application basis. Access to this storage location is guaranteed through the user identity and the application identity.

The other type of access for isolated storage is based on the site. In this case, you can have multiple applications using the same isolated storage as long as the applications reside from the same site.

Reading and Writing from Isolated Storage

As an example of writing and reading from isolated storage, create a new Silverlight application and produce a UI that is similar what is shown in Figure 16-20.

For this, there are really two operations — one to save items to isolated storage and another to read the settings out. The save operation is presented in Listing 16-21.

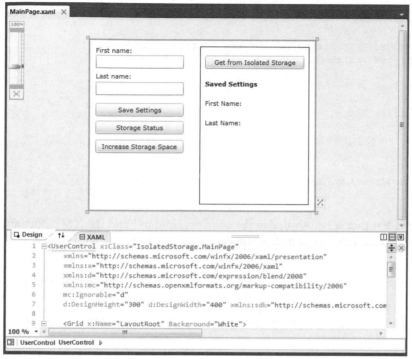

FIGURE 16-20

Available for
download on
Wrox.com

LISTING 16-21: Save settings to isolated storage

```csharp
private void btnSave_Click(object sender, RoutedEventArgs e)
{
    using (IsolatedStorageFile isf =
        IsolatedStorageFile.GetUserStoreForApplication())
    {
        using (IsolatedStorageFileStream isoStream =
            new IsolatedStorageFileStream("MainSettings.xml",
            FileMode.Create, isf))
        {
            XmlWriterSettings settings = new XmlWriterSettings();
            settings.Indent = true;

            using (XmlWriter writer = XmlWriter.Create(isoStream, settings))
            {
                writer.WriteStartElement("UserSettings");

                writer.WriteStartElement("firstName");
                writer.WriteString(txtFirstName.Text);
                writer.WriteEndElement();

                writer.WriteStartElement("lastName");
```

continues

```
                writer.WriteString(txtLastName.Text);
                writer.WriteEndElement();

                writer.WriteEndElement();

                writer.Flush();
            }
        }
    }

    MessageBox.Show("Settings applied.");
}
```

There is a bit of code here, but that is mainly due to the code required to build the XML document that is then placed within isolated storage. The first important thing happening with this code is presented here:

```
using (IsolatedStorageFile isf = IsolatedStorageFile.GetUserStoreForApplication())
{
        using (IsolatedStorageFileStream isoStream =
            new IsolatedStorageFileStream("MainSettings.xml", FileMode.Create,
            isf))
        {
```

Here, an instance of an `IsolatedStorageFile` is created using a user and application type of access. A stream is then created using the `IsolatedStorageFileStream` object, which creates the virtual `MainSettings.xml` file.

From there, an `XmlWriter` object is created to build the XML document and the XML contents are written to the `IsolatedStorageFileStream` object instance:

```
XmlWriterSettings settings = new XmlWriterSettings();
settings.Indent = true;

using (XmlWriter writer = XmlWriter.Create(isoStream, settings))
{
    // code removed for clarity
}
```

After the `XmlWriter` object is created, all the values are written to the XML document node by node. When everything is written to the XML document, everything is closed and is stored in the isolated storage.

Reading from isolated storage is done through the other button-click event. This is demonstrated in Listing 16-22.

LISTING 16-22: Reading data from isolated storage

```
private void btnGet_Click(object sender, RoutedEventArgs e)
{
```

```
using (IsolatedStorageFile isf =
    IsolatedStorageFile.GetUserStoreForApplication())
{
    StreamReader storStream =
        new StreamReader(new IsolatedStorageFileStream("MainSettings.xml",
            FileMode.Open, isf));

    XmlReaderSettings xmlReaderSettings = new XmlReaderSettings();

    xmlReaderSettings.IgnoreWhitespace = true;
    xmlReaderSettings.IgnoreComments = true;
    xmlReaderSettings.CheckCharacters = true;

    XmlReader xmlReader = XmlReader.Create(storStream, xmlReaderSettings);

    while (xmlReader.Read())
    {
        if (xmlReader.NodeType == XmlNodeType.Element &&
            "firstName" == xmlReader.LocalName)
        {
            lblFirstName.Content = "First Name: " +
                xmlReader.ReadElementContentAsString();
        }

        if (xmlReader.NodeType == XmlNodeType.Element &&
            "lastName" == xmlReader.LocalName)
        {
            lblLastName.Content = "Last Name: " +
                xmlReader.ReadElementContentAsString();
        }
    }

    xmlReader.Close();
}
```

Using this button-click event, the `MainSettings.xml` document is pulled from the isolated storage and then placed into a stream and parsed using the `XmlReader` object:

```
using (IsolatedStorageFile isf = IsolatedStorageFile.GetUserStoreForApplication())
{
    StreamReader storStream =
        new StreamReader(new IsolatedStorageFileStream("MainSettings.xml",
        FileMode.Open, isf));

    // code removed for clarity
}
```

After the XML document is contained within the `IsolatedStorageFileStream` object, it is parsed using the `XmlReader` object:

```
XmlReaderSettings xmlReaderSettings = new XmlReaderSettings();

xmlReaderSettings.IgnoreWhitespace = true;
```

```
xmlReaderSettings.IgnoreComments = true;
xmlReaderSettings.CheckCharacters = true;

XmlReader xmlReader = XmlReader.Create(storStream, xmlReaderSettings);
```

After the document is pulled from the stream via the `XmlReader`, the element values are then pushed back into the application.

Understanding Space Constraints

Isolated storage is a limited resource. When you are running a standard Silverlight application, the default limit is set at 1MB. If you are running your Silverlight application in an out-of-browser mode, you actually have a much larger space to work with — 25 MB.

Through your application, you can determine how much space the end user actually has on the machine and, if required, you can request more space than the default allotment. Listing 16-23 shows an example of understanding the space utilized on the end user's machine.

LISTING 16-23: Understanding space constraints

```csharp
private void btnStatus_Click(object sender, RoutedEventArgs e)
{
    try
    {
        using (var isf = IsolatedStorageFile.GetUserStoreForApplication())
        {
            string spaceUsed = (isf.Quota - isf.AvailableFreeSpace).ToString();
            string spaceAvailableFreeSpace = isf.AvailableFreeSpace.ToString();
            string quota = isf.Quota.ToString();
            MessageBox.Show(
                String.Format("Used: {1} bytes\nAvailable: {2} bytes\nQuota: {0}
                        bytes", quota, spaceUsed, spaceAvailableFreeSpace));
        }
    }
    catch (IsolatedStorageException)
    {
        MessageBox.Show("Unable to access store.");
    }
}
```

Here, you can see that the `IsolatedStorageFile` object allows you to get at the quota and the amount of available space. This information, along with some minor math to figure out the amount of space utilized, is then presented in a message box dialog as shown in Figure 16-21.

If you don't have enough space, you need to request more from the end user (see Listing 16-24).

FIGURE 16-21

LISTING 16-24: Requesting more space from the end user

```csharp
private void btnIncrease_Click(object sender, RoutedEventArgs e)
{
    try
    {
        using (var isf = IsolatedStorageFile.GetUserStoreForApplication())
        {
            Int64 spaceRequested = 1048576; // 1mb
            Int64 spaceAvailableFreeSpace = isf.AvailableFreeSpace;

            if (spaceAvailableFreeSpace < spaceRequested)
            {
                if (!isf.IncreaseQuotaTo(store.Quota + spaceRequested))
                {
                    MessageBox.Show("Sorry you don't want the additional space!");
                }
                else
                {
                    MessageBox.Show("Great! Thanks for the extra space!");
                }
            }
            MessageBox.Show("You already have 1mb available.");
        }
    }
    catch (IsolatedStorageException ex)
    {
        MessageBox.Show("Something went wrong in assigning more space.\n\n" +
            ex.Message);
    }
}
```

In this example, an additional 1 MB of space is requested from the end user using the
`isf.IncreaseQuotaTo()` method call. In this case, it is only done if there is not even that
amount of space available to the application. It is important to understand that your application
can request only additional space. You cannot decrease the amount of space available.

Creating Directories in Isolated Storage

So far, you have been working with files in isolated storage that are stored in the root location that
you are working with. In the space provided to your Silverlight application, you can treat this as if
it were a filesystem that you can work with (in fact, that's what it really is). This means that you are
able to create things like directories and subdirectories quite easily.

Listing 16-25 shows an example of creating a directory in isolated storage.

LISTING 16-25: Creating a directory in isolated storage

```csharp
using (var isf = IsolatedStorageFile.GetUserStoreForApplication())
{
    isf.CreateDirectory("MyDirectory1");
```

continues

LISTING 16-25 *(continued)*

```
        isf.CreateDirectory("MyDirectory2");
        isf.CreateDirectory("MyDirectory3");
        isf.CreateDirectory("MyDirectory4");
    }
```

In this example, four distinct directories are created with the names of MyDirectory1, MyDirectory2, and so on. To use your file within one of these directories, use a construct similar to what is presented in Listing 16-26.

LISTING 16-26: Saving a file within your directory

```
using (IsolatedStorageFile isf = IsolatedStorageFile.GetUserStoreForApplication())
{
        string directoryPath = "MyDirectory1";

        using (IsolatedStorageFileStream isoStream =
          new IsolatedStorageFileStream(Path.Combine(directoryPath,
            "MainSettings.xml"), FileMode.Create, isf))
        {
           // code removed for clarity
        }
}
```

You can then create subdirectories as presented in Listing 16-27.

LISTING 16-27: Creating subdirectories

```
using (var isf = IsolatedStorageFile.GetUserStoreForApplication())
{
    isf.CreateDirectory("MyDirectory1");
    isf.CreateDirectory("MyDirectory2");
    isf.CreateDirectory("MyDirectory3");
    isf.CreateDirectory("MyDirectory4");

    isf.CreateDirectory(Path.Combine("MyDirectory1", "MySubDirectory1"));
}
```

You end up using the exact same method, `CreateDirectory()`, to create sub-directories.

Deleting Your Store

Now that you have looked at creating your isolated store, you need to know how to delete the store. You do this by simply using the `Remove()` method as illustrated in Listing 16-28.

LISTING 16-28: Deleting your store

```
isf.Remove()
MessageBox.Show("Your isolated store has been deleted.");
```

SUMMARY

In this chapter, you examined how to use the .NET base classes to access the filesystem from your application code. You have seen that in both cases the base classes expose simple, but powerful, object models that make it very simple to perform almost any kind of action in these areas. For the filesystem, these actions are copying files; moving, creating, and deleting files and folders; and reading and writing both binary and text files.

This chapter also reviewed isolated storage and how to use this from your applications to store them in the application state.

17

Using Graphics and Visuals

WHAT'S IN THIS CHAPTER?

➤ Working with shapes and paths

➤ Referencing images and media

➤ Defining and applying custom effects

➤ Transforming elements in 2D and 3D

Silverlight includes all of the core primitive elements you would expect in a platform designed to provide a compelling visual experience. These basic elements include the `Rectangle`, `Ellipse`, `Path`, `Image`, and `MediaElement` controls. Expression Blend 4 introduces a new library of shape elements, empowering you to easily create stars, hexagons, talk bubbles, arrows, and arcs. In addition to these shapes and controls, Silverlight includes bitmap effects, support for HLSL shaders, and Perspective 3D. These last three items can empower a limitless array of visual effects in your applications. This chapter starts by covering the basic building block controls and how they are defined in XAML to provide a firm foundation of understanding. Along the way, you see how to use Expression Blend to save some time by creating these elements on the design surface. Finally, you see how both effects and 3D can fit into your application and look at the tooling that supports them.

THE BASICS

This section starts by looking at the core Silverlight controls at your disposal to create visuals. It looks at each control individually and covers XAML composition of that control. Along the way, I'll try to point out things you need to be aware of when working with particular controls.

Working with Rectangles and Borders

The Rectangle control can serve as a foundation for many UI elements. Most controls that you interact with on a daily basis are rectangular in nature: buttons, scrollbars, header element backgrounds, and so forth. Generally, these controls are not composed of a single rectangle, but multiple layered rectangles, each with varying shades of opacity, margins, and fills. Together these rectangles form the visuals you have come to expect from modern operat-

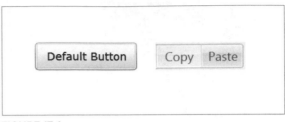

FIGURE 17-1

ing systems and applications. Figure 17-1 calls out the nested rectangles used to create the Office 2007 Ribbon control and the default Silverlight button.

The following XAML defines a lime-green Rectangle that is 100 pixels wide by 20 pixels tall:

```
<Rectangle Width="100" Height="20" Fill="#FFCCFF00" />
```

Applying Rounded Corners

You might have noticed in Figure 17-1 that both examples had rounded corners. This is easily achieved in Silverlight by setting the RadiusX and RadiusY properties on the Rectangle control. The following XAML defines a Rectangle with uniformly rounded corners, each with a 5-pixel corner radius:

```
<Rectangle Height="20" Width="80" Fill="#CCFF00" RadiusX="5" RadiusY="5" />
```

Both the RadiusX and RadiusY properties have the same value as in the previous example. These values do not have to be the same, however. By increasing the value on either axis, you'll see that the corner begins to skew either horizontally or vertically, depending on which property value is greater. Figure 17-2 demonstrates the effect on each axis when one corner radius value is greater than the other.

FIGURE 17-2

Understanding Pixel-Based Values

It's important to note once again that the corner radius values are pixel-based and not percentage-based. So, if you set the corner radius to 5, the amount of curvature on each corner will remain the same whether your rectangle is 100 pixels wide or 100 pixels high. Some design programs store the corner radius as a percentage of the object's size, so a corner radius of 10 would be 10 pixels for a rectangle 100 pixels wide and 100 pixels for a rectangle 1,000 pixels wide. That is always frustrating for me, so I'm glad Silverlight implements these as pixel values rather than percentage values.

Comparing Rectangles to Borders

You may be wondering why `Border` is included in a discussion about drawing primitives. The `Border` control is actually a `FrameworkElement`-derived control that can accept child content, and not a primitive drawing element. The `Border` control provides a key feature that the `Rectangle` control does not — individual control over each corner's radius! This means that you can have a "rectangle" whose top-left and top-right corners are rounded, while its bottom corners remain square. With the `Rectangle` control, it's an all-or-nothing proposition. The following XAML defines a lime-green `Border` that is 100 pixels wide by 20 pixels tall, with its top-left and top-right corners rounded on a 5-pixel radius:

```
<Border
    Width="80" Height="20"
    Background="#CCFF00"
    CornerRadius="5,5,0,0"/>
```

The Border's `CornerRadius` property provides the corner-by-corner flexibility that makes this control so useful. The `CornerRadius` property has four properties that let you specify the corner radius for each corner: `TopLeft`, `TopRight`, `BottomRight`, and `BottomLeft`. The preceding XAML demonstrates how these properties can be set inline with comma-delimited values. The following pseudo-XAML represents the order in which these values are applied to each corner:

```
<Border CornerRadius="TopLeft, TopRight, BottomRight, BottomLeft" />
```

Nesting Borders

The `Border` element, unlike the `Rectangle`, has a `Child` property and supports nested content. This means that you can create a series of nested `Border`s housed by a single parent `Border`. You set the `Padding` property on each `Border` to create inset effects with each child `Border`. The following XAML demonstrates how three nested `Border`s can be used to create a shiny button, as shown in Figure 17-3:

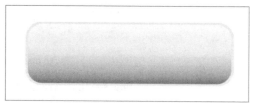

FIGURE 17-3

Available for download on Wrox.com

```
<Border
    Opacity="1"
    HorizontalAlignment="Left"
    VerticalAlignment="Top"
    Margin="281.031005859375,250,0,0"
    CornerRadius="14.805,14.805,14.805,14.805"
    Background="#ccff00" Width="208" Height="63" Padding="2,2,2,2">
    <Border
        Opacity="1"
```

```
            HorizontalAlignment="Stretch"
            VerticalAlignment="Stretch"
            CornerRadius="14.1,14.1,14.1,14.1">
            <Border.Background>
                <LinearGradientBrush
                    StartPoint="0.5098039215686274,0.35"
                    EndPoint="0.5098039215686274,1.0478118896484374">
                    <LinearGradientBrush.GradientStops>
                        <GradientStopCollection>
                            <GradientStop
                                Color="#00ccff00"
                                Offset="0" />
                            <GradientStop
                                Color="#FF5e7500"
                                Offset="1" />
                        </GradientStopCollection>
                    </LinearGradientBrush.GradientStops>
                </LinearGradientBrush>
            </Border.Background>
            <Border
            Opacity="1"
            HorizontalAlignment="Stretch"
            VerticalAlignment="Stretch"
            Margin="0,0,0,27"
            CornerRadius="13.8,13.8,13.8,13.8">
            <Border.Background>
                <LinearGradientBrush
                    StartPoint="0.3872549019607843,-0.08571428571428572"
                    EndPoint="0.3872549019607843,1.2612723214285715">
                    <LinearGradientBrush.GradientStops>
                        <GradientStopCollection>
                            <GradientStop
                                Color="#FFffffff"
                                Offset="0" />
                            <GradientStop
                                Color="#00ffffff"
                                Offset="1" />
                        </GradientStopCollection>
                    </LinearGradientBrush.GradientStops>
                </LinearGradientBrush>
            </Border.Background>
        </Border>
    </Border>
    </Border>
</Border>
```

Brushes.xaml

So, you now have two tools in your arsenal to create rectangle-based shapes. The Rectangle is a lighter control, so you'll probably want to go with it for most cases, but, when you need to specifically target individual corners, the Border is your best friend.

Using the Ellipse

The `Ellipse` control is used to define both circles and ellipses and is just as easy to define as the `Rectangle`. In fact, the following XAML is the same XAML you started with for `Rectangle` but with the term *Ellipse* instead of *Rectangle*:

```
<Ellipse Width="100" Height="20" Fill="#FFCCFF00" />
```

This XAML results in an oval 100 pixels wide by 20 pixels high, as shown in Figure 17-4.

FIGURE 17-4

To create a circle, just set the `Height` and `Width` to the same value.

Using the Path

Whereas the `Rectangle` and `Ellipse` controls are used to customize predefined, familiar shapes, the `Path` control is used to represent *any* shape. Like the `Rectangle` and `Ellipse`, the `Path` control includes `Height` and `Width` properties, but unlike `Rectangle` or `Ellipse`, the `Path` control has a `Data` property that is used to define the point data that makes up the shape. And although you can hand-code the path data, you'll likely do that only in the most basic of cases and instead rely on a tool like Expression Blend to actually define artwork.

Defining and Understanding Path Data

Start by looking at simple path data, then you can move on to additional properties on the `Path` control that define the way the shape is ultimately rendered. The following XAML defines a 10×10 square purely using path data, also known as the path mini-language:

```
<Path
       HorizontalAlignment="Left" VerticalAlignment="Top"
       Stroke="#FF000000" Data="M0,0 L10,0 L10,10 L0,10 L0,0 z"/>
```

Figure 17-5 shows this `Path` rendered in Expression Blend.

FIGURE 17-5

The path data `"M0,0 L10,0 L10,10 L0,10 L0,0 z"` may look a little cryptic at first, but once you know the basic structure, I think you'll find it quite readable. All paths consist of a starting point (defined by an X,Y-coordinate pair), followed by a series of subsequent points. In the data string for this rectangle path, think of *M* as "MoveTo" and *L* as "LineTo." The result reads more like a sentence: `"MoveTo 0,0 LineTo 10,0 LineTo 10,10 LineTo 0,10 LineTo 0,0 z"`. The z closes the path.

The next XAML defines a circle purely using path data:

```
<Path Fill="#FFCCFF00" Stretch="Fill" Stroke="#FF000000"
    Data="M50.147999,25.323999 C50.147999,39.033916 39.033916,50.147999
        25.323999,50.147999 C11.614083,50.147999 0.5,39.033916
        0.5,25.323999 C0.5,11.614083 11.614083,0.5 25.323999,0.5
        C39.033916,0.5 50.147999,11.614083 50.147999,25.323999 z" />
```

Figure 17-6 shows this path rendered in Expression Blend.

Whereas the rectangle's path data consists of a series of straight lines, the circle consists of a series of curves. Instead of a simple X,Y pair representing each point on the path, the circle's points are represented by three X,Y pairs to define a Bezier point. The first and third X,Y pairs define the tension handles, and the second pair defines the anchor point. Figure 17-7 shows a selected point in Expression Blend. The selected point is solid, with its two tension points denoted by circles drawn at the end of the tangent line.

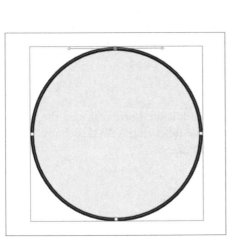

FIGURE 17-6

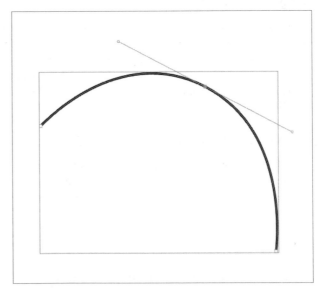

FIGURE 17-7

The path data `"M50.147999,25.323999 C50.147999,39.033916 39.033916,50.147999 25.323999,50.147999 C11.614083,50.147999 0.5,39.033916 0.5,25.323999 C0.5,11.614083 11.614083,0.5 25.323999,0.5 C39.033916,0.5 50.147999,11.614083 50.147999,25.323999 z"` for the circle is a bit more complex than that of the rectangle, but again with a little string substitution the data will read like a sentence. This time, think of *M* as "MoveTo" and *C* as "CurveTo." You'll end up with a sentence that reads like `"MoveTo x,y CurveTo x,y x,y x,y CurveTo x,y x,y x,y..."`.

The following XAML mixes things up a bit by combining both `LineTo` and `CurveTo` points:

```
Data="M74.833336,76.333336 L85.5,76.333336 C85.5,76.333336
    87.666351,83.250168 80.083427,83.250168 C72.500504,83.250168
    74.833336,76.333336 74.833336,76.333336 z"
```

With your new understanding of the path data syntax, you can now recognize that this path starts with a line segment, followed by two Bezier points. However, unless you're some type of savant, you probably can't read the data and immediately picture the path that will be rendered. That's why, as I said before, you'll likely use a design tool to define paths.

Try removing the closing z and see what your `Path` *looks like. Its absence will be more noticeable if you've set both the* `Stroke` *and* `StrokeThickness` *properties and if your last point is a considerable distance away from your starting point.*

Defining the Path Resize Behavior

When you defined the rectangle as a `Path`, the first point of your path data was (0,0). However, when you drew the circle, the starting point was approximately (75,76). When the circle was rendered on the screen, it didn't actually start at the point (75,76). Instead, Silverlight drew the circle artwork based on several properties on the `Path` control, taking into account the `Path`'s `Width`, `Height`, `HorizontalAlignment`, `VerticalAlignment`, and `Margin`. The underlying path data was normalized to the top-left corner of the `Path` control.

When the `Path` control is resized, the actual size of the control will differ from that of the underlying path data. You can define how the underlying data is rendered by setting the `Stretch` property. The `Stretch` property accepts one of the following values:

> `Fill` (Default) — The artwork is stretched both vertically and horizontally, filling the `Path` control. This is the behavior you most likely expect if you are coming to Silverlight from the design world.

> `None` — The underlying artwork does not stretch at all.

Expression Blend strives to create a design-time experience that is consistent with other design tools. As you resize and move `Paths` *on the stage, the underlying path data is sometimes modified, along with the height, width, and alignment properties. This results in a* `Stretch` *property that does not always behave the way you would expect if you were hand-coding all of your XAML.*

> `Uniform` — The underlying artwork maintains its original shape and aspect ratio while scaling to fit within the control. With this mode the shape is always drawn in its entirety.

➤ UniformToFill — The underlying artwork maintains its original shape and aspect ratio, although if the aspect ratio of the containing Path control differs from the underlying path data, the path will be clipped.

Figure 17-8 demonstrates how these different stretch modes affect the final rendering of a Path.

FIGURE 17-8

Using Geometries

You spent some time looking at the path mini-language to define a Path and came to the conclusion that you probably wouldn't be hand-coding this data very often. In cases where do you want to hand-code paths, you can use alternative Geometry classes via XAML to make this process less abstract.

The Path's Data property is actually of type Geometry. At run time, the path mini-language is interpreted and converted to the geometries you're about to take a look at. Start with the RectangleGeometry class. Using the mini-language to define a 20×10 rectangle, the Data would look like "M0,0 L20,0 L20,10 L0,10 C". You can achieve the same result using a RectangleGeometry:

```
<Path
    Fill="#FFB5DA40"
    UseLayoutRounding="False"
    Stretch="Uniform">
    <Path.Data>
        <RectangleGeometry Rect="0,0,20,10"/>
    </Path.Data>
</Path>
```

The Rect property accepts four parameters (Left, Top, Width, and Height), so this code tells the RectangleGeometry to draw a rectangle that is 20 pixels wide by 10 pixels tall, positioned at (0,0). Though more verbose than the path mini-language, this XAML is much easier to read and understand. In addition to the RectangleGeometry class, the following Geometries are available for you to work with:

➤ EllipseGeometry

➤ LineGeometry

➤ PathGeometry

Both the `EllipseGeometry` and `LineGeometry` are used by themselves like the `RectangleGeometry`. The following XAML defines a circle, centered at (100,100) with a radius of 50:

```
<EllipseGeometry Center="100,100" RadiusX="50" RadiusY="50"/>
```

With similar simplicity, the `LineGeometry` expects start and end points:

```
<LineGeometry StartPoint="0,0" EndPoint="100,100"/>
```

And that's how you define a line that starts at (0,0) and runs diagonally to (100,100).

Defining Complex Shapes

Once your geometry needs grow beyond basic rectangles, ellipses, and straight lines, you'll need to turn to the `PathGeometry` object. The `PathGeometry` object accepts a collection of `PathFigure` objects, which in turn accept a collection of any number and order of `PathSegment` objects:

- ➤ `ArcSegment`

- ➤ `BezierSegment`

- ➤ `LineSegment`

- ➤ `PolyBezierSegment`

- ➤ `PolyLineSegment`

- ➤ `PolyQuadraticBezierSegment`

- ➤ `QuadraticBezierSegment`

The following XAML uses three `LineSegment`s to create a triangle:

```
<Path Fill="Black">
    <Path.Data>
        <PathGeometry>
            <PathGeometry.Figures>
                <PathFigure StartPoint="50,0" IsClosed="True">
                    <PathFigure.Segments>
                        <LineSegment Point="100,100"/>
                        <LineSegment Point="0,100"/>
                    </PathFigure.Segments>
                </PathFigure>
            </PathGeometry.Figures>
        </PathGeometry>
    </Path.Data>
</Path>
```

This sample is intentionally simple so that you can see the basic structure of a `PathGeometry`. You can add additional `PathFigure` objects to the Figures collection and combine any of the available `PathSegment` objects in the `PathFigure.Segments` collection to achieve the final illustration.

Expression Blend will not preserve your hand-coded PathGeometries. Any time you interact with a path on the design surface, hand-coded PathGeometry *syntax will be replaced with the mini-language syntax.*

Why Use PathGeometries?

PathGeometries are generally used procedurally (in code-behind) rather than in XAML. In fact, when working with Paths in Expression Blend, any hand-coded PathGeometries you've created will be blown away and replaced with the path mini-language. This is rarely a problem, because you're simply not creating complex geometries by hand. It doesn't make sense when you have a design surface and design tools at your disposal.

However, if you're dynamically generating masks or creating an application that itself has a design surface (like a simple paint program) you'll definitely become intimately involved with the PathGeometry classes.

Using Clipping/Masking Elements

When you want to prevent areas of an element from showing you can use what is known as a clipping mask. In Silverlight, this is achieved by setting the Clip property. Like the Data property of the Path, the Clip property is of type Geometry, which means you can use either the path mini-language or the full PathGeometry syntax to define a clipping path. The following XAML clips a Viewbox using an EllipseGeometry, resulting in the visual shown in Figure 17-9:

FIGURE 17-9

```
<Grid Height="213" Width="318">
    <Ellipse Fill="#FF3F3F3F" Height="211" Width="314"
        VerticalAlignment="Top"
        HorizontalAlignment="Left"/>
    <Viewbox Width="314" HorizontalAlignment="Left" VerticalAlignment="Top"
        Margin="4,4,0,0" >
        <Viewbox.Clip>
            <EllipseGeometry RadiusX="150" RadiusY="100" Center="150,100"/>
        </Viewbox.Clip>
        <Image Source="Images/PikesPlace.jpg" Stretch="Fill"
            Height="2023" Width="3038"/>
    </Viewbox>
</Grid>
```

Geometries.xaml

Just like working with `Paths`, it's much easier to use Expression Blend to do the heavy lifting for you when clipping objects. Simply define a path using the Expression Blend drawing tools, then size and position the path over the object you want to clip. Once you have the path positioned, select both the `Path` and the target object (hold down the Shift key to select multiple objects), then from the main menu, select Object ➪ Path ➪ Make Clipping Path. Figure 17-10 shows both a `MediaElement` and `Path` selected on the design surface with the command exposed on the main menu.

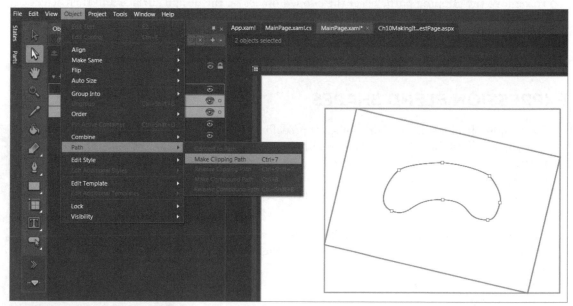

FIGURE 17-10

Notice that the `Path` is positioned directly over the `MediaElement` that I want to clip. You need to position the `Path` exactly where you want the visible area of the object to be before using the Make Clipping Path command. Expression Blend normalizes the values of the `Path` data to be relative to the top-left corner of the element being clipped. With clipping masks, (0,0) represents the top-left corner of the object being clipped, not the top-left corner of the design surface. Figure 17-11 shows the `MediaElement` after it has been clipped.

FIGURE 17-11

In the following XAML, you can see that the `Clip` property accepts the same path mini-language that you should be vaguely familiar with now. Try hand-editing a few points to see how the clipping mask is affected.

```
<MediaElement
    Width="320"
    Height="240"
    x:Name="meSampleVideo"
    Source="/SampleVideo.wmv"
    RenderTransformOrigin="0.5,0.5"
    Clip="M89.626343,47.989033 C89.626343,47.989033 1.9381521,109.92341
```

```
                    54.496151,126.16163 C107.05415,142.39984 88.938194,90.738899
                    141.32475,105.99192 C193.71132,121.24493 205.15047,87.790825
                    202.15236,82.222031 C199.15424,76.653236 186.56322,39.257092
                    151.01031,33.257763 C115.45742,27.258436 89.626343,47.989033
                    89.626343,47.989033 z">
        </MediaElement>
```

To remove the clipping path, select the clipped object on the design surface and then select Object ⇨ Path ⇨ Release Clipping Path from the main menu. To edit an existing clipping path on the design surface, you'll need to release the clipping path, edit the path, and then use the Make Clipping Path command once again.

EXPRESSION BLEND SHAPES

Expression Blend 4 ships with a number of predefined shapes that you can drag directly from the Asset Library to the design surface. This library adds to the simple `Rectangle` and `Ellipse` more complex shapes like `Star`, `Triangle`, `Ring`, `Pie`, and `Pentagon`. Figure 17-12 shows the new Shapes category selected in the Asset Library.

Although 18 shapes are listed in this library, there are actually only 5 underlying controls that have been preconfigured in 18 distinct ways:

FIGURE 17-12

> ➤ `Arc`

> ➤ `BlockArrow`

> ➤ `Callout`

> ➤ `LineArrow`

> ➤ `RegularPolygon`

The 18 preconfigured options represent a core set of desirable shapes, but you can create a much wider array of looks simply by adjusting a few properties on each control. For example, the `Star`, `Pentagon`, and `Hexagon` shapes are all created by adjusting the `InnerRadius` and `PointCount` properties of the `RegularPolygon` shape. Figure 17-13 shows the variety of shapes that can be created simply by dragging these preconfigured shapes onto the design surface.

When you create an instance of one of these new shapes, Expression Blend automatically adds a reference to the `Microsoft.Expression.Drawing` assembly and adds a new `ed` (Expression Design) namespace definition to your page. Figure 17-14 shows three customized `RegularPolygon` controls, and Listings 17-1 and 17-2 represent the underlying XAML. Note the required `<ed:/>` namespace prefix for these new shapes.

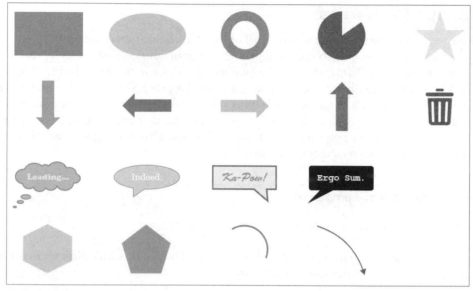

FIGURE 17-13

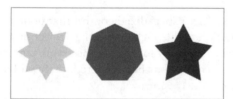

FIGURE 17-14

LISTING 17-1: Expression Design namespace definition

```
xmlns:ed="http://schemas.microsoft.com/expression/2010/drawing"
```

LISTING 17-2: Defining the RegularPolygon

```
<StackPanel Height="100" Orientation="Horizontal">
    <ed:RegularPolygon Fill="#FFB9E04B" InnerRadius="0.71" PointCount="8"
        Stretch="Fill" Width="100" Margin="0,0,20,0" StrokeThickness="4"/>
    <ed:RegularPolygon Fill="#FF6B4424" InnerRadius="1" PointCount="7"
        Stretch="Fill" Width="100" Margin="0,0,20,0"/>
    <ed:RegularPolygon Fill="#FF302D23" InnerRadius="0.652" PointCount="5"
        Stretch="Fill" Width="100" Margin="0,0,20,0"/>
</StackPanel>
```

RegularPolygon.xaml

Binding to Shape Properties

Because these custom shapes are actually controls, all of their customization points can be DataBound, which can open the door to some unique design opportunities. For example, suppose you want to show a progress indicator while you're loading something in the background. You can start with a `Pie` shape (actually a customized `Arc`) and bind a progress value to the `EndAngle` property of the `Arc`. The `EndAngle` range is 0 to 360, so you'll have to coerce your underlying percentage into a value in that range (where 50% == 180), but that's easily done. Listing 17-3 shows the `EndAngle` property bound to a property named `LoadProgress`. This binding assumes that the `DataContext` of my layout is set to a custom `ViewModel` object.

LISTING 17-3: Binding to shape properties

```
<ed:Arc EndAngle="{Binding LoadProgress}" StartAngle="0" />
```

This listing required a value of 360 to represent 100% progress. Though this isn't difficult to achieve programmatically, it does require additional manipulation.

IMAGES AND MEDIA

Images and media are dealt with similarly in Silverlight. Each has a specialized control that points to a source image or media file. The image or media can be either a file included in the project or an external file, possibly residing on a remote server. This section starts by looking at the `Image` control, then moves on to the `MediaElement` control. Once the `Image` control has been covered, there will just be a few more things to add to bring you up to speed with `MediaElement`.

Displaying Images

Even though Silverlight provides a vector-based rendering and layout engine, you're likely to use `Images` in your Silverlight applications. Whether you're creating a photo-browser, using an existing image-based icon library, or working with artwork from your design team, I'm sure you'll encounter the need to use an image at some point in your Silverlight career.

Using the Image Control

The `Image` control is used to display bitmap images in your Silverlight applications. The following XAML demonstrates how to display a photo that is 640×480 pixels in dimension, positioned 25 pixels from the left and top of its parent `Grid`:

```
<Image
    Source="myPhoto.jpg"
    HorizontalAlignment="Left"
    VerticalAlignment="Top"
    Margin="25,25,0,0"
    Stretch="Uniform" Width="640" />
```

Notice that the `Image` control has a `Stretch` property, just like the `Path` control. And, like the `Path` control, the available values for `Stretch` are `Fill`, `None`, `Uniform`, and `UniformToFill`. See the previous section, "Defining the Path Resize Behavior," to understand how these values affect the way the Image is resized.

 If the Height *and* Width *are not set or other sizing constraints (such as* Margins*) are not in place, the* Image *will be displayed at the native size of the underlying source image.*

Referencing Images

Images referenced via the Image control can be images compiled into the containing assembly, images that live inside the XAP file as siblings to your compiled assembly, images compiled as resources in other assemblies, loose images on your server (outside of the XAP), or images on a remote server. The following sections look at how each of these approaches is achieved and the pros and cons of each.

Compiling Images

An image is compiled into your project's assembly when its Build Action is set to Resource. This is the default approach taken by Expression Blend when you first reference an image.

 This is the same behavior you see in Flash when an image is imported and dragged onto the stage. It is compiled into the SWF file and does affect file size.

Adding an Image in Expression Blend

The Image control in Expression Blend is not exposed in the main Toolbox. You have to open the Asset Library, expand Controls, and select All, as shown in Figure 17-15. Select Image to make it the active control. You can now draw an Image control on the canvas, just like you create a rectangle, or you can double-click the Image icon to add a default-sized Image to the canvas.

Setting the Image Source

Once you've added an Image control to the surface, you need to set its Source property using the Properties panel. The Source property is located in the Common Properties category. If you've already added images to your project, those images should appear in the Source combo box. In Figure 17-16, you can click the ellipses to launch a File Browser dialog.

Once you've selected an image, that image will be copied to your project directory and added to the root folder of your project. Behind the scenes, the file's Build Action will be set to Resource. This is not something that you can change via the Expression Blend interface, but you can do so in Visual Studio. Figure 17-17 highlights both the Build Action and the Copy to Output Directory properties that are available in Visual Studio's Properties window when a file is selected. The scenarios that follow will require that you change these properties.

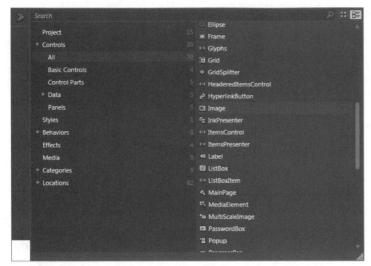

FIGURE 17-15

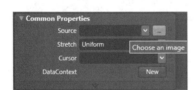

FIGURE 17-16

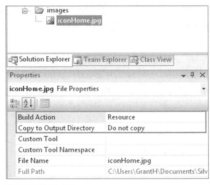

FIGURE 17-17

You reference an embedded image using a relative URL. If the image is in the root folder of your project, simply type its name. If the image is in a subfolder, such as Images, include the entire relative path. For example, the following XAML references an image stored in the Images/Icons subfolder of the project directory:

```
<Image HorizontalAlignment="Left" Margin="10,10,0,0" Width="72"
  Source="images/icons/iconHome.jpg"/>
```

You can also use a path that explicitly references the assembly in which this image is housed. If your Silverlight project name is MyProject, the previous XAML could be replaced by the following:

```
<Image HorizontalAlignment="Left" Margin="10,10,0,0" Width="72"
  Source="/MyProject;component/images/icons/iconHome.jpg"/>
```

The text in bold is key: /*MyProject*;component/.

The text /*MyProject* should be replaced with the name of your project, but ;component/ should remain at all times.

➤ **Pros** — Image is available immediately; simple relative path references; no security issues.

➤ **Cons** — Large images or large numbers of small images can bloat the assembly size and increase page load time.

Using XAP File Images

An image is included in the XAP file and is not compiled into the assembly when its Build Action is set to Content. When configured as Content, image files do not bloat the size of your project assembly, but they do continue to bloat the size of the XAP file. You might want to do this if you will be reusing the project assembly, but not the resources.

To reference the image in XAML, when images are included this way, you need to add a forward slash (/) before the path to the image:

```
<Image HorizontalAlignment="Left" Margin="10,10,0,0" Width="72"
  Source="/images/icons/iconHome.jpg"/>
```

➤ **Pros** — Image is available immediately; simple relative path references; no security issues; assembly size is reduced.

➤ **Cons** — Large images or large numbers of small images can bloat the XAP size and increase page load time.

Adding Loose Images

You can add images to your project that are not compiled into the project assembly or added to the XAP file. These files do not bloat either the assembly or the XAP file. To achieve this scenario, set the Build Action of your image to None and set Copy to Local Directory to Copy Always or Copy if Newer.

To reference the image in XAML, use the same syntax that you used with XAP file images, adding a forward slash to the URI:

```
<Image HorizontalAlignment="Left" Margin="10,10,0,0" Width="72"
  Source="/images/icons/iconHome.jpg"/>
```

➤ **Pros** — Assembly size is reduced; XAP size is reduced (faster page load time).

➤ **Cons** — Image is not loaded at page load; image loads asynchronously after the XAP is downloaded.

Use this scenario when you want to create a very lightweight, quick-loading application. You can then use the WebClient to download the image asynchronously and provide a "loading" experience.

Compiling Images in Other Assemblies

Just as images can be compiled in your main project assembly, images can be compiled in additional resource assemblies. These could be assemblies that you create yourself or they could be third-party assemblies. And, just like referencing images embedded in the project assembly, images in other assemblies can be referenced in XAML using a special syntax.

The following XAML references an image named `alienFace.png` defined in an assembly named `AlienImages.dll`:

```
<Image HorizontalAlignment="Left" Margin="10,10,0,0" Width="72"
  Source="/AlienImages;component/images/alienFace.png"/>
```

This syntax should look familiar to you — it's the same *alternative* syntax shown previously in the "Compiling Images" section. The only thing that has changed is the assembly name. It should be comforting to know that the URI for referencing resources is the same whether it is defined in the main project assembly or a referenced assembly.

➤ **Pros** — Assembly size is reduced; XAP size is (potentially) increased, as referenced assemblies grow in size; separates visuals from application logic.

➤ **Cons** — Images can be renamed or removed if you are not in control of the resource assembly; increases the number of projects you must maintain (if you are in control of the resource assembly).

Accessing Images on Other Domains

When you want to access an image on a remote server (like flickr or photobucket, or a friend's site), you can use the fully qualified URL to access the image:

```
<Image HorizontalAlignment="Left" Margin="10,10,0,0"
  Source="http://www.remotewebsite.com/images/targetImage.png"/>
```

However, Silverlight's security policies will prevent the remote image from loading if the remote site does not have a security manifest file in place that grants you access. For all the gory details on security policies, see Chapter 14.

➤ **Pros** — Enables your cross-domain needs.

➤ **Cons** — Cannot rely on image being at URI; requires security policies.

Which Build Action you choose is ultimately up to the priorities and reliance on images of your application. If you are using just a few images that are relatively small in size, embedding the images in your assembly probably makes sense. If your project is image-intensive and intended to load gracefully for users with limited bandwidth, going with a loose image solution is probably the right move for you. It will let you create a fast startup experience that then relies on asynchronous image-loading.

Displaying Media

Adding video to your Silverlight application is just as easy as adding an image using the `Image` control. However, instead of using the `Image` control, you use the `MediaElement` control. With the exception of a few additional properties and methods, working with media is practically the same as working with images. In fact, you can pretty much re-read the previous section about images and replace `Image` with `MediaElement`.

As was the case with the `Image` control, the `MediaElement` control is accessed by launching Expression Blend's Asset Library, expanding Controls, and selecting All. Figure 17-18 shows the `MediaElement` control in the Asset Library.

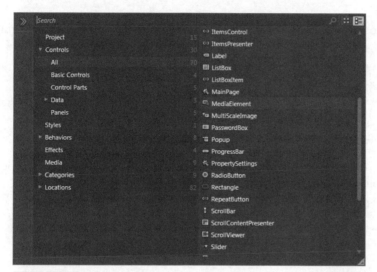

FIGURE 17-18

Create an instance of the `MediaElement` by dragging a rectangle on the design surface or double-clicking the control's icon once selected. With the `MediaElement` selected on the design surface, you can select a Source file by clicking the ellipsis next to the `Source` property. Figure 17-19 shows the `Source` property in Expression Blend's Media category.

FIGURE 17-19

Once you've selected a supported media file, it will be added to your project with a Build Action of *Content* and a Copy to Output Directory setting of *Copy if Newer.* You can modify these settings in Visual Studio to meet your needs. See the previous section, "Referencing Images," to understand the various options afforded to you by changing the values of these two properties.

This section on MediaElement just touches on adding a MediaElement to your page. For a much more in-depth look at this control, see Chapter 20.

BRUSHES

In Silverlight, brushes are used to paint elements on your page. These brushes can be solid color values, linear or radial gradients, or even images. This section looks at the base XAML definitions for each of these, then looks at how you can define and edit brushes in Expression Blend.

Painting with Solids

The SolidColorBrush is used to paint elements with a (surprise, surprise) solid color. The following XAML shows how to define a SolidColorBrush and set its color property:

```
<SolidColorBrush Color="#FFCCFF00"/>
```

Generally, when applying a solid color to an object, just set its appropriate Brush property (Fill, Stroke, Background, or Border) inline:

```
<Rectangle Height="20" Width="100" Fill="#CCFF00" />
```

You need to use the full SolidColorBrush definition only when you are creating Resources of type SolidColorBrush. However, you can use the full syntax:

```
<Rectangle Height="20" Width="100">
   <Rectangle.Fill>
      <SolidColorBrush Color="#FFCCFF00"/>
   </Rectangle.Fill>
</Rectangle>
```

Painting with Linear Gradients

Gradients are used in applications of every flavor (desktop, Web, mobile) to create a modern, polished experience. Through skilled techniques, artists can create glass effects, reflection effects, and subtle transitions that draw the eye from one area to the next. In Silverlight, you use the LinearGradientBrush to achieve such feats. The following XAML defines a (boring) black-to-white, vertical gradient:

```
<LinearGradientBrush StartPoint="0.5,0" EndPoint="0.5,1">
    <GradientStop Color="#FF000000" Offset="0"/>
    <GradientStop Color="#FFFFFFFF" Offset="1"/>
</LinearGradientBrush>
```

 When two GradientStops *share the same* Offset *value, the Silverlight renderer relies on the order in which the* GradientStops *appear in XAML when drawing the gradient.*

To define the direction of the gradient, you must specify both a StartPoint and an EndPoint. The value of each of these properties is an ordered pair that specifies a point in a normalized 1×1 square, where 1 actually represents 100 percent. When the control is rendered, this imaginary square stretches from the top-left corner of the object's bounding box (0,0) to the lower-right corner of the object's bounding box (1,1).

Figure 17-20 shows what the directional handles look like for the previous LinearGradientBrush.

In addition to defining the StartPoint and EndPoint for the brush, you also define a collection of GradientStops. Each GradientStop consists of a Color and Offset. The Color property accepts a Color using the #AARRGGBB notation, just like the SolidColorBrush, and the Offset accepts a double-precision value between 0 and 1. The Offset is used to define the order of the each GradientStop.

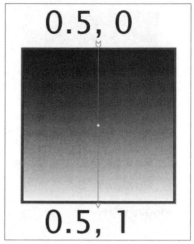

FIGURE 17-20

Painting with Radial Gradients

The RadialGradientBrush can be used to define both radial and elliptical gradients. Like the LinearGradientBrush, the RadialGradientBrush accepts a collection of GradientStops. The following XAML creates a radial gradient that goes from blue in the center to white:

```
<RadialGradientBrush>
    <GradientStop Color="#FF65BADA" Offset="0"/>
    <GradientStop Color="#FFFFFFFF" Offset="1"/>
</RadialGradientBrush>
```

By default, the radial gradient is drawn from the center of the object it is being applied to in a symmetrical fashion. However, by adjusting the following properties, you can achieve a wide range of variations:

➤ Center

➤ RadiusX

➤ RadiusY

➤ GradientOrigin

The first three properties work together to define an ellipse within which a gradient is drawn. Just like the LinearGradientBrush, you need to imagine a 1×1 normalized box that starts at the top-left corner of the target object's bounding box and stretches to the lower-right corner of the target object's bounding box. The values of all four of these properties lie within the 0 . . . 1 range and are applied across this imaginary box. Figure 17-21 demonstrates how changing the values of Center, RadiusX, and RadiusY affect the ellipse within which the gradient is drawn.

By default, Center is set to 0.5,0.5, and both RadiusX and RadiusY are set to 0.5. This is the first example shown in Figure 17-21. Once you've defined the ellipse, you need to specify a GradientOrigin.

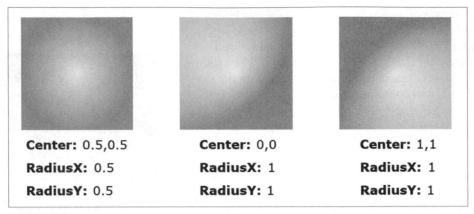

FIGURE 17-21

You can think of the GradientOrigin almost like a light source, with the GradientStops radiating from the GradientOrigin to the edge of the ellipse defined by the Center, RadiusX, and RadiusY properties. Each *ray* is drawn from the GradientOrigin (offset 0) to the edge of the ellipse (offset 1). Figure 17-22 shows how various values of GradientOrigin affect the final rendering.

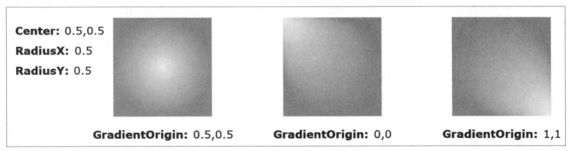

FIGURE 17-22

Painting with Images

The ImageBrush is used to paint objects with images. You can use an ImageBrush for any Brush-derived property, like the Path's Fill property or the TextBlock's Foreground property. When applied, the image referenced by the ImageBrush is painted within the bounds of the object. The following XAML defines an ImageBrush resource whose ImageSource property references a wood-textured image:

```
<Grid
    Height="Auto"
    Background="{x:Null}"
    VerticalAlignment="Top" HorizontalAlignment="Left"
    Margin="29,30,0,0" Width="Auto">
    <Grid.Resources>
        <ImageBrush
```

```
            x:Key="Brush1"
            Stretch="UniformToFill"
            ImageSource="wood.png"
    />
  </Grid.Resources>
  <Border
    Opacity="1"
    HorizontalAlignment="Left"
    VerticalAlignment="Stretch"
    Margin="0,0,0,0"
    Background="{StaticResource Brush1}" Width="125" Height="125" />
  <Ellipse HorizontalAlignment="Left" Margin="147,0,-126,-1"
    Width="125" Fill="{StaticResource Brush1}" Stroke="#FF000000"
    Height="125"/>
  <TextBlock HorizontalAlignment="Left" Margin="285,62,0,0"
    VerticalAlignment="Center" FontFamily="Arial Black" FontSize="48"
    Text="WOOD" TextWrapping="NoWrap"
    Foreground="{StaticResource Brush1}"/>
</Grid>
```

Figure 17-23 shows the result of the preceding XAML — an `ImageBrush` applied to `Border`, `Ellipse`, and `TextBlock` objects.

Just like the `Image` control, the `ImageBrush` control has a `Stretch` property that defines the way the source image is rendered when the object being painted is not the same size as the underlying image. As you've seen before, the values for `Stretch` can be `None`, `Fill`, `Uniform`, and `UniformToFill`.

FIGURE 17-23

Painting with Video

Just as you can paint an object with an image, you can paint an object with video! Though a lot of the samples demonstrating this may seem a bit frivolous (like animated text with video painted on it), being able to paint elements with video can enable some really interesting visual effects. Just for fun, I'll show you how to paint text with video anyway.

Instead of simply setting a `Source` property on the `VideoBrush` (as you did with `ImageBrush`), you first have to define a `MediaElement` and give it a name. You then consume the `MediaElement` with the `VideoBrush` by setting its `SourceName` property to the name of the `MediaElement` you just created. You can then apply the `VideoBrush` to your target object just like any of the previous brushes you've looked at.

The following XAML defines a `MediaElement` and sets its name to `sourceMediaElement`:

```
<MediaElement
    x:Name="sourceMediaElement"
    Source="SampleVideo.wmv" IsMuted="True" Opacity="0"
    IsHitTestVisible="False" />
```

In addition to giving the `MediaElement` a name, I also set `Opacity` to 0, `IsHitTestVisible` to `False`, and `IsMuted` to `True`. Together these properties ensure that the `MediaElement` itself is neither seen nor heard nor able to intercept mouse clicks. The following XAML defines a `VideoBrush` that references this `MediaElement`. The `VideoBrush` is then applied to the `Foreground` of a `TextBlock`:

```
<TextBlock
    FontFamily="Arial Black" FontSize="48" Text="VIDEO"
    TextWrapping="NoWrap">

    <TextBlock.Foreground>
        <VideoBrush SourceName="sourceMediaElement"
            Stretch="UniformToFill" />
    </TextBlock.Foreground>
</TextBlock>
```

Editing Brushes in Expression Blend

You've seen how to define the various brush types by hand. Now it's time to take a look at how these same brushes can be created using Microsoft Expression Blend. Expression Blend provides a brush-editing experience similar to other design programs you may have experienced before, reducing the labor of hand-typing `GradientStops` to simple, familiar user-interface conventions. Don't feel that the previous XAML-focused exercise was a waste, however — you now have a solid understanding of what's happening behind the scenes, and you're prepared to hand-tweak the designer-generated brushes when they just don't follow your every need.

Using the Brush Editor

Properties such as `Fill`, `Background`, `Stroke`, and `Foreground` all accept values of type `Brush`. You've just seen how Silverlight supports brushes of type `SolidColorBrush`, `LinearGradientBrush`, `RadialGradientBrush`, `ImageBrush`, and `VideoBrush`. A simple text field will obviously not work for this type of property. Enter the Brush editor, a tool that should look familiar to users of modern design programs.

In Figure 17-24, a rectangle is selected on the canvas whose `Fill` property is set to a `LinearGradientBrush`. On the right, the Brushes category is expanded (select the Properties tab in Expression Blend if you haven't already). Notice the list of brush properties at the very top of this category. You'll see the `Fill`, `Stroke`, and `OpacityMask` brush properties listed. You can tell that `Fill` is the active property because it's highlighted with a light-gray background. Pay attention to two other details here also: the brush preview drawn adjacent to the property name, and the white marker directly next to the preview.

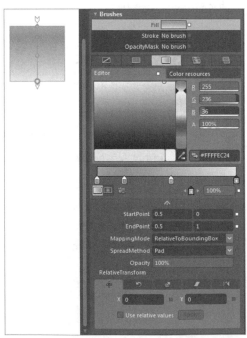

FIGURE 17-24

You can use the preview to glance and quickly determine the brush values that are applied to the currently selected object. The white box is known as a *marker* and launches a context menu for the property. Clicking it reveals a menu that lets you reset the property value, among other things. You can see that neither the Stroke nor the OpacityMask properties in Figure 17-24 have values set because their markers are both grayed out.

Applying a Brush Value

The Brush editor is divided into four tabs, one for each brush type available. Click the first tab to clear the brush value. Click the second tab to specify a SolidColorBrush, click the third tab to specify a GradientBrush, and click the fourth tab to select a brush resource.

Applying Solid Color Brushes

When you specify a SolidColorBrush, the Brush editor interface appears as shown in Figure 17-25.

Although this editor may appear a little complicated at first glance, it is actually quite simple and just provides multiple ways to achieve the same task. You can quickly change the color by clicking anywhere in the large color area, indicated by the mouse cursor in Figure 17-25. Change the hue by dragging the Hue slider or clicking anywhere along the hue range.

As you change the hue or choose different colors, the R, G, and B values will be updated accordingly. These are the Red, Green, and Blue color components of the selected color, respectively. Each component has a range from 0 to 255. The "A" entry listed beneath R, G, and B stands for *Alpha* (Transparency) and has a value range from 0 percent to 100 percent, where 0 represents fully transparent and 100 represents fully opaque. You can also specify the color by typing in an #AARRGGBB hexadecimal representation. The hexadecimal box will accept RRGGBB values if you paste in from a paint program that doesn't include an Alpha value, so it's a quick way to bring over color values if you have them elsewhere.

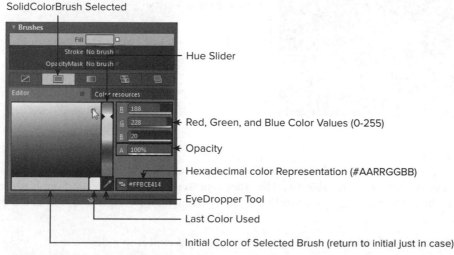

FIGURE 17-25

You can switch between RGB, HSL, HSB and CMYK color modes by clicking on the R, G, or B letters in the color editor.

Applying Gradient Brushes

Click the third tab in the Brush editor to specify a `GradientBrush`. By default, a `LinearGradientBrush` will be applied to your selected object. You can toggle between `LinearGradientBrush` and `RadialGradientBrush` by clicking either of the two Gradient Type buttons located in the lower-left corner of the editor (as shown in Figure 17-26).

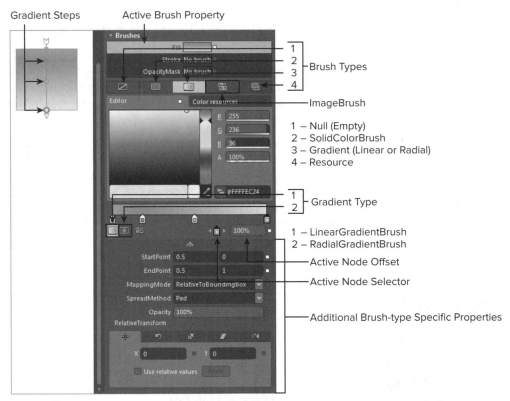

FIGURE 17-26

The `GradientBrush` editor builds on the `SolidColorBrush` editor by adding a gradient preview rectangle. The preview includes draggable swatches that represent `GradientStops`. Simply click a swatch to make it the active swatch. In Figure 17-26, the rightmost swatch is active, indicated by its black border.

The gradient editor supports all the key editing actions you would expect in a design tool:

➤ **Adding Stops** — Add additional `GradientStops` by clicking anywhere in the preview rectangle that does not already include a stop.

➤ **Moving Stops** — Change the position and order of stops by pressing and dragging the target stop.

➤ **Deleting Stops** — Remove GradientStops by dragging the stop down and away from the rectangle preview. Release when the stop disappears.

➤ **Precision Editing** — When editing gradients that require extreme precision, such as the sharp highlight shown in Figure 17-27, you can step through stops by clicking the left and right arrow, next to the selected stop icon. Specify offsets using the selected gradient stop offset editor next to the selected stop icon.

In Figure 17-28, the second stop from the left is actually two stops. Their offsets are so close that they appear to be a single stop. Achieving this level of precision can be achieved using the *Precision Editing* method described above, or by directly editing the XAML. Jump directly to the XAML for your selected rectangle by right-clicking it in the Object tree and selecting View XAML from the context menu.

FIGURE 17-27

FIGURE 17-28

The following code shows the XAML used to define the gradient shown in Figure 17-28:

```
<Rectangle
        Opacity="1"
        Canvas.Left="689"
        Canvas.Top="114"
        Width="128"
        Height="35t">
        <Rectangle.Fill>
                <LinearGradientBrush
                        StartPoint="0.9334821701049805,0.05263148716517857"
                        EndPoint="0.9334821701049805,0.9473685128348214">
                        <LinearGradientBrush.GradientStops>
                                <GradientStopCollection>
                                        <GradientStop
                                                Color="#FFd3ddab"
                                                Offset="0" />
                                        <GradientStop
                                                Color="#FF819d35"
                                                Offset="0.49" />
                                        <GradientStop
                                                Color="#FF739221"
                                                Offset="0.49" />
                                        <GradientStop
                                                Color="#FF678822"
                                                Offset="0.79" />
                                        <GradientStop
```

```
                                                    Color="#FFBBC749"
                                                    Offset="0.92t" />
                                    <GradientStop
                                                    Color="#FFdbde58"
                                                    Offset="1" />
                                    </GradientStopCollection>
                                </LinearGradientBrush.GradientStops>
                        </LinearGradientBrush>
                </Rectangle.Fill>
        </Rectangle>
```

Notice the two stops with `Offset` values of 0.49. Remember, when two stops have the same `Offset` value, they are rendered in the order in which they're defined in XAML. This gives you the ability to create sharp lines in your gradients. Any time you find yourself having trouble getting your gradient to look exactly right using the editor, you can jump to the XAML and manually tweak the `Offset` values.

Using the Gradient Tool

The Expression Blend Gradient Tool can be used to edit the gradient direction and gradient stops directly on the design surface. If you flip back to Figure 17-24, you'll see an arrow adorner drawn on the surface of the selected rectangle. This adorner is visible when you press G on your keyboard, or select the Gradient tool directly from the Tools palette.

You can drag either the head or the tail of the adorner to change the direction of the gradient, and you can even edit `GradientOffsets` directly by dragging the circle nodes on the adorner. Double click the node to launch a color editor on the design surface.

Creating ImageBrushes

`ImageBrushes` can be quickly created from existing `Images` on the design surface in Expression Blend. First, create an instance of the `Image` control and set its `Source` property to an image you want to use as an `ImageBrush`. With the `Image` selected, navigate to Make ImageBrush Resource on the main menu, as shown in Figure 17-29.

After selecting Make ImageBrush Resource, you will be prompted to specify both a Key and a location for the `ImageBrush` resource. In Figure 17-30, I gave my brush the name `tiledImageBackgroundBrush` and selected `UserControl` as the location where I want the resource defined.

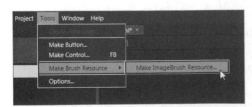

FIGURE 17-29

FIGURE 17-30

After clicking OK, it appears as if nothing has happened. The selected control is still an `Image`, and your design surface remains unchanged. Behind the scenes, a new `ImageBrush` resource was created in the location you specified, either in `App.xaml` or in the current `Page`'s resources collection (`UserControl.Resources`).

You can now apply this new resource using the fourth tab of the Expression Blend Brush editor. First, draw a `Rectangle` on the stage, and then switch to the Properties tab if you have not already done so. With the rectangle selected, click the `Fill` property in the Brush editor to make it the active brush property. Now, select the Brush Resources tab, the fourth tab next to the Gradient Brush tab. Figure 17-31 shows the Brush Resources tab selected.

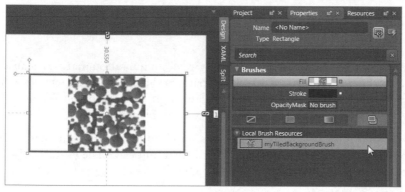

FIGURE 17-31

With the rectangle selected, clicking the name of the `ImageBrush` you just defined applies the brush to the active brush property (in this case, `Fill`). By default, the image used by the `ImageBrush` is scaled uniformly within the object to which it is being applied. But, just like the `Image` and several other controls you've looked at along the way, the `ImageBrush` has a `Stretch` property that lets you define the stretching and scaling behavior of the image.

To edit the `Stretch` property of the `ImageBrush`, you have to switch to the Resources tab of Expression Blend. Figure 17-32 shows the Resources tab selected and `UserControl` expanded to reveal the `ImageBrush` named `myTiledBackgroundBrush`.

Click the down arrow next to the brush preview to reveal the Brush editor and set the `Stretch` property, as shown in Figure 17-33.

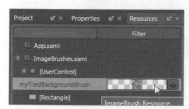

FIGURE 17-32

FIGURE 17-33

The two other important properties of the `ImageBrush` — `ViewportUnits`, and `Viewport` — are not exposed in the version of Expression Blend available at the time of this writing. You'll have to jump to XAML to edit those properties. (See, I told you the XAML section wasn't a waste!)

Expression Blend does not currently provide authoring support for `VideoBrush`. For now, you'll have to define your `VideoBrush` resources by hand. See the "Painting with Video" section earlier in this chapter.

FONTS AND FONT EMBEDDING

Silverlight ships with several "system" fonts built-in. I put "system" in quotation marks, because these are included in the Silverlight run time and do not fall back to the operating system, so you can count on these core fonts whether you are running your Silverlight application on Windows, OS X, or Linux. Figure 17-34 shows a preview of these always-available fonts.

These fonts should all be familiar to you — they've shipped as standard fonts with Windows since Windows XP. Well, maybe not *Portable User Interface*. What is that, anyway? The Portable User Interface designation is really a fallback to the default Lucida Sans Unicode. It's the font you get when you don't specify a `FontFamily`.

If you've selected a `TextBlock` in Expression Blend, you'll see these default fonts listed at the top of the FontFamily drop-down (see Figure 17-35). The blue Silverlight logo next to these fonts indicates that they are embedded.

FIGURE 17-34

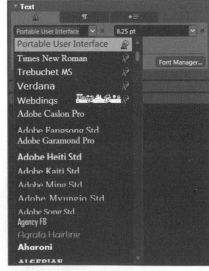

FIGURE 17-35

If you want to use a font other than one of the defaults, you'll have to embed that font in your project (or a referenced assembly). This is easy in Expression Blend: Simply select the font you want to apply and check the Embed box in the Text Properties panel. Expression Blend will automatically create a Fonts folder, copy the required fonts files to that folder, and set their Build Action. It will also write the FontFamily syntax required for referencing embedded fonts so you can go about your business designing. If you're not using Expression Blend you'll have to do these steps manually, as described next.

To get started, find a font file on your system that you want to use in your Silverlight application. In Expression Blend, you can add the font to the project by right-clicking either the project itself or a folder within the project and selecting Add Existing Item, as shown in Figure 17-36.

As with images, when Expression Blend adds external font files, it automatically sets the Build Action to Resource. If you add the file using Visual Studio, you need to manually set the Build Action to Resource (see Figure 17-37).

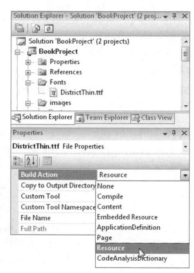

FIGURE 17-36   **FIGURE 17-37**

Once the font is included in your project as a resource, apply it via XAML by setting the FontFamily property:

```
<TextBlock FontFamily="Fonts/DistrictThin.ttf#DistrictThin"
  Text="Custom Font: District Thin" />
```

Here's a breakdown of FontFamily's value so that you understand exactly how this works. First, specify the actual font file path within your project. In this case, it's "Fonts/DistrictThin.ttf". Next, you specify the actual name of the font, preceded by the # symbol. Here, it's "#DistrictThin". It's important to note that the *name* of the font may be different from the *filename* of the font. An easy way to find the *name* of the font is by double-clicking the font file in Windows Explorer and taking a look at the Font Name declaration at the top of the preview window. Figure 17-38 shows this preview window for the example font DistrictThin.

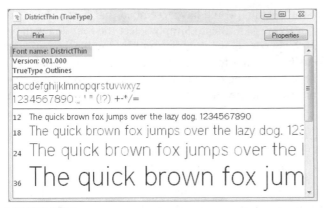

FIGURE 17-38

In the previous XAML, the font file was referenced just like you reference image resources in the project. And, just as you saw with image references, you can add a notation to the `FontFamily` font source path that specifies which assembly the font file resides in. The following XAML explicitly declares the project (assembly) name:

```
<TextBlock FontFamily="/BookProject;component/Fonts/DistrictThin.ttf#DistrictThin"
    Text="Custom Font: District Thin" />
```

This means that you can embed font resources in other assemblies and still reference them via XAML, using a familiar syntax that is consistent with the syntax used by other controls.

EFFECTS

Effects are used throughout the design industry — from print to the Web to desktop applications to motion video. These effects are used to add realism (subtle glows), create a sense of depth (drop shadows), simulate a real-world phenomenon (rippling water), and achieve a wide variety of additional visualizations. The core Silverlight run time includes a couple of common effects (`Blur` and `DropShadow`) but also supports custom PixelShader-based effects. This support essentially delivers the potential for an infinite number of effect possibilities.

Applying Effects

All objects derived from `UIElement` have a property of type `Effect` that also happens to be named `Effect`. To apply an effect to an object, you simply set the value of this property to an object that derives from `Effect`. The following sample XAML defines two buttons, one with and one without a `BlurEffect` applied:

```
<StackPanel Orientation="Horizontal" HorizontalAlignment="Center">
    <Button Content="I'm Not Blurred"
        HorizontalAlignment="Center"
        VerticalAlignment="Center"
```

```
        Margin="0,0,10,0">
    </Button>
    <Button Content="I'm Blurred"
        HorizontalAlignment="Center"
        VerticalAlignment="Center">
        <Button.Effect>
            <BlurEffect Radius="4" />
        </Button.Effect>
    </Button>
</StackPanel>
```

This XAML results in a layout that looks like that shown in Figure 17-39.

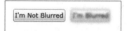

FIGURE 17-39

 Currently only a single effect can be applied to an object at a time. To apply multiple effects to the same visual, you will need to wrap the target element with additional panels (such as a Border*) and progressively apply effects to each wrapper panel.*

Using Native Effects

Silverlight includes two native effects that are included as part of the core run time — BlurEffect and DropShadowEffect. These two effects alone may not seem like much, but the DropShadowEffect can also be used to create what is traditionally known as a glow effect as well. Together, these three effects are probably the most commonly used effects when creating user interface artwork.

Applying the BlurEffect

Using the BlurEffect is extremely simple and includes only a single customization property — Radius. The radius is used to determine how blurry the target element is: the higher the radius value, the blurrier your target. The default value for this property is 5 (in device-independent units of 1/96 of an inch).

Figure 17-40 shows the same target element with varying degrees of blur applied.

Common uses for the BlurEffect include the following:

FIGURE 17-40

➤ Blur the main body of your application to draw focus to modal dialogs in the foreground.

➤ Apply BlurEffects over time in animations to simulate motion blur.

➤ Emphasize disabled items by slightly blurring them.

➤ Create a sense of depth by applying varying degrees of blur to layers in your application.

Applying the DropShadowEffect

The DropShadowEffect can be used to create both drop shadow and glow effects. Unlike the BlurEffect, this effect includes more than one property for customization. The following XAML defines a DropShadowEffect that results in a green glow around a custom button (Style is defined in Chapter 21):

```xaml
<Button Style="{StaticResource ButtonWithDropShadow}"
    Width="130" Content="GLOW" Height="45">
    <Button.Effect>
        <DropShadowEffect ShadowDepth="0" BlurRadius="20" Opacity="1"
            Color="#FF25DFCE" Direction="315"/>
    </Button.Effect>
</Button>
```

It's by setting the ShadowDepth property to 0 that this effect essentially becomes a glow effect. The other properties all affect the way the final "shadow" is drawn. Figure 17-41 shows several DropShadowEffect configurations and their resulting visuals. The first sample shown is the result of the preceding XAML.

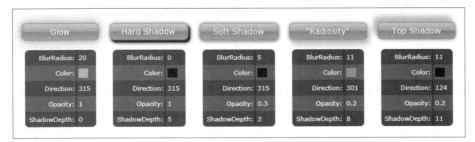

FIGURE 17-41

When using the DropShadowEffect for user interfaces, I generally find subtle techniques, such as the *Soft Shadow* or *Radiosity* samples in the figure, more effective than "in your face" options like *Hard Shadow* and *Top Shadow*. I hope you see that a wide variety of visualizations can be achieved with this single effect.

Applying Effects in Expression Blend

You don't have to manually apply effects in XAML if you're using Expression Blend 4. Figure 17-42 shows the Asset Library expanded with the Effects tab selected.

To apply an effect, press and hold your mouse over the effect you want to apply and drag the effect to the target object either on the design surface or in the Object tree. The effect will appear in the Object tree as shown in Figure 17-43.

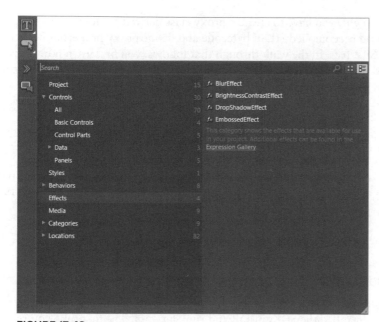

FIGURE 17-42

FIGURE 17-43

Editing the properties of an effect is no different from editing the properties of any other selected object on the stage. You can either select the effect in the Object tree directly and edit the effect's properties in the Properties panel, or you can select the parent object (in this case `Image`) and expand the `Effect` property in the Properties panel. Figure 17-44 shows the Properties panel when the effect is selected directly (on the left) and shows the `Effect` property expanded when the parent `Image` is selected.

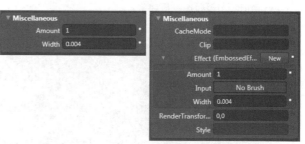

FIGURE 17-44

Using Custom Effects

Silverlight opens up a world of creativity possibilities by supporting custom High Level Shading Language (HLSL)–based effects. HLSL is the shader language used to define DirectX effects and was introduced with DirectX 8. Because HLSL has been around for a while, you can find a large number of articles and free resources (read: "free effects") that you can take advantage of. Start by visiting `http://msdn.microsoft.com/en-us/library/bb509561(VS.85).aspx` to learn more about HLSL, then do a Web search on *HLSL* to find a wealth of resources on this topic.

To use HLSL-based effects in Silverlight, you have to create a proxy class derived from `ShaderEffect`. It's in this derived class that you load precompiled HLSL bytecode and define proxy properties between your class and the underlying HLSL effect. In the walk-through that follows, you first learn how to use freely available tools to tweak and compile HLSL shaders, and then see how to consume those effects in custom classes that can be used in your Silverlight projects in the same way as native effects.

Getting the Tools

To compile HLSL shaders, you'll need the DirectX SDK, freely available on the Microsoft website. In addition to the SDK, I also recommend downloading Walt Ritscher's Shazzam Shader Editing Tool, updated in early 2010 with native support for Silverlight code generation. Shazzam is delivered as a WPF ClickOnce application and provides a nice interface for editing and testing HLSL shaders.

> ➤ **DirectX SDK** — `http://msdn.microsoft.com/en-us/directx/aa937788.aspx`

> ➤ **Shazzam** — `http://shazzam-tool.com/publish.htm`

Viewing and Compiling Shaders with Shazzam and the DirectX SDK

Start by downloading and installing the latest version of the DirectX SDK. (Be warned, it's a fairly hefty 400+ MB download.) Once you've installed the SDK, install and run Shazzam. The first time you run Shazzam, you'll probably need to update its settings to ensure that it knows the correct location of the DirectX FX compiler. Do this by expanding the Settings panel and clicking the Browse button, shown expanded in Figure 17-45.

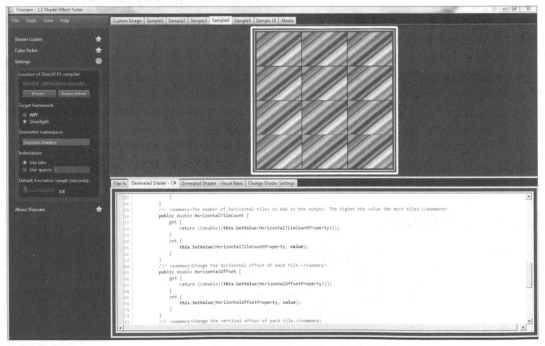

FIGURE 17-45

The default installation path required by Shazzam will be something like `C:\Program Files\Microsoft DirectX SDK (March 2009)\Utilities\bin\x86\fxc.exe`. This path will vary slightly based on the version of the SDK you've installed and whether or not you've changed the default installation path. Be sure to select Silverlight as the Target Framework on the Settings panel as well. Once you've addressed these settings, you can move on to the fun stuff — testing and compiling shaders.

Shazzam ships with several default shaders that you can play with by expanding the Shader Loader panel. Click the Sample Shaders button, and then select a shader from the list. The shader will be loaded in an uncompiled state as the first tab. Press F5 or select Tools ➪ Apply from the main menu to compile and test the results. When you compile a shader in Shazzam, several important things happen:

➤ `ShaderEffect`-derived classes are auto-generated in both C# and Visual Basic for use in your own projects.

➤ The Change Shader Settings tab is either added or updated, providing you with an interface for modifying the shader input values.

➤ The new effect is applied to all of the sample images in the tabbed preview area.

Figure 17-46 shows the Embossed.fx shader selected, compiled, and applied to the Sample5 image.

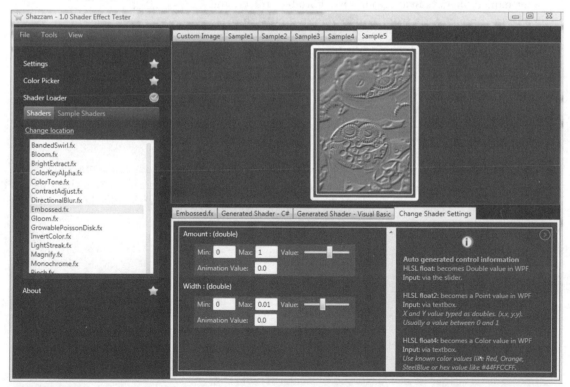

FIGURE 17-46

I've set the value of the `Amount` parameter to .57 and the value of the `Width` parameter to .004. For many of the sample effects, the default value range of the sliders is not effective. For example, I changed the Max value of `Width` to .01 for this Embossed effect. If you compile a shader and feel like it's not working, it's likely that you just haven't found an appropriate combination of input values yet.

Creating a Custom Shader Effect

With the custom shader tweaked and compiled, it's now time to create a custom `ShaderEffect` class that can be consumed by your Silverlight applications. Shazzam has already taken a lot of the guesswork out of the process by compiling the .fx shader and generating a starter effect class for you. You now have to add the compiled effect to your Visual Studio project and customize the starter class for Silverlight. (Shazzam currently generates WPF code.)

Adding the Compiled Shader to Visual Studio

Select Tools ⇨ View Compiled Shaders from the main menu in Shazzam. This opens the GeneratedShaders folder in Windows Explorer. You will see a number of `.ps` files, one for each Sample Shader you've compiled and tested. In this sample, I'm going to use the Embossed shader. Create a folder named Shaders inside your Visual Studio project, and then drag `Embossed.ps` from Windows Explorer to the Visual Studio folder. Figure 17-47 shows the file `Embossed.ps` added to the Shaders folder inside the Visual Studio project. Make sure you set the Build Action of your shader file to Resource.

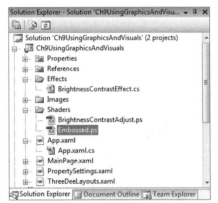

FIGURE 17-47

Creating the Effect Class

With the shader in place in the project, it's now time to create your proxy effect class. Start by creating an Effects folder in Visual Studio. Add an empty class to that folder with the filename `EmbossedEffect.cs`. Now, switch back to Shazzam and select the Generated Shader — C# tab (or Visual Basic if you're trying this in VB). Copy all of the auto-generated code to the new `EmbossedEffect` class you just added to Visual Studio.

Following is the initial code generated by Shazzam:

```
using System;
using System.Windows;
using System.Windows.Media;
using System.Windows.Media.Effects;
using System.Windows.Media.Media3D;


namespace Ch17Graphics.Shaders
{
    /// <summary>An effect that embosses the input.</summary>
    public class EmbossedEffect : ShaderEffect
    {
        public static readonly DependencyProperty InputProperty =
```

```
      ShaderEffect.RegisterPixelShaderSamplerProperty("Input",
      typeof(EmbossedEffect), 0);
  public static readonly DependencyProperty AmountProperty =
      DependencyProperty.Register("Amount", typeof(double),
      typeof(EmbossedEffect), new PropertyMetadata(((double)(0.5)),
      PixelShaderConstantCallback(0)));
  public static readonly DependencyProperty WidthProperty =
      DependencyProperty.Register("Width", typeof(double),
      typeof(EmbossedEffect), new PropertyMetadata(((double)(0.003)),
      PixelShaderConstantCallback(1)));
  public EmbossedEffect()
  {
      PixelShader pixelShader = new PixelShader();
      pixelShader.UriSource = new
      Uri("/Ch17Graphics;component/Shaders/Embossed.ps", UriKind.Relative);
      this.PixelShader = pixelShader;

      this.UpdateShaderValue(InputProperty);
      this.UpdateShaderValue(AmountProperty);
      this.UpdateShaderValue(WidthProperty);
  }
  public Brush Input
  {
    get
    {
      return ((Brush)(this.GetValue(InputProperty)));
    }
    set
    {
      this.SetValue(InputProperty, value);
    }
  }
  /// <summary>The amplitude of the embossing.</summary>
  public double Amount
  {
    get
    {
      return ((double)(this.GetValue(AmountProperty)));
    }
    set
    {
      this.SetValue(AmountProperty, value);
    }
  }
  /// <summary>The separation between samples (as a fraction of input
  size).</summary>
  public double Width
  {
    get
    {
      return ((double)(this.GetValue(WidthProperty)));
    }
    set
    {
```

```
            this.SetValue(WidthProperty, value);
        }
    }
}
}
```

The generated code includes a class derived from `ShaderEffect` and dependency properties for each of the shader's input fields. If you didn't customize the namespace in Shazzam's settings panel, now is a good time to update the namespace manually. Here, you'll see `Ch17Graphics.Shaders` as the namespace.

The `PixelShader` property (defined on `ShaderEffect`) is initialized to a new instance of `PixelShader` whose `UriSource` references the compiled `.ps` file you added to the project previously. This is the magic hookup that ties the HLSL shader to a Silverlight-supported `ShaderEffect`. The last three lines of this constructor ensure that the shader values are initialized the first time it is applied.

Before moving on to actually applying the custom effect, I want to recap what is a fairly simple process:

1. Test and compile the shader in Shazzam.

2. Add a compiled `.ps` file to Visual Studio and set its Build Action to Resource.

3. Add a new *x*Effect-named class to your project.

4. Copy the Shazzam-generated effect code to your new class.

5. Update the namespace (if necessary).

6. Update the `Uri` reference to the `.ps` file you added.

Applying the Custom Effect

With the custom effect defined, you can now apply it via XAML just like you apply the `Blur` and `DropShadow` effects. The only additional thing required is a namespace mapping to your custom effects namespace. The following XAML defines a `localEffects` namespace and applies the `EmbossedEffect` to a sample image:

```
<UserControl
    xmlns:localEffects="clr-namespace:Ch17Graphics.Effects"

<Image Source="Images/sampleImage.jpg">
    <Image.Effect>
        <localEffects:EmbossedEffect Width=".003" Amount="1" />
    </Image.Effect>
</Image>
```

Figure 17-48 shows the sample image with and without the `EmbossedEffect` applied.

You can easily enable real-time adjustments of the effect input values by binding `Slider` controls to the effect instance itself, just as Shazzam generates automatically. The following XAML adds

an x:Name attribute to the EmbossedEffect instance and binds a Slider's Value property to the
EmbossedEffect's Width property:

```
<Image Source="Images/sampleImage.jpg">
    <Image.Effect>
        <localEffects:EmbossedEffect x:Name="EmbossedEffect"
            Width=".003" Amount="1" />
    </Image.Effect>
</Image>
<Slider Value="{Binding ElementName=EmbossedEffect, Path=Width, Mode=TwoWay}"
        Minimum="0" SmallChange=".001" Maximum=".01" />
```

Effects.xaml

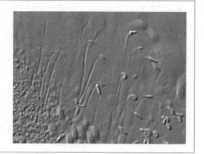

FIGURE 17-48

When you compile and run, you can drag the slider and adjust the Width parameter of the
EmbossedEffect in real time — Nice!

No doubt you are now starting to see the power of shader-based custom effects in Silverlight. There are
so many creative possibilities here. If you're interested in seeing more effects than those that ship with
Shazzam, be sure to check out the open-source WPF/Silverlight Shader Effects Library at Codeplex:
http://wpffx.codeplex.com. In addition to providing a large number of predefined effects, this solution also demonstrates how to share a code base between Silverlight and WPF projects.

> *The use of effects does incur a performance hit, as pixel shader effects are ren-
> dered in software. Any objects that have an effect applied to them will also be
> rendered in software, so be sure to keep this in mind when working with effects
> and apply them strategically.*

TRANSFORMS

Using the Silverlight Transform classes, you can rotate and position (in 2D and 3D), scale, and
skew any object on the design surface. Together, these transforms are used to add interactivity
and motion to your applications. For example, you can apply and animate both a ScaleTransform

and a `RotateTransform` in the `MouseOver` state of a `Button`'s style. You define the underlying `Button`, without rotation or scaling, and then independently apply the transform(s) to achieve the desired effect.

Silverlight offers both 2D and 3D manipulation capabilities. You can apply a single 2D transform, a single 3D transform, a collection of 2D transforms, or both 2D and 3D transforms at the same time. All of the properties of these transforms can be animated via Storyboards, or directly manipulated via code at run time, which provides you with a great deal of creative freedom. This section starts by looking at the 2D transform classes.

Using 2D Transforms

Here are the four core `Transform` classes that you will use most frequently:

➤   `RotateTransform`

➤   `ScaleTransform`

➤   `SkewTransform`

➤   `TranslateTransform`

Transforms are applied by setting the `RenderTransform` property of any `UIElement`. The following XAML shows a `RotateTransform` applied to a simple `Button` instance:

```
<Button
    Content="Rotated"
    HorizontalAlignment="Center"
    VerticalAlignment="Center">
    <Button.RenderTransform>
        <RotateTransform Angle="35"/>
    </Button.RenderTransform>
</Button>
```

Take a look at each of these transforms in a little more detail. For the most part, each of these transforms is extremely easy to work with and consists of just a couple of key properties to manipulate.

 To apply more than one transform at a time, you'll need to either use a `CompositeTransform` *(new to Silverlight 4) or a* `TransformGroup`. *These are covered in the "Applying Multiple Transforms" section later in this chapter.*

Using the RotateTransform

Elements are rotated by applying a `RotateTransform`. The following XAML demonstrates how to apply a rotation of –75 degrees to an object. The final result is shown in Figure 17-49.

```
<Rectangle
    Fill="#FF3FA9F5"
    HorizontalAlignment="Left" Margin="0,0,0,5"
```

```
        Width="88" RadiusY="18" RadiusX="18"
        RenderTransformOrigin="0.5,0.5">
        <Rectangle.RenderTransform>
            <RotateTransform Angle="-75"/>
        </Rectangle.RenderTransform>
    </Rectangle>
```

Though not commonly used, and not even exposed by Expression Blend, the `RotateTransform` includes `CenterX` and `CenterY` properties that can be used to adjust the origin of the rotation that is applied to the underlying object. These values are pixel-based and not percentage based, which means you'll need to know the exact size of your target object when setting these values. The more common approach to modifying the rotation origin is by adjusting the `RenderTransformOrigin`.

By default, when you apply a transform the translation is anchored to the top-left corner of the object at (0,0). In some cases this has the desired result (if you want to simulate a stack of photos that are pinned together at their top-left corner and fanned out); however, in most cases you'll expect the transform to be applied from the center of the object. To do this you'll need to set the `RenderTransformOrigin` to (0.5,0.5). Expression Blend does this for you automatically when you apply a transform to an object.

Test this out by first drawing a rectangle on the design surface and then rotating it. Note that the `RenderTransformOrigin` property has automatically been set (either by viewing the XAML or expanding the Miscellaneous category in the Expression Blend Properties panel). Figure 17-50 demonstrates how various values of `RenderTransformOrigin` alter the final effect.

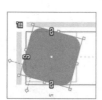

FIGURE 17-49

(0.5,0.5)   (0,0)   (0,1)

FIGURE 17-50

Using the ScaleTransform

The `ScaleTransform` lets you increase or decrease the size of a target object on a percentage basis. For example, to double the size of an object, set the `ScaleX` and `ScaleY` properties of the `ScaleTransform` to 2. This effect is commonly used either by itself or in combination with the `RotateTransform` to add interactivity to buttons. The following XAML shows a `TextBlock` being scaled by 150 percent, with the final result shown in Figure 17-51.

FIGURE 17-51

```
<TextBlock
    HorizontalAlignment="Left" Margin="30,31,0,-5" TextWrapping="Wrap"
    Text="X" Foreground="White" FontSize="64" FontFamily="ChunkFive"
    RenderTransformOrigin="0.5,0.5">
    <TextBlock.RenderTransform>
        <ScaleTransform ScaleX="1.5" ScaleY="1.5"/>
    </TextBlock.RenderTransform>
</TextBlock>
```

Using the SkewTransform

Elements can be skewed either on the X-axis, the Y-axis, or both by setting the `AngleX` and `AngleY` properties. The following XAML creates an *italic* effect by skewing a `TextBlock` on its X-axis. Figure 17-52 shows the final result.

FIGURE 17-52

```
<TextBlock Text="Transforms" Foreground="#FFA1A1A1" FontSize="64"
    FontFamily="ChunkFive" HorizontalAlignment="Left"
    RenderTransformOrigin="0.5,0.5"
    <TextBlock.RenderTransform>
        <SkewTransform AngleX="-8"/>
    </TextBlock.RenderTransform>
</TextBlock>
```

Using the TranslateTransform

The `TranslateTransform` is used to move elements on the X- and Y-axis, "translating" them from their original positions. The `X` and `Y` properties are pixel-based, so the following XAML moves the original object 87 pixels to the right and 26 pixels down (shown in Figure 17-53).

```
<TextBlock HorizontalAlignment="Left" Text="AML" Foreground="#FFFD832D"
    FontSize="64" FontFamily="ChunkFive" RenderTransformOrigin="0.5,0.5">
    <TextBlock.RenderTransform>
        <TranslateTransform X="87" Y="26"/>
    </TextBlock.RenderTransform>
</TextBlock>
```

You may be wondering why you would use a `TranslateTransform` if you have so many positioning capabilities at your disposal already (Margins, Canvas.Top, Canvas.Left, and so on). More so than the previous transforms, the `TranslateTransform` is used predominantly for animation or interactivity. For example, when you create an "opening" Storyboard in Expression Blend to animate elements into place, the `X` and `Y` properties of the `TranslateTransform` are animated rather than the `Canvas.X` and `Canvas.Y` (or left and right margins plus `HorizontalAlignment` and `VerticalAlignment`) properties.

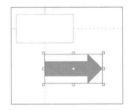

FIGURE 17-53

The translation is applied to elements after they have been positioned and sized by the Silverlight rendering engine so you're guaranteed that the spacing and layout is not altered as the elements are re-positioned.

Using the MatrixTransform

The `MatrixTransform` can be used to achieve additional custom transformations that cannot be achieved using the core set of transforms just discussed. This particular transform is not tooled by Expression Blend and is beyond the scope of this book. A number of examples and guided tutorials are available online that you can use to dig into this more abstract transform.

Applying Multiple Transforms

All of the previous samples demonstrate how to apply a single transform by setting the `RenderTransform` property. In real-world layouts, you'll often need to apply more than one transform at a time, and though the `RenderTransform` property accepts only a single value, that doesn't mean you can't apply more than one transform.

In previous versions of Silverlight, you would have used the `TransformGroup` to define a collection of transforms. Silverlight 4 introduces the `CompositeTransform`, the new preferred method of applying multiple transforms to elements. This section starts by looking at the `TransformGroup`, then moves on to the `CompositeTransform`.

Using the TransformGroup

The `TransformGroup` accepts a collection of transform objects, letting you apply any number of transforms to the target element. The following XAML scales, skews, rotates, and translates the target object:

```xml
<local:Fly x:Name="transformViaGroup" Height="150" Width="150">
    <local:Fly.RenderTransform>
        <TransformGroup>
            <ScaleTransform ScaleX="0.75" ScaleY="0.85" />
            <SkewTransform AngleX="-18" />
            <RotateTransform Angle="33" />
            <TranslateTransform X="46" />
        </TransformGroup>
    </local:Fly.RenderTransform>
</local:Fly>
```

Transforms.xaml

With the `TransformGroup`, the order in which transforms are applied affects the final rendering. The order used in the preceding code is the preferred order and is what Expression Blend 3 (and earlier) generated automatically any time you applied a transform to an element. Try changing the order of the transforms and note how the final result changes.

Using the CompositeTransform

The `CompositeTransform` is new to Silverlight 4 and is the preferred method of applying multiple transforms. In fact, Expression Blend 4 now renders a `CompositeTransform` any time you apply a transform to an element, where previous versions used the `TransformGroup`. This new transform brings several advantages to the table:

➤ Simplifies XAML by uniting all transform properties on a single object.

➤ Applies transforms in the recommended order (guaranteeing consistent transform results).

➤ Simplifies code manipulation of transforms.

The following XAML uses a `CompositeTransform` to achieve the exact same render result as the `TransformGroup` of the previous section:

```
<local:Fly x:Name="transformViaComposite" Width="150" Height="150">
    <local:Fly.RenderTransform>
        <CompositeTransform
            SkewX="-18"
            Rotation="33"
            ScaleX="0.75"
            ScaleY="0.85"
            TranslateX="46"/>
    </local:Fly.RenderTransform>
</local:Fly>
```

Transforms.xaml

Though most of the `CompositeTransform`'s properties were used, the following is a complete list of the available properties:

➤ `CenterX`

➤ `CenterY`

➤ `Rotation`

➤ `ScaleX`

➤ `ScaleY`

➤ `SkewX`

➤ `SkewY`

➤ `TranslateX`

➤ `TranslateY`

Figure 17-54 shows the final composite of the individual transforms seen throughout this section and shows the `TransformGroup` and `CompositeTransform` side-by-side, demonstrating the identical rendering of these two approaches.

FIGURE 17-54

Using Perspective 3D

Silverlight gives you the ability to rotate every UIElement in your application in its own three-dimensional (3D) space simply by setting the Projection property. Unlike true 3D environments wherein multiple elements live in a shared 3D space, objects in Silverlight each have their own space. In Silverlight, 3D is really a 3D transform applied to individual objects and not a true all-encompassing 3D environment that supports 3D objects and materials. For example, you can't import a .3DS model of a fighter jet and have it fly across the screen, but you *can* flip a configuration panel up from the bottom of the screen or rotate an image into view.

Though this level of support may sound limited compared to a full 3D environment, it actually supports a wide array of user interface scenarios and is more flexible than you might at first think. Start by looking at a simple sample, then you can move on to some of the configuration options that demonstrate flexibility. The following XAML defines two images. The first is displayed normally, and the second is rotated about the X- and Y-axes:

```
<Image Height="116" Margin="241,317,0,0" VerticalAlignment="Top"
    Source="Images/sampleImage.jpg" Stretch="Fill" Width="154"
    HorizontalAlignment="Left"/>
<Image Source="Images/sampleImage.jpg" Stretch="Fill" Width="154"
    VerticalAlignment="Top" Height="116" HorizontalAlignment="Left"
    Margin="421,317,0,0">
    <Image.Projection>
        <PlaneProjection RotationX="-17" RotationY="-34"/>
    </Image.Projection>
</Image>
```

All you had to do was set the Projection property of the Image to an instance of the PlaneProjection object. It's on the PlaneProjection where you customize all of the rotation properties. This sample uses an Image, but Image could just as easily have been a Button, Grid, Border, Rectangle, or any other control you felt needed to be rotated. Figure 17-55 shows the Image both with and without the transform.

FIGURE 17-55

By default, the image is rotated about its center on all three axes. You can customize the center of rotation by adjusting the CenterOfRotationX, CenterOfRotationY, and CenterOfRotationZ properties on the `PlaneProjection` object. The following XAML sets both the X and Y center to 0 (top, left corner) of the image and rotates −60 degrees about the Y-axis:

```
<Image Height="116" Margin="241,317,0,0" VerticalAlignment="Top"
    Source="Images/sampleImage.jpg" Stretch="Fill" Width="154"
    HorizontalAlignment="Left"/>
<Image Source="Images/sampleImage.jpg" Stretch="Fill" Width="154"
    VerticalAlignment="Top" Height="116" HorizontalAlignment="Left"
    Margin="421,317,0,0">
    <Image.Projection>
        <PlaneProjection RotationX="0" RotationY="-60" CenterOfRotationX="0"
            CenterOfRotationY="0" CenterOfRotationZ="0"/>
    </Image.Projection>
</Image>
```

In Figure 17-56, you can see how the image appears to be swinging back, almost like a door on its hinge.

You can simulate a true 3D environment by synchronizing the initial position of a number of objects and synchronizing their `CenterOfRotation` properties. Figure 17-57 shows 200 procedurally generated `Rectangle`s, all positioned in the center of a container `Grid`, with a `CenterOfRotationZ` property set to −300. When the `RotationX` and `RotationY` properties are set, it's as if these images are being moved around the surface of a sphere.

FIGURE 17-56

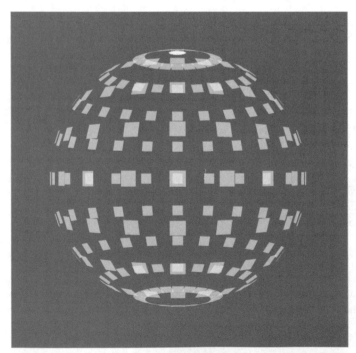

FIGURE 17-57

Each rectangle has its own PlaneProjection and is rotated in its own 3D space, but synchronizing the initial positions and CenterOfRotationZ property has achieved a deceptive result. The following code shows how this visual was created:

```
public ThreeDee()
{
    // Required to initialize variables
    InitializeComponent();

    GenerateSphere();
    this.LayoutRoot.MouseMove += new MouseEventHandler(OnMouseMove);
}

int rowCount = 10;
int columnCount = 20;
int rectHeightWidth = 50;

Random rand = new Random(23496321);

private void GenerateSphere()
{
  for (var i = 0; i < rowCount; i++)
  {
    for (var j = 0; j < columnCount; j++)
    {
      // Create Rectangle
      Fly rect = new Fly();
      rect.Height = rect.Width = rectHeightWidth;
      rect.Opacity = 0.3;

      // Create PlaneProjection and Initialize CenterOfRotationZ
      PlaneProjection projection = new PlaneProjection();
      projection.CenterOfRotationZ = -300;

      // Set RotationX and RotationY based on current row and column
      projection.RotationX = -90 + ((180 / rowCount) * i);
      projection.RotationY = (360 / columnCount) * j;
      projection.RotationZ = rand.Next(5, 360);

      // Assign PlaneProject to Rectangle's Projection property
      rect.Projection = projection;

      // Add the Rectangle to a XAML-defined Grid (named "sphere")
      this.sphere.Children.Add(rect);
    }
  }
}
```

ThreeDee.xaml.cs

This sample just defines and applies a 3D transformation to a collection of rectangles. You could extend this sample and make it more interactive by responding to mouse position and updating all of the 3D transforms, creating a sense of interactive 3D space. I'll leave that up to you, though; you are now armed with the basic understanding of what is required to take it further.

Adjusting PlaneProjections in Expression Blend

Expression Blend includes support in the Properties panel for adjusting the values of a `PlaneProjection` applied to an object. Select an object on the stage and then scroll to the Transform category of the Properties panel. By default, the `Projection` property is hidden in the Advanced Properties section. Click the down arrow to reveal the editor shown in Figure 17-58.

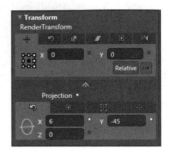

FIGURE 17-58

You can manually define rotation values for the X-, Y-, and Z-axes, or you can click and drag the circle-based sphere icon to do a freeform rotation. Additional tabs in this editor expose the Center of Rotation, Global Offset, and Local Offset property categories. We did not look at these last two property groups in the previous exercise. These additional value categories let you adjust the positions of items in 3D space, much like applying a `TranslateTransform` in 2D space. These properties can be used to further simulate a true 3D environment much as the previous sphere example demonstrated.

SUMMARY

This chapter started by examining the core set of controls at your disposal for creating interesting visuals in Silverlight. You were exposed to the XAML syntax first so that you would have a solid understanding of what's happening behind the scenes. After covering the XAML, you jumped to Expression Blend and used a design surface to do the same things you had just done by hand. In some cases, Expression Blend was able to do everything for you (and was practically necessary for tasks such as creating complex paths). In other cases, Expression Blend didn't provide tooling for certain control features (such as setting `ViewportUnits` on an `ImageBrush`), and you had to return to the XAML to achieve just what you wanted.

You also looked at how to reference and include binary assets (images, fonts, videos, and so on) and how to use Visual Studio to set the Build Action. You also learned that Expression Blend doesn't provide a way to change the Build Action itself and that you *have* to use Visual Studio (or edit the `.csproj` file by hand). Focus then shifted to effects and 3D support offered by Silverlight and even stepped through creating your own custom effect. You should now have an understanding of how the various tools at your disposal — whether raw XAML, design tools such as Expression Blend, or development environments such as Visual Studio — all have their place in the Silverlight ecosystem and are really co-dependent. You can use one or two exclusively, but ultimately you need to be familiar with a number of design and development tools.

18
Working with Animations in Silverlight

WHAT'S IN THIS CHAPTER?

➤ Performing storyboard animation

➤ Creating complex animations using keyframes

➤ Rendering animations with the CompositionTarget.Rendering event

➤ Animating sprites

As software becomes a greater part of our lives, our experience with it becomes ever more important. Part of this experience can mean adding animation to applications. From Silverlight-based games to basic Line-of-Business applications, Silverlight includes a variety of ways you can add animation to an application.

This chapter looks at the animation capabilities available in Silverlight and the support provided by Visual Studio and Expression Blend to create animations both in XAML and in code. You learn how to use the `Storyboard` and `Animation` objects to create basic and keyframe animations, using Expression Blend to configure them. You also review more advanced techniques such `CompositionTarget` rendering.

Note that although this chapter provides information on animation techniques that can be useful for creating Silverlight games, it is not intended to be a complete guide for creating games and game animations. For more information on creating games, check out the Wrox title *Professional XNA Programming: Building Games for Xbox 360 and Windows with XNA Game Studio 2.0, 2nd Edition* by Benjamin Nitschke (Wiley, 2008). Additionally, you can find information specific to creating Silverlight-based games, including leveraging the XNA framework to build Silverlight games, on this website:

www.bluerosegames.com/silverlight-games-101/

STORYBOARD ANIMATIONS

Storyboard animations allow you to animate object properties over a certain duration. Silverlight supports two variants of storyboard animations: From/To and keyframe. From/To animations allow you to create a linear animation between two values (From/To) or by a set amount (From/By).

Listing 18-1 shows a basic From/To storyboard animation that changes the position of an ellipse over a period of two seconds using a `CompositeTransform`.

LISTING 18-1: Animating an ellipse using a basic animation

```
<sdk:Page xmlns="http://schemas.microsoft.com/winfx/2006/xaml/presentation"
    xmlns:x="http://schemas.microsoft.com/winfx/2006/xaml"
    xmlns:d="http://schemas.microsoft.com/expression/blend/2008"
    xmlns:mc="http://schemas.openxmlformats.org/markup-compatibility/2006"
    mc:Ignorable="d" x:Class="Chapter18.Listing1801"
    xmlns:sdk="http://schemas.microsoft.com/winfx/2006/xaml/presentation/sdk"
    Title="Listing1801 Page" d:DesignWidth="640" d:DesignHeight="480">
    <sdk:Page.Resources>
        <Storyboard x:Name="Storyboard1">
            <DoubleAnimation Duration="0:0:2" To="198"
                Storyboard.TargetProperty="(UIElement.RenderTransform).
                                           (CompositeTransform.TranslateY)"
                Storyboard.TargetName="ellipse" d:IsOptimized="True"/>
        </Storyboard>
    </sdk:Page.Resources>

    <Grid x:Name="LayoutRoot" >
        <Ellipse x:Name="ellipse" Fill="#FF0000BA" Margin="256,170,251,187"
            Stroke="#FF000558" Width="100" Height="100" StrokeThickness="3"
            RenderTransformOrigin="0.5,0.5">
            <Ellipse.RenderTransform>
                <CompositeTransform/>
            </Ellipse.RenderTransform>
        </Ellipse>
    </Grid>
</sdk:Page>
```

As you can see in the listing, the animation consists of a `DoubleAnimation` object inside of a `Storyboard`. The `Storyboard` is responsible for executing the animation, and the `DoubleAnimation` defines the animation's `Duration`, the value to animate to, and the target element and element property on which the animation will act.

You can manually enter this XAML in Visual Studio or you can use the animation tools in Expression Blend. Figure 18-1 shows the basic sample loaded in Expression Blend.

To animate the ellipse using Expression Blend, locate the Objects and Timeline panel in Expression Blend. The panel is shown in Figure 18-2.

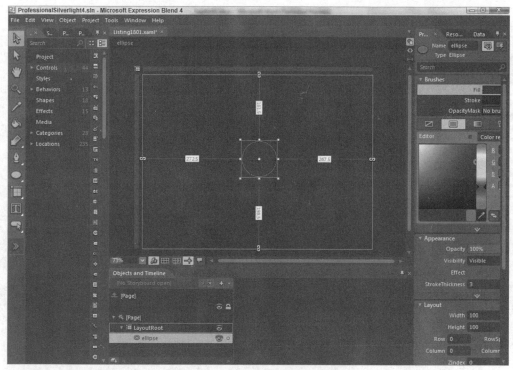

FIGURE 18-1

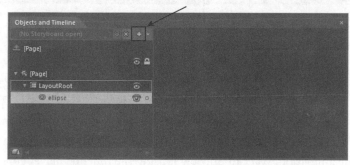

FIGURE 18-2

Click the New Storyboard button and enter a name for the storyboard in the dialog. Once the dialog closes, Expression Blend creates a new storyboard in XAML and enters storyboard record mode, as shown in Figure 18-3.

As you can see, while in storyboard record mode, Expression Blend changes its UI. The Objects and Timeline panel now shows the storyboard timeline. The currently recording storyboard and target element is shown with a red sphere. The design surface is surrounded by a red border and includes a message indicating timeline recording is on.

Recording Storyboard Message   Storyboard Recording Border

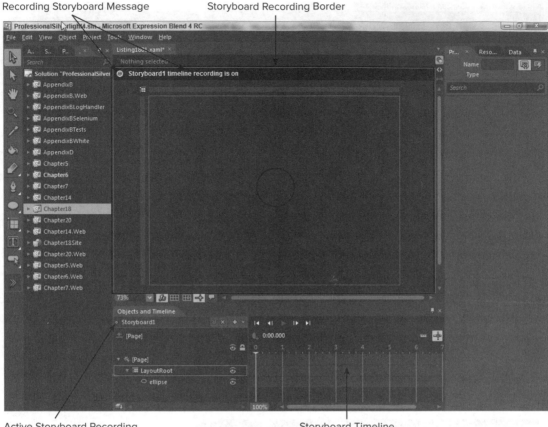

Active Storyboard Recording   Storyboard Timeline

FIGURE 18-3

To create the animation shown in Listing 18-1, select the ellipse in the Objects tree, move the play-head to two seconds, and then on the design surface, move the ellipse. This is shown in Figure 18-4.

Moving the playhead sets the animation's `Duration` property and moving the ellipse sets the animation's `To` property, which tells the animation what value to change the target property to.

Once you've completed setting up the animation, you can preview it using the timeline player controls. These controls not only allow you to play the animation, they also allow you to step frame-by-frame and to move to the first and last frames.

If you review the XAML generated by Expression Blend, you will notice that when it created the animation, it automatically used a `DoubleAnimation` as the animation type. It chose this based on the property changed when you moved the ellipse. Silverlight includes three types of animation objects that Expression Blend can use based on the type of property changed. The animation object types are shown in Table 18-1.

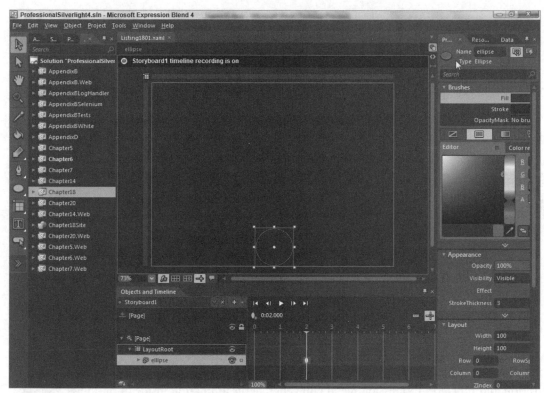

FIGURE 18-4

TABLE 18-1

ANIMATION TYPE	DESCRIPTION
DoubleAnimation	Animates the value of a `Double` property between two target values using linear interpolation over a specified `Duration`.
ColorAnimation	Animates the value of a `Color` property between two target values using linear interpolation over a specified `Duration`.
PointAnimation	Animates the value of a `Point` property between two target values using linear interpolation over a specified `Duration`.

Listing 18-2 shows an example of using the sample ellipse with a `ColorAnimation`.

Available for download on Wrox.com

LISTING 18-2: Animating the color of an ellipse

```
<sdk:Page.Resources>
    <Storyboard x:Name="Storyboard1">
        <ColorAnimation Duration="0:0:2" To="#FF158F0B"
```

continues

LISTING 18-2 *(continued)*

```
                Storyboard.TargetProperty="(Shape.Fill).(SolidColorBrush.Color)"
                Storyboard.TargetName="ellipse" d:IsOptimized="True"/>
        </Storyboard>
    </sdk:Page.Resources>
```

You can animate multiple properties in a single storyboard. For example, you can combine the animations shown in Listing 18-1 and Listing 18-2 into a single storyboard, shown in Listing 18-3.

LISTING 18-3: Animating both the color and position in a single storyboard

```
<sdk:Page.Resources>
    <Storyboard x:Name="Storyboard1">
        <ColorAnimation Duration="0:0:2" To="#FF158F0B"
            Storyboard.TargetProperty="(Shape.Fill).(SolidColorBrush.Color)"
            Storyboard.TargetName="ellipse" d:IsOptimized="True"/>
        <DoubleAnimation Duration="0:0:2" To="198"
            Storyboard.TargetProperty="(UIElement.RenderTransform).
                                       (CompositeTransform.TranslateY)"
            Storyboard.TargetName="ellipse" d:IsOptimized="True"/>
    </Storyboard>
</sdk:Page.Resources>
```

To do this in Expression Blend, while you are editing the storyboard, simply change the ellipse's position and fill color. Expression Blend will generate the animation inside of the single storyboard.

Storyboards include a number of other properties that you can use to control the storyboard play behavior. Some of the properties can be configured using Expression Blend's property panel, whereas others must be set directly in XAML.

To view the Storyboard properties in Expression Blend's property panel, simply select the storyboard from the Objects and Timeline panel. When you do this, Expression Blend exposes the AutoReverse and RepeatBehavior properties. The AutoReverse property allows you to tell the storyboard to automatically play the animation in reverse once it reaches the end of the duration. The RepeatBehavior allows you to configure the storyboard to repeat the animation a set number of times. You can also select the Forever value to have the storyboard repeat indefinitely.

In XAML you can set several other storyboard properties. The SpeedRatio allows you to set the rate at which the animation's time progresses. The BeginTime allows you to set a time that the animation should begin. The FillBehavior allows you to dictate how the animation behaves once it ends.

Because the storyboard and animation objects are all derived from the Timeline class, you can set any of these properties on the storyboard or on the animation objects.

Listing 18-4 demonstrates using several of these properties in a single animation.

LISTING 18-4: Using AutoReverse and RepeatBehavior properties in an animation

```
<sdk:Page.Resources>
    <Storyboard x:Name="Storyboard1" AutoReverse="True" RepeatBehavior="Forever">
        <DoubleAnimation Duration="0:0:1.7" To="282.32"
            Storyboard.TargetProperty="(UIElement.RenderTransform).
                                       (CompositeTransform.TranslateY)"
            Storyboard.TargetName="ellipse" d:IsOptimized="True"/>
        <DoubleAnimation BeginTime="0:0:0.3333333" SpeedRatio="2"
            Duration="0:0:1.7" To="282.32"
            Storyboard.TargetProperty="(UIElement.RenderTransform).
                                       (CompositeTransform.TranslateY)"
            Storyboard.TargetName="ellipse1"/>
        <DoubleAnimation BeginTime="0:0:0.6666667" SpeedRatio="4"
            Duration="0:0:1.7" To="282.32"
            Storyboard.TargetProperty="(UIElement.RenderTransform).
                                       (CompositeTransform.TranslateY)"
            Storyboard.TargetName="ellipse2" d:IsOptimized="True"/>
    </Storyboard>
</sdk:Page.Resources>
```

As shown in the listing, three ellipses are animated by a single storyboard, each with a different `BeginTime` and `SpeedRatio`. The storyboard has the `AutoReverse` property set to `true` and the `ReverseBehavior` set to `Forever`.

Note that even though two of the `Ellipse` elements have `BeginTime` values, this does not affect the overall duration of the animation. It simply delays the start of the animation for those elements.

To play the animation you simply call its `Begin` method. Storyboards also include `Pause`, `Resume`, and `Stop` methods that allow you to programmatically control the animation. Listing 18-5 shows how you can use several buttons to control a storyboard's animation.

LISTING 18-5: Programmatically controlling an animation

```
private void btnPlay_Click(object sender, System.Windows.RoutedEventArgs e)
{
    Storyboard1.Begin();
}

private void btnPause_Click(object sender, System.Windows.RoutedEventArgs e)
{
    Storyboard1.Pause();
}

private void btnResume_Click(object sender, RoutedEventArgs e)
{
    Storyboard1.Resume();
}

private void btnStop_Click(object sender, System.Windows.RoutedEventArgs e)
{
    Storyboard1.Stop();
}
```

Note that if you are using the `Pause` method, you should use the `Resume` method to resume the storyboard (as opposed to using the `Play` method, which can have undesired effects on the storyboard). To see this, pause the animation from Listing 18-1, then click the Play button. You will see that the ellipses transform origin has changed to the location the ellipse was when the play method was called, affecting how the storyboard runs.

Additionally, calling storyboard members in the page constructor causes the Storyboard to silently fail.

Animations can also be created and played completely programmatically. Listing 18-6 shows how you can create and play the animation shown in Listing 18-1 completely in code.

LISTING 18-6: Creating animations completely programmatically

```
protected override void OnNavigatedTo(NavigationEventArgs e)
{
    Storyboard1 = new Storyboard();

    DoubleAnimation doubleAnimation = new DoubleAnimation();
    doubleAnimation.Duration = TimeSpan.FromSeconds(2);
    doubleAnimation.To=198;
    Storyboard1.Children.Add(doubleAnimation);

    Storyboard.SetTargetName(doubleAnimation, "ellipse");
    Storyboard.SetTargetProperty(doubleAnimation,
                            new PropertyPath("(UIElement.RenderTransform).
                                        (CompositeTransform.TranslateX)"));

    this.Resources.Add("Storyboard1", Storyboard1);

    Storyboard1.Begin();
}
```

As shown in the listing, to programmatically create animations, simply create an instance of a new storyboard and an instance of the animation type you want to use. Set the animation type's properties and add it as a child of the storyboard. Finally, set the target element and property using the storyboard's attached properties and add the storyboard to the page's resources so that it will be included in the applications visual tree.

By default when Expression Blend creates an animation it uses the `To` property to set the ending value of the animation, but you can also use the `By` property to set this value. The `By` property tells the animation to change the target property by a certain value. This can be useful when you are not certain of the starting position of the element, but you want to move a specific amount.

Applying Easing Functions

Standard animations in Silverlight run at a uniform speed throughout the duration of the animation, but this does not usually accurately represent the motion that we as humans are used to. In the real world, objects do not move at uniform rates; they tend to accelerate and decelerate as they move. You can simulate this in animations by applying an `Easing` function to the animation.

Silverlight 4 includes a set of predefined easing functions described in the Table 18-2.

TABLE 18-2

EASING FUNCTION	DESCRIPTION
Back	Represents an easing function that retracts the motion of an animation slightly before it begins to animate in the path indicated.
Bounce	Represents an easing function that creates an animated bouncing effect.
Circle	Represents an easing function that creates an animation that accelerates and/or decelerates using a circular function.
Cubic	Represents an easing function that creates an animation that accelerates and/or decelerates using the formula $f(t) = t3$.
Elastic	Represents an easing function that creates an animation that resembles a spring oscillating back and forth until it comes to rest.
Exponential	Represents an easing function that creates an animation that accelerates and/or decelerates using an exponential formula.
Power	Represents an easing function that creates an animation that accelerates and/or decelerates using the formula $f(t) = tp$, where p is equal to the Power property.
Quadratic	Represents an easing function that creates an animation that accelerates and/or decelerates using the formula $f(t) = t2$.
Quartic	Represents an easing function that creates an animation that accelerates and/or decelerates using the formula $f(t) = t4$.
Quintic	Represents an easing function that creates an animation that accelerates and/or decelerates using the formula $f(t) = t5$.
Sine	Represents an easing function that creates an animation that accelerates and/or decelerates using a sine formula.

To apply an easing to an animation simply set the animation's `EasingFunction` property as shown in Listing 18-7.

LISTING 18-7: Applying an easing function to an animation

```
<sdk:Page.Resources>
    <Storyboard x:Name="Storyboard1">
        <DoubleAnimation Duration="0:0:2" To="198"
            Storyboard.TargetProperty="(UIElement.RenderTransform).
                                (CompositeTransform.TranslateY)"
```

continues

LISTING 18-7 *(continued)*

```
            Storyboard.TargetName="ellipse" d:IsOptimized="True">
            <DoubleAnimation.EasingFunction>
                <BounceEase EasingMode="EaseOut" />
            </DoubleAnimation.EasingFunction>
        </DoubleAnimation>
    </Storyboard>
</sdk:Page.Resources>
```

You can also use Expression Blend to set the `Easing` function of an animation. Simply place the storyboard into record mode and then expand and select the `RenderTransform` under the ellipse as shown in Figure 18-5.

Once the transform is selected, you can use the Properties panel to select and configure an easing function. The Properties panel with a `BounceOut` function selected is shown in Figure 18-6.

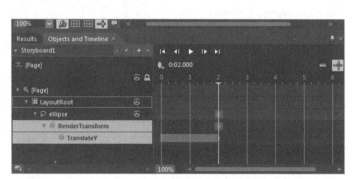

FIGURE 18-5

FIGURE 18-6

Easing functions allow you to configure how they should be applied to an animation using the `EasingMode` property, which includes three values: `EaseIn`, `EaseOut`, or `EaseInOut`. Figure 18-7 shows how the `BounceEase` animation changes based on the value of the `EasingMode` property.

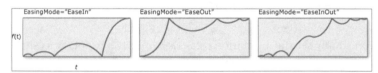

FIGURE 18-7

Additionally, each easing includes properties specific to its own function. For example, the `BounceEase` class exposes properties that allow you to control the number of bounces and the elasticity of the bounces.

Controlling Storyboards Using Behaviors

Expression Blend 4 includes a new `ControlStoryboardAction` behavior that allows you to easily add the ability to control storyboards without writing any code. To use the behavior, add a `Button` to your application and then locate the `ControlStoryboardAction` behavior in the Expression Blend Assets. Select the behavior and drop it into the `Button`.

Once you have added the behavior, locate and select it in the Objects and Timeline panel. You can now configure the behavior using the Properties panel, which is shown in Figure 18-8.

To configure the behavior to start the animation, create a new `TriggerType` from the Properties panel, select the Button as value of the `SourceObject` property, and then select Click from the `EventName` property.

FIGURE 18-8

Now you simply select the Action you want the `Button` to execute, and the storyboard it should target.

Nesting Storyboards

You can nest storyboards inside of other storyboards, allowing you to create more complex storyboard animations. Listing 18-8 shows a single storyboard that contains three nested storyboards, each animating a separate ellipse.

LISTING 18-8: Nesting multiple storyboards together

```
<sdk:Page.Resources>
    <Storyboard x:Name="Storyboard1">
        <Storyboard x:Name="Storyboard1a">
            <DoubleAnimation Duration="0:0:1.7" To="282.32"
            Storyboard.TargetProperty="(UIElement.RenderTransform).
                                       (CompositeTransform.TranslateY)"
            Storyboard.TargetName="ellipse" d:IsOptimized="True"/>
        </Storyboard>
        <Storyboard x:Name="Storyboard1b">
            <DoubleAnimation BeginTime="0:0:0.3333333" SpeedRatio="2"
            Duration="0:0:1.7" To="282.32"
            Storyboard.TargetProperty="(UIElement.RenderTransform).
                                       (CompositeTransform.TranslateY)"
            Storyboard.TargetName="ellipse1"/>
        </Storyboard>
        <Storyboard x:Name="Storyboard1c">
                <DoubleAnimation BeginTime="0:0:0.6666667" SpeedRatio="4"
            Duration="0:0:1.7" To="282.32"
            Storyboard.TargetProperty="(UIElement.RenderTransform).
                                       (CompositeTransform.TranslateY)"
            Storyboard.TargetName="ellipse2" d:IsOptimized="True"/>
        </Storyboard>
    </Storyboard>
</sdk:Page.Resources>
```

Starting the parent storyboard automatically runs each child storyboard but allows you the flexibility to run each storyboard independent of any others.

Using Storyboards as Timers

Storyboards can also be used as timers in your application. Storyboards run on a separate thread. To create a timer using a storyboard, simply add an empty storyboard to your application, set a duration, and handle the storyboard's `Completed` event. Listing 18-9 shows the empty storyboard created in XAML.

LISTING 18-9: Setting up an empty storyboard to use as a timer

```
<sdk:Page.Resources>
    <Storyboard x:Name="Storyboard1" Duration="0:0:1"
                Completed="Storyboard1_Completed" />
</sdk:Page.Resources>
```

In the storyboard's `Completed` event, shown in Listing 18-10, you can perform the timed action, which in this case is incrementing a counter and updating a `TextBlock`.

LISTING 18-10: Responding to the animation's Completed event

```
private void Storyboard1_Completed(object sender, EventArgs e)
{
    seconds++;
    this.txtSeconds.Text = seconds.ToString();
    Storyboard1.Begin();
}
```

Using a storyboard for a timer also allows you to create animations that use vector movement. Listing 18-11 shows how a simple storyboard can be used as a vector movement timer to animate an ellipse in a `Canvas`.

LISTING 18-11: Creating simple vector animation using a storyboard

```
protected override void OnNavigatedTo(NavigationEventArgs e)
{
    Storyboard1 = new Storyboard();
    Storyboard1.Completed+=new EventHandler(Storyboard1_Completed);

    doubleAnimation = new DoubleAnimation();
    doubleAnimation.Duration = TimeSpan.FromMilliseconds(1);
    doubleAnimation.By = 5;
    Storyboard1.Children.Add(doubleAnimation);

    Storyboard.SetTargetName(doubleAnimation, "ellipse");
    Storyboard.SetTargetProperty(doubleAnimation,
        new PropertyPath("(Canvas.Left)"));

    this.Resources.Add("Storyboard1", Storyboard1);

    Storyboard1.Begin();
}
```

Using the storyboard's `Completed` event, you can change the animation parameters. Listing 18-12 show how you can add a test to see if the ellipse has reached the left or right edge of the canvas, and if so, you can reverse its direction by multiplying the `By` value by –1.

LISTING 18-12: Changing the vector animation direction

```
private void Storyboard1_Completed(object sender, EventArgs e)
{
    double left = Canvas.GetLeft(ellipse);

    if ( ((left+ellipse.ActualWidth) >= this.ActualWidth) || (left <=0) )
    {
        doubleAnimation.By = doubleAnimation.By * -1;
    }

    Storyboard1.Begin();
}
```

Of course, in this simple sample only a single attribute is being tested and updated. But you can imagine how, by adding additional animations and tests, you could create some very complex animations.

KEYFRAME ANIMATION

The second mechanism of creating animations in Silverlight is keyframe animation. Keyframe animations are more powerful than standard storyboard animations. They allow you to create more complex animations by changing multiple values over a period of time and controlling the interpolation method used.

Silverlight includes four keyframe animation types, as shown in Table 18-3.

TABLE 18-3

ANIMATION TYPE	DESCRIPTION
`DoubleAnimationUsingKeyFrames`	Animates the value of a `Double` property along a set of `KeyFrames`.
`ColorAnimationUsingKeyFrames`	Animates the value of a `Color` property along a set of `KeyFrames` over a specified `Duration`.
`PointAnimationUsingKeyFrames`	Animates the value of a `Point` property along a set of `KeyFrames`.
`ObjectAnimationUsingKeyFrames`	Animates the value of an `Object` property along a set of `KeyFrames` over a specified `Duration`.

Notice that the available keyframe animation types are similar to the standard animation types, with the addition of the `ObjectAnimationUsingKeyFrames` type.

Listing 18-13 demonstrates the use of a keyframe animation, converting the code from Listing 18-1 from a standard storyboard animation to a keyframe animation.

LISTING 18-13: Using a keyframe animation to animate an ellipse

```
<sdk:Page xmlns="http://schemas.microsoft.com/winfx/2006/xaml/presentation"
    xmlns:x="http://schemas.microsoft.com/winfx/2006/xaml"
    xmlns:d="http://schemas.microsoft.com/expression/blend/2008"
    xmlns:mc="http://schemas.openxmlformats.org/markup-compatibility/2006"
    mc:Ignorable="d" x:Class="Chapter18.Listing1813"
    xmlns:sdk="http://schemas.microsoft.com/winfx/2006/xaml/presentation/sdk"
    Title="Listing1813 Page" d:DesignWidth="640" d:DesignHeight="480">
    <sdk:Page.Resources>
        <Storyboard x:Name="Storyboard1">
            <DoubleAnimationUsingKeyFrames
                    Storyboard.TargetProperty="(UIElement.RenderTransform).
                                        (CompositeTransform.TranslateY)"
                    Storyboard.TargetName="ellipse">
                <EasingDoubleKeyFrame KeyTime="0" Value="0"/>
                <EasingDoubleKeyFrame KeyTime="0:0:2" Value="198"/>
            </DoubleAnimationUsingKeyFrames>
        </Storyboard>
    </sdk:Page.Resources>

    <Grid x:Name="LayoutRoot" >
        <Ellipse x:Name="ellipse" Fill="#FF0000BA" Margin="256,170,251,187"
            Stroke="#FF000558" Width="100" Height="100" StrokeThickness="3"
            RenderTransformOrigin="0.5,0.5">
            <Ellipse.RenderTransform>
                <CompositeTransform/>
            </Ellipse.RenderTransform>
        </Ellipse>
    </Grid>
</sdk:Page>
```

In this listing notice that rather than a `DoubleAnimation`, the storyboard contains a `DoubleAnimationKeyFrames` object, which itself contains two `EasingDoubleKeyFrame` objects. The `EasingDoubleKeyFrame` objects define the time and values that the animation should interpolate between as well as the style of interpolation.

You can create this example in Expression Blend by opening the storyboard in the Objects and Timeline panel; within the timeline, add keyframes at the appropriate points using the Record Keyframe button, shown in Figure 18-9.

As with creating standard animations, when you create the animation using Expression Blend, Expression Blend automatically chooses an appropriate `KeyFrames` object to use based on the properties being animated. Within the KeyFrames object, you can change the specific type of KeyFrame objects used to interpolate between keyframes by using the Properties panel.

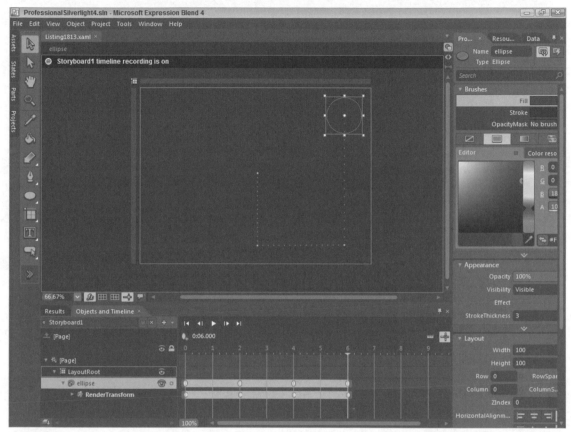

FIGURE 18-9

To change the EasingDoubleKeyFrame shown in Listing 18-13 to a different keyframe type, select the RenderTransform from the Objects and Timeline panel. On the Properties panel, change the Easing selection. The Properties panel is shown in Figure 18-10.

As you can see, Expression Blend exposes three easing types, KeySpline, EasingFunction, and Hold In. These different types correspond to the SplineDoubleKeyFrame, EasingDoubleKeyFrame, and DiscreteDoubleKeyFrame objects, respectively.

The different types of KeyFrame objects available in Silverlight are described in Table 18-4.

FIGURE 18-10

TABLE 18-4

KEYFRAME TYPE	DESCRIPTION
LinearDoubleKeyFrame	Animates from the `Double` value of the previous keyframe to its own `Value` using linear interpolation.
DiscreteDoubleKeyFrame	Animates from the `Double` value of the previous keyframe to its own `Value` using discrete values.
SplineDoubleKeyFrame	Animates from the `Double` value of the previous keyframe to its own `Value` using splined interpolation.
EasingDoubleKeyFrame	Defines a property that enables you to associate an easing function with a `DoubleAnimationUsingKeyFrames` key frame animation.

`KeyFrame` objects like those described in Table 18-4 exist for each of the keyframe animation types shown previously in Table 18-3.

To create more complex animations using multiple keyframes, simply add additional keyframe objects to the animation object. You can do this manually in XAML or you can use Expression Blend.

To add additional keyframes to Listing 18-13 in Expression Blend, place the storyboard into recording mode, move the playhead to the new position in the timeline, click the Create Keyframe button to insert a new keyframe, and then move the ellipse to a new location. Listing 18-14 shows how the XAML is changed by Expression Blend.

LISTING 18-14: Adding multiple keyframes to an animation

```xaml
<sdk:Page.Resources>
    <Storyboard x:Name="Storyboard1">
        <DoubleAnimationUsingKeyFrames
            Storyboard.TargetProperty="(UIElement.RenderTransform).
                                      (CompositeTransform.TranslateY)"
            Storyboard.TargetName="ellipse">
            <EasingDoubleKeyFrame KeyTime="0" Value="0"/>
            <EasingDoubleKeyFrame KeyTime="0:0:2" Value="198"/>
            <EasingDoubleKeyFrame KeyTime="0:0:4" Value="196.5"/>
            <EasingDoubleKeyFrame KeyTime="0:0:6" Value="-157.5"/>
        </DoubleAnimationUsingKeyFrames>
        <DoubleAnimationUsingKeyFrames
            Storyboard.TargetProperty="(UIElement.RenderTransform).
                                      (CompositeTransform.TranslateX)"
            Storyboard.TargetName="ellipse">
            <EasingDoubleKeyFrame KeyTime="0:0:2" Value="0"/>
            <EasingDoubleKeyFrame KeyTime="0:0:4" Value="241.5"/>
            <EasingDoubleKeyFrame KeyTime="0:0:6" Value="241.5"/>
        </DoubleAnimationUsingKeyFrames>
    </Storyboard>
</sdk:Page.Resources>
```

You can see the keyframes added by Expression Blend. Additionally, because the animation changes both the `TranslateX` and `TranslateY` properties of the `CompositeTransform`, an additional double animation was added by Expression Blend.

Rendering CompositionTargets

In the previous section you learned how you can use keyframe animations to animate sprites. Silverlight offers an even higher resolution method for rendering animations with the `CompositionTarget.Rendering` event. The `CompositionTarget.Rendering` event is fired before each frame is rendered and is generally the highest priority loop in Silverlight.

Listing 18-15 shows how to modify the visuals in Silverlight before they are rendered using the `Rendering` event.

LISTING 18-15: Using the CompositionTarget Rendering event to alter Silverlight visuals

```
public partial class Listing1815 : Page
{
    public Listing1815()
    {
        InitializeComponent();
    }

    // Executes when the user navigates to this page.
    protected override void OnNavigatedTo(NavigationEventArgs e)
    {
        CompositionTarget.Rendering +=
            new EventHandler(CompositionTarget_Rendering);
    }

    bool reverseHeight = false;
    bool reverseWidth = false;
    void CompositionTarget_Rendering(object sender, EventArgs e)
    {
        RenderingEventArgs args = e as RenderingEventArgs;
        TimeSpan time = args.RenderingTime;

        double left = Canvas.GetLeft(ellipse);
        double top = Canvas.GetTop(ellipse);

        if (reverseHeight)
        {
            top--;
            if (top <= 0)
                reverseHeight = false;

            Canvas.SetTop(ellipse, top);
        }
        else
        {
            top++;
```

continues

LISTING 18-15 *(continued)*

```
        if (top + ellipse.ActualHeight >= this.ActualHeight)
            reverseHeight = true;

        Canvas.SetTop(ellipse, top);
    }

    if (reverseWidth)
    {
        left--;
        if (left <= 0)
            reverseWidth = false;

        Canvas.SetLeft(ellipse, left);
    }
    else
    {
        left++;
        if (left + ellipse.ActualWidth >= this.ActualWidth)
            reverseWidth = true;

        Canvas.SetLeft(ellipse, left);
    }
  }
}
```

In this listing, the `Rendering` event is used to modify the position of the ellipse. When the ellipse reaches the edge of the canvas, its direction is reversed.

Note that because the `Rendering` event takes such a high priority in the Silverlight application, to avoid performance problems in your application you should avoid putting long-running or performance-intensive logic in the event.

Animating Visibility

A common task in applications is toggling the visibility of UI elements as users navigate the applications. In Silverlight, it's common to see this toggling performed using an animation to add a smooth fade-in/fade-out transition rather than simply toggling an element's `Visibility` property.

Listing 18-16 shows an example of how to use keyframe animation to create an animation that changes an element's opacity and then toggles its `Visibility`.

LISTING 18-16: Toggling element visibility using an animation

```
<sdk:Page.Resources>
    <Storyboard x:Name="Storyboard1">
        <DoubleAnimationUsingKeyFrames
            Storyboard.TargetProperty="(UIElement.Opacity)"
            Storyboard.TargetName="ellipse">
            <EasingDoubleKeyFrame KeyTime="0" Value="1"/>
```

```xml
                <EasingDoubleKeyFrame KeyTime="0:0:1" Value="0"/>
            </DoubleAnimationUsingKeyFrames>
            <ObjectAnimationUsingKeyFrames
                Storyboard.TargetProperty="(UIElement.Visibility)"
                Storyboard.TargetName="ellipse">
                <DiscreteObjectKeyFrame KeyTime="0">
                    <DiscreteObjectKeyFrame.Value>
                        <Visibility>Visible</Visibility>
                    </DiscreteObjectKeyFrame.Value>
                </DiscreteObjectKeyFrame>
                <DiscreteObjectKeyFrame KeyTime="0:0:1">
                    <DiscreteObjectKeyFrame.Value>
                        <Visibility>Collapsed</Visibility>
                    </DiscreteObjectKeyFrame.Value>
                </DiscreteObjectKeyFrame>
            </ObjectAnimationUsingKeyFrames>
        </Storyboard>
        <Storyboard x:Name="Storyboard2">
            <DoubleAnimationUsingKeyFrames
                Storyboard.TargetProperty="(UIElement.Opacity)"
                Storyboard.TargetName="ellipse">
                <EasingDoubleKeyFrame KeyTime="0" Value="0"/>
                <EasingDoubleKeyFrame KeyTime="0:0:1" Value="1"/>
            </DoubleAnimationUsingKeyFrames>
            <ObjectAnimationUsingKeyFrames
                Storyboard.TargetProperty="(UIElement.Visibility)"
                Storyboard.TargetName="ellipse">
                <DiscreteObjectKeyFrame KeyTime="0">
                    <DiscreteObjectKeyFrame.Value>
                        <Visibility>Visible</Visibility>
                    </DiscreteObjectKeyFrame.Value>
                </DiscreteObjectKeyFrame>
            </ObjectAnimationUsingKeyFrames>
        </Storyboard>
    </sdk:Page.Resources>
```

As shown in the listing, two storyboards were created:

➤ One that changes the ellipse Opacity to 0 over two seconds and then changes its Visibility to Collapsed.

➤ One that performs the opposite animation.

Notice that that the visibility value is changed using a `DiscreteObjectKeyFrame` inside of an `ObjectAnimationUsingKeyFrames` animation. The `DiscreteObjectKeyFrame` object allows you to animate properties whose value is a complex object type as opposed to a simple type. As shown in the previous listing, you can set the target value of the keyframe by defining an instance of the object as its `Value` property.

If you are animating the opacity of an element (as shown in the previous listing), you should consider setting the `CacheMode` on the element, which allows the animation to render in the GPU. Listing 18-17 shows you how to add the `CacheMode` property to the ellipse.

LISTING 18-17: Caching elements to improve animation performance

```
<Ellipse x:Name="ellipse" Fill="#FF0000BA" Margin="256,170,251,187"
    Stroke="#FF000558" Width="100" Height="100" StrokeThickness="3"
    RenderTransformOrigin="0.5,0.5">
    <Ellipse.CacheMode>
        <BitmapCache />
    </Ellipse.CacheMode>
    <Ellipse.RenderTransform>
        <CompositeTransform/>
    </Ellipse.RenderTransform>
</Ellipse>
```

You can see the results of setting the `CacheMode` property by enabling GPU acceleration on the Silverlight plug-in, then setting the application's `EnableCacheVisualization` property to `true`.

If you run the application now, Silverlight shades any non-accelerated area in red. You should see that the ellipse is not shaded because the `CacheMode` property has been set on it, indicating that when it is animated, it will be hardware-accelerated.

Animating Sprites

Sprite animation is a great example of keyframe animation. Sprites are two-dimensional images or graphics that are integrated into a larger scene and are commonly used in games for animation. Similar to an old-fashioned flipbook, sprite animation relies on showing and hiding a sequence of images over a short period of time so that Silverlight appears to animate the image.

> *The rate at which images are shown is called the frame rate. The frame rate is typically measured as the number of images shown per second or the number of frames per second (FPS). You can set the maximum number of frames per second on the Silverlight plug-in by setting its* `MaxFrameRate` *property.*

Creating sprite animations in Silverlight is easy using Expression Blend. To get started, add the sprite images to your project and place them onto the design surface, aligning them vertically and/or horizontally. Select all of the images from the Objects and Timeline panel and then change their `Visibility` property to `Collapsed`.

Now you can start creating the animation. Begin by creating a new storyboard. While the storyboard is in record mode, select the first sprite image. Place a keyframe at zero in the timeline and change the first image's `Visibility` property to `Visible`.

Next move the playhead ahead to the next time increment and insert another keyframe. The specific time increment will depend on the number of sprite images you are animating. For example, if you have 30 sprite images, the time each image is displayed is 0.333333 seconds.

With the playhead at the first interval, set the first image's `Visibility` back to `Collapsed`. Select the second sprite image and change its `Visibility` property to `Visible`.

Move the playhead forward to the next interval (0.666667 if you have 30 sprite images) and insert a new keyframe. Set the second image's `Visibility` property to `Collapsed`.

Listing 18-18 shows the animation XAML generated by Expression Blend for the first and second images.

LISTING 18-18: Animating sprites using keyframes

```xml
<ObjectAnimationUsingKeyFrames
        Storyboard.TargetProperty="(UIElement.Visibility)"
        Storyboard.TargetName="image00">
    <DiscreteObjectKeyFrame KeyTime="0">
        <DiscreteObjectKeyFrame.Value>
            <Visibility>Visible</Visibility>
        </DiscreteObjectKeyFrame.Value>
    </DiscreteObjectKeyFrame>
    <DiscreteObjectKeyFrame KeyTime="0:0:0.0333333">
        <DiscreteObjectKeyFrame.Value>
            <Visibility>Collapsed</Visibility>
        </DiscreteObjectKeyFrame.Value>
    </DiscreteObjectKeyFrame>
</ObjectAnimationUsingKeyFrames>
<ObjectAnimationUsingKeyFrames
        Storyboard.TargetProperty="(UIElement.Visibility)"
        Storyboard.TargetName="image01">
    <DiscreteObjectKeyFrame KeyTime="0:0:0.0333333">
        <DiscreteObjectKeyFrame.Value>
            <Visibility>Visible</Visibility>
        </DiscreteObjectKeyFrame.Value>
    </DiscreteObjectKeyFrame>
    <DiscreteObjectKeyFrame KeyTime="0:0:0.0666667">
        <DiscreteObjectKeyFrame.Value>
            <Visibility>Collapsed</Visibility>
        </DiscreteObjectKeyFrame.Value>
    </DiscreteObjectKeyFrame>
</ObjectAnimationUsingKeyFrames>
```

Continue this process for each of the remaining sprite images in your animation, incrementing the `KeyTime` for each animation. Once completed, you can run the animation and see the sprites animate.

SUMMARY

This chapter introduced you to the variety of ways that you can create animations in a Silverlight application. Using storyboards and animation objects or keyframes, you can easily add animations as simple as making a `Button` fade out to animations as complex as sprite animations. Leveraging the animation tools in Expression Blend makes adding animations even easier.

19

Working with Text

WHAT'S IN THIS CHAPTER?

➤ Using TextBlock and RichTextBox

➤ Supporting and rendering text and fonts

Although the graphical browser has made the Web a powerful platform for expressing ideas using complex imagery, a core function of the Web remains to disseminate information, and text remains a primary mechanism to achieve this function. The basic text capabilities of HTML and CSS have improved dramatically, giving you significant control over the layout and appearance of the text displayed in your website. Silverlight provides you with many of the same powerful capabilities of HTML and CSS and extends those basic capabilities with even more functionality that can dramatically enhance your ability to control, to a fine point, the way your website delivers textual information.

This chapter looks at the features included in Silverlight for inputting, displaying, and formatting text using the `TextBlock` and `RichTextBox` controls. The chapter also covers the different font support options included in Silverlight and how transformations can be used to alter the look of text.

 Although this chapter covers the `RichTextBox` *control, you can find additional content on other text input controls like the* `TextBox` *and* `AutoComplete` *box in Chapter 6.*

DISPLAYING AND INPUTTING TEXT

Silverlight includes a variety of ways to display and input text. The easiest way to display text in your application is to use the `TextBlock` control. If you need more advanced display of text, such as rich text display, you can use the `RichTextBox` control.

Using the TextBlock Element

The basic mechanism for displaying text in Silverlight is the `TextBlock` element. This basic element encapsulates text display and serves as the core means of manipulating the text display. Listing 19-1 shows the most basic use of the `TextBlock` element in Silverlight.

LISTING 19-1: Adding content to a TextBlock

```
<TextBlock>Lorem ipsum dolor sit amet, consectetuer adipiscing
    elit. Fusce porttitor, tellus id tristique viverra, ligula pede
    pulvinar purus, nec hendrerit urna justo et nulla. Cras
    condimentum nulla at ipsum. Nullam nulla. Sed elit lectus,
    hendrerit rhoncus, gravida id, tristique quis, justo. Vivamus
    et enim. Nunc accumsan. Curabitur ultrices dui ac tortor. Nunc
    mollis, turpis quis consequat laoreet, nisl quam laoreet justo,
    a euismod magna nisi sed orci. Etiam nec dui egestas elit
    pretium sodales. Etiam felis.</TextBlock>
```

Figure 19-1 shows this `TextBlock` rendered in a default Silverlight `UserControl`.

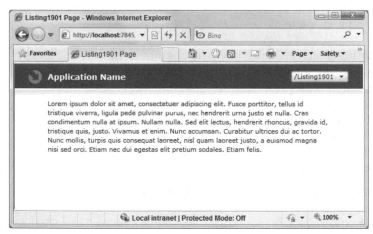

FIGURE 19-1

The `TextBlock` control also includes a `Text` property, shown in Listing 19-2, that you can use to provide the element's content.

LISTING 19-2: Using the TextBlock's Text property

```
<TextBlock Text="Lorem ipsum dolor sit amet, consectetuer adipiscing elit.
    Fusce porttitor, tellus id tristique viverra, ligula pede pulvinar purus,
    nec hendrerit urna justo et nulla. Cras condimentum nulla at ipsum. Nullam
    nulla. Sed elit lectus, hendrerit rhoncus, gravida id, tristique quis,
    justo. Vivamus et enim. Nunc accumsan. Curabitur ultrices dui ac tortor.
```

```
Nunc mollis, turpis quis consequat laoreet, nisl quam laoreet justo, a
euismod magna nisi sed orci. Etiam nec dui egestas elit pretium sodales.
Etiam felis."></TextBlock>
```

 There is a slight difference in the behavior of the TextBlock, *depending on whether you provide the text content using the* Text *property or as inline content. Starting in Silverlight 4, when you use the* Text *property, the Silverlight parser will honor any whitespace that may be present in the text; however, this same whitespace is ignored by the Silverlight parser when using the content inline.*

You can force the parser to honor the whitespace in inline content by adding xml:space="preserve" *to the* TextBlock.

 You may notice that the Silverlight design surface does not always render text content identically to the Silverlight run time. Because of a bug in the design surface, it doesn't always correctly render TextBlock *and* RichTextBox *content that contains embedded tags or spaces. At run time, the Silverlight plug-in renders the content correctly.*

You can force the design surface to honor the whitespace in inline content by adding xml:space="preserve" *to the control.*

The TextBlock includes a variety of properties that allow you to control various font-related properties such as the family, weight, style, and size. Listing 19-3 shows the TextBlock with additional font-related properties set.

LISTING 19-3: Setting font properties on the TextBlock

```
<TextBlock FontFamily="Times New Roman" FontSize="24"
    FontStyle="Italic" FontWeight="Bold">Lorem ipsum dolor sit amet,
    consectetuer adipiscing elit. Fusce porttitor, tellus id tristique
    viverra, ligula pede pulvinar purus, nec hendrerit urna justo et
    nulla. Cras condimentum nulla at ipsum. Nullam nulla. Sed elit
    lectus, hendrerit rhoncus, gravida id, tristique quis, justo.
    Vivamus et enim. Nunc accumsan. Curabitur ultrices dui ac tortor.
    Nunc mollis, turpis quis consequat laoreet, nisl quam laoreet justo,
    a euismod magna nisi sed orci. Etiam nec dui egestas elit
    pretium sodales. Etiam felis.</TextBlock>
```

The FontFamily property allows you to specify the family of fonts that the TextBlock should use to display the text. A *font family* is a group of typefaces with the same name but differing in features such as Bold or Italic.

You can provide a list of fallback fonts by providing a comma-delimited list of font family names:

```
<TextBlock FontFamily="My Favorite Font, Times New Roman" FontSize="24">
```

In the preceding sample, if the font family named My Favorite Font cannot be found on the client, Silverlight automatically falls back to using Times New Roman as the font for this TextBlock. It is also possible to use custom fonts by specifying the font name. This is described later in this chapter.

The FontStyle property allows you to specify a style to apply to the font. Currently, Silverlight supports two FontStyle values: Normal, which is the default, and Italic.

The FontWeight property allows you to specify that a font be displayed as bold.

Silverlight also includes the ability to algorithmically render italic and bold fonts, when a true italic or bold font set is not available. If the FontStyle is set to Italic or the FontWeight is set to Bold, Silverlight first attempts to locate an italic or bold font set on the local system. If none is found, it falls back to algorithmic font rendering and generates Italic and/or Bold glyphs for display. Unlike most applications, which measure font size in points, the FontSize property in Silverlight is a numeric value that represents the font size in pixels. This is done to maintain compatibility with Windows Presentation Foundation (WPF); however, it can cause some confusion if you try to compare a font size set in an application like Microsoft Word against the font size rendered by Silverlight. For example, setting the FontSize property to 24 doesn't render a font of 24 *points* as you might expect; instead, this value represents 24 *pixels*, which Silverlight converts to a point value. This is shown in Figure 19-2, which shows a 24-point font rendered in Word (top) and a 24-pixel font rendered in Silverlight (bottom).

> This is a font size of 24
> This is a font size of 24

FIGURE 19-2

Notice how much smaller the 24-pixel font appears in Silverlight because of the pixels-to-points conversion. Silverlight renders text at a default 14.666 pixels, which converts to exactly 11 points.

 The calculation from pixels to points is one of the few areas of Silverlight that contains a fixed value. To run this conversion, Silverlight needs to know a dots-per-inch (dpi) value, which is hard-coded at 96 dpi.

In addition to font properties, the TextBlock also allows you to set the foreground of its text. Unlike many other platforms, where you are limited to simply setting the foreground color of the font, Silverlight allows you to provide any standard Brush type as the Foreground property value. The following sample demonstrates using a simple SolidColorBrush to change the foreground color:

```
<TextBlock Foreground="Green">
```

Notice that you can simply provide the property with a named color, and it automatically converts it to the appropriate brush.

If you want to get more complex, you can provide more complex brushes such as a gradient brush or even image or video brushes. Listing 19-4 demonstrates how to provide a LinearGradientBrush for the TextBlock's foreground property.

LISTING 19-4: Setting the TextBlock's Foreground to a GradientBrush

```
<TextBlock TextWrapping="Wrap" >
    <TextBlock.Foreground>
        <LinearGradientBrush EndPoint="0,0" StartPoint="1,1">
            <GradientStop Color="#FFFF2300"/>
            <GradientStop Color="#FFFB00FF" Offset="1"/>
            <GradientStop Color="#FFF0FF00"
                Offset="0.25900000333786011"/>
            <GradientStop Color="#FF1CFF00"
                Offset="0.51800000667572021"/>
            <GradientStop Color="#FF0B07FF"
                Offset="0.75900000333786011"/>
        </LinearGradientBrush>
    </TextBlock.Foreground>
    Lorem ipsum dolor sit amet, consectetuer adipiscing elit. Fusce
    porttitor, tellus id tristique viverra, ligula pede pulvinar purus,
    nec hendrerit urna justo et nulla. Cras condimentum nulla at ipsum.
    Nullam nulla. Sed elit lectus, hendrerit rhoncus, gravida id,
    tristique quis, justo. Vivamus et enim. Nunc accumsan. Curabitur
    ultrices dui ac tortor. Nunc mollis, turpis quis consequat laoreet,
    nisl quam laoreet justo, a euismod magna nisi sed orci. Etiam nec
    dui egestas elit pretium sodales. Etiam felis.
</TextBlock>
```

Figure 19-3 shows what your text will look like after setting the Foreground to a LinearGradientBrush.

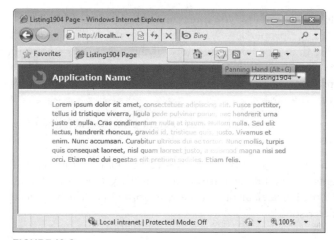

FIGURE 19-3

Using Text Element Layout Properties

The TextBlock element also includes a series of properties that allow you to influence the layout of text in the TextBlock. TextWrapping, LineHeight, and LineStackingStrategy are all properties that give you fine-grained control over the layout of the TextBlock's text.

The `TextWrapping` property allows you to indicate whether you want the text within the `TextBlock` to automatically wrap based on the size of the `TextBlock`. As you have seen in previous samples in this chapter, by default, if your `TextBlock`'s text exceeds its container, it is simply clipped. To instead set the text to wrap, simply set the `TextWrapping` property to `Wrap`, as shown in Listing 19-5.

LISTING 19-5: Setting the TextBlock's TextWrapping property

```
<TextBlock TextWrapping="Wrap">Lorem ipsum dolor sit amet,
    consectetuer adipiscing elit. Fusce porttitor, tellus id
    tristique viverra, ligula pede pulvinar purus, nec hendrerit
    urna justo et nulla. Cras condimentum nulla at ipsum. Nullam
    nulla. Sed elit lectus, hendrerit rhoncus, gravida id, tristique
    quis, justo. Vivamus et enim. Nunc accumsan. Curabitur ultrices
    dui ac tortor. Nunc mollis, turpis quis consequat laoreet, nisl
    quam laoreet justo, a euismod magna nisi sed orci. Etiam nec dui
    egestas elit pretium sodales. Etiam felis.</TextBlock>
```

Enabling text wrapping allows the `TextBlock` to intelligently wrap the text to fit it within the width of its container.

Note that even though the `TextBlock` wraps text horizontally, if the wrapped text exceeds the vertical height available to the `TextBlock`, the text continues to be clipped.

For East Asian text, Silverlight correctly uses Kinsoku line-breaking rules when wrapping is enabled.

Also keep in mind that when you enable text wrapping, you alter the values returned from the `TextBlock`'s `ActualWidth` and `ActualHeight` properties. When text wrapping is disabled, the `ActualWidth` property returns a value that is equal to the width of the `TextBlock`'s container. When text wrapping is enabled, the `ActualWidth` will be the length of the longest wrapped line in the `TextBlock`. The `TextWrapping` property is honored even if the `TextBlock` is given infinite width, such as when it is contained in a `StackPanel`.

`LineHeight` and `LineStackingStrategy` give you control over the height given to each line of text and how lines are stacked when wrapped.

`LineStackingStrategy` offers two options. `MaxHeight` says that Silverlight should use the smallest value that contains all of the inline elements on that line that are aligned properly. `BlockLineHeight` says that the stack height is determined by the block element's `LineHeight` property, which by default is determined according to the font characteristics.

Using Text Trimming

A new feature of Silverlight 4 is Text Trimming. This simple feature allows you to tell Silverlight to automatically trim words that exceed the bounds of the `TextBlock`. To enable Text Trimming, use the `TextTrimming` property:

```
<TextBlock TextTrimming="WordEllipsis">
```

As indicated by the property value, trimmed text is indicated to the end user by the insertion of an ellipsis at the end of the text, as shown in Figure 19-4.

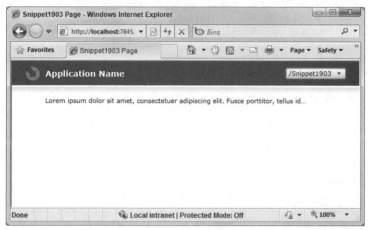

FIGURE 19-4

Using Text Decorations

TextBlock also allows you to supply a text decoration. *Text decorations* are visual ornaments that can be applied to text (such as underline, overline, or strikethrough). Whereas in WPF you can apply any of these different types of text decorations, in Silverlight you are limited to only the underline text decoration. To apply the decoration, simply use the TextDecorations property and provide it with a value of Underline, as shown in the following sample:

```
<TextBlock TextDecorations="Underline">
```

Formatting Inline Text

So far in this chapter, you have looked at how changing the different formatting properties on a TextBlock affects the format of the text within; however, many times you want to format only a portion of a larger block of text. Thankfully, Silverlight supports formatting blocks of text within a larger body of text.

TextBlock allows you to specify specific runs of Text that need unique formatting options by using the Run element. Listing 19-6 demonstrates using the Run element within a TextBlock to create three discrete text sections, each of which has its own unique font styling.

LISTING 19-6: Using Run elements for inline text formatting

```
<TextBlock TextWrapping="Wrap">
    Lorem ipsum dolor sit amet, consectetuer adipiscing elit.
    <Run FontFamily="Courier New">Fusce porttitor, tellus id
```

continues

LISTING 19-6 *(continued)*

```
tristique viverra, ligula pede pulvinar purus, nec hendrerit
urna justo et nulla.</Run> Cras condimentum nulla at ipsum.
<Run Foreground="Red">Nullam nulla.</Run> Sed elit lectus,
hendrerit rhoncus, gravida id, tristique quis, justo. Vivamus
et enim. Nunc accumsan. <Run FontWeight="Bold">Curabitur
ultrices dui ac tortor.</Run> Nunc mollis, turpis quis
consequat laoreet, nisl quam laoreet justo, a euismod magna nisi
sed orci. Etiam nec dui egestas elit pretium sodales.
Etiam felis.</TextBlock>
```

Figure 19-5 shows the output of this TextBlock.

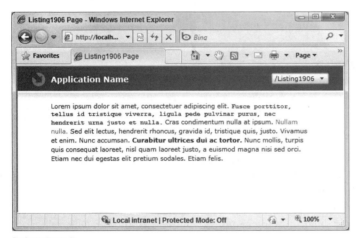

FIGURE 19-5

Setting styling properties in a discrete Run element overrides the style properties set on the TextBlock for that specific Run.

The TextBlock also allows you to explicitly insert line breaks into the text content using the LineBreak element. Using the LineBreak element gives you explicit control over the location where the TextBlock breaks a line of text, as shown in Listing 19-7.

LISTING 19-7: Using LineBreaks in a TextBlock

```
<TextBlock TextWrapping="Wrap">
    Lorem ipsum dolor sit amet, consectetuer adipiscing elit.
    <Run FontFamily="Courier New">Fusce porttitor, tellus id
    tristique viverra, ligula pede pulvinar purus, nec hendrerit
    urna justo et nulla.</Run>
    <LineBreak />
    Cras condimentum nulla at ipsum.
```

```
<Run Foreground="Red">Nullam nulla.</Run> Sed elit lectus,
hendrerit rhoncus, gravida id, tristique quis, justo. Vivamus
et enim. Nunc accumsan. <Run FontWeight="Bold">Curabitur
ultrices dui ac tortor.</Run>
<LineBreak />
Nunc mollis, turpis quis
consequat laoreet, nisl quam laoreet justo, a euismod magna nisi
sed orci. Etiam nec dui egestas elit pretium sodales.
Etiam felis.</TextBlock>
```

Figure 19-6 shows the text rendered with the line breaks.

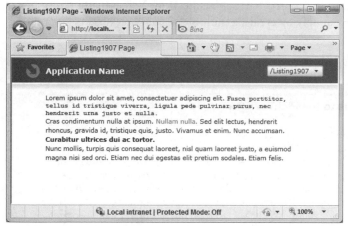

FIGURE 19-6

Using `Run` and `LineBreak` still allows the `TextBlock` to control the rendering of the text as a single unified object; therefore, as your application is resized, the `TextBlock` can intelligently reorganize the text it contains, regardless of how that text may be formatted.

Using the RichTextBox Control

Silverlight 4 introduces a new `RichTextBox` control, which provides a means to display and edit rich content in your Silverlight application. Rich content includes text formatted using font face, italics, underline, bold, and color, controlling the layout and arrangement of content as well as inserting other UI elements directly into text. The control also includes basic text editing features like selection, copy and paste, and undo/redo.

Creating Rich Content

By default, the `RichTextBox` exists in an editable mode, allowing end users to add and remove content. You can change this by using the `IsReadOnly` property. While in read-only mode, the content of the `RichTextBox` remains selectable and programmatic changes can still be made, but no end-user input or edits are accepted. Additionally, interactive inline elements like the

`Hyperlink` and `InlineUIContainer` (both discussed later in this chapter) are active only while the control is read-only.

To add content to a `RichTextBox`, there is no `Text` or `Value` property. Instead the control exposes a `Blocks` collection. A `Block` is the outer-most content container in the `RichTextBox` and Silverlight includes two types of `Block` objects: `Paragraph` and `Section`. As its name suggests, the `Paragraph` object groups `RichTextBox` content into paragraphs. The `Section` object represents some section of content that is typically accessed only by selecting content in the control, which is discussed later in this chapter.

Typically when you define content to be added to the control, that content will be contained inside of a `Paragraph`, which is then added to the control's `Blocks` collection. You can add multiple paragraphs of content to the `RichTextBox` simply by creating multiple `Paragraph` objects and adding them to the `Blocks` collection.

Listing 19-8 shows how to create several paragraphs of text within the `RichTextBox`.

LISTING 19-8: Adding paragraphs to the RichTextBox

```xml
<RichTextBox x:Name="RichTextBox1">
    <Paragraph>Lorem ipsum dolor sit amet, consectetuer adipiscing elit.
        Fusce porttitor, tellus id tristique viverra, ligula pede pulvinar
        purus, nec hendrerit urna justo et nulla. Cras condimentum nulla
        at ipsum. Nullam nulla. Sed elit lectus, hendrerit rhoncus, gravida
        id, tristique quis, justo. Vivamus et enim. Nunc accumsan. Curabitur
        ultrices dui ac tortor. Nunc mollis, turpis quis consequat laoreet,
        nisl quam laoreet justo, a euismod magna nisi sed orci. Etiam nec
        dui egestas elit pretium sodales. Etiam felis.</Paragraph>
    <Paragraph>Lorem ipsum dolor sit amet, consectetuer adipiscing elit.
        Fusce porttitor, tellus id tristique viverra, ligula pede pulvinar
        purus, nec hendrerit urna justo et nulla. Cras condimentum nulla
        at ipsum. Nullam nulla. Sed elit lectus, hendrerit rhoncus, gravida
        id, tristique quis, justo. Vivamus et enim. Nunc accumsan. Curabitur
        ultrices dui ac tortor. Nunc mollis, turpis quis consequat laoreet,
        nisl quam laoreet justo, a euismod magna nisi sed orci. Etiam nec
        dui egestas elit pretium sodales. Etiam felis.</Paragraph>
    <Paragraph>Lorem ipsum dolor sit amet, consectetuer adipiscing elit.
        Fusce porttitor, tellus id tristique viverra, ligula pede pulvinar
        purus, nec hendrerit urna justo et nulla. Cras condimentum nulla
        at ipsum. Nullam nulla. Sed elit lectus, hendrerit rhoncus, gravida
        id, tristique quis, justo. Vivamus et enim. Nunc accumsan. Curabitur
        ultrices dui ac tortor. Nunc mollis, turpis quis consequat laoreet,
        nisl quam laoreet justo, a euismod magna nisi sed orci. Etiam nec
        dui egestas elit pretium sodales. Etiam felis.</Paragraph>
</RichTextBox>
```

Because the default content container of the `RichTextBox` is the `Blocks` collection, the `Paragraphs` are added directly to the control. Also note that of the two `Block` types, `Paragraph` is the only one that can be used from XAML. Figure 19-7 shows the results of adding the paragraphs to the `RichTextBox`.

The `Paragraph` object exposes a set of basic font formatting properties that allow you to control font styling. These properties apply to all content in the `Paragraph`.

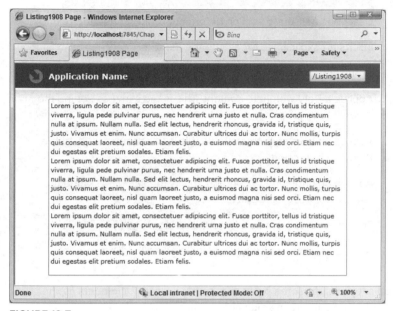

FIGURE 19-7

Because content elements of the `RichTextBox`, including `Paragraph`, all derive from the abstract `TextElement` class (which includes properties for basic text formatting, including the font family, size, style, weight, and foreground color), you have to set these font properties on any content object in the `RichTextBox`.

Also note that although you can change the foreground color of an individual `TextElement`, currently there is no way to change the background color of an individual run of content in the control.

The `Paragraph` also allows you to set the text alignment for its content using the `TextAlignment` property. Like the text alignment for the `TextBlock`, you can align `Paragraph` content Center, Left, or Right. The `Paragraph` `TextAlignment` property also allows you to align content in a Justified format.

The easiest and most flexible way to style individual sections of a paragraph is using inline formatting elements. Inline formatting elements allow you to apply a variety of formatting to `Paragraph` content and to insert more complex rich content. The inline formatting elements included in Silverlight are described in the Table 19-1.

TABLE 19-1

FORMAT OBJECT	DESCRIPTION
Run	Describes a discrete section of formatted or unformatted text.
LineBreak	Inserts an explicit line break into the content.
Span	Groups multiple inline content elements into a single section.
Bold	Applies a Bold weight to content. This is the same as setting the `FontWeight` property.
Italic	Applies an Italic style to content. This is the same as setting the `FontStyle` property.
Underline	Applies an underline to content. This is the same as setting the `TextDecoration` property.
Hyperlink	Formats text content as a hyperlink using a `HyperlinkButton`.
InlineUIContainer	A generic container for adding UI elements to inline content.

As you can see, the `Paragraph` supports the same basic `Run` and `LineBreak` elements as the `TextBlock` but adds a number of other formatting elements.

To apply formatting to content within a paragraph, simply wrap the content in a formatting object. Listing 19-9 shows how you can use the `Bold`, `Italic`, `Underline`, and `Hyperlink` objects in a `Paragraph`.

LISTING 19-9: Adding inline formatting elements to RichTextBox content

```
<RichTextBox x:Name="RichTextBox1">
    <Paragraph>
        <Bold>Lorem ipsum dolor sit amet, consectetuer adipiscing
        elit.</Bold> Fusce porttitor, tellus id tristique viverra,
        <Italic>ligula pede pulvinar purus</Italic> ,
        nec hendrerit urna justo et nulla. Cras
        <Hyperlink>condimentum</Hyperlink> nulla at ipsum. Nullam nulla.
        Sed elit lectus, hendrerit rhoncus, gravida id, tristique quis,
        justo. <Underline>Vivamus et enim. Nunc accumsan.</Underline>
        Curabitur ultrices dui ac tortor. Nunc mollis, turpis quis
        consequat laoreet, nisl quam laoreet justo, a euismod magna nisi
        sed orci. Etiam nec dui egestas elit pretium sodales. Etiam felis.
    </Paragraph>
</RichTextBox>
```

As noted in the previous table, the `Bold`, `Italic`, and `Underline` formatting objects are simply markup-friendly ways of setting the standard font properties. The `Hyperlink` is a friendly way of inserting a `HyperlinkButton` within the `RichTextBox`. The `Hyperlink` object exposes the same properties as the `HyperlinkButton`, including `NavigationUri` and `TargetName`. There are also properties for altering the style of the link.

You can use the `Span` object to group together multiple sections of text within a paragraph and apply formatting to them. Listing 19-10 shows how you can use the `Span` object to create a group of content with a specific font face and use additional formatting elements within the span.

LISTING 19-10: Grouping rich content using the Span element

```
<RichTextBox x:Name="RichTextBox1">
    <Paragraph FontFamily="Comic Sans MS">
        Lorem ipsum dolor sit amet, consectetuer adipiscing elit.
        Fusce porttitor, tellus id tristique viverra, ligula pede
        pulvinar purus, nec hendrerit urna justo et nulla.
        <Span Foreground="Red" FontFamily="Courier New"
        FontSize="16">Cras condimentum nulla at ipsum. <Bold>
        Nullam nulla.</Bold> Sed elit lectus, hendrerit rhoncus,
        gravida id, <Italic>tristique</Italic> quis, justo.
        </Span> Vivamus et enim. Nunc accumsan. Curabitur ultrices
        dui ac tortor. Nunc mollis, turpis quis consequat laoreet,
        nisl quam laoreet justo, a euismod magna nisi sed orci.
        Etiam nec dui egestas elit pretium sodales. Etiam felis.
    </Paragraph>
</RichTextBox>
```

Finally, the `InlineUIContainer` allows you to add arbitrary UI Elements like `Buttons`, `Images`, or even a `DataGrid` to the `RichTextBox` content.

Listing 19-11 demonstrates how you can add a `Button` to the `RichTextBox` content using the `InlineUIContainer`.

LISTING 19-11: Adding a Button to rich content

```
<RichTextBox x:Name="RichTextBox1" Grid.Row="1">
    <Paragraph>
        <Bold>Lorem ipsum dolor sit amet, consectetuer adipiscing elit.
        </Bold>Fusce porttitor, tellus id tristique viverra, <Italic>
        ligula pede pulvinar purus</Italic>, nec hendrerit urna justo
        et nulla. Cras <Hyperlink>condimentum</Hyperlink> nulla at ipsum.
        Nullam nulla. Sed elit lectus, hendrerit rhoncus, gravida id,
        tristique quis, justo. <Underline>Vivamus et enim. Nunc accumsan.
        </Underline> Curabitur ultrices dui ac tortor. Nunc mollis, turpis
        quis consequat laoreet, nisl quam laoreet justo, a euismod magna
        nisi sed orci. Etiam nec dui egestas elit pretium sodales. Etiam.
    </Paragraph>

    <Paragraph TextAlignment="Center" >
        <InlineUIContainer>
            <Button x:Name="Button1" Content="Chapter 19"
                    Margin="10" Click="Button1_Click" />
        </InlineUIContainer>
    </Paragraph>
</RichTextBox>
```

Figure 19-8 shows the `RichTextBox` containing a variety of text elements.

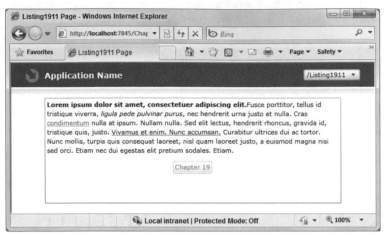

FIGURE 19-8

If you decide to use the `InlineUIContainer` in the `RichTextBox`, you should be aware of several restrictions:

➤ Use of the `InlineUIContainer` is not supported within the `Hyperlink` element. An exception will be raised by Silverlight if it finds an `InlineUIContainer` within a `Hyperlink`'s content.

➤ The content of the `InlineUIContainer` is always bottom-aligned with its surrounding content. This is not currently configurable.

➤ `InlineUIElements` are not included in the content exposed by the `RichTextBox`'s `Xaml` property. If you intend to allow users to save the control's content, and restore it at a later point, the content of any `InlineUIContainers` will be converted to empty `Run` objects.

➤ `InlineUIElements` are not included in Cut/Copy/Paste operations.

➤ As mentioned earlier, `InlineUIElements` are active only when the `RichTextBox` is in read-only mode. This means that elements like `Buttons` will remain disabled while the `RichTextBox` is editable.

In addition to content formatting the `Paragraph` allows you to set the alignment of its content using the `TextAlignment` property. As you would expect you can set the alignment of the content to be `LeftAligned`, `RightAligned`, `Centered`, or `Justified`.

Adding content at design time is one way to provide content to the `RichTextBox`. You can also provide content dynamically at run time using the control's `Xaml` property, which accepts a string of XAML content.

Note that currently the `Xaml` property is not a dependency property; therefore, you cannot use normal XAML data binding syntax to set this property. Setting it at run time must be done in code-behind.

Listing 19-12 demonstrates how you can read in some XAML stored in a file and load that into the RichTextBox using the Xaml property.

LISTING 19-12: Providing XAML to the RichTextBox

```
protected override void OnNavigatedTo(NavigationEventArgs e)
{
    Uri url = new Uri("Listing1920.xml", UriKind.Relative);
    WebClient client = new WebClient();
    client.DownloadStringCompleted +=
        new DownloadStringCompletedEventHandler(
                client_DownloadStringCompleted);
    client.DownloadStringAsync(url);
}

void client_DownloadStringCompleted(object sender,
    DownloadStringCompletedEventArgs e)
{
    this.RichTextBox1.Xaml = e.Result;
}
```

As mentioned earlier, some restrictions exist around what will be included in the XAML returned by the Xaml property. Only attributes that can be represented as a string will be included. For example, if you have an element's foreground property set to a complex brush like a gradient brush, this will not be included in the XAML.

If enough content is entered into the RichTextBox that it begins to overflow the control bounds, the control will begin to show scrollbars to allow end users to scroll the content. By default the control shows scrollbars only when its content begins to exceed the bounds of the control, but you can control the visibility of scrollbars using the HorizontalScrollbarVisibility and VerticalScrollbarVisibility properties.

Finally, as the end user inputs content into the control or the Block's property is changed, or formatting changes occur in the control, its ContentChanged event is raised. This event allows you to add custom application logic that reacts to changes in the content.

Working with RichTextBox Default Behaviors

As stated earlier, by default the content within the RichTextBox is editable by the end user. To assist in editing this content, the RichTextBox includes a set of editing behaviors beyond the basic inline editing experience. These behaviors are all enabled by default.

First, the ability to cut, copy, and paste text using the default platform shortcut keys is included. This means that users can simply select a section of text and use Ctrl+X to copy, Ctrl+C to cut, and Ctrl+V to paste (Command+X, Command+C, Command+V on a Mac). End users can also copy and paste using the standard select and drag mouse gestures.

The cut/copy/paste commands in the RichTextBox leverage Silverlight 4's new ability to access the system's Clipboard. Like using the Clipboard APIs directly, cutting, copying, or pasting from the RichTextBox causes a security prompt to be shown to the end user asking for permission to access the Clipboard.

You can of course add your own user interface to perform the same action should you want to. Adding a series of buttons and using Silverlight Clipboard APIs allows you to create an "editing" toolbar for the `RichTextBox`. Listing 19-13 shows how to use the `RichTextBox` selection APIs and Silverlight's Clipboard APIs to add cut, copy, and paste buttons to your application.

LISTING 19-13: Using the Clipboard APIs to save and restore content

```
private void btnCopy_Click(object sender, RoutedEventArgs e)
{
    if (this.RichTextBox1.Selection != null)
    {
        Clipboard.SetText(this.RichTextBox1.Selection.Text);
    }
}

private void btnPaste_Click(object sender, RoutedEventArgs e)
{
    string content = Clipboard.GetText();
    this.RichTextBox1.Selection.Xaml = content;
}
```

This listing shows how in an event such as a `Button`'s click event you can access the `RichTextBox`'s currently selected content using the `Selection` object, which is discussed in greater detail later in this section. The listing also shows how you can insert content stored on the Clipboard back into the control.

If you create your own custom cut/copy/paste user interface, it is important to know about and plan for a number of limitations. Currently the public Clipboard APIs in Silverlight place only text into the Clipboard. There are no APIs that allow you to place content in XAML form into the Clipboard. This can be problematic if you allow users to use both the keyboard commands as well as a custom user interface to set or get `RichTextBox` content to and from the Clipboard.

For example, if you include a button that copies XAML content from the `RichTextBox` to the Clipboard using the `SetText` method, if the user subsequently uses the Ctrl+V command to paste that content from the Clipboard back into the `RichTextBox`, the content is pasted as plain text. This will expose the raw XAML, even though when originally copied it was understood by the `RichTextBox` to be XAML.

Conversely, if the user copies rich content to the Clipboard using the Ctrl+X or Ctrl+C commands, using the `GetText` Clipboard API returns only the plain text content, not the XAML.

It is possible via a custom user interface to paste XAML content stored on the Clipboard back into the `RichTextBox`. To do this you must load the content using the `XamlReader`, then because you cannot load a `Section` directly into the control, walk the resulting `TextElements` and manually insert `Paragraphs` into the control's `Blocks` collection.

As stated earlier, select and copy behaviors are enabled regardless of the `RichTextBox`'s read-only state. But as you would expect, cut and paste behaviors require the control to be in an editable state.

The `RichTextBox` also includes an Undo/Redo stack, which end users can access using the standard Ctrl+Z and Ctrl+Y commands (Command+Z and Command+Y on a Mac). Note that there is currently no public API for the Undo/Redo stack; therefore you cannot programmatically cause an undo or redo action, or access the items in the stack. Additionally, undo/redo behavior can be disabled only by placing the `RichTextBox` into read-only mode.

Selecting and Navigating Content

Once you have content in the `RichTextBox`, users can begin to select and navigate the content using the cursor. The control includes APIs that allow you to determine the currently selected content as well as change the position of the cursor and the selection.

Users can select content by using standard selection mouse gestures, placing the cursor at some position in the content and using mouse drag gestures to select a section of content.

When a section of content is highlighted, while the `RichTextBox` has focus, the section will be shown with a blue background. Currently this is hard-coded into the control and cannot be changed. A section of selected content is shown in Figure 19-9.

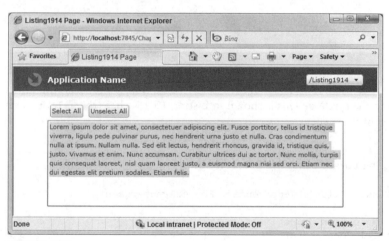

FIGURE 19-9

You can also programmatically select text using the `RichTextBox` APIs. The control includes a simple `SelectAll` method, which simplifies programmatically selecting all of the content in the control. Listing 19-14 shows how you can use this method.

LISTING 19-14: Using the SelectAll method to select all content

```
private void btnSelectAll_Click(object sender, RoutedEventArgs e)
{
    //Make sure you focus on order to get the text to highlight
    this.RichTextBox1.Focus();
    this.RichTextBox1.SelectAll();
}
```

Note that before the `SelectAll` method is called the control's `Focus` method is called. As described earlier, the selection highlight is shown only while the control has focus, so this listing makes sure to return focus from the `Button` to the `RichTextBox`.

You can also programmatically select sections of content using the control's `Selection` property. This property returns a `TextSelection` object that provides a `Select` method that allows you to set the specific section of content you want selected.

The `Select` method accepts two `TextPointer` objects as input. A `TextPointer` represents a specific point in the `RichTextBox` content, and is used to navigate the content of the `RichTextBox`. When using `TextPointers` with the `Select` method you need to provide one that represents the selection starting point and one that represents the selection end point. Listing 19-15 shows how you can use the `Select` method to select all content in the `RichTextBox`.

LISTING 19-15: Selecting a section of RichTextBox content

```
private void btnSelectAll_Click(object sender, RoutedEventArgs e)
{
    this.RichTextBox1.Selection.Select(
        this.RichTextBox1.ContentStart,
        this.RichTextBox1.ContentEnd);
}
```

It is also possible to use the `Select` method to position the cursor. To do this, simply pass the same start and end `TextPointer` into the method. This is shown in Listing 19-16 where the `Select` method positions the cursor at the start of the content.

LISTING 19-16: Positioning the cursor using the Select method

```
private void btnMoveCursor_Click(object sender, RoutedEventArgs e)
{
    this.RichTextBox1.Selection.Select(
        this.RichTextBox1.ContentStart,
        this.RichTextBox1.ContentStart);
}
```

You can use the `ContentStart` and `ContentEnd` properties to get `TextPointers`, which represent the content's starting point and end point. A number of other of ways also exist to get `TextPointers` from the `RichTextBox` that represent other locations in the content.

The control's `GetPositionFromPoint` method allows you to get the `TextPointer` from a `Point`. Listing 19-17 shows how you can use the `GetPositionFromPoint` method to select a word in the control's content based on the current mouse position.

LISTING 19-17: Getting a TextPointer based on mouse position

```
void RichTextBox1_MouseMove(object sender, MouseEventArgs e)
{
    Point mouse = e.GetPosition(this.RichTextBox1);
```

```
    TextPointer originationPosition =
        RichTextBox1.GetPositionFromPoint(mouse);
}
```

As you can see, the code in the listing uses the MouseMove event's GetPosition method to get a Point that represents the current mouse position. To get the corresponding TextPointer, simply pass the Point in to the GetPositionFromPoint method.

Finally, you can use the GetPositionFromOffset method to get a TextPointer based on an offset from another TextPointer. The method accepts as input an integer representing the offset, and a LogicalDirection value that dictates the direction of the offset. Listing 19-18 demonstrates using the method to position the cursor at a specific location in the content.

LISTING 19-18: Getting a TextPointer based on an offset value

```
private void btnFind_Click(object sender, RoutedEventArgs e)
{
    int offset = int.Parse(this.txtPosition.Text);

    TextPointer position =
        this.RichTextBox1.ContentStart.
            GetNextInsertionPosition(LogicalDirection.Forward).
            GetPositionAtOffset(offset, LogicalDirection.Forward);

    if (position != null)
    {
        this.RichTextBox1.Selection.Select(position, position);
        this.RichTextBox1.Focus();
    }
}
```

As you can see, an offset TextPointer is created based on the control's ContentStart TextPointer position. In this case the listing uses the GetNextInsertionPoint method to determine the position of the first valid insertion point forward of the ContentStart position. This is done because the actual ContentStart position is not a valid insertion point, and therefore using it directly would cause the curser to be positioned incorrectly.

Once selection of content has been made, you can use the TextSelection object and get and set formatting properties of the selection, as well as get the actual selection content.

The TextSelection object exposes the current selection both as Xaml and as Text. As its name implies the Xaml property returns the currently selected content's XAML. The XAML returned is in the form of a Section. By using a Section, the RichTextBox is able to resolve selections that begin in the middle of content elements, and cross paragraph boundaries.

The Text property returns the plain text content of the currently selected content.

Listing 19-19 shows how you can use the Xaml property to get the current selection and Listing 19-20 shows the XAML that is returned.

LISTING 19-19: Accessing the current selection's XAML

```
private void btnSave_Click(object sender, RoutedEventArgs e)
{
    if (this.RichTextBox1.Selection!=null)
    {
        string content = this.RichTextBox1.Selection.Xaml;
    }
}
```

LISTING 19-20: An example of a Section's XAML

```
<Section xml:space="preserve"
    HasTrailingParagraphBreakOnPaste="False"
    xmlns="http://schemas.microsoft.com/winfx/2006/xaml/presentation">
    <Paragraph FontSize="11" FontFamily="Portable User Interface"
        Foreground="#FF000000" FontWeight="Normal" FontStyle="Normal"
        FontStretch="Normal" TextAlignment="Left">
            <Bold FontWeight="Bold">
                <Run Text="consectetuer adipiscing elit." />
            </Bold>
            <Run Text=" Fusce porttitor, tellus id tristique viverra, " />
            <Italic FontStyle="Italic">
                <Run Text="ligula pede pulvinar purus" />
            </Italic>
            <Run Text=" , nec hendrerit urna justo et nulla. Cras " />
            <Hyperlink Foreground="#FF337CBB" TextDecorations="Underline"
                MouseOverForeground="#FFED6E00">
                <Run Text="condimentum" />
            </Hyperlink>
            <Run Text=" nulla at ipsum. Nullam nulla. Sed elit lectus,
                hendrerit rhoncus, gravida id, tristique quis, justo. " />
            <Underline TextDecorations="Underline">
                <Run Text="Vivamus et enim. Nunc accumsan." />
            </Underline>
            <Run Text=" Curabitur ultrices dui ac tortor. Nunc mollis,
                            turpis quis consequat laoreet, nisl quam laoreet
                            justo, a euismod magna nisi sed orci. Etiam nec dui
                            egestas elit pretium sodales. Etiam felis." />
    </Paragraph>
</Section>
```

The TextSelection object also includes methods that allow you to access and change the property values assigned to the selection. Using the GetPropertyValue method, you can check the value of currently applied properties. Using the ApplyPropertyValue method, you can change the value of those properties. Listing 19-21 shows how you can use these methods to check if the selection is currently Bold and change its state based on that.

LISTING 19-21: Setting selection format properties

```
private void btnBold_Click(object sender, RoutedEventArgs e)
{
    if (this.RichTextBox1.Selection != null)
    {
        object obj = this.RichTextBox1.Selection.GetPropertyValue(
                                   Section.FontWeightProperty);

        if (obj != DependencyProperty.UnsetValue)
        {

            FontWeight currentWeight = (FontWeight)obj;

            if (currentWeight == FontWeights.Bold)
                this.RichTextBox1.Selection.ApplyPropertyValue(
                    Section.FontWeightProperty, FontWeights.Normal);
            else
                this.RichTextBox1.Selection.ApplyPropertyValue(
                    Section.FontWeightProperty, FontWeights.Bold);
        }
    }
}
```

Note that in the preceding listing, once the property value is retrieved from the Selection, it is checked to see if it is equal to DependancyProperty.UnsetValue. UnsetValue is a value used by the property system instead of null, and will be returned by the GetPropertyValue method if the TextSelection extends across more than one value for the property being retrieved. In the preceding example, if the selection contains both Bold and Normal text, the method will return UnsetValue.

Finally, the TextSelection object includes an Insert method, which allows you to programmatically insert content into the control at the current cursor position. The Insert method accepts any content derived from the base TextElement class as input.

Note that because the Insert method accepts TextElement objects, it cannot be used to directly insert XAML content that has been previously copied to the Clipboard. As described earlier, using the GetText method to retrieve content from the Clipboard returns the content as plain text, not true XAML.

To insert content retrieved from the Clipboard's GetText method into the RichTextBox, you can either:

➤ Set the plain XAML content to the Selection's Xaml property.

➤ Load the content using the XamlReader's Load method.

If you choose to use the XamlReader to load the content, you need to walk the resulting Section object's Paragraphs and copy them to the RichTextBox's Blocks collection.

FONT SUPPORT AND RENDERING

Silverlight continues to improve its already excellent support for text and font rendering. Silverlight 4 adds support for additional languages including use of Indic scripts in an application. Also added to Silverlight 4 is the `FlowDirection` property, which allows you to render text in right-to-left orientation. Figure 19-10 shows an example of a Silverlight `TextBlock` displaying Arabic script in right-to-left orientation.

FIGURE 19-10

By default, Silverlight uses a special font called the Portable User Interface (PUI) font, which is a composite font that uses several different fonts to implement characters for the full range of international languages supported by Silverlight. The font is primarily composed of Lucida Grand, which is used for most Western writing systems, and many other fonts used for East Asian support.

 The PUI font is actually not really a font at all. It is just a logical definition of how Silverlight does font fallback. This definition ultimately maps to real OS fonts.

Starting in Silverlight 4, Silverlight removes the font "whitelist" restriction that was present in previous versions. This restriction limited Silverlight support for the local system fonts to only 10 local system Latin fonts and 31 different East Asian fonts. But, starting with Silverlight 4, you are free to use any font available on the local system.

You can get a list of the typefaces available on the local system by using the static `Fonts`
`.SystemTypefaces` property, which returns a collection of `TypeFace` objects. A typeface is a single variation of a font within a font family, for example, the italic version of Times New Roman is an example of a specific typeface within a family.

Listing 19-22 shows how you can create a `FontSource` from a `Typeface` and assign it to a `TextBlock`.

LISTING 19-22: Accessing local system typefaces

```
protected override void OnNavigatedTo(NavigationEventArgs e)
{
    List<Typeface> typefaces = Fonts.SystemTypefaces.ToList<Typeface>();

    List<GlyphTypeface> glyphtypefaces = new List<GlyphTypeface>();

    foreach (Typeface t in typefaces)
    {
        GlyphTypeface glyph;

        if (t.TryGetGlyphTypeface(out glyph))
        {
            try
            {
                FontSource source = new FontSource(glyph);
                Glyphs testGlyphs = new Glyphs() {
                                UnicodeString = glyph.FontFileName,
                                FontSource = source,
                                FontRenderingEmSize = 11.0,
                                Fill = new SolidColorBrush(Colors.Black) };

                this.fontslist.Children.Add(testGlyphs);
            }
            catch (NullReferenceException exc)
            {
                /* This typeface is not supported by Silverlight */
            }

        }
        else
        {
            System.Diagnostics.Debug.WriteLine("No Glyph found");
        }
    }
}
```

In this listing, the `SystemTypefaces` property is used to get the list of local typefaces, which is then converted to a `List<T>`. The list of typefaces is then converted to a list of glyph typefaces using the `TryGetGlyphTypeface` method. A `GlyphTypeface` is a low-level text object that represents a single face of a font in a font family. The `GlyphTypeface` is what actually ties the `Typeface` to a physical font file on disk.

Finally, the list of `GlyphTypeface` objects is enumerated and a `Glyphs` object is created that displays the names of the available typefaces.

You might think the next logical step from listing the fonts would be to allow your end users to select a font to apply to text in something like a TextBlock. *Unfortunately in Silverlight 4 this is not a simple task. In order to tell the* TextBlock *to render a font, you need to set both its* FontFamily *and* FontSource *properties. In the preceding listing you can see that you can create a* FontSource *from the* GlyphTypeface, *but then there is no way to determine the* FontFamily. *You would need to find some way to divine the font family based on the glyph's font filename.*

Using Embedded Fonts

In addition to local system fonts, Silverlight also supports embedding fonts directly into an application, allowing you to use any font you want in your application design.

To use an embedded font with the TextBlock, simply provide the FontFamily property with a special font URI that tells Silverlight the name of the TrueType font file you want to use and the specific TypeFace from that file to use. This is shown in the following sample:

```
<TextBlock FontFamily="[FontFile]#[TypeFace]" />
```

So, for example, if you want to use the font file named *MyFavoriteFont.ttf*, which contains a typeface named *My Favorite Font Normal*, configure a TextBlock to use this font using this syntax:

```
<TextBlock FontFamily="segoesc.ttf#Segoe Script" />
```

Figure 19-11 shows the text in the TextBlock using the embedded font.

Note that if you are embedding fonts in your Silverlight application, this may be considered distributing a font with your application. If you are using a licensed font, you may need to ensure that you have the appropriate distribution rights.

Blend provides a set of advanced properties editors that make managing fonts in your application easy. Figure 19-12 shows the font selection list of the Text property editor. The list not only includes the list of available fonts, but uses icons to indicate if a font is a built-in Silverlight font or a font that has been embedded in the application.

When you select a font, if it is not a built-in font, you can choose to have Blend automatically embed the font in your application by checking the Embed checkbox, shown in Figure 19-13.

Checking the Embed checkbox tells Blend to add the font as a resource in your application's XAP file, which ensures that all of the users of your application will be able to see the font even if they do not have it installed. Note, this does also increase the size of your XAP file.

Icons indicating the source of the font

FIGURE 19-11

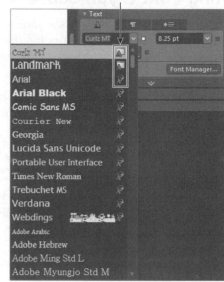

FIGURE 19-12

The Text property editor also includes a button to launch the Font Manager dialog, shown in Figure 19-14. Note that the Font Manager can also be accessed from the Expression Blend Tools menu.

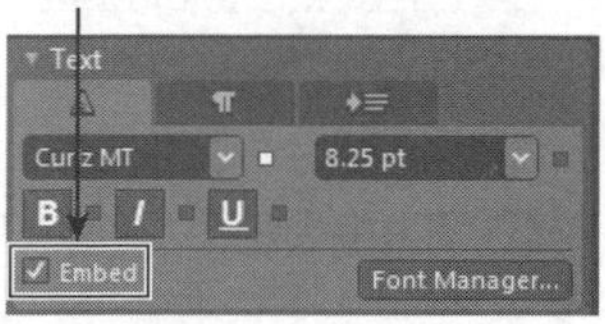

FIGURE 19-13

FIGURE 19-14

The Font Manager gives you a single location to manage all the fonts embedded in your application and also lets you create a font subset by selecting only specific glyphs from the font to include.

Creating Font Glyph Subsets

Silverlight also allows you to render individual font glyphs. The advantage of using glyphs is that you do not have to embed an entire font file into your application. Instead, you create a subset of the font that includes only the specific characters you need.

The easiest way to create a font subset is to use Expression Blend's Font Manager dialog, which was shown in the previous section. The dialog allows you to create font subsets by specifying the exact glyphs you want to use and includes a number of common selection options such as selecting only upper- or lowercase characters. You can explicitly set the specific characters you want to include.

Once you select the characters you want to include in the font subset, Expression Blend automatically generates the appropriate TTF files and adds them to a compressed ZIP file. This ZIP file is included in your project as a resource.

To use the font subset you use the same syntax as shown in the previous section for accessing embedded fonts.

```
<TextBlock TextWrapping="Wrap"
           FontFamily="/Chapter19;component/Fonts/Fonts.zip#Curlz MT" >
    Font Subset
</TextBlock>
```

If the `TextBlock` contains characters that are not included in the font subset, Silverlight will automatically fall back to the default Portable User Interface font to display those characters.

You can also use the `Glyphs` element to display specific font glyphs. While the `Glyphs` object is a low-level object and in most cases you should simply use the `TextBlock`, using `Glyphs` can be useful if you are creating XPS documents at run time because XPS uses glyphs to display text.

Listing 19-23 shows using the `Glyphs` element to render specific glyphs contained in a font.

LISTING 19-23: Displaying font glyphs

```
<Glyphs FontUri="="/Chapter19;component/Assets/LANDMARK.ttf"
     Fill = "SteelBlue" FontRenderingEmSize = "36"
     UnicodeString = "Chapter 19">
</Glyphs>
```

In the preceding sample, only the glyphs necessary to render the `UnicodeString` are retrieved from the font that is specified by the `FontUri` property. Also note that, unlike `TextBlock`, the default `Fill` value for `Glyphs` is null and the `FontRenderingEmSize` is zero; therefore, you should make sure to provide values for both of these properties in order to render the text.

You can use the `Glyphs` element's `Indices` property to specify specific glyph indices in the font. You can also use the `Indices` property to control the spacing of characters in the `UnicodeString`. The `Indices` property accepts a semicolon-delimited list of glyph indices and spacing information. Each index can be defined using the following format:

```
[GlyphIndex][,[Advance][,[uOffset][,[vOffset]]]]
```

Although the Glyphs FontUri *property accepts a URI object as its value, the object only works with URIs that resolve to an embedded resource. Absolute URIs and URIs that are relative to the server location will not work as the* FontUri *of the* Glyphs *object. If you want to load the font from a remote location, you can download the font using the WebClient APIs and set the resulting stream as the* Glyphs *font using its* FontSource *property.*

Each portion of this format is optional. You can find more information on using the Indices property to control font spacing at http://msdn.microsoft.com/en-us/library/ms748985.aspx.

Rendering Text

Since Silverlight 3, Silverlight has included ClearType as its default mechanism for rendering text. Although in most cases the use of ClearType is transparent to you, some situations can cause the run time to fall back to grayscale antialiasing for text rendering.

The basic rule of thumb is if during rendering Silverlight cannot determine the background color that the text should be blending with, it falls back to grayscale antialiasing. This may happen in the following scenarios:

➤ The application uses Cached Composition (Bitmap Caching).

➤ The application uses Writable Bitmap.

➤ The Silverlight plug-in's Windowless property is set to true, and the plug-in has a transparent background.

➤ You are using the DropEffect class.

SUMMARY

As the Internet moves toward even more rich media content, text still remains a central way to convey information to end users. Silverlight puts significant new capabilities into the hands of web developers and frees web designers from many of the constraints imposed on them by traditional HTML text displays.

This chapter looked at the core mechanisms used to display text in Silverlight, the TextBlock and RichTextBox. These versatile elements give you amazing power to style and display text. Choose from the local system fonts or provide your own font set to differentiate your site from others.

The chapter also explored more advanced text options such as using the Glyphs element to display individual font glyphs.

20

Making It Richer with Media

WHAT'S IN THIS CHAPTER?

➤ Examining Silverlight's media support and DRM

➤ Working with the MediaElement Control

➤ Setting up playlists

Silverlight supports MP3 audio, H.264 Video, AAC Audio, and several Windows Media Audio and Windows Media Video formats, giving you the ability to create media-rich, web-based experiences. And even if you're not creating a photo browser or interactive video application, you can use Silverlight's media capabilities to add subtle `MouseOver` sound effects to buttons in your application to add that next level of polish. In this chapter, you'll learn the capabilities of the Silverlight `MediaElement` control and the file formats it supports. You'll see how to define the control both in XAML and in Expression Blend and see how to respond to the events it raises. You'll also be introduced to Expression Media Encoder 3 and learn how to prepare your media for use in your Silverlight app.

SUPPORTED FORMATS

Before we even take a look at including media in our Silverlight apps, let's take a look at the file formats and codecs supported natively by the Silverlight player. Media can be encoded using several of the Windows Media Video and Windows Media Audio codecs, as well as the MP3 and AAC audio codecs and H.264 video codec. Windows Media Audio and Video are more than just two codecs. Both of these formats include various versions and use-specific codecs (such as Windows Media Screen and Windows Media Voice). Silverlight supports a subset of the broad array of Windows Media codecs. Listed next are the versions supported by the player. These formats are supported, regardless of the file extension of the encoded file. Silverlight ignores the file extension when the source media file is referenced.

Video

➤ **Raw Video**

➤ **YV12** — YCrCb(4:2:0)

➤ **RGBA** — 32-bit Alpha Red, Green, Blue

➤ **WMV1** — Windows Media Video 7

➤ **WMV2** — Windows Media Video 8

➤ **WMV3** — Windows Media Video 9

> ➤ Supports Simple and Main Profiles.

> ➤ Supports only progressive (non-interlaced) content.

➤ **WMVA** — Windows Media Video Advanced Profile, non-VC-1

➤ **WVC1** — Windows Media Video Advanced Profile, VC-1

> ➤ Supports Advanced Profile.

> ➤ Supports only progressive (non-interlaced) content.

➤ **H264 (ITU-T H.264 / ISO MPEG-4 AVC)**

> ➤ Supports H.264 and MP43 codecs.

> ➤ Supports Base, Main, and High Profiles.

> ➤ Supports only progressive (non-interlaced) content.

> ➤ Supports only 4:2:0 chroma subsampling profiles.

> ➤ Supports PlayReady DRM with Mp4 (H264 and AAC-LC).

Audio

➤ **1** — This is Linear 8- or 16-bit Pulse Code Modulation. Roughly speaking, this is WAV format.

➤ **353** — Microsoft Windows Media Audio v7, v8 and v9.x Standard (WMA Standard)

➤ **354** — Microsoft Windows Media Audio v9.x and v10 Professional (WMA Professional)

> ➤ Supports full fidelity decoding of WMA 10 Professional Low Bit Rate (LBR) modes in the 32–96-Kbps range.

> ➤ Multichannel (5.1 and 7.1 surround) audio content is automatically mixed down to stereo.

➤ 24-bit audio will return silence.

➤ Sampling Rates beyond 48,000 return an invalid format error code in same-domain and a 4001 in cross-domain scenarios.

➤ 85 — ISO MPEG-1 Layer III (MP3)

➤ 255 — ISO Advanced Audio Coding (AAC)

> ➤ Supports Low Complexity (AAC-LC) decoding at full fidelity (up to 48 kHz).
>
> ➤ High Efficiency (HE-AAC) encoded content will decode only at half-fidelity (up to 24 kHz).
>
> ➤ Multichannel (5.1 surround) audio content is not supported.

UNSUPPORTED WINDOWS MEDIA FORMATS

The following Windows Media–based formats are *not* supported by the Silverlight `MediaElement` control:

➤ Interlaced video content

➤ Windows Media Screen

➤ Windows Media Audio Professional

➤ Windows Media Voice

➤ Combination of Windows Media Video and MP3 (WMV video + MP3 audio)

➤ Windows Media Video using odd (not divisible by 2) dimensioned frames; for example, 127 × 135

➤ VC-1 in MP4

H.264 AND AAC SUPPORT

H.264 is a popular codec for encoding high-definition video. This format is used widely across several devices and applications and has been made popular by the iTunes Store and family of supported devices. Many consumer camcorders now encode video natively to H.264 so that the video can be immediately uploaded to media-sharing websites such as `YouTube.com` and `Vimeo.com`. The Silverlight player can access H.264 videos directly via the `MediaElement` or via IIS7 Smooth Streaming (enabled through the Media Services 3.0 extension for IIS7 available at `www.iis.net/extensions/SmoothStreaming`).

AAC is the audio codec counterpart to H.264; most videos encoded with the H.264 codec have an accompanying audio stream encoded using the AAC codec. AAC is also the audio format natively used by iTunes.

DIGITAL RIGHTS MANAGEMENT

Silverlight 4 has introduced a robust Digital Rights Management (DRM) capability to help you deliver audio and video content that is more secure and better protected from unauthorized capture and redistribution. The scenarios for DRM include:

- ➤ **Online Scenarios** — Live Streaming and Progressive Download are scenarios that require a user to be online while they play protected content.

  - ➤ **Live Streaming** — Live streaming (or *true streaming*) sends content directly to the computer or device without saving the file to a hard disk and is played immediately.

  - ➤ **Progressive Download** — Progressive download lets users play back the media while it is downloading. In this scenario, the data that is downloaded is temporarily stored on the user's computer before playback.

- ➤ **Offline Scenarios** — Download Offline, Rental, and Subscription are three scenarios that allow users to be offline while they play the content. There must be an initial connection to validate the user's rights to the content.

  - ➤ **Download File Offline** (onetime purchase) — The user downloads the content from the Internet and later plays it by using an offline Silverlight player.

  - ➤ **Rental** — You can specify time limits in your DRM licenses in order to limit playback of content, such as a 24-hour or 30-day viewing period.

  - ➤ **Subscription** — Customers can play back content based on a subscription.

USING THE MEDIAELEMENT CONTROL

Media is displayed in Silverlight applications by using the `MediaElement` control. Just like the `Image` control, the `MediaElement` control has a `Source` property that points to the source media. The source media can be an internal resource, compiled into your Silverlight assembly, a resource compiled into a referenced assembly, a loose file sitting on the host server, a file residing on a remote server, or a playlist served up from a local or remote server. In short, the `MediaElement` can reference a file that resides just about anywhere.

The following XAML defines a `MediaElement` control and references a loose video on the server, located as a sibling to the XAP file:

```
<MediaElement
   Width="320"
   Height="240"
   HorizontalAlignment="Left"
   VerticalAlignment="Bottom"
   Margin="50,50,0,0"
   Source="SampleVideo.wmv" />
```

This particular `MediaElement` is 320 pixels wide × 240 pixels tall and is aligned to the top-left corner of the page with both a top and left margin of 50 pixels (`Margin="50,50,0,0"`, where `Margin="TL, TR, BR, BL"`). It's as easy as that to get video or audio in your Silverlight application.

Review Chapter 5 to understand the layout principles like Margin.

Build Actions and Referencing Media

Just like images or other binary files, media files can reside just about anywhere and can even be included in your project in a number of ways. Let's take a look at the various approaches available, examine the pros and cons of each, and see how the approach alters the way the media is referenced via XAML.

Each of the following sections mentions the term *Build Action*. Build Action refers to a property available in Visual Studio (and not available in Expression Blend) that dictates how the file is treated when the project is compiled. Figure 20-1 shows the Visual Studio Property panel when a media file has been selected in Solution Explorer.

The Build Actions that are important to understand and are covered in detail in the next section are:

➤ Resource

➤ Content

➤ None

FIGURE 20-1

Assembly Resource Media

A media file is compiled into your project's assembly when its Build Action is set to *Resource*. This should only be done for short clips that you want to be available immediately when your application or assembly is loaded. Files included as Resources are compiled into the application assembly and can greatly increase the assembly's file size, which will increase the amount of time to download and load the XAP file to start your application.

You reference an embedded media file using a relative URL. If the file is in the root folder of your project, you simply type its name. If the file is in a subfolder, such as Media, include the entire relative path. For example, the following XAML (Listing 20-1) references a video stored in the Media/Stockfootage subfolder of the project directory:

Available for download on Wrox.com

LISTING 20-1: Referencing an embedded media file

```xml
<MediaElement
    Width="320"
    Height="240"
    HorizontalAlignment="Left"
    VerticalAlignment="Bottom"
    Margin="50,50,0,0"
    Source="media/stockfootage/Bear.wmv" />
```

You can also use a path that explicitly references the assembly that the video is housed in. If your Silverlight project name is *MyProject*, then the previous XAML could be replaced by the following (Listing 20-2):

LISTING 20-2: Referencing media embedded in an assembly

```
<MediaElement
    Width="320"
    Height="240"
    HorizontalAlignment="Left"
    VerticalAlignment="Bottom"
    Margin="50,50,0,0"
    Source="MyProject;component/media/stockfootage/Bear.wmv" />
```

The text in bold is key: `MyProject;component/`.

The text *MyProject* should be replaced with the name of your project, but `;component/` should remain at all times.

➤ Pros

   ➤ Media is available immediately.

   ➤ Simple relative path references

   ➤ No security issues

➤ Cons

   ➤ Large media files can bloat the assembly size and increase page load time.

XAP File Media

A media file is included in the XAP file and is not compiled into the assembly when its Build Action is set to *Content*. When configured as `Content`, media files do not bloat the size of your project assembly, but they do continue to bloat the size of the XAP file. You might take this approach if you want your media files available immediately but do not want to bloat the size of your assembly.

When media is included this way, you must add a forward slash (/) before the path to the file (Listing 20-3):

LISTING 20-3: Referencing media when Build Action set to Content

```
<MediaElement
    Width="320"
    Height="240"
    HorizontalAlignment="Left"
    VerticalAlignment="Bottom"
    Margin="50,50,0,0"
    Source="/media/stockfootage/Bear.wmv" />
```

> ➤ Pros

>> ➤ Media is available immediately.

>> ➤ Simple absolute path references

>> ➤ No security issues

>> ➤ Assembly size is reduced.

> ➤ Cons

>> ➤ Large media files can bloat the XAP size and increase page load time.

Loose Files

You can add media files to your project that are not compiled into the project assembly or added to the XAP file. These files bloat neither the assembly nor the XAP file. To achieve this scenario, set the Build Action of your file to *None*, and "Copy to Local Directory" to *Copy Always* or *Copy if Newer*.

Use the same syntax as you used with XAP File Images, adding a forward slash to the URI (Listing 20-4):

LISTING 20-4: Referencing media file when Build Action set to None

Available for
download on
Wrox.com

```
<MediaElement
    Width="320"
    Height="240"
    HorizontalAlignment="Left"
    VerticalAlignment="Bottom"
    Margin="50,50,0,0"
    Source="/media/stockfootage/Bear.wmv" />
```

> ➤ Pros

>> ➤ Assembly size is reduced.

>> ➤ XAP size is reduced (faster page load time).

> ➤ Cons

>> ➤ Media is not loaded at page load; instead, it loads asynchronously after the XAP is downloaded.

Use this scenario when you want to create a very lightweight, quick-loading application. The media begins streaming from the server to the MediaElement control as soon as it is referenced.

Media in Other Assemblies

Media does not have to be housed in your main project's assembly for you to reference it. Media files can be compiled as resources into separate assemblies created either by you or a third party. When referencing images in assemblies other than the main project, you are required to use the "ProjectName;component/" syntax introduced a couple of sections back.

The following XAML (Listing 20-5) references a video named *cloudTexture.wmv* defined in an assembly named *BackgroundVideoTextures.dll*:

LISTING 20-5: Referencing media in another assembly

```
<MediaElement
    Width="320"
    Height="240"
    HorizontalAlignment="Left"
    VerticalAlignment="Bottom"
    Margin="50,50,0,0"
    Source="BackgroundVideoTextures;component/cloudTexture.wmv" />
```

➤ Pros

➤ Assembly size is reduced.

➤ XAP size is (potentially) increased; as referenced assemblies grow in size, separates visuals from application logic.

➤ Cons

➤ Media cannot be renamed or removed if you are not in control of the resource assembly.

➤ Increases the number of projects you must maintain (if you are in control of the resource assembly).

Media on Other Domains

When you want to access audio or video on a remote server, you can use the fully qualified URI to access the image (Listing 20-6):

LISTING 20-6: Referencing media on another server

```
<MediaElement
    Width="320"
    Height="240"
    HorizontalAlignment="Left"
    VerticalAlignment="Bottom"
    Margin="50,50,0,0"
    Source="http://www.remotewebsite.com/publicvideo.wmv" />
```

However, Silverlight's security policies prevents the remote file from loading if the remote site does not have a security manifest file in place that grants you access.

➤ Pros

➤ Allows you to host media on remote, high-capacity servers.

➤   Cons

>   ➤   You don't have control of the remote server.

>   ➤   The integrity of the application is dependent on third-party server performance.

>   ➤   Requires security policies.

Adding a MediaElement in Blend

While it's important to know how to define `MediaElement` by hand in XAML, it's also quite likely that you'll use Visual Studio 2010 or Expression Blend to add, position, and size media. In this section, we'll cover working with the `MediaElement` in Blend. There are a couple of nice features in Blend that help manipulating the `MediaElement` easier than in Visual Studio 2010. Either way, everything you see here can be achieved in Visual Studio 2010, although some of it you'll need to code yourself in XAML. The `MediaElement` control is accessed from Expression Blend's Asset Library and clicking the "All" tree node under Controls. Figure 20-2 shows the `MediaElement` control in the Asset Library.

FIGURE 20-2

Create an instance of `MediaElement` by first selecting the `MediaElement` control from the Asset Library and then dragging a rectangle on the design surface to define its initial position and size. You can also double-click on the control's icon in the toolbar. With "MediaElement" selected on the design surface, you can specify a Source file by either clicking the drop-down arrow or clicking the ellipsis next to the `Source` property. Clicking the drop-down arrow reveals any media files already added to the project.

Clicking the ellipsis launches a File Browser dialog. Once you've selected a supported media file, i's added to your project with a Build Action of *Content* and a "Copy to Output Directory" setting of *Copy if Newer*. You can modify these settings in Visual Studio to meet your needs.

FIGURE 20-3

Figure 20-3 shows the `Source` property in Blend's Media category.

Sizing Video and Setting the Stretch Behavior

The `MediaElement` control does not have to be the same size as the source video. Just like any element in your Visual Tree, you are in charge of its positioning and size. Just like the `Image` and `Path` controls that we examined earlier, the `MediaElement` control has a `Stretch` property that dictates the way the underlying video is drawn as its container `MediaElement` control is sized and resized. The following values can be set on `MediaElement.Stretch`:

➤ `Fill` — The video is stretched both vertically and horizontally, filling the `MediaElement` control. With this setting, video can feel distorted.

➤ `None` — The underlying artwork does not stretch at all.

 In practice, the behavior when set to `None` *is the same as when set to* `Fill`.

➤ `Uniform (Default)` — The underlying video maintains its original aspect ratio while scaling to fit within the control. With this mode, the video is always drawn in its entirety.

➤ `UniformToFill` — The underlying video maintains its original aspect ratio; although unlike `Uniform`, it always scales to fit the longest axis. The resulting video is never distorted, although it may be clipped.

Figure 20-4 demonstrates how the various values of `Stretch` affect the final rendering of the `MediaElement`.

None

Fill   **Uniform**

UniformToFill

FIGURE 20-4

The `Stretch` property lets you control the behavior of the `MediaElement` when the source video is a different size from the `MediaElement` control. What if you always want to draw the `MediaElement` at the exact same size as the underlying video? Fortunately, the `MediaElement` control provides a couple of properties that expose the native height and width of the loaded file. You can use `NaturalVideoHeight` and `NaturalVideoWidth` to get the original height and width of the source video, then update the `Height` and `Width` properties (and any additional layout properties) of your `MediaElement` to display your video in the size it was intended to be viewed.

The following method (Listing 20-7) handles the `MediaOpened` event for our sample video. Once this event has been raised, we have access to the `NaturalVideoHeight` and `NaturalVideoWidth` properties. This event handler uses these two properties to update the `Height` and `Width` properties of the `MediaElement` that raised the event:

LISTING 20-7: Handling the MediaOpened event

```
<MediaElement
    Width="320"
    Height="240"
    x:Name="meSampleVideo"
    MediaOpened="SetNaturalDimensions"
    Source="/SampleVideo.wmv" />

private void SetNaturalDimensions(object sender, RoutedEventArgs e)
{
    MediaElement media = sender as MediaElement;
    media.Height = media.NaturalVideoHeight;
    media.Width = media.NaturalVideoWidth;
```

Transforming Video

Just like any `FrameworkElement`-derived object, the `MediaElement` can be positioned, sized, transformed, and clipped in a myriad of ways to meet your layout needs. I'll show you a few examples here, just to get your creative juices flowing, but this is in no way an exhaustive demonstration of what can be achieved.

Let's start by rotating a `MediaElement`. On the Blend design surface, shown in Figure 20-5, I can simply mouse over one of the corners of my selected `MediaElement` until I get the rotate icon, then rotate to the desired angle.

FIGURE 20-5

Figure 20-6 shows the RenderTransform Editor in the Blend Properties panel that lets you adjust rotation (and all of the other transform properties) with numerical precision.

Behind the scenes, the `RenderTransform` property of the `MediaElement` has been set. When editing any of the transform properties in Blend, a `TransformGroup` containing each of the transform types is applied to the `RenderTransform` property. The following XAML (Listing 20-8) shows what Blend has applied behind the scenes:

LISTING 20-8: Setting a RenderTransform on a MediaElement

```xaml
<MediaElement
    Width="320"
    Height="240"
    HorizontalAlignment="Left"
    VerticalAlignment="Stretch"
    x:Name="meSampleVideo"
    Source="/SampleVideo.wmv" RenderTransformOrigin="0.5,0.5" >
        <MediaElement.RenderTransform>
            <TransformGroup>
                <ScaleTransform/>
                <SkewTransform/>
                <RotateTransform Angle="9.862"/>
                <TranslateTransform/>
            </TransformGroup>
        </MediaElement.RenderTransform>
</MediaElement>
```

Rotating Video in 3D

After realizing that you can apply a RenderTransform to video, it's only natural to consider rotating the video in three-dimensional (3D) space. Fortunately, 3D transformations can be applied to `MediaElements` just as easily as they can be applied to other `UIElements`, by setting the `Projection` property. The following XAML (Listing 20-9) *swings* the video back. Refer to Figure 20-6 to see the Projection in the Properties panel.

LISTING 20-9: Setting a Projection on a MediaElement to perform a 3D transformation

```xaml
<Image Source="Images/sampleImage.jpg" Stretch="Fill" Width="154"
    VerticalAlignment="Top" Height="116" HorizontalAlignment="Left"
    Margin="421,317,0,0">
    <Image.Projection>
        <PlaneProjection RotationX="0" RotationY="-60" CenterOfRotationX="0"
            CenterOfRotationY="0" CenterOfRotationZ="0"/>
    </Image.Projection>
</Image>
```

Figure 20-7 shows the resulting `MediaElement`.

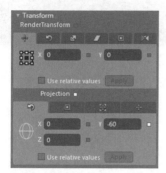

FIGURE 20-6

FIGURE 20-7

With the ability to apply true 3D transformations to video, Silverlight is empowering creative and media professionals to create truly stunning interfaces that were previously only capable on desktop and gaming platforms. And it's easy to do, too!

 Performing operations, such as 3D transforms, using PlaneProjection on your video could impact performance at run time depending on the hardware your application is running on.

Clipping Video

Again, just like any `FrameworkElement`-derived object, the `MediaElement` can be clipped using a clipping path. To clip the `MediaElement`, you set the `Clip` property using the same path data syntax you were introduced to in Chapter 7. Blend makes creating clipping paths easy. Simply define a path using the Blend drawing tools, and then size and position the path over the `MediaElement` you want to clip. Once you have the path where you want it, select both the `Path` and the `MediaElement` (hold down the Shift key to select multiple objects); then, from the main menu, select Object ➪ Path ➪ Make Clipping Path. Figure 20-8 shows both a `MediaElement` and a `Path` selected on the design surface with the command exposed on the main menu.

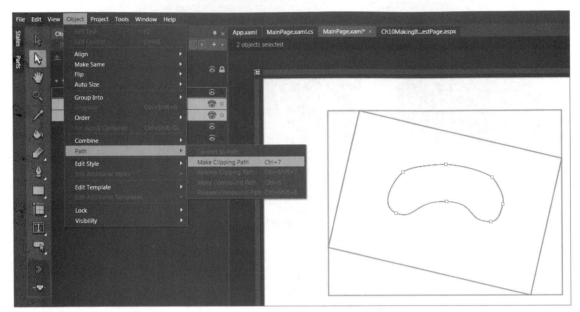

FIGURE 20-8

Notice that the Path is positioned directly over the MediaElement that I want to clip. You must position the Path exactly where you want the visible area of the video to be before using the Make Clipping Path command. Expression Blend normalizes the values of the Path data to be relative to the top-left corner of the element being clipped. With clipping masks, (0,0) represents the top-left corner of the object being clipped, not the top-left corner of the design surface. Figure 20-9 shows the MediaElement after it has been clipped.

FIGURE 20-9

In the following XAML (Listing 20-10), you can see that the Clip property accepts the same path data syntax that you should be vaguely familiar with now. Try hand-editing a few points to see how the clipping mask is affected:

Available for download on Wrox.com

LISTING 20-10: Clipping video using a Path on the MediaElement Clip property

```
<MediaElement
    Width="320"
    Height="240"
    x:Name="meSampleVideo"
    Source="/SampleVideo.wmv"
    RenderTransformOrigin="0.5,0.5"
    Clip="M89.626343,47.989033 C89.626343,47.989033 1.9381521,109.92341
54.496151,126.16163 C107.05415,142.39984 88.938194,90.738899 141.32475,105.99192
C193.71132,121.24493 205.15047,87.790825 202.15236,82.222031 C199.15424,76.653236
186.56322,39.257092 151.01031,33.257763 C115.45742,27.258436 89.626343,47.989033
89.626343,47.989033 z" >
</MediaElement>
```

Painting Elements with the VideoBrush

Using the `VideoBrush`, you can paint any element on your design surface with video. The classic example is text painted with video; however, you can paint any custom artwork with a video brush to create a variety of really interesting effects. You could, for example, have cloud-shaped paths, painted with subtly moving fluffy textures, floating across your page. Let's stick with convention, though, and paint some text with video!

The `VideoBrush` is not completely self-contained. Instead, it needs a reference to an existing `MediaElement` defined within your page. The following XAML (Listing 20-11) defines a `MediaElement` that references a WMV file named *texture.wmv*:

LISTING 20-11: Working with Properties on the MediaElement

```
<MediaElement
    Width="320"
    Height="240"
    x:Name="textureVideo"
    Opacity="0"
    IsMuted="True"
    IsHitTestVisible="False" />
```

I've bolded several properties in the preceding code that you'll likely want to set when defining a `MediaElement` for use by a `VideoBrush`. First, I've set `Opacity` to `0` so that the source video won't be seen except when used by the `VideoBrush`. Second, I've set `IsMuted` to `True`. I don't really want to hear any audio playing in the background if this video has an audio track. I just want the video. Last, I've set `IsHitTestVisible` to `False` so that the `MediaElement` doesn't erroneously capture my mouse clicks. These three properties together keep the `MediaElement` quiet and prevent it from making itself known in ways other than how I've intended.

The following XAML (Listing 20-12) defines a `TextBlock` and sets its `Foreground` property with a `VideoBrush` that references the `MediaElement` just defined. Note that the name of the `MediaElement` is "textureVideo" (x:Name="textureVideo").

LISTING 20-12: Applying a VideoBrush on a MediaElement

```
<TextBlock
    Text="VideoBrush"
    FontFamily="Arial"
    FontSize="72"
    FontWeight="Bold">
    <TextBlock.Foreground>
        <VideoBrush
            SourceName="textureVideo" Stretch="UniformToFill" />
    </TextBlock.Foreground>
</TextBlock>
```

The `VideoBrush` is applied just as you apply a `SolidColorBrush`, `LinearGradientBrush`, or `ImageBrush`. I've bolded the `SourceName` property in the previous code listing. The `SourceName` property accepts a string with the name of the source `MediaElement`, in this case, *textureVideo*. Because `VideoBrush` is derived from `TileBrush` (like `ImageBrush`), it has a `Stretch` property. Use the `Stretch` property to define how the video is applied as it fills the target element.

Simulating Video Reflections

It's likely you've seen Silverlight media samples that simulate reflected video. This technique is easy and fast to achieve once you know the basics. You can apply this same technique to any other element in your Page as well. To achieve the effect, we'll use:

➤ Two `MediaElement`s, both using the same `Source`

➤ `ScaleTransform`

➤ `OpacityMask`

First, start by creating two `MediaElement`s and set their `Source` property to the same video. Then, position them one on top of the other as shown in Figure 20-10.

You can use whatever layout panel works best for you here — positioning absolutely using the `Canvas` control, or via the `StackPanel` with its `Orientation` set to `Vertical`. Next, we need to flip the bottom video using a `ScaleTransform`. The following XAML (Listing 20-13) shows how to do this by setting the `ScaleY` property to `-1` to *flip* the video on the Y-axis:

FIGURE 20-10

LISTING 20-13: Setting up for video reflection by adding a flip on the ScaleY property

Available for
download on
Wrox.com

```xaml
<MediaElement
    Height="320"
    Width="240"
    x:Name="videoReflection"
    Source="/SampleVideo.wmv" RenderTransformOrigin="0.5,0.5">
    <MediaElement.RenderTransform>
        <TransformGroup>
            <ScaleTransform ScaleY="-1"/>
        </TransformGroup>
    </MediaElement.RenderTransform>
</MediaElement>
```

You can achieve this with a single button click in the Expression Blend transform editor. Just select the second video and select the last tab in the transform editor. Figure 20-11 shows the "Flip Y axis" button that automatically applies the `ScaleTransform` for you.

FIGURE 20-11

The last step in simulating a reflection is applying a `LinearGradientBrush` as an `OpacityMask` to the second video. The following XAML (Listing 20-14) defines a vertical `LinearGradientBrush` that starts at 50 percent opacity (4C in Hexadecimal) and fades to 0 percent opacity (00 in Hexadecimal):

LISTING 20-14: Adding a LinearGradientBrush to simulate video reflection

```xml
<MediaElement
    Height="320"
    Width="240"
    x:Name="videoReflection"
    Source="/SampleVideo.wmv" RenderTransformOrigin="0.5,0.5">
    <MediaElement.RenderTransform>
        <TransformGroup>
            <ScaleTransform ScaleY="-1"/>
        </TransformGroup>
    </MediaElement.RenderTransform>
    <MediaElement.OpacityMask>
        <LinearGradientBrush EndPoint="0.5,1" StartPoint="0.5,0">
            <GradientStop Color="#00FFFFFF"/>
            <GradientStop Color="#4CFFFFFF" Offset="1"/>
        </LinearGradientBrush>
    </MediaElement.OpacityMask>
</MediaElement>
```

The order of the stops feels reversed, with the first stop representing 0 percent opacity and the second stop representing 30 percent opacity. This is because the OpacityMask is applied to the MediaElement before it is flipped.

So, that's all there is to it! Create two videos. Position them. Flip the second. Apply an OpacityMask. Easy, easy! Now you can spend time adjusting the OpacityMask until you achieve the final effect you're after. Try wrapping the two MediaElements with a container panel (such as Grid) and apply a 3D transform — reflected, 3D-rotated video in just a few steps!

Enabling GPU Hardware Acceleration

When rendering high-definition video (or any video for that matter), you may want to enable hardware acceleration to offload the processing to your GPU. You set these parameters using the <param /> tag when adding the <object /> tag for the Silverlight plugin to your HTML page (Listing 20-15):

LISTING 20-15: Setting EnableCacheVisualization and EnableGPUAcceleration in the Silverlight plugin

```html
<object data="data:application/x-silverlight-2,"
    type="application/x-silverlight-2" width="100%" height="100%">
    <param name="source" value="ClientBin/Ch10MakingItRicherWithMedia.xap"/>
    <param name="EnableGPUAcceleration" value="true" />
    <param name="EnableCacheVisualization" value="true" />
    <param name="background" value="white" />
    <param name="minRuntimeVersion" value="3.0.40307.0" />
</object>
```

The first parameter, `EnableGPUAcceleration`, enables the option of GPU acceleration at the plug-in level. Note that at this point no elements in the player are actually GPU-accelerated. The second parameter, `EnableCacheVisualization`, applies a red overlay to all elements *not* GPU-accelerated. If you run your project at this point, everything should be red because you haven't explicitly turned on acceleration for any objects. `EnableCacheVisualization` is a great tool for understanding what is actually being offloaded to the GPU.

Now that you've enabled GPU acceleration at the plug-in level, you have to turn on GPU acceleration for specific elements in your application. The following XAML (Listing 20-16) enables GPU acceleration by setting the `CacheMode` property to `BitmapCache` on a `MediaElement`:

LISTING 20-16: Setting CacheMode on the MediaElement

```
<MediaElement x:Name="sampleVideo"
    Source="media/sampleVideo.m4v"
    CacheMode="BitmapCache"
/>
```

If you test now, you should see that your video is no longer red (meaning that the GPU is rendering it). When you're satisfied with your caching settings, either delete the `EnableCacheVisualization` parameter or set its value to `false`.

Audio Settings

The Blend interface exposes some of the common properties you might want to set when initializing your media. Three of the properties shown in Figure 20-3 deal with audio: `Balance`, `IsMuted`, and `Volume`. These properties can be set via XAML, via the Blend Property panel, or at run time via code.

➤ `Balance` — The `Balance` property accepts a value between –1 and 1, where –1 represents the left channel of audio, and 1 represents the right channel. By default, this value is centered with a value of 0.

➤ `IsMuted` — Toggle the value of this property to turn the volume of the `MediaElement` on or off, while preserving the value of the `Volume` property.

➤ `Volume` — The `Volume` property accepts a value between 0 and 1, where 0 represents no volume, and 1 represents full volume.

Buffering

By default, the `MediaElement` buffers five seconds of the target source file before playback starts. You can adjust this value by setting the `BufferingTime` property. This property is of type `TimeSpan` and accepts a value in the following format:

```
[days.]hours:minutes:seconds[fractionalSeconds]
```

Both `days` and `fractionalSeconds` are optional. The following XAML (Listing 20-17) instructs the `MediaElement` to buffer 1 minute and 30.5 seconds of video:

LISTING 20-17: Setting the BufferingTime on a MediaElement

```
<MediaElement
    Width="320"
    Height="240"
    BufferingTime="00:01:30.5"
Source="/media/stockfootage/Bear.wmv" />
```

As the buffer is loaded, the `BufferingProgress` property of the `MediaElement` is updated. The value of this property, like other properties representing a percentage, is 0 to 1. When this value reaches 1, it means that 100 percent of the media specified by the `BufferingTime` has been downloaded, not 100 percent of the media itself. Every time the `BufferingProgress` value is updated by 0.05 or more, the `MediaElement` raises the `BufferingProgressChanged` event. The following XAML (Listing 20-18) demonstrates how to specify an event handler for the `BufferingProgressChanged` event:

LISTING 20-18: Setting the BufferingProgressChanged event handler

```
<MediaElement
    x:Name="meSampleVideo"
    BufferingProgressChanged="meSampleVideo_BufferingProgressChanged"
    Width="320"
    Height="240"
    BufferingTime="00:01:30.5"
Source="/media/stockfootage/Bear.wmv" />
```

The following code (Listing 20-19) represents the `meSampleVideo_BufferingProgressChanged` event handler, referenced by the previous XAML. When called, this method sets the `Text` property of the `TextBlock` named `tbBufferProgress` with a meaningful message, based on the value of the `MediaElement`'s `BufferingProgress` value:

LISTING 20-19: Handling the BufferingProgressChanged event

```
private void meSampleVideo_BufferingProgressChanged(object sender,
                        RoutedEventArgs e)
{
    tbDownloadProgress.Text = (meSampleVideo.BufferingProgress *
                            100).ToString() + "% Buffered";
}
```

Detecting Download Progress

Just as you can detect the amount of video that has been buffered, you can detect the amount of the total video that has been downloaded. The MediaElement's DownloadProgress property represents the percentage of video that has been downloaded in the value range of 0 to 1. As the value of this property increases by 0.05, the DownloadProgressChanged event is raised by the MediaElement. The following XAML (Listing 20-20) demonstrates how to specify an event handler for the DownloadProgressChanged event:

LISTING 20-20: Setting the DownloadProgressChanged event handler

```
<MediaElement
    x:Name="meSampleVideo"
    DownloadProgressChanged="meSampleVideo_DownloadProgressChanged"
    Width="320"
    Height="240"
    BufferingTime="00:01:30.5"
Source="/media/stockfootage/Bear.wmv" />
```

The following code (Listing 20-21) represents the meSampleVideo_DownloadProgressChanged event handler referenced by the previous XAML. When called, this method sets the Text property of the TextBlock named *tbDownloadProgress* with a download status message based on the MediaElement's DownloadProgress property:

LISTING 20-21: Handling the DownloadProgressChanged event

```
private void meSampleVideo_DownloadProgressChanged(object sender,
    RoutedEventArgs e)
{
    tbDownloadProgress.Text = (meSampleVideo.DownloadProgress *
                        100).ToString() + "% Downloaded";
}
```

Notice that I'm multiplying the DownloadProgress value by 100 to obtain a percentage-based value.

Detecting Playback Quality

The MediaElement control exposes two properties, DroppedFramesPerSecond and RenderedFramesPerSecond, that you can use to detect the video quality being rendered at any point in time. If the frame rate has dropped to a really low number or the number of frames being dropped per second is close to the frame rate of your video, you could choose to change the Source of the MediaElement to a stream encoded at a lower bit rate.

Controlling Playback

The MediaElement exposes several common methods that you can use to control the playback of the loaded media.

Pause()

When called, the Pause method pauses playback at the current position. Playback can be resumed from the Pause position by calling the Play method. If Pause is called but not available, the call is simply ignored. The MediaElement exposes a Boolean CanPause property that you can access to determine whether or not pausing is available for the currently loaded media. Even though the Pause method is ignored when CanPause is false, you can take advantage of this property to update your user interface, potentially disabling or hiding your Pause button.

The following code (Listing 20-22) represents the Click event handler for a Button named btnPause:

LISTING 20-22: Checking the CanPause property

Available for download on Wrox.com

```
private void btnPause_Click(object sender, RoutedEventArgs e)
{
  if (meSampleVideo.CanPause)
      meSampleVideo.Pause();
}
```

Play()

When the Play method is called, the media is either started (if media was loaded with AutoPlay set to false) or playback resumes from the current position (if paused). If the media is already playing, calling this method has no effect. The following code (Listing 20-23) represents the Click event handler for a Button named btnPlay:

LISTING 20-23: Calling the Play method on a MediaElement

Available for download on Wrox.com

```
private void btnPlay_Click(object sender, RoutedEventArgs e)
{
    meSampleVideo.Play();
}
```

Stop()

When called, the Stop method stops playback and resets the Position property to 00:00:00. If the media was paused when Stop was called, the Position is simply reset. If playback was already stopped, the method is ignored. The following event handler (Listing 20-24) stops playback of the `MediaElement` named `meSampleVideo`:

LISTING 20-24: Calling the Stop method on a MediaElement

```
private void btnStop_Click(object sender, RoutedEventArgs e)
{
    meSampleVideo.Stop();
}
```

SetSource()

Generally, you set the value of the `MediaElement`'s `Source` property directly, specifying a valid URI. However, if you already have access to a media file via a `Stream` or `MediaSourceStream` (potentially obtained asynchronously using the `WebClient`), you can use the `SetSource` method to change the media stream. The following code hints at how this might be achieved:

```
private void btnLoadStream_Click(object sender, RoutedEventArgs e)
{
    // Load media using a stream obtained via WebClient
    // meSampleVideo.SetSource(WebClient stream here);
}
```

Seeking

The `MediaElement` does not expose a method for seeking to a particular location within the loaded media. You can, however, set the value of the `Position` property, which achieves the desired result. Just like pausing, seeking is not available when the media source is a live stream. You can detect whether or not seeking is available for the loaded media by accessing the `CanSeek` property.

The following XAML (Listing 20-25) specifies an event handler for the `MediaElement`'s `MediaOpened` event:

LISTING 20-25: Setting the MediaOpened event handler

```
<MediaElement
    Width="320"
    Height="240"
    x:Name="meSampleVideo"
    MediaOpened="UpdateScrubberVisibility"
    Source="/SampleVideo.wmv" />
```

The following code (Listing 20-26) handles the `MediaOpened` event and toggles the visibility of a `Slider` named *Scrubber* based on the value of the `MediaElement`'s `CanSeek` property:

LISTING 20-26: Handling the MediaOpened event

```
private void UpdateScrubberVisibility(object sender, RoutedEventArgs e)
{
```

```
    MediaElement media = sender as MediaElement;

    if (media.CanSeek)
    {
        Scrubber.Visibility = Visibility.Visible;
    }
    else
    {
        Scrubber.Visibility = Visibility.Collapsed;
    }
}
```

Responding to Video Markers

Windows Media files can be encoded with *markers* throughout their timelines that can represent either text or some type of script at a specified point on the timeline. You can use these markers to create a higher level of interactivity with the media currently playing. For example, consider a recorded presentation that includes a set of coordinating slides. As the video plays, you would like to change the active slide at different points in the video to coincide with the appropriate narration. You can achieve this by encoding your video with markers at each point along the timeline where you want the slide to change. The section "Encoding Media with Expression Encoder" later in this chapter describes how to add markers to video.

The Markers Property

When media is loaded via the `MediaElement` control, the `MediaElement.Markers` property is cleared and then loaded with any markers defined in the currently loaded media. This property is available once the `MediaOpened` event is raised.

The `Markers` property is of type `TimelineMarkerCollection`, a collection of `TimelineMarker` objects. Each timeline marker has a `Text`, a `Time`, and a `Type` property. Generally, with video encoded for Silverlight applications, the value of the `Type` property will be `"Name"`, with the value of `Text` representing the *Name* of the particular marker. The `Time` property is of type `TimeSpan` and represents the location along the media's timeline where the marker occurs.

Using the Markers collection, you can retrieve all of the names of each marker for the currently loaded video and create an interface that lets you jump directly to a particular scene. The following code (Listing 20-27) loops through all of the markers for a `MediaElement` that has just been opened and writes the value of each marker's `Text` property to the Debug window:

Available for download on Wrox.com

LISTING 20-27: Iterating the Markers collection in a MediaElement

```
private void TraceMarkers(object sender, RoutedEventArgs e)
{
    MediaElement mediaElementWithMarkers = sender as MediaElement;
    foreach (TimelineMarker marker in mediaElementWithMarkers.Markers)
    {
        Debug.WriteLine("Marker Found: " + marker.Text);
```

continues

LISTING 20-27 *(continued)*

```
        Debug.WriteLine("                > " + marker.Time.ToString());
    }
}
```

You can also use the `Time` property of a particular marker to seek a position in the loaded media. The following code (Listing 20-28) jumps to the position of the last marker in the Markers collection:

LISTING 20-28: Setting a MediaElement position with the Time property of a Marker

```
private void SeekLastMarker(MediaElement mediaElement)
{
    // Get Index of Last Marker
    int lastMarkerIndex = mediaElement.Markers.Count - 1;

    // Seek to Position of Last Marker
    mediaElement.Position = mediaElement.Markers[lastMarkerIndex].Time;
}
```

Remember, the `MediaElement` does not contain a `Seek()` method; instead, you simply set the value of the `Position` property directly.

The MarkerReached Event

The `Markers` property gives you all of the information you need to jump directly to a predefined point in your media. However, if you want to enable the synchronized video + slideshow scenario described at the beginning of this section, you'll need to respond to the `MarkerReached` event of the `MediaElement`. The `MarkerReached` event is raised any time a marker is reached during playback. The following XAML (Listing 20-29) demonstrates how to assign an event handler to the `MarkerReached` event:

LISTING 20-29: Setting the MarkerReached event handler

```
<MediaElement
    Width="320"
    Height="240"
    x:Name="meSampleVideo"
    MarkerReached="OnMarkerReached"
    Source="/SampleVideo.wmv" />
```

Similar to the `TraceMarkers` method we saw earlier, the following `OnMarkerReached` method (Listing 20-30) displays the `Text` and `Time` of the marker that was just reached:

LISTING 20-30: Handling the MarkerReached event

```
private void OnMarkerReached(object sender,
        TimelineMarkerRoutedEventArgs e)
```

```
    {
        Debug.WriteLine("Marker Reached: " + e.Marker.Text);
        Debug.WriteLine("               > " + e.Marker.Time.ToString());
    }
```

The `TimelineMarkerRoutedEventArgs` object includes a `Marker` property that you use to get information about the marker that has just been reached. The previous simple event handler just writes the `Text` and `Time` to the Debug window. A more realistic sample might update an image and modify the text of a label. The following example (Listing 20-31) does just that:

LISTING 20-31: Updating controls in the MarkerReached event handler

```
private void OnMarkerReached(object sender, TimelineMarkerRoutedEventArgs e)
{
    // Set Slide Title
    txtSlideTitle.Text = e.Marker.Text;

    // Update Slide Image
    imgSlide.Source = new BitmapImage(new Uri("images\\"
                        + e.Marker.Text
                        + ".png", UriKind.Relative));
}
```

In the previous example, we created a new `BitmapImage` (`System.Windows.Media.Imaging` namespace), assuming that there is a PNG image available that matches the string contained within the `Marker.Text` property. In practice, you could have some type of data structure that matches the marker's text or offset with the source video file and provides any number of fields you need to support your UI.

> *Windows Media files support multiple streams, each of which can have its own set of markers. The* `MediaElement.Markers` *property only contains the markers embedded in the main file header, not the additional streams. However, the* `MediaElement` *still raises the* `MarkerReached` *event as these additional markers are reached.*

Handling Failed Media

We'd all like to think that nothing we create will ever fail, but you and I both know that's just not reality. When you're setting the source file of the `MediaElement` to a URL on a remote website, you can only hope that it will always be there. If you're not in control of the server, you can never truly count on its existence, or the availability of the server, for that matter. Fortunately, the `MediaElement` control lets us know when a referenced media file doesn't load, isn't supported, or *errors out* during playback.

The following XAML (Listing 20-32) demonstrates how to assign an event handler to the `MediaFailed` event:

LISTING 20-32: Setting the MediaFailed event handler

```
<MediaElement
    Width="320"
    Height="240"
    MediaFailed="OnMediaFailed"
    Source="/SampleVideo.wmv" />
```

When this unfortunate event occurs, you can either try to load another file or present the user with some type of meaningful message or experience. The following code (Listing 20-33) updates a `TextBlock` and displays an error image:

LISTING 20-33: Handling the MediaFailed event

```
private void OnMediaFailed(object sender, RoutedEventArgs e)
{
    // Set Slide Title
    txtSlideTitle.Text = "An error occurred while trying to load the
                          selected video.";

    // Update Slide Image
    imgSlide.Source = new BitmapImage(new Uri("images\\errorSlide.png",
                                              UriKind.Relative));
}
```

Responding to State Changes

The `MediaElement` has a `CurrentState` property that can be accessed at any point during the life of the control to determine its state. The `CurrentState` property is of type `MediaElementState`, an enum type with the following values:

➤ `Closed`

➤ `Opening`

➤ `Individualizing`

➤ `AcquiringLicense`

➤ `Buffering`

➤ `Playing`

➤ `Paused`

➤ `Stopped`

The MediaElement also raises a CurrentStateChanged event that you can handle and respond to. The following XAML (Listing 20-34) demonstrates how to assign an event handler to this event:

Available for download on Wrox.com

LISTING 20-34: Setting the CurrentStateChanged event handler

```
<MediaElement
    Width="320"
    Height="240"
    CurrentStateChanged="OnCurrentStateChanged"
    Source="/SampleVideo.wmv" />
```

The following code (Listing 20-35) handles this event and writes the current state of the MediaElement to the Debug window:

Available for download on Wrox.com

LISTING 20-35: Handling the CurrentStateChanged event

```
private void OnCurrentStateChanged(object sender, RoutedEventArgs e)
{
    MediaElement media = sender as MediaElement;
    Debug.WriteLine("Current State: " + media.CurrentState);
}
```

You can use your knowledge of the current state of the MediaElement to update playback controls in your application. For example, if the current state changes to Playing, you probably want to show a Pause button and vice versa.

MEDIA PLAYLISTS

In certain scenarios, playing a single media file is not enough. Consider an online news program that consists of several news segments interspersed with commercials. Or consider on online radio program that consists of several audio tracks, framed at the beginning and the end with commentary. In both of these scenarios, a media playlist is desirable.

Silverlight supports both Server Side Playlist (SSPL) and Advanced Stream Redirector (ASX) playlist files to enable the scenarios described previously.

Server-Side Playlist (SSPL) Files

SSPL files are XML-based and use the .wsx file extension. These files are used by a Microsoft Media Server of some flavor (Windows Server 2003, Windows Server 2008, Windows Web Server 2008, etc.). Microsoft has a server comparison guide to help illustrate the differences between their different server offerings at the following URL: www.microsoft.com/windows/windowsmedia/forpros/server/version.aspx.

You'll see that the Standard Edition of Windows Server 2003 does not support Advanced Fast Start or Advanced Fast Forward/Rewind, whereas the Enterprise and Datacenter versions of those servers do. There are several other features such as this that you don't get with the non-Enterprise version of the servers.

Why Use a Media Server and SSPL?

Below are some common advantages offered by the Media Server technologies. Access the previously referenced website to get a full understanding of the capabilities offered by Microsoft Media Servers.

➤ **Dynamic Generation** — SSPL files can be created either statically or, more attractively, dynamically. This means that you can serve up a dynamic playlist based on a user's authentication level or the time of day the playlist is being requested. You can even edit the playlist after it has been accessed by a client, giving you an extreme level of control over the served-up content.

➤ **Loading/Startup Experience** — When broadcasting a live event, it's common for users to sign in before the event has started. To provide a better experience for the early birds, you can specify a media file to loop prior to the broadcast.

➤ **Fine-Grained Control** — The SSPL supports various configuration options that give you a high level of control over each media file in your playlist. For example, you can define alternative video streams or files should another video fail. You can also display a subclip of a video instead of the entire video, by setting the `clipBegin` and `clipEnd` properties.

Creating and Consuming a WSX File

The `.wsx` file is an XML-based file that can be easily defined by hand. Once defined and saved, the file must be published using a Windows Media Server. When a `.wsx` file is published, a *publishing point* will be defined. It is this publishing point that will be consumed by the `MediaElement` control, just like a standard media file:

```
myCustomPlaylist.wsx => publish => mms://MyMediaServer:8081/myCustomPlaylist
```

The following (Listing 20-36) shows a simple WSX file definition:

LISTING 20-36: A WSX file definition

```
<?wsx version="1.0"?>
<smil>
  <seq id="debateSeq">
   <media id="introVideo" src="intro.wmv" />
   <media id="debate" src="debate.wmv" />
   <media id="summaryVideo" src="summary.wmv" />
  <seq>
</smil>
```

Consuming the WSX is just as easy as consuming a single media file. You simply set the Source property of MediaElement to the URI of your published playlist (see Listing 20-37):

LISTING 20-37: Setting the MediaElement Source property to consume a server side playlist

```
<MediaElement
    Width="320"
    Height="240"
    HorizontalAlignment="Left"
    VerticalAlignment="Bottom"
    Margin="50,50,0,0"
    Source="mms://MyMediaServer:8081/myCustomPlaylist" />
```

The SSPL currently supports a number of features that Silverlight *does not* support. To see the latest list of Silverlight-supported attributes, visit the Audio and Video ➪ Server-Side Playlists section of the Silverlight Developer Center (http://msdn.microsoft.com/en-us/library/cc645037(VS.95).aspx).

Advanced Stream Redirector (ASX) Files

In addition to SSPL files, Silverlight supports ASX-based playlist files. Like WSX files, ASX files are XML-based and can be easily defined by hand or programmatically on the server. Unlike WSX files, ASX files can reside on a standard web server and do not have to be published via Windows Media Server. This capability may make ASX files more attractive to you when the power (and extra overhead) of Windows Media Server is too much for your needs. The following URL covers all aspects of the ASX file format in depth: http://msdn.microsoft.com/en-us/library/ms925291.aspx.

Key Features of ASX

The following are a few key features of the ASX playlist that may help you decide between SSPL and ASX:

➤ **Server-Independent** — ASX files do not require a Windows Media Server. They are standalone files that can reside loosely on a server or as part of your Silverlight project.

➤ **Dynamic Generation** — ASX files can be created either statically or, more attractively, dynamically. This means that you can serve up a dynamic playlist based on a user's authentication level or the time of day the playlist is being requested. You could achieve this dynamic approach by creating an ASPX page that returns ASX content. Set the Source property of your MediaElement to the ASPX page's path.

➤ **Fine-Grained Control** — The ASX file format offers various configuration options for each entry in the playlist. For example, the STARTMARKER attribute lets you specify the start time of a particular entry. Most of these features of ASX are not currently supported by Silverlight 3, although I wanted to call this ASX feature out should they be implemented at some point in the future.

Creating and Consuming an ASX File

A simple ASX file contains a single root `ASX` element and a list of child `Entry` elements. Each `Entry` represents an item in the playlist. Listing 20-38 is a simple example that defines a playlist with a single item:

LISTING 20-38: An ASX file definition

```
<ASX version = "3.0">
<!--A simple playlist with entries to be played in sequence.-->
    <Title>Playlist Title</Title>
    <Entry>
        <Title>Sample Show Title</Title>
        <Author>ABC Video</Author>
        <Copyright>(c) 2008 ABC Video</Copyright>
        <Ref href="Bear.wmv" />
    </Entry>
</ASX>
```

Reference the ASX playlist just as you would a single media element (Listing 20-39):

LISTING 20-39: Setting the MediaElement Source property to an ASX file

```
<MediaElement
    Width="320"
    Height="240"
    HorizontalAlignment="Left"
    VerticalAlignment="Bottom"
    Margin="50,50,0,0"
    Source="MyCustomPlaylist.asx" />
```

Not all of the capabilities of the ASX format are supported by Silverlight. Table 20-1 identifies those features and describes the behavior of the player when unsupported features are encountered.

TABLE 20-1

ASX FEATURE	DESCRIPTION
`PreviewMode` attribute	This attribute is found on the root ASX object. It is not supported and will raise a `MediaError` with `AG_E_ASX_UNSUPPORTED_ATTRIBUTE`.
`BannerBar` attribute	This attribute is found on the root ASX object. It is not supported and will raise a `MediaError` with `AG_E_ASX_UNSUPPORTED_ATTRIBUTE`.
`SkipIfRef`	This attribute is found on the root `ENTRY` object. It is not supported and will raise a `MediaError` with `AG_E_ASX_UNSUPPORTED_ATTRIBUTE`.

ASX FEATURE	DESCRIPTION
REPEAT element	This is not supported and will raise a MediaError with AG_E_ASX_UNSUPPORTED_ELEMENT.
EVENT element	This is not supported and will raise a MediaError with AG_E_ASX_UNSUPPORTED_ELEMENT.
STARTMARKER element	This is not supported and will raise a MediaError with AG_E_ASX_UNSUPPORTED_ELEMENT.
ENDMARKER element	This is not supported and will raise a MediaError with AG_E_ASX_UNSUPPORTED_ELEMENT.
Invalid content	If a valid ASX tag has content that is not accepted (e.g., a MOREINFO tag contains a REF tag), a MediaFailed error is raised.
Fallback URLs	If an ENTRY tag has multiple REF children, only the first one is read. Unlike WMP, Silverlight will not attempt to open additional REF URLs in case the first one fails, and a MediaFailed error is raised.

Encoding Media with Expression Encoder

Now that you know how to do practically everything you can with the MediaElement, let's take a look at how to prepare media for use by the MediaElement. We'll use Microsoft Expression Encoder 3 (available as a trial download from www.microsoft.com/expression/products/Encoder_Overview.aspx). Expression Encoder is designed with Silverlight exporting in mind. It lets you quickly record videos, trim videos, add markers, and render to a format natively supported by Silverlight. It even includes publishing templates that generate Silverlight-based layouts (that include MediaElements, of course) to quickly present your media on the Web.

In this walk-through, I'll step you through a common encoding scenario to get you up-and-running quickly, but I won't cover Expression Encoder in full detail. If you really need to dig deep, the Expression website has complete video training that can get you really immersed into the product. Check that out here: http://expression.microsoft.com/en-us/cc197144.aspx.

Here's a quick glance at what we'll cover:

➤ Importing a media file

➤ Trimming the media

➤ Adding markers

➤ Setting encoder settings

➤ Defining metadata

➤ Publishing the video

Let's get started. Figure 20-12 shows Expression Encoder right after it's been launched.

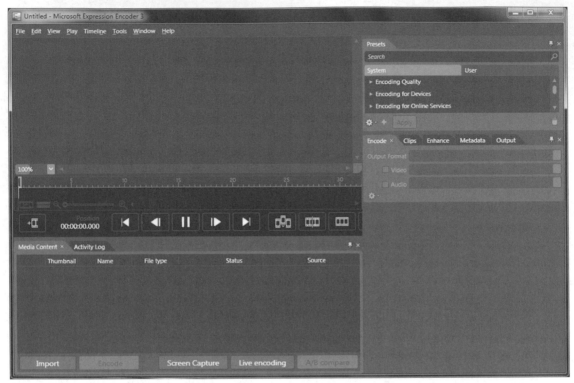

FIGURE 20-12

The default workspace is mostly disabled at startup. To get going, click on the Import button in the lower-left corner of the screen or select File ➪ Import from the main menu.

Clicking Import launches the "File Browser" dialog and let you select a file of any of the supported media types, a fairly exhaustive list that should meet most of your needs.

Once you've selected a media file, it's added to the Media Content panel, shown in Figure 20-13. I selected the file Wildlife.wmv from the Windows 7 Videos folder as an example.

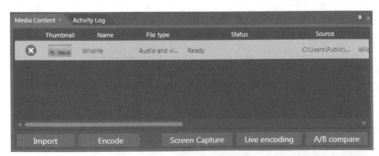

FIGURE 20-13

Once you've imported the file, Expression Encoder detects some features of the file, such as File type, duration, file size, and dimensions. These are displayed inline as a quick reference for you and are demonstrated in Figure 20-14. You can import any number of media files by clicking on the Import button again. Just select the media element in the Content panel's list to make it the active element on the edit surface, as seen in Figure 20-14.

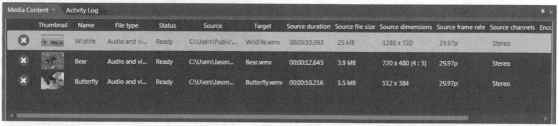

FIGURE 20-14

Timeline Controls

The Timeline and Transport controls appear directly beneath a video once it is selected. The interface is broken into six key regions, highlighted in Figure 20-15:

- ➤ Timeline
- ➤ Timeline Viewing controls
- ➤ Playback controls
- ➤ Editing buttons
- ➤ "Add leader" button
- ➤ "Add trailer" button

FIGURE 20-15

Timeline

The Timeline is where you trim the beginning and ending of your video, cut segments from your video, and add media markers. You navigate the Timeline by dragging the *playhead* (orange box icon) to a desired position. As you drag (or *scrub*, as it's also known), the position indicator and video preview updates (see Figure 20-16).

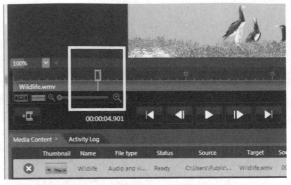

FIGURE 20-16

Trimming Video

Mouse over the beginning or ending of the Timeline until your cursor changes, and you'll see the icons shown in Figure 20-17. Once you see the icon, press and drag to the right or left to trim the beginning or ending of the video.

Cutting Video/Editing along the Timeline

You can cut segments from the middle of the Timeline by adding an *edit*. Do this by positioning the scrubber at the location where you want to make the edit, then click the "Add an edit at the playhead" button, as shown in Figure 20-18.

Once you've added an edit, you can trim the beginning or ending of the new segment just like you trimmed the entire Timeline (see Figure 20-19).

FIGURE 20-17

FIGURE 20-18

FIGURE 20-19

The third of the editing buttons lets you remove the segment currently beneath the playhead. This lets you cut out an entire segment of video. If you want to control your edits with an extra level of precision, select the Clips tab on the Properties panel. Figure 20-20 shows the "Start time" and "End time" for all of the edits you've added.

FIGURE 20-20

Adding Markers

Markers can be added to the Timeline by right-clicking at the location of the playhead and selecting "Add Marker," or by positioning the playhead and pressing Ctrl+M on your keyboard. Once you've added a marker, it appears on the Timeline as a white rectangle (see Figure 20-21).

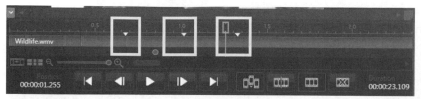

FIGURE 20-21

Once you've added markers on the Timeline, you can edit their properties using the Markers panel, available on the Metadata tab (Window ➪ Metadata). Figure 20-22 shows the Markers tab open with three markers added.

You can hand-tweak the time, provide a `Value`, specify whether or not to encode this as a key frame, and specify whether or not to generate a thumbnail for this particular marker. When you click on the Thumbnail checkbox, a JPG image is created from the video at the position of the marker. This is useful if you want to create a DVD-style navigation that displays images for different jump points in your media.

FIGURE 20-22

Timeline Viewing Controls

The Timeline Viewing controls are directly beneath the start of the Timeline, on the left side of the screen. The first item in this set is a toggle button that lets you toggle the visibility of segments in the video that have been cut. In Figure 20-23, this feature is turned on, revealing a section in red (though this book doesn't show the color) that has been cut. The second button toggles between the current zoom level (set by the Zoom slider at the end of this set) and a zoom level that shows the Timeline in its entirety. Use the Zoom slider to set the zoom factor, sliding it to the right to zoom in for more precise editing.

FIGURE 20-23

Playback Controls

The Playback controls are positioned right in the middle of the Timeline area, making it easy to navigate your Timeline quickly. The leftmost and rightmost buttons, commonly used to navigate to the previous and next track on a media player, are here used to navigate from edit point to edit point or marker to marker. The next set of buttons, second from the left and second from the right, lets you step through your video frame-by-frame. The middle button lets you toggle between Play and

Pause. If you ever forget the meaning of practically any element in the interface, just hover for a few moments to see the control's tooltip.

Editing Buttons

See the previous section, "Cutting Video/Editing along the Timeline."

"Add Leader"/"Add Trailer" Buttons

Expression Encoder lets you quickly set an opening (*leader*) and closing (*trailer*) video to your currently selected media by clicking on either the "Add leader" or the "Add trailer" button. This is useful if you have a standard branding that you want to apply to the beginning, end, or both of all of the videos you produce.

 You cannot edit or trim either the leader or trailer. You'll have to edit those separately, encode them, and then set them as a leader or trailer if you need to perform any editing on those videos.

Editing Metadata

Select the Metadata tab (Window ➪ Metadata) to edit properties such as `Title`, `Author`, `Copyright`, `Rating`, and the like that will be included with your encoded media file. If the encoded file is opened with Windows Media Player, this information is displayed. The metadata properties listed by default are only the most commonly used fields. Click the down arrow beneath the Description field to see all of the supported fields. You can access this metadata in Silverlight using the `MediaElement.Attributes` property (see Figure 20-24).

Encoding Settings

Select the Encode tab (Window ➪ Encode) to customize the way your video and audio will be encoded. At the beginning of this chapter, we looked at a list of codecs supported by Silverlight. Now, we actually encounter them. Figure 20-25 shows the Profile panel of the Encode tab. The first two sections let you specify a video profile and an audio profile by selecting from a drop-down list of options. You can think of these as presets, each of which sets a codec, bit rate, height, width, and several other properties.

When you click the down arrow beneath the Video combo box, you'll see all of the properties each item in the combo box is setting. Try changing your combo box selection to see how property settings are updated.

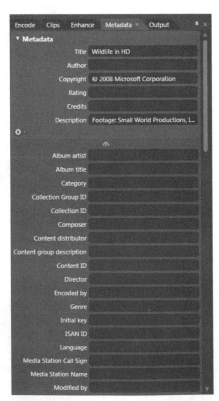

FIGURE 20-24

If you want to get a feeling for how your video looks with your current encoding settings, click the A/B compare button in the lower-right corner of the Media Content area, as shown in Figure 20-26.

When you click A/B compare, the video preview area goes into a Split mode, with the original video on the left and a preview of the encoding video on the right. You first have to click the Generate preview link positioned in the right area of the video. When the preview area goes blank, don't worry — the preview is being rendered. You will see a progress bar in the Media Content List for the currently selected item.

Exit the Preview mode by clicking on the same A/B button you pressed to enter this mode. Its label has changed to Exit A/B compare.

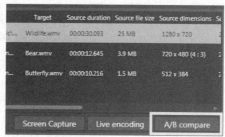

FIGURE 20-25

FIGURE 20-26

Additional Encoding Features

The Encode tab also includes two other panels: Video and Audio. Each panel lets you further customize the individual settings of the video and audio output.

Adding a Video Overlay

You can quickly add an overlay image to your encoded video. This could be useful if you wanted to watermark your video with a transparent logo, or even if you wanted to simulate a television-style footer. You can supply either a static overlay, in the form of an image, or a motion overlay, in the form of another video file or even XAML!

To add an overlay, select the Enhance tab (Window ➪ Enhance) and then scroll down to the Overlay panel, as shown in Figure 20-27.

Click on the ellipsis button to the right of the File box to browse for an overlay file. For still-image overlays, you can use a JPG, BMP, PNG, or GIF file. I recommend using a 32-bit PNG file, as it supports a full alpha channel (meaning

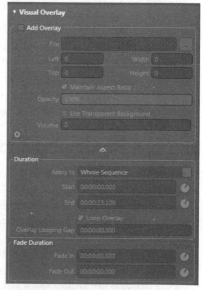

FIGURE 20-27

real transparency). When you want to use a video overlay, select any of the many video types that Expression supports for encoding. Expression also supports QuickTime files with full alpha channels, giving you the ability to add animated overlays with full alpha-channel transparency.

As mentioned earlier, you can also provide XAML-based overlays. This puts the full power of the Silverlight rendering and animation engine at your disposal for creating video overlays.

 You'll need to use a `Canvas`*-based layout when creating your overlay.*

Output Settings

The Output tab (Window ➪ Output) lets you customize thumbnail encoding options (file type, image dimensions, etc.) and, most importantly, lets you specify where you want to render your media and whether or not you want to publish using a Silverlight template. Figure 20-28 shows the Job Output panel. The first property listed is Template. By default, *(None)* is selected. If you wish to publish your video with a Silverlight Media Player template, select an item from the drop-down list. As you change your selection, the preview below the drop-down changes. Selecting one of these presets does not affect your render settings; it just adds to the number of files that are generated and copied to your destination folder. With *None* selected, only the .wmv or .wma is generated. With a template, the .wmv or .wma *plus* several supporting files are generated.

Encoding Media

Once you've finished customizing the Output Settings, Encoding Options, and optional overlay, you're ready to encode. So, click on the large Encode button in the lower-left corner of the screen, and watch the progress bar work its way to 100 percent. That's it! (See Figure 20-29.)

FIGURE 20-28

FIGURE 20-29

Smooth Streaming and IIS 7

Smooth Streaming is an IIS Media Services extension, available for download at www.iis.net/extensions/ SmoothStreaming. This technology dynamically switches between various encodings of the same media content based on the detected bandwidth of the requesting PC. Via this dynamic switching, Smooth Streaming can enable near-instant seeking of video: A low-quality version of the video is immediately sent to the PC upon seeking so that playback can begin. In the background, the next-higher-quality feed is being cached. When available, the video steps up to the next level of quality. This process continues until the PC's bandwidth no longer supports the next-higher encoding.

In order to deliver Smooth Streaming video, the video must be encoded at several target quality levels to support the various levels of bandwidth encountered. To generate a collection of files to enable Smooth Streaming, select the "Adaptive Streaming" profile from the Video drop-down, and select "Adaptive Streaming Audio" from the Audio drop-down.

Like any of the other presets, you can customize individual properties once the preset has been selected. Once you're satisfied with your settings, you can complete the Publish section to publish your rendered files directly to a Smooth Streaming IIS 7 server. Select "WebDAV" from the "Publish To" drop-down in the Publish category.

Finally, click the Encode button and step away for a coffee or a good night's rest, depending on the length of your footage.

SUMMARY

The media capabilities offered by the Silverlight player empower you to create true multimedia experiences. You now know how to respond to all of the events raised by the `MediaElement` and interact with its properties to create interactive, media-rich applications. You learned how to use Microsoft Expression Media Encoder to prepare media files for consumption by your Silverlight applications and saw how the Microsoft Silverlight Streaming service can be used to help carry your bandwidth burden. I hope your mind is now racing with ideas for exciting media applications!

21

Styling and Themes

WHAT'S IN THIS CHAPTER?

➤ Defining core terminology

➤ Defining and using resources

➤ Creating keyed styles

➤ Re-templating controls

➤ Creating implicit styles

➤ Using themes

➤ Styling with Expression Blend

Creating beautiful, highly styled web-based applications is a core promise of the Silverlight platform. Rarely have you seen Microsoft promote ugly Silverlight applications. Generally, they have been through the user experience and visual design machines of top-notch companies that specialize in creating beautiful software. However, learning to take advantage of the power of the platform and thus deliver on the promise of the platform starts at a technical, and somewhat *unbeautiful*, level. This chapter does not try to teach you to create a thing of great beauty — it's just going to empower you to apply your artistic talents to a platform that embraces them.

In this chapter, you learn how to customize the look and feel of the core controls you were introduced to in previous chapters. You see how you can target controls for styling, gain insight into approaches for organizing your styles and resources, and learn what a *resource* actually is. When you are finished, you should have a solid understanding of how to make your application look the way you want it to.

GETTING STARTED

Before you jump into styling, this section defines a small set of core terminology that will be used throughout this chapter, and also defines a testing environment that you can use to follow the examples that are coming up.

Defining a Core Terminology

The following are five key concepts that are used throughout this discussion. Many more concepts are covered along the way, but these will provide you with just enough common ground to move ahead.

➤ **Brush** — A `Brush` object in Silverlight is used to paint elements with solid colors, linear gradients, radial gradients, and images. The brush can be applied to elements such as rectangles, circles, text, and panels.

➤ **Resource** — A resource is a static instance of some type of object. Brush-based types are frequently defined as resources for use within an application.

➤ **ResourceDictionary** — A `ResourceDictionary` contains a collection of resources. A `ResourceDictionary` can be defined inline in a Silverlight page (for example, `Page.xaml`) or externally as a stand-alone XAML file.

➤ **Style** — A `Style` is a special type of object that contains a collection of property `Setters`. A `Style` is defined within a `ResourceDictionary` and targets a particular type of control, like a `TextBox`. It is commonly used to set properties like `Foreground`, `FontStyle`, and `FontFamily`. Remember and repeat to yourself: *A Style is a collection of Setters*.

➤ **ControlTemplate** — A `ControlTemplate` is the `VisualTree` of elements that make up the look of a control. These elements can range from a series of nested `Borders` (like the default button) to a combination of paths with complex gradient fills. A `ControlTemplate` is generally applied by a `Style` in a `Setter` that sets the `Template` property.

The term "styling" encompasses many ideas, from the `Foreground` color and `FontStyle` of a `TextBlock`, to the default hover animation applied to a button. You will start from the ground up, first learning how to set visual properties inline, at the control level. You'll then learn how resources, such as `SolidColorBrushes`, are defined and consumed by elements in a `Page`, then move on to defining `Styles` that set multiple properties on a particular type of control. Finally, you will learn how to re-template controls to completely customize their appearance. In the end, you should understand the "big picture" of styling in Silverlight.

Defining the Working Environment: A XAML-Based Approach

As you start your styling journey, it's important to establish a common working environment so that you can easily follow the examples. Either you can work in Visual Studio 2010 or in Expression Blend 4; the environment you choose is really not important at this point. (Expression Blend was used as the primary authoring tool during the creation of this chapter, so the screenshots you see will likely be taken in the Expression Blend environment.)

Create a new Silverlight 4.0 Project and add a `UserControl` to your project. Figure 21-1 demonstrates how to do this in both Expression Blend and Visual Studio by right-clicking the Project node in Solution Explorer. Once you have added the `UserControl`, double-click its XAML file to make it the active document, and then switch to XAML view.

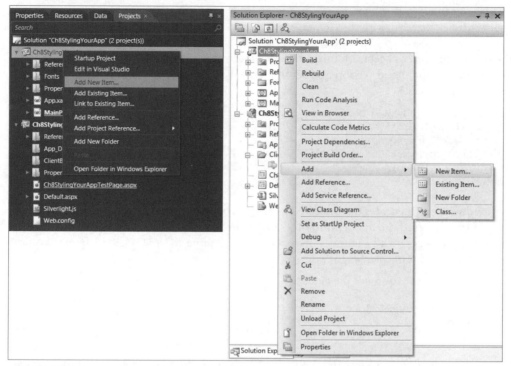

FIGURE 21-1

To ensure that your new `UserControl` is the page that you see when you debug, open `App.xaml.cs` and edit the `Application_Startup` method created by the Silverlight Project starter template. Change the line bolded in the following code to match the name of your new `UserControl`:

```
private void Application_Startup(object sender, StartupEventArgs e)
{
  // Load the main control here
  this.RootVisual = new UserControl1(); // Change this control
}
```

Now, with that little bit of housecleaning out of the way, you can get started.

DEFINING LOCAL STYLING (INLINE STYLING)

Local styling is no more than setting properties on an instance of a control. This may sound a bit obvious, but it is crucial that you see this basic piece of the bigger puzzle. Assume that you want to customize the look of a `TextBlock`, setting its `Foreground` to red (#FF0000 in hexadecimal), its

`FontStyle` to Arial, and its `FontWeight` to bold. The following code demonstrates how to do this in XAML:

```
<TextBlock
  Text="My Red Bold Arial Label"
  Foreground="#FF0000"
  FontFamily="Arial"
  FontWeight="Bold" />
```

The `Foreground` property accepts an inline hexadecimal value that represents a `SolidColorBrush`. You can also use the longhand version and set the `Foreground` property by explicitly declaring a `SolidColorBrush` object:

```
<TextBlock Text="My Red Bold Arial Label" FontFamily="Arial"
  FontWeight="Bold">
  <TextBlock.Foreground>
    <SolidColorBrush Color="#FF0000" />
  </TextBlock.Foreground>
</TextBlock>
```

This longhand version illustrates the underlying object type needed to set the `Foreground` property. You have just encountered the first definition — *Brush*, in this case, the `SolidColorBrush`. Suppose now that you want to create a `Rectangle`, painted with the same red `SolidColorBrush`. You can do it inline just as you did with the `TextBlock`:

```
<Rectangle Width="100" Height="100">
  <Rectangle.Fill>
    <SolidColorBrush Color="#FF0000" />
  </Rectangle.Fill>
</Rectangle>
```

Now assume that you always want your `TextBlock` Foreground to match the `Fill` of this `Rectangle`, and pretend that your mood just changed from red to green. Also, add to your layout ten additional `TextBlocks` and three additional `Rectangles` and demand that they abide by the same color rules. You could step through your XAML (or Expression Blend or Visual Studio) and manually change property values every time you change your mind . . . or you can use resources.

STYLING WITH RESOURCES

You can resolve your color-sync nightmare through the use of resources. First, define the resource and then reference that resource inline on each of your `TextBlocks` and `Rectangles`. The following XAML snippet shows your `UserControl` prior to defining any resources:

```
<UserControl
  xmlns="http://schemas.microsoft.com/winfx/2006/xaml/presentation"
  xmlns:x="http://schemas.microsoft.com/winfx/2006/xaml"
  xmlns:d="http://schemas.microsoft.com/expression/blend/2008"
  xmlns:mc="http://schemas.openxmlformats.org/markup-compatibility/2006"
  mc:Ignorable="d"
  x:Class="Ch21StylesAndThemes.MainPage"
```

```
        d:DesignWidth="640" d:DesignHeight="480">

        <Grid x:Name="LayoutRoot" Background="White" >
          <Rectangle
            Height="84"
            HorizontalAlignment="Left"
            Margin="8,35,0,0"
            VerticalAlignment="Top"
            Width="84"
            Fill="#FFFF0000"
            Stroke="#FF000000"/>
          <TextBlock
            HorizontalAlignment="Left"
            VerticalAlignment="Top"
            Text="TextBlock"
            TextWrapping="Wrap"
            Margin="8,12,0,0"/>
        </Grid>
      </UserControl>
```

Resources are housed in a `ResourceDictionary`, commonly in the outermost element of your XAML file. All `UIElement`-derived classes have a `Resources` property of type `ResourceDictionary`, and `UserControl` is no exception. The following code shows a new `SolidColorBrush` added to the `UserControl.Resources` ResourceDictionary:

```
<UserControl
  xmlns="http://schemas.microsoft.com/winfx/2006/xaml/presentation"
  xmlns:x="http://schemas.microsoft.com/winfx/2006/xaml"
  xmlns:d="http://schemas.microsoft.com/expression/blend/2008"
  xmlns:mc="http://schemas.openxmlformats.org/markup-compatibility/2006"
  mc:Ignorable="d"
  x:Class="Ch21StylesAndThemes.MainPage"
  d:DesignWidth="640" d:DesignHeight="480">
  <UserControl.Resources>
      <SolidColorBrush x:Key="SharedBrush" Color="#FFFF0000"/>
  </UserControl.Resources>
```

Notice that the definition of the brush is exactly the same as the inline definition, only it now includes an `x:Key` property value. When applying this resource, you will reference it by the key value *SharedBrush*. To reference a resource in XAML, use the `{StaticResource keyName}` markup extension. The following shows both the `Rectangle`'s `Fill` property and the `TextBlock`'s `Foreground` property referencing the new resource named `SharedBrush`:

```
<UserControl
  xmlns="http://schemas.microsoft.com/winfx/2006/xaml/presentation"
  xmlns:x="http://schemas.microsoft.com/winfx/2006/xaml"
  xmlns:d="http://schemas.microsoft.com/expression/blend/2008"
  xmlns:mc="http://schemas.openxmlformats.org/markup-compatibility/2006"
  mc:Ignorable="d"
  x:Class="Ch21StylesAndThemes.MainPage"
  d:DesignWidth="640" d:DesignHeight="480">
  <UserControl.Resources>
    <SolidColorBrush x:Key="SharedBrush" Color="#FFFF0000"/>
```

```
    </UserControl.Resources>

    <Grid x:Name="LayoutRoot" Background="White" >
      <Rectangle
        Height="84"
        HorizontalAlignment="Left"
        Margin="8,35,0,0"
        VerticalAlignment="Top"
        Width="84"
        Fill="{StaticResource SharedBrush}"
        Stroke="#FF000000"/>
      <TextBlock
        HorizontalAlignment="Left"
        VerticalAlignment="Top"
        Text="TextBlock"
        TextWrapping="Wrap"
        Margin="8,12,0,0"
        Foreground="{StaticResource SharedBrush}"/>
    </Grid>
  </UserControl>
```

The key thing to notice in the XAML is the statement `Fill="{StaticResource SharedBrush}"`. This statement reads, "Assign the resource named `SharedBrush` to the `Fill` property."

 The curly braces are required when referencing a resource.

You have now seen how to define a resource and reference that resource. Try changing the `Color` property of your `SharedBrush` resource and re-run your application. You should see that both the foreground of the text and the fill of the rectangle have been updated, reflecting your new color value.

As pointed out in the *Defining a Core Terminology* section at the beginning of the chapter, a resource is a static instance of *some type* of object. You are not limited to creating `Brush` resources. The following code shows two additional resources, `CornerRadiusX` and `CornerRadiusY`, both of type `System:Double` (note that a namespace definition has been added for `System`). These are referenced by the `Rectangle`'s `CornerX` and `CornerY` properties.

```
  <UserControl
    xmlns="http://schemas.microsoft.com/winfx/2006/xaml/presentation"
    xmlns:x="http://schemas.microsoft.com/winfx/2006/xaml"
    xmlns:d="http://schemas.microsoft.com/expression/blend/2008"
    xmlns:mc="http://schemas.openxmlformats.org/markup-compatibility/2006"
    xmlns:System="clr-namespace:System;assembly=mscorlib"
    mc:Ignorable="d"
    x:Class="Silverlight2BookSamples.UserControl1"
    d:DesignWidth="640" d:DesignHeight="480">
    <UserControl.Resources>
      <SolidColorBrush x:Key="SharedBrush" Color="#FFFF0000"/>
      <System:Double x:Key="CornerRadiusX">9</System:Double>
      <System:Double x:Key="CornerRadiusY">9</System:Double>
```

```
          </UserControl.Resources>

          <Grid x:Name="LayoutRoot" Background="White" >
            <Rectangle
              Height="84"
              HorizontalAlignment="Left"
              Margin="8,35,0,0"
              VerticalAlignment="Top"
              Width="84"
              Fill="{StaticResource SharedBrush}"
              Stroke="#FF000000"
              RadiusX="{StaticResource CornerRadiusX}"
              RadiusY="{StaticResource CornerRadiusY}"/>
            <TextBlock
              HorizontalAlignment="Left"
              VerticalAlignment="Top"
              Text="TextBlock"
              TextWrapping="Wrap"
              Margin="8,12.4,0,0"
              Foreground="{StaticResource SharedBrush}"/>
          </Grid>
        </UserControl>
```

If you are keeping your local project in sync with this running sample, your
UserControl should now look like Figure 21-2.

Carrying this idea further, you can define resources for the FontFamily,
FontSize, FontWeight, and FontStyle properties of your TextBlock.
Though this approach still satisfies your goal of centralizing shared
values, the following code demonstrates how messy this approach
can become:

FIGURE 21-2

```
        <UserControl.Resources>
          <SolidColorBrush x:Key="SharedBrush" Color="#FFFF0000"/>
          <System:Double x:Key="CornerRadiusX">9</System:Double>
          <System:Double x:Key="CornerRadiusY">9</System:Double>
          <FontFamily x:Key="SharedFont">Portable User Interface</FontFamily>
          <System:Double x:Key="SharedFontSize">14.666666984558106</System:Double>
          <FontWeight x:Key="SharedFontWeight">Normal</FontWeight>
          <FontStyle x:Key="SharedFontStyle">Normal</FontStyle>
        </UserControl.Resources>


        <TextBlock
          HorizontalAlignment="Left"
          VerticalAlignment="Top"
          Text="TextBlock"
          TextWrapping="Wrap"
          Margin="8,12.4630002975464,0,0"
          Foreground="{StaticResource SharedBrush}"
          FontFamily="{StaticResource SharedFont}"
          FontSize="{StaticResource SharedFontSize}"
          FontWeight="{StaticResource SharedFontWeight}"
          FontStyle="{StaticResource SharedFontStyle}"/>
```

You are now referencing resources for a large number of properties on this `TextBlock` control. You will have to do the same thing for every other `TextBlock` in your layout that you want to share this same look. Not only will this make your XAML hard to read, but it will also become a nightmare to maintain. What if you decide to synchronize another property, such as `TextWrapping`? With this model, you will need to define another resource and update all of your `TextBlocks` to point to this new resource. This is quickly becoming a problem. Fear not — the `Style` object is here to save the day!

WORKING WITH THE STYLE OBJECT

In defining *Style* at the beginning of this chapter, you were asked to remember that *a Style is a collection of Setters*. Furthermore, a `Style` is a resource that contains a collection of `Setters` that target properties and specify values for a particular type of control (such as `TextBlock`). The previous code block shows what can happen when you try to centralize values for several different properties on a control. A large number of resources are defined, one for each property. Then, on each instance of the control (`TextBlock` in the example), you have to use a `StaticResource` reference for each centralized property value. It becomes a real mess! The following code shows you how this problem is solved, using a `Style` object defined in the same `ResourceDictionary`:

```
<UserControl.Resources>
  <Style x:Key="TextBlockStyle" TargetType="TextBlock">
    <Setter Property="FontFamily" Value="Verdana"/>
    <Setter Property="FontSize" Value="14"/>
    <Setter Property="FontWeight" Value="Bold"/>
    <Setter Property="FontStyle" Value="Normal"/>
    <Setter Property="Foreground" Value="#FFFF0000"/>
  </Style>
</UserControl.Resources>

<Grid x:Name="LayoutRoot" Background="White" >
  <TextBlock
    HorizontalAlignment="Left"
    VerticalAlignment="Top"
    Text="TextBlock" TextWrapping="Wrap"
    Style="{StaticResource TextBlockStyle}"/>
</Grid>
```

See how much cleaner your `TextBlock` has become? All of the individual property settings (and `StaticResource` references) have been replaced by a single `Style` property setting. Additionally, all of your resources have been rolled into a single resource of type `Style`. With all of these resources rolled into a single `Style`, keeping several `TextBlocks` in sync is no longer a problem. You simply set the `Style` property.

Now, look a little more closely at the details of this `Style` object. First, and not surprisingly, the `Style` resource has a key. In addition to the `Key` property, the `Style` object also has a property named `TargetType`. When defining a `Style`, you must specify the type of control the `Style` is going to target, and you do this by setting the `TargetType` property. If you are coming to Silverlight from Windows Presentation Foundation (WPF), you will note the omission of curly braces when setting the target type. This value is simply a string. If you were targeting a control in a custom assembly, you would need to preface the control name with the correct namespace mapping (that is, `TargetType="customNamespace:customControl"`).

The previous code sample demonstrated clearly the *collection of Setters* idea. Where once you had four individual resources, you now have five Setter objects. Each Setter has a property/value pair that must be set. The value of the Property property (not a typo) is set to the name of a property on the TargetType control. The first Setter defined previously sets the default value of TextBlock.FontFamily to "Verdana". Any property defined on the TargetType control can be set in the Style, using a Setter. Applying the Style is just as easy as pointing the Foreground property to a StaticResource: You set the Style property of the control using the {StaticResource Syntax}. The following snippet highlights how this is set one more time for you:

```
<TextBlock
    Text="TextBlock" TextWrapping="Wrap"
    Style="{StaticResource TextBlockStyle}"/>
```

If you want to synchronize the TextWrapping property of all TextBlocks using this Style, you simply add another Setter to the Style:

```
<Setter Property="TextWrapping" Value="Wrap" />
```

You have gone from a large number of cumbersome resource references to a single resource reference, all thanks to the Style object.

Understanding Value Resolution

When defining and applying a custom Style to a control, it is important to understand how the values defined in that style are resolved with local values set on the control itself and with values set in the default Style for the control. When a custom Style is applied, the property settings in the custom style are combined with the property settings of both the default style and the local control instance. Each property set in a custom Style overrides the default value defined in the control's default Style, and properties set at the control-instance level override values set in the custom Style. The following demonstrates the order of resolution, with the highest priority on the right:

```
Default Control Style > Custom Style > Local Values
```

If FontSize is set in the default style of TextBlock to 14 and the custom Style does not include a Setter for FontSize, 14 will still be applied to the TextBlock.FontSize property, unless the TextBlock explicitly sets its own FontSize property inline.

It is important to remember that custom Styles do not completely replace all of the default property settings, but instead override the default property settings. Test this out for yourself by creating a simple Style that targets a Button. Define a single Setter that targets the FontWeight property and set its value to Bold. When you apply this Style to a Button, the button looks exactly like the default button, only the text is bold. All of the other property settings defined by the control's default Style are still intact — you have simply overridden the FontWeight property.

Creating BasedOn Styles

The Style object has a BasedOn property that can be used to reference another Style. This can be a real time-saver when you want to create Styles that have subtle derivations from a master Style.

When the `BasedOn` property is set, the referenced `Style` is essentially injected into the resolution order shown in the previous section:

```
Default Control Style > BasedOn Style > Custom Style > Local Values
```

It should come as no surprise that the `BasedOn` property is set using the `{StaticResource keyName}` markup syntax. The following XAML shows two `Button` styles, the second based on the first:

```xml
<Style x:Key="ButtonBaseStyle" TargetType="Button">
  <Setter Property="Foreground" Value="#FF0000" />
</Style>

<Style x:Key="ButtonBasedOn"
       BasedOn="{StaticResource ButtonBaseStyle}"
       TargetType="Button">
  <Setter Property="FontWeight" Value="Bold" />
</Style>
```

It is important to note that the order in which resources are defined in XAML makes a difference when they're being referenced by other resources. For example, if you move the `ButtonBasedOn` style so that it is defined before `ButtonBaseStyle`, you will get a run time error because the `ButtonBaseStyle` will not have been created yet. It is also important to note that the `Style` you derive from should have the same `TargetType` as your new `Style` or have a `TargetType` matching one of the current `Styles`'s base classes.

Changing the Look of a Control with a Custom ControlTemplate

You have now seen how you can set multiple properties of a particular type of control using the `Style` object. These properties all affect the look of the control in some way, often by changing the `FontStyle`, the `Foreground`, or perhaps the default `Height` or `Width`. When your customization needs outgrow simple property settings, you need to customize the `ControlTemplate`.

Overriding the `ControlTemplate` is achieved in the `Style` by setting the `Template` property. Remember, *a Style is just a collection of Setters*, and the `Template` property is the most powerful property you can set.

What Is a ControlTemplate?

At the beginning of this chapter, you learned that a `ControlTemplate` is the `VisualTree` of elements that make up the look of a control. These elements can range from a series of nested `Borders` (like the default `Button`) to a combination of paths with complex gradient fills. A `ControlTemplate` is generally applied by a `Style`. In Silverlight, just like WPF, controls are said to be *lookless*. The definition of a control's properties is independent from the actual look of the control. The look of the control is defined in XAML and is applied at compile time.

Why Define a Custom Template?

Acknowledging that Silverlight controls are devoid of style is one thing, but understanding *why* they are without style is another. Because a control is without style, you can completely replace its visual appearance. Consider the `Button` for a moment. The `Button` control is probably the most commonly re-templated control in both Silverlight and WPF. Consider the immersive web experiences or applications you have encountered over the years. A core action of your experience is clicking. You click, click, click — text, images, custom artwork — anything is fair game. Generally, the item you are clicking responds to the MouseOver and MousePressed events, providing you with visual feedback to your interaction.

If you are asked to picture different button styles that you've encountered, your mind probably fills with different shapes, colors, and textures — imprints left by the many visually diverse experiences you've had in your travels. If your mind did not fill with images, at least consider the differing appearance between a Windows Vista button and an OS X button. The two buttons react to the same interaction (MouseOver, MousePressed, Disabled) and generally fire the same events for developers (for example, Click), but their appearance is markedly different.

Your application will likely need the functionality provided by Buttons, ListBoxes, RadioButtons, and CheckBoxes, but your *brand* may require a look other than the default look provided by Silverlight. By re-templating the controls, you get the same functionality provided out-of-the-box with the added benefit of having your custom look applied.

Defining and Applying a Custom Template

Before you re-template the Button, add a default-styled Button to the page for comparison. Figure 21-3 shows the default Silverlight Button on the stage in Expression Blend.

FIGURE 21-3

All of the visual elements that make up the look of the button reside in the Button's default template. Later, you will look at the XAML that makes up the default button; for now, you should be aware of a few key elements. Notice the single-pixel gray border with rounded corners — that is defined by a Border element. In the foreground of that Border element is another border with a gradient fill. In the foreground of that element is a rounded piece of artwork that simulates a highlight. Finally, there is an element that displays the Content you have specified on the button. It is center-aligned both vertically and horizontally.

A custom template is defined using the same layout panels and controls you have been introduced to throughout this book. Everything in your Silverlight arsenal is fair game for a control's template. The following code shows a simple Style that sets the Template property of a Button control, replacing the default template with a Grid containing a nested red Rectangle:

```
<Style x:Key="customStyle" TargetType="Button">
    <Setter Property="Template" >
        <Setter.Value>
            <ControlTemplate TargetType="Button">
                <Grid>
                    <Rectangle Fill="#FF0000" />
                </Grid>
            </ControlTemplate>
        </Setter.Value>
    </Setter>
</Style>
```

Here, for the first time in this chapter, you are seeing the more verbose way of setting the Value property of a Setter. Because the value you are supplying is much more complex than a single string value, you have to set the Value property by using <Setter.Value />. The value of the Template property is always a ControlTemplate object whose TargetType property matches the value of the Style object within which it is defined. The ControlTemplate object accepts a single child element whose value is always some type of Panel; in this case, it's a Grid.

 Unlike WPF, the value of the TargetType *property is just a string and does not require the* {x:Type ControlName} *syntax.*

Applying this Style to a Button is achieved by setting the Style property, just like you did for the TextBlock example before:

```
<Button
  Style="{StaticResource customStyle}"
  Content="Click Me!"
  HorizontalAlignment="Center"
  VerticalAlignment="Center"/>
```

Applying this Style to a Button results in a button that looks like a flat, red rectangle like the button depicted in Figure 21-4. You have completely replaced the default template of the button with a single rectangle.

FIGURE 21-4

Not too exciting, eh? Moreover, where is the text "Click Me!" as specified on the Content property? Because you have completely replaced the template of the Button with a Grid and nested Rectangle, you have eliminated the Button's ability to display its own content! See, the Template property really *is* the most powerful property of all. As you define the template of a control, you have to think about how you want the control's property values to affect the way the control actually looks. You will deal with the content issue first.

Using the ContentPresenter

The ContentPresenter control, just as its name indicates, is used to display *content*. All controls derived from ContentControl have a Content property. Button happens to be derived from ContentControl, which is why you set its Content property instead of its Text property. The Content property is of type UIElement, which means pretty much any visual element can be thrown at it, even another Button.

To display the text "Click Me!" as set on your Button's Content property, you need to add a ContentPresenter to your custom template defined in customStyle. The following XAML shows this ContentPresenter in place:

```
<Style x:Key="customStyle" TargetType="Button">
    <Setter Property="Template" >
        <Setter.Value>
            <ControlTemplate TargetType="Button">
```

```
            <Grid>
               <Rectangle Fill="#FF0000" />
                  <ContentPresenter Margin="5,5,5,5" />
            </Grid>
         </ControlTemplate>
      </Setter.Value>
   </Setter>
</Style>
```

That is all there is to it. It is actually deceptively simple. The ContentPresenter, when dropped into a ContentControl, automatically detects the type of content that has been set and displays it accordingly. When the content is text, as in this example, a TextBlock is automatically created whose Text property is set to the value specified.

Try setting the Content of the button to different types of objects (Circles, Rectangles, ComboBoxes, and so on) and notice how each of these objects is displayed inside the custom template. Figure 21-5 shows some of the variations available. Remember you can affect the layout of the ContentPresenter by using the HorizontalAlignment, VerticalAlignment, and Margin properties (or any other layout properties) as with any other control.

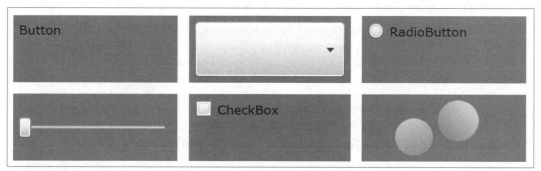

FIGURE 21-5

Using the TemplateBinding Markup Extension

In the previous section, you learned how to present the Content of a ContentControl by using a ContentPresenter. In this section, you learn how you can use other properties defined on the control you are templating, using the TemplateBinding markup extension.

TemplateBinding is a special type of binding that lets you access the value of properties defined on a control from within the template you are authoring. The first template you created consisted of a Grid with a nested Rectangle. At run time, all Buttons whose Style was set to customStyle looked exactly the same, regardless of their property settings. If the Background property was set to green, the Rectangle in the template was still red. In fact, those buttons could not even present their own content. You took care of the content situation by adding a ContentPresenter to the template. You now want to take advantage of the Background property, empowering the template to set the Rectangle's color to the value of the Button's Background property.

The following XAML demonstrates how to use the `TemplateBinding` Markup Extension (`TemplateBinding` from this point on) syntax to assign values set on the control to elements within its template:

```xaml
<Style x:Key="customStyle" TargetType="Button">
    <Setter Property="Template" >
        <Setter.Value>
            <ControlTemplate TargetType="Button">
                <Grid>
                    <Rectangle Fill="{TemplateBinding Background}" />
                        <ContentPresenter />
                </Grid>
            </ControlTemplate>
        </Setter.Value>
    </Setter>
</Style>
```

The `Rectangle`'s `Fill` property is now bound to the `Button`'s `Background` property. This example uses the `Background` property, but it could just as easily have used the `BorderBrush` property, because they are both of type `Brush`. If you were authoring a template for another control that defined more `Brush` properties, you could have chosen those properties as well.

Try creating several instances of `Button`, setting each instance's `Style` property to `customStyle`, and then set each `Button`'s `Background` property to a different color value. When you run the sample, you should see your `Background` properties honored on each `Button` instance. It is important to note that the value supplied by the `TemplateBinding` is the run time value of each control's instance. `TemplateBinding` does not synchronize values across controls; it just gives you a way to pump property values into your control's template.

Embracing TemplateBinding throughout the ControlTemplate

In the previous example, you used `TemplateBinding` to bind the `Button`'s `Background` property to the `Fill` property of a `Rectangle` nested within the `Button`'s `ControlTemplate`. Every single property defined on `Button` can be bound to an element within the template using `TemplateBinding`. It is through `TemplateBinding` that the properties of this lookless control come to life and start to have meaning.

Attach a few more properties. Start with `Padding`. *Padding* is typically used to define the amount of space surrounding an object's content. In comparison, an object's *margin* is the amount of space preserved around the control itself. Both the `Margin` and `Padding` properties are of type `Thickness` and are defined using four `Double` values that represent Left, Top, Right, and Bottom. The most meaningful way to use the `Padding` property is by applying it as the `Margin` of the `ContentPresenter`. The following code demonstrates how this is achieved:

```xaml
<Style x:Key="customStyle" TargetType="Button">
    <Setter Property="Template" >
        <Setter.Value>
            <ControlTemplate TargetType="Button">
                <Grid>
                    <Rectangle Fill="{TemplateBinding Background}" />
                        <ContentPresenter Margin="{TemplateBinding Padding}" />
                </Grid>
```

```
            </ControlTemplate>
          </Setter.Value>
       </Setter>
   </Style>
```

KeyedStyles.xaml — line 97

```
   ...
   <!--Red Button with 5 Pixel Margin on All Sides-->
   <Button
       Style="{StaticResource customStyle}"
       Content="Click Me!"
       Background="#FF0000"
       HorizontalAlignment="Left"
       VerticalAlignment="Top"
       Margin="10,10,0,0"
       Padding="5,5,5,5" />

   <!--Green button with 5 pixel Margin on Top and Bottom-->
   <Button
       Style="{StaticResource customStyle}"
       Content="Click Me!"
       Background="#00FF00"
       HorizontalAlignment="Left"
       VerticalAlignment="Top"
       Margin="10,60,0,0"
       Padding="0,5,0,5" />

   <!--Blue Button with 5 pixel Margin on Left and Right-->
   <Button
       Style="{StaticResource customStyle}"
       Content="Click Me!"
       Background="#0000FF"
       HorizontalAlignment="Left"
       VerticalAlignment="Top"
       Margin="10,120,0,0"
       Padding="5,0,5,0" />
```

KeyedStyles.xaml — line 121

The preceding code defines a custom `Style` that is then used by three subsequent `Buttons`. Figure 21-6 demonstrates how the local values set on the individual `Buttons` are represented by the underlying `ContentTemplate` through `TemplateBinding`. Note how the space around the content changes as the `Padding` value changes.

Now add `HorizontalAlignment` and `VerticalAlignment` property settings to the `ContentPresenter` and set their values to `HorizontalContentAlignment` and `VerticalContentAlignment` using `TemplateBinding`. The following XAML demonstrates the updated `Style`:

```
   <Style x:Key="customStyle" TargetType="Button">
       <Setter Property="Template">
          <Setter.Value>
```

```
<ControlTemplate TargetType="Button">
    <Grid>
        <Rectangle Fill="{TemplateBinding Background}" />
            <ContentPresenter
                Margin="{TemplateBinding Padding}"
                HorizontalAlignment="{TemplateBinding
                HorizontalContentAlignment}"
                VerticalAlignment="{TemplateBinding
                VerticalContentAlignment}" />
    </Grid>
</ControlTemplate>
        </Setter.Value>
    </Setter>
</Style>
```

KeyedStyles.xaml — line 97

Now that you've hooked these properties up in the template, they actually have an effect when set on each `Button` instance. You can now specify both the padding and internal alignment of the content of each `Button` that uses the `customStyle` style.

You can continue this process for other properties on `Button`, repeating the same `TemplateBinding` process, experimenting to your heart's content. One thing you should know, however, is that you can `TemplateBind` to the same property multiple times in a template. For example, you could have two nested `Borders`, each of whose `Padding` property is bound to the `Button`'s `Padding` property. Similarly, you could have multiple `TextBlocks`, each of whose `Text` property is bound to the `Button`'s `Content` property, achieving the drop-shadow effect shown in Figure 21-7.

FIGURE 21-6

FIGURE 21-7

Without `TemplateBinding`, properties set on individual control instances would have no visual effect at all. `TemplateBinding` provides a path into the template of a control by means of simple property settings at the control-instance level. The `Styles` and `Templates` defined for the default Silverlight controls have made extensive use of `TemplateBinding`. Try changing the `Background`, `BorderBrush`, `HorizontalContentAlignment`, and `Padding` properties of the default `Button`. As you change these properties, the button's appearance changes accordingly. The author(s) of the default `Styles` had to employ `TemplateBinding` throughout the default `Styles` to enable the behavior that you expect when interacting with the control.

Preserving the Essence of Your Style

If you have experimented with the default Silverlight `Button` control, you should have noticed that as you set its `Background` property, the overall look and feel, or *essence*, of the control remains the same. For example, if you set the `Background` property to a green `SolidColorBrush`, the button does not actually appear flat green. Instead, it looks almost the same, only now it has a green hue. The oval highlight in the foreground remains, and the background color appears to fade vertically to white. Figure 21-8 shows the default Silverlight button, without a custom background color, and two additional buttons, each of whose `Background` property has been set.

FIGURE 21-8

To achieve this effect, the `Template` must include more than a single rectangle, as you have been using up to this point. The default template employs several elements, layered in the foreground of a base element that is template-bound to the `Background` property. The foreground elements are partially transparent to allow the base element to shine through. As the `Style` author, it is up to you to define how various property settings affect the final look of your control. You can choose to completely ignore local settings, by not using `TemplateBinding` at all, or you can choose to strategically apply `TemplateBinding` to elements within your `Template` to maintain the essence of your design, while providing a degree of flexibility.

Listing 21-1 displays the XAML for the default Silverlight button. Comments have been added throughout the template to hopefully shed some light on the techniques employed.

LISTING 21-1: Default Silverlight button style

```xml
<Style x:Key="DefaultButtonStyle" TargetType="Button">
  <!-- ====================================== -->
  <!-- Default Brushes Defined At Style Level  -->
  <!-- ====================================== -->
  <Setter Property="Background" Value="#FF1F3B53"/>
  <Setter Property="Foreground" Value="#FF000000"/>
  <Setter Property="Padding" Value="3"/>
  <Setter Property="BorderThickness" Value="1"/>
  <Setter Property="BorderBrush">
    <Setter.Value>
```

continues

LISTING 21-1 *(continued)*

```xml
        <LinearGradientBrush EndPoint="0.5,1" StartPoint="0.5,0">
          <GradientStop Color="#FFA3AEB9" Offset="0"/>
          <GradientStop Color="#FF8399A9" Offset="0.375"/>
          <GradientStop Color="#FF718597" Offset="0.375"/>
          <GradientStop Color="#FF617584" Offset="1"/>
        </LinearGradientBrush>
      </Setter.Value>
    </Setter>
    <Setter Property="Template">
      <Setter.Value>
        <ControlTemplate TargetType="Button">
          <Grid>
          <!-- ============================================================
               VisualStateManager Defined as Child of First Template Element
               ============================================================ -->
            <vsm:VisualStateManager.VisualStateGroups>
              <vsm:VisualStateGroup x:Name="CommonStates">
                <vsm:VisualState x:Name="Normal"/>
                <!-- =============== -->
                <!-- MouseOver State -->
                <!-- =============== -->
                <vsm:VisualState x:Name="MouseOver">
                  <Storyboard>
                    <DoubleAnimationUsingKeyFrames
                      Storyboard.TargetName="BackgroundAnimation"
                      Storyboard.TargetProperty="Opacity">
                      <SplineDoubleKeyFrame KeyTime="0" Value="1"/>
                    </DoubleAnimationUsingKeyFrames>
                    <ColorAnimationUsingKeyFrames
                      Storyboard.TargetName="BackgroundGradient"
                      Storyboard.TargetProperty="(Rectangle.Fill)
                      .(GradientBrush.GradientStops)[1]
                      .(GradientStop.Color)">
                      <SplineColorKeyFrame KeyTime="0"
                        Value="#F2FFFFFF"/>
                    </ColorAnimationUsingKeyFrames>
                    <ColorAnimationUsingKeyFrames
                      Storyboard.TargetName="BackgroundGradient"
                      Storyboard.TargetProperty="(Rectangle.Fill).(GradientBrush
                      .GradientStops)[2]
                      .(GradientStop.Color)">
                      <SplineColorKeyFrame KeyTime="0"
                        Value="#CCFFFFFF"/>
                    </ColorAnimationUsingKeyFrames>
                    <ColorAnimationUsingKeyFrames
                      Storyboard.TargetName="BackgroundGradient"
                      Storyboard.TargetProperty="(Rectangle.Fill).(GradientBrush
                      .GradientStops)[3]
                      .(GradientStop.Color)">
                      <SplineColorKeyFrame KeyTime="0"
                        Value="#7FFFFFFF"/>
                    </ColorAnimationUsingKeyFrames>
                  </Storyboard>
```

```
    </vsm:VisualState>
    <!-- ============== -->
    <!-- Pressed State  -->
    <!-- ============== -->
    <vsm:VisualState x:Name="Pressed">
      <Storyboard>
        <ColorAnimationUsingKeyFrames
          Storyboard.TargetName="Background" Storyboard.TargetProperty=
          "(Border.Background).(SolidColorBrush.Color)">
          <SplineColorKeyFrame KeyTime="0"
            Value="#FF6DBDD1"/>
        </ColorAnimationUsingKeyFrames>
        <DoubleAnimationUsingKeyFrames
          Storyboard.TargetName="BackgroundAnimation"
          Storyboard.TargetProperty="Opacity">
          <SplineDoubleKeyFrame KeyTime="0" Value="1"/>
        </DoubleAnimationUsingKeyFrames>
        <ColorAnimationUsingKeyFrames
          Storyboard.TargetName="BackgroundGradient"
          Storyboard.TargetProperty="(Rectangle.Fill).(GradientBrush
          .GradientStops)[0]
          .(GradientStop.Color)">
          <SplineColorKeyFrame KeyTime="0"
            Value="#D8FFFFFF"/>
        </ColorAnimationUsingKeyFrames>
        <ColorAnimationUsingKeyFrames
          Storyboard.TargetName="BackgroundGradient"
          Storyboard.TargetProperty="(Rectangle.Fill).(GradientBrush
          .GradientStops)[1]
          .(GradientStop.Color)">
          <SplineColorKeyFrame KeyTime="0"
            Value="#C6FFFFFF"/>
        </ColorAnimationUsingKeyFrames>
        <ColorAnimationUsingKeyFrames
          Storyboard.TargetName="BackgroundGradient"
          Storyboard.TargetProperty="(Rectangle.Fill).(GradientBrush
          .GradientStops)[2]
          .(GradientStop.Color)">
          <SplineColorKeyFrame KeyTime="0"
            Value="#8CFFFFFF"/>
        </ColorAnimationUsingKeyFrames>
        <ColorAnimationUsingKeyFrames
          Storyboard.TargetName="BackgroundGradient"
          Storyboard.TargetProperty="(Rectangle.Fill).(GradientBrush
          .GradientStops)[3]
          .(GradientStop.Color)">
          <SplineColorKeyFrame KeyTime="0"
            Value="#3FFFFFFF"/>
        </ColorAnimationUsingKeyFrames>
      </Storyboard>
    </vsm:VisualState>
    <!-- =============== -->
    <!-- Disabled State  -->
    <!-- =============== -->
    <vsm:VisualState x:Name="Disabled">
```

continues

LISTING 21-1 *(continued)*

```xml
        <Storyboard>
          <DoubleAnimationUsingKeyFrames
            Storyboard.TargetName="DisabledVisualElement"
          Storyboard.TargetProperty="Opacity">
            <SplineDoubleKeyFrame KeyTime="0" Value=".55"/>
          </DoubleAnimationUsingKeyFrames>
        </Storyboard>
      </vsm:VisualState>
    </vsm:VisualStateGroup>
    <vsm:VisualStateGroup x:Name="FocusStates">
      <!-- =============== -->
      <!-- Focused State  -->
      <!-- =============== -->
      <vsm:VisualState x:Name="Focused">
        <Storyboard>
          <DoubleAnimationUsingKeyFrames
            Storyboard.TargetName="FocusVisualElement"
            Storyboard.TargetProperty="Opacity">
            <SplineDoubleKeyFrame KeyTime="0" Value="1"/>
          </DoubleAnimationUsingKeyFrames>
        </Storyboard>
      </vsm:VisualState>
      <vsm:VisualState x:Name="Unfocused"/>
    </vsm:VisualStateGroup>
  </vsm:VisualStateManager.VisualStateGroups>
<!-- ==============================================================
    Base Border (BorderBrush and BorderThickness TemplateBound)
    ==============================================================  -->

  <Border x:Name="Background" Background="White"
  BorderBrush="{TemplateBinding BorderBrush}"
  BorderThickness="{TemplateBinding BorderThickness}" CornerRadius="3">
    <!-- ===================================================== -->
    <!-- Grid (Background TemplateBound to Button.Background) -->
    <!-- ===================================================== -->
    <Grid Margin="1" Background="{TemplateBinding Background}">
      <Border x:Name="BackgroundAnimation" Opacity="0"
        Background="#FF448DCA"/>
      <Rectangle x:Name="BackgroundGradient">
        <Rectangle.Fill>
          <LinearGradientBrush EndPoint=".7,1"
            StartPoint=".7,0">
            <GradientStop Color="#FFFFFFFF" Offset="0"/>
            <GradientStop Color="#F9FFFFFF"
              Offset="0.375"/>
            <GradientStop Color="#E5FFFFFF"
              Offset="0.625"/>
            <GradientStop Color="#C6FFFFFF" Offset="1"/>
          </LinearGradientBrush>
        </Rectangle.Fill>
      </Rectangle>
    </Grid>
```

```
        </Border>
        <!-- ============================================= -->
        <!-- ContentPresenter (Content and ContentTemplate
        <!-- Property Settings Not Necessary)          -->
        <!-- ============================================= -->
        <ContentPresenter x:Name="contentPresenter"
          HorizontalAlignment="{TemplateBinding HorizontalContentAlignment}"
          Margin="{TemplateBinding Padding}"
          VerticalAlignment="{TemplateBinding VerticalContentAlignment}"
          Content="{TemplateBinding Content}"
          ContentTemplate="{TemplateBinding ContentTemplate}"/>
        <Rectangle x:Name="DisabledVisualElement" Fill="#FFFFFFFF"
          RadiusX="3" RadiusY="3" IsHitTestVisible="false"
          Opacity="0"/>
        <Rectangle x:Name="FocusVisualElement" Stroke="#FF6DBDD1"
          StrokeThickness="1" RadiusX="2" RadiusY="2" Margin="1"
          IsHitTestVisible="false" Opacity="0"/>
      </Grid>
    </ControlTemplate>
  </Setter.Value>
 </Setter>
</Style>
```

If you look at the first grid defined in the template, you'll see that its Background property is set to {TemplateBinding Background}:

```
<!-- ===================================================== -->
<!-- Grid (Background TemplateBound to Button.Background) -->
<!-- ===================================================== -->
<Grid Margin="1" Background="{TemplateBinding Background}">
```

The second child of that grid is a rectangle that uses a LinearGradientBrush as its Fill. The Color values of each GradientStop are white, each with varying shades of opacity. This lets the containing grid's background brush bleed through. The foreground rectangle is used to create a shading effect. When the Background property of the control is set, the essence of the button remains the same because it's really the foreground rectangle that's responsible for creating the gradient effect.

Try replacing the white foreground gradient with a black-based gradient. You should see that the template still responds to the Background setting, only now the button is much darker than the default Silverlight version.

Understanding the Limitations of TemplateBinding

You just learned that the default button lets you change its background color by allowing you to specify a custom value for its Background property. However, what if you want to change the button's hover color? There is not a BackgroundHover property. Likewise, if you want the HorizontalContentAlignment to change when the button is in a hover state, you will not find a property specific to the hover state. Or maybe you just want to turn off the default button's oval highlight artwork — it's in these cases of interaction and customization where the control author can either choose to add additional properties (such as a DisplayHighlight property) or require you to edit the default template. In most cases, you will need to edit the default template.

You can see that once your customization needs step beyond just the basics, you have to create a custom `Style` and override the default template. To anticipate even a minor level of template-level customization, a large number of properties would need to be added to the control. Consider once again, just for a moment, the ways you might want to customize the button when it is in a hover state. How about turning off the highlight and changing the border color, the background color, the foreground color of the text, and the text's `FontWeight`? This would all require custom properties to be defined on the control that you could then `TemplateBind` to. In addition, what if the template itself had no highlight artwork? What good would your highlight-based property(ies) be then?

Hopefully you see that properties defined simply to point directly into the template can be quite arbitrary in nature and often won't hold up across the many uses a control might find itself in. There are certainly cases in which it makes sense to add properties (such as an `AlternateRowBackground` brush property for a grid), but they should not be added on a whim. Fortunately, Silverlight provides a model that allows you to react to state changes from within the template itself.

Visual State Manager: Reacting to State Changes within a Template

So far, you have seen how to define the look of a control by creating a custom `ControlTemplate`. However, the examples so far result in a static visual, with no interaction whatsoever. The control looks the same whether it has focus or does not have focus, whether or not the mouse is over it, and even whether or not it is pressed. For a personal project, this may be fine, but for interactive Silverlight applications, your users are going to expect visual feedback. Enter the `VisualStateManager`.

In the previous code listing, you may have noticed the `VisualStateManager` definition (`<vsm:VisualStateManager />`) defined within the button's `ControlTemplate`. The `VisualStateManager` is used to define how controls react visually to changes in state, such as `MouseOver` or `Pressed`. You use the `VisualStateManager` (VSM) to define different `VisualStates` for the control whose template you are authoring.

It is up to the control author to define both the control's `VisualStateGroups` and the `VisualStates` of each group. The control author is also responsible for transitioning from state to state throughout the life of the control. The default Silverlight controls all employ this *State Model* and use the `TemplateVisualState` attribute:

```
[TemplateVisualState(Name = "MouseOver", GroupName = "CommonStates")]
```

Expression Blend looks for this attribute on controls and presents all `VisualStateGroups` and `VisualStates` defined when in Template-editing mode. Figure 21-9 shows how Expression Blend exposes these states.

Editing state transitions is most commonly done in Expression Blend, but the default button's `VisualStateManager` is broken down in XAML here so that you have a firm grasp of what is being generated behind the scenes. The following XAML defines two `VisualStateGroups` — `CommonStates` and `FocusStates`:

```
<vsm:VisualStateManager.VisualStateGroups>
    <vsm:VisualStateGroup x:Name="CommonStates"></vsm:VisualStateGroup>
    <vsm:VisualStateGroup x:Name="FocusStates"></vsm:VisualStateGroup>
</vsm:VisualStateManager.VisualStateGroups>
```

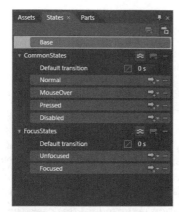

FIGURE 21-9

To the `VisualStateGroups`, add `VisualStates`:

```
<vsm:VisualStateManager.VisualStateGroups>
    <vsm:VisualStateGroup x:Name="CommonStates">
        <vsm:VisualState x:Name="Normal" />
        <vsm:VisualState x:Name="MouseOver" />
        <vsm:VisualState x:Name="Pressed" />
        <vsm:VisualState x:Name="Disabled" />
    </vsm:VisualStateGroup>
    <vsm:VisualStateGroup x:Name="FocusStates">
        <vsm:VisualState x:Name="Focused" />
        <vsm:VisualState x:Name="Unfocused" />
    </vsm:VisualStateGroup>
</vsm:VisualStateManager.VisualStateGroups>
```

These are all of the states that have been defined for the `Button` control by the Silverlight engineering team. You can add additional `VisualStates` to the XAML, but they will never be accessed because the control is not looking for them. This is another reason it is a good idea to start from the default control XAML when skinning controls.

Now that you have the default `VisualStateGroups` and `VisualStates` defined, add a simple `Storyboard` to the `MouseOver` state:

```
<vsm:VisualStateManager.VisualStateGroups>
    <vsm:VisualStateGroup x:Name="CommonStates">
        <vsm:VisualState x:Name="Normal" />
        <vsm:VisualState x:Name="MouseOver">
          <Storyboard>
            <ColorAnimation
              Storyboard.TargetName="LinearBevelDarkEnd"
              Storyboard.TargetProperty="Color"
              To="#000000" Duration="0"/>
          </Storyboard>
        </vsm:VisualStatep>
        <vsm:VisualState x:Name="Pressed" />
        <vsm:VisualState x:Name="Disabled" />
```

```
        </vsm:VisualStateGroup>
        <vsm:VisualStateGroup x:Name="FocusStates">
            <vsm:VisualState x:Name="Focused" />
            <vsm:VisualState x:Name="Unfocused" />
        </vsm:VisualStateGroup>
    </vsm:VisualStateManager.VisualStateGroups>
```

The `ColorAnimation` added targets a `GradientStop` with the name `"LinearBevelDarkEnd"` defined
in the default button's XAML and animates the value of the `GradientStop`'s `Color` property to black
(#FF000000). This `Storyboard` starts when the control enters the `MouseOver` state. The `Duration` of
the `ColorAnimation` is set to 0, which essentially means "Take 0 seconds to get to your destination." If
you wanted the `GradientStop` value to slowly change to black, you could have entered `"00:00:05.00"`
for a 5-second animation. The animation continues to have an effect even after the `Duration` has
been reached and remains at the destination value until another animation is started. In this case, the
`GradientStop` value remains black until the control changes state.

A control can be in only one state *per* `VisualStateGroup` at a time. Therefore, based on the preceding
XAML, this means that the `Button` cannot be in both a `Normal` state and a `MouseOver` state at once.
If you look at the states that have been defined, you will see this makes sense. However, a control *can*
be in multiple states across `VisualStateGroups`. For example, the `Button` can be in both a `MouseOver`
and `Focused` state at the same time.

Empty `VisualStates` *have an effect on the control: As a control changes state,
if a matching* `VisualState` *is found, any previous animations that were started
as a result of previous* `VisualStates` *are stopped. Empty* `VisualStates` *essentially reset a control to its base state when triggered.*

Defining Transitions

The `VisualStateManager` lets you define `Transition` `Storyboard`s that are played as the control
transitions between states. The animations do not replace the `VisualState` `Storyboard`s; they just
serve as interludes between them. The XAML shown in Listing 21-2 adds to the `VisualStateManager`
a `VisualTransition` that will be played as the control leaves the `MouseOver` state and enters the
`Normal` state:

LISTING 21-2: Defining state transitions

```
<vsm:VisualStateManager.VisualStateGroups>
    <vsm:VisualStateGroup x:Name="CommonStates">
        <vsm:VisualStateGroup.Transitions>
            <vsm:VisualTransition From="MouseOver" To="Normal"
                Duration="0:0:0.2">
                <Storyboard>
                    <ColorAnimation
                        Storyboard.TargetName="LinearBevelDarkEnd"
                        Storyboard.TargetProperty="Color" To="#FFFFFFFF" />
```

```
            </Storyboard>
          </vsm:VisualTransition>
       </vsm:VisualStateGroup.Transitions>

       <vsm:VisualState x:Name="Normal" />
       <vsm:VisualState x:Name="MouseOver">
         <Storyboard>
           <ColorAnimation Storyboard.TargetName="LinearBevelDarkEnd"
             Storyboard.TargetProperty="Color" To="#FF000000" Duration="0" />
         </Storyboard>
       </vsm:VisualStatep>
       <vsm:VisualState x:Name="Pressed" />
       <vsm:VisualState x:Name="Disabled" />
    </vsm:VisualStateGroup>
    <vsm:VisualStateGroup x:Name="FocusStates">
       <vsm:VisualState x:Name="Focused" />
       <vsm:VisualState x:Name="Unfocused" />
    </vsm:VisualStateGroup>
 </vsm:VisualStateManager.VisualStateGroups>
```

Over a period of 0.2 seconds, the same GradientStop you have been targeting animates to a white color before returning to its base state. Because the "Normal" VisualState is empty, all previously applied Storyboards are stopped. The final result of this VisualStateManager definition: Mousing over the Button will result in the GradientStop named LinearBevelDarkEnd animating to black immediately (Duration: 0). As the mouse leaves the control, the same GradientStop animates to white over a 0.2-second duration, then immediately returns to its original, base state.

The default Button XAML defines additional Storyboards and transitions that were not covered here. It is really just more of the same, but now you can read the XAML and actually decipher what you see!

Using Text-Related Properties

Text properties in Silverlight behave differently than their fellow non-text properties. Unlike properties such as Fill and HorizontalAlignment, the following properties cascade from the top down in the VisualTree:

➤ FontFamily

➤ FontWeight

➤ FontStyle

➤ FontSize

➤ FontStretch

When set at any level, these property settings are inherited by all children in the VisualTree of the element where the properties are set. Only set these properties locally when you want to intercept this inheritance and override those values. Keep this in mind when you are defining styles for controls — font settings on the Style will take precedence over those defined at an application or page level, intercepting application-level font settings.

DEFINING AND USING IMPLICIT STYLES

Up to this point, you have looked at defining keyed styles and learned how to reference those styles using the StaticResource keyword. This model works well when you want to target individual controls with custom styles, but what if you want to target every instance of a particular control type? New to Silverlight 4 are implicit styles, or un-keyed styles. By omitting the x:Key attribute of a Style, you can *implicitly* apply a Style to all controls whose TargetType matches that of your Style.

The XAML in Listing 21-3 defines a simple Style that targets the Button control along with a layout that includes a couple of buttons:

LISTING 21-3: Defining an implicit button style

```
<UserControl x:Class="Ch21StylesAndThemes.MainPage"
    xmlns="http://schemas.microsoft.com/winfx/2006/xaml/presentation"
    xmlns:x="http://schemas.microsoft.com/winfx/2006/xaml"
    xmlns:d="http://schemas.microsoft.com/expression/blend/2008"
    xmlns:mc="http://schemas.openxmlformats.org/markup-compatibility/2006"
    mc:Ignorable="d"
    d:DesignHeight="300" d:DesignWidth="400">
  <UserControl.Resources>
  <!-- Style All Buttons -->
  <Style TargetType="Button">
   <Setter Property="Template">
     <Setter.Value>
      <ControlTemplate TargetType="Button">
       <Grid
          Background="{x:Null}"
          HorizontalAlignment="Left"
          VerticalAlignment="Top">
        <Rectangle Opacity="1" HorizontalAlignment="Stretch"
          VerticalAlignment="Stretch" RadiusX="12" RadiusY="12">
         <Rectangle.Fill>
          <LinearGradientBrush StartPoint="0.05,-2.45"
             EndPoint="0.05,-1.45">
            <LinearGradientBrush.GradientStops>
             <GradientStopCollection>
              <GradientStop Color="#FF7a7a7a" Offset="0"/>
              <GradientStop Color="#FF000000" Offset="0.99"/>
             </GradientStopCollection>
            </LinearGradientBrush.GradientStops>
          </LinearGradientBrush>
         </Rectangle.Fill>
        </Rectangle>
        <Rectangle Opacity="1" HorizontalAlignment="Stretch"
         VerticalAlignment="Stretch" Margin="4" RadiusX="8"
         RadiusY="8" Stroke="#ffffff" StrokeThickness="1"
         Fill="#000000"/>
        <TextBlock
         HorizontalAlignment="Center"
         VerticalAlignment="Center"
         Opacity="1"
```

```
            TextWrapping="Wrap"
            FontSize="31"
            FontFamily="ChunkFive"
            TextAlignment="left"
            Text="{TemplateBinding Content}" Margin="15,17,15,15" >
            <TextBlock.Foreground>
             <LinearGradientBrush EndPoint="0.5,1" StartPoint="0.5,0">
               <GradientStop Color="White"/>
               <GradientStop Color="#FF727272" Offset="1"/>
             </LinearGradientBrush>
            </TextBlock.Foreground>
           </TextBlock>
         </Grid>
       </ControlTemplate>
      </Setter.Value>
    </Setter>
   </Style>
  </UserControl.Resources>

  <Grid x:Name="LayoutRoot" Background="White">
   <Button Content="ACCEPT" HorizontalAlignment="Left" Margin="28,52,0,0"
    x:Name="btnAccept" VerticalAlignment="Top" />
   <Button Content="CANCEL" HorizontalAlignment="Right" Margin="0,52,37,0"
    x:Name="btnCancel" VerticalAlignment="Top" />
  </Grid>
</UserControl>
```

Because the `Style` is defined at the `UserControl`
level, and because the `x:Key` attribute is not
set, all `Button`s defined in the `UserControl`
pick up this `Style` automatically, as shown in
Figure 21-10.

Using implicit styles does not prevent you from
using explicit styles. You can redefine the default
look and feel of the buttons (or any other control) in your application and still set the `Style`
property on any individual, unique button. Later
in this chapter, the "Using Themes" section discusses how implicit styles can be used to define
application-wide themes.

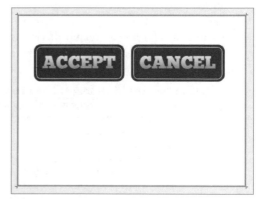

FIGURE 21-10

DEFINING AND ORGANIZING RESOURCES

Resources can be defined almost anywhere. Because all `FrameworkElement`-derived objects
have a `.Resources` collection, you can dangle resources off your base `UserControl` (`UserControl`
`.Resources`), in nested `Grid`s (`Grid.Resources`), in nested `Button`s (`Button.Resources`), and any
number of other elements. In addition to defining resources within a single `UserControl`, resources
can also be defined in `App.xaml` and in external `ResourceDictionaries`. With all of these locations

capable of housing resources, it is important to define some best practices and understand how these resources are scoped.

Defining Stand-alone ResourceDictionaries

Silverlight provides you with a mechanism for housing resources outside of `UserControls`. These stand-alone `ResourceDictionaries` are simply XAML files whose outermost element is a `ResourceDictionary`. Both Expression Blend and Visual Studio have `ResourceDictionary` templates that can be accessed by right-clicking the project, selecting Add New Item, and selecting `ResourceDictionary` from the dialog that appears. In both applications, you are prompted to provide a name for the new `ResourceDictionary`. The following XAML shows a simple stand-alone `ResourceDictionary` with a single `SolidColorBrush` resource defined:

```
<ResourceDictionary
    xmlns="http://schemas.microsoft.com/winfx/2006/xaml/presentation"
    xmlns:x="http://schemas.microsoft.com/winfx/2006/xaml">
    <SolidColorBrush x:Key="SharedBrush" Color="#FFFF0000"/>
</ResourceDictionary>
```

Loading ResourceDictionaries (via the Merged Dictionaries Collection)

Much like CSS's `@import` statement for referencing additional CSS files, Silverlight's `ResourceDictionary.MergedDictionaries` collection lets you reference external `ResourceDictionaries`. Each `ResourceDictionary` has a `MergedDictionaries` collection, so you can reference external dictionaries from any location where resources can be defined. The following XAML demonstrates how a `ResourceDictionary` containing button resources (`Resources/Buttons.xaml`) can be referenced at the `UserControl` level:

```
<UserControl x:Class="SilverlightBookSamples.Resources"
    xmlns="http://schemas.microsoft.com/winfx/2006/xaml/presentation"
    xmlns:x="http://schemas.microsoft.com/winfx/2006/xaml"
    Height="300" Width="300">
    <UserControl.Resources>
        <ResourceDictionary>
          <ResourceDictionary.MergedDictionaries>
             <ResourceDictionary Source="Resources/Buttons.xaml" />
             <!-- Additional Resource Definitions Here -->
          </ResourceDictionary.MergedDictionaries>
        </ResourceDictionary>
    </UserControl.Resources>
    <Grid>

    </Grid>
</UserControl>
```

When using the `MergedDictionaries` collection, you have to explicitly declare a `ResourceDictionary` object within the container `.Resources` collection. If you refer to previous resource definitions in the chapter, the `<ResourceDictionary />` tag was not required.

Understanding Resource Scope

The location where a resource is defined and/or referenced determines the scope within which it can be used. The following are the locations where resources may be defined:

➤ `App.xaml`

➤ `Themes/generic.xaml` (for defining custom controls)

➤ Custom `UserControl.xaml`

➤ External `ResourceDictionaries` (`.xaml` files within the project)

Defining Application-Wide Resources

Resources defined or referenced at the `App.xaml` level can be used anywhere in your Silverlight application. When you are synchronizing the look of an application across multiple `UserControls`, you will want to define your resources here. Any external `ResourceDictionaries` referenced at this level will also be available throughout your application.

Defining Styles for Custom Controls

In projects in which you define custom controls, a `myButton` control, for example, the default style for that custom control is defined in `Themes/generic.xaml`. Both Expression Blend and Visual Studio automatically add this file to your project when you add a custom control to the project using their starter templates. When your project is compiled and your control is used either in the same project or another project, the style defined in `Themes/generic.xaml` is applied. You should not house application-level styles or resources in this file as this `ResourceDictionary` is reserved for custom control-specific resources.

Scoping Resources to a Single UserControl or Element

When you do not need your resources to have a full application-wide scope, you can define them within the current `UserControl` you're authoring. In these cases, you will likely add the resources to `<UserControl.Resources>`:

```
<!-- Add Resources Here -->
</UserControl.Resources>
```

All resources defined in `<UserControl.Resources />` will be available throughout your `UserControl`. If you want to further scope your resource definitions to a particular area within your `UserControl`, this is a possibility as well. Each `FrameworkElement`-derived object in Silverlight has a `Resources` collection, so just as you can access the `UserControl`'s resources collection via `UserControl.Resources`, you can access the `Grid`'s resources collection via `Grid.Resources`:

```
<Grid x:Name="LayoutRoot">
  <Grid.Resources>
    <!-- Add Local Resources Here. Only items within this Grid have
         access to these resources -->
  </Grid.Resources>
</Grid>
```

Littering your `UserControl` with localized `Resources` is generally not the best approach. You will end up with resources scattered throughout your page and have a hard time tracking down your styling bugs. However, for those times when you need to scope your resources, you now know that you have localized resources at your disposal.

Thus, the discussion of organization is really a discussion of scope. If you want your entire Silverlight application to have access to a resource, you need to add that resource to `App.xaml`. Every page loaded in your Silverlight application will have access to resources defined in `App.xaml`.

Understanding External ResourceDictionary Scope

External `ResourceDictionaries` do not have an inherent scope. Their scope is determined by the scope of the `MergedDictionaries` collection to which they are added. If they are referenced in `App.xaml`, they will have an application-wide scope. Likewise, if they are referenced by a `Grid` defined within `UserControl2.xaml`, they will be scoped to that `Grid`.

Organizing Resources

You have already looked at where resources can be defined; now look at one approach for organizing your resources within those locations. Often, the organization of resources is an afterthought, something that you come back to as part of your cleanup phase once you have everything working. When you choose to organize your resources is dependent on your workflow requirements. If you are a single developer working on a project, the resource organization is more for your own sanity than the sanity of others, so you can do this when you please. If you are a member of a team, collaborating with both designers and developers, it makes sense to organize your resources early, providing both consistency and clarity for team members.

In applications with a large number of resources, it generally makes sense to organize your resources into external `ResourceDictionaries`. Start by creating a Resources folder in your project and then group your resources by shared type or shared purpose:

➤ Define common brushes in one `ResourceDictionary`.

➤ Define non-`Style` or non-`Template` related resources (that is, `CornerRadius`, `Thickness`, and so on) in their own `ResourceDictionary`.

➤ Define `Styles`, grouped by control type (that is, all `Buttons` together).

➤ Define `Styles` for related controls (that is, `ComboBox` and its subcontrols).

The following sample folder structure gives you a better idea:

```
\[ProjectName]\
    \Resources
        \Brushes.xaml
        \Buttons.xaml
        \CommonControls.xaml
        \MainMenuBrushes.xaml
        \MainMenuControls.xaml
```

It is important to get into the habit of creating centralized styles and brushes for use throughout your application. It may feel like extra work at first, but in the end, it empowers you and your team to refine the application much more quickly than they could if everything were defined inline.

Naming Resources

Just as there are best practices for naming variables within an application, there are best practices for naming resources. In addition, just like strategies for naming variables, with a little Web searching, you can find some heated debates as to which approach is the best. As was the case in the previous section on organization, this section is just going to present you with a few guidelines to get you started. How you evolve this and make this work within your organization is entirely up to you.

Naming Brushes: Template/Style-Specific Brushes

When naming brushes that are specific to certain `Styles` and `Templates`, try to tie the name of the brush to the `Style`, to elements within the `Style`, and to the state of the control represented by the brush. For example:

```
ControlNameStateElementNameFill
```

Here are three hypothetical brushes used by the `PlayButton` style:

```
PlayButtonNormalOuterBorderFill
PlayButtonHoverOuterBorderFill
PlayButtonPressedOuterBorderFill
```

Here are three additional brushes that will be applied to the `BorderBrush` of the `OuterBorder` element contained within the `PlayButton` template:

```
PlayButtonNormalOuterBorderBorderBrush
PlayButtonHoverOuterBorderBorderBrush
PlayButtonPressedOuterBorderBorderBrush
```

Naming Brushes: Non-Template Brushes

Name brushes for elements within your applications in a way that makes sense to you and your team. For example, using the name `BackgroundBrush` is quite vague. Instead, use the name `ApplicationBackgroundBrush` or `MainMenuBackgroundBrush`. It is important that your brush naming maps to the element-naming conventions you have decided on for your application. Consistency here is key. If you have a `UserControl` named `MenuArea`, do not name the brush that is applied as the `MenuArea`'s background `BackgroundRegionMenu`; instead, name it `MenuAreaBackground`. Furthermore, name additional `MenuArea` brushes and resources with the `MenuArea` prefix: `MenuAreaForeground`, `MenuAreaCornerRadius`, and so forth.

Again, consistency is paramount here. Define a naming convention that is logical for your team, that is repeatable, and that is readable; and follow that convention religiously.

Naming Styles/Templates

When naming styles, include the control's `TargetType` in your key (`PlayButtonStyle`, `PlayButtonTemplate`, `VolumeSliderStyle`). This lets you quickly identify the control type without having to rely on additional information that the IDE might provide you with (via an icon or additional label).

USING THEMES

A theme in Silverlight is a collection of styles that redefine the way all of the controls in your application look. The Silverlight Toolkit (`http://silverlight.codeplex.com`) includes a number of predefined themes and originally included a control known as the `ImplicitStyleManager`. Prior to Silverlight 4's introduction of implicit style support, the `ImplicitStyleManager` was the only way to target all controls of a specific type without having to explicitly set the `Style` property.

Now, you can create a `ResourceDictionary` that targets all of the control types in your application, then reference that `ResourceDictionary` anywhere in your application. To scope the resources to your entire application, simply reference the `ResourceDictionary` within `App.xaml`:

```xml
<Application
  xmlns="http://schemas.microsoft.com/winfx/2006/xaml/presentation"
  xmlns:x="http://schemas.microsoft.com/winfx/2006/xaml"
  x:Class="Ch21StylesAndThemes.App">
  <Application.Resources>
   <ResourceDictionary>
    <ResourceDictionary.MergedDictionaries>
      <ResourceDictionary
        Source="/Ch21StylesAndThemes;component/AppThemes/CustomTheme.xaml" />
    </ResourceDictionary.MergedDictionaries>
   </ResourceDictionary>
  </Application.Resources>
</Application>
```

App.xaml

Any resources defined within `CustomTheme.xaml` will be applied automatically to all controls throughout your application.

Using Silverlight Toolkit Themes

The Silverlight Toolkit (`http://silverlight.codeplex.com`) includes both loose XAML `ResourceDictionaries` and custom `Theme` controls, the effects of which are shown in Figure 21-11.

Referencing via the MergedDictionaries Collection

After downloading the Toolkit, you will find the loose XAML in the Themes\Xaml folder, shown in Figure 21-12.

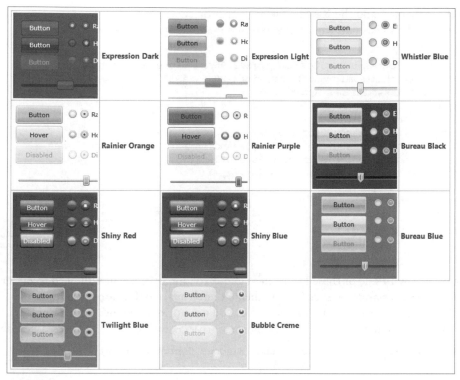

FIGURE 21-11

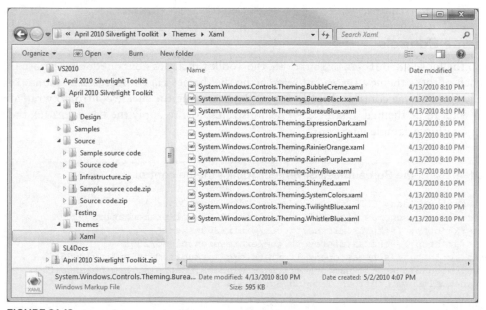

FIGURE 21-12

To apply any of these themes, add the XAML file to your project with a `Build Action` of `Page`. You can now reference the file as you would any external `ResourceDictionary`:

```
<Application
  xmlns="http://schemas.microsoft.com/winfx/2006/xaml/presentation"
  xmlns:x="http://schemas.microsoft.com/winfx/2006/xaml"
  x:Class="Ch21StylesAndThemes.App">
  <Application.Resources>
   <ResourceDictionary>
    <ResourceDictionary.MergedDictionaries>
      <ResourceDictionary Source="/Ch21StylesAndThemes;component/AppThemes/
        System.Windows.Controls.Theming.BureauBlack.xaml" />
    </ResourceDictionary.MergedDictionaries>
   </ResourceDictionary>
  </Application.Resources>
</Application>
```

App.xaml

To compile your project with one of these theme `ResourceDictionaries`, you will need to either add all of the assemblies that are referenced in the theme's namespace definitions or manually remove `Styles` that target controls found in assemblies you are not referencing. For example, the `dataPrimitives` namespace definition references the `System.Windows.Controls.Data` assembly:

```
xmlns:dataPrimitives="clr-namespace:System.Windows.Controls.Primitives;
                     assembly=System.Windows.Controls.Data"
```

You need to either a) add a project reference to the `System.Windows.Controls.Data` assembly or b) remove this namespace definition and remove all styles whose `TargetType` includes `dataPrimitives:controlName`.

Using the Theme Controls

In addition to the loose `ResourceDictionaries`, the Toolkit includes `ContentControl`-based versions of each of these themes. Instead of referencing the themes via the `MergedDictionaries` collection, add these theme controls directly to your layout, using the theme control to wrap any elements you want to be themed. Listing 21-4 demonstrates how to apply the `BureauBlack` theme to all elements within a sample `UserControl`.

LISTING 21-4: Using the BureauBlack Silverlight Toolkit theme control

```
<UserControl x:Class="Ch21StylesAndThemes.UsingThemeControl"
    xmlns="http://schemas.microsoft.com/winfx/2006/xaml/presentation"
    xmlns:x="http://schemas.microsoft.com/winfx/2006/xaml"
    xmlns:d="http://schemas.microsoft.com/expression/blend/2008"
    xmlns:mc="http://schemas.openxmlformats.org/markup-compatibility/2006"
    xmlns:bureauBlack="clr-namespace:System.Windows.Controls.Theming;assembly=
      System.Windows.Controls.Theming.BureauBlack"
```

```
   mc:Ignorable="d"
   d:DesignHeight="300" d:DesignWidth="400">
   <bureauBlack:BureauBlackTheme>
     <StackPanel Orientation="Horizontal" Margin="20,20,0,0">
        <Button Content="Accept" Margin="0,0,10,0" x:Name="btnAccept"/>
        <Button Content="Cancel" x:Name="btnCancel"/>
     </StackPanel>
   </bureauBlack:BureauBlackTheme>
</UserControl>
```

Again, the same results could be achieved by manually referencing the ResourceDictionary via the UserControl.Resources collection, as shown in Listing 21-5.

LISTING 21-5: Loading the BureauBlack theme ResourceDictionary

```
<UserControl x:Class="Ch21StylesAndThemes.ReferencingThemeRD"
   xmlns="http://schemas.microsoft.com/winfx/2006/xaml/presentation"
   xmlns:x="http://schemas.microsoft.com/winfx/2006/xaml"
   xmlns:d="http://schemas.microsoft.com/expression/blend/2008"
   xmlns:mc="http://schemas.openxmlformats.org/markup-compatibility/2006"
   xmlns:bureauBlack="clr-namespace:System.Windows.Controls.Theming;assembly=
      System.Windows.Controls.Theming.BureauBlack"
   mc:Ignorable="d"
   d:DesignHeight="300" d:DesignWidth="400">
   <UserControl.Resources>
    <ResourceDictionary>
     <ResourceDictionary.MergedDictionaries>
       <ResourceDictionary Source="/Ch21StylesAndThemes;component/AppThemes/
          System.Windows.Controls.Theming.BureauBlack.xaml" />
     </ResourceDictionary.MergedDictionaries>
    </ResourceDictionary>
   </UserControl.Resources>
   <StackPanel Orientation="Horizontal" Margin="20,20,0,0">
    <Button Content="Accept" Margin="0,0,10,0" x:Name="btnAccept"/>
    <Button Content="Cancel" x:Name="btnCancel"/>
   </StackPanel>
</UserControl>
```

When the ResourceDictionary is referenced directly (instead of using the Theme control) a default background isn't applied. The Theme controls have background fills applied to their root elements.

The Silverlight Toolkit Themes required modification out-of-the-box in order to get them working correctly with my Silverlight 4 project. I had to remove a couple of Styles from the XAML file and recompile the theme assembly before it would work at run time. Be prepared for a little work when using these Themes because they are not officially supported.

Creating Custom Themes

At this point, it should be clear that a *Theme* is just a collection of `Styles` and other resources stored in an external `ResourceDictionary`. When creating your own theme for a specific application, you really need only to target the controls that are used by your application. If you are not using `RadioButtons`, there is no need to re-style the `RadioButton` control. Similarly, if your application includes custom controls (like a `SuperIconButton`), you'll want to include custom styles for those controls.

If you're creating a set of Themes to be deployed across your development team, you'll definitely want to target all of the system controls as well as custom controls defined within your organization. When creating a custom theme, you should start with one of the Silverlight Toolkit themes. A lot of the organization work has already been taken care of for you.

Distributing Your Theme

Once you have created your theme, you'll need a way to distribute it to your development team or throughout your organization. Either you can pass around the loose XAML `ResourceDictionaries`, or you can compile these `ResourceDictionaries` into an assembly that can be shared. By creating a custom assembly, you can maintain tighter control over the underlying `Styles` and version the deployed assemblies.

If you choose to compile the resources, the `ResourceDictionaries` can still be referenced directly using `/AssemblyName;component` syntax:

```
<Application.Resources>
  <ResourceDictionary>
    <ResourceDictionary.MergedDictionaries>
      <ResourceDictionary Source="/ThemeAssembly;component/Path/To/
        ResourceDictionary.xaml" />
    </ResourceDictionary.MergedDictionaries>
  </ResourceDictionary>
</Application.Resources>
```

EDITING STYLES AND TEMPLATES IN EXPRESSION BLEND

This chapter has focused on the fundamentals of styling and tried to illuminate the concepts through XAML. This section departs from this pure XAML approach and demonstrates how Expression Blend simplifies the creation of custom `Styles` and `ControlTemplates`. This will not be an exhaustive Expression Blend tutorial but will instead tie some of the concepts you've just covered to the tool. You will start, as always, with a custom `Button Style`.

Editing the Default Button Style

You can take two approaches when creating a custom button in Expression Blend. In the first approach, simply drag a button to the Stage and then select Edit Template ⇨ Edit a Copy from the Style Breadcrumb shown in Figure 21-13.

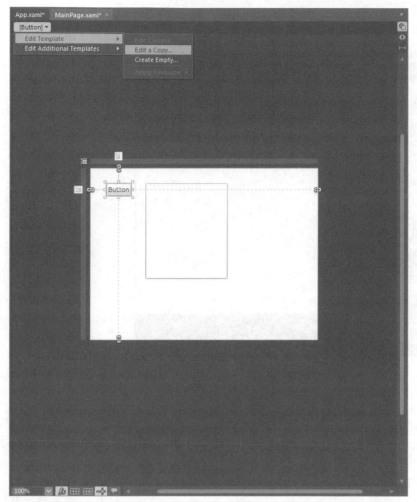

FIGURE 21-13

In the resulting Create Style Resource dialog (Figure 21-14), you can choose whether to define a Key for this resource or to select Apply to all, which creates an un-keyed (Implicit) `Style` that will be applied to all `Button`s within the new resource's scope. The Define in section lets you choose where this resource will be defined. Don't worry; you can always move the `Style` later, either via the Resources pane in Expression Blend or manually via XAML.

FIGURE 21-14

After clicking OK in this dialog, you are taken directly into Template-editing mode within Expression Blend, shown in Figure 21-15.

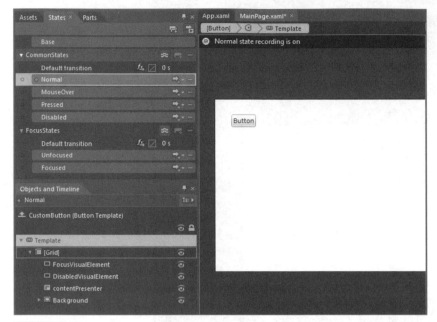

FIGURE 21-15

You are now editing an exact copy of the default Silverlight `Button`. This is a great way for you to really gain an understanding of how elements and states come together to create production-ready control `Style`s. There are several key things that you need to notice when in Template-editing mode. First, note how the Breadcrumb has changed. There are now three pieces:

➤ **[Button]** — The Type and/or name of the control you're editing

➤ **Style Icon** — Click this icon to scope the Object tree to the Style itself, not the Template.

➤ **Template Icon** — This element changes as you select different elements in the Object tree. By default, the root-level Template node will be selected in the tree.

It is important to understand the functionality this breadcrumb provides. You can quickly switch between Style editing and Template editing. When in Style-editing mode, you are simply setting default values for properties (like `Foreground` or `Background` or `Margin`). When in Template-editing mode, you are actually editing the underlying `ControlTemplate`.

Using the Property Panel to Define TemplateBindings

A number of elements in the default `Button` use `TemplateBinding`. Figure 21-16 shows the Properties panel when the `ContentPresenter` has been selected in the object tree.

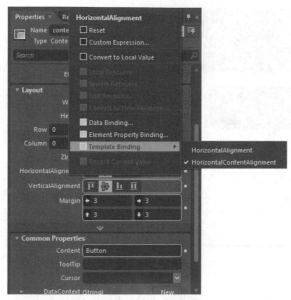

FIGURE 21-16

Any property that uses `TemplateBinding` is highlighted in orange. To change the binding, click the property Marker (small square button) to the right of the property name to display the Advanced property options menu. In Figure 21-16 the `HorizontalAlignment` menu is opened with the Template Binding submenu selected. To bind to a property, just click an available property from the Template Binding menu. Expression Blend will show only properties whose type matches the current property you are editing. Once you have bound to a property, you can switch back to Style-editing mode (via the Breadcrumb) to change the default value for that property.

Editing Control States

When you are in Template-editing mode, use the States panel to edit the `VisualStates` of a control. Expression Blend automatically shows you all of the `VisualStateGroups` and their child `VisualStates`, whether or not you have defined them in XAML. With the default Button template open, step through the different states by selecting them in the States panel. When a particular state is active, you'll see a red icon indicating "state recording" is on.

Any changes you make to elements within the Object tree during state recording will be applied only when the control finds itself in the selected state at run time.

Creating a Custom Button

You can quickly convert any artwork on the stage to a custom `Button`, or any control for that matter, using the Make Into Control command. Figure 21-17 shows a `Grid` on the stage with a `TextBlock` and two child `Rectangles`.

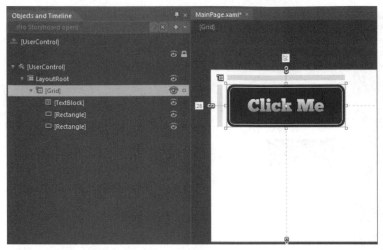

FIGURE 21-17

With the root `Grid` selected, click Tools ➪ Make Into Control to launch the dialog shown in Figure 21-18.

FIGURE 21-18

You first need to select a target Control type. `Button` is selected here, but you can select any control type available within your project. Like the Create Style Resource dialog you saw earlier, you must choose whether to key this resource and define where the resource lives.

After clicking OK in this dialog, several things happen behind the scenes. A new `Style` is created whose `Template` property is set with a copy of the elements you selected on the Stage. The elements you selected on the Stage are replaced with a `Button` whose `Style` property is set to `{StaticResource StyleName}`. If the elements you selected contain a `TextBlock`, that `TextBlock` will likely be converted to a `ContentPresenter` with the `Font` properties of the `TextBlock` promoted to the `Style` level as `Property Setters`. If the elements you selected did not contain a `TextBlock`, a `ContentPresenter` is automatically added to the Object tree. It's up to you to jump in and tweak the positioning of the `ContentPresenter`.

Now that your elements have been converted into a `ControlTemplate`, you need to step through and apply `TemplateBinding` where necessary and edit the various states of the control using the States panel.

 Some controls have specific, named parts that are required to be defined in the `ControlTemplate` to function properly. Select the Parts panel (Window ⇨ Parts) any time you create a `ControlTemplate` from scratch like this to make sure the control works. The Progress bar is an example of a control that has required parts. Try editing a copy of the default Progress bar template then select the Parts panel to see how Expression Blend highlights these requirements.

SUMMARY

You should now have a solid mental image of what the term "styling" means in the context of Silverlight. In this chapter, you started by learning a very basic approach of setting properties on controls, and then you learned how to replace those property values with Resources that represented the property type (a `SolidColorBrush` Resource was the first). From there, you learned how to set more and more properties with inline `StaticResource` references and welcomed the clarity, and brevity, that the `Style` object provides. With all of your property `Setters` moved to a centralized `Style`, you learned the highest degree of control customization possible: template editing. You saw how powerful template editing is and learned how `TemplateBinding` ties specific elements within the template to the properties of your *lookless* control.

You saw how the absence of an `x:Key` attribute lets you target all controls of a specific type (implicit styling), and then you learned how the location of resource definitions and references define resource scope. From there you looked at Silverlight Themes and learned how implicit styles empower this capability. The chapter concluded in Expression Blend, tying XAML theory to design surface practice.

As we mentioned at the start of this chapter, learning to style Silverlight apps starts at a technical, and somewhat unbeautiful, level. This chapter has laid the groundwork for your technical understanding; it is now up to you to make something of it!

XAML Primer

Chapter 1 exposed you to the fundamentals of building Silverlight applications. You were introduced to XAML, which is the glue between the interactive user interfaces you create and the managed code you write. This appendix explores more details of XAML and gives you a primer on XAML that can serve as a reference as you work through the book.

INTRODUCING XAML

As you learned in Chapter 1, XAML finally provides a unified markup that can describe not only what a control is and how it fits into a page, but also how layout and, more importantly, the overall look and feel of the controls on a page are defined. A designer can use XAML to create a mockup of a page or an application, and a developer can take that XAML markup and use it directly in his project files. Because partial classes and code-behind files in Visual Studio allow you to separate the code logic from the layout and control definitions, using XAML gives the opportunity to have this separation of the design from the code. Look at the following XAML example, which demonstrates an animation on a `TextBlock` element:

```
<Canvas
    Width="640" Height="480"
    Background="White">
        <Canvas.Triggers>
            <EventTrigger RoutedEvent="Canvas.Loaded">
                <BeginStoryboard>
                    <Storyboard x:Name="Timeline1"/>
                </BeginStoryboard>
            </EventTrigger>
        </Canvas.Triggers>

        <TextBlock Width="349" Height="67"
            Canvas.Top="140" Text="Hello World"
            TextWrapping="Wrap"
            RenderTransformOrigin="0.5,0.5"
            x:Name="textBlock">
            <TextBlock.RenderTransform>
```

```
                <TransformGroup>
                    <ScaleTransform ScaleX="1" ScaleY="1"/>
                </TransformGroup>
            </TextBlock.RenderTransform>
        </TextBlock>
    </Canvas>
```

This XAML may seem daunting, but learning XAML is like learning HTML; there are a lot of details, but for most of your applications, you are using tools to build the XAML and not hand-coding it yourself. The reason why it is important to understand XAML is the same reason why it is important to know HTML if you are a web developer. There are times when you need to inspect the HTML of a file to understand or debug a page, just as there will be times when you are looking at XAML and you need to understand why something is happening in your Silverlight application.

Microsoft Expression Blend and Visual Studio are both Rapid Application Development (RAD) tools that you can use to create the XAML in your Silverlight applications. Both applications give you the ability to drag-and-drop controls onto the design surface and switch between the designer view and the XAML view as you design your user interface.

Before you delve deeper into XAML, there is an issue that's important to understand: When using XAML in Silverlight versus using XAML in WPF, not all things are created equal. Because Silverlight is optimized for speed and the fast delivery of rich, interactive applications to the browser, the XAML available to Silverlight applications is a subset of the XAML that can be used in a full desktop-based WPF application. In WPF, each XAML element maps directly to a corresponding class in the .NET Framework. In Silverlight, the XAML parser is part of the Silverlight player, so there is no dependency on the .NET Framework for it to run. With Silverlight 4, the distinction between the XAML objects in Silverlight and WPF is becoming smaller; however, you will still run in to areas where the XAML in WPF has no equivalent in Silverlight.

SILVERLIGHT XAML BASICS

XAML is a case-sensitive declarative language based on XML that lets you design the user interface of a Silverlight application in descriptive markup. Similar to the way ASP.NET or Windows Forms work with the concept of a code-behind file, XAML files map to managed-code partial classes where you can write in your language of choice. XAML is important for the evolution of how you create the user interface because the user interface is separate from the code files. This means that a designer using tools like Expression Blend can create a UI using XAML, and that same XAML can be used in Visual Studio and integrated into a larger project. As a matter of fact, Expression Blend and Visual Studio share the same project structure, so the .csproj and .vbproj files can be opened by either tool. The ability for a designer to express a user interface and have it directly used without alteration in an application is something that has never been possible with Microsoft tools. There has always been a large amount of throwaway art work, because developers would get a mockup and try to duplicate it.

XAML files have a .xaml extension and, at first glance, might be confused with an XML data file. This makes sense, because XML (Extensible Markup Language) is the basis for XAML (Extensible Application Markup Language). The following code shows the default Silverlight XAML file when you create a new Silverlight application using Visual Studio, which is also broken down in the table that follows the code:

```
<UserControl x:Class="XamlTestApp.MainPage"
    xmlns="http://schemas.microsoft.com/winfx/2006/xaml/presentation"
    xmlns:x="http://schemas.microsoft.com/winfx/2006/xaml"
    xmlns:d="http://schemas.microsoft.com/expression/blend/2008"
    xmlns:mc=http://schemas.openxmlformats.org/markup-compatibility/2006
    mc:Ignorable="d"
    d:DesignHeight="300" d:DesignWidth="400">

    <Grid x:Name="LayoutRoot" Background="White">

    </Grid>
</UserControl>
```

Table A-1 describes the preceding code.

TABLE A-1

XAML	DESCRIPTION
`<UserControl x:Class="XamlTestApp.MainPage"`	Opening object tag of the root `UserControl`
`xmlns="http://schemas.microsoft.com/winfx/2006/xaml/presentation"`	Default Silverlight namespace mapping
`xmlns:x="http://schemas.microsoft.com/winfx/2006/xaml"`	Default XAML namespace mapping
`xmlns:d="http://schemas.microsoft.com/expression/blend/2008"`	Designer namespace for design-time support
`xmlns:mc="http://schemas.openxmlformats.org/markup-compatibility/2006"`	Markup Compatibility prefix for sharing data between Blend and Visual Studio
`mc:Ignorable="d"`	Directive to ignore the "d" namespace at runtime
`d:DesignHeight="300" d:DesignWidth="400">`	Default design-time `Height` and `Width` properties of the `UserControl`
`<Grid x:Name="LayoutRoot" Background="White">`	Opening tag for the `Grid` layout element
`</Grid>`	Closing tag for the `Grid` layout element
`</UserControl>`	Closing tag for the root `UserControl` object

In Chapter 1, you learned about the namespace declaration in Visual Studio for assemblies other than the core Silverlight and core Silverlight XAML namespaces. If you had a compiled user control or class file that you wanted to include in your opening `UserControl` declaration, you would use a custom prefix and point to the fully qualified namespace and object you are adding to the page. For example, if you need to access features in the `System.Windows` assembly, add the following namespace declaration to your page:

```
xmlns:vsm="clr-namespace:System.Windows;assembly=System.Windows"
```

where `vsm` is your custom prefix (which can be whatever prefix you would like), the `clr-namespace` you are using is `System.Windows`, and the actual assembly name is `System.Windows`. Later in this appendix, you learn about the XAML namespace, whose objects are prefixed with the default `x:` identifier.

DECLARING OBJECTS IN XAML

You can use either the object element syntax or the attribute syntax to declare objects in XAML:

➤ **Object Element Syntax** — Uses opening and closing tags to declare an object as an XML element. You can use this syntax to declare root objects or set complex property values.

➤ **Attribute Syntax** — Uses an inline value to declare an object. You can use this syntax to set the value of a property.

Object or Content Element Syntax

Most elements are created using the object (or content) element syntax, which is used in the "Introducing XAML" section earlier in this chapter to create the `TextBlock` object:

```
<TextBlock>Hello World</TextBlock>
```

This syntax maps to:

```
<ObjectName> … </ObjectName>
```

where `ObjectName` is the name of the object that you are trying to instantiate. The following example uses object element syntax to declare a `Canvas`:

```
<Canvas>
</Canvas>
```

Some objects, such as `Canvas`, can contain other objects, such as `Rectangle` or `TextBlock`:

```
<Canvas>
    <TextBlock>
    </TextBlock>
</Canvas>
```

If an object does not contain other objects, you can declare it using one self-enclosing tag instead of two:

```
<Canvas>
    <Rectangle />
</Canvas>
```

When you are creating objects, there really is no bad or good way. The hierarchy of the XAML documents, which is covered later in this appendix, does not change.

Attribute Element Syntax

XAML also supports the less verbose attribute syntax for setting properties. The following markup creates a rectangle that has a green background (or Fill as the attributed property is named):

```
<Rectangle Fill="Green" Height="100" Width="100" />
```

Property Element Syntax

Attribute syntax is not possible on certain object properties because the object or information necessary to provide the property value cannot be adequately expressed as a simple string. For these cases, the property element syntax can be used. Property element syntax sets the referenced property of the containing element with a new instance of the type that the property takes as its value, for example:

```
<objectName>
    <objectName.property>
        <setter propertyValue = "" />
    </objectName.property>
</objectName>
```

The following code uses property element syntax to add a Stroke with a LinearGradientBrush to a Rectangle element:

```
<Rectangle Width="485" Height="60"
    Canvas.Left="99" Canvas.Top="55">
    <Rectangle.Stroke>
        <LinearGradientBrush EndPoint="1,0.5" StartPoint="0,0.5">
            <GradientStop Color="#FF483333" Offset="0.308"/>
            <GradientStop Color="#FF514C4C" Offset="0.1070303"/>
        </LinearGradientBrush>
    </Rectangle.Stroke>
    <Rectangle.Fill>
        <LinearGradientBrush EndPoint="1,0.5" StartPoint="0,0.5">
            <GradientStop Color="#FF000000" Offset="0"/>
            <GradientStop Color="#FFFFFFFF" Offset="1"/>
        </LinearGradientBrush>
    </Rectangle.Fill>
</Rectangle>
```

You can set properties on objects declared using object element syntax. You have three ways to set properties in XAML:

➤ Using implicit collection syntax

➤ Using attribute syntax

➤ Using property element syntax

Setting a Property Using Implicit Collection Syntax

When a property takes a collection, you can omit the collection element and simply specify its contents instead. This is known as *implicit collection syntax*. The following code shows how you can omit the GradientStopCollection for a LinearGradientBrush and simply specify its GradientStop objects. The GradientStopCollection is included in the first LinearGradientBrush but omitted from the second.

```
<Rectangle Width="100" Height="100"
              Canvas.Left="0" Canvas.Top="30">
    <Rectangle.Fill>
        <LinearGradientBrush>
            <LinearGradientBrush.GradientStops>

                <!-- Here the GradientStopCollection tag is used. -->
                <GradientStopCollection>
                    <GradientStop Offset="0.0" Color="Red" />
                    <GradientStop Offset="1.0" Color="Blue" />
                </GradientStopCollection>
            </LinearGradientBrush.GradientStops>
        </LinearGradientBrush>
    </Rectangle.Fill>
</Rectangle>


<Rectangle Width="100" Height="100"
              Canvas.Left="100" Canvas.Top="30">
    <Rectangle.Fill>
        <LinearGradientBrush>
            <LinearGradientBrush.GradientStops>

                <!-- Notice that the GradientStopCollection
                    tag is omitted. -->
                <GradientStop Offset="0.0" Color="Red" />
                <GradientStop Offset="1.0" Color="Blue" />
            </LinearGradientBrush.GradientStops>
        </LinearGradientBrush>
    </Rectangle.Fill>
</Rectangle>
```

There are times when the property collection indicates the type of collection being parsed. In these cases, you can omit both the collection element and the property element tags, as the following code demonstrates:

```
<Rectangle Width="100" Height="100"
                    Canvas.Left="200" Canvas.Top="30">
    <Rectangle.Fill>
        <LinearGradientBrush>
            <GradientStop Offset="0.0" Color="Red" />
            <GradientStop Offset="1.0" Color="Blue" />
        </LinearGradientBrush>
    </Rectangle.Fill>
</Rectangle>
```

Deciding When to Use Attribute or Property Element Syntax to Set a Property

So far, you have learned that all properties support either the attribute or property element syntax. Some properties, however, support other syntax, which is dependent on the type of object property it accepts.

Primitive types, such as a `Double`, `Integer`, or `String`, support only the attribute element syntax. The following example uses attribute element syntax to set the width of a rectangle. The `Width` property supports attribute syntax because the property value is a `Double`.

```
<Rectangle Width="100" />
```

Whether or not you can use attribute syntax to set a property depends on whether the object you use to set that property supports attribute syntax. The following example uses attribute syntax to set the fill of a rectangle. The `Fill` property supports attribute syntax when you use a `SolidColorBrush` to set it because `SolidColorBrush` supports attribute syntax.

```
<Rectangle Fill="Blue" />
```

Whether or not you can use property element syntax to set a property depends on whether the object you use to set that property supports object element syntax. If the object supports object element syntax, the property supports property element syntax. The following example uses property element syntax to set the fill of a rectangle. The `Fill` property supports attribute syntax when you use a `SolidColorBrush` to set it because `SolidColorBrush` supports attribute syntax.

```
<Rectangle>
    <Rectangle.Fill>
        <SolidColorBrush Color="Blue" />
    </Rectangle.Fill>
</Rectangle>
```

XAML HIERARCHY

When you add XAML objects to the Silverlight control, you are defining a hierarchical tree structure with a root object. All XAML files have a root element. In Silverlight, the root element is always the container that has the x:Class attribute. The following XAML example creates an object hierarchy containing a root UserControl object in the XamlTestApp namespace Page class. When the XAML is parsed by the player, the Canvas object, which has Rectangle and TextBlock elements, is resolved, as well as the additional TextBlock element in the file. When the parsing is complete, there is a tree-structured hierarchy of the elements in the file.

```
<!-- The top-most object in the XAML hierarchy is -->
<!-- referred to as the root object. -->
<UserControl x:Class="XamlTestApp.MainPage"
    xmlns="http://schemas.microsoft.com/winfx/2006/xaml/presentation"
    xmlns:x="http://schemas.microsoft.com/winfx/2006/xaml"
    xmlns:d="http://schemas.microsoft.com/expression/blend/2008"
    xmlns:mc="http://schemas.openxmlformats.org/markup-compatibility/2006"
    mc:Ignorable="d"
    d:DesignHeight="300" d:DesignWidth="400">

    <Grid x:Name="LayoutRoot" Background="White" Height="337" Width="626">
        <!-- Canvas objects can be a child of another Canvas object. -->
        <Canvas
      Canvas.Left="20" Canvas.Top="20">
            <Rectangle
          Width="200" Height="35"
          Fill="Red" />
            <TextBlock
          Canvas.Left="25" Canvas.Top="5"
          Foreground="White" FontFamily="Verdana"
          FontSize="18" FontWeight="Bold"
          Text="Child Canvas TextBlock" />
        </Canvas>

        <TextBlock
      Canvas.Left="40" Canvas.Top="60"
      Foreground="Black" FontFamily="Verdana"
      FontSize="18" FontWeight="Bold"
      Text="Hello Silverlight" />

    </Grid>
</UserControl>
```

When the Silverlight player attempts to render the XAML content, it is converted into a hierarchical tree structure with a root object. The tree structure determines the rendering order of Silverlight objects. The order of traversal starts with the root object, which is the topmost node in the tree structure — in this case, the UserControl object. The root object's children are then traversed, from left to right. If an object has children, its children are traversed before the object's siblings. This means the content of a child object is rendered in front of the object's own content.

EVENTS AND THE SILVERLIGHT CONTROL

The Silverlight object model defines a set of objects that allow you to create a Silverlight application. In the managed code programming model of Silverlight you have a rich set object that you interact with in code. The events for these objects are handled in the code-behind of the partial class that is associated with the XAML file your objects are in. All interaction with the browser is handled through the normal interaction processing of the browser, where inputs are accepted client-side. In the case of Silverlight, the player responds to events and routes them to the appropriate event handler that you have defined.

This section discusses the Silverlight objects; how you reference them; and how you handle, add, and remove events on those objects. Because you cannot create fully interactive applications in XAML alone, it is important to understand how all of the elements — the objects in XAML, the HTML, and your code-behind — work together to deliver the richness that Silverlight offers.

Event Handlers and Partial Classes

In Silverlight, the association of the XAML file with a code-behind file is set up with the `x:Class` attribute at the top of your XAML files. The `x:` prefix indicates that the `Class` object is part of the XAML namespace, and the `Class` object is declared as an attribute off the root element of a XAML file. The `x:Class` attribute cannot be used on child elements in a page hierarchy; it can only be declared once and on the root element. The syntax for declaring the `x:Class` is the same as for any other type declaration in Silverlight:

```
<object x:Class="namespace.classname;assembly=assemblyname"...>
   ...
</object>
```

In default cases when you add new pages to your application, the `assembly` is left off and assumed to be the current project's assembly.

```
<UserControl x:Class="SilverlightApplication1.Page"
```

When you build your Silverlight application, the compiler builds the XAML, parses the XAML, and creates instance objects of all of the uniquely identified elements in the file using `x:Name`. The association of the class defined in the `x:Class` attribute and its partial class occur during the compile, and the references for all of the objects with an `x:Name` are created so that they can be referenced at run time. The `x:Name` attribute is used as a unique identifier to the elements you define. Similar to HTML, where the `id` attribute denotes the uniqueness of an element, Silverlight needs a way to isolate and reference elements in XAML so that they can be referenced in the code-behind files. In Silverlight 1.0, there were no code-behind files because all coding was handled via JavaScript. But by using `<script>` tags in HTML pages, you can define what code files should be able to access DOM for the page in which you are running the Silverlight control. In Silverlight, the partial class files contain your managed code, and thus they contain your event handlers. Objects are defined in XAML with an `x:Name` attribute, and corresponding fields are created in the partial class, which can have event handlers that respond to the input event.

The naming rules for the x:Name, x:Class, and x:Key attributes are:

➤ They can contain numbers, letters, or underscores.

➤ They cannot begin with a number.

➤ Unicode characters are not supported.

The x:Key attributes are used in the child elements of ResourceDictionary objects. The child elements are basically keyed by the XAML processor and can be used by the StaticResource markup extension, which is covered later in this appendix.

The following XAML demonstrates a file where a button element has a unique identifier. Although both x:Name and x:Key enforce uniqueness, you will get a compile error if you have an x:Name and x:Key object using the same name.

```
<Grid x:Name="LayoutRoot" Background="White">
    <Button x:Name="button1" Click="button1_Click"></Button>
</Grid>
```

In the code-behind for this XAML file, the event handler looks like this:

```
private void button1_Click(object sender, RoutedEventArgs e)
{

}
```

In Visual Studio, the XAML Editor will give you hints for the attributes for the object that you are typing against, including the object's corresponding events. This makes it easier to wire events from XAML to your code-behind. You can also manually wire events to objects:

```
button1 += new MouseButtonEventHandler(button1_Click);
```

In Visual Basic, you can use the Handles keyword to associate XAML elements with class functions:

```
Private Sub button1_Click(ByVal sender As Object, _
        ByVal e As System.Windows.RoutedEventArgs) _
        Handles button1.Click

End Sub
```

Your event handlers can be public or private. Objects with the x:Name attribute are scoped to the page they are in. Similar to the way events are handled in ASP.NET or Windows Forms, the event handlers in Silverlight have two parameters:

➤ sender — Identifies the Silverlight object that generated the event. You can retrieve the type value of the object by calling the object's API.

➤ args — Identifies the set of argument values for the specific event. An event, such as the Loaded event, does not define any event arguments, so the value of eventArgs is null.

Table A-2 shows an example of the event parameters for the KeyDown event of the Silverlight player. This example is typical of how you will see events described in Silverlight 4.

TABLE A-2

EVENT PARAMETER	DESCRIPTION
sender	The object that invoked the event
KeyEventArgs	keyEventArgs.key — Integer that indicates that a key is pressed. This value is not operating-system-specific.
	keyEventArgs.platformKeyCode — Integer that indicates that a key is pressed. This value is operating-system-specific.
	keyEventArgs.shift — Boolean value that indicates whether the [Shift] key is down
	keyEventArgs.ctrl — Boolean value that indicates whether the [Ctrl] key is down

As an example of the KeyDown event, the following code demonstrates how to define the event on the TextBox element in XAML:

```
<TextBox Height="100" Width="200"
        KeyDown="TextBox_KeyDown"></TextBox>
<TextBlock x:Name="results"></TextBlock>
```

Next, the code here demonstrates the code-behind in Visual Basic that is used to handle the KeyDown event on the TextBox object:

```
Private Sub TextBox_KeyDown(ByVal sender As System.Object, _
        ByVal e As System.Windows.Input.KeyEventArgs)

        results.Text = e.Key & "-" & e.PlatformKeyCode
End Sub
```

When you wire the event directly in the XAML to the method in your code-behind, the approach is no different than if you were building a Windows Forms application.

Defining Events in JavaScript

If you choose not to use a managed programming model, which is the case if you omit the x:Class attribute on your XAML file, you must handle all events in JavaScript. When adding or removing event handlers via JavaScript, you will use the AddEventListener and RemoveEventListener methods on the elements on which you want to add or remove events. You use the following syntax:

```
Element.addEventListener("EventName", "EventHandler");
```

For example, the following code demonstrates adding the onMouseEnter and onMouseLeave event handlers to the TextBlock element named Status.

```
function onLoaded(sender, eventArgs)
{
    textBlock = sender.findName("Status");
    textBlock.addEventListener("MouseEnter", "onMouseEnter");
    textBlock.addEventListener("MouseLeave", "onMouseLeave");
}
```

To remove an existing event handler function, use the `RemoveEventListener` method, as demonstrated next:

```
function removeEvents()
{
    textBlock.removeEventListener("MouseEnter", "onMouseEnter");
    textBlock.removeEventListener("MouseLeave", "onMouseLeave");
}
```

Finding a XAML Object Using findName

In JavaScript, you use the `findName` method and reference the object's `x:Name` attribute value. The `findName` function searches the entire object hierarchy of the DOM running in the Silverlight control, so the location of an element in the hierarchy does not matter. If the element passed to the `findName` function cannot be found, a null value is returned. The following code demonstrates using the `findName` function as well as how to properly check whether the object being sought exists:

```
function onLoaded(sender, eventArgs)
{
    // Retrieve the object corresponding to the x:Name attribute value.
    var canvas = sender.findName("rootCanvas");

    // Determine whether the object was found.
    if (canvas != null)
    {
        alert(canvas.toString());
    }
    else
    {
        alert("Object not found");
    }
}
```

Event Bubbling

Because Silverlight supports the same routed event model that WPF uses, the concept of *event bubbling* becomes important for some events. A *routed event* is an event that traverses the object hierarchy from the root element that triggers the event up to each of its parent objects. Events are *bubbled* up.

The framework elements that support routed events are:

➤ KeyDown

➤ KeyUp

➤ GotFocus

➤ LostFocus

➤ MouseLeftButtonDown

➤ MouseLeftButtonUp

➤ MouseMove

- MouseWheel

- BindingValidationError

- DragEnter

- DragLeave

- DragOver

- Drop

The following code demonstrates an example in which event bubbling might come into play. Notice there are MouseMove events on the root UserControl, as well as the child elements in the user control:

```
<UserControl x:Class="XamlTestApp.MainPage"
    xmlns="http://schemas.microsoft.com/winfx/2006/xaml/presentation"
    xmlns:x="http://schemas.microsoft.com/winfx/2006/xaml"
    xmlns:d="http://schemas.microsoft.com/expression/blend/2008"
    xmlns:mc="http://schemas.openxmlformats.org/markup-compatibility/2006"
    mc:Ignorable="d"
    d:DesignHeight="300" d:DesignWidth="400"
    Loaded="onLoaded"
    MouseMove="rootCanvasMouseMove">

<Grid x:Name="LayoutRoot" Background="White">
    <Rectangle
    x:Name="rect1"
    MouseMove="rect1MouseMove"
    Width="100" Height="100"
    Fill="PowderBlue" />

    <Rectangle
    x:Name="rect2"
    MouseMove="rect2MouseMove"
    Canvas.Top="50" Canvas.Left="50"
    Width="100" Height="100"
    Fill="Gold" Opacity="0.5" />

    <TextBlock
    x:Name="statusTextBlock"
    Canvas.Top="180" />
</Grid>
</UserControl>
```

Event bubbling means that multiple MouseMove events are defined for an object and its ancestors. The event is received by each object in the ancestor hierarchy, starting with the object that directly receives the event.

The next code demonstrates this in a different fashion. Because both Rectangle elements have a MouseMove event defined and the Canvas element has a MouseMove event defined, if the mouse is moved over either rectangle, the onRectMouseMove event is fired. And because the Canvas is looking for a `MouseMove` event, the mouse move over the rectangles is bubbled up through the object hierarchy to the `Canvas` element.

```
<Canvas
    MouseMove="onCanvasMouseMove"
    Loaded="onLoaded">

    <Rectangle
    x:Name="RectA"
    MouseMove="onRectMouseMove"
    Width="100" Height="100" Fill="Red" />

    <Rectangle
    x:Name="RectB"
    MouseMove="onRectMouseMove"
    Width="100" Height="100" Fill="Blue"
    Canvas.Top="25" Canvas.Left="25" Opacity="0.5" />
</Canvas>
```

MARKUP EXTENSIONS

Because you can create static or instance objects in XAML, you need a way to use those objects as properties on other XAML elements. This is where XAML markup extensions come in. Using an opening and a closing curly brace ({}) syntax, you can reference static object resources created elsewhere in your application using an attribute or property element syntax. For example, if you created a static `Style` resource that you planned to use to target multiple elements in your application, use the markup extension syntax to set the style property on the target element. The following code is an example of a static style resource:

```
<Style x:Key="MainButton" TargetType="Button">
    <Setter Property="Width" Value="80" />
    <Setter Property="Height" Value="35" />
    <Setter Property="FontSize" Value="18" />
</Style>
```

To apply this resource to a target element, in this case the `TargetType Button`, use the attribute syntax shown here:

```
Button x:Name="Button1" Style="{StaticResource MainButton}" ... />
<Button x:Name="Button2" Style="{StaticResource MainButton}" ... />
```

When the XAML is parsed, the presence of the curly brace indicates that this is an extension and to process the type of markup extension and the string value that follows the type. Silverlight supports four markup extensions:

➤   `Binding` — Supports data binding, which defers a property value until it is interpreted under a data context.

➤   `StaticResource` — Supports referencing resource values that are defined in a `ResourceDictionary`.

➤ `TemplateBinding` — Supports control templates in XAML that can interact with the code properties of the templated object.

➤ `RelativeSource` — Enables a particular form of template binding.

We look at `Binding` and `StaticResource` in this appendix and `TemplateBinding` in Chapter 21.

Binding Markup Extensions

In Chapter 7, you learned the details of data binding. This section looks at the basic XAML syntax. To understand the binding markup extension, you'll need to understand how data retrieved in a managed function ends up being displayed in XAML. Before we go into an example, let's go over the basic syntax. You can set binding in several ways using the `Binding` markup extension:

```
<object property="{Binding}" .../>

<object property="{Binding propertyPath}" .../>

<object property="{Binding oneOrMoreBindingProperties}" .../>

<object property="{Binding propertyPath, oneOrMoreBindingProperties}" .../>
```

In all cases, `object` is an element such as a `TextBlock`, and `property` is an attribute property on that element, such as `Text`. The remaining options are how you specify the properties of the binding, such as the binding `Mode` (`OneTime`, `OneWay`, or `TwoWay`), `Converter`, `Path`, and so forth.

When you retrieve or build data, you normally set the data source to the `DataContext` of a XAML element, such as a `Canvas` or `Grid` object, so it can be used by the containers' child elements. For example, if you had a basic `Grid` element named `LayoutRoot`, it would look something like this:

```
<Grid x:Name="LayoutRoot" Background="White">

    <!-- grid definition, XAML children -->

</Grid>
```

In your code-behind, to bind data to the child elements of `LayoutRoot`, set the data source in your code-behind to the `DataContext` of `LayoutRoot`:

```
LayoutRoot.DataContext = dataRecords;
```

In this case, `dataRecords` is a custom object that has various properties like `Name`, `Address`, and `Email` that I set through code. Once the `DataContext` is set, the child elements have access to fields on the data context of the parent element, as the following code demonstrates:

```
<Grid x:Name="LayoutRoot" Background="White">

    <!-- Grid definition -->

    <Grid.RowDefinitions>
        <RowDefinition MaxHeight="30" />
```

```xaml
            <RowDefinition MaxHeight="30" />
            <RowDefinition MaxHeight="70" />
            <RowDefinition MaxHeight="30" />
            <RowDefinition MaxHeight="40" />
            <RowDefinition MaxHeight="50" />
        </Grid.RowDefinitions>
        <Grid.ColumnDefinitions>
            <ColumnDefinition MaxWidth="150"/>
            <ColumnDefinition MaxWidth="200" />
        </Grid.ColumnDefinitions>

        <!-- XAML children -->

        <TextBlock x:Name="NameLabel" Text="Name:   "
    VerticalAlignment="Bottom"
    HorizontalAlignment="Right"
    Grid.Row="0"  Grid.Column="0" />

        <TextBlock x:Name="Name"
    Text="{Binding Name, Mode=OneWay }"
    VerticalAlignment="Bottom"
    HorizontalAlignment="Left"
    Grid.Row="0" Grid.Column="1" />

        <TextBlock x:Name="AddressLabel" Text="Address: "
    VerticalAlignment="Bottom"
    HorizontalAlignment="Right"
    Grid.Row="1"  Grid.Column="0" />

        <TextBlock x:Name="Address"
    Text="{Binding Address, Mode=OneWay }"
    VerticalAlignment="Bottom"
    HorizontalAlignment="Left"
    Grid.Row="1" Grid.Column="1" />

        <TextBlock x:Name="EmailLabel" Text="Email:   "
    VerticalAlignment="Bottom"
    HorizontalAlignment="Right"
    Grid.Row="2" Grid.Column="0"  />

        <TextBlock x:Name="Email"
    Text="{Binding  Email, Mode=OneWay}"
    VerticalAlignment="Bottom"
    HorizontalAlignment="Left"
    Height="60" Width="200"
    Grid.Row="2" Grid.Column="1" />
    </Grid>
```

When the application runs, the data from the custom object is bound to the Grid element, and the grid's child TextBlock elements consume the available data by using the binding markup extension.

StaticResource Markup Extensions

The `StaticResource` markup extension is used to set the `x:Key` attribute on an object that is defined in a `ResourceDictionary` object.

```
<Style x:Key="MainButton" TargetType="Button">
    <Setter Property="Width" Value="80" />
</Style>
```

The `x:Key` attribute is applied to the `Style` object to give it the unique name `MainButton`. This `Style` object is in a `ResourceDictionary`, which in Silverlight is normally the outermost XAML element of your XAML file:

```
<UserControl.Resources>
    <Style x:Key="MainButton" TargetType="Button">
        <Setter Property="Width" Value="80" />
        <Setter Property="Height" Value="35" />
        <Setter Property="FontSize" Value="18" />
    </Style>
</UserControl.Resources>
```

`x:Key` gives the resource its uniqueness, so it can be applied to objects in the XAML file using the `StaticResource` markup extension syntax you learned about earlier:

```
<Button x:Name="Button1" Style="{StaticResource MainButton}" ... />
```

In this case, the properties defined in the `MainButton` `Style` will be applied to any `Button` object using the `StaticResource` markup extension.

SUMMARY

This appendix gave you a good foundation for the various aspects of using XAML in Silverlight. Here are a few takeaways about Silverlight XAML that you need to remember:

➤ Silverlight XAML is a subset of WPF XAML, so theoretically an application in Silverlight can move up to WPF.

➤ The Silverlight player is an ActiveX browser plug-in, so the XAML you are using is built into the player; it is not based on .NET Framework objects.

➤ XAML alone cannot build Silverlight applications. You need HTML to host the Silverlight player, which, in turn, hosts the XAML, and you need to use the managed coding model in Silverlight 2 or greater or the unmanaged coding model in Silverlight 1.0 to interact with the XAML.

➤ XAML opens the doors for designers and developers to work closely together, because the same language (XAML) that is used to style applications is also used to define the user interface.

➤ The X in XAML stands for extensible, so as Silverlight matures, with the capabilities of the player such that you can add your own extensions, your applications will become more powerful.

Testing Silverlight Applications

As software applications become more sophisticated and increasingly part of our daily lives, they are also becoming more complex. It therefore becomes all that more important that we focus on the quality of the software we produce. Fantastic progress has been made in both the development processes and development tools we use to create software, including advances in how we think about quality and testing as we develop applications. Processes like unit testing ingrain testing and quality into a developer's daily life.

A variety of testing platforms are currently available for Silverlight, each with its own pros and cons, but remember that in general, anything that helps you test is good. Some testing tools focus exclusively on unit testing, and others focus on UI automation, though as you may find out when evaluating these tools, the lines between the different types of testing are not always clear. This appendix looks at three different testing tools that can help you unit test your application and create recorded UI automation tests.

Because software testing is an enormous topic all on its own, this appendix is not intended to be a guide on how you should test your software. Nor is this appendix intended to cover every commercial and free testing tool available. Instead, it reviews a selection of popular tools that you can use to help test your applications. The good news is that even though Silverlight is a relatively new platform, a wide variety of tools are already available to help you test your application.

CREATING THE SAMPLE APPLICATION

To demonstrate the various Silverlight testing frameworks, this appendix uses a very simple Silverlight application that allows the end user to add two numbers together and display a sum. The sample application includes a simple user interface defined in XAML, showing in Listing B-1.

LISTING B-1: Sample application user interface markup

```xml
<UserControl x:Class="AppendixB.MainPage"
    xmlns="http://schemas.microsoft.com/winfx/2006/xaml/presentation"
    xmlns:x="http://schemas.microsoft.com/winfx/2006/xaml"
    xmlns:d="http://schemas.microsoft.com/expression/blend/2008"
    xmlns:mc="http://schemas.openxmlformats.org/markup-compatibility/2006"
    mc:Ignorable="d"
    d:DesignHeight="300" d:DesignWidth="400">

    <Grid x:Name="LayoutRoot" Background="White">
        <StackPanel Orientation="Vertical" HorizontalAlignment="Center"
                    VerticalAlignment="Center">
            <StackPanel Orientation="Horizontal" Margin="3"
                        HorizontalAlignment="Right">
                <TextBlock Text="A: " VerticalAlignment="Center" />
                <TextBox x:Name="txtA" Width="50" />
            </StackPanel>
            <StackPanel Orientation="Horizontal" Margin="3"
                        HorizontalAlignment="Right">
                <TextBlock Text="B: " VerticalAlignment="Center" />
                <TextBox x:Name="txtB" Width="50" />
            </StackPanel>
            <Button x:Name="btnAdd" Margin="3" Width="50"
                    Click="btnAdd_Click">Add</Button>
            <StackPanel Orientation="Horizontal" Margin="3">
                <TextBlock Text="Sum: " VerticalAlignment="Center" />
                <TextBlock x:Name="lblSum" Width="50" />
            </StackPanel>
        </StackPanel>
    </Grid>
</UserControl>
```

When the button is clicked, the event creates a new Calculator object, whose Add method is used to sum the values and produce a result that is shown in a TextBlock. This is shown in Listing B-2.

LISTING B-2: Executing the Calculators Add method in a button click

```csharp
internal void btnAdd_Click(object sender, RoutedEventArgs e)
{
    Calculator calc = new Calculator();

    int a = int.Parse(this.txtA.Text);
    int b = int.Parse(this.txtB.Text);

    this.lblSum.Text = calc.Add(a, b).ToString();
}
```

This simple application shows you how the various test frameworks can be used to test application logic like the Calculator class, as well as test UI interaction like clicking the Sum button.

USING THE SILVERLIGHT UNIT TEST FRAMEWORK

The Silverlight Unit Test Framework is a derivation of Microsoft's standard unit testing framework that has shipped with Visual Studio since 2005. It leverages the same API names as the standard unit testing framework, allowing you to share tests between platforms. And it includes project and item templates that are integrated directly into Visual Studio.

To get started with the framework, create a new Silverlight Unit Test Application project, as shown in Figure B-1.

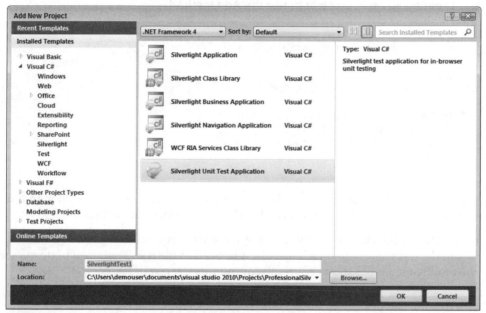

FIGURE B-1

This project template sets up a typical Silverlight application, but adds two additional project references shown in Figure B-2.

The project template also changes the default `RootVisual` to the Framework's test page as shown in Listing B-3.

FIGURE B-2

Available for
download on
Wrox.com

LISTING B-3: Changing the RootVisual to the Unit Test Frameworks test page

```
private void Application_Startup(object sender, StartupEventArgs e)
{
    RootVisual = UnitTestSystem.CreateTestPage();
}
```

Changing the `RootVisual` allows the test framework to generate a default application harness in which tests are executed.

Once the project is created, you can start creating unit tests. Listing B-4 shows a basic unit test that has been created to test the methods of the sample application's `Calculator` class. As the test class name describes, this test is compatible with the standard CLR test framework. If the `Calculator` class were a shared class, being used in both a Silverlight application as well as a full CLR application (such as a WPF application), this same test could be reused between the two platforms.

LISTING B-4: Creating a simple unit test to test the Add method

```
[TestClass]
public class VisualStudioTestCompatibleTests
{
    [TestMethod]
    public void CalculatorAddReturnsTwo()
    {
        Calculator calc = new Calculator();
        int result = calc.Add(1, 1);
        Assert.AreEqual<int>(2, result);
    }
}
```

In this test, a new instance of the `Calculator` class is created and its `Add` method called with the test providing two known values. The test asserts that the result of the `Add` method should be `2`.

To run the test, simply set the Unit Test Application as the startup project and run it as a normal application. When the test harness application loads, it runs all of the tests contained in the project and reports the results. Figure B-3 shows the results of running the test in Listing B-4.

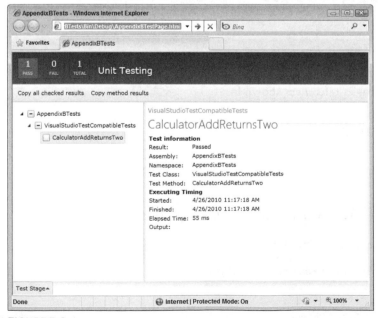

FIGURE B-3

As you can see, the one test in the project has passed successfully.

The test harness user interface shows a list of the tests that were run, their completion status, and allows you to copy the results to the Clipboard so that they can be shared with others. Should a test fail, the UI allows you to drill into the test to see why it failed. Figure B-4 shows a failed test.

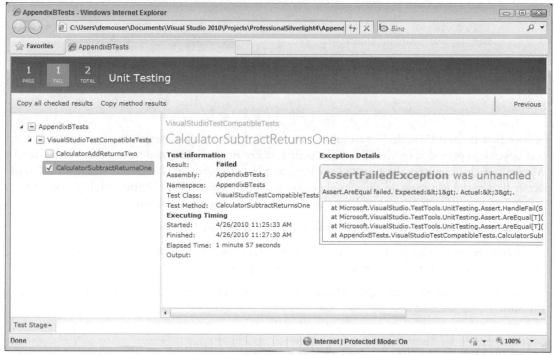

FIGURE B-4

In this case the `CalculatorSubtractReturnsOne` test has failed. The details can be seen on the left side of the screen, which tell you that the `Assert` failed because a value of 1 was expected, but the method actually returned 3.

It is also possible to test UI aspects of an application using the Silverlight Unit Test Framework, but because of the asynchronous nature of Silverlight, it requires you to code tests slightly differently. Listing B-5 shows a test that checks to make sure a `Button` exists in the UI.

LISTING B-5: Using a PresentationTest to check for the existence of a UI Element

```
[TestClass]
public class PresentationTests : PresentationTest
{
    MainPage mainPage;

    [TestInitialize]
    public void PreparePage()
```

continues

LISTING B-5 *(continued)*

```
    {
        mainPage = new AppendixB.MainPage();
        TestPanel.Children.Add(mainPage);
    }

    [TestMethod]
    public void AddButtonExists()
    {
        Assert.IsNotNull(((FrameworkElement)mainPage).FindName("btnAdd"),
                        "btnLogin not found");
    }
}
```

Notice that the test class derives from the `PresentationTest` class. `PresentationTest` is a special test base class provided by the Silverlight Unit Test Framework designed to simplify testing the UI. Also notice this test uses the `TestInitialize` attribute to perform some setup actions that need to occur before the test runs. In this case because you are testing the application's UI, you need to create an instance of that UI and add it to the Unit Test Framework's test panel.

Once that is done, the test can be run and can check to ensure the existence of that button.

The `PresentationTest` base class also provides a set of methods that allow you to queue commands that the test framework will execute at the appropriate time.

Listing B-6 demonstrates using the enqueue methods to verify that the correct value is assigned to the Sum `TextBlock`.

LISTING B-6: Simulating a button click in a unit test

```
[TestMethod, Asynchronous]
public void AddExecutesWhenButtonClicked()
{
    Assert.IsNotNull(((FrameworkElement)mainPage).FindName("txtA"),
                    "txtA not found");
    Assert.IsNotNull(((FrameworkElement)mainPage).FindName("txtB"),
                    "txtB not found");
    Assert.IsNotNull(((FrameworkElement)mainPage).FindName("lblSum"),
                    "txtSum not found");
    Assert.IsNotNull(((FrameworkElement)mainPage).FindName("btnAdd"),
                    "btnAdd not found");

    EnqueueCallback(() => mainPage.txtA.Text = "1");
    EnqueueCallback(() => mainPage.txtB.Text = "1");
    EnqueueCallback(() => mainPage.btnAdd_Click(mainPage.btnAdd,
                    new RoutedEventArgs()));

    EnqueueCallback(() => Assert.IsTrue(mainPage.lblSum.Text=="2"));

    EnqueueTestComplete();
}
```

The test first checks to make sure that all of the UI elements exist, then simulates the button click by executing the button's click handler method, checking the value of the Sum TextBlock, and finally indicating that the test is complete.

Note that to execute the button's click handler method, you must make the method visible by changing its accessor, which is private by default. To prevent the method from being publicly exposed, you can change its accessor to Internal and then apply the InternalsVisibleTo assembly attribute to your application project:

```
[assembly: InternalsVisibleTo("AppendixBTests")]
```

This allows the test project to see the internal members.

Once you have developed a set of tests, you may want to begin to incorporate those into your normal automated build process. Starting with Silverlight 4, the Silverlight Unit Test Framework harness is able to be run as an out-of-browser application (for in-depth discussion of Silverlight out-of-browser applications see Chapter 9). This means that you can launch the test harness from the command line using the sllauncher.exe application:

```
sllauncher /emulate:xapfilename /origin:uri
```

Additionally, although the test harness is not integrated directly into Visual Studio, it does have the ability to output its results to the test results format (.trx) used by Visual Studio. By using the VisualStudioLogProvider class as one of the framework's Log Providers, the framework will output its results to a service address. Setting up the Log Provider is shown in Listing B-7.

LISTING B-7: Using the VisualStudioLogProvider to log unit test results

Available for
download on
Wrox.com

```
private void Application_Startup(object sender, StartupEventArgs e)
{
    UnitTestSettings settings = UnitTestSystem.CreateDefaultSettings();
    settings.TestService.UniqueTestRunIdentifier = Guid.NewGuid().ToString();
    settings.LogProviders.Add(new VisualStudioLogProvider());

    RootVisual = UnitTestSystem.CreateTestPage(settings);
}
```

As you can see in the listing, the UnitTestSystem method contains a static CreateDefaultSettings method that returns a UnitTestSettings object. On this object you can set a unique test run identifier and then add the Log Provider.

By default the log provider outputs the log file to http://localhost:8000/externalInterface. An example of an ASP.NET MVC website that can capture the log provider content is included in the downloadable code for this appendix.

USING THE SELENIUM TEST FRAMEWORK

Selenium is a popular testing application that uses managed code to drive JavaScript, which automates testing of web applications. An add-in called Silverlight-Selenium (or Silvernium) can be used to automate Silverlight applications running in the browser. To set up the Selenium test environment needed to execute tests and record test results, you need to download and install a number of applications (see Table B-1).

TABLE B-1

APPLICATION	URL	DESCRIPTION
Selenium Remote Control (RC)	`http://seleniumhq.org/`	Provides the test harness that knows how to execute the Selenium tests in the browser.
NUnit or MbUnit	`http://www.nunit.org` or `https://launchpad.net/nunitv2`	The unit test runner application.
Silverlight-Selenium	`http://code.google.com/p/silverlight-selenium/`	The Selenium extension that allows you to automate Silverlight using Selenium commands and the Selenium test harness.

Once you have these applications downloaded and installed you need to think about the application code you are going to test. As stated earlier, Selenium works by driving the browser through JavaScript. The Silvernium plug-in extends the basic functionality so that you can execute commands using the Silverlight plug-in's JavaScript API, or against managed code that has been exposed via Silverlight's HTML Bridge (see Chapter 13 for details on using the HTML Bridge to expose managed types).

For example, to test the `Add` method of the `Calculator` class in the sample application, you need to apply the `ScriptableType` and `ScriptMember` attributes to the top of the class and its members as shown in Listing B-8.

LISTING B-8: Marking the Calculator class and methods as Scriptable

Available for
download on
Wrox.com

```
[ScriptableType]
public class Calculator
{
    [ScriptableMember(ScriptAlias="Add")]
    public int Add(int a, int b)
    {
        return a + b;
    }

    [ScriptableMember(ScriptAlias = "Subtract")]
```

```
    public int Subtract(int a, int b)
    {
        return a + b;
    }
}
```

Next you need to register this class as a scriptable object by using the `RegisterScriptableObject` method:

```
HtmlPage.RegisterScriptableObject("Calculator", new Calculator());
```

Notice the script key parameter provided to the `RegisterScriptableType` method. This will be the name of the JavaScript class exposed by Silverlight and will be provided to the Silvernium plug-in when you write tests.

Finally, before you start writing tests, when Silvernium runs, it attempts to locate the Silverlight plugin in the browser DOM by using its Object tag's ID property. If your Silverlight application is being hosted by the default test pages created by the Visual Studio project templates, you need to add an ID to the Object tag.

```
<object data="data:application/x-silverlight-2," type="application/x-silverlight-2"
        width="100%" height="100%" id="silverlightControl">
```

Now that you have configured the test environment and modified your Silverlight application to expose methods via JavaScript, you can begin to create tests. Start by creating a new Class Library project.

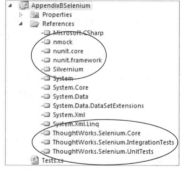

Note that this should be a full CLR class library, not a Silverlight class library and that it should target the full .NET 4 Framework, not the .NET 4 Client Profile.

Once the project is set up, you need to add a number of new references, shown in Figure B-5.

FIGURE B-5

Next you need to add `Setup` and `Teardown` actions to your test class. The `Setup` action is used to configure Selenium to look for the Remote Control server at the address `http://localhost:4444` and then start the test runner and open the test page. Finally, the Silvernium object is created using the Selenium object, the ID of the HTML Object tag hosting the Silverlight plug-in, and the script key that represents the managed object. The setup is shown in Listing B-9.

LISTING B-9: Initializing Silvernium in a unit test

```
[TestFixture]
public class Tests
{
    private const string URL = "http://localhost:6565/AppendixBTestPage.aspx";
```

continues

LISTING B-9 *(continued)*

```
    private const string OBJECTID = "silverlightControl";
    private const string SCRIPTKEY = "Calculator";
    private ISelenium selenium;
    private Silvernium silvernium;


    [SetUp]
    public void Setup()
    {
        selenium = new DefaultSelenium("localhost", 4444, "*iexploreproxy", URL);
        selenium.Start();
        selenium.Open(URL);
        silvernium = new Silvernium(selenium, OBJECTID, SCRIPTKEY);
    }

    [TearDown]
    public void TearDown()
    {
        selenium.Stop();
    }
}
```

Note that when configuring the browser parameter, you should specify the *iexplorerproxy value if you have a pop-up block running with the browser. Selenium also supports running tests in Firefox, Safari, Opera, and Chrome.

Now you are ready to create tests that exercise the Add and Subtract methods. To do this, you use the normal NUnit test attributes along with the Silvernium methods as shown in Listing B-10.

LISTING B-10: Creating a unit test using the Silvernium Call method

```
[Test]
public void AddTwoNumericValues()
{
    Assert.AreEqual("2", silvernium.Call("Add", new string[] { "1", "1" }) );
}
```

This test ensures that the Add method returns a value of 2.

Once you have written your tests, you are ready to run them using Selenium and NUnit. First, start the Selenium server by running the following command at the Windows command prompt:

```
java -jar server\selenium-server.jar -interactive
```

Now open the NUnit application, load your test project, and run your tests. NUnit runs the test, instantiating the Selenium test runner, which in turn executes the test against your Silverlight application in the browser. Figure B-6 shows NUnit in the foreground running a batch of Selenium tests, with the Selenium running in the background.

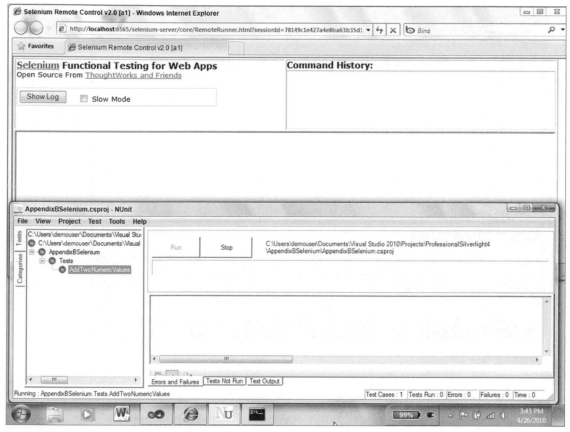

FIGURE B-6

As is the case with most unit test runners, if the tests succeed, NUnit will show a green banner; if any tests fail, NUnit will show red.

AUTOMATED UI TESTING USING WHITE

White is an automated testing framework designed to leverage Microsoft's new UI Automation APIs. These APIs are integrated into both Silverlight and WPF controls and allow you to simulate user interface interaction programmatically.

To get started using White, download and extract the assemblies from the White Codeplex site at `http://white.codeplex.com/`.

Once you have White downloaded, you can start to create tests with it. To start, create a new Test Project in Visual Studio. The Test Project template is located under the Test category as shown in Figure B-7.

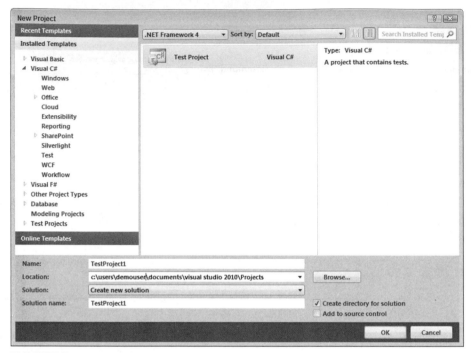

FIGURE B-7

Once the project is created, add new project references to the White assemblies as shown in Figure B-8.

Now you are ready to start writing tests. Listing B-11 shows how you can create a test using White that launches Internet Explorer, accesses and changes properties of the UI objects in the application, and then simulates clicking the button.

FIGURE B-8

Available for
download on
Wrox.com

LISTING B-11: Simulating a button click in a unit test using White

```
[TestMethod]
public void TestMethod1()
{
    InternetExplorerWindow browseWindow =
        InternetExplorer.Launch(@"http://localhost:6565/AppendixBTestPage.aspx",
                            "AppendixB - Windows Internet Explorer");
    SilverlightDocument document = browseWindow.SilverlightDocument;

    TextBox txtA = document.Get<TextBox>("txtA");
    TextBox txtB = document.Get<TextBox>("txtB");
    Button btnAdd = document.Get<Button>("btnAdd");
    Label lblSum = document.Get<Label>("lblSum");


    txtA.Text = "1";
```

```
    txtB.Text = "1";

    btnAdd.Click();

    Assert.AreEqual("2", lblSum.Text);
}
```

White uses the `InternetExplorerWindow` object to indicate that you want to launch a test inside Internet Explorer.

At the time of this writing, Firefox was also partially supported. See the White website site for updates on Firefox support.

Once the browser is loaded and the document obtained, you can start accessing `UIItems`. `UIItems` are essentially proxies on top of the actual UI controls in the applications. White includes a selection of `UIItems`, but you can also extend White, creating custom `UIItems` by deriving from `White.Core` `.UIItems.Custom.CustomUIItem`.

An advantage to White is that it is well integrated into Visual Studio's test system, therefore you can use the normal test execution and report features to run and view test results.

Figure B-9 shows the results of the test in Listing B-11.

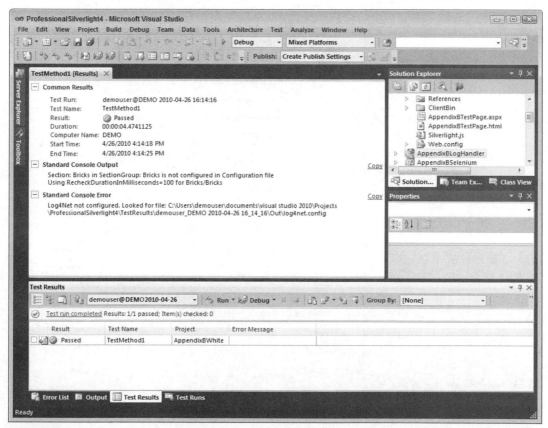

FIGURE B-9

Note that you should make sure you close your existing browser windows before running the White tests, or tests will fail to run properly.

As previously mentioned, White uses the Microsoft UI Automation APIs to manipulate UI elements and simulate user interactions. But how do you know if a control or application implements these interfaces correctly? Microsoft provides another tool for this called UIA Verify, which you can download from Codeplex (`http://uiautomationverify.codeplex.com/`).

To use UIAVerify, simply run your application, then run the `VisualUIAVerify.exe` application. When UIAVerify opens, you will see a list of all running applications on the left side of the application, a list of UIA Verification tests in the center, and a property grid on the right.

To test a specific Silverlight control or application, locate the browser instance running your application in the Automation Elements tree and then begin to drill into the tree nodes. Notice that as you drill down, UIAVerify begins to highlight areas of the application that correspond to the currently selected tree node.

Figure B-10 shows UIAVerify running with the Add button in your application set as the selected element.

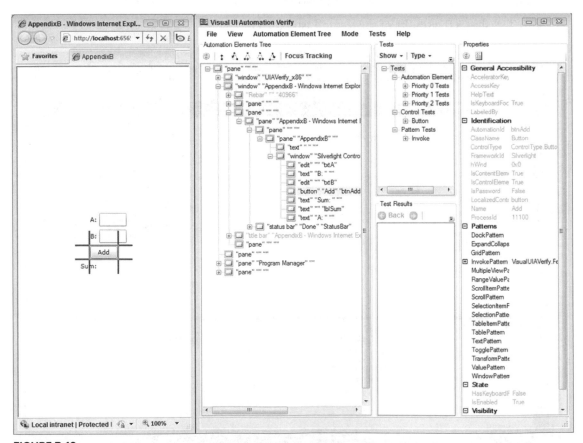

FIGURE B-10

Once you have reached the application or control, simply right-click the tests you want to run, or from the Tests menu select the Run Selected Test(s) on Selected Element menu option. The results of the test appear in the Test Results pane.

MOCKING FRAMEWORKS

A mock object is a stand-in for a real object, used while an application is being unit tested. Mock objects allow you to create unit tests that are narrowly focused and predictable, enabling you to pinpoint problems by removing the additional layers of complexity that your real objects might introduce to the application.

Mock objects are typically used for calls that return unpredictable results, calls to databases or other external systems, or calls to long-running processes.

Many mocking frameworks are available for .NET and two of the most popular open source frameworks have ported their frameworks to Silverlight:

➤ RhinoMocks (http://ayende.com/projects/rhino-mocks.aspx)

➤ Moq (http://code.google.com/p/moq/)

SUMMARY

This appendix looked at some of the different tools available to you to help you test your Silverlight applications, from unit testing to record UI testing. Each testing tool has its own unique pros and cons, so you should evaluate each carefully and remember that you are not limited to using just one tool.

To start, the appendix looked at the Silverlight Unit Testing Framework that ships with Silverlight tools and integrates through project and file templates into Visual Studio. Using this framework, you can share some tests across different platforms.

Next you looked at using Selenium to test your application via JavaScript. Selenium is a proven and powerful web application testing tool and is a fantastic way to test Silverlight applications that exist as part of a larger website.

Finally, you looked at using White to execute automated UI tests. White uses the UI Automation provider APIs to allow you to simulate user interface actions like button clicks to test the application UI.

Whichever tool (or tools) you choose, it is important to realize that software testing is an important part of the development process and that tools can make it easier for you to produce quality software release after release.

Building Facebook Applications with Silverlight

You can create an application that accesses the Facebook API in several ways. If you do a quick search on Bing you'll see a variety of open source projects and Visual Studio project templates that will help you access Facebook information and display it, or add your own games or social media experiences to Facebook. This appendix looks at using the Facebook API to interact with your own Facebook data in a unique Silverlight user interface hosted in an ASP.NET web application.

CREATING A NEW APPLICATION ON FACEBOOK

To access your Facebook data, you need an API Key and Secret value. To generate these, you need to create a Facebook application:

1. Sign up for a Facebook account at www.facebook.com.

2. Enable Developer access by navigating to http://www.Facebook.com/developers/ (see Figure C-1) and clicking the Allow button. The Developer page displays.

3. On the Developer page (see Figure C-2), click the Set Up New Application button. The Create Application page displays.

4. As shown in Figure C-3, type the name of your new Facebook application (SilverlightDemo in our example) and agree to the Terms of Service. Then click Create Application.

5. On the Edit Silverlight page that displays (see Figure C-4), make sure you make a note of the API Key and the Secret values for your application. You'll need to input the values for the API Key and Secret into your Web.config in your ASP.NET website later, so copy them to Notepad for later use.

6. Click the Canvas tab on the left, and update the following settings to configure your application:

➤ **Canvas Page URL** — This is the unique URL for your application on Facebook. Logically, this maps directly to the callback URL. Set the value to `silverlightdemo`.

➤ **Render Method** — For a Silverlight app that you want to debug locally, you'll need to use an iFrame. For this example, choose iFrame.

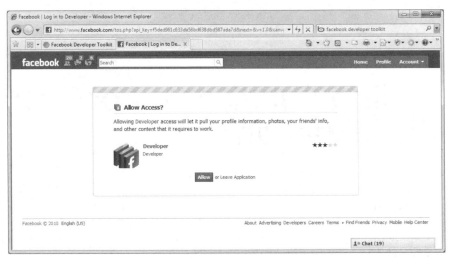

FIGURE C-1

FIGURE C-2

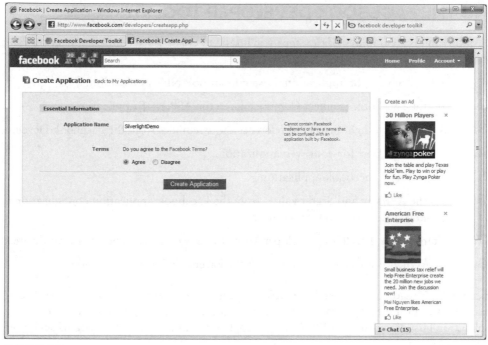

FIGURE C-3

7. Click Save Changes to save your configured application. At this point, you have the API Key and Secret values that you'll need to use in the application you create in the next section to access your Facebook content.

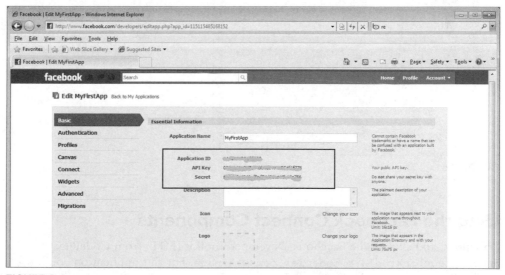

FIGURE C-4

USING THE FACEBOOK DEVELOPER TOOLKIT

The following is a summary of the steps you'll take to create a Facebook application using the Facebook API:

1. Create a Silverlight application, hosted in an ASP.NET application.

2. Add the Facebook Connect Components to the ASP.NET application.

3. Set up the Silverlight project to reference the assemblies from the Facebook Developer Toolkit.

4. Set the static port for your web application.

5. Create a new Facebook application.

6. Add the API Key and Secret values from the Facebook application configuration to the `Web.config` of your web application.

7. Instantiate the Facebook Developer Toolkit `BrowserSession` object and authenticate the user.

8. Use Asynchronous API Requests with the Facebook Developer Toolkit.

Since you've already created the Facebook application to generate the API Key and Secret values, the next step is to build the application that will use these values. To get started, create a new Silverlight application hosted within an ASP.NET web application and name it SilverlightFacebookDemo as shown in Figure C-5.

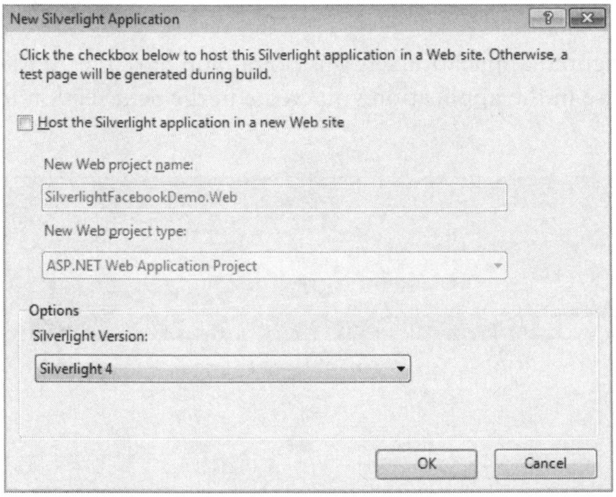

FIGURE C-5

Adding the Facebook Connect Components

Download and extract the Facebook Developer Toolkit (FDT) from CodePlex at `http://facebooktoolkit.codeplex.com/wikipage`. For this application you'll use the 3.1 Beta version of the Facebook Developer Toolkit.

To set up the host website application for communication with Facebook, add the following script references, shown in Listing C-1, to the web page that will host the Silverlight .xap (i.e., default.aspx).

LISTING C-1: Adding the Facebook API script reference

```
<head runat="server">
            <script
src=
"http://static.ak.connect.Facebook.com/js/api_lib/v0.4/FeatureLoader.js.php"
            type="text/javascript">
            </script>
            <script type="text/javascript" src="fblogin.js"></script>
            <!-- Other header info -->
</head>
```

Add a new Jscript file to your root of the web application named fblogin.js.

Open fblogin.js and replace the entire file with the code in Listing C-2.

LISTING C-2: Facebook Login script

```
// Verify this variable matches the Silverlight plugin ID
var silverlightPluginId = 'Silverlight1';

function Facebook_init(appid) {
    FB.init(appid, "/xd_receiver.htm");
}

function isUserConnected() {
    FB.ensureInit(function () {
        FB.Connect.get_status().waitUntilReady(function (status) {
            var plugin = document.getElementById(silverlightPluginId);
});
    });
}

function Facebook_login() {
    FB.ensureInit(function () {
        FB.Connect.requireSession(Facebook_getSession, true);
    });
}

function Facebook_logout() {
    FB.Connect.logout(Facebook_onlogout);
}

function Facebook_getSession() {

    FB.Facebook.get_sessionState().waitUntilReady(function () {
        var session = FB.Facebook.apiClient.get_session();
        var plugin = document.getElementById(silverlightPluginId);
```

continues

LISTING C-2 *(continued)*

```
        plugin.Content.FacebookLoginControl.LoggedIn
        (session.session_key, session.secret, session.expires, session.uid);
    });
}

function Facebook_onlogout() {
    var plugin = document.getElementById(silverlightPluginId);
    plugin.Content.FacebookLoginControl.LoggedOut();
}

function Facebook_onpermission(accepted) {
    var plugin = document.getElementById(silverlightPluginId);
    plugin.Content.FacebookLoginControl.PermissionCallback(accepted);
}

function Facebook_prompt_permission(permission) {
    FB.ensureInit(function () {
        FB.Connect.showPermissionDialog(permission, Facebook_onpermission);
    });
}
```

Edit the `fblogin.js` file's `silverlightPluginId` variable value to match the ID of the Silverlight plug-in in your hosting web page. This variable is used to locate the plug-in during authentication.

Next, in Visual Studio, add a reference to the `Facebook.Silverlight.dll` assembly into the Silverlight project (by browsing to the location to which the Toolkit was extracted). Once the assembly reference is added, you need to set the development server to a specific port, so in the Properties window for the project, set the Specific Port to 48282 as shown in Figure C-6.

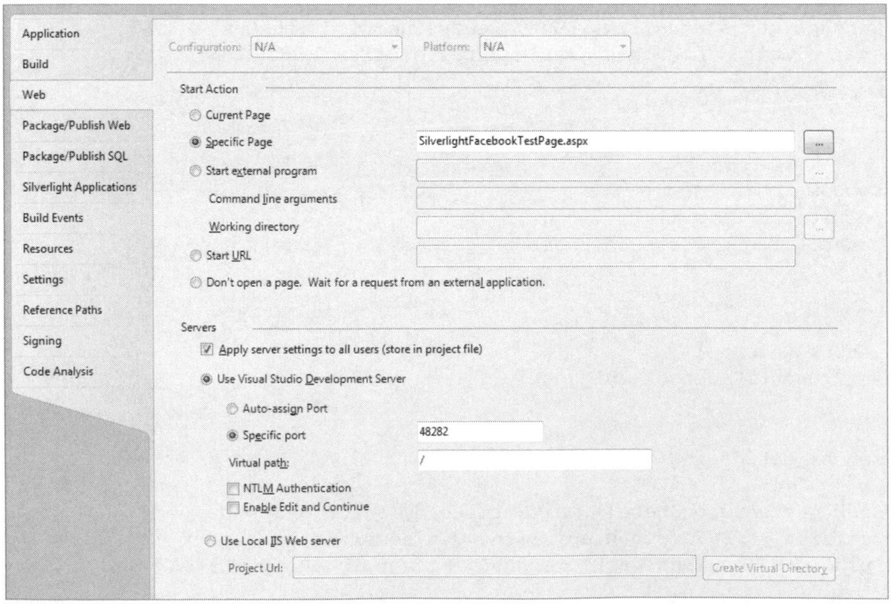

FIGURE C-6

Now that the web application is set up, you need to write code that instantiates the Facebook Developer Toolkit `BrowserSession` object and authenticates the user. In your Silverlight application's main page code-behind, add the following private members, shown in Listing C-3, to the class.

Storing the API Secret within Silverlight code (which runs on the client) is not recommended because this code can be viewed by third-party tools. The BrowserSession API requires only the API Key as shown in the following code snippet.

Available for download on Wrox.com

LISTING C-3: Private members for MainPage.cs

```
#region Private Members
private Api _fb;
readonly BrowserSession _browserSession;

private const string ApplicationKey = "add your key here";
private const string ApplicationSecret = "add your key here";

#endregion Private Members
```

Add the code in Listing C-4 to the constructor of the class.

Available for download on Wrox.com

LISTING C-4: MainPage.cs constructor

```
public MainPage()
{
    InitializeComponent();

    _browserSession = new BrowserSession(ApplicationKey);
    _browserSession.LoginCompleted += BrowserSession_LoginCompleted;
    _browserSession.LogoutCompleted += BrowserSession_LogoutCompleted;
}
```

Add a login button to the XAML markup and attach a click event handler as shown in Listing C-5. In the handler, issue a login call to the Facebook Developer Toolkit `BrowserSession` object. When the user clicks the button, the `BrowserSession` launches the Facebook authentication popup window.

Available for download on Wrox.com

LISTING C-5: Login_Click code behind

```
private void Login_Click(object sender, RoutedEventArgs e)
{
    _browserSession.Login();
}
```

Add a logout button to the XAML markup and attach a click event handler as shown in Listing C-6.

LISTING C-6: Logout_Click code behind

```
private void Logout_Click(object sender, RoutedEventArgs e)
{
    _browserSession.Logout();
}
```

In the `BrowserSession_LoginCompleted` event handler referenced in the constructor, add code to handle a completed user authentication (see Listing C-7). Once the `_fb` object is assigned, the application has everything needed to access and integrate with Facebook data.

LISTING C-7: BrowserSession_LoginCompleted code behind

```
private void BrowserSession_LoginCompleted
        (object sender, AsyncCompletedEventArgs e)
{
    _fb = new Api(_browserSession);
}
```

Using an Asynchronous API Request

Silverlight applications are required to issue all service requests in an asynchronous manner. It prevents service calls from locking the user interface. Because of this, the Facebook Developer Toolkit's Silverlight version (`Facebook.Silverlight.dll`) exposes only asynchronous API methods.

The following example shows a simple implementation of an asynchronous call to Facebook and displays the result in a user control.

Authenticating and Initiating a Session (BrowserSession.Login() Method)

To initiate a session with Facebook, you need to have a `BrowserSesson` object that is initialized in the constructor as shown in Listing C-8.

LISTING C-8: BrowserSession and ApplicationKey local variables

```
readonly BrowserSession _browserSession;
private const string ApplicationKey = "enter you app key here";
```

The `AppKey` from your Facebook application is required to initialize a browser session (see Listing C-9).

LISTING C-9: Initializing a BrowserSession

```
public MainPage()
{
    InitializeComponent();
```

```
        _browserSession = new BrowserSession(ApplicationKey);
        _browserSession.LoginCompleted += BrowserSession_LoginCompleted;
    }
```

Clicking the button brings up the Facebook Authentication screen (see Listing C-10).

LISTING C-10: Logging in to a BrowserSession

```
private void Login_Click(object sender, RoutedEventArgs e)
{
    _browserSession.Login();
}
```

Click the Login button, fill in your credentials, and click the Connect button. After a successful authentication, the LoginCompleted event handler is called. It should look like Listing C-11.

LISTING C-11: Getting user information after the login is completed

```
private void BrowserSession_LoginCompleted
        (object sender, AsyncCompletedEventArgs e)
{
    _fb = new Api(_browserSession);
    this.RefreshInfo();
}
private void RefreshInfo()
{
    _fb.Users.GetInfoAsync(new Users.GetInfoCallback(GetUserInfoCompleted), null);
    _fb.Friends.GetUserObjectsAsync(new
        Users.GetInfoCallback
          (GetFriendsInfoCompleted), null);
}

private void GetUserInfoCompleted
    (IList<user> users, Object state, FacebookException e)
{
    if (e == null)
    {
        _currentUser = users.First();
        if (_currentUser.pic != null)
        {

            Uri uri = new Uri(_currentUser.pic);
            Dispatcher.BeginInvoke(() =>
            {
                ProfilePhoto.Source = new BitmapImage(uri);
                ProfileStatus.Text = _currentUser.status.message;
                ProfileName.Text =
                  _currentUser.first_name +
                   " " + _currentUser.last_name +
                   " Birthday:" + _currentUser.birthday;
            });
```

continues

LISTING C-11 *(continued)*

```
        }
    }
    else
    {
        Dispatcher.BeginInvoke(() => MessageBox.Show("Error: " + e));
    }
}
```

Once a successful authentication occurs, the GetUserObjectsAsync asynchronously calls the GetInfoCallback delegate (shown in Listing C-12), which gets the list of friends of the current user. Information for each friend is stored in Facebook.Schema.user class.

LISTING C-12: The GetFriendsInfoCompleted event

```
private void GetFriendsInfoCompleted
    (IList<user> users, Object state, FacebookException e)
{
    if (e == null)
    {
        Dispatcher.BeginInvoke(() => ListFriends.ItemsSource = users);
    }
    else
    {
        Dispatcher.BeginInvoke(() => MessageBox.Show("Error: " + e.Message));
    }
}
```

Before you can test the application, you need to update the MainPage.xaml. The XAML in Listing C-13 should be added to the root Grid element in MainPage.

LISTING C-13: MainPage.xaml user interface

```
<ListBox x:Name="ListFriends" Grid.Row="1" Background="LightGray"
        HorizontalAlignment="Stretch"
        VerticalAlignment="Stretch" Margin="0,5,0,0">
    <ListBox.ItemTemplate>
        <DataTemplate>
            <Grid Background="Transparent" Margin="0, 0, 0, 10">
<StackPanel Orientation="Vertical"
        HorizontalAlignment="Stretch"
        VerticalAlignment="Stretch">
                <Grid HorizontalAlignment="Stretch" VerticalAlignment="Stretch">
<Image x:Name="coverImage" Width="150"
        Source="{Binding pic}" Stretch="Uniform" Tag="pic"/>
                </Grid>
                <Grid HorizontalAlignment="Stretch" VerticalAlignment="Stretch">
                    <Grid.RowDefinitions>
                        <RowDefinition/>
```

```
                        <RowDefinition/>
                    </Grid.RowDefinitions>
    <TextBox x:Name="firstName" Grid.Row="0"
            Background="Transparent"
            BorderThickness="0" Text="{Binding first_name}"/>
    <TextBox x:Name="lastName" Grid.Row="1"
            Background="Transparent"
            BorderThickness="0" Text="{Binding last_name}"/>
                    </Grid>
                </StackPanel>
            </Grid>
        </DataTemplate>
      </ListBox.ItemTemplate>
    </ListBox>
```

Now you can run and test your application; you should see something similar to Figure C-7.

Once you log in, you should see the friend information, as shown in Figure C-8.

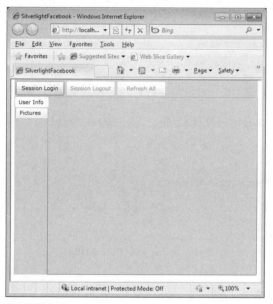

FIGURE C-7

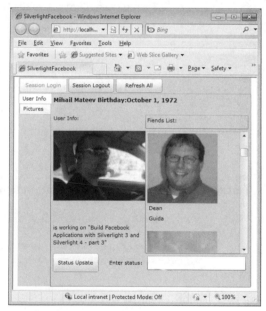

FIGURE C-8

Adding Features from the Facebook API

In this section, you will add more features to your application based on the capabilities of the Facebook API, including setting your status in Facebook and retrieving photo albums and displaying them in the ItemsControl.

To set your status, use the method call in Listing C-14.

LISTING C-14: Setting the Facebook status

```
Api.Status.SetAsync( string status, Status.SetCallback callback, object state);
_fb.Status.SetAsync(TxtStatus.Text, SetStatusCompleted, null);
```

The `Status.SetCallback` delegate maintains the result and exceptions when the status update is complete, as shown in Listing C-15.

LISTING C-15: SetStatusCompleted event

```
private void SetStatusCompleted(bool result, Object state, FacebookException e)
{
    if (e == null)
    {
        if (result == false)
        {
            Dispatcher.BeginInvoke(() => MessageBox.Show("call failed"));
        }
    }
    else
    {
        Dispatcher.BeginInvoke(() => MessageBox.Show("Error: " + e.Message));
    }
}
```

To retrieve the photo albums and photos of a user, implement the `GetAlbumsByUser` function (as shown in Listing C-16).

LISTING C-16: GetAlbumsByUser funtion to retrieve user albums

```
private void GetAlbumsByUser(long userId)
{
    // Issue async request for user albums via the Facebook Developer Toolkit
    _fb.Photos.GetAlbumsAsync(userId, GetUserAlbumsCompleted, UserAlbums);
}

private ObservableCollection<album> _userAlbums;

public ObservableCollection<album> UserAlbums
{
    get
    {
        return _userAlbums;
    }
    set
    {
        _userAlbums = value;
        NotifyPropertyChanged("UserAlbums");
    }
}
```

```
private void GetUserAlbumsCompleted
    (IList<album> albums, object state, FacebookException exception)
{
    // Marshall back to UI thread
    Dispatcher.BeginInvoke(() =>
    {
        // Verify albums returned
        if (albums == null) return;

        // If existing collection is null, new up collection ObservableCollection
        <album>
        UserAlbums = state as ObservableCollection<album> ??
            new ObservableCollection<album>();

        // Iterate result set
        foreach (var a in albums)
        {
            if (!UserAlbums.Contains(a))
            {
                UserAlbums.Add(a);
            }
        }
    });
}
```

Next, add a ListBox to the page and bind the objects to the ListBox (see Listing C-17).

LISTING C-17: Albums Listbox for displaying retrieved albums

```
<ListBox Width="200" Height="270" x:Name="ListAlbums"
        ItemsSource="{Binding UserAlbums,
            ElementName=MainWindow}" SelectionChanged="AlbumList_SelectionChanged">
    <ListBox.ItemTemplate>
        <DataTemplate>
            <StackPanel Orientation="Horizontal">
                <TextBlock Text="{Binding Path=name}"></TextBlock>
            </StackPanel>
        </DataTemplate>
    </ListBox.ItemTemplate>
</ListBox>
```

Set the AlbumList_SelectionChanged event to set the album properties and call the GetAlbumPhotos method (see Listing C-18).

LISTING C-18: SelectionChanged event on the AlbumList control

```
private void AlbumList_SelectionChanged(object sender, SelectionChangedEventArgs e)
{
    // Clear any album photo captions
    AlbumPhotoCaption.Text = string.Empty;
    AlbumPhotoCacheCaption.Text = string.Empty;
```

continues

LISTING C-18 *(continued)*

```
    this.CurrentAlbum = e.AddedItems[0] as album;

    this.UserAlbumCaption.Text = string.Format("User Albums: {0}",
            UserAlbums.Count);

    GetAlbumPhotos();

    if (AlbumPhotos != null)
    {
        // Set cache loaded and async loaded album photo counts
        AlbumPhotoCacheCaption.Text =
            string.Format("Original Load Album Photos: {0}", AlbumPhotos.Count);

        AlbumPhotos.CollectionChanged += delegate
        {
            // Set album photo total count
            AlbumPhotoCaption.Text =
                string.Format("Total Album Photos: {0}", AlbumPhotos.Count);
        };
    }

}
private void GetAlbumPhotos()
{
    // Issue async request for all photos in the current album
    if (CurrentAlbum == null || CurrentAlbum.aid == null) return;
    _fb.Photos.GetAsync(null, CurrentAlbum.aid, null,
        GetAlbumPhotosCompleted, AlbumPhotos);

}
private void GetAlbumPhotosCompleted
        (IList<photo> photos, object state, FacebookException exception)
{

    // Marshall back to UI thread
    Deployment.Current.Dispatcher.BeginInvoke(() =>
    {

        // Verify photos returned
        if (photos == null) return;

        // If stateful (existing) collection is null, new up collection
        // if you want to add new photos to list without lost the old photos use:
        // ObservableCollection<photo> statefulPhotos = state as
        ObservableCollection<photo> ??
            new ObservableCollection<photo>();
        ObservableCollection<photo>
            statefulPhotos = new ObservableCollection<photo>();

        // Iterate result set
        foreach (var p in photos)
```

```
        {
            // Set flag to determine existence
            var photoExistsInCollection = false;

            // Iterate existing photo cache
            foreach (var existingPhoto in statefulPhotos)
            {
                // Check for matching photo IDs
                if (existingPhoto.pid == p.pid)
                {
                    // This is a duplicate, ignore and break
                    photoExistsInCollection = true;
                    break;
                }
            }

            // Check if photo does not exist in cache
            if (!photoExistsInCollection)
            {
                // Add to photo collection
                statefulPhotos.Add(p);
            }
        }

        this.AlbumPhotos = statefulPhotos;
    });
}
#endregion //GetAlbumPhotosCompleted
```

The `AlbumPhotos` collection, shown in Listing C-19, is used to store a collection of photos from the selected photo album.

LISTING C-19: AlbumPhotos collection to hold the albums list

```
private ObservableCollection<photo> _currentAlbumPhotos;
public ObservableCollection<photo> AlbumPhotos
{
    get
    {
        return _currentAlbumPhotos;
    }
    set
    {
        _currentAlbumPhotos = value;
        NotifyPropertyChanged("AlbumPhotos");
    }
}
```

To finish, bind the `PhotoAlbums` to the `DataTemplate` in an `ItemsControl`, shown in Listing C-20.

LISTING C-20: ItemsControl DataTemplate which binds to PhotoAlbums

```
<DataTemplate x:Key="photoItemsTemplate">
    <Grid Background="Transparent" Margin="0, 0, 0, 10">
        <StackPanel Orientation="Vertical"
            HorizontalAlignment="Stretch" VerticalAlignment="Stretch">
            <Grid HorizontalAlignment="Stretch" VerticalAlignment="Stretch">
                <Image x:Name="coverImage" Width="180"
                    Source="{Binding src}" Stretch="Uniform" Tag="src"/>
            </Grid>
        </StackPanel>
    </Grid>
</DataTemplate>

<ScrollViewer BorderThickness="0"
    VerticalScrollBarVisibility="Visible" HorizontalScrollBarVisibility="Hidden"
Height="300" Width="190" HorizontalAlignment="Stretch" VerticalAlignment="Stretch">
    <ItemsControl x:Name="ScrollPhoto"
         VerticalAlignment="Stretch" HorizontalAlignment="Stretch"
ItemTemplate="{StaticResource photoItemsTemplate}"
        ItemsSource="{Binding AlbumPhotos, ElementName=MainWindow}">
        <ItemsControl.ItemsPanel>
            <ItemsPanelTemplate>
                <StackPanel />
            </ItemsPanelTemplate>
        </ItemsControl.ItemsPanel>
    </ItemsControl>
</ScrollViewer>
```

Finally, to upload a new photo to an album, add this code (Listing C-21) to the UploadPhoto event handler.

LISTING C-21: Uploading a photo to Facebook

```
private void UploadButton_Click(object sender, RoutedEventArgs e)
{
    OpenFileDialog openfile = new OpenFileDialog { Multiselect = false };
    openfile.ShowDialog();

    System.IO.Stream fileStream = openfile.File.OpenRead();
    byte[] data;
    using (BinaryReader reader = new BinaryReader(fileStream))
    {
        TxtUploadStatus.Text = "Uploading...";
        data = reader.ReadBytes((int)fileStream.Length);
    }
    fileStream.Close();

    _fb.Photos.UploadAsync(null, "Myphoto", data, "image/jpeg",
                        OnUploadPhoto, null);

}
```

Once this is all completed, you have a working Facebook application written in Silverlight that allows you to view friends, look at photo albums, and upload new photos to an album. Your completed project should look like Figure C-9.

FIGURE C-9

SUMMARY

In this appendix, you learned how to create a Silverlight Facebook application using the Facebook Developer Toolkit from CodePlex. Using this Toolkit, you learned how to list your friends, how to view albums, and how to upload new photos to albums. You also learned how to configure a Facebook Developer application on the Facebook website.

Integrating Silverlight into SharePoint 2010

Since its release, Microsoft's SharePoint platform has exploded as a hugely popular collaboration and communication platform. It allows organizations to easily get up-and-running fast with a rich set of out-of-the-box features and includes an expansive set of extensibility points that allow developers to customize just about every part of it. Starting with the 2010 release, Microsoft has renamed what was formerly known as Windows SharePoint Services to SharePoint Foundation 2010. Additionally, Microsoft has continued to make significant investments in both the experience and the extensibility that the platform offers, including a significant improved way of integrating Silverlight into SharePoint.

This appendix shows you how to use the new features of SharePoint Foundation 2010 to seamlessly integrate Silverlight applications into SharePoint.

Note that because SharePoint is a vast and highly extensible platform, it would be impossible for this appendix to cover every aspect of extending SharePoint. This appendix specifically focuses on integrating Silverlight into SharePoint, but you can find more in-depth information on SharePoint 2010 in the Wrox title *Professional SharePoint 2010 Development*.

THE SAMPLE APPLICATION

To demonstrate how easy it is to integrate Silverlight applications into SharePoint, this appendix uses a small sample application that displays weather information in SharePoint. Figure D-1 shows the application running as a Web Part on a SharePoint page.

The application is a standard Silverlight application built using an MVVM style architecture. It uses Yahoo Pipes as the source of its weather data, receiving back from the Yahoo service JSON-formatted data. The `DataContractSerializer` and `JsonObject` classes are used to transform this data into managed objects whose data is then displayed by the application.

The application also stores data on the locations to get weather in a SharePoint list and uses the SharePoint Foundation 2010 Silverlight Object Model to retrieve that data.

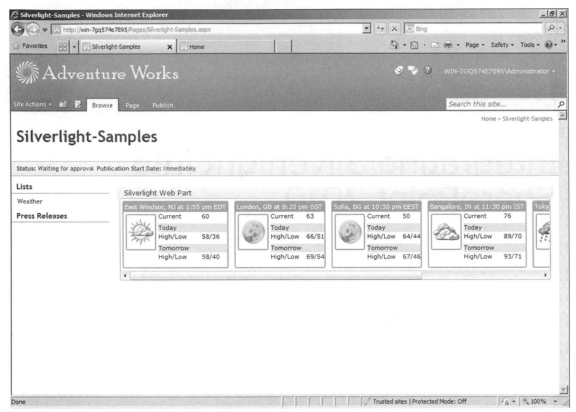

FIGURE D-1

 Although this appendix focuses specifically on the SharePoint integration portions of the sample application, the complete source is available as part of the downloadable code for this book on www.wrox.com.

USING THE SHAREPOINT FOUNDATION 2010 SILVERLIGHT OBJECT MODEL

As stated in the previous section, the sample application stores the names of the locations for which it should retrieve data in a SharePoint list. It uses the new SharePoint Foundation 2010 Silverlight Object Model to programmatically retrieve the data.

To do this, you first need to add references to the following object model assemblies to your Silverlight project:

➤ `Microsoft.SharePoint.Client.Silverlight.dll`

➤ `Microsoft.SharePoint.Client.Silverlight.Runtime.dll`

These assemblies provide a set of managed Silverlight APIs that allow you to interact with SharePoint Foundation 2010. You can find the assemblies on your SharePoint server at `C:\ Program Files\Common Files\Microsoft Shared\Web Server Extensions\14\TEMPLATE\ LAYOUTS\ClientBin`.

Once you have added the project references you can begin to write code using them. In the sample application, the APIs are used to read data from a SharePoint list.

You can find the full API documentation for the SharePoint Foundation 2010 Silverlight Object Model on the MSDN website at `http://msdn.microsoft .com/en-us/library/ee536622(office.14).aspx`.

Listing D-1 demonstrates using the API's from the SharePoint Foundation 2010 Silverlight Object Model assemblies to connect to SharePoint and retrieve the list data.

Available for
download on
Wrox.com

LISTING D-1: Using the Silverlight Object Model API's to connect to and retrieve data from a SharePoint list

```
ClientContext spContext = ClientContext.Current;

if (spContext == null)
{
    spContext = new ClientContext("http://sharepoint-demo");
}

var spWeb          = spContext.Web;
var spList         = spWeb.Lists.GetByTitle("Weather");
var spQuery        = new CamlQuery { ViewXml = "<View></View>" };

//Gets a ListItemCollection containing the List items
_spItems = spList.GetItems(spQuery);

spContext.Load(spWeb);
spContext.Load(spList);
spContext.Load(_spItems);

spContext.ExecuteQueryAsync(OnSharePointGetRequestSucceeded,
                            OnSharePointGetRequestFailed);
```

To start, the listing attempts to retrieve the current client context, which is the context for SharePoint objects and operations. If there is no current context, a new context is created using the URL of the SharePoint server.

Once the context is retrieved, you can start accessing SharePoint objects. First you need to get the website that is associated with the current client context. Once you have the website, you can access objects within that website like Lists, Folders, Features, or sub-Webs. For the sample application, you want to get the contents of a List, so you can use the `GetByTitle` method to access the content of a specific list. Once you have the list, you can now begin to execute CAML queries against the list. In this case you want to select all of the `Location` items in the list so the query asks for the entire view.

> *Collaborative Application Markup Language (CAML) is an XML-based language used by SharePoint to define fields and views used by Sites and Lists. Using CAML you can query SharePoint for specific information about Sites or Lists. You can find a full reference to the CAML language on Microsoft's MSDN website at* `http://msdn.microsoft.com/en-us/library/ms462365(office.14).aspx`.

Note that as you are using the APIs, no calls are actually being executed against SharePoint yet. The Silverlight Object Model uses a batching architecture that allows you to create multiple commands and execute them as a single batch. You can see this in the next few lines of code, which take the SharePoint objects created just prior and loads them in the context using its `Load` method. This essentially adds them to the execution queue.

Once you are ready to execute the commands, you call the `ExecuteQueryAsync` method, passing in two event delegates: one used if the asynchronous call succeeds, and one used if it fails.

The sample application's query success event delegate is shown in Listing D-2.

LISTING D-2: Handling a successful asynchronous query

```
private void OnSharePointGetRequestSucceeded(object sender,
                                    ClientRequestSucceededEventArgs e)
{
    Locations.Clear();

    foreach (ListItem item in _spItems)
    {
        string location;

        // Try to find the correct column
        try
        {
            location = item["Location"].ToString();
```

```
        }
        catch
        {
            // If that doesn't work, let's try the Title column
            location = item["Title"].ToString();
        }

        Locations.Add(location);
    }

    RaiseCallback();
}
```

If the asynchronous call is successful, the list items collections will contain the list of Location values, which you can loop through and add to a local Locations collection. Because the sample needs to update the UI with the results, it must do this using the BeginInvoke method. This is because the success event delegate is run on a non-UI thread. Trying to update the UI directly from it will raise an exception.

In the sample application, at the end of the event delegate method, the RaiseCallback method is called, which is where the application executes the BeginInvoke method. This is shown in Listing D-3.

LISTING D-3: Updating the UI from the asynchronous execution thread

```
private void RaiseCallback()
{
    if (_callback == null) return;

    Action<Settings> a = x => _callback(x);

    Deployment.Current.Dispatcher.BeginInvoke(a, this);
}
```

In the previous listing, you can see a member variable called _callback of type System.Action<T> is used. The Action<T> object allows you to wrap a delegate. In the sample application, the delegate contains a reference to the method on the UI thread that will be called in order to marshal the data retrieved in the asynchronous SharePoint query handler back to the UI thread.

Finally, you must also create the event delegate to handle the asynchronous call failing. This is shown in Listing D-4.

LISTING D-4: Handling a failed asynchronous query

```
private void OnSharePointGetRequestFailed(object sender,
                                ClientRequestFailedEventArgs e)
{
    throw new Exception(e.Message, e.Exception);
}
```

DEPLOYING A SILVERLIGHT APPLICATION INTO SHAREPOINT

Once you have your Silverlight application completed, you need to deploy it into SharePoint. To do this, you begin by uploading the application's XAP file into a document library.

For the sample application shown in this appendix, once the XAP file is in SharePoint, you need to create a custom list that contains the list of locations. Figure D-2 shows a list containing the locations for which the application should retrieve weather data.

FIGURE D-2

At this point you are ready to add the Silverlight application to a SharePoint page by using the new Silverlight Web Part that is included with SharePoint 2010. To add the Web Part, start by placing the SharePoint page in Edit mode and selecting the Web Part Zone to which you want to add the application.

Once you select the Silverlight Web Part, a dialog (shown in Figure D-3) appears, prompting you to enter the location of the Silverlight application.

Though in the case of the sample application the location is local to SharePoint, it is possible to provide any valid URL to the Web Part. Note, however, that you may have to resolve cross-domain access issues if the Silverlight application is hosted in a different domain. Once the URL is provided, you can access the Web Part settings via the Web Part context menu as you would any other Web Part.

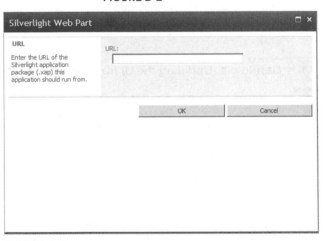

FIGURE D-3

Once you have configured the Web Part settings, simply click OK to close the editor. The web page refreshes, and you should see the application loaded in the page. Figure D-4 shows the completed sample application running in SharePoint.

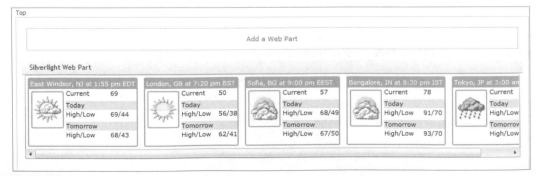

FIGURE D-4

SUMMARY

This appendix introduced you to the new SharePoint Foundation 2010 Silverlight Object Model. Using a simple sample application, the appendix demonstrated how you can use these managed APIs in a Silverlight application to execute commands against SharePoint, retrieving data and other information about SharePoint.

Finally, the appendix walked you through deploying and configuring a Silverlight application, allowing you to easily integrate Silverlight into your SharePoint pages.

Silverlight Control Assemblies

Table E-1 provides a reference which can help you locate the assembly that contains a specific control.

TABLE E-1

CONTROL NAME	ASSEMBLY
Accordian	System.Windows.Controls.Layout.Toolkit.dll
AutoCompleteBox	System.Windows.Controls.Input.dll
BusyIndicator	System.Windows.Controls.Toolkit.dll
Button	System.Windows.dll
Calendar	System.Windows.Controls.dll
Chart	System.Windows.Controls.DataVisualization.Toolkit.dll
CheckBox	System.Windows.dll
ChildWindow	System.Windows.Controls.dll
ComboBox	System.Windows.dll
ContextMenu	System.Windows.Controls.Input.Toolkit.dll
DataForm	System.Windows.Controls.Data.DataForm.Toolkit.dll
DataGrid	System.Windows.Controls.Data.dll
DataPager	System.Windows.Controls.Data.dll
DatePicker	System.Windows.Controls.dll
DockPanel	System.Windows.Controls.Toolkit.dll

continues

TABLE E-1 *(continued)*

CONTROL NAME	ASSEMBLY
Expander	System.Windows.Controls.Toolkit.dll
Frame	System.Windows.Controls.Navigation.dll
GlobalCalendar	System.Windows.Controls.Toolkit.dll
GridSplitter	System.Windows.Controls.dll
HyperlinkButton	System.Windows.dll
Image	System.Windows.dll
Label	System.Windows.Controls.Data.Input.dll
ListBox	System.Windows.dll
MediaElement	System.Windows.dll
MultiScaleImage	System.Windows.dll
NumericUpDown	System.Windows.Controls.Input.Toolkit.dll
Page	System.Windows.Controls.Navigation.dll
PasswordBox	System.Windows.dll
ProgressBar	System.Windows.dll
RadioButton	System.Windows.dll
Rating	System.Windows.Controls.Input.Toolkit.dll
RichTextBox	System.Windows.dll
ScrollViewer	System.Windows.dll
Slider	System.Windows.dll
TabControl	System.Windows.Controls.dll
TextBlock	System.Windows.dll
TextBox	System.Windows.dll
TimePicker	System.Windows.Controls.Input.Toolkit.dll
TimeUpDown	System.Windows.Controls.Input.Toolkit.dll
ToggleButton	System.Windows.dll
ToolTip	System.Windows.dll
TreeMap	System.Windows.Controls.DataVisualization.Toolkit.dll

CONTROL NAME	ASSEMBLY
TreeView	System.Windows.Controls.dll
ValidationSummary	System.Windows.Controls.Data.Input.dll
ViewBox	System.Windows.dll
WebBrowser	System.Windows.dll
WrapPanel	System.Windows.Controls.Toolkit.dll

INDEX

G

H